This second edition of Sidney I. Landau's landmark work offers a comprehensive and completely up-to-date description of how dictionaries are researched and written, with particular attention to the ways in which computer technology has changed modern lexicography. A completely new chapter has been added and every chapter has been updated and reorganized to reflect the changes. Landau has an insider's practical knowledge of making dictionaries and every feature of the dictionary is examined and explained, with frequent examples given from the latest dictionaries of the US and Britain. A history of English lexicography is also included. The book is both practically grounded and soundly based on current lexicographic scholarship. Written in a readable style, free of jargon and unnecessary technical language, it will appeal to readers who are simply interested in dictionaries – with no special knowledge of the field – as well as to professional lexicographers.

SIDNEY I. LANDAU is former Editorial Director of the North American Branch of Cambridge University Press and has been engaged in lexicography since 1961. He has contributed widely to professional journals in the field and is editor of the three-volume *International Dictionary of Medicine and Biology* (1986) and the *Cambridge Dictionary of American English* (2000).

DICTIONARIES

The Art and Craft of Lexicography

SECOND EDITION

SIDNEY I. LANDAU

PUBLISHED BY THE PRESS SYNDICATE OF THE UNIVERSITY OF CAMBRIDGE
The Pitt Building, Trumpington Street, Cambridge, United Kingdom

CAMBRIDGE UNIVERSITY PRESS
The Edinburgh Building, Cambridge CB2 2RU, UK
40 West 20th Street, New York, NY 10011–4211, USA
10 Stamford Road, Oakleigh, VIC 3166, Australia
Ruiz de Alarcón 13, 28014 Madrid, Spain
Dock House, The Waterfront, Cape Town 8001, South Africa

http://www.cambridge.org

First published by Charles Scribner's Sons 1984
First published by Cambridge University Press 1989
Second edition 2001

Typeface Baskerville MT 11/12½   *System* QuarkXPress™   [SE]

A catalogue record for this book is available from the British Library

Library of Congress Cataloguing in Publication data

Landau, Sidney I.
Dictionaries: the art and craft of lexicography / Sidney I. Landau. – 2nd edn.
p.   cm.
Includes bibliographical references and index.
ISBN 0 521 78040 3 (hardback) – ISBN 0 521 78512 X (paperback)
1. Lexicography.   2. Encyclopedias and dictionaries – History and criticism.   I. Title.

P327.L3   2001
413′.028 – dc21   00-064146

ISBN 0 521 78040 3 hardback
ISBN 0 521 78512 X paperback

Transferred to digital printing 2004

For Sarah

Contents

Illustrations

Preface to the second edition and acknowledgments

Revision of one's own work puts one in the uncomfortable position of judging oneself as an outsider, as indeed one is after a span of nearly twenty years. I understand that every nine years' time, on average, every cell of a person's body has been replaced, so I have undergone two complete transformations in this period and am working on a third. Perhaps the more significant changes are in one's view of the world and of one's own place within it. Both mentally and physically I am not the same person I was when I wrote this book in 1981–82. Although I could have had the text optically scanned, I elected to retype all of it, as this would compel me to review every word. I have not regretted the decision.

An honest appraisal of one's book, as of one's self, makes one realize how one's views of what is important have in some cases changed. One's capacity for indignation about some things especially, like one's capacity to race upstairs two at a time, is mysteriously weakened without one knowing precisely when the change took effect. I have been surprised at the vigor of some of my criticisms over what now strike me as fairly trivial matters, and have not been reluctant to excise such comments entirely or modify them as the case seemed to warrant. On the other hand, I remain convinced that my willingness to express a personal point of view and a style of writing that permitted such expression have been instrumental in giving the first edition whatever success it has had in the select world of dictionary people and in the wider public interested in dictionaries. I was determined not to change the style or character of the book, and I have not.

Some critics of the first edition said the book had its virtues but was not methodical enough; it wasn't organized systematically and failed to cover everything in a logical way. They were probably right. But if I were to dissect the dictionary structure in a completely calm and logical way, if I were to write a string of endless, numbered paragraphs, 3.1.5.6 followed by 3.1.5.7 followed by 3.1.5.8, and so on, one passive-voice sentence dribbling away into the next, the system might be improved but the book would be unreadable, and worse, unread. Writing is hard work, and I have never been motivated to write a book that no one will read, even if it wins critical acclaim. One has to have some passion to write a book when one isn't doing it to earn a living. Yet I have no constitutional antagonism towards coherent organization and do not regard chaotic or incongruent structure as essential for sustaining reader interest. I have indeed found in the first edition organizational superfluities, odd repetitions, and peculiar transitions, and I have tried to correct these by judicious deletion, by moving passages from one chapter to another or within a chapter, or by rewriting, but I have not disabled, I hope, the essential appeal of the book. This I take to be the result of its having been written by someone with a committed, first-hand experience of editing a wide range of dictionaries over many years, one who is willing to give his honest report of how it is done and what can go wrong and who is not afraid to comment on what is good, what could be better, and what is deplorable. When making a criticism, I have always tried to offer a constructive proposal along with it. On balance my voice in this edition is raised in contention less often. I have no points I want to score. Whatever hurts or disappointments I had have long since been absorbed into my system and, though still a presence that no doubt shape my views of dictionaries (and of much else!), are no longer catalysts for acerbic comment. Their effects are physiological, more profound and more lasting perhaps, but less exigent.

It is a pleasure to acknowledge again, as in the first edition, the patient help of my principal tutor at Funk & Wagnalls many years ago, Sam Davis; the generosity and wisdom of that formidable scholar, Albert H. Marckwardt; and the encouragement and kind attention given me by Randolph Quirk – all offered at a time when I was virtually a mere recruit in lexicography. I should also like to acknowledge with gratitude Robert L. Chapman, who gave me my first dictionary job at Funk & Wagnalls, helped me acquire the skills of a good lexicographer, and aided my career in ways large and small. The omission of his name from the first edition was an oversight that I regret.

A number of people offered constructive criticism of the first edition and pointed out errors and omissions of one sort or another. On some of these criticisms I have acted; on others I have not. But I thank all those who took the trouble to write or e-mail me about ways to improve the book. I want to thank particularly Edward Gates, Tom McArthur,

Dušan Gabrovšek, and Włodzimierz Sobkowiak for their specific criticisms and corrections. A number of active lexicographers were willing to take time out from their busy schedules to reply to my queries about practical issues involved in dictionary making today or in the current marketplace. I am grateful to the following for their generous help: Frank Abate, Michael Agnes, Robert K. Barnhart, David Jost, Erin McKean, Wendalyn Nichols, and Joseph Pickett. For his advice on legal issues in the European Union, I am most grateful to Alan Hughes. I thank Patrick Hanks for his kindness in making available to me his unpublished lecture on Samuel Johnson and to Edward Gates for sending me a copy of an article he had written and which I could not otherwise obtain.

A number of my former colleagues at Cambridge University Press, expert in particular areas of corpus use, lexicography, or language research, agreed to look at portions of the manuscript for this edition and give me the benefit of their comments, or steered me to others who could provide needed advice. For such services I am pleased to express my thanks to Patrick Gillard, Andrew Harley, Paul Heacock, Alan Harvey, Christine Bartels, and Penny Carter. I also wish to thank Joan Houston Hall, Chief Editor of the *Dictionary of American Regional English*, for her gracious help in reviewing my coverage of *DARE*, correcting mistakes, and answering any and all questions I had about the dictionary. Any errors that remain on any of the subjects discussed in this book are entirely my responsibility.

The dictionary entries and maps (Figures 15–19) that appear in Chapter 5 from the *Dictionary of American Regional English*, ed. Frederic G. Cassidy and Joan Houston Hall, are reprinted by permission of the publishers, the Belknap Press of Harvard University Press, Cambridge, Mass.: Volume I, A–C, Copyright © 1985 by the President and Fellows of Harvard College; Volume II, D–H, Copyright © 1991 by the President and Fellows of Harvard College; Volume III, I–O, Copyright © 1996 by the President and Fellows of Harvard College; Volumes IV and V, forthcoming.

Anyone reading this edition will see how central to the task of dictionary making the use of a corpus has become. In order to revise the book, it was therefore absolutely necessary to have access to a first-rate lexicographical corpus, and I am pleased to acknowledge using the Cambridge International Corpus and the Cambridge Corpus Tools (the unique software that enables one to make use of the Corpus), which were used with the permission of Cambridge University Press. The CIC is a computerized database of contemporary spoken and written

English, which currently stands at over 300 million words. It includes British English, American English, and other varieties of English. Cambridge University Press has built up the CIC to provide evidence about language use that helps to produce better language teaching materials.

Abbreviations

(The full titles of dictionaries are usually given when first mentioned in any discussion, along with their abbreviations; abbreviations are used in the text immediately following to avoid repeating the full title.)

ACD	*American College Dictionary*
AHCD3	*American Heritage College Dictionary*, Third Edition
AHD	*American Heritage Dictionary of the English Language*
AHD4	*American Heritage Dictionary of the English Language*, Fourth Edition
CDAE	*Cambridge Dictionary of American English*
CED	*Collins English Dictionary*
CIDE	*Cambridge International Dictionary of English*
Cobuild	*Collins Cobuild English Dictionary*, Second Edition
Cobuild ELD	*Collins Cobuild English Language Dictionary*
DAE	*Dictionary of American English*
DARE	*Dictionary of American Regional English*
DMAU	*Dictionary of Modern American Usage*
EWD	*Hamlyn Encyclopedic World Dictionary*
EWED	*Encarta World English Dictionary*
LAAD	*Longman Advanced American Dictionary*
LDAE	*Longman Dictionary of American English*
LDOCE	*Longman Dictionary of Contemporary English*
LDOCE3	*Longman Dictionary of Contemporary English*, Third Edition
MW10	*Merriam-Webster's Collegiate Dictionary*, Tenth Edition
NID2	*Webster's New International Dictionary of the English Language*, Second Edition
NID3	*Webster's Third New International Dictionary*
NODE	*New Oxford Dictionary of English*
NTC	*NTC's American English Learner's Dictionary*
OALD	*Oxford Advanced Learner's Dictionary*
OALD6	*Oxford Advanced Learner's Dictionary*, Sixth Edition

OED	*Oxford English Dictionary*
OED2	*Oxford English Dictionary*, Second Edition
RHD2	*Random House Dictionary of the English Language*, Second Edition
RHWCD	*Random House Webster's College Dictionary*
WBD	*World Book Dictionary*
WDEU	*Webster's Dictionary of English Usage*
WNW	*Webster's New World Dictionary of the American Language*, College Edition
WNWCD	*Webster's New World College Dictionary*, Fourth Edition

Introduction

The first edition of this book appeared in 1984, the year that George Orwell chose to represent his vision of an unpleasant futuristic world in which individual freedom was suppressed by the manipulations of an authoritarian state. This edition is appearing in 2001, the year Arthur C. Clarke chose as the time for a space adventure marked by a deranged and dangerous computer. These two books, both improbably visionary when they were written, have not predicted exactly what the world would be like in those years, but they represent with astonishing accuracy how the things in life which most concern us have changed. In 1984 it was political freedom for the individual; in 2001 it is the control of technology to advance a human agenda. Computers existed in 1984 and earlier, but they had not changed the world. Now they have and, among other things, they have changed the way dictionaries are done. That is the overriding reason for the need for a second edition.

It has been my good fortune to have been intimately involved from 1994 to 2000 with the preparation of a new dictionary for foreign learners, the *Cambridge Dictionary of American English*. In the course of this work, I became familiar at first hand with many of the changes in lexicography wrought by computer technology. I had had some acquaintance with computers and lexicography in an earlier work, a multivolume medical dictionary, the *International Dictionary of Medicine and Biology* (John Wiley, 1986), but that experience was rudimentary compared to the more recent one. As I was in the midst of editing a medical dictionary when the first edition of this book was written, there were many references to technical, and specifically medical, lexicography in it. Some of the examples of technical definitions have been cut in this edition, but by and large I have maintained the detailed coverage of technical lexicography.

Since my more recent experience has been in the field of ESL (for "English as a second language") lexicography, this edition contains many more examples from that branch of dictionary work than the earlier edition. Britain has led the way in developing dictionaries for foreign learners and still has the largest and most advanced line of dictionaries in this field; therefore I had to become thoroughly familiar with the leading British ESL dictionaries. I was pleased in my first edition to give more attention to British lexicography than had commonly been given in books by Americans; but in this edition I have considerably expanded the coverage of British lexicography, especially in the ESL area, but not exclusively. Nonetheless, I confess to having a more intimate knowledge of American dictionaries, and I cannot claim to give equal coverage to British dictionaries in every area of lexicography.

In the decade from 1985 to 1995 the world of dictionaries underwent a dramatic change because of the vastly greater power first of file servers and then of hard drives in individual desktop computers. The greatest and most far-reaching impact of this change has been in the development of huge electronic collections of naturally occurring language (called *corpora*, singular *corpus*, meaning "body" in Latin). Such corpora are used to study and analyze language use in ways that were not possible before, and the use of corpora has led to major changes in the way dictionaries are researched and written. Chapter 6, "The corpus in lexicography," is entirely new to this edition, and describes the history of corpus development, how the corpus is used in modern lexicography, and how a corpus is compiled. I also speculate on the future of corpus use.

Computer technology has also dramatically changed the way dictionaries are written and edited. Dictionaries are written on-line, and the editors do not have to work together in the same place. The corpus is used continually in various ways during the day-to-day editing of a dictionary, and elaborate computer software has simplified some aspects of dictionary work, such as cross-reference checking. Planning a dictionary is now a very different process than formerly, involving computer experts and the necessity to acquire computer hardware. Chapter 7, "Dictionary making," reflects these changes. Much of it is new.

Because of the revolutionary effects of the corpus in lexicography, the role of the citation file – a collection of quotations clipped from periodicals, books, etc., or retyped – which had been the only original source for definition, has been changed. The latter part of Chapter 4, "Definition," has therefore been completely rewritten to introduce the concept of the corpus and to differentiate it from the citation file. Because of the wide-ranging effect of the corpus, I felt that it was necessary to describe the corpus in general terms here, rather than wait until Chapter 6 to introduce it. (In fact, the corpus is mentioned even in the first three chapters, but only in passing.) The first part of Chapter 4 deals with the nature of meaning and the principles of defining, as in the previous edition. It also includes practical advice on defining and shows examples of various defining styles, drawing upon recent innovations especially in the field of dictionaries for foreign learners.

The changes in lexicography have not *all* been caused by the development of more powerful computers. Some innovations, such as those in ESL defining styles mentioned above, were originally an outgrowth of corpus use, but have ramifications in lexicography that have led to changes that have nothing essentially to do with corpus research. Many new dictionaries and even new kinds of dictionaries have been published in the last two decades of the twentieth century, and all of these had to be reflected in this edition. New research had to be recognized. Even in those chapters in which the computer is not the leading cause of change, there are many changes: Chapter 1, "What is a dictionary?"; Chapter 2, "A brief history of English lexicography"; and Chapter 3, "Key elements of dictionaries and other language references." The influence of computer technology is pervasive, however, even when not dominant. For example, in Chapter 1, more attention is given to nonalphabetic dictionaries. In Chapter 2, I have added sections on dictionaries for foreign learners and describe the demise of the unabridged dictionary, discuss the American college dictionaries and their British cousins, and conclude with a section on electronic dictionaries and the Internet.

When the first edition was published, *Webster's Third New International Dictionary (NID3)* was already twenty-three years old, but the controversy that had surrounded its publication in 1961 was still fresh in memory, and as the only unabridged dictionary of contemporary language, it merited extensive treatment. I have deleted some of the detailed discussions of *NID3* definitions in Chapter 4, though the reader will still find frequent reference to *NID3* throughout the text, as it is still a benchmark in contemporary lexicography in spite of its age. In particular, Chapter 5, "Usage," includes a revised treatment of the critical reception given *NID3* because of its treatment of usage labeling. The sections on sexual and scatological taboo and on insult have been thoroughly rewritten in the light of changes in lexicographical practice. The discussion of modern usage guides has been updated to reflect more recent publications.

Chapter 8, "Legal and ethical issues in lexicography," has been almost completely rewritten and made more coherent by focusing on legal and ethical matters not dealt with elsewhere, and includes much new material, such as a discussion of the history of the use of the name *Webster* in American lexicography and a set of approved guidelines for giving credit to lexicographers for work done on dictionaries. The concluding section, dealing with the role of dictionaries in reflecting social values, has also been thoroughly revised to take into account more recent studies.

The first edition of my book included two bibliographies: "A critical bibliography of selected monolingual dictionaries" and "A selective bibliography of nondictionary sources." The second, updated, has been retained. The first has been replaced by "Dictionaries mentioned in the text, from Johnson (1755) to the present: a bibliography and index." The critical bibliography of the first edition often repeated comments made within the text proper and was therefore repetitious. By combining the new bibliography with index references – critical references appear in boldface, other mentions in light face – repetition is avoided. Critical commentaries are easily accessible by this means, and the reader will have at his or her disposal a complete list of all dictionaries of this period mentioned in the text.

This second edition, like the first edition, is written in a style intended to make it accessible to anyone interested in dictionaries. The level of detail, however, is sufficient to reward the attention of lexicographers and would-be lexicographers as well: compilers of or contributors to dictionaries, lexicons, glossaries, and other language reference books. The book is suitable as a text for a course on English lexicography or as a supplement to one on the history of the English language. It should also be of especial interest to librarians. As in the previous edition, this edition is for those, too, who would never dream of making a dictionary but would just like to know more about such works and how they are made. Some attention is also given to bilingual dictionaries, but chiefly as a means of contrasting the problems of bilingual lexicography with those of monolingual.

A number of books dealing with lexicography have appeared since the first edition, notably Bo Svensén's *Practical Lexicography: Principles and Methods of Dictionary-Making* (Oxford University Press, 1993), translated from the Swedish; and Henri Béjoint's *Tradition and Innovation in Modern English Dictionaries* (Oxford University Press, 1994). Robert Burchfield's edited collection, *Studies in Lexicography* (Oxford: Clarendon Press, 1987), is also worth noting. On a popular level, Jonathon Green's *Chasing the Sun: Dictionary Makers and the Dictionaries They Made* (Jonathan Cape (UK), Henry Holt (US), 1996) provides a wealth of information not formerly available to a wide audience. For professional lexicographers Ladislav Zgusta's *Manual of Lexicography* (The Hague: Mouton, 1971) remains the seminal work in the field, and I acknowledge my debt to it, particularly with reference to bilingual lexicography. As valuable as these works are in their several ways, none combines the particular qualities of the first edition of this book that made it singular and that I have endeavored to maintain in this edition. These are the point of view of a seasoned lexicographer with broad practical experience in planning, managing, and editing dictionaries; an individual writing style devoid of pretentiousness or condescension that speaks from one person to another, not to a crowd of assembled acolytes or to a roomful of robed academics; and comprehensive, in-depth coverage of the field of English lexicography.

CHAPTER 1

What is a dictionary?

Dictionary is a powerful word. Authors and publishers have found that if they call a reference book a dictionary it tends to sell better than it would if called by another name because the word suggests authority, scholarship, and precision. It should come as no surprise, then, that all kinds of books are described as dictionaries. There are dictionaries of silk and cinematography, of drink and dance, of fashion, taxes, and chivalry. There is a dictionary of poker, a dictionary of movie terminology, and a dictionary of motor bike slang. Had Ambrose Bierce called his book *Bierce's Aphorisms* instead of *The Devil's Dictionary*, the book would have suffered the neglect it deserved, but I suppose one must give the devil his due.

To most people, dictionaries and encyclopedias are closely linked and are sometimes considered interchangeable, but they are essentially different kinds of reference works with different purposes. A dictionary is a text that describes the meanings of words, often illustrates how they are used in context, and usually indicates how they are pronounced. Dictionaries in the traditional form of books usually have their words listed in alphabetic order. Modern dictionaries often include information about spelling, etymology (word derivation), usage, synonyms, and grammar, and sometimes include illustrations as well. An encyclopedia is a collection of articles about every branch of knowledge. Although some articles include definitions, their descriptions go far beyond the information given in a dictionary.

Dictionary definitions are usually confined to information that the reader must have to understand an unfamiliar word. The emphasis is on the word, and all the information given bears directly on the meaning, pronunciation, use, or history of the word. Encyclopedic articles are essentially topical, dealing with the entire subject represented by the article's title. An encyclopedia article on religion does not merely say what the word *religion* means or has meant in the past or how it is pronounced or used; it systematically describes the religions of the world: their histories, doctrines, and practices. The difference is sometimes stated, perhaps a bit too simply, by the apophthegm, "Dictionaries are about words, encyclopedias are about things." This is true enough if we look at dictionaries and encyclopedias as a whole, but it admits of many exceptions if we try to apply it to every entry in each type of work.[1]

It is difficult to make grand generalizations about dictionaries. They are not encyclopedias, but what are they? They are protean in form, so that any generalization that may apply to one or several types of dictionaries may not apply at all to others. It will therefore be necessary, before we proceed much further, to analyze the various types of dictionaries and related language books.

A SURVEY OF TYPES OF DICTIONARIES AND OTHER LANGUAGE REFERENCES

Dictionaries can be classified by many criteria, some of them obvious to everyone, such as size, but there is no standard, agreed-upon taxonomy for dictionaries. A few intrepid souls have, however, made an attempt to construct an organized scheme of classification, or typology; before we start our own survey, it will be worth taking a look at a thoughtful and discriminating typology devised by the linguistic scholar Yakov Malkiel.[2]

Malkiel says dictionaries can be distinguished by three categories: range, perspective, and presentation. Range refers to the size and scope of the dictionary: how well does it cover the entire lexicon? He calls this quality density. When dealing with an entire language, range is almost impossible to establish; who knows the total extent of the lexicon? But when the designated lexicon is limited to a specific work, the range can be comprehensive. Another aspect of range is the number of languages covered – whether it is monolingual, bilingual, or multilingual (including more than two languages). The third aspect of range is the extent of concentration on lexical data; in other words, how encyclopedic is the work?

Perspective is based on how the compiler views the work and what approach is taken. First, is the work *diachronic* (covering an extended time) or *synchronic* (confined to one period)? Second, how is it organized – alphabetically, by sound (as in rhyming dictionaries), by concept (as in some thesauruses), or by some other means? Third, is the level of tone detached, preceptive (or didactic), or facetious?

Presentation signifies how material of a given perspective is presented; specifically, how full are the definitions? For example, monolingual dictionaries tend to have fuller definitions than bilingual works.

Compared to native-speaker dictionaries, dictionaries for foreign learners have simpler definitions and more illustrative examples. What form of verbal documentation is employed? One type of dictionary may rely on cited quotations, another may give invented phrases, a third may list bibliographic references. Are graphic illustrations included? Finally, what special features, such as pronunciations and usage information, are included?

Malkiel's classification is valuable because it suggests relationships between types. For example, diachronic dictionaries tend to have few or no pictorial illustrations; bilingual dictionaries are seldom diachronic and usually alphabetic in arrangement. Virtually every type of dictionary can be analyzed with reference to the three categories of range, perspective, and presentation.[3] Malkiel's system, while elegant, is not very serviceable as a teaching tool. Accordingly, I offer my own less elegant survey, which is not intended to be a formal typology but merely a convenient way to highlight significant differences among dictionaries. The categories are not exclusive. This arrangement will give the opportunity to explain in what ways types of dictionaries differ and are alike.

Number of languages

Dictionaries differ in the number of languages they contain. The difference between a monolingual dictionary and a bilingual one consists not only in the number of languages in which they are written but in their essential purpose. A bilingual dictionary consists of a list of words or expressions, in alphabetical order when in printed form, in one language (the *source language*), for which, ideally, exact equivalents are given in another language (the *target language*). The purpose is to provide help to someone who understands one language but not the other. More, the presumption is that one of the languages is the user's native language.

A monolingual dictionary, written entirely in one language, may be intended for the native speakers of that language, for people learning it as a second language in a country where the language is widely spoken either as a native language or a lingua franca, or for people learning it as a foreign language. It provides many kinds of information about its entry words but most importantly gives definitions; that is, each of the entry words or expressions is rephrased in words of the same language as the entry word. (The principles of defining are discussed in Ch. 4.) The chief purpose of a monolingual dictionary is to explain, in words likely to be understood, what other words mean, and, especially in a learner's dictionary, how to use them. Thus, whereas bilingual dictionaries provide equivalents of their entry words in another language, monolingual dictionaries provide periphrastic definitions in the same language.

Bilingual dictionaries may be unidirectional (monodirectional) or bidirectional; that is, they may go in one direction only, from English, let us say, to French, or be combined with another dictionary that goes from French to English. In studies of bilingual lexicography, the languages included are often designated as *L1* and *L2*. Bidirectional dictionaries really consist of two dictionaries, L1→L2 and L2→L1. There are also dictionaries in which the entry words are translated into two other languages (trilingual dictionaries) or more than two other languages (multilingual dictionaries).

There are two main purposes for using a bilingual dictionary: for comprehension, as in reading, of the source language, by a person who knows the target language; or as an aid in expression, as in writing, of the target language, by a person who knows the source language. A dictionary that is intended to be used in the latter way – for translation from a person's native language to a foreign language – is sometimes called an *active* dictionary, and one used for translation from a foreign language to a person's native language is called a *passive* dictionary.[4] A speaker of English, for example, will consult a French–English dictionary for "passive" help in understanding unfamiliar French words encountered in reading. On the other hand, a French speaker who must write an essay in English may consult a French–English dictionary for "active" help in finding the right words to express himself. Many bilingual lexicographers have observed that it is next to impossible to construct a unidirectional bilingual dictionary for speakers of both languages. The compiler has, or ought to have, one group in mind, else the dictionary is likely to be satisfactory for neither. But rarely does a bilingual dictionary identify the user for whom it is intended.[5] As one linguist comments, "Book-publishers can scarcely be expected to take kindly to the thought, but it is nevertheless true that bilingual dictionaries should be titled in such a way that the language of the intended user is made clear, e.g., *French–English Dictionary for Americans* as against *French–English Dictionary for Frenchmen*."[6]

Why is this so? First of all, there is often no equivalent in the target language for entry words in the source language, not only in the obvious instances of indigenous flora and fauna but for many common words as well. Ladislav Zgusta cites the English word *girlhood* as an example that poses problems in providing an exact French equivalent. *État de fille* is an explanatory equivalent, but it will be of no use to the English speaker who wants to translate *girlhood* into French in a sentence such as, "In her girlhood, she used to read Tennyson."[7]

Many words, too, are culture specific (or culture bound, as some linguists prefer). For example, American and Canadian football terms like *tackle* have no equivalents in countries where this sport is not played.[8] Many social terms (such as those referring to family relationships), culinary words, political and legal terms, and religious words have no equivalent in the target language and require explanations instead of or in addition to some approximate translation.[9] Terms relating to historical events and to health care are also often culture specific. The lack of equivalence is particularly acute, of course, when the two languages are used in cultures that differ greatly in cultural background, but it occurs with surprising frequency even in cultures with a similar heritage.

In a paper particularly rich in examples of culture-specific items, the Slavic scholar Morton Benson observes that because of such cultural anomalies, the bilingual lexicographer cannot just reverse the direction of translations to obtain a word list for a companion volume. "Lexical gaps" occur when a thing or concept in the culture of the source language does not exist in the culture of the target language; Benson cites as examples the English items "advance man," "dial-a-joke," and "exit poll." Some items have partial equivalents in the target language but no exact parallel; "assistant professor" and "health maintenance organization" are examples of this type. Sometimes the concept exists in the target language, although there is no term to describe it; Benson mentions "gridlock," "double-park," and "moving violation," as falling into this category.[10]

It is crucial for the lexicographer to decide in advance whether an L1→L2 dictionary is intended to help L2 speakers comprehend L1 or to help L1 speakers express themselves in L2. If the dictionary also includes an L2→L1 dictionary, the same questions must be asked: is the dictionary intended to help L1 speakers comprehend L2 or to help L2 speakers express themselves in L1? Thus there are four possible purposes of every bidirectional, bilingual dictionary. The decision on exactly for which speakers the dictionary is intended will affect not only the kind of translational equivalents given and the fullness of the equivalents, but the choice of entries themselves. For example, in an English–French dictionary for French speakers, the inclusion of culture-specific words like *tackle* in football use would make sense; the French speaker would be puzzled by this unfamiliar word. But if the dictionary is intended to help an English speaker express himself in French, *tackle* has no place in the dictionary. Moreover, for the English speaker, many uncommon or difficult words, such as *circumnavigate*, would be unnecessary, for if the English speaker wanted a French equivalent he could seek the same sense under simpler entry words, such as *sail around*.[11] Yet for the French speaker, uncommon and difficult English words are of considerable importance. If the equivalent of a common word in the source language (English) is an uncommon or difficult word in the target language (French), the disparity is of less consequence to the French speaker than to the English speaker, who may use the uncommon French word in an altogether unsuitable context unless the dictionary specifies its limited usage. Few dictionaries have space for such information.

Mary R. Haas lists a number of desiderata for a bilingual dictionary, including the following:

1. It provides a translation for each word in the source language.
2. Its coverage of the source language lexicon is complete.
3. Grammatical, syntactic, and semantic information is provided.
4. Usage guidance is given.
5. Names are included.
6. It includes special vocabulary items, such as scientific terms.
7. Spelling aids and alternative spellings are indicated.
8. Pronunciation is included.
9. It is compact in size – which obviously limits its coverage of items 1–8.[12]

Given the complexities of accurate translation, which I have barely touched upon but which give some idea of the difficulties, one can see that the compilers of multilingual dictionaries face formidable problems. First of all, such dictionaries are necessarily passive; that is, they are used for translating from a known language into a foreign language for purposes of comprehension only. Translating into two or more other languages makes any sophisticated equivalences among the languages impossible. Linguists use the word *anisomorphic* (from *an* = not + *iso* = same + *morph* = form) to describe languages composed of lexical forms that are not parallel. Trilingual dictionaries are comparatively rare, but those that do exist generally consist of two widely understood languages, such as English and French – or, in the past, Latin and English or a Romance language – plus one language that was very dissimilar, from a completely different language family, such as a Bantu language. Such dictionaries were often created by European missionaries to help them communicate with prospective converts in an unknown language having no relation to their own. Thus these dictionaries had in effect two source languages and one target language, a language largely anisomorphic to their own language. Needless to say, such dictionaries are necessarily elementary and practical, more closely resembling travelers' word guides than bilingual dictionaries. The more languages included, the more difficult the problems become. Zgusta remarks that multilingual dictionaries are justified only for technical terminology, when other meanings can be ignored.[13]

Variety of English

English dictionaries vary according to the variety of English they represent. David Crystal has estimated that nearly one fourth of the world's population is fluent or competent in English – 1.2 to 1.5 billion people.[14] English is spoken as a native language in the UK, the US, Ireland, Canada, Australia, New Zealand, and in the Caribbean. As Crystal reports, it has official status or special status of some sort in over seventy other countries, which use it as a lingua franca (in other words, as a second language), and it is very widely taught as a foreign language throughout the world.[15] As English has become more widely used in disparate places, it has developed distinctive features, just as American English developed a number of distinctive features in the period following the settlement of the American colonies. In the eighteenth and nineteenth centuries, however, air travel was nonexistent and communication of news was slow. In the twentieth and twenty-first centuries, communication of all kinds has become amazingly swift. Through television and print periodicals, the Internet and electronic mail, movies and popular music, tourism, scientific research and educational programs, the internationalization of business organizations and the growth of international trade, there is a huge and steady volume of interaction in English (and, of course, in many other languages). One can argue that this interaction will put a brake on divergences, but that remains to be seen. Exposure to so much more English gives users a greater opportunity to attach new meanings or connotations to these words in adapting them to conditions in their own countries. Although rapid and massive international communication of language may retard some kinds of changes, I believe it acts mainly to accelerate the spread and popularity of new vocabulary, particularly in the realms of media, popular music, and commercial advertising. So far, the various Englishes spoken throughout the world are mutually intelligible, even if some pronunciations and expressions may momentarily puzzle a speaker of a different variety.

Noah Webster, as we shall see in the next chapter, emphasized – some would say, exaggerated – the unique nature of American English, but differences there surely were. Others apart from Webster were well aware of the development of new words or new meanings in America – called *Americanisms* – and began collecting them to publish as specialized dictionaries. John Bartlett's *Dictionary of Americanisms* (1848) was an early alphabetical dictionary of this type, and went through a number of editions over many years. A notable early collection is Schele de Vere's *Americanisms: The English of the New World* (1871). This is not an alphabetical dictionary but a discursive treatment of Americanisms organized by their sources. Thus, there are sections on The Indian, Immigrants from Abroad (including the Dutch, French, Spanish, German, Negro, and Chinese), the West, the Church, etc. In 1919, the first edition of H. L. Mencken's *The American Language* appeared, and was successively revised and enlarged, appearing in several volumes, until 1936. It has never really gone out of print; the language section of almost every used bookstore in America is likely to have some edition of Mencken on its shelves, and in 1967 Raven I. McDavid, Jr., edited an abridged, annotated version in one volume, along with new material.[16] As a journalist and writer Mencken was popular for his sardonic wit and blunt opinions about American life and mores, but he was also a first-rate scholar of the English language. Mencken's work is not a dictionary but has an extensive word index, so it can be used as one. Another major work, also not a dictionary, is George Philip Krapp's two-volume *The English Language in America* (1925), which gives a thorough, scholarly account of the differences in vocabulary, pronunciation, and spelling in American English as compared to British English.[17]

In an effort to fill the gaps in the *OED*'s coverage of American English, William A. Craigie, one of the *OED*'s editors, with James R. Hulbert, edited *A Dictionary of American English* in four volumes (1938–44). It included words first arising in the United States and also words revealing the cultural life of the American people. In 1951, Mitford M. Mathews' *A Dictionary of Americanisms* appeared. This work was limited to Americanisms, i.e., to words that originated in the United States; but as Allen Walker Read has observed, Mathews unfortunately excluded those terms that had survived in the United States while becoming obsolete in

Britain, simply on the grounds that they had not originated in the United States.[18]

A Dictionary of Canadianisms – consisting of that part of Canadian English "which is neither British nor American" – was published in 1967, under the chief editorship of Walter S. Avis.[19] This one-volume dictionary is modeled after the *OED*, with dated, attributed quotations illustrating each entry and each definition. *The Canadian Oxford Dictionary* (1998), edited by Katherine Barber, is a large, general dictionary that gives special attention to the preferences and usages of Canadians. The *Macquarie Dictionary* of Australia (1981, rev. 1985, 1987), edited by Arthur Delbridge, has a similar purpose; it is a massive, general, synchronic dictionary of the English language as used in Australia, giving special attention to Australian usage. *The Australian National Dictionary* (1988), edited by W. S. Ramson, on the other hand, *is* a dictionary of Australianisms "on historical principles," and follows the *OED* format of dated, attributed quotations showing the historical development of each word and sense. *The Dictionary of New Zealand English: A Dictionary of New Zealandisms on Historical Principles*, edited by H. W. Orsman, appeared in 1997. Still another dictionary on historical principles, *A Dictionary of South African English*, edited by Penny Silva, was published in 1996. "Begun in 1969 during the height of the apartheid era," the dictionary was completed at the end of 1994, "the year of the country's first democratic elections."[20] The dictionary had to include many words formerly (and perhaps still) used by whites that were and are offensive to blacks, words like *hottentot* and *kaffir*, and to deal with these words in a sensitive but accurate way. It devotes ten columns of dense type to the first of these, and eight full pages (twenty-four columns) to the second, owing in part to the large number of compounds formed with it.[21] This illustrates the peculiar difficulties of dealing with a variety of English during a period of dramatic political change.

From the Caribbean region, F. G. Cassidy and R. B. LePage's *Dictionary of Jamaican English*, Second Edition (1980), is a pioneering work; its first edition was published in 1967. The *Dictionary of Caribbean English Usage* (1996), edited by Richard Allsopp, draws upon this and numerous other sources, including field research; it is a complex dictionary because it must deal with eighteen different islands or territories, each with its own variety of language, and must deal with words that derive from various African languages, from Spanish, and from other languages.

There are now many varieties of English, not only among those countries where English is the mother tongue but also in countries or territories where it is widely spoken as a second or foreign language, such as India and Pakistan, Hong Kong and Singapore, Nigeria and Zimbabwe. There is still wide disagreement as to how profound the differences are among the varieties of English, but increasing attention is being given them by lexicographers and linguists, who are making collections of naturally occurring text for language study in many of these varieties. (See Ch. 6, "National and specialized corpora," p. 292).

There are also dictionaries that in the fashion of bilingual dictionaries attempt to translate from one variety of English into another, such as *British English A to Zed* (1987) by Norman Schur. Designed for the bewildered American who encounters distinctively British forms in his reading or travels, this dictionary is one-way, from British to American, advising us that *flex* refers to an electric extension cord and that *snookered* means *up the creek* or *in a tight spot.*

If, in the past, British dictionaries, and to a lesser extent American dictionaries, could assume that the language they represented was simply English, without qualification, those days are gone. Not only do these dictionaries, quite naturally, give special attention to the variety that their audience uses and mainly encounters, but the defining vocabulary (in linguistic terms, the *metalanguage*) employs the particular variety as well. For example, in American English one agrees to (or with) a proposal, in British English one agrees a proposal. Such uses find their way into definitions, usage notes, and synonym discussions. Even dictionaries that trumpet their international coverage reflect a single variety of English in their metalanguage and can give only a superficial treatment to other varieties. Although most of the differences between American and British English are known, economic considerations preclude giving the amount of space that would be required in an American dictionary for adequate coverage of British English, and vice versa. Neither Americans nor British are that interested in the minutiae of each other's varieties, especially if that means omitting information relating to their own variety. Other varieties have not been as fully studied as British and American English and may be in the process of rapid change; there is even less likelihood that they will be represented adequately in British or American dictionaries. Therefore, all English dictionaries should acknowledge, either in their titles or in their prefatory matter, what variety of English they represent, or at least which variety is primary, even if their variety happens to be one used by many more speakers as a mother tongue than as a second or foreign language. I do not think American dictionaries will find this especially traumatic, as some American dictionaries, notably in the ESL field, already use "American English" in their titles to distinguish them from dictionaries based on British English. For the British, whose appreciation of their language is proprietary and deeply felt as part of their country's history, it may be impossible. No one disputes the historical priority of British English; we cannot reasonably expect its speakers to acquiesce to a status merely equivalent to every other. But whether they acknowledge it or not, their brand of English is no longer the single standard by which all other varieties are measured.

Primary language of the market

Monolingual dictionaries differ in the primary language of their intended users. Some monolingual English dictionaries are intended for native speakers of English, and others are designed for foreign learners, a market that is divided pedagogically into *English as a second language* (ESL) and *English as a foreign language* (EFL). ESL is English taught to speakers of languages other than English who need to know it because they are living in an English-speaking country or because their country has adopted English as an official language or because it is used there unofficially but widely as a lingua franca. EFL is English taught to speakers of languages other than English who do not live in an English-speaking country but believe it would be useful to know, even though it may not be a practical necessity. Dictionaries for foreign learners are intended for both of these groups. The degree-granting organization called TESOL stands for "teachers of English to speakers of other languages," which also applies to both groups. For the sake of simplicity but somewhat inaccurately, dictionaries for foreign learners, especially in the US, are sometimes called "ESL dictionaries," a practice I will adopt in this book. In Britain, *English language teaching* (ELT) is often used to cover both ESL and EFL instruction. So much for acronyms.

ESL dictionaries include some of the features of foreign-language dictionaries, such as providing more information than native-speaker dictionaries on grammar, phrasal verbs, and idiomatic usages. Many ESL dictionaries use a simplified, controlled vocabulary for their definitions, generally limited to 2,000 or 3,000 words (but often including derivative forms as well, thus stretching the total). ESL dictionaries devote a substantial amount of space to exemplifying definitions with illustrative phrases or sentences; unlike native-speaker dictionaries but like some bilingual dictionaries, ESL dictionaries are designed to enable the foreign learner to produce utterances in English (the *encoding* function), not just to comprehend them (the *decoding* function). Like children's dictionaries, ESL dictionaries have an essentially pedagogical purpose, and there are ESL dictionaries – as there are school ones – for students at various levels, from "low intermediate" to advanced. However, since these works are for adults, the tone of the definitions and the selection of entries differ from those of school dictionaries. Some ESL dictionaries include sexually taboo words and racial epithets, for instance. ESL dictionaries at the advanced level are as large as American college dictionaries, containing 1,500 to 2,000 pages. As English has grown in importance in the world of commerce and as international travel has vastly increased, ESL lexicography in English has been transformed from a minor offshoot of mainstream lexicography into a huge field in its own right, every bit as large, remunerative, and competitive as native-speaker lexicography. David Crystal has written convincingly of the rapid growth of English as an international language since 1950. He cites the British Council, an organization promoting cultural, educational, and technical cooperation in over 100 countries, as having estimated that over 1 billion people will soon be learning English.[22] Unlike dictionaries for native speakers, which for the entire latter half of the twentieth century remained, with one or two exceptions, completely impervious to meaningful innovation, ESL dictionaries eagerly embraced new technology for research. Drawing upon advances in computational linguistics to use the technology of the electronic corpus, they are leading the way in making dictionaries more reliably accurate and comprehensive. (See Ch. 6, "The corpus in lexicography," p. 273.)

The advanced-level ESL dictionaries, all of British origin as of this writing, are an impressive lot, more sophisticated and more demanding of the user than most native-speaker dictionaries. For example, ESL dictionaries include codes that distinguish between nouns that are countable (called count nouns, which can be made plural, like *shoe*) and nouns that cannot (called mass nouns, like *contempt*). They tell readers not only whether verbs are transitive or intransitive but what sort of objects they take if they are transitive. Sometimes they indicate whether a verb is followed by a complement beginning with *that* or with an adverb used to begin a question such as *why* or *what*. They may indicate whether adjectives are apt to occur before a noun or after a verb. They give much more coverage to collocations (words that tend to occur together, such as *good news* or *answer the door*). Many ESL dictionaries are used in conjunction with courses in English-language teaching and are assigned along with textbooks, but many are bought by people studying independently. Most ESL dictionaries use the International Phonetic Alphabet (IPA) for pronunciations because it is based on phonetic articulation and is not ambiguous, whereas native-speaker dictionaries often use a system linked to "key words" in English which the user is expected to know how to pronounce. For the history of ESL lexicography, see Ch. 2, p. 74.

In 1992 two new learner's dictionaries with substantial encyclopedic content appeared on the scene: the *Longman Dictionary of the English Language and Culture* and the *Oxford Advanced Learner's Encyclopedic Dictionary*. Both were based on previously published ESL dictionaries, but with numerous names of people, places, organizations, etc., added. Although native-speaker dictionaries traditionally include short entries for many encyclopedic terms, ESL dictionaries had generally not done so. Moreover, there were more encyclopedic entries in the two new dictionaries and they were more expansive than those in native-speaker dictionaries. The idea was to meld the language with the culture. The idea sounds good on paper but in practice the choice of cultural items to be included is often arbitrary and the encyclopedic material becomes dated very quickly.[23]

Form of presentation

Dictionaries and other language reference books differ in the manner in which access to their information is provided, specifically as to whether their word lists are arranged alphabetically or thematically, and, allied to this, whether they are produced in books or exist in electronic form. We think now of dictionaries as being necessarily alphabetical, but as we shall see in Ch. 2, some early dictionaries were arranged by subject. A number of modern language reference books, notably thesauruses and some innovative works designed to help foreign learners in expressing themselves, have made use of thematic approaches.

The proliferation of electronic dictionaries has meant that access to the lexicon does not depend – at least from the user's point of view – on the alphabet; he just has to key in a word and the computer finds it for him. Indeed, even in printed dictionaries, reliance on alphabetical order has often deviated from a strict or uniform application. Many technical dictionaries, such as medical dictionaries, are arranged by entry and subentry and are therefore not in exact alphabetical order; they are alphabetized by the governing noun. Thus, *infectious hepatitis* appears as a subentry under *hepatitis*, not under *infectious*. Some ESL dictionaries also depart from strict alphabetization by including multiword phrasal items and compounds under the headword of the first element, so that *dog-eat-dog* and *doghouse* appear under the entry for *dog* rather than as separate headwords in their own alphabetic positions. If one broadens the scope of dictionaries to include other word reference books such as thesauruses, there are quite a variety of works arranged nonalphabetically. (See "Conceptually vs. alphabetically arranged thesauruses," Ch. 3, p. 138.) In fact, a slavish devotion to strict alphabetization is a comparatively modern phenomenon. Early editions of Johnson's *Dictionary* contain a number of places where strings of words fall out of alphabetic sequence and no one seemed to mind very much. Perhaps the growing use of electronic dictionaries presages a period of decreasing reliance on the alphabet, and as many youths now have difficulty doing simple arithmetic calculations without the aid of automatic calculators, perhaps in time the knack of letter-by-letter alphabetization – not a simple matter for children to master – will also be forgotten. Tom McArthur, who has written widely about thematic word reference books, has commented:

In the electronic culture of the late 20th century people are acclimatizing quickly to thematic order and complex cross-referencing. In the process, these devices are losing their low peripheral status and in tandem with the PC are gaining high cultural value. In effect, the pendulum is swinging back again from an era in which alphabetic order . . . attained high status in print culture.[24]

Named after the German philologist Konrad Duden (1829–1911), the many Duden books are semantically arranged and depend on illustrations that are elaborately labeled to convey the names of real objects. A multitude of different things – the parts of a bicycle or of a motorcar, types of screws and tools, the layout of a modern kitchen with all of its appliances – are depicted and labeled. The original Duden was a monolingual work for German speakers. Oxford University Press now publishes a number of bilingual, pictorial "Oxford-Dudens" for English speakers. As a bilingual work, the Duden is one-way. For example, in *The Oxford-Duden Pictorial Spanish and English Dictionary* (1995), each label is given in Spanish, the target language, with the corresponding English word below it. Alphabetic indexes in both languages are usually provided in such works, with numerical references to the page and drawing in which the labels appear. Dudens are most useful for identifying technical or mechanical things that can be illustrated, such as machine tools, kitchen utensils, the parts of a horse, or items of clothing. They are not designed to cope with words like *justice, mercy, taxation,* or *sorrow.*

The *Longman Lexicon of Contemporary English,* by Tom McArthur, is an unusual thematic dictionary "produced with paper, pencil, pen and typewriter," without any computer database, in 1981.[25] It includes 15,000 general (chiefly nonscientific) terms arranged by subject and an alphabetic index (which includes pronunciations) along with an alphanumeric reference to each sense covered. Extremely successful, this innovative book is still in print as of this writing. Unlike a thesaurus, which assumes that the reader knows the meanings of the included words, the *Longman Lexicon* is designed for people who do not know the meanings of related words and has set up an apparatus to teach them what they are. It is essentially a vocabulary builder divided into hierarchies of meaning, with definitions drawn from the *Longman Dictionary of Contemporary English* (1978) and with many composite pictures (as in those of a pictorial Duden) in which implements, kinds of apparel, and the like, are labeled. A number of other features common to ESL dictionaries are also included; it is rich in illustrative examples, for instance, and gives elaborate grammatical information.

In the same vein, but more specifically to aid intermediate-level foreign learners in expressing themselves, the purpose of the *Longman Essential Activator* (1997) is aptly stated in the book's subtitle: "Put Your Ideas Into Words." This is a book that *was* created from a database (derived from the more advanced *Longman Language Activator* (1994)), and that draws upon the Longman language corpus and the British National Corpus to provide examples of authentic usage. It is actually a thematic thesaurus with many built-in aids for foreign learners (including many illustrations) to help them distinguish between synonyms and related words, with examples and usage advice freely given. For example, *happy* is divided into six senses: (1) "feeling happy," under which *happy, cheerful,* and *be in a good mood* are distinguished, with examples of each; (2) "happy because something good has happened," under which *happy, pleased, glad, delighted,* and *satisfied* appear; (3) "a happy feeling," under which *happiness, pleasure, satisfaction,* and *joy* are given; (4) "happy because you are no longer worried about something," under which *relieved* and *relief* appear; (5) "to make someone feel happy," under which *make sb [somebody] happy, please, satisfying,* and *cheer up* are given; and (6) "to feel happy again after feeling sad," under which *cheer up* appears. All of these words are also accessible from an index. The dictionary also contains many cross-references to related words and to "opposites" and often indicates whether a particular word used in a specific way is usually spoken or usually written. A separate thematic listing titled "Essential Communication" gives advice about language to be used in various social interactions, such as "permission," "complaining," "apologizing," "saying Yes" or "saying No." This kind of information is commonly used in ESL instructional courses in texts and videos, but the *Longman Essential Activator* is one of the first to attempt to integrate interactional language use within the framework of a monolingual dictionary/thesaurus. This would not be possible without using a corpus of spoken English. (For further information about the use of a corpus, see Ch. 6, "The corpus in lexicography.")

There are similar thematic dictionaries for encoding in bilingual lexicography as well. The *Cambridge Word Selector* (1995), for example, is designed to help Spanish speakers learn how to express themselves in English. Illustrated with Duden-type pictures with labels in both the target language (English) and in Spanish, groups of synonyms and near-synonyms are listed together under an English word, with its Spanish equivalent. For example, one finds a heading *Remember (Recordar)*, and entries for *recall, recollect, memory*, and *memorable*, with definitions in Spanish and with illustrative examples in English, followed by their Spanish equivalents. As in the *Longman Essential Activator*, there is also a section providing advice on linguistic behavior in interactional situations, such as *Persuading, Making Arrangements*, and *Praising*. English expressions are given, qualified if necessary with usage labels in Spanish (e.g., to indicate informality), followed by the equivalent Spanish expression.

The *Random House Webster's Word Menu*, by Stephen Glazer, is an unusual thematically arranged word-reference book. Published originally in 1992, it resembles a thesaurus, since it is arranged according to a thematic hierarchy, but is in other respects a dictionary, because within each subject category one finds a list of terms that are conventionally defined. For example, *Part Three – Domestic Life* is subdivided into *The Home, The Family, Eating*, and *Clothing*. Under *The Home* one finds further subdivisions into *Buildings, Exterior Structure, Interior Structure, Furnishings*, and *Ornamental and Functional Articles*. Each of these subdivisions is subdivided once again. *Buildings* is subdivided into *Living Places* and *Types of Buildings*. Under *Living Places* we find an alphabetical list of words with definitions: *abode, accommodations, apartment*, etc.; under *Types of Buildings* we find entries such as *barn, barracks, basilica,* etc. – quite a disparate group of buildings! There is an exhaustive index at the back of the book where every word can be located. Because the organization of the *Word Menu* is based on things rather than concepts, it is more like a Duden than like a standard thesaurus, but instead of depicting objects graphically it gives written definitions of them. Moreover, it is not entirely confined to describing actual things; it also contains many lists, as of countries, and of plants and animals. Like the *Longman Essential Activator,* the *Word Menu* is designed to help the user who has an idea find the word to express it, but it is a very different sort of book, seeking to invest structure on the entire universe of material things and encyclopedic subjects, and it is intended for the native speaker, not the foreign learner. The *Longman Essential Activator* is a much more focused and more consistently structured book, produced at a high level of professional lexicographic skill. The *Word Menu* has the earmarks of an immensely dedicated but eccentric individual effort, filled with oddities that are peculiar to it and that no doubt make it endearing to some of its users.

There are still other kinds of nonalphabetic dictionaries. Crossword puzzle dictionaries are often arranged by the number of letters in each word. All three-letter words are listed together alphabetically, followed by all four-letter words (used as a phrase, not as a lexical unit!), five-letter words, and so on. Thus the harried crossword-puzzler can more easily find the answer to his quest. Rhyming dictionaries, which are very old, are arranged according to the sound of the ultimate syllables of each word. John Walker produced a rhyming dictionary in 1775 that went through countless editions and was still in print in the early twentieth century.

Note that even most thematically organized word-reference books include an alphabetical index to the words included. Because it taps a universal skill among the literate, alphabetization is the only sure way of arranging words for quick access in print, although alphabetization itself is not always as routine as it may appear. There are many ways to alphabetize, and in scientific and technical vocabularies in particular the decisions that must be made in alphabetizing are by no means simple, as we shall see in Ch. 3. Once we leave the world of books, however, and rely on electronic products, alphabetization – though it may be the basis of computerized indexing – plays no visible role for the user. Soon we shall be able to talk to our computers – say a word or phrase – and receive an immediate graphic and audible response, and then the alphabet will have been completely vanquished.

Manner of financing

Dictionaries differ in how they are financed and in the expectation of profit. Scholarly dictionaries, such as the *Dictionary of American Regional English* at the University of Wisconsin or the *Middle English Dictionary* at the University of Michigan, are usually funded by government agencies or foundation grants in addition to university support, supplemented by individual donations, and are not designed to make money for investors. Such long-term projects often run into financial difficulties, and some have been aborted and abandoned after years of work. Often the editors of scholarly dictionaries have to devote much of their time and effort to fund-raising rather than lexicography, thus prolonging the duration of the project. Commercial dictionaries, such as the Random House or Merriam-Webster line of dictionaries in the US and Longman or Collins in the UK, are supported by private investors who expect to make money.

In market appeal, scholarly dictionaries resemble specialized commercial dictionaries, such as a dictionary of building terms or electrical engineering. In both cases the market is sharply defined, but within that cross section of the public, interest in the dictionary is likely to be high. In the jargon of publishers, the market is vertical. General commercial dictionaries, on the other hand, appeal to a broad spectrum of the population, but this spectrum's attachment to the particular work is relatively weak; the market for it is horizontal. The primary purpose of the scholarly dictionary is to describe data and communicate knowledge; a secondary purpose may be to promote the name of the supporting institution or to acquire prestige for it by publishing a major work. The primary purpose of a commercial dictionary is to make money, although to the people writing it the day-to-day purpose is usually indistinguishable from that of a scholarly dictionary. The real difference is that the commercial lexicographer is in the business of communicating knowledge, whereas the scholarly lexicographer is not engaged in business, though he is often enough engaged in raising funds.

Scholarly dictionaries may take many years to complete. The field work for the *Dictionary of American Regional English* was conducted in 1965–70, and the first volume was published in 1985; by 1996, two additional volumes had been published, taking the dictionary through the letter O. The *Middle English Dictionary* began publishing parts in 1952 and by the end of the millennium was nearing completion in print, though an electronic version had by then been made available. Commercial dictionaries are done at a much accelerated rate, though often not fast enough to satisfy their publishers. However, the pressure to produce quickly is not confined to commercial lexicographers:

When one thinks of tying up $2 million for five or six years and imagines what one could do with that money by investing it, one can see why scheduling is so important, and what an unusual act of faith it is to put so much money into the making of a dictionary. During all those years of preparation, no money is coming in. Voices have been known to be raised at board of directors' meetings about whether this is the best use of such a large amount of money. The pressure gets transmitted, ultimately, to the editor in chief. Anyone who has read *Caught in the Web of Words*, the biography of James A. H. Murray, the chief editor of the *Oxford English Dictionary*, knows what severe pressure even so distinguished a lexicographer as Murray was placed under, and what ignominious explanations he was forced to make to defend himself. And the *OED* is hardly a commercial dictionary. His situation was all too typical. Every working lexicographer has had similar experiences.[26]

Commercial lexicographers often resist intense pressures, sometimes even at the threat of losing their jobs, to maintain the standards they feel they must. The argument is seldom represented as an ethical imperative, which would compel any corporate financial officer to regard one as a lunatic, but on the safe, hard-headed, practical grounds of keeping the quality on a level with the competition in order to preserve sales. Only in the privacy of one's own home is one free to indulge in good intentions. In any event, the wonder is that the level of commercial dictionary making is so high on both sides of the Atlantic in spite of these pressures. Competition in the marketplace often depends upon superficial editorial features or the physical appearance of the dictionary rather than any genuine merit. In the US dictionary market, competition has done more to suppress innovation than to encourage excellence, but, in spite of this, the top American college dictionaries are of relatively high quality.[27] One can only conclude that the quality of dictionary making depends to a great extent on the traditions that some key lexicographers working in the field continue to maintain. The development of electronic corpora (described in Ch. 6) will require new, major investments by US dictionary publishers to keep pace with their British counterparts, who have the benefit of the British National Corpus, and without making that commitment they may well begin a long, slow, but inescapably fatal decline into mediocrity.

Age of users

Dictionaries differ in the age of the intended user: some are aimed at children, others at adults. Many of the Latin–English dictionaries of the sixteenth century and earlier were designed to help students. Indeed, as Ch. 2 will make clear, monolingual English lexicography developed from such dictionaries, and some of the earliest monolingual dictionaries were compiled by schoolmasters for the edification of young scholars and other untutored people. In this sense school dictionaries are as old as lexicography; the pedagogical purpose was original, and broader purposes developed from it. But school dictionaries as we know them, with simplified and graded vocabularies, large type, and attractive graphics, are strictly a modern development. In the early twentieth century and before, any small-sized dictionary was considered suitable for schoolchildren; no concession to simplicity was made in the treatment of vocabulary.

The pioneer in children's dictionaries was Edward L. Thorndike, who "applied the principles of the psychology of learning to dictionary making" in the 1930s.[28] Thorndike edited a series of Thorndike-Century dictionaries in the 1930s and '40s for three levels of school-age children. An educational psychologist before he was a lexicographer, Thorndike had compiled the *Teacher's Word Book* in 1921 and enlarged it in 1931 to 20,000 words. The words were listed according to their frequency of occurrence in a large corpus of material examined for this purpose. Subsequently combined with word counts of Irving Lorge and expanded to 30,000 words, the list was published in 1944 as *The Teacher's Word Book of 30,000 Words* and, in spite of its imperfections (such as the failure to discriminate between different meanings of the same word in making a count of its occurrences), the work remained for many years an extremely valuable tool for teachers, psychologists, and lexicographers. The editor of the *American College Dictionary* (1947), Clarence L. Barnhart, has said that "without the basic research that had been done on the *Thorndike-Century Senior Dictionary* . . . it would have been impossible to produce the *ACD* in the two years of its actual production."[29]

Whole series of dictionaries have now been produced, in a highly competitive market, for children of ages ranging from eight or nine years – third or fourth grade level – through senior high school. The dictionaries are usually divided into three tiers: elementary school (or beginners' dictionaries), for grades 3–5, ages 8–10; middle school, for grades 6–9, ages 11–14 or 15; and secondary school, for grades 9–12, ages

14–18. There are also various levels of "picture dictionaries" for children who are in the process of learning to read; these are often thoughtful introductions to dictionary use, but until users have acquired the skills necessary to look up a word independently and to read its definition, they are not using a dictionary, whatever it may be called.

The skills required to use a dictionary are often taken for granted by adults; teachers, however, know very well that they must be taught and are not easily mastered by everyone. One's grasp of the alphabet must be secure, and, more, one must understand conceptually the sequential way in which alphabetizing is done. Even if children can perform the operation of finding the word they seek, if it is a great chore filled with false starts they are likely to give up the battle. This is a pity, because the habit of using a dictionary is formed early in life, and if the skills to use it are neglected, the student may never be comfortable using dictionaries. Dictionary publishers have accordingly made their school dictionaries as inviting as possible. The type is large, the format attractive, and color illustrations abound. In fact, it has been suggested that children's dictionaries have been made so attractive and simplified that they do not prepare children adequately for adult dictionaries. Some critics have claimed that the use of school dictionaries actually discourages children from using adult dictionaries, which by comparison are formidable books filled with small type and small, spare illustrations.

The theory underlying school dictionaries, begun by Thorndike's analysis of the frequency of word use, is that dictionaries for children should be written in words that children can understand. This may appear to be a truism, but it is not. One learns new words by encountering them, either in speech or writing, and by making a shrewd guess, based on the context in which they occur and one's knowledge of similar words in similar contexts, as to what they mean. It is therefore not self-evident that a dictionary or any other book for children should avoid using words that challenge readers to add new words to their vocabularies. On the other hand, users of dictionaries are presumably already on the track of a new word and would be ill served by spicing the special context of definition with another word they don't know.

If one accepts the latter view, it follows that the children's dictionary should have a controlled vocabulary. Now in one sense every dictionary's vocabulary is controlled; every word used in a definition is, or ought to be, itself defined as an entry. But some children's dictionaries go further, confining the defining vocabulary to a more limited range than that embraced by the entry words. (Some dictionaries for foreign learners also use limited defining vocabularies.) Moreover, some children's dictionaries have graded vocabularies; that is, they assign a grade level to each vocabulary entry and attempt to define that entry in words presumably understood by most children at that grade level. I say "attempt" advisedly, because the vocabulary skills of children at any grade level are highly variable, and the state of knowledge of these skills is still very imperfect. As a practical matter, it would be impossible to define every term by other words at the same or a lower grade level, even if we knew what they were. (See Ch. 6, pp. 283–4, for a discussion of the *American Heritage Word Frequency Book* (1971), one of the first computerized studies of graded vocabularies.)

Although there may be some justice to the charge that school dictionaries retard the rate at which some children acquire adult dictionary skills, surely this is overbalanced by the benefit to the far greater number of children who would otherwise find dictionary use a daunting experience. Too, a good teacher will encourage bright students to use adult dictionaries as soon as their skills are equal to the task.

Period of time covered

Dictionaries differ in the period of time covered by their lexicons. Diachronic, or historical, dictionaries deal with an extended period of time, often centuries, with the chief purpose of tracing the development of forms and meanings of each headword over the period covered. Etymology is thus an integral part of such a work, since it illustrates how form and meaning have changed. Indeed, etymological dictionaries are specialized diachronic dictionaries. Synchronic dictionaries, by contrast, deal with a narrow band of time and attempt to represent the lexicon as it exists or existed at a particular point in time – not necessarily the present. Almost all the commercial, one-volume dictionaries available in the US and Britain are synchronic, including the unabridged *Webster's Third New International Dictionary* (*NID3*). Of course, no dictionary can be purely synchronic, since it takes years to produce any dictionary, and even synchronic dictionaries include some archaic forms.[30] Larger synchronic dictionaries such as *NID3* take in a broader band of time than smaller works. As a rule, archaic and obsolete words are the first to go when a dictionary is abridged. Thus in synchronic dictionaries etymology is less important, and the representation of neologisms, current slang, and scientific and technical terms is more important than it is in diachronic works.

Major diachronic dictionaries are chiefly of scholarly interest. They are therefore usually undertaken by universities or their presses, and they often take a very long time to complete. The *Oxford English Dictionary* (*OED*) was originally planned to take ten years but actually took nearly fifty (1879–1928); nor does this include the twenty years before, during which the millions of citations forming the basis of the definitions were collected. Zgusta cites two other diachronic dictionaries, one Dutch and the other Swedish, that took sixty-five years each to produce, and a Danish work that took forty-nine years. In each case they were planned to take one quarter or less of the actual time required.[31] The *Dictionary of the Older Scottish Tongue*, a historical dictionary of the Scots language up to 1700, was first proposed in 1915 by Sir William Craigie, one of the *OED*'s editors. Work began before 1921, and the first fascicle was published ten years later; by the end of 1999, seven volumes had been published, and the dictionary had reached part way into the letter S. If the remainder of the schedule is met, the dictionary will have taken about seventy years. This would hardly set a record. The *Deutsches Wörterbuch* begun by Jacob and Wilhelm Grimm – known popularly for their fairy tales but to students of language for their discoveries of systematic sound change in philology – was not completed until 1960, over a century after it was begun.

Size

Dictionaries differ in how fully they cover the lexicon. Since the size of the lexicon varies from language to language, the number of entries in a dictionary is a measure only of its relative size compared with other dictionaries of the same language. As Zgusta has observed, only dead languages can be exhaustively described in a dictionary, because "no new sentences are produced in a dead language."[32] Whenever the possibility exists of new utterances being generated, there is the likelihood that new senses and new words will also be generated.

How large is the English lexicon? Allen Walker Read has estimated its extent at about 4 million words.[33] He adduces this figure by citing 700,000 words in the Merriam-Webster files (in the early 1970s) and at least 1 million words in the scientific vocabulary. There are in addition nonce words (words coined for a particular occasion), regional expressions, slang, neologisms (new words), exotic words (words introduced from other languages and not yet naturalized), trade names, and words derived from place names, such as *New Yorker* or *Michigander*. Read's was as good a guess as any, but even so it is not very meaningful. Does one include all obsolete words and all forms (or spellings) of each of them? If one admits lexical units larger than words, where does one draw the line? How shall we define *word*? Scholars have long disputed the answer to this question, and the best answer anyone has come up with so far is "a string of letters with a space at the beginning and end," which is serviceable for computerized studies but not very satisfactory conceptually, as it does not include many meaningful units of language that, according to this definition, consist of more than one word. When we ask how many words there are in the English language, surely we do not mean to exclude phrasal verbs like *make up* (as in, "She made up the story") or compounds like *middle class*. Are proper nouns to be considered words? Read's estimate of the extent of the scientific vocabulary was far too low even when he made it, and it is much larger now. For example, the website of Chemical Abstracts Service informs us that its databases, *Chemical Abstracts* and *Registry*, include "about 15 million document records and more than 21 million substance records respectively." Every year the list grows larger. Are these lexical units? Many chemical compounds are of great importance in industry and medicine, and some, like *sodium bicarbonate* and *potassium nitrate*, are included in general dictionaries. Current medical terms – excluding chemical compounds used in medicine, and excluding obsolete terms – probably add up to about 200,000. These include many Latin anatomical words and expressions; are these to be considered English? They are when used in medicine and they're not when used otherwise.

The question, "How many words are there in English?" cannot be answered in any satisfactory way. It depends on what one means by "words" and by "English," and even if one could decide the limits to each, the answer would be little more than a guess.

It is widely but erroneously believed that an unabridged dictionary includes all the words in the language. The last synchronic, unabridged dictionary of the English language was *Webster's Third New International Dictionary* (*NID3*), published in 1961.[34] It contains 450,000 words, and as its editor, Philip Babcock Gove, explains in the Preface, it omitted all those terms that had become obsolete by 1755 "unless found in well-known major works of a few major writers," a comment that echoes Samuel Johnson's criterion for including obsolete words in his *Dictionary* of 1755. Gove also remarks that "the number of words available is always far in excess of . . . the number that can possibly be included."[35] The only other dictionary of English that might be called unabridged is the *OED*, which, with the publication of the *Supplements* (1971–86) and, in 1989, of the *Second Edition* (*OED2*), substantially increased its coverage of the vocabulary of the modern period, especially of scientific terms. Even so, there are many gaps in the coverage of *OED2*; indeed, nobody is more aware of this than the current editors of *OED2*, who are hard at work preparing a major new edition. "Most of the current edition [i.e., the Second Edition, 1989] is completely unchanged since the Dictionary was first published between 1884 and 1928," writes John Simpson, its chief editor.[36] In spite of the nonpareil status of the *OED2*, it cannot be said to do the work of an unabridged dictionary of the current period.

As we shall see in the next chapter, the unabridged dictionary was a late nineteenth-century to mid-twentieth-century American phenomenon, having no parallel in Britain. As a genre, the unabridged dictionary is one that gives full coverage to the lexicon in general use at a particular time in the history of a language and substantial coverage to specialized lexicons, with quotations given to support its definitions, illustrate context, and suggest typical varieties of usage. By "general use" I mean in common use in the public press and in ordinary speech in both informal and reserved styles (such as those used in business), as distinguished from specialized lexicons such as those of law, medicine, or the physical sciences. In practice, *unabridged* has meant a dictionary of 400,000 to 600,000 entries. (See "The unabridged dictionary in America: the passing of an era," Ch. 2, p. 84.) In the sense of "not abridged," *unabridged* is a misnomer, since many smaller dictionaries are also not abridged from a larger work. They may be based, for example, on a collection of glossaries, or be derived from several other dictionaries.

The next recognized category is that of US college dictionaries, which currently claim to have between 160,000 and 180,000 entries. These are by far the most popular hardcover dictionaries in the US. There is a comparable stratum in the UK, but it is not as well defined and it has never been specifically linked to university students. Dictionaries are still an optional purchase for many people in the UK, whereas in the US the publishing industry has succeeded in convincing every family that their continuing literacy depends crucially on owning a dictionary. Entry counts matter more in the US than in Britain, but there are worrisome signs that statistical claims are gaining ground in the UK as well. Each new competitor who enters the market asserts his superiority by putting big numbers on his dictionary's dust jacket, and venerable dictionary

houses have found they cannot rely on their names alone to sell dictionaries as they once did. As we shall see in Ch. 3 (see p. 109), almost anything in bold type can count as an entry. Modest exaggeration is to be
expected, but in evaluating a publisher's claims for entry totals, one must
always take into account the possibility of plain prevarication.[37] This
caution applies, by the way, to claims of corpus size (see Ch. 6) as well as
of entry count. In the US, college dictionaries have inexorably slipped
upward in entry count, like gliders wafting on hot air. (See Ch. 2,
"American college dictionaries and their British cousins," p. 90.)

Dictionaries intermediate in size between college and unabridged,
like the *Random House Dictionary, Second Edition*, with 315,000 entries
(including many names and encyclopedic entries), have been called
"semi-unabridged." The *Encarta World English Dictionary* and the *New
Oxford Dictionary of English* claim between 350,000 and 400,000 "references" or "words, phrases and definitions" adding up to that total, using
a system of counting, I suspect, that is other than decimal, and which in
any case is never explained. Are entries counted separately or in addition to the definitions contained within them? This is rather like claiming a tax exemption for a family as well as for each member of it. My
guess is that these dictionaries all have only slightly more entries than
college dictionaries and are in the 180,000–200,000 range, mostly
because they include many more encyclopedic entries, but they are
printed in a larger, 3-column format and include other features that
make them look more like an unabridged dictionary. The *Random House
Dictionary* has considerably more text than any of them.

One step below the college dictionaries are the desk dictionaries –
hard-covered books but with substantially fewer entries (and a lower
price to match) than college dictionaries, generally in the range of
60,000 to 80,000 entries. They not only have fewer entries but their
definitions are briefer and fewer senses are given for each word.
Etymologies, if given at all, are in telescoped form. Pronunciations are
usually included. Often, as in school dictionaries, vulgar and taboo
words are omitted.

The next step takes us to the paperback dictionaries. Trade paperbacks, which may be identical to a hardcover edition or abridged from
it, are usually about 6 by 9 inches. Many thesauruses have trade paperback editions, and this size is often used for specialized dictionaries, such
as for astronomy or the computer sciences. Though cheaper than corresponding hardcover editions, they are not necessarily cheap. The least

expensive dictionaries are mass-market paperbacks, usually about 4 by 6 inches or smaller. If one's primary need is for a spelling book they are a good buy, but their definitions are often little more than strings of synonyms. They may include pronunciations but seldom etymologies; given their size, this is a sensible omission. They often include useful encyclopedic information such as small maps, population statistics, and the like. Because of the cheap paper used and the massive print runs employed in their manufacture, the quality of printing tends to vary greatly. They are very popular with students because they are light, cheap, and easy to carry about.

Scope of coverage by subject

Dictionaries differ in scope in respect to the subjects they cover. I make a distinction between dictionaries confined to a special subject, such as law or medicine, and dictionaries limited to an aspect of language, such as a pronouncing dictionary or a slang dictionary. The latter will be addressed in the next section.

"Special-field" dictionaries, to use Barnhart's term, have been with us for a long time. Medical and legal dictionaries in Latin, and dictionaries of military and nautical science, in particular, existed long before the development of English monolingual dictionaries. Today's interest in specialized vocabularies is by no means unique but rather carries on the tradition of earlier English dictionaries such as *Cocker's English Dictionary* of 1704, which boasted of the inclusion of many military and commercial terms. John Harris' *Lexicon Technicum*, also of 1704, was an early subject-field dictionary, in Latin, devoted to terms in the sciences and the arts and is of considerable importance in the history of English lexicography.

Subject-field dictionaries, like scholarly dictionaries, are directed to a vertical and restricted market. Unlike scholarly dictionaries, however, which as a rule are entirely descriptive and lexical, subject-field dictionaries often have a normative purpose as well as an informative one, and they tend to be more encyclopedic in content. It is instructive to draw a distinction between the way general words and scientific words are defined:

General words are defined on the basis of citations illustrating actual usage: the meanings are EXTRACTED from a body of evidence. . . . The meanings of scientific entries, on the other hand, are IMPOSED on the basis of expert advice. The experts may have sources apart from their own knowledge and experience, but their sources are informative or encyclopedic rather than lexical, that is, they are likely to consist of authoritative definitions composed by other experts whose concern is maintaining the internal coherence of their discipline rather than faithfully recording how terms are used. Their goal is ease and accuracy of communication between those versed in the language of science.[38]

On the other hand, it is not true to say that usage plays no part in the dictionary treatment of a scientific vocabulary. When a dozen or so terms are used to describe exactly the same concept – a common circumstance in medicine – usage is the most important criterion for determining what the preferred term should be. The problem is that it is very difficult to determine which of the variants is most widely used. Citation files for technical terms do not exist. Although electronic searches may shed light on preferred terms in subject-field databases, often the specialist is forced to rely on his own experience, which is necessarily limited in both time and place, and in cases of disputed usage is apt to be parochial. Furthermore, even if usage can determine the preferred term, it has a limited role in determining its meaning. That is usually imposed, as I have said, by the demands of the discipline rather than extracted from evidence of actual usage. For example, *Stedman's Medical Dictionary* (1995) defines *normal* as follows:

1. Typical; usual; according to the rule or standard. 2. In bacteriology, nonimmune; untreated; denoting an animal, or the serum or substance contained therein, that has not been experimentally immunized against any microorganism or its products. 3. Denoting a solution containing 1 equivalent of replaceable hydrogen or hydroxyl per liter . . . 4. In psychiatry and psychology, denoting a level of effective functioning which is satisfactory to both the individual and his social milieu.

Definition 1 is the general sense extracted from ordinary usage. Definitions 2–3 are imposed and are peculiar to bacteriology and chemistry. Definition 4 corresponds more or less to an extracted meaning in general use but is here labeled as applying to particular disciplines. It seems to be a case where the ordinary meaning of a word has been gussied up in fancy dress to look scientific.

What has changed since the mid-twentieth century is the proportion of entries in general dictionaries devoted to scientific and technical vocabulary. It is a commonplace that the specialized vocabularies of science have increased enormously in this period, but what is not so often realized is the increased weight given them in relative importance in our dictionaries, compared to the general vocabulary. I have estimated that more than 40% of the entries in *NID3* are scientific or technical, and 25–35% of those in college dictionaries.[39] Clarence Barnhart has estimated that almost 40% of the contents in college dictionaries are scientific or technical.[40] Perhaps these estimates made in the 1970s were a bit high, but the proportion of scientific and technical entries has certainly not gotten any smaller since then. The larger general dictionaries are becoming a collection of subject-field dictionaries merged with a general dictionary, which is being compressed into an ever smaller proportion of the entire work.

Why is this so? The answer is twofold. First, the growth in the vocabulary of our language has been disproportionately in the scientific and technical vocabulary. A glance at any dictionary of new words will prove the point. A typical page from *12,000 Words: A Supplement to Webster's Third New International Dictionary* contains words like *monoamine oxidase* (an enzyme), *monoclonal, monoploid*, etc. Second, and more profoundly, the greater space provided technical terms in our dictionaries mirrors the prevailing cultural view in our society that science and technology are of the highest importance.

General dictionaries have always relied chiefly on subject-field dictionaries for technical definitions. Therefore, although the chief market for specialized dictionaries is relatively restricted, their influence is in reality much broader. The inclusion of specialized scientific terms in such large numbers in our dictionaries diminishes the force of the claim that definitions are based on actual usage as revealed by a collection of quotations exemplifying particular words and meanings (a citation file) or by an examination of a corpus of texts. (See Ch. 4, p. 189.) It also introduces, even in the most determinedly descriptive work, a normative element, since such definitions often have a prescriptive purpose. The descriptive nature of the dictionary is thus substantially compromised.

There are subject-field dictionaries in almost every subject one can think of. Among the most widely used are those of law, medicine and other branches of biology, electronics, computing, and architecture. Some specialized works, however, though called dictionaries, are entirely encyclopedic in content, depending on concepts rather than terms for classifying their information. Many of the smaller dictionaries are amateurish, compiled by people who may be expert in their subjects but who are often ignorant of the basic principles for writing definitions. These works, sometimes little more than glossaries, may be entertaining but are seldom useful for the serious student. Among the notable exceptions – specialized dictionaries produced by professional lexicographers – are

Funk & Wagnalls Cook's and Diner's Dictionary: A Lexicon of Food, Wine, and Culinary Terms (1968), edited by Samuel Davis, and *Davies' Dictionary of Golfing Terms* (1980), which includes dated citations going back to the nineteenth century and which was written entirely by one man, Peter Davies, the editor-in-chief of the Second Edition of the *American Heritage Dictionary* (1982), in what was surely a labor of love. Both of these special-subject dictionaries are expertly illustrated with drawings that supplement the text.

Some special-field dictionaries are sponsored by professional organizations that appoint committees to study the nomenclature of the field, resolve cases of conflicting and disputed usage, settle on preferred terms, and write official definitions for them. The differences in international usage of the same concept, even in English, but much more so when different languages are involved, are very difficult to resolve and have confounded the experts in many disciplines, especially in medicine, for at least a century. Indeed, there is even considerable confusion over what to call reference works that attempt to classify or define technical terms. As one medical lexicographer says in despair, "Some of the names given to terminological reference works – particularly 'glossary,' 'vocabulary,' and 'dictionary' – have been so misused that there is complete confusion, and the title on the cover of a book is no safe guide to its content."[41] Figure 1 (p. 36), "Reference works dealing with concepts," is one attempt to define these troublesome terms. I would only note that the word *lexicon* is often used interchangeably with *vocabulary* in all three of the senses in which it is defined, and is so used in this book.

Limitations in the aspects of language covered

Dictionaries differ in scope in respect to the aspect of language covered. Dictionaries limited to one aspect of language are called special-purpose dictionaries by Barnhart and restricted (or special) dictionaries by Zgusta. Neither name is entirely satisfactory, but Barnhart's term is preferable because less ambiguous.

Special-purpose dictionaries range from scholarly works, such as Joseph Wright's monumental *English Dialect Dictionary* in six volumes (1898–1905), to "pop-up" picture dictionaries for preschoolers; from Charles Talbut Onions' *Oxford Dictionary of English Etymology* (1966) to popular, commercial books designed to help people increase their vocabularies or improve their style of writing or harness their usage to prescribed models of correctness – or to lure them into buying such books

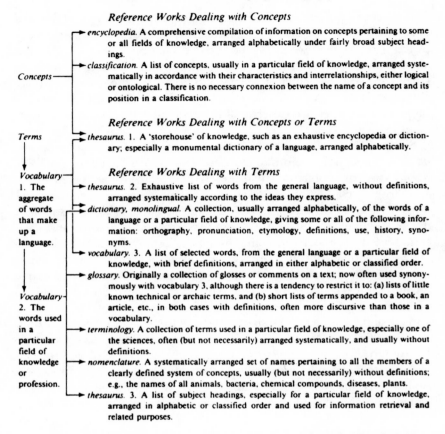

Reference Works Dealing with Concepts

→ *encyclopedia.* A comprehensive compilation of information on concepts pertaining to some or all fields of knowledge, arranged alphabetically under fairly broad subject headings.

→ *classification.* A list of concepts, usually in a particular field of knowledge, arranged systematically in accordance with their characteristics and interrelationships, either logical or ontological. There is no necessary connexion between the name of a concept and its position in a classification.

Reference Works Dealing with Concepts or Terms

→ *thesaurus.* 1. A 'storehouse' of knowledge, such as an exhaustive encyclopedia or dictionary; especially a monumental dictionary of a language, arranged alphabetically.

Reference Works Dealing with Terms

→ *thesaurus.* 2. Exhaustive list of words from the general language, without definitions, arranged systematically according to the ideas they express.

→ *dictionary, monolingual.* A collection, usually arranged alphabetically, of the words of a language or a particular field of knowledge, giving some or all of the following information: orthography, pronunciation, etymology, definitions, use, history, synonyms.

→ *vocabulary.* 3. A list of selected words, from the general language or a particular field of knowledge, with brief definitions, arranged in either alphabetic or classified order.

→ *glossary.* Originally a collection of glosses or comments on a text; now often used synonymously with vocabulary 3, although there is a tendency to restrict it to: (a) lists of little known technical or archaic terms, and (b) short lists of terms appended to a book, an article, etc., in both cases with definitions, often more discursive than those in a vocabulary.

→ *terminology.* A collection of terms used in a particular field of knowledge, especially one of the sciences, often (but not necessarily) arranged systematically, and usually without definitions.

→ *nomenclature.* A systematically arranged set of names pertaining to all the members of a clearly defined system of concepts, usually (but not necessarily) without definitions; e.g., the names of all animals, bacteria, chemical compounds, diseases, plants.

→ *thesaurus.* 3. A list of subject headings, especially for a particular field of knowledge, arranged in alphabetic or classified order and used for information retrieval and related purposes.

Concepts

Terms

Vocabulary
1. The aggregate of words that make up a language.

Vocabulary
2. The words used in a particular field of knowledge or profession.

1 Reference works dealing with concepts, terms, or both. From A. Manuila (ed.), *Progress in Medical Terminology* (Basel: S. Karger, 1981), p. 58

in the hope that they will. Such books – for here we must enlarge our survey to include reference works other than dictionaries – may deal with etymology, pronunciation, spelling, vocabulary, usage, synonymy, offensive and taboo words, slang, dialect, neologisms, and many other subjects.[42] There are scores of different types of such works, represented by many hundreds, perhaps thousands, of different titles. Although I will discuss a number of these works in various parts of this book, no systematic survey of all types is possible. Nonetheless, it may be useful to describe some major varieties.

Etymological dictionaries are alphabetic lists of words showing how the current forms were derived from older ones (called *etyma*, singular *etymon*) in the same or another language. If the earlier form had a meaning different from that of the current form, the older form is translated by an equivalent word or brief phrase in English (called a *gloss*). The current English word usually is briefly defined, merely to identify it, in each important sense. In English, the *OED* is without parallel as a source of reliable, scholarly etymologies. Onions' work, previously cited, is an excellent one-volume dictionary; it is based on the *OED* (of which Onions was one of the editors) but with many additions and corrections. It is an exemplary work, giving the century in which each sense of each word originated. *The Barnhart Dictionary of Etymology* (1988) is a welcome addition to this field, containing many words not found elsewhere. Written in a style virtually devoid of abbreviations, it is delightfully easy to understand. Walter W. Skeat's *An Etymological Dictionary of the English Language* (1879–82) is also still of value, but now mainly of historical interest. Other major etymological works are Ernest Weekley's *An Etymological Dictionary of Modern English* (1921), Eric Partridge's *Origins: A Short Etymological Dictionary of Modern English* (1958), and Ernest Klein's *A Comprehensive Etymological Dictionary of the English Language* (1971). Klein's work gives particular attention to words of Semitic origin.

Pronouncing dictionaries provide transcriptions of the sounds of speech corresponding to an alphabetic list of words so that the reader can understand how each word is usually pronounced. The classic modern works of this kind, one British and one American, are Daniel Jones' *An English Pronouncing Dictionary* (First Edition 1917) and John S. Kenyon and Thomas A. Knott's *A Pronouncing Dictionary of American English* (1944), respectively. The latter has never been revised, but Jones' book, revised by A. C. Gimson in 1967, has gone through many editions. It is intended chiefly for foreign learners and like all such books uses the International Phonetic Alphabet. A new pronouncing dictionary (1997) based on the Jones book but incorporating many new entries and including American English pronunciations is *English Pronouncing Dictionary*, edited by Daniel Jones, Peter Roach, and James Hartman. The *Longman Pronunciation Dictionary* (1990), edited by John Wells, is a leading work in British English for learners. *NID3* is still the best source of American English pronunciations for the general lexicon. A useful compendium of all kinds of names is the *Pronouncing Dictionary of Proper Names*, edited by John Bollard; it provides two transcriptions for each entry, one in the IPA and the other in a simplified respelling. Dictionaries available in CD form often include the capacity to give audible pronunciations. This is clearly superior to having to interpret a transcription; however, as of now, audible dictionary pronunciations do not give variant pronunciations. Perhaps they are the future.

Books about usage are discussed in Ch. 5. (See p. 261.)

Synonym dictionaries have existed in English since the second half of the eighteenth century. William Taylor's *English Synonyms Discriminated* (1813) and George Crabb's *English Synonymes Explained* (1816) are two early examples; a revised edition of Crabb's work was reprinted as late as 1917. In 1852, Peter Mark Roget's *Thesaurus of English Words and Phrases* appeared. Unlike earlier synonym books, it was not alphabetically arranged but organized conceptually according to an elaborate philosophical scheme. So successful was the idea that it spawned a number of similarly organized works, and the word *thesaurus*, which had until then meant an exhaustive dictionary or survey of the entire lexicon of a language (literally "storehouse"), now usually refers to a synonym dictionary, whether conceptually organized or alphabetic. Incidentally, the term *Roget's*, like *Webster's*, is in the public domain and can be used with impunity by any publisher. (See Ch. 3, "Dictionaries of synonyms," p. 134 and *Roget's* Thesaurus, p. 137.)

What is slang? Slang is usually defined as words or expressions that originated in cant (the familiar, nontechnical vocabulary restricted to a particular occupation, age group, or any group sharing a special interest), jargon (a technical vocabulary restricted to a particular occupation or special-interest group), or argot (the vocabulary peculiar to thieves and other criminals) but that have become more widely known and are used by some segments of the general population. Most slang is colorful, irreverent, or facetious, but it is not to be confused with taboo words. Although slang is often meant to shock the staid or discomfort the pretentious, it is not intended essentially to violate the proprieties of common decency, although it may, depending upon what one's proprieties are. Many taboo words are not slang, and most slang expressions do not deal with sexually or scatologically offensive concepts. As Stuart Berg Flexner has pointed out, "Many so-called bedroom words are not technically slang at all, but are sometimes associated with slang only because standard speech has rejected them as taboo."[43]

The two standard, one-volume slang dictionaries for British and American English are Eric Partridge's *A Dictionary of Slang and Unconventional English* (Eighth Edition revised by Paul Beale, 1984), which describes British slang from a historical point of view, and Wentworth and Flexner's *Dictionary of American Slang* (Second Supplemented Edition,

1975), which was based on material originally compiled by Harold Wentworth, whose *American Dialect Dictionary* (1944) was derived from these collections. Flexner added much new material and brought the work to completion. More recently, this work has been used as the basis for a substantially new though somewhat shorter dictionary, *Dictionary of American Slang* (Third Edition, 1995), edited by Robert L. Chapman. Jonathon Green's *The Cassell Dictionary of Slang* (1998) is a recent addition to this genre, impressively comprehensive in scope, though unfortunately lacking citations of actual usage. By far the most exhaustive and scholarly of slang dictionaries to date is Jonathan Lighter's multivolume *Random House Historical Dictionary of American Slang* (1994–), which includes dated citations like those of the *OED* based on an extraordinary amount of research. The extent of coverage and citational evidence is incomparably greater than any other source. The first volume appeared in 1994, the second, through the letter O, in 1997. (For more information on slang, see Ch. 5, p. 237.)

In dialect studies, the *Dictionary of American Regional English* (*DARE*) is the most important work being done in English today. Sponsored by the American Dialect Society, which had been gathering materials since 1889, it was begun in 1963 when it was placed in the capable hands of Frederic G. Cassidy as chief editor. *DARE* conducted a survey of native speakers in all parts of the United States and compiled over 1,000 lengthy questionnaires that were personally collected by fieldworkers, mostly graduate students. Projected to run to five volumes (with a sixth to include the responses to the questionnaires, plus the bibliography, maps, addenda, and corrections), three volumes have been published to date, through the letter O. Cassidy, a remarkable man revered by every lexicographer, continued to work regularly to the age of 92 until his death in June 2000. In October 2000, Joan Houston Hall, who had been listed as co-editor on volumes II and III, and who as associate editor had taken over the day-to-day management of the dictionary, was formally appointed chief editor. *DARE* is already an invaluable aid to linguistic scholarship, and its completion will be a signal event in the history of lexicography. In American dialect studies, no work based on original research of this scope had ever before been attempted, and if the work had not been undertaken when it was, much of the questionnaire data based on the recollections of old people, often in remote rural areas, would have been lost forever. (See Ch. 5, p. 221, for further information about *DARE*.)

In British dialect studies, Joseph Wright's *English Dialect Dictionary* is the outstanding work. There are also a number of linguistic atlases in both

Britain and the United States that map the geographic distribution of uses of particular vocabulary items or features of pronunciation. These are for the specialist and scholar rather than for the general public.

Collections of new words (neologisms) vary from flippant newspaper glossaries to extensive dictionaries with illustrative quotations documenting each new term. In the US, the Barnhart dictionaries of new words, published since 1963, have been leading sources. The most recent collection is *The Third Barnhart Dictionary of New English* (1990). Extensive quotations for each new word or sense are included, as well as etymological and usage information. Merriam-Webster has also issued a series of supplements to *NID3*, the latest of which is *12,000 Words* (1986). A high percentage of the new words in this collection (as in the Barnhart dictionaries) are scientific and technical. The journal *American Speech* has published for many years a feature called "Among the New Words," which chronicles new word forms, including definitions and copious citations from a variety of sources. A collection of the first fifty years of these articles was published with definitions and an index compiled by John Algeo as *Fifty Years Among the New Words: A Dictionary of Neologisms, 1941–1991*. The *OED* has issued three volumes of "additions" – items being prepared for the next edition – called *Oxford English Dictionary Additions Series*; the last volume was published in 1997.

Dictionaries of idioms are limited to expressions that in more or less fixed combination convey distinctive meanings. In the history of this genre, *The Kenkyusha Dictionary of Current English Idioms* (1964) plays a prominent role as one of the earliest historical, scholarly dictionaries of this type. It is an impressive work, organized by key words, with clear, accurate definitions and extensive citations illustrating each idiom. Its coverage is now dated, however, and incomplete. One of the earliest collections published in the US was *A Dictionary of Idioms for the Deaf*, edited by Maxine Tull Boatner, which first appeared in 1966. It was subsequently revised and enlarged by Adam Makkai; the Third Edition (1995), retitled *A Dictionary of American Idioms*, appears under the editorship of Makkai, Boatner, and J. Edward Gates, and contains over 8,000 entries. It is intended mainly for foreign learners. Another large collection of idioms, unusual in not being targeted especially at foreign learners, is Christine Ammer's *The American Heritage Dictionary of Idioms* (1997), which claims nearly 10,000 entries.

One of the most comprehensive and thorough collections of idioms is the *Oxford Dictionary of Current Idiomatic English* (in two volumes, 1975 and 1983). Volume I, edited by A. P. Cowie and R. Mackin, deals entirely with idioms consisting of verbs with prepositions and particles; volume II, edited by Cowie, Mackin, and I. R. McCaig, deals with phrase, clause, and sentence idioms. Both volumes are densely packed with grammatical and other information, and both draw upon extensive citations of actual usage to illustrate their entries. They are not the easiest books to use if one wants to exploit all they have to offer – the explanatory introduction runs to eighty-one pages – but they are easy enough to use for basic lexical information, and the level of comprehensiveness and sheer lexicographic invention are very impressive.

Less comprehensive but much easier to use are the dictionaries of idioms published by virtually every ESL publishing house, usually as fairly inexpensive paperbacks, for a wide range of learners, not just those at an advanced level. These idioms dictionaries are intended to help learners use these expressions, not just to understand them. The better dictionaries, such as the *Collins Cobuild Dictionary of Idioms* (1995), are derived from a corpus of texts and are based on the authentic use of language rather than made-up examples. (See Ch. 6, "The corpus in lexicography," p. 273.)

There are also dictionaries of foreign words and phrases, dictionaries of acronyms, and dictionaries of abbreviations. The chief difficulty with such works is that the criteria for selecting entries are often uncertain. Presumably a dictionary of foreign words should include only those terms that are in the process of becoming assimilated but are not yet accepted as English. Admittedly, the decision is often difficult, but in practice such dictionaries routinely include patently foreign terms.

An abbreviation is a shortened form for a word or phrase, consisting of part of the word or the first letter of each of the words in the phrase, or sometimes the first two letters. An acronym is a form of abbreviation composed of the first or the first two letters, or a syllable, from each of the words in a compound term or phrase, so ordered that the resulting series of letters is usually pronounced as a word. The distinction between abbreviations and acronyms is often arbitrary because the same designation may be pronounced by some as a word and by others by reciting the names of the letters, as the military term *AWOL* for absent without leave. Some dictionaries of abbreviations and acronyms are limited to a particular field, such as medicine or law, and these may be particularly useful, since their narrower focus would theoretically suggest more complete coverage. In practice, however, many of these works are haphazardly put together; one finds common abbreviations in the discipline missing and numerous abbreviations that one has reason to doubt ever existed. My guess is that the compilers of abbreviation and acronym dictionaries tend to copy from one another, sometimes uncritically, and that "ghost" abbreviations are thus created.

A *ghost word* is a word that has never existed in actual usage but that appears in dictionaries through the lexicographer's error. Ghost words are introduced in dictionaries iatrogenically, so to speak, as diseases are sometimes introduced in well patients by the physician's treatment. Once a term is in a dictionary it acquires the quiet authority of print and may spread to other innocent dictionaries, thus acquiring more authority, until it appears by virtue of its ubiquitous representation to be firmly established in the language. The medical literature abounds with mistranslations of diseases into expressions that had never been used in the target language but for which meanings were invented based on the mistranslations. These ghost terms were subsequently adopted as genuine by other works in the target language until they gained widespread currency, much to the confusion of all concerned.[44]

Another fertile branch of lexicography owes its existence to the study of names (*onomastics*). In this field *A Dictionary of Surnames* (1988), edited by Patrick Hanks and Flavia Hodges, stands out as an exemplary work, providing explanations for the origins of names when this is possible, and conjectures when it is not, and listing many variant spellings. The same editors have also compiled *A Dictionary of First Names* (1990). With the help of many advisers and a huge databank of names, Hanks is now engaged in editing a large dictionary of American family names; given the immigration history of the US and the range of nationalities represented, the task will not be easy, but Hanks promises that every name borne by more than one hundred families in the US will get an entry.[45]

CHAPTER 2

A brief history of English lexicography

The history of English lexicography usually consists of a recital of successive and often successful acts of piracy. Representing what may be the least inspiring of all seminal works, Robert Cawdrey's *A Table Alphabeticall* . . . of 1604 is generally accounted to be the first English dictionary.[1] It incorporated almost 90% of the words of Edmund Coote's *English Schoole-Master*, a grammar, prayer book, and lexicon with brief definitions published in 1596. Moreover, about half of Cawdrey's three thousand entries were taken from a Latin-English dictionary of 1587, Thomas Thomas' *Dictionarium Linguae Latinae et Anglicanae*. The early history of English lexicography is little more than a record of judicious or flagrant copying from one's predecessors, sometimes with grudging acknowledgment, more often (at least in the seventeenth century) without.

Some of the eighteenth- and nineteenth-century lexicographers publicly acknowledged their indebtedness to specific predecessors. Sad to say, such honesty disappeared in the twentieth century and is not likely to be restored in the twenty-first. The pressures of the marketplace dictate that every dictionary be "new." A really new dictionary would be a dreadful piece of work, missing innumerable basic words and senses, replete with absurdities and unspeakable errors, studded with biases and interlarded with irrelevant provincialisms. Fortunately, very few dictionaries are really new, and none of the general, staff-written, commercial dictionaries published by major dictionary houses are. One would think any historian mad who claimed that his new general history was entirely new, spun freshly from his brain without being firmly based on the accumulated store of histories preceding his. Yet the public expects general dictionaries – which are, even if synchronic, histories of the usage of language – to be new in this sense. They are not. They never were and they never will be.

Modern lexicographers look very carefully at each other's work. The working lexicographer simply does not have time to redo the work of hundreds of years of lexicography and analyze the meanings of *set*, for example, which take up more than eighteen pages in the *OED*. Working with an enormous collection of actual usages of *set* in all of its senses could take a highly skilled lexicographer two months or more of uninterrupted work to sort them out and define them. Listen to James A. H. Murray, the chief editor of the *OED*, who worked with thousands of slips of paper (called *citations*), each consisting of a quoted passage containing the word under consideration:

> Only those who have made the experiment know the bewilderment with which an editor or sub-editor, after he has apportioned the quotations for such a word as *above* . . . among 20, 30 or 40 groups, and furnished each of these with a provisional definition, spreads them out on a table or on the floor where he can obtain a general survey of the whole, and spends hour after hour in shifting them about like the pieces on a chess-board, striving to find in the fragmentary evidence of an incomplete historical record, such a sequence of meanings as may form a logical chain of development. Sometimes the quest seems hopeless; recently, for example, the word *art* utterly baffled me for several days: something *had* to be done with it: something was done and put in type; but the renewed consideration of it in print, with the greater facility of reading and comparison which this afforded, led to the entire pulling to pieces and reconstruction of the edifice, extending to several columns of type . . . those who think that such work can be hurried, or that anything can accelerate it, except more brain power brought to bear on it, had better try.[2]

And this was said by the man who was possibly the finest lexicographer in the entire history of English dictionary making. Few modern commercial publishers have an instinct for scholarship so pure that they will spend millions of dollars to redo what other, better scholars have done before them. Although the use of an electronically stored collection of texts (called *corpora*, singular *corpus*), as we shall see in Chapter 6, has replaced many of the functions of the old paper citation files and dramatically improved the capacity of the lexicographer to examine and analyze words in their contexts, it has not lessened the amount of work to be done in defining words like *set* in a large dictionary. The lexicographer, facing a computer display of thousands of uses of *set* (or *art*), will have no easier time than Murray, and may find it even harder to limit the extent of his search than Murray did, since the corpus evidence for such a word will be potentially huge and easily accessible. On the other hand, the ordinary word-processing functions of a computer give modern lexicographers (and all writers) the ability to see what they have written "in type" when it can be easily changed, avoiding the delay and the expense of using printed galley proofs, which were used in dictionary work in Murray's time and for nearly a century after it.

Before we begin to fulminate at the supposed chicanery of the early English lexicographers, we had best reflect that modern lexicographers, though more discreet, depend heavily on their predecessors as well, and often the line between using another dictionary as a source or reference and copying its definition with trivial changes is a fine one.

EARLY BILINGUAL DICTIONARIES

The earliest word reference books for English-speaking people were bilingual glossaries that provided English equivalents for Latin or French words. In the Middle Ages, as early as the eighth century, difficult words in manuscripts were sometimes glossed, just as current editions of Shakespeare annotate obsolete words for the modern student, with easier Latin words or with the Old English (Anglo-Saxon) equivalent. The practice continued through the sixteenth century. Schoolmasters sometimes collected the glosses and listed them together; the resulting collection, called a *glossarium*, is today called a *glossary*. Although the word *dictionarius* was used as early as 1225 for a list of Latin words, no such term was applied to anything we would recognize as a dictionary until the sixteenth century. Sir Thomas Elyot's Latin-English work of 1538 was originally called *Dictionary*, then *Bibliotheca Eliotae*.

English-Latin dictionaries also appeared very early as teaching aids. The *Promptorium Parvulorum, sive Clericorum* ("storehouse [of words] for Children or Clerics"), the earliest known English-Latin dictionary, may have been written as early as 1440.[3] Caxton introduced printing in England in 1476, and in 1480 he printed a French-English glossary without a title. The *Promptorium* appeared in print in 1499 and is one of the earliest printed books in England. In 1553 John Withals published a little English-Latin teaching manual called *A Shorte Dictionarie for Yong Begynners*, which proved to be very popular and went through many editions. It is arranged thematically rather than alphabetically.

In 1500, the first printed Latin-English dictionary appeared, *Hortus Vocabularum* ("garden of words"), bearing on its title page "Ortus Vocabularum," by which name it is also known. This is an alphabetically arranged collection of glossaries, falsely claiming to include all of the terms in four different glossaries. Gabriele Stein remarks, "It is interesting to note that we find this hyperbolic feature already in the first printed [Latin-]English dictionary: to claim that the *Ortus* contains all the meanings listed in the four dictionaries . . . is simply absurd."[4] Sir Thomas Elyot's *Dictionary* of 1538, also a Latin-English dictionary, was absorbed in 1565 by a much larger and more important work by Thomas Cooper, *Thesaurus Linguae Romanae et Britannicae* ("thesaurus of the Roman tongue and the British"), which influenced seventeenth-century monolingual dictionaries. As related in Aubrey's *Lives*, Cooper's wife, apparently a woman of volatile temper,

> was irreconcileably angrie with him for sitting-up late at night so, compileing his Dictionary . . . When he had half-donne it, she had the opportunity to gett into his studie, tooke all his paines out in her lap, and threw it into the fire, and burnt it. Well, for all that, that good man had so great a zeale for the advancement of learning, that he began it again, and went through with it to that Perfection that he hath let it to us, a most usefull Worke.[5]

Although Latin was the most commonly preferred second language in bilingual dictionaries, the Renaissance inspired interest in other languages as well, and Spanish, French, and Italian were not ignored. In 1598, John Florio's massive *A Worlde of Wordes* appeared. This Italian-English dictionary, intended for speakers of English, was far ahead of its day in many respects, and by comparison the early English dictionaries are mean affairs. Florio was "the first compiler of a modern-language dictionary to have listed the sources from which his headword list had been drawn."[6] He included citations for contemporary Italian authors in illustration of some definitions, a practice that was not adopted in any systematic way in English lexicography until the time of Johnson 150 years later. He included slang and even what we would now call taboo words, such as *pesca* (peach) in the sense of a "yoong man's bum" and *fava* (bean) as a vulgar word for penis. In his definition of *fottere*, Florio's work includes one of the earliest printed records of *fuck*: "to iape, to sard, to fucke, to swiue, to occupy."[7]

EARLY ENGLISH DICTIONARIES AND THE "HARD WORDS" TRADITION

Although Cawdrey's dictionary is most often accepted as the first dictionary, in truth the right of primacy in English lexicography is a dubious and feeble privilege. The history of lexicography includes no breathtaking innovations or bursts of creativity that leave us in awe, as do some discoveries in the sciences and some masterpieces of art. It is rather a succession of slow and uneven advances in vocabulary and methodology, tempered always in its early stages by outrageous promotional blather consisting in equal parts of self-deification and attacks on the very predecessors whose works one has systematically rifled and without which one's own dictionary would have been impossible. The first English dictionary occurred almost inevitably as a modification of bilingual dictionaries, some of them of far greater importance. The only importance in being first in this case is that of providing an answer to the question, What was the first English dictionary?

The entire stock of English words in the fifteenth century was a mere fraction of what it is today, and it sometimes became necessary to turn to other languages to provide descriptions of things for which no English word existed. The interest in Renaissance learning naturally made the classical languages, particularly Latin, a favorite source. For those unacquainted with Latin, dictionaries were needed to translate into the English vernacular a multitude of "hard words" based on Latin. Later called contemptuously *inkhorn* terms, not without justification, since the coinages went far beyond what was necessary for utility or clarity, they often represented little more than the writer's desire to appear elegant and sophisticated at the expense of the reader's understanding.

Most of the early lexicographers were schoolmasters who compiled glossaries or dictionaries as teaching aids for their students, since there was little else available. In this tradition, Richard Mulcaster listed some 8,000 English words without definitions in his *Elementarie* (1582), which he considered worthy of inclusion in a dictionary. Mulcaster was an unusually independent thinker. He defended the use of foreign terms in English but insisted they be completely Anglicized and assimilated by the language. For him, English was primary, and he made no apologies for it. He defined the power and serviceability of English at a time when such sentiments were not commonplace, and expressed the need for a dictionary of the English language.[8] Thomas Thomas' *Dictionarium Linguae Latinae et Anglicanae* of 1587, which drew substantially from Cooper's *Thesaurus Linguae* of 1565, was as noted a primary source for Cawdrey and others and probably spread the idea of including certain kinds of encyclopedic material in dictionaries. Early seventeenth-century dictionaries included many of Thomas' Latin terms with slight changes (as "inkhorn terms") to make them appear Anglicized, mainly as a pretext to increase the number of vocabulary entries and give their work a competitive edge over that of their rivals.

Specialized dictionaries of law, religion, military science, and other subjects appeared in the sixteenth and seventeenth centuries as well, some of them remaining in print for many years.

Robert Cawdrey's dictionary of 1604 is a small octavo volume of some 3,000 vocabulary entries. Its title is usually abbreviated to *A Table Alphabeticall* because the full title, like that of many works of its day, filled the title page. It does specify that it deals with "hard usuall English wordes, borrowed from the Hebrew, Greeke, Latine, or French, &c . . . gathered for the benefit & helpe of Ladies, Gentlewomen, or any other unskilfull persons." Because women ordinarily received much less schooling than men, they were more likely to need help in deciphering "hard" words derived from Latin, or so Cawdrey and other lexicographers thought, for it was not uncommon to specify women as their chief audience. Cawdrey gives some rudimentary etymological information by marking some words derived from Greek with a small "g." His word list, as noted, is based almost entirely on two previous works.[9] It is notable that Joseph Worcester, an eminent American lexicographer of the nineteenth century, writing a detailed, scholarly account of the history of English lexicography as part of the introductory material for his dictionary of 1846, does not mention Cawdrey. He comments,

The object of the first lexicographical labors in England was to facilitate the study of the Latin language, afterwards that of the Greek, and also of foreign modern languages . . . The early dictionaries, which were designed for mere English readers, were very limited and meagre productions, their chief object being to explain what were styled the "hard words" of the language.[10]

A close comparison between Cawdrey, Coote, and Thomas shows that Cawdrey used many of their definitions with little or no change. His work was wholly unoriginal. He may have derived the idea from Mulcaster and, capitalizing on the tradition of bilingual dictionaries in explaining "hard words," quietly adopted their substance as well as their method.[11] All we can say about Cawdrey is that he had the industry and sense to do it.

The next English dictionary, *An English Expositor* (1616), was that of John Bullokar and was more of a "hard word" dictionary than Cawdrey's, containing about twice as many words. As was the custom, he lifted many terms from Cawdrey as well as from Thomas Thomas' *Dictionarium Linguae Latinae et Anglicanae*, which Cawdrey had apparently not fully exploited. Bullokar thus included more foreign terms (from Thomas) and more obsolete ones. It is really a question whether these early dictionaries, consisting mainly of Latin words somewhat

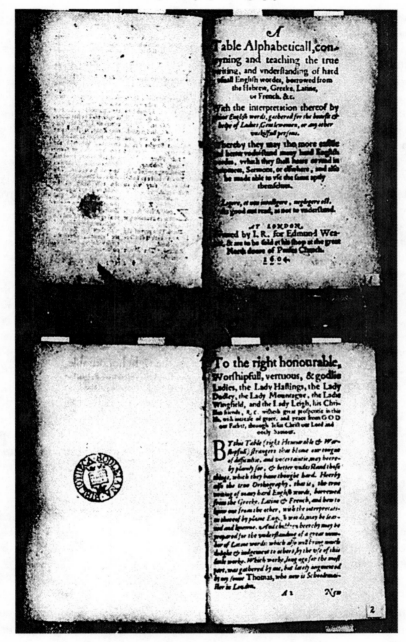

2 Title page of a facsimile edition of Robert Cawdrey's 1604 dictionary, *A Table Alphabeticall*

Anglicized in form, were truly English dictionaries or whether they were a subspecies of the Latin-English dictionaries they so closely resembled. In this respect Cawdrey's work was more English than Bullokar's. Bullokar was a doctor of physic (medicine) and included terms not only from medicine but from logic, philosophy, law, astronomy, and heraldry. He sometimes identified such terms as specialized by saying "A terme of Herauldrie," etc. Cawdrey's dictionary is exceedingly rare, with few reprintings, but Bullokar's was reprinted many times, the last in 1731, more than a century after the first printing.

In 1623, Henry Cockeram's *The English Dictionarie: or, An Interpreter of Hard English Words* appeared. Cockeram was not noted for his modesty. In his Introduction he stated, "what any before me in this kinde have begun, I have not onely fully finished, but thoroughly perfected."[12] Cockeram's was the "hard word" dictionary par excellence, containing words like *abequitate, bulbulcitate,* and *sullevation.* Cockeram mercilessly raided Bullokar for word lists and definitions, and anything that Bullokar had neglected in Cawdrey was seized upon by Cockeram. His dictionary is arranged in three parts. The first lists "hard words" with simple equivalents, as in a Latin-English dictionary. The second gives simple words with their fancy equivalents, i.e., English-Latin. The third is an encyclopedic section listing gods and goddesses, mythological creatures, birds and beasts, rivers, trees, and so on, a section drawn largely from earlier Latin dictionaries, especially that of Thomas. Thus the tradition of including encyclopedic entries began with the earliest of English dictionaries. Cockeram was much criticized for including many terms that had probably never been used in English. For example, what might be listed as *Necessitudo* in Thomas' Latin dictionary would be listed as *Necessitude* in Cockeram. His definitions were brief and sometimes unintentionally funny. *Commotrix* is defined as "A Maid that makes ready and unready her Mistris." *Parentate* is "To celebrate one parents funerals." *Phylologie* is "Love of much babling."[13] Cockeram did attempt "to distinguish among choice words of current usage, vulgar words, and refined and elegant terms," and, however imperfectly done, such usage information does anticipate the labeling that became the standard practice in later dictionaries.[14]

On the principle that turnabout is fair play, Bullokar's edition of 1663 included encyclopedic entries copied from Cockeram, who in *his* subsequent editions lifted even more material from Bullokar. Copyright laws were, of course, nonexistent. Anything published was fair game, and copying was widespread. Exclusive ownership of published material, though doubtless cherished, was not a reasonable expectation if its commercial value was likely to be great. The indignation sometimes expressed by early lexicographers did not make them stint from copying from others. In our day copyright is once again increasingly under challenge as a result of technological advances – the xerographic photocopier and the Internet – that have made copying easy and cheap. We should therefore be able to understand the justifications that might have been used to appropriate someone else's work without credit, as, for example, the argument that since everyone is doing it, one would be a fool to scruple using the work of others. Why should one put oneself at a disadvantage?

The next English dictionary to be published (1656) was Thomas Blount's *Glossographia: or, A Dictionary Interpreting all such Hard Words . . . as are now used in our refined English Tongue*. This was a much more ambitious and somewhat more original work than any of its predecessors, although Blount took more than half of his terms from Thomas and from Francis Holyoke's *Dictionarium Etymologicum*, a Latin-English dictionary. Blount's use of Thomas and Holyoke represented many new Anglicized Latin words as English; although some of them would never become English, many Latin words were by such means assimilated in English. Though Blount's judgment of what constituted a suitable entry was sometimes suspect, Blount did collect words from his own reading and cited some of his sources (though not the main ones); he also was the first to attempt etymologies. More importantly, Blount recognized the changing nature of language and endorsed the process by which new words became assimilated through use by respected authors. He broke new ground among English dictionaries by including two woodcuts in illustration of heraldic terms. Blount, like his predecessors, relied heavily on other works for the great majority of his terms, yet he showed a measure of discrimination in rejecting some of their terms and in altering, often expanding, many of their definitions.[15]

Two years after Blount's *Glossographia*, in 1658, Edward Phillips' *The New World of English Words* appeared in a small folio edition of 300 pages. Although Phillips, who was Milton's nephew, gave no credit to Blount and even publicly disparaged him, his dictionary is a close copy of Blount's, with a number of encyclopedic entries added. His dictionary contained some 11,000 words, including proper names and historic and mythological terms taken from earlier sources. Blount, enraged, published *A World of Errors Discovered in the New World of Words* (1673), in which he attacked Phillips and catalogued numerous mistakes in his dictionary.

He listed Phillips' incomplete or ambiguous definitions, obviously carelessly abridged from Blount, sometimes uncritically repeating Blount's own mistakes, at other times introducing his own, to which Blount frequently appended sarcastic comments. However, in spite of the unscrupulous character of the work, *The New World of Words* did initiate several ideas. Phillips included a long list of prominent specialists and gave the impression that they had contributed to or approved certain definitions, a claim that Blount disputed. There is no evidence to confirm Phillips' claim and it is doubtful that the specialists actually contributed to his dictionary.[16] Nonetheless, the idea of enlisting the support of specialists was a new one in English lexicography. Phillips indicated the subject field of each term and also gave, as others had before him, the language of origin.

In 1671, the *Etymologicon Linguae Anglicanae* was published. Its compiler was Stephen Skinner who, taking a leaf out of Phillips' own book, attacked Phillips while borrowing much of his dictionary. Skinner devoted most of his attention to etymology, as his title suggests, and for this reason his work influenced a number of successors, including Johnson.

Another work based on Phillips' but much expanded was Elisha Coles' *An English Dictionary* of 1676. Still in the "hard words" tradition, Coles, a schoolmaster, included thousands of "old words," obsolete ones from Chaucer's day. His dictionary contained 25,000 words, 8,000 more than the last, augmented revision of Phillips. He shortened Phillips' already brief definitions in order to include more words and more etymological information. Coles did break new ground in including cant (thieves' argot) and dialectal terms. These, taken from other specialized dictionaries, had never before been included in a general English dictionary.[17]

THE BEGINNING OF MODERN DICTIONARY PRACTICE: THE EIGHTEENTH CENTURY

In the early eighteenth century the "hard words" tradition finally began to give way before the more useful philosophy of serving the reader's more general need to know the meanings of all sorts of words. John Kersey, regarded by Allen Walker Read as the first professional lexicographer, was reputedly the editor of *A New English Dictionary* (1702).[18] It was the first English dictionary to attempt systematic coverage of common words as well as difficult ones.[19] Though small in size, the dictionary contained about 28,000 words, many of them included for the first time in any English dictionary. The work marked a new direction in English lexicography, for Kersey deliberately set out to make the book a dictionary of English words, rejecting doctored Latin terms, obsolete terms, and the too specialized vocabularies of the arts and sciences. The work thus parts company with the bilingual Latin-English dictionaries which, up to this time, English dictionaries had taken as their model. His work is more closely allied to spelling books, which had included common words but without definitions.[20] Although Kersey's definitions were brief and often inadequate, his work in this and in his subsequent compilations was a turning point in English lexicography. *A New English Dictionary* was very popular and remained in print for seventy years.

Kersey next thoroughly revised Phillips' *The New World of English Words*. In 1706 the new volume appeared, almost twice the size of Phillips' original dictionary. Kersey added some 20,000 words to bring the word list to 38,000. Many of the new words were scientific terms, which he obtained chiefly from an influential work of 1704 by John Harris, *Lexicon Technicum: Or, An Universal English Dictionary of the Arts and Sciences*. Harris had produced an excellent illustrated compilation of technical and scientific terms. Kersey was only the first of a long line of lexicographers to use Harris' work as a source of technical terms, together with rephrasings of Harris' definitions. Kersey also improved and expanded Phillips' definitions. He was one of the first English lexicographers to recognize and list multiple meanings (polysemy) of the same word. His etymologies represented no advance, however, over those of his predecessors.[21]

An Universal Etymological English Dictionary (1721), by Nathan Bailey, represents another major advance in English lexicography. Bailey, like so many of his predecessors, was a schoolmaster, but he seems to have become a professional lexicographer, for his achievements were prodigious. The *Universal* contained about 40,000 words, even more than the Kersey-Phillips, and unlike that work gave great attention to etymology. Bailey listed not only the immediate source of the English word (etymon), but often earlier forms in other languages, a practice now commonplace in dictionaries but then a novelty. As is to be expected, many of the etymologies appear wildly speculative from our vantage point, but Bailey was working a century before the great advances in Germanic philology.

The word list of the *Universal* was borrowed from a number of sources, including Kersey's *Dictionarium Anglo-Britannicum* of 1708.[22] Bailey included cant, dialect terms, and obsolete terms used in literature, and cited expressions used by Spenser, for example. He certainly had no clear idea of the distinction between a dictionary and an encyclopedia or, if he did, suppressed it in the interests of satisfying his customers, for his dictionaries contain many entries that have no lexical relevance. For example, he included discussions of proverbs. The following disquisition appears under "A Rolling Stone gathers no Moss":

There are a Set of People in the World of so unsettled and restless a Temper, and such Admirers of Novelty, that they can never be long pleased with one Way of living, no more than to continue long in one Habitation; but before they are long entered upon one Business dip into another; so that they are always busily beginning to live, but by reason of Fickleness and Impatience, never arrive at a Way of Living: Such Persons fall under the Doom of this Proverb, which is designed to fix the Volatility of their Tempers, by laying before them the ill Consequences of such Fickleness and Inconstancy.[23]

Then follow Latin, Greek, French, and Italian versions of the proverb. Such a profligate use of space strikes us today as very odd in a dictionary, where space is always at a premium.

Bailey's dictionary proved to be immensely popular and remained in widespread use throughout the eighteenth century. Its thirty editions spanned a period of over eighty years, from 1721 to 1802. Bailey's dictionaries were the chief competitors of Johnson's great work and were probably more popular.

Subsequent editions of Bailey's work included indications of word stress. The verb *descend* was represented as DESCEND', *describe* as DESCRI'BE, *fraction* as FRAC''TION. Unfortunately, Bailey used full capitals for all of his entry words. The placement of the stress mark (beginning with the 1740 edition) was supposed to do double duty by indicating vowel quality. A mark that followed immediately after a vowel, as in *describe*, indicated a long or "open" vowel, whereas one that followed a consonant, as in *fraction*, indicated that the preceding vowel was short or "closed." No attempt was made to indicate vowel quality beyond this rough guide, and no other pronunciation aid was provided.[24]

In 1727, Bailey issued a supplementary volume, sometimes called Volume II, to the original edition. The supplementary volume was divided into two parts: one part contained words ostensibly omitted from Volume I (though in fact some were included in some editions), and the other part contained a miscellany of encyclopedic information: names, places, theological and mythological terms, and so on. It also gave some usage guidance by marking some words with symbols that signified

An Univerſal Etymological

Engliſh Dictionary:

COMPREHENDING

The Derivations of the Generality of Words in the *Eng-liſh* Tongue, either Antient or Modern, from the Antient *Britiſh*, *Saxon*, *Daniſh*, *Norman*. and Modern *French*, *Teutonic*, *Dutch*, *Spaniſh*, *Italian*, *Latin*, *Greek*, and *Hebrew* Languages, each in their Proper Characters.

AND ALSO

A Brief and clear Explication of all difficult Words derived from any of the aforeſaid Languages ; and Terms of Art relating to Anatomy, Botany, Phyſick, Pharmacy, Surgery, Chymiſtry, Philoſophy, Divinity, Mathematicks, Grammar, Logick, Rhetorick, Muſick, Heraldry, Maritime Affairs, Military Diſcipline, Horſemanſhip, Hunting, Hawking, Fowling, Fiſhing, Gardening, Husbandry, Handicrafts, Confectionary, Carving Cookery, &c.

Together with

A Large Collection and Explication of Words and Phraſes us'd in our Antient Statutes, Charters, Writs, Old Records, and Proceſſes at Law ; and the Etymology and Interpretation of the Proper Names of Men, Women, and Remarkable Places in *Great Britain*: Alſo the Dialects of our different Countries.

Containing many Thouſand Words more than either *Harris*, *Phillps*, *Kerſey*, or any *Engliſh* Dictionary before Extant.

To *which is Added* a Collection of our moſt Common Proverbs, with their Explication and Illuſtration.

The whole WORK compil'd and Methodically digeſted, as well for the Entertainment of the Curious, as the Information of the Ignorant, and for the Benefit of young Students, Artificers, Tradeſmen and Foreigners. who are deſirous thorowly to underſtand what they Speak, Read, or Write.

By N. BAILEY, Φιλολόγ. ↗

LONDON:

Printed for E. BELL, J. DARBY, A. BETTESWORTH, F. FAYRAM, J. PEMBERTON, J. HOOKE, C. RIVING-TON, F. CLAY, J. BATLEY, and E. SYMON. 1721.

3 Title page of Nathan Bailey's *An Universal Etymological English Dictionary* (1721)

either that the term should be used with care or that it was certifiably good usage. The second volume was much modified in later editions to prune it of some of its encyclopedic excesses, though it remained a curious mixture of thieves' argot, specialized terms, and names of people and places. The 1731 edition was much expanded and improved and was the basis for numerous future editions.

Bailey made a genuine attempt to represent the language as it was used and to represent as much of it as he could. Kersey deserves much credit for making a start in that direction, but Bailey's treatment of definition reflects a much greater degree of sophistication. Although Bailey continued the tradition of including many obsolete and rare terms, he also took pains to include the common words of the language, including vulgar and taboo words. For example, *shite* is defined as "to ease Nature, to discharge the Belly." *Fuck* is also entered with a full etymology, but defined only in Latin: "*Foeminam subagitare.*" Other common taboo words that were excluded from English dictionaries throughout the nineteenth century and for most of the twentieth also appear in Bailey.

In 1730, Bailey's great folio dictionary, *Dictionarium Britannicum*, was published. It is this dictionary that Johnson used as a working base for his own dictionary.[25] A massive work by the standards of its time, it contained 48,000 terms, 10,000 more than Kersey-Phillips, and represented an amalgam of the two volumes of *An Universal Etymological Dictionary* with additional material. It was illustrated with many woodcuts but omitted some of the more extravagantly encyclopedic material, such as proverbs and legendary names. It did, however, include some encyclopedic articles based on Ephraim Chambers' *Cyclopaedia: Or, An Universal Dictionary of Arts and Sciences* (1728), such as one on "Gothick Building," which discussed the history of this architectural style, denouncing it, of course, as "incorrect."[26] Chambers, like Harris before him, was to provide a veritable army of lexicographers with scientific and technical terms to increase their vocabulary coverage. Bailey's *Dictionarium Britannicum* of 1730 was, after the Kersey-Phillips work of 1706, the standard bearer in English lexicography until 1755 when Samuel Johnson's dictionary appeared.

SAMUEL JOHNSON'S *PLAN*

"The triumphant completion of the *Dictionnaire de l'Académie française* in 1694," say Starnes and Noyes, "made the English uncomfortably aware of their backwardness in the study of their own tongue, and from then on the air was full of schemes for improving the English language and giving it greater prestige."[27] Daniel Defoe and Jonathan Swift made proposals for establishing authoritative standards that would halt language change and fix it in its present "pure" form forever. Addison proposed a dictionary with quotations from literature, a proposal Johnson knew of. Pope was also much interested in the proposed dictionary. The time was ripe for a great literary figure to undertake the task of establishing the standard by making a dictionary that attempted to survey and record the language, especially the literary language, as it had never been recorded. It was Samuel Johnson who undertook the task, and his *Plan of a Dictionary of the English Language,* published in August 1747 and addressed to the Earl of Chesterfield, is a masterful analysis of what would be required to do it. Although a number of his specific proposals as outlined in the *Plan* would be changed or abandoned as unworkable in the face of the punishing realities of putting together a massive dictionary virtually single-handedly, the *Plan* remains a remarkable document. For someone who had never before compiled a dictionary, Johnson's grasp of the lexicographic problems he would be confronted with is extraordinary. What the rest of us are forced to learn through years of experience, Johnson realized at once through the brilliance and originality of his mind. With characteristic humility, though in this instance somewhat artfully contrived to enlist the sympathetic attention of Lord Chesterfield, his would-be patron, Johnson described the lowly status of the lexicographer:

I knew, that the work in which I engaged is generally considered as drudgery for the blind, as the proper toil of artless industry, a task that requires neither the light of learning, nor the activity of genius, but may be successfully performed without any higher quality than of bearing burthens with dull patience, and beating the track of the alphabet with sluggish resolution.

He continues in the same vein, suggesting that the occupation of lexicography, "tho' not splendid, would be useful," and goes on to examine the difficulty of selecting terms. In a memorable passage he argues that usefulness is the prime consideration:

The value of a work must be estimated by its use: It is not enough that a dictionary delights the critic, unless at the same time it instructs the learner; as it is to little purpose, that an engine amuses the philosopher by the subtilty of its mechanism, if it requires so much knowledge in its application, to as be of no advantage to the common workman.

THE

PLAN

OF A

DICTIONARY

OF THE

ENGLISH LANGUAGE;

Addreſſed to the Right Honourable

PHILIP DORMER,

Earl of *CHESTERFIELD*;

One of His MAJESTY's Principal Secretaries
of State.

LONDON:

Printed for J. and P. KNAPTON, T. LONGMAN and
T. SHEWELL, C. HITCH, A. MILLAR, and
R. DODSLEY.   MDCCXLVII.

4 Title page of Samuel Johnson's *Plan of a Dictionary* (1747)

On this basis, it is unwise to exclude terms of science and art. Johnson draws a distinction between naturalized terms and foreign ones, which he will exclude as a rule, although even some foreign terms must be included as a practical matter. The use of technical terms in nontechnical contexts, he says, justifies their inclusion in a general dictionary. He discusses the criteria for inclusion of specialized terms of war and navigation, law and industry; the necessity for including common words like *dog* and *cat* and the difficulty of defining them. He discusses by turns orthography (he will follow traditional spelling and shun innovation), pronunciation (where his ambitious and impractical plan to list words rhyming with the entry words was never fully implemented), etymology, grammar (the treatment of verbs and adjectives and their inflections and comparative forms), what he calls "syntax" but what we should now call collocation or context, and idiomatic expressions. He also intended to enlist the aid of experts to include encyclopedic material under some terms. His *Dictionary* did indeed include encyclopedic material, but for the most part he relied on Chambers' *Cyclopedia* and Harris' *Lexicon Technicum* rather than on contributors.

Johnson's views on the question of whether language can or should be "fixed" in a presumably pure state have been variously interpreted, partly because his position changed markedly from the time of the *Plan* (1747) to the publication of his *Dictionary* (1755), but partly because his own position was inconsistent. About whether it is desirable for language to be stabilized, there is no doubt: Johnson thought it desirable and wished that change could be retarded or stopped. But by the time the *Dictionary* was published, he seems to have realized that achieving such a goal was impossible. The *Plan*, on the other hand, is rife with expressions of determination to fix the language much as the French Academy was setting about to fix the standard in French. We must remember that the strength of Johnson's views of the role of authority may well have been influenced by his awareness that Chesterfield clearly favored such an approach.[28] Nonetheless, his position must be taken as his own. "The chief intent of . . . [the *Dictionary*] is to preserve the purity and ascertain the meaning of our English idiom," he says. And again, in connection with pronunciation: "one great end of this undertaking is to fix the English language." And again, in connection with etymology: "By . . . not admitting, but with great caution, any [word] of which no original can be found, we shall secure our language from being over-run with *cant*, from being crouded with low terms." Wistfully, he asks, "who . . . can forbear to wish, that these fundamental atoms of our speech might

obtain the firmness and immutability of the primogenial and constituent particles of matter." And again: "With regard to questions of purity,
or propriety, I was once in doubt whether I should not attribute too much
to myself in attempting to decide them. . . ; but I have been since determined to your Lordship's opinion, to interpose my own judgment." In
summary he says this is his idea of an English dictionary, "a dictionary
by which the pronunciation of our language may be fixed, and . . . by
which its purity may be preserved." As part of the same goal of moral
uplift, Johnson proposes to prefer quotations from writers of the "first
reputation to those of an inferior rank," and hopes to convey "some elegance of language, or some precept of prudence, or piety," in his illustrative quotations.

Yet even in 1747 he hinted at the futility of attempting to fix an arbitrary standard. "And though, perhaps, to correct the language of nations
by books of grammar, and amend their manners of discourses of moral-
ity, may be tasks equally difficult" suggests as much.

Though ingenious, the *Plan* was far too ambitious. The stated goal was
nothing less than to survey the whole of the English language and to
show the history of every word. "[T]he reader will be informed of the
gradual changes of the language, and have before his eyes the rise of
some words, and the fall of others," a description that sounds more like
that of the *OED* than of Johnson's *Dictionary*, though Johnson sensibly
adds that such observations are "to be desired rather than expected."
Indeed, as critics of the *Dictionary* were quick to observe, he did not meet
such expectations, but it was unreasonable to expect any one man to do
more.

JOHNSON'S *DICTIONARY* AND ITS COMPETITORS

Two years after Johnson's *Plan*, Benjamin Martin's *Lingua Britannica
Reformata* appeared. Martin's work, unlike most of his predecessors',
dealt at length in his Preface with definition and proffered a theory by
which the senses of words ought to be arranged. In some ways Martin's
treatment resembles that of Johnson's *Plan*, and may have influenced
Johnson. His comments about the inevitability of language change fore-
shadow Johnson's maturer judgments in the Preface to his *Dictionary*.
Martin wrote (in 1749): "The pretence of fixing a standard to the purity
and perfection of any language . . . is utterly vain and impertinent," and
"what is deem'd polite and elegant in one age, may be accounted
uncouth and barbarous in another."[29] Martin's plan was well thought

out, and he tried to put his theories into practice before Johnson. Basing his sense division on a French and Latin dictionary, he divided senses into numbered definitions and put more effort into such distinctions of meaning than anyone had before him. In practice, however, Martin's definitions are sometimes too brief to make clear the distinctions in meaning he attempts to make.[30] Martin's use of the bilingual dictionary treatment of polysemy is an interesting step backward since, as we have seen, Kersey and Bailey had moved away from that tradition. Yet it was a sensible and fruitful one, for in this respect bilingual lexicography was far advanced over monolingual English dictionaries.

The booksellers of Bailey's dictionary – in those days the booksellers were also publishers – knew from 1747 that Samuel Johnson's *Dictionary* would be formidable competition and set about improving the *Dictionarium Britannicum*. Called the Scott-Bailey after Joseph Nicol Scott, a well-known scholar in the worlds of religion and science (he was a practicing medical doctor and an accomplished author of sermons), the revised dictionary was really a pastiche of the *Dictionarium Britannicum* and Johnson's *Dictionary*, which was freely pirated for definitions and quotations (often in shortened form), and combined with additional material obtained elsewhere. Entitled *A New Universal English Dictionary* (1755), it was a multiauthored work, of which Scott was only one of the contributors, but the best-known. It attempted to provide a cheaper alternative to the expensive two-volume Johnson *Dictionary*. Accordingly, Scott-Bailey was printed in small type in one large folio and contained many more terms than Johnson, perhaps 65,000 as compared to Johnson's 40,000.[31] Johnson had deliberately excluded many obsolete and foreign terms as well as most scientific terms, and did not include names. The Scott-Bailey was designed to appeal to common people who wanted a basic tool without frills, as distinguished from the literary appeal of Johnson's work, with its extended quotations from great writers of past and present.

Johnson's *Dictionary* was published nine years after he had signed a contract (on June 18, 1746) to produce it. It was a prodigious achievement. Remarking on the impossibility of resolving many questions without unduly delaying the project, Johnson wrote eloquently in his Preface of the necessity for setting limits to scholarly inquiry.

To deliberate whenever I doubted, to enquire whenever I was ignorant, would have protracted the undertaking without end, and, perhaps, without much improvement; for I did not find by my first experiments, that what I had not of my own was easily to be obtained: I saw that one enquiry only gave occasion to another, that book referred to book, that to search was not always to find, and to find was not always to be informed; and that thus to pursue perfection, was, like the first inhabitants of Arcadia, to chace the sun, which, when they had reached the hill where he seemed to rest, was still beheld at the same distance from them.

All dictionary makers are sometimes faced with the necessity of making decisions without full information, which is sometimes impossible to obtain. Of course, Johnson's problem was particularly acute compared to that of an established publishing house which can call upon specialists to provide information and guidance. But so vast is the scope of the subjects covered by any large dictionary that experts cannot be found in every branch of every field without an effort out of all proportion to the likely benefit. Truly, one would need an army of specialists to cover every definition expertly. Such is not practicable, and it is not done, even today. Many decisions in current dictionaries are still made as Johnson made them in his. In Johnson's words, "he, whose design includes whatever language can express, must often speak of what he does not understand." Unlike most of his predecessors, Johnson acknowledged his debt to other dictionaries, citing in particular Bailey, Phillips, and Ainsworth.[32]

Johnson discusses in his Preface the principles of defining and the purposes of illustrative quotations. He acknowledges the difficulty of defining common words without using more difficult words in their definitions. Definitions are to be given in historical sequence to show the development of meaning. (In practice he was not consistent in applying this principle, and some critics rightly took him to task.) The illustrative quotations are designed to elucidate shades of meaning, show examples of "pure" English, and illustrate the range of usage and ordinary context of the words described. Johnson noted the prevalence of phrasal verbs in English and may have been the first to draw attention to them as a common feature of English.[33] He was even mindful of their particular importance for foreigners. Whether Johnson was the first to recognize the peculiar nature of phrasal verbs, he was certainly the first to take them seriously as an integral part of the language and to seek to give them full treatment in his dictionary. "In methodology at least," Noel Osselton observes, "Johnson's sheer boldness as a lexicographer is perhaps better measured by his treatment of the phrasal verb than by any other feature in the dictionary."[34]

On usage Johnson remains ambivalent. He still believes it is the task of the lexicographer "to correct or proscribe . . . improprieties and absurdities," and feels it his obligation to rescue English from corruption by Gallicisms. On the other hand, he says plainly that it is not his task to "form, but register the language. . .; not [to] teach men how they should think, but relate how they have hitherto expressed their thoughts." His most celebrated statement on "fixing" the language clearly shows a considerable evolution of thought from the views expressed in the *Plan*:

Those who have been persuaded to think well of my design, require that it should fix our language, and put a stop to those alterations which time and chance have hitherto been suffered to make in it without opposition. With this consequence I will confess that I flattered myself for a while; but now begin to fear that I have indulged expectation which neither reason nor experience can justify. When we see men grow old and die at a certain time one after another, from century to century, we laugh at the elixir that promises to prolong life to a thousand years, and with equal justice may the lexicographer be derided, who being able to produce no example of a nation that has preserved their words and phrases from mutability, shall imagine that his dictionary can embalm his language, and secure it from corruption and decay, that it is in his power to change sublunary nature, or clear the world at once from folly, vanity, and affectation.

In his next breath he speaks of commerce corrupting the language. He urges struggle against linguistic change even while acknowledging the futility of such a struggle. He opposes the formation of an English academy modeled after the French Academy as contrary to "the spirit of English liberty." His final advice is that, though language change cannot be stopped, "we retard what we cannot repel, . . . we palliate what we cannot cure."

Johnson's profound commitment to tradition would not permit him to accept linguistic change philosophically; it ran counter to everything he believed in. But he was never one to turn his back on the real world. He was neither naive nor so ideological as to be unable to face unpleasant facts. He accepted the role of the lexicographer as the recorder of actual usage, but nonetheless felt it his duty to expose "barbarous" expressions and infelicities, for even though such an effort might have no influence on the course of actual usage, it was the only honorable course of action to take. Johnson always viewed the *Dictionary* as not only an educational enterprise but in part a moral one, and just as he reprimanded himself for idleness he felt it was his responsibility to act morally, for the good of his own soul, in instructing others in correct usage. Though the explanation sounds quixotic, and Johnson was preeminently practical-minded, it was characteristic of Johnson to act on the basis of personal moral conviction even when it came into conflict with practical effect.

The Preface is a remarkable piece of writing: humble without being false to Johnson's own estimate of the magnitude of his achievement, honest in recognizing the limited influence of lexicography on language, moving in its dignified allusion to the personal hardships and suffering he endured while carrying on his work. He acknowledges ruefully that "I have not always executed my own scheme, or satisfied my own expectations." Nonetheless, "when it shall be found that much is omitted, let it not be forgotten that much likewise is performed." Although the world is little interested, he notes, in what caused the faults its critics condemn, "the *English Dictionary* was written with little assistance from the learned, and without any patronage of the great; not in the soft obscurities of retirement, or under the shelter of academick bowers, but amidst inconvenience and distraction, in sickness and in sorrow." He alludes to the failure of the Earl of Chesterfield to contribute to his support, and the hardship this caused him; to his lifelong battle with debilitating, chronic illnesses (scrofula, nervous disorders, bronchitis); and to the death in 1752 of his beloved wife, Tetty. He concludes the Preface with these words: "I have protracted my work till most of those whom I wished to please have sunk into the grave, and success and miscarriage are empty sounds: I therefore dismiss it with frigid tranquillity, having little to fear from censure or from praise."

Johnson's *Dictionary* is often cited as the first to include illustrative quotations, a claim that is not justified. As already noted, John Florio's Italian-English dictionary of 1598 included such quotations, as had Greek and Latin dictionaries of the sixteenth century. In fact, some of these dictionaries – with which Johnson was certainly familiar – were more copious and various in their selections and more precise in their quotations than was Johnson's but, of course, they were the works of academies such as the Accademia della Crusca, not of one man.[35] Johnson is also often credited with being the first to divide and number different senses of a word, but Benjamin Martin had already elaborated such a system in 1749, and Latin-English and French-English dictionaries had already used such discriminations. In fact, Johnson's *Dictionary* is not distinguished by its innovations in the use of either illustrative quotations or divided and numbered senses, but by the skillful and original execution of these methods. What Johnson did he did supremely well. It is no criticism to say that he was thoroughly conversant with the practices of contemporary and earlier bilingual dictionaries, and wise enough to draw upon their established methods to make his own *Dictionary* more useful and up to date than any prior English dictionary.

In his treatment of pronunciation, Johnson made some advances over the past. Although as a rule he showed only stress, without indicating vowel quality, he did sometimes indicate pronunciation by citing a word with the same vowel quality (as he said he would in the *Plan*) and, less often, when the sound was "irregular," by respelling. There is some disagreement among scholars on how innovative these steps were and how important Johnson was in the development of pronunciation systems used in dictionaries.[36]

Critically, the reception of Johnson's *Dictionary* was mixed. It was said to have too many quotations, sometimes from writers "of no authority." (Such criticism eerily evokes the reception of *NID3* in 1961, which was denounced because it quoted popular radio and television personalities and musical comedy stars.) The etymologies were attacked and even ridiculed, but much of the criticism was undeserved. As one twentieth-century lexicographer put it, "Everyone remembers Macaulay's snap verdict: 'Johnson was a wretched etymologist.' He does not tell us who knew any better. Who *should* etymologize, beyond the limits of the obvious, in that pre-Copernican age before philology was born?"[37]

Johnson was criticized for not including more specialized terms of the arts and commerce and for including too many artificial or purely literary words. However, on the whole his *Dictionary* was praised, his choice of spellings recognized as authoritative, and his definitions much admired.[38] Later, in America, the two great nineteenth-century lexicographers, Noah Webster and Joseph E. Worcester, would take diametrically opposite views, with Webster attacking virtually every aspect of Johnson's work (at the same time that he relied heavily on it in his own dictionaries) and Worcester praising Johnson with equal vigor. Worcester's judgment was much the soberer, less biased, and historically more accurate. In 1846, in the Introduction of his own dictionary, Worcester pointed out that Johnson's *Dictionary*, "from the time of its first publication, has been, far more than any other, regarded as a standard for the language. It has formed substantially the basis of many smaller works, and, as Walker remarks, it 'has been deemed lawful plunder by every subsequent lexicographer.'"[39]

Although Johnson's choice of illustrative quotations and his finely crafted definitions are justly regarded as major advances in the practice of lexicography, his real achievement lay in his success in fulfilling –

grandly – the expectations of the English literary establishment, and through its influence of a much wider segment of the public, that the English language was every bit as worthy of study as the French or German. Johnson's *Dictionary* was mighty and tangible evidence that English was sufficiently developed to be analyzed and studied with sophistication and informed historical judgment. In this sense it paved the way for the *Oxford English Dictionary* (*OED*). Without Johnson's *Dictionary*, it is doubtful that Dean Trench, a century later, would ever have set his goals so high for the historical survey of the development of English, or seen the deficiencies in earlier English dictionaries so clearly.[40]

By the force of his reason, his wide reading and the excellent memory with which he put it to use, and his masterly command of the art of lucid expression, Johnson fashioned a work that engendered such respect that for well over a century it was without peer as the most authoritative dictionary in English. Revised by Henry John Todd in 1818 and again in 1827, Todd-Johnson, as it came to be known, was esteemed the best of dictionaries in both England and America until well into the nineteenth century. Indeed, it was Webster's ambition, to which he devoted the better part of his life, to supplant Todd-Johnson's place in America as the standard work.

PRONOUNCING DICTIONARIES OF THE EIGHTEENTH AND NINETEENTH CENTURIES

The latter part of the eighteenth century saw the publication of a number of dictionaries devoted principally to pronunciation. There was throughout this century and much of the next a lively interest in "correct" pronunciation promoted by "elocutionists" – presumed authorities on pronunciation. But it was not until the publication of Thomas Sheridan's *A General Dictionary of the English Language* in 1780 that a major advance was made in the dictionary treatment of pronunciation.[41]

Although Bailey had already used the stress mark in 1740 to indicate whether the preceding vowel were "long" or "short," James Buchanan, in *Linguae Britannicae* (1757), was the first to attempt actual pronunciations rather than simply indicating stress. William Johnstone's *Pronouncing and Spelling Dictionary* (1764), a guide to pronunciation without definitions, included an elaborate diacritic system to indicate every sound, but the system was so elaborate that it was difficult to follow. The most popular way to indicate pronunciation proved to be that of William Kenrick in *A New Dictionary of the English Language* (1773); he used tiny numbers placed over individual letters, or sometimes following them, to indicate phonetic quality. So did Sheridan and his successors. Examining a dictionary with diacritic numbers, one can only conclude that eighteenth-century dictionary users had marvelously acute vision. The numerals can easily be mistaken for insect droppings, shredded dots dumped across the page, or the hallucinatory effect of too many brandies. Kenrick's system had diacritic numbers from 0 to 16.

Thomas Sheridan is the first lexicographer who consistently respelled the entry words to indicate pronunciation. His diacritic numbers were used with the respellings rather than with the entry words themselves. Though the idea of respelling was not new – Johnson and earlier lexicographers had sometimes done it – it had been used only exceptionally and in systems that were relatively crude. Sheridan pronounced every word, even simple ones, indicated stress as well as sound in his respellings, and gave greater attention to the hitherto neglected consonants than ever before.

John Walker's *Critical Pronouncing Dictionary and Expositor of the English Language* (1791) was one of the most popular and influential dictionaries ever published. It went through countless editions and remained in widespread use well into the nineteenth century. The work had an incalculably great effect on the treatment of pronunciation in other dictionaries as well as on schoolbooks, and many pronunciations still taught as correct in our schools can be traced to Walker's dictionary. Walker's prescription for popularity was simple. He used, with due acknowledgment – "I have scrupulously followed Dr. Johnson," he says in his Introduction – Johnson's definitions. He omitted all illustrative quotations and etymologies, added some words that had been inadvertently neglected, and employed his detailed pronunciation system. A key to the system, which is fully explained in the front matter, appears at the head of every page. It is a fairly simple but adequate system, and it is easy to use.

Walker's system, a refinement of Sheridan's, is not much different from those used even today in abridged dictionaries, except for the modern replacement of Walker's numerals with diacritic marks. Walker respelled, showed primary (but not secondary) stress, syllabication, and vowel quality, and used special symbols to distinguish pairs of voiced and voiceless consonants, as the *th* of *that* and *throw*. Whereas Sheridan generally tried to follow actual usage in rendering his pronunciations, Walker wanted to "correct" certain pronunciations and often included monitory notes to the reader. For example, under *decrepit*, he says: "This word is frequently mispronounced, as if spelled *decrepid*." (Interestingly, *NID3* of 1961 still gives the voiceless /-ət/ ending as preferred, but adds, | usu. əd· + V |, which means, usually /-əd/ if followed by a vowel without pause, as in "a decrepit old house." This is a very conservative treatment which still shows Walker's influence. I wonder how many people use /-ət/ in "a decrepit person." To my ear the /-əd/ is no less likely in this frame than if followed by a vowel.) Sheldon cites Walker's insistence that unstressed syllables be pronounced precisely and that every syllable be given its due weight. For example, Walker deplored the pronunciation of /med'sin/ for *medicine*, which Sheridan had accurately given. Walker preferred /med'de-sin/, which remains the usual pronunciation in the United States, whereas /med'sin/ remains the usual one in England. For Walker, a word's spelling and etymology were more important criteria than its actual usage, even among educated speakers. It was Walker who preferred the /sju/ pronunciation in words like *suicide* and *super*, which in the eighteenth century were commonly pronounced with initial /ʃ/ as in *sugar* and *sure* today. If usage clearly favored a form of which Walker disapproved, he would indicate the actual usage but include a note warning the reader not to use it. For the millions of linguistically insecure immigrants pouring into the United States in the early nineteenth century and for the legions of upwardly mobile middle-class people, Walker's advice was a much appreciated help. Walker urged them to say inter*e*sting, not *intristing*; laboratory, not *labratory*; boundary, not *boundry*.[42]

I should not be surprised if Walker's strictures are still being applied in oral instruction in many schools. Every time I have served on jury duty in New York County (Manhattan), I have been struck by the unusual and emphatic pronunciation of the second syllable of *juror* when uttered by lawyers and judges. It receives equal stress with the first (/'dʒu'rɔr/ rather than /'dʒʊrə/), as though equivalent stress on every syllable, like the measured pace in a ceremonial procession, is the only fit manner of expression for the dignity of a court of law. The same measured kind of Gilbert and Sullivan pronunciation is heard also for the last syllable of *defendant*, which leaves no doubt as to the -*ant* spelling. Perhaps these pronunciations have long traditions in the legal profession, but I wonder whether they are not uttered, by way of many intermediaries, in obedience to Walker's admonitions in 1791 against the "slurring" of unaccented syllables. The reluctance to pronounce part of an important word as unstressed is analogous to the reluctance to use lower-case initial letters in writing nouns like *Hope, Charity, Love,* or *Nation,* which were traditionally capitalized and still are in some formal documents.

WEBSTER AND THE NINETEENTH CENTURY

Noah Webster's name became famous because of his "blue-backed speller," *The American Spelling Book,* first published in 1783 as part of *A Grammatical Institute of the English Language.* It went through many editions and at least 260 impressions from 1783 to Webster's death in 1843, becoming one of the most widely used books in America after the Bible and the most popular schoolbook ever published.[43] By 1850, when the US population was scarcely more than 23 million, Webster's *Spelling Book* sold the phenomenal total of about 1 million copies annually.[44] It has been estimated that by the end of the nineteenth century, 100 million copies had been sold.

In 1806, Webster's first dictionary appeared, a modest effort entitled *A Compendious Dictionary of the English Language.* It was based, by Webster's own acknowledgment, on John Entick's *Spelling Dictionary,* published in London in 1764, though reprinted many times and widely used in America. Even at this time, Webster had ambitious plans to produce a much larger dictionary, one that would excel Johnson's and establish himself as first among lexicographers.[45] Webster improved Entick's definitions and added about 5,000 terms, many of them scientific and technical or Americanisms. Unlike Johnson, Webster had no desire to "fix" the language but welcomed change as an invigorating force. Although the *Compendious* had no etymologies, it included certain features that have since become more or less standard in American dictionaries, such as the inclusion of the past tense and past participle of strong verbs and the inclusion of appendixes of weights and measures and of US population figures.

Webster attacked Johnson for including rare and difficult terms and for including vulgar words that Johnson had included because of their use in literary works. Webster omitted *fart* and *turd,* for instance, and any term having sexual or excretory meaning. He maintained an abhorrence of indelicate words throughout his life and never entered them in his dictionaries. (Such was the difference between the eighteenth and nineteenth centuries!)

Originally, Webster opposed any spelling change, and with characteristic exuberance ridiculed the omission of *u* from *favour* and *e* from *judgement.* By 1789 he had changed his mind and had gone to the other extreme, endorsing *bred* for *bread* and *tuf* for *tough*, spellings advocated by Benjamin Franklin. But by 1806 his position had moderated and he endorsed certain changes in conformity with the principle of analogy and, if illustrative, of etymology. Although not entirely consistent, he dropped the final *k* from *musick, logick,* etc., used the *-er* ending in words like *theater* and *meter,* dropped the *u* in *honor, favor,* etc., used *check* and *mask* for *cheque* and *masque* and *defense* for *defence.* He also dropped the final *e* from words like *determine, examine,* etc., the only change that did not last.

The *Compendious* did not take the world by storm. Some Americans were offended by Webster's brash assertions of the inadequacies of Johnson and of his own superiority, and British conventions in language were still considered proper and safe. "Johnson, Walker, and Company still had, if not a monopoly, something comfortably close to one, on both sides of the Atlantic."[46]

In 1818, Henry Todd's edition of Johnson appeared. Todd revised Johnson's etymologies, added to the vocabulary, and corrected errors, but did not alter the definitions much. In 1820, Albert Chalmers issued an abridged edition of Todd-Johnson with Walker's pronunciations, and, in 1828, Joseph E. Worcester edited Chalmers' work.

Noah Webster was seventy years old when his great two-volume quarto work, *An American Dictionary of the English Language*, was published in 1828. It contained about 70,000 words, as compared to about 58,000 in Todd-Johnson. Webster's work was superior to Todd-Johnson in its coverage of scientific and technical terms, thousands of which were added. Webster also included many eponymous words like *Newtonian* and gave encyclopedic information on the bearer of the name. Webster was a brilliant definer, although sometimes he lapsed into provinciality or wordiness or became too encyclopedic. Like everyone else, he owed the substance of many of his definitions and citations of authority to Johnson, whom he attacked for including so many illustrative quotations.[47] Webster included very few and was himself severely rebuked by Dean Trench on this account. Webster believed that illustrative quotations were unnecessary in most instances, and he invented an illustrative phrase in those contexts where a quotation was deemed useful. His definitions were, however, fuller than Johnson's and well divided into senses.

Always the patriot, Webster included many new terms and senses that had originated or been changed by usage in America. In spite of his excessive claims for American English and his exaggeration of the differences between British and American English, many of his observations on the need for recognizing a distinctively American English were sensible, informed, and foresighted. American culture, customs, and political institutions differed from the British, and different words were used to describe them in each country. Moreover, the same word, such as *congress* or *plantation*, often took on quite different meanings in America from those in Britain. Thus, he argued, America needed an American dictionary. The same argument, and with equal justification, has been made subsequently by others about Canada, Australia, and other English-speaking countries. (See Ch. 1, "Variety of English," p. 12.)

Webster's spellings were only slightly adjusted from his 1806 dictionary. The final *e* was restored to words like *doctrine*; the final consonant in words like *worship* was not doubled in the past tense and present participle, a practice never adopted by the British and in recent years often eschewed in America; -*ize* was used in preference to -*ise* in most words having such an ending. "There is a retreat to conventional spelling in a number of instances."[48]

Webster's provinciality showed through markedly in his pronunciations, which were those of New England. The rest of the country was ignored or was considered to speak incorrectly. His pronunciation system was not even as sophisticated as Walker's of 1791, and the pronunciations were not based on actual usage but on what one would suppose a pronunciation ought to be because of its correspondence to another word of similar form.

Webster's etymologies, for which he had taken ten years to study the world's languages, were sadly deficient, even for his own time. It was Webster's ill fortune to publish his dictionary at a time of great ferment and rapid progress in the understanding of linguistic change. The major discoveries of the German philologists, especially Jacob Grimm, were just becoming widely known, but Webster's natural arrogance, contentiousness, and contempt for any theory that controverted his own blinded him to the significance of even those discoveries with which he was familiar. Many of his etymologies were fantastic speculations, devoid of any value save that of historical curiosity.

Webster's *Dictionary* was not a great commercial success. It suffered from the same disadvantage – high price – that Johnson's had. Although the *Dictionary* was important in its day, apart from its influence on American spelling and a few other minor conventions of lexicography it would have had no lasting effect had it not been vigorously promoted and extensively revised by Webster's publishers. George Philip Krapp commented, "If it were not for elaborate publishers' revisions of

Webster's work, revisions with which he had nothing to do but which nevertheless did retain what was genuinely good in the dictionary of 1828, Webster's name would probably now be unknown in the land."[49]

In 1830, Joseph Worcester's *Comprehensive Pronouncing and Explanatory Dictionary* was published, and several years later Webster accused Worcester of having plagiarized his *American Dictionary* of 1828. Worcester had formerly worked for Webster and had revised the *American Dictionary*, abridging definitions but adding vocabulary entries and deleting most of the etymologies for an octavo edition. Webster, then in his seventies, did not approve of many of the changes, but apparently Webster's son-in-law, Chauncey Goodrich, did, and Goodrich was directing the work. One can understand Webster's feeling, then, if one year after the publication of the octavo edition of the *American Dictionary* another dictionary by Worcester appeared under his own name. The charge, however, was unfounded, since Worcester had been working on his own dictionary before he began abridging Webster's, and he was able to point to many differences between his work and Webster's. Of course, a relationship between the two works is undeniable, but anyone who has read this brief history of lexicography is by now aware of how much each lexicographer owes to his predecessors. This is as true of Webster as of Worcester. Both borrowed from other sources, but neither did so systematically and egregiously, as had commonly occurred in the early days of English lexicography in the seventeenth century.

Worcester's dictionary contained about 43,000 entries in 400 pages, included no etymologies, but had a better pronunciation system than Webster's, showing more variants. His approach was more detached and objective than Webster's in that he sought to establish what the cultivated pronunciation was rather than saying what it ought to be on the basis of analogy or etymology. Worcester included a number of neologisms of his day but, like Webster, omitted vulgar and taboo words.

A new edition of Webster's *Dictionary* was published in 1841, two years before his death. In 1846, Worcester's *Universal and Critical Dictionary of the English Language* appeared and the battle was joined. Joseph Friend comments: "What had begun as a personal quarrel in print between rival lexicographers and their partisans was now clearly a fight for the market between publishing firms as well as a linguistic dispute involving regional, class, and academic antagonisms."[50] Webster was identified with Yale University, Worcester with Harvard. Webster was brash, cocky, contemptuous of tradition, and 100 percent American; Worcester was staid, solid, scholarly, and admired the British tradition in lexicography.

As a modern lexicographer observes, "To conservative people of the time, Worcester's books seemed preferable to Webster's because of their closer approximation to British standards, their use of what seemed a more refined type of pronunciation . . . and their preference for established usage in spellings."[51] Although some of these differences were reflected in the works themselves, one wonders how much the different outlooks were exaggerated by publishers eager to play upon the prejudices of the marketplace.

Worcester's *Dictionary* of 1846 includes an extensive discussion of pronunciation; the traditional English grammar; a brief history of the English language; archaisms, provincialisms, and Americanisms; and a scholarly and accurate history of English lexicography, including a catalog of dictionaries and encyclopedias. Worcester is disinterested enough to credit Noah Webster's 1828 dictionary as "a work of great learning and research, comprising a much more full vocabulary of the language than Johnson's Dictionary, and combining many and great improvements with respect both to the etymology and definitions of words" – an assessment much too kind in respect to etymology – then adds: "but the taste and judgment of the author are not generally esteemed equal to his industry and erudition."

The scholarly nature of Worcester's work is illustrated by his notes on orthography. For example, under the entry for *judgment*, so spelled in the quotation above and in the text of his dictionary, there is a long note tracing Johnson's usage (without the intermediate *e*) to Todd's (inserting it), up to the present, and ending with the reasonable statement that usage remains divided and is still undergoing change.

The "war of the dictionaries," as it is called, lasted from 1830 to 1864 and was filled with charges and countercharges, endorsements by authorities, invidious publicity releases, and unscrupulous marketing tactics by both publishers, who put pressure on booksellers to stock only their own dictionary. In 1860, Worcester's magnum opus, *A Dictionary of the English Language*, appeared. It was the culmination of his life's work and was seen as an immediate threat by Webster's publishers. Worcester's *Dictionary* was impressive. A large quarto, it included 104,000 entries in 1,800 pages and was illustrated with 1,000 woodcuts (in response to an illustrated edition of Webster's issued the previous year). Its pronunciations, developed from Worcester's 1846 work, were far fuller and more accurate than Webster's. Though its definitions were on the whole briefer, its coverage of the vocabulary was better and its preferred spellings remained traditional. The etymologies, though less speculative and pretentious than Webster's, were unexceptional but adequate. Worcester introduced illustrative quotations in this work to support definitions and, while acknowledging his debt to earlier works comparing synonyms, included thousands of discussions in which groups of synonyms were discriminated, a feature that has become standard in modern dictionaries.

Although Worcester's new dictionary was widely acclaimed as the best and most comprehensive since Johnson's and occasioned another exchange of pamphlets from each side, it was in fact Worcester's last hurrah. Webster's son-in-law, Chauncey Goodrich, had commissioned the German philologist C. A. F. Mahn to redo Webster's etymologies, and in 1864 the new work, edited by Noah Porter but known as the Webster-Mahn, or "the unabridged," was published. Its official title was *A Dictionary of the English Language.* It ended the war of the dictionaries, ironically by abandoning everything characteristic of Webster and adopting Worcester's virtues: in the words of Joseph Friend, "neatness, precision, caution, moderation, and elegance, together with his handling of synonymy and . . . divided usage, and idiomatic phrases . . . Worcester deserves a considerable share of the credit so unjustly monopolized by Webster's popular reputation."[52] The line of dictionaries now known as Merriam-Webster dictionaries evolved from the Webster-Mahn of 1864.[53]

DICTIONARIES FOR FOREIGN LEARNERS

The earliest English dictionaries for foreign learners were an outgrowth of English language teaching by British educators in Japan. They were developed in the 1930s from the vocabulary studies of Harold E. Palmer, Michael West, and A. S. Hornby of the UK and Edward L. Thorndike of the US. (See also Ch. 6, pp. 273–75.) *The New Method English Dictionary* of 1935, edited by Michael West and James Endicott, was the first dictionary for foreign learners. It is a small volume of about 300 pages, containing 24,000 entries and using a controlled defining vocabulary, a practice still employed by many ESL dictionaries.[54] In 1942 A. S. Hornby's seminal work, the *Idiomatic and Syntactic English Dictionary*, appeared, later published as *A Learner's Dictionary of Current English* (1948) and again as *The Advanced Learner's Dictionary of Current English* (1952). For many years Hornby's name was synonymous with dictionaries for foreign learners just as the Webster name in America was regarded as synonymous with dictionaries for native speakers.[55] Subsequent *Oxford* editions of the *Advanced Learner's Dictionary* (*OALD*) would become larger and larger, and were not seriously challenged until the appearance in 1978 of the *Longman Dictionary of Contemporary English* (*LDOCE*).

LDOCE was an innovative work in a number of ways. Hornby's dictionaries had grown to the point where they tried to cover so much ground in so many different areas that they had become difficult to use. Though indisputably authoritative, they were too detailed, particularly in grammatical description (as of verb patterns), and the choice of vocabulary and style of defining gave the impression of an imperturbable propriety bordering on stodginess. In this climate, *LDOCE*, with a completely modern approach to vocabulary selection (as suggested by its title), with many current idioms, slang, and colloquialisms, was received by learners and teachers alike with considerable excitement. It gave much more attention to American English than the contemporary edition of *OALD*. Arriving just before the rapid development of large corpora, it nonetheless did draw upon Randolph Quirk's Survey of English Usage for examples of authentic speech and writing. (See Ch. 6, p. 280.) It simplified the presentation of grammar, employed a defining vocabulary limited to about 2,000 words, and was printed in an attractive, readable style. Suddenly the door was open for other ESL dictionaries.[56] It was not long before others seized upon the opportunity to compete in this growing market.

There are special-purpose ESL dictionaries, dealing only with phrases, collocations, or idioms, as well as general dictionaries, and the development of these phraseological dictionaries (as this genre is called) has had a strong influence on the development of general ESL dictionaries. Palmer and Hornby were well aware of the importance of collocations, and in the 1930s they had collaborated in producing a report on English collocations. But, as A. P. Cowie has observed, it was the work of Russian lexicographers from the mid-1970s and throughout the 1980s that refined the analysis of types of phrases and that led to some notably innovative dictionaries, such as I. Mel'čuk and A. Zholkovsky's *Explanatory Combinatorial Dictionary of Modern Russian* (1984). The second volume of the *Oxford Dictionary of Current Idiomatic English* (1983), though belonging to "a tradition stemming from the work of Palmer and Hornby . . . owes much to Russian influences as well."[57] In 1986 *The BBI Combinatory Dictionary of English*, edited by Morton Benson (a Slavic scholar familiar with Russian lexicography), Evelyn Benson, and Robert Ilson, appeared, since revised under the title *The BBI Dictionary of English Word Combinations* (1997). Though not based on corpus research, these dictionaries are the most comprehensive dictionaries of collocations in English and have been extremely successful. *The BBI Dictionary* includes both *grammatical collocations* (containing a preposition or a grammatical structure such as an infinitive or clause) and many *lexical collocations* (such as "fly a kite"). Examples of grammatical collocations are a*ngry at, bored with, a pleasure to do (something), surprised that. The BBI Dictionary* describes eight types of grammatical collocation and seven types of lexical collocation.

Following the publication of *LDOCE* in 1978, the rapid development of linguistic corpora (discussed in Ch. 6) resulted in two major new ESL dictionaries – *Collins Cobuild English Language Dictionary* in 1987 and *Cambridge International Dictionary of English* (*CIDE*) in 1995 – to join *LDOCE* and *OALD*, which both came out with new editions in 1995, as did *Cobuild*. In 2000, Oxford produced yet another new edition (the sixth) (*OALD6*), which is a substantial revision of the Fifth Edition.

ESL lexicography is an area in which the British have always been far ahead of America because historically the teaching of English throughout the world was largely a product of British colonialism and the role of British missionaries to spread the word of the English Bible. The English taught was British English, and it is still the dominant form of English taught throughout the world, though American English is preferred in some regions and is important in many others. Both in theory and practice, ESL lexicography had been led by British and other European scholars (particularly the Dutch and German) of the English language. The last few years, however, have seen a dramatic change in the North American market, with no fewer than five new ESL dictionaries appearing. In the past Oxford and Longman produced ESL dictionaries for the American market, supposedly in American English, but both were small in size and were obviously closely based on their British progenitors. As far as coverage of many common American usages went, they were grossly inadequate.

The publication of the *Longman Dictionary of American English* (*LDAE*) (Second Edition, 1997) marks a turning point in the history of ESL lexicography in America, as this is the first corpus-based, soundly edited ESL dictionary giving extensive coverage of American English. It was followed in 1998 by the *Oxford American Wordpower Dictionary*, and in late 1999 by the *Cambridge Dictionary of American English* (*CDAE*), which was based on a large corpus of current American English. These three, all published under the imprints of British publishers but edited by American lexicographers, have raised the quality of ESL lexicography in America to a higher level. As the reader will see in Chapter 6, I believe that, other things being equal, any new dictionary not based on a linguistic corpus is bound to be inferior to one that is. The three abovementioned dictionaries have been joined by a raft of other dictionaries, none of which, however, is corpus-based, and therefore not nearly as reliable in representing actual usage, although they are not without their individual merits. The other American ESL dictionaries are *The Newbury House Dictionary of American English* (1996, with a new edition every year), *Random House Webster's Dictionary of American English* (1997), and the following, all published in 1998: *NTC's American English Learner's Dictionary*, *Webster's New World Basic Dictionary of American English*, and *The American Heritage English as a Second Language Dictionary*. Now that American publishers have discovered there is an ESL market for American English, we can expect a continuing stream of dictionaries, but they have a long way to go before they will be able to match the British-made ESL dictionaries, especially at the advanced levels. The chief market for advanced-level dictionaries for foreign learners is outside the US. In 2000, Longman published the first advanced-level dictionary of American English for learners, the *Longman Advanced American Dictionary (LAAD)*, based on the third edition of *LDOCE*. *LAAD* is clearly designed as an EFL dictionary, mainly for speakers of America English in Japan, Korea, and Latin America.

The Oxford English Dictionary *and other historical dictionaries*

A remarkable and unique work in the history of lexicography appeared serially from 1818 on. First published as part of *Encyclopaedia metropolitana*, it consisted of a great many illustrative quotations drawn from literature, but with relatively few and brief definitions. It was compiled by Charles Richardson, a disciple of John Horne Tooke, who had been one of Johnson's severest critics. Tooke had elaborate and rather fantastic theories on the importance of etymology; Sledd and Kolb, not usually given to wild overstatement, describe him as "one of the most systematically frantic etymologists who ever lived. By pure reasoning a priori he reached certain conclusions about language, which he then attempted to support – naturally with complete success – by the appeal to etymology."[58] Richardson's approach was based on the notion that quotations alone, if sufficient in number, could serve to elucidate "true etymological meaning." He went far beyond Johnson in collecting quotations, beginning at the fourteenth century. In *A New Dictionary of the English Language*, collected and published in book form in 1837, Richardson sought by his vast collection of quotations to justify the theory of John Horne Tooke that each word had a single immutable meaning.[59] He wrote lengthy essays attacking Johnson for attributing many different meanings to ordinary words. In his own work, each word and its derivatives were given one etymology and one meaning. His etymologies were as preposterous as his theories, but his dictionary was of great interest to lexicographers because it foreshadowed the historical collections of quotations that were later to form the basis of the *Oxford English Dictionary*.

In November 1857, Richard Chenevix Trench, Dean of Westminster, presented two papers before the Philological Society that are widely credited with inspiring the undertaking of the finest dictionary in the English language. The papers, published by the Society under the title *On Some Deficiencies in Our English Dictionaries*, were specific, informed, thoughtful, and notably devoid of pettiness. Before then most criticisms of dictionaries had been made by partisan lexicographers whose arguments were always colored by the fact or suspicion of self-interest. Dean Trench was clearly an observer and his criticisms, though firm and unequivocal, were never harsh or contemptuous – such as Webster's, for example, were wont to be – but addressed themselves always to the issues, and always with some expression of respect for what had been accomplished.

Trench lists seven ways in which past dictionaries had been defective, and gives examples for each. The seven areas are:

1. They failed to include obsolete terms by any consistent method.
2. Families and groups of words were inconsistently entered in dictionaries.
3. Earlier and later examples of illustrative quotations could be found other than those listed in dictionaries.
4. Coverage of important early meanings was defective, especially important for understanding the historical development of the word.
5. Synonym discriminations were neglected.
6. The literature had been inadequately surveyed for apt quotations to illustrate the first use of a word, its etymology, and its meaning.
7. A miscellany of irrelevant and redundant information – mythological characters, encyclopedia articles, and so on – was cluttering up dictionaries needlessly.

The history of lexicography is not studded with perceptive criticisms of this order, nor are they any more common today. For this reason, and because many of Trench's criticisms apply still to current dictionaries, it will be worth our while to take a closer look at what the dean was saying.

His idea of a dictionary is straightforward and simple: a dictionary is "an inventory of the language"; "It is no task of the maker of . . . [a dictionary] to select the *good* [his italics] words of a language . . . He is an historian of . . . [the language] not a critic." The public "conceive of a Dictionary as though it had this function, to be a standard of the language." But that is a misconception, which he blames the French Academy for fostering. Echoing Johnson, Trench demands to know how anyone with a spark of "vigour and vitality" would allow "one self-made dictator, or forty, determine for him what words he should use, and what he should forbear from using." This suggests not just a linguistic objection to prescription but a philosophical and political objection: it is repugnant to the English tradition of individual freedom. He does, however, go on to assert linguistic objections as well, namely, that omitting disapproved forms would diminish the value of the work by falsely representing the language. Instead, he advises the lexicographer to include all words but to state his objections to those deemed affected, pedantic, or otherwise objectionable. "A Dictionary," he says, "is an historical monument, the history of a nation contemplated from one point of view, and the wrong ways into which a language has wandered . . . may be nearly as instructive as the right ones."

Although some of Trench's specific likes and dislikes can be questioned with hindsight – such as his gullible admiration for Richardson's etymologies and his unduly harsh criticisms of Webster – seen in their entirety, Trench's remarks constitute a profound *raison d'être* for historical lexicography. The role of the lexicographer as a recorder of actual usage – *all* actual usage – is clearly and unequivocally delineated. It is a curiously modern credo, one that would even today evoke cries of derision and outrage among linguistic conservatives if recast in contemporary idiom and printed on the op-ed page of the *New York Times*.

The massive task of perusing the whole of English literature is far beyond the power of any man, Trench says, and must be "the combined action of many." Although he does not call for a new dictionary, he calls for a concerted effort by the members of the Philological Society to contribute to an inventory of the whole of the English language to supplement existing dictionaries and to aid future dictionaries.[60] Given this purpose, it is easy to see why Trench admired Richardson, who had compiled a prodigious number of quotations. By providing an example of the value of historically ordered quotations, Richardson was indeed important, however misguided his underlying theories were. The example of Jacob and Wilhelm Grimm, who in 1852 had issued the first part of the great historical dictionary of the German language, *Deutsches Wörterbuch*, was also on Trench's mind. The Grimm brothers had a large group of volunteer readers to assist them. Dean Trench provided the descriptive, inclusive rationale for the collection of quotations and their use that had been missing in English lexicography up to this time. Once such an inventory of the language was seen as a desideratum, it was just a matter of time before the proposal would turn into a call for a new dictionary.

The history of the origin of the *Oxford English Dictionary*, fully described in the Introduction to that work, apparently began with a suggestion from F. J. Furnivall to Dean Trench that resulted in his analysis of the deficiencies in English dictionaries. Following Trench's talks, the Philological Society decided that rather than merely supplementing the dictionaries of Johnson or Richardson, a new dictionary was needed – hence the work's original title: *A New Dictionary on Historical Principles*. The first editor, Herbert Coleridge, was appointed in 1859. Though able and industrious, he lived but a short time, dying in 1861 at the age of thirty-one. Through the efforts of Furnivall and Coleridge, volunteer readers were organized to inventory the entire literature of the English language as Dean Trench had urged. Furnivall, colorful, dynamic, and indomitably cheerful, took over the editorship at the age of thirty-six.[61] He was instrumental in greatly expanding the reading and enlisting aid of the English Text Society, which compiled invaluable Middle English material for the dictionary.

The real beginning of the dictionary can be placed at 1879, when James A. H. Murray, a Scottish schoolmaster and an active member of the Philological Society, was persuaded to take over the editorship. Murray had the patient and scholarly temperament ideally suited for the position. At that time the dictionary was supposed to take ten years to complete; in fact it would take fifty. The length of the project was not occasioned by any laxness in pursuit of its completion. On the contrary, Murray and his assistants worked rapidly and efficiently; the scope of the project was simply enormous. By the time of its completion the dictionary, published in fascicles from 1882 to 1928, ran to 15,487 unnumbered pages, each of which contained three columns of type. Based on a file of 5 million citations, it printed more than 1.8 million. It included more than 240,000 headwords and, counting subordinate words and combinations, contained over 400,000 entries.

Each of the 5 million citations had to be painstakingly collected – a process conducted largely from 1858 to 1881 – subsorted (i.e., alphabetized and divided in a preliminary way by sense); analyzed by assistant editors and defined, with representative citations chosen for inclusion; and checked and redefined by Murray or one of the other supervising editors.[62] Even this sketchy summary omits many other necessary steps. Far from being surprised at the time required to complete the project, we should be amazed that it was ever completed at all. That the first fascicle was published in 1882, only three years after Murray assumed the editorship, is impressive testimony to the diligence of Murray and his staff.

In 1888, Henry Bradley was invited to become an editor of the dictionary with his own staff to speed the progress of the work. In 1901, William Alexander Craigie was enlisted in a similar capacity, and in 1914 Charles Talbut Onions was added as a fourth editor. Murray, who died in 1915, had spent thirty-eight years of his life working on the dictionary and was responsible for editing nearly half of the entire work. Bradley and Craigie were each responsible for very large segments, with Onions, who joined the group much later, for substantially less. The *Oxford English Dictionary*, as it came to be called, is a monumental achievement, without parallel in the English language and in all but a very few others. Every dictionary thereafter is indebted to it. It is the basis that every other dictionary uses as the essential support, the ultimate reference point, from which to build new dictionaries.

The *OED* not only provides a historical record of the development of meaning of each word, with illustrative quotations and definitions for each sense. It also shows the changes in spelling, the different forms each word assumed during its history. It gives by far the most complete and authoritative etymologies that existed up until that time, a body of information that is still unchallenged as a whole. The divisions of sense are the most detailed and exacting, the definitions the most precise and clearly substantiated, of any English dictionary.

Even with such great merits, the original *OED* was not without its defects. Its pronunciation system was adequate but not as sophisticated as it might have been. More serious, its coverage of words native to North America was notably deficient. Words considered vulgar or taboo were not admitted, in clear violation of Trench's philosophy. The scientific and technical vocabulary was largely ignored. In this case the policy accords with Trench's criticism of including such terms, which he considered extraneous. Given the increasingly common usage of many such terms, it was nonetheless unfortunate.

The English tradition in lexicography, as opposed to the American, depended upon the educated generalist, the University of Oxford or

5 James A. H. Murray, the chief editor of the *Oxford English Dictionary*

Cambridge scholar who was in the best sense of the word an amateur. The army of volunteer readers was largely composed of such people. The ideal of the educated gentleman or woman of broad knowledge and exquisite taste was vitiated by narrowly specialized expertise such as that required in the sciences. The absence of scientific terms from the

OED was due not only to the limitations of space – for in spite of its huge size the *OED* editors were pressed to omit many quotations – or to the theoretical objections of Dean Trench, but also to a distaste for such special subjects, as for commerce and industry, as being profoundly incompatible with the generalist orientation of the upper classes. The years of the 1840s and afterward were a time of rapid industrialization in Britain and elsewhere, and periods of rapid social change generate strong sentiments of rejection of the changes, just as in our own time – also a period of rapid change – issues like the loss of privacy (resulting from Internet technology) and genetically altered food are generating a climate of rejection of scientific and technological advances. Writing of the early 1860s, one historian observes that "The most obvious example of the [English] public schools' detachment from the modern world was the virtual absence of science of any sort from their curricula. In the teaching of science the public schools lagged far behind schools of lesser social standing."[63] This tradition, reflected in British lexicography, was not really breached until the 1970s. In this respect it was far behind American lexicography, which had long recognized the importance of the scientific and technical vocabulary.

Because the volumes of the *OED* were published over a period of forty years, from 1888 to 1928, by the time the last volumes appeared the earliest needed revision, and a supplementary volume was therefore issued in 1933 to record changes in the earlier volumes. Even the supplement was soon outdated, and in 1957 a New Zealand-born Oxonian scholar, Robert W. Burchfield, was asked to edit a multivolume supplement not only to fill in the gaps of the historical record but to correct errors, add the sexual and scatological words that had been omitted, and try to capture at least the basic lexicon of science and technology. For the first time, the *OED* staff drew upon the specialized knowledge of experts. A concerted effort was made also to report uses of English in Australia, New Zealand, and elsewhere as well as in the United States and Canada.

A Supplement to the Oxford English Dictionary was published in four large volumes from 1972 to 1986. They are admirable works of a quality commensurate with that of the *OED* itself. However, using the original *OED* with the *Supplements* requires one to check for a word in two places, and comparing the additions of definitions, citations, and compound words in the *Supplements* to entries in the original *OED* makes for an awkward and time-consuming process. The editors of the *OED* therefore resolved to undertake the enormous (and enormously expensive) task of rekeyboarding the entire text of the *OED* and of the *Supplements*, at a cost reported to be $10 million, in order to have a machine-readable database that could be used to integrate the *Supplements* with the original *OED* and make future revisions and editions technologically feasible. This was accomplished, and the resulting work, called the Second Edition (*OED2*), was published in twenty volumes in 1989. Along the way, other significant improvements and additions were also made. All the pronunciations were retranscribed in the International Phonetic Alphabet for greater consistency and accuracy. Some 5,000 new entries, not in the *Supplements*, were added. Many of the additions were concentrated in areas of weakness that the *Supplements* had already specifically aimed to address: scientific and technical entries, vulgarisms and taboo expressions, and usages of varieties outside Britain. Once digitized, *OED2* could be made available in CD form, providing a range of tools for searching the text in ways that were impossible in print. For example, one can find all etymologies referring to a particular language, or search for a particular word throughout the entire text (which includes, of course, citations for other words), thus finding new citations of the word in question that even the original *OED* editors had been unaware of. Early in the year 2000, *OED2* went online, with new batches of revised entries added every quarter as work progresses towards the eventual publication of an entirely revised edition, *OED3*, scheduled for completion in 2010.

THE UNABRIDGED DICTIONARY IN AMERICA: THE PASSING OF AN ERA

From 1828 when Noah Webster published *An American Dictionary of the English Language*, to 1864, when the so-called Webster-Mahn, generally regarded as the first unabridged (though not the first dictionary to be called unabridged), was published, each new dictionary was larger than the last.[64] The war of the dictionaries that raged from 1830 between Webster and his successors and Joseph Worcester established the pattern of larger and ever more comprehensive dictionaries. The Webster-Mahn of 1864 had 114,000 entries, which is today a paltry number, about what we should expect in a high school dictionary.

In 1850, John Ogilvie's *The Imperial Dictionary* . . . was published, acknowledged even in its long title to be based on Webster's *Dictionary* of 1828. In 1882, Charles Annandale greatly enlarged Ogilvie's dictionary, which came to be the basis for *The Century Dictionary*, an American work modeled on the *OED*. William Dwight Whitney, a well-known Sanskrit scholar and linguist, was the editor. Published in six volumes from 1889 to 1891, it was subsequently issued in ten volumes, along with two volumes of names and an atlas, as *The Century Dictionary and Cyclopedia*. It includes much encyclopedic material even in its A-Z section, many thousands of illustrative quotations, and numerous fine pictorial illustrations. Beautifully printed and bound, it is surely one of the handsomest dictionaries ever made. In spite of the competition of other large but less expensive dictionaries – the 1890 Webster's unabridged, the Funk & Wagnalls *Standard* – it was highly successful, but unfortunately was never revised. A three-volume abridgment (later issued in two volumes), *The New Century Dictionary*, appeared in 1927. Both the *New Century* and the *Century* were important sources for the celebrated *American College Dictionary* (1947), discussed below.

During the latter half of the nineteenth century a number of influences contributed to making dictionaries extraordinarily popular among great masses of people in America. The growth of linguistic knowledge marked by the studies of Franz Bopp, Rasmus Rask, Jacob and Wilhelm Grimm, and others was rapid and in some ways revolutionary. For example, Grimm's Law (after Jacob Grimm) accounted for correspondences of certain sounds between the Germanic languages and Greek and Latin; at one stroke it rendered earlier theories of sound correspondences, such as those used by Webster, obsolete. The rapid growth of industrialization and technology spawned a new vocabulary and gave it greater importance than ever before. The growth of population and of public education as a means of self-improvement in a free society created an enormous demand for books that would teach immigrants and others how to speak and write correctly. Advancement depended on how one behaved rather than on the advantages of birth. Breeding could be acquired through education and hard work. Dictionaries naturally assumed large importance as authorities to be relied on to settle questions of usage, pronunciation, and etymology. If a word wasn't in the dictionary, it wasn't a word. Whatever was in the dictionary was venerated as the unquestioned truth. To a considerable extent these generalizations still obtain, more so in the United States than in Britain, where tradition dictated more independence and less linguistic insecurity among all classes than in America.

The period from 1890 to 1913 was one of intense rivalry between the two publishers of unabridged dictionaries: G. & C. Merriam Company, publishers of the Webster dictionaries, and Funk & Wagnalls, the publishers of the *Literary Digest*, as popular in its day as the *Reader's Digest* would become to later generations of Americans. In 1890 the first

Webster's *International* dictionary appeared, with a vocabulary of 175,000 words. Three years later the Funk & Wagnalls *Standard Dictionary* burst on the scene with 304,000 entries. In 1895 an edition of the *Standard* appeared in two splendid, leather-bound volumes with gold stamping, stippled pages, and thumb indexes. They looked like bibles, and they were expected to generate in users the same trust in authority that bibles evoked in believers. In many ways the *Standard* marks the maturity of the unabridged as a genre. It was also a direct challenge to the supremacy of Webster's dictionary. The Merriam Company responded in 1900 by expanding its *International*, and in 1909 the first of its *New International* dictionaries was published. Based on the *International* but greatly enlarged, it contained 350,000 entries, including many scientific and technical terms. Its etymologies were scholarly, its pronunciations conservative, and encyclopedic appendixes were included.

Funk & Wagnalls fought back with the giant-sized *New Standard* in 1913, with 450,000 entries in 2,800 pages. It included 65,000 proper names, many biblical. The Funk & Wagnalls dictionaries of 1893 and 1913 introduced lasting changes in dictionary practice. The etymology was placed at the end of the entry rather than at the beginning; definitions were presented with the most common meaning first rather than in historical order. Etymology was thus recognized as less important than meaning and pronunciation. These innovations have been maintained by other dictionaries, though not by all. Less enduring were the attempts to introduce simplified spelling – a pet project of Theodore Roosevelt – which played a conspicuous part in Funk & Wagnalls dictionaries until the 1940s, and unquestionably contributed to the relative lack of success of their line of smaller dictionaries.

The second edition of *Webster's New International Dictionary* (*NID2*) appeared in 1934 and takes the prize as the largest lexicon in English, with 600,000 vocabulary entries. Its pronunciations retained Webster's conservative, eastern bias. Its coverage of both current and obsolete and rare terms was immense, and for many years it was regarded by many – even after the third edition of 1961 was published – as the dictionary *par excellence*. Funk & Wagnalls never responded to the challenge of *NID2* but kept issuing anemic updates of its 1913 unabridged, and as a consequence eventually ceased to be serious competition.

Reversing the pattern of ever larger and more comprehensive dictionaries, *Webster's Third New International Dictionary* (*NID3*) (1961), edited by Philip Babcock Gove, cut back on its vocabulary coverage to 450,000.

Of this total, about 100,000 entries were new; thus no fewer than a quarter of a million entry words were dropped from the second edition. One of the compelling reasons for the limitation in size of the third edition was the staggering cost of hand-bound books. No machinery could bind books with a bulk (the extent of a book measured horizontally across the spine) of five inches, such as *NID2*, and the cost of labor had gone up precipitately from the mid-1930's to the 1960s. Accordingly, by trimming the number of entries substantially, the new edition's bulk was reduced to less than four inches, and the books could be bound largely by machine, at great savings in cost. Another reason *NID3* had to cut so much was that it had to add so much, and much of what it had to add was the vocabulary of science and technology, which had long been a problem – or an opportunity, depending upon how one chose to look at it – for lexicographers.

In 1889 William Dwight Whitney wrote that one of the basic purposes of *The Century Dictionary* was to provide "a more complete collection of the technical terms of the various sciences, arts, trades, and professions than has yet been attempted."[65] Isaac Funk, editor of the *Standard* of 1893, complained in his introduction that "developments in the arts and sciences, now wonderfully rapid, are originating so many new terms as to make it difficult for dictionaries to keep vocabularies complete. In the *Standard*, for example, are recorded 4,000 terms that refer to electricity or its multifarious applications."[66] *NID3*'s decision to cut its encyclopedic and other categories was taken not only to preserve and enlarge its coverage of the basic lexicon, but to give expanded coverage to the scientific and technical vocabulary.

There are two aspects to the growth of scientific terminology. First, from 1934 to 1961 it grew enormously and of course continues to grow, though probably not at the same pace. There are many millions of chemical compounds, as I have already noted, hundreds of thousands of which have medical significance. Allen Walker Read has pointed out that more than 2 million insects have been identified and named by entomologists.[67] Burchfield has written of his decision to omit the name of a genus of corals from the *Supplements* when he discovered there were 6,000 genus names for corals alone.[68] Along with the growth of the scientific vocabulary has come an expansion of its use: it laps over at the margins into the common vocabulary, so that, increasingly, scientific terms have developed extended or metaphoric senses. Even if it were willing to omit the original scientific meanings, how could any dictionary afford to omit *osmosis, parameter, metastasize, black hole, clone,* or *nanosecond?* We are more tolerant of scientific terms even in publications of general interest than we were in the past, and as their range of use expands they tend to acquire new meanings, often ones, incidentally, that scientists denounce in very much the same terms that critics like Edwin Newman and John Simon have used to denounce extended senses of other words.

NID3, therefore, had little choice but to expand its coverage of scientific and technical vocabulary, and the resulting omissions in other areas provided an opportunity for critics to attack it as having abandoned the principles of the much larger *NID2*. *NID3* was neither as innovative as its detractors claimed nor as traditional as some defensive comments from Gove and others have made it appear. Encyclopedic entries were dropped, as were many thousands of rare and obsolete terms (all those before 1755), but in spite of some imperfections and some overelaboration, the quality and completeness of its sense discrimination remains unmatched by any other dictionary apart from the *OED*. The treatment of pronunciations by Edward Artin was a great improvement over those of *NID2*. It is no exaggeration to say that for the first time in any general English dictionary the great advances in phonological research of the twentieth century were systematically utilized. In spite of these great virtues, *NID3* was widely attacked, in part for its decision to omit encyclopedic entries. (For a discussion of the critical reaction to *NID3*, particularly with respect to its handling of usage, see Ch. 5, pp. 254–60.) Recent trends in general dictionaries on both sides of the Atlantic have only strengthened the role of encyclopedic entries of all types: every new dictionary boasts about having large numbers of geographical and biographical entries as well as scientific and technical entries (along with new words). Any new unabridged dictionary would have to devote a high percentage of its space to cover science and technology and would run the risk of being nothing more than a collection of specialized dictionaries.

Future unabridged dictionaries might be available only on CDs or by subscription to a database maintained on the Internet. (The latter method is how the *OED3* has been made available while in preparation.) But they will still cost many millions of dollars to research, write, and edit. Some clue as to the cost is given by the estimate by the *OED2* editors that the revision of the next edition would take 500 person-years.[69] That strikes me as a conservative estimate, but even so it translates to between $15 and $20 million. In the early 1990s one reviewer even doubted whether Oxford University Press would spend the money to produce *OED3*, noting that the cost of simply updating the CD "would not be exorbitant."[70] Subsequent events have laid those fears to rest, and no one doubts that we will in time have an *OED3*. But this is a unique situation. The British government rightly regards the *OED* as a national resource and has made contributions to the editorial effort. The very fact that a seasoned observer could question whether the most comprehensive and respected dictionary in the English language would ever be thoroughly revised attests to the difficulties attending the revision of an unabridged work without the commitment and prestige of a national government behind it.

The fate of the *World Book Dictionary* (*WBD*) is instructive in this connection. Edited by Clarence L. Barnhart and his son Robert K. Barnhart, *WBD* was originally published in 1963 and was sold with the *World Book Encyclopedia* in two volumes. It therefore excluded all biographical and geographical entries, and, with 170,000 lexical entries, in America it was second only to *NID3* in the extent of its coverage. Based on the Thorndike-Barnhart line of dictionaries and on the *Century Dictionary* files, along with millions of citations in the Barnharts' own collection, this dictionary is one of the finest available, containing copious illustrative quotations and full definitions. It went through many editions, growing with each, but by 1998, with 265,000 entries, it was being marketed chiefly in CD form.[71]

In 1999, *Encyclopaedia Britannica*, the owner of Merriam-Webster, announced that it was putting its entire encyclopedia on the Internet and that it would be freely available to everyone, in effect conceding that the printed volumes by which the *Britannica* name had become famous throughout the English-speaking world were no longer marketable.

We may take it as a general rule of business that if a technology exists that can reduce costs substantially for the dissemination of a product, it will be used unless the new product is so fundamentally different from the old that it is likely to be rejected by the intended market. Unlike the print medium, which is discontinuous and lends itself to periodic but thorough revisions to minimize the substantial costs of paper, printing, and binding, the electronic medium is continuous and encourages small but frequent updatings, since the cost of transmission is trivial and the promotional value of anything new is considerable. The temptation will be to adopt a policy of allegedly continuous updating rather than of a thorough reconsideration of the entire synchronic use of English. Because the editorial effort is so time-consuming and expensive, I am afraid that the unabridged dictionary as a genre is obsolete, whether in print or in electronic form. It may survive in name only as an electronic database, but I doubt that it will have the same quality of content. A century after the creation of the genre, the unabridged is doomed by the staggering costs of a thorough revision of the general lexicon (much more difficult than adding encyclopedic material), the proliferation and growing importance of scientific vocabulary, and – the final nail in the coffin – the emergence of a cheaper and more flexible alternative to print, an alternative in which it is easy to fake improvement. The effort and expense that formerly went into a complete editorial revision in print will henceforth be deflected into investment in technological improvement of the electronic format to promote easier and more flexible access to the text. Such new products may well be promoted as new editions, but the changes are likely to be more technological than editorial. The advantages of electronic distribution of dictionaries are manifold, but exquisitely refined sense discrimination is not likely to be one of them. As ease of access improves, the value of the material accessed will decline.

AMERICAN COLLEGE DICTIONARIES AND THEIR BRITISH COUSINS[72]

The phenomenal success of the college dictionary in the United States – about 2 million are sold each year – cannot be understood without appreciating the peculiar conditions that encouraged their acceptance by the American public. When G. & C. Merriam published *Webster's Collegiate Dictionary* in 1898, there were fewer than 240,000 students enrolled at institutions of higher education in the United States, which then had a population of 76 million. In other words, about 0.3% of the population were college students.[73] In the academic year 1995–96, by contrast, there were about 14.3 million students enrolled at a time when the population stood at 263 million; 5.4% of the population were students, or 18 times the ratio that existed in 1898.[74] The audience for college dictionaries, of course, extends far beyond college students, although they remain the core market; yet the fact that so many millions of Americans experienced a college education during this century and were thus generally disposed to react favorably to the word "college," which, in America at any rate, has at least as much to do with pleasure as with higher education, accounts in no small part for the success of this genre of books. To many Americans the most memorable part of a college experience is not intellectual enlightenment but exposure to a new and privileged society of one's peers marked by a high level of tolerance for youthful exuberance, play, and sexual adventure. Although not everyone flourishes in such an atmosphere, and, of course, not all colleges encourage or tolerate it, most do and most people look back fondly on their college days.

The second element in the success of the college dictionary is the name *Webster*. The blue-backed speller made Webster famous, and the success of his dictionaries, particularly the Webster-Mahn of 1864, reinforced the authority of *Webster* in the American consciousness, an association G. & C. Merriam exploited, promoting its dictionaries as "the ultimate authority." The Webster name was from then on nonpareil among American dictionary makers, a position it retains to this day. By 1949 the Merriam company had lost the exclusive right to use *Webster* for its dictionaries, and the word is now in the public domain. So powerful is the commercial benefit of the Webster name that all of the main competitors of Merriam-Webster (the new name of G. & C. Merriam) publish dictionaries with *Webster* in the title.[75] Random House added *Webster* to the title of its college dictionary in 1990, precipitating a lawsuit by Merriam-Webster on the particular way *Webster* was displayed on its dust jacket. (For an account of the legal history of the name *Webster* in American dictionaries, see Ch. 8, p. 410.)

Although Merriam's *Webster Collegiate Dictionary* of 1898 was the first of the type now called "college dictionaries," the dictionary that has come to define the modern genre was not published until nearly half a century later. This was Random House's *American College Dictionary* (*ACD*) of 1947, edited by Clarence L. Barnhart, the doyen of American lexicographers, who after a lifetime of immense productivity died in 1993 at the age of ninety-two. Whereas earlier college dictionaries had been promoted as abridgments of better-known larger dictionaries, the *ACD* was represented as a new dictionary in its own right, one prepared with the assistance of leading linguists and psychologists, and of specialists in many other fields. Kemp Malone was in charge of etymologies, W. Cabell Greet of pronunciations; Leonard Bloomfield, Irving Lorge, and Charles C. Fries rounded out the Editorial Advisory Committee. It is difficult to imagine a more celebrated group of linguistic scholars of the period. What distinguishes the *ACD* most from its predecessors is that it drew upon the best available scholarship and linguistic studies of its time, such as that of Irving Lorge and Edward Thorndike in *A Semantic Count of English Words* (1938), and applied them in its dictionary. It was the first general, adult dictionary to use the schwa (ə) in pronunciations, now a standard feature of almost all dictionaries.[76] It included a large number of technical terms and used a team of experts to check its definitions in these fields. Indeed, the title page of the first edition bears the information, under Barnhart's name, "*With the assistance of 355 Authorities and Specialists.*" This is in marked contrast to the Merriam-Webster dictionaries, which have always been resolutely self-contained. The Preface of *Merriam-Webster's Collegiate Dictionary*, Tenth Edition (1993), makes no mention of obtaining the help of any outside experts and instead pays homage to its "trained, experienced, permanent staff."

Although much of the success of the *ACD* can be attributed to its merits, the timing of its first publication could scarcely have been better. The only other major competitor apart from Merriam was Funk & Wagnalls, which had not revised its unabridged, the *New Standard*, since 1913, and continued to muddle along with college dictionaries of indifferent quality that captured a far smaller percentage of the market than Merriam's line of *Webster's* dictionaries. More significantly, the end of World War II in 1945 released hundreds of thousands of war veterans (almost all men) from the military, and the GI Bill of Rights presented many who otherwise would never have thought of going to college with an opportunity not to be missed. University attendance skyrocketed. In the academic year 1939–40, about 1.5 million students attended institutions of higher education. In 1949–50, 2.6 million were students. Moreover, most of the increase was among men. Whereas the number of women students increased from 601,000 to 806,000, an increase of 34%, the number of male students more than doubled, with almost a million more men enrolled at colleges and universities than before the war, rising from 893,000 to 1,853,000, an increase of 107%. The *ACD* found itself not only competing against a weak Funk & Wagnalls but with a vastly expanded market, moreover, a cohort of men somewhat older and more serious-minded than those in earlier (and later) periods. Many were married and had children to support and were working at full-time jobs while attending college. Most felt they had to make up for time lost in the service and any ready reference that would help them improve their skills would be welcome. As Laurence Urdang has observed, "In those days, every college freshman was required to have such a dictionary."[77] This is true, although, as we know, not every requirement is met. But this group of freshmen was more highly motivated than most. It is therefore no surprise that the *ACD* was immensely successful, immediately establishing itself as a major presence in the dictionary field. From the outset, *ACD* stressed its coverage of "special vocabularies," which we would today call scientific and technical terms, embracing everything from accounting to zoology (and including, among its many experts, an expert on swine).

ACD's phenomenal success was not to go unchallenged for long. A Funk & Wagnalls college dictionary, the *New College Standard*, edited by Charles Earle Funk, was also published in 1947; but though larger in vocabulary – 145,000 to the *ACD*'s 132,000 – it was no match for the *ACD* in popularity. In 1953, *Webster's New World Dictionary of the American Language*, College Edition (*WNW*) appeared. Edited by David B. Guralnik and Joseph H. Friend, it simplified its technical definitions to make them more understandable to the layperson, gave full etymologies, and used no undefined (or "run on") derivatives, a policy changed in later editions. Buoyed by the vastly enlarged university market, the *WNW* made an immediate impact and through the years has proved to be a formidable competitor to Merriam. The Second College Edition (1970) introduced the now familiar identification of Americanisms, and was for a time the only college dictionary to do so.

In response to the uproar following the publication of *NID3* in 1961, the president of the American Heritage Publishing Company, James Parton, convinced that Merriam-Webster had abandoned the standards of traditional lexicography and sold out to a bunch of radical descriptivists who would trample all our principles of correct usage, determined to rescue English from the academic long-hairs and other apologists for the creeping rot infecting our language by creating a wholesome new unabridged dictionary that would set matters right. At one time he considered buying the Merriam-Webster company in order to destroy all copies of *NID3*, but Merriam had been uncooperative. The Great Task was abandoned after an enormous expenditure of funds when it was finally realized that the means to produce a new unabridged dictionary from scratch were beyond even the capacity of an indignant and determined multimillionaire. But a new college dictionary was reckoned still possible, and with shrewd marketing American Heritage (now owned by Houghton Mifflin) has always managed to represent its bread-and-butter dictionary as something more than a college dictionary. It has done this chiefly by superior graphic design and illustration rather than by enlarging the scope or depth of the lexical content. The one extraordinary feature of the American Heritage dictionaries apart from their design has been the introduction of a usage panel of putative "good writers" whose judgments about disputed usages are supposed to provide guidance for the rest of the benighted English-speaking world. It was hoped that this would redress the mischief done by *NID3*'s permissiveness, as detected by Mr. Parton. The usage panels for the early editions were composed disproportionately of older men, mainly writers, critics, and academics.[78] (See Ch. 5, p. 244.)

We can see clearly from this survey that the Webster dictionaries emanating from G. & C. Merriam influenced by example or opposition, by name or by content, every other American college dictionary. *Webster's New World* (*WNW*) took the name as its own; Random House felt compelled to do likewise a half a century later; and the American Heritage dictionaries came into existence in reaction to the presumed errors of *NID3*. By the same token, all of the other college dictionaries have made distinctive contributions, often in a deliberate effort to set themselves apart from their competitors and from Merriam-Webster in particular. In so doing, they have inevitably forced their competitors, including Merriam-Webster, to take note of their innovations and often to adapt their own presentations accordingly. The *American Heritage Dictionary* (*AHD*) reintroduced taboo words like *fuck* – generally excluded from general dictionaries since Bailey's time in the eighteenth century.[79] This was an important and courageous step in reporting the actual usage of commonly used words, and now every other college dictionary in America, even *Webster's New World,* for years the lone holdout, includes taboo words, as do all the British desk dictionaries. *AHD* also gave greater attention to etymology, providing in its first edition an index to Indo-European roots. The Fourth Edition of *AHD* (*AHD4*) (2000) retains this feature, and includes an index to Semitic roots as well. Random House dictionaries gave special attention to scientific and technical terms and to current slang. *WNW* dictionaries emphasized their coverage of Americanisms and endorsed a generalist approach to technical definitions, arguing that understandability was more important than scientific precision. These traditions have been maintained in the current crop of American college dictionaries: *Merriam-Webster's Collegiate Dictionary,* Tenth Edition (*MW10*) (1993); *Random House Webster's College Dictionary*, Second Edition (1997); *Webster's New World College Dictionary*, Fourth Edition (1999); and *The American Heritage College Dictionary*, Third Edition (1997).

In recent years the British desk dictionaries, which were once very different from the American college dictionaries, have come to resemble them. Early British desk dictionaries such as the *Chambers* line of dictionaries (from 1901) and the *Concise Oxford Dictionary* (from 1911) and its successors saw themselves as appealing to a more restricted and exclusive educated public than even the earliest American college dictionaries. Their definitions used a sophisticated vocabulary. The Fourth Edition of the *Concise Oxford* of 1951, the first dictionary I ever owned, begins its definition of *horn* by saying it is a "non-deciduous excrescence." Learning how to use such a dictionary took some practice and trial-and-error, but one often found the effort was worthwhile. The style of presentation was dense but efficient, to cram as much information as possible into the least space. Thus, entries were generally nested rather than listed separately. There were few or no numbered senses; often only a semicolon separated definitions. Stress and vowel quality were sometimes indicated by diacritics in the headword, and no respelling was offered. No encyclopedic information was given, and there was little coverage of the scientific and technical vocabulary. No pictorial illustrations were included; in this respect only, the British dictionaries have held the line, continuing to omit illustrations. Many of the other features persisted in British dictionaries until the 1980s. Since then, probably because of the success of the *Collins English Dictionary* (1979), which had many of the qualities of an American college dictionary, all have changed in varying degrees to follow suit.[80]

The *Collins English Dictionary*, Fourth Edition (1998), is still the leading American-style, British desk dictionary. Even thumb-index tabs, that useless American appurtenance that disfigures the edges of a book's pages, is now a standard feature of British desk dictionaries. The latest *Concise Oxford Dictionary*, Ninth Edition (1995), has them. Even *Chambers 21st Century Dictionary* (1996) has them. Only the somewhat larger work, the *New Oxford Dictionary of English* (1998), has resisted this trend.

ELECTRONIC DICTIONARIES AND THE INTERNET

Will print dictionaries become a thing of the past, to be replaced by hand-held electronic dictionaries, CDs, or dictionary databases accessed on the Internet? Some will – some already have – and some won't. Unabridged dictionaries in print will largely become a thing of the past; if produced at all in print form, they will be limited editions for collectors and libraries. Desk dictionaries, which include the American college dictionaries, will remain attractive commodities in print, as will shorter versions, but will suffer from increased competition from electronic alternatives produced by the print publishers themselves or by others whom they license.[81]

In bilingual lexicography, hand-held electronic dictionaries are already making an impact, and will very likely grow in popularity as they become more powerful and as their pricing becomes more competitive with books. Some of these devices are already quite sophisticated and able to produce extensive lists of phrasal verbs in the target language, for example, along with illustrations of their use. They are easy to operate and produce information very quickly. The main limitation is in their vocabulary coverage, but that is improving and is not likely to be a serious problem for anyone but advanced students. I believe there will still be a very large market for travelers' guides of every description, but that electronic hand-held dictionaries will be bought in addition to small print dictionaries and guides. This type of electronic dictionary may have more of an impact among beginning and intermediate-level students, who may elect not to buy a print dictionary unless instructed to by their teachers. Advanced students will still feel the need to have print dictionaries, because I doubt that it will be economically feasible, even if technologically possible, to manufacture hand-held electronic dictionaries that have the capacity of large dictionaries.

Many dictionaries are already available via the Internet, but in most cases accessibility is limited to looking up particular words. This kind of access is a selling tool rather than an information service, designed to entice the user to buy a book, CD, or electronic access to text on the Internet. More and more dictionary texts are likely to be accessible on the Internet, although some large, specialized dictionaries may, like the *OED*, demand that the user register and pay a fee to acquire the freedom to access the entire text.

A number of dictionaries are available on CD, notably the "unabridged" *Random House Dictionary* and the *Encarta World English Dictionary*. Every major dictionary house has or will have some of its dictionaries available in CD form. This format clearly provides some significant advantages over print. Pronunciations, which users often have difficulty understanding when given in printed transcriptions, can be heard audibly. If there is a word in a definition one doesn't understand, one can usually click on it and get the definition of that word, a process perhaps easier than flipping the pages of a book. One can usually search a dictionary text on CD for every occurrence of a word or phrase, and sometimes search on other parameters (such as language labels) as well. Access to an electronic database enables one to avoid having to look up two terms, if the first should be a cross-reference, to find a definition. The database will present the definition and its preferred term immediately, regardless of the variant under which it is sought. Many electronic texts also use a dictionary as an ancillary component. If one is reading a text and wants a definition of a word, one simply clicks on it to see the dictionary definition. (See also Ch. 7, p. 394.)

Still, a book is a marvelous device for random access to short entries. If the amount of information it yields is often slight, the time and effort needed to find the information is likewise insignificant. But if one has to keyboard *oscillation* or *indefatigable*, let alone *plexus venosi vertebrales anteriores*, is it worth it?[82] Most search systems have shortcuts. Before one has finished typing *indefatigable*, the computer will display a set of words beginning with those letters so that one can stop typing and make a selection from the set. But this takes additional time. To my mind, hearing the pronunciation is the only unarguable improvement of a CD over a book, and, even in this case, variant pronunciations are generally ignored. A book has portability and a solid independent existence. It is not plugged into anything. It is more satisfying to read black print on white paper than to read electronic images against a backlit background. The text of a book is also more accessible, to my way of thinking, than an electronic database, because unless one has created all the programs of the database one really doesn't know by what means the text can be fully explored, whereas everyone who has experience in reading books understands perfectly how to exploit the content of a book. One can be taught how to use a database or software program to one's advantage, but there remain many possible uses of it that one doesn't know, that one isn't expected to know, that, perhaps, no one knows, not even the original programmers, who were probably succeeded by other teams of programmers who made innumerable modifications and adjustments. The new electronic world of information assumes a greater tolerance for ignorance on the part of the user than book readers are accustomed to. We have to accept that we are using only a sliver of the capability of a tool, that vast regions of information and potential uses are hidden from us for our own benefit. I do not know if this bothers anyone else, but it bothers me. I am suspicious of what I do not understand. I feel I understand a book, though, I must admit, I am composing this book using a computer and a program I do not fully understand.

CHAPTER 3

Key elements of dictionaries and other language references

THE ENTRY TERM

We turn now to a discussion of the elements that make up a dictionary entry, beginning with the alphabetized headword, or main entry, by which the word or expression being defined (the lexical unit) is identified. The canonical form, sometimes called the *lemma*, is the form chosen to represent a paradigm; most headwords, with the exception of cross-references and names, are canonical forms. (For a discussion of the selection of entries in dictionaries, see Ch. 7, p. 356.) This section will deal with the question of determining the form and placement of the headword for each lexical unit.

In order to have canonical forms, forms that the speakers of a language recognize as representative of grammatical paradigms, there must be a standard language. If there are competing forms with exactly the same meaning, one must arrive at some basis for deciding which of the various usages is to be represented in the dictionary as the canonical form. Thus, before a dictionary can be written for a language, the language must have developed more or less standard spellings or, in a language with various dialects, have a preferred dialect. Variant spellings and dialectal forms can, of course, be given, and for the larger (and especially the historical) dictionaries should be given; but a single form must be chosen as the canonical one.

In English, the standard, which emerged during the fifteenth century, was that of the East Midland district that included London. Spelling remained variable throughout the sixteenth century, one of the chief aims of the early English lexicographers, such as William Bullokar and Richard Mulcaster, being to bring about greater uniformity in spelling. Though they directed attention to the problem, they did not succeed in resolving it. In the early eighteenth century individual variations in spelling were widely denounced as intolerable, but it was not until Bailey's dictionaries of the 1730s and more particularly Johnson's of

1755 that the spellings of many words became fixed. In America, Noah Webster was an active and influential spelling reformer, as already noted.[1]

"The first task of the editor of a dictionary," writes James R. Hulbert, "is to decide on the spelling of his word-entry. Usually on a modern dictionary this affords no difficulty, as usage has fixed a single spelling."[2] Spelling, however, is not the only problem. In bilingual dictionaries, for example,

One of the traditions of Western lexicography is to use the so-called "infinitive" form for both the entry heading and the translation of verbs . . . In many parts of the world, verbs are usually entered under the plain present (or non-past) form, and it is misleading to translate such headings with English *to* + construc-tions. Japanese *suru* does not mean "to do"; it means "(someone) does" or "will do." The one advantage of the *to* + translation is that it clearly marks the word as a verb, and in English many verb forms are homonymous with nouns.[3]

Because the users of bilingual and ESL dictionaries may not know the canonical forms used as headwords, it is particularly important in these dictionaries that inflected forms that differ markedly from the canonical forms, such as *is* and *went*, be listed as headwords in their own alphabet-ical positions with cross-references to the canonical forms (*be* and *go* in the examples cited). If space permits, even more closely related inflections, such as *made* (*make*) and *tried* (*try*) should also be listed.

The traditional practice of large, comprehensive dictionaries, whether historical like the *OED* or synchronic like the American unabridged dictionaries of the nineteenth to mid-twentieth century, was to list virtually all canonical forms as main entries. Even if a word had the same form in more than one part-of-speech, each part-of-speech appeared as a separate headword. College-level and shorter dictionar-ies, pressed to conserve space, often combine all parts-of-speech within a single dictionary entry, the notable exception being the Merriam-Webster college dictionaries, which do not.

Some linguists call the overall organization of the dictionary, as deter-mined by the headwords (or lemmas), the *macrostructure* of a dictionary, and the organization of the information within each dictionary article the *microstructure*.[4] The particular way in which definitions and other fea-tures of the dictionary article are presented comprise the microstructure. Are definitions arranged by part-of-speech? Are definition numbers used? Are subsenses distinguished by alphabetic letters also included? Are examples included? If so, in what form? How are cross-references indicated?

Homonymy and polysemy

One aspect of the decision as to whether or not to list a lexical unit as a headword has to do with whether it is perceived as belonging to the same cluster of meanings as other lexical units of the same form, or whether it has a completely different meaning. If the form and grammatical function of two lexical units are the same but the meanings are different, are we dealing simply with two different meanings of the same word (*polysemy*) or with two different words? *Homonymy* is the condition of two words that are pronounced alike or have the same spelling, irrespective of grammatical function, but that differ significantly in other respects. *Wind* (a current of air) and *wind* (to turn something around) are homonyms, as are *lie* (to say something untrue) and *lie* (to place oneself in a reclining position). Homonyms are further distinguished by whether they are spelled the same (*homographs*) or pronounced the same (*homophones*). Thus, both pairs of words cited above are homographs, but only the second pair (*lie*) are homophones. In alphabetically arranged dictionaries, spelling rules when determining headword status, so as a practical matter lexicographers are concerned with only with those homonyms spelled alike, not with homophones that are spelled differently, like *way* and *weigh*. They are concerned about words like *light*, which as a noun means a source of illumination and as an adjective means weighing comparatively little. How does one determine homonymy and distinguish it from polysemy?

Determining homonymy is important because most dictionaries accord homonyms separate headword status, whereas definitions in a polysemous entry are usually listed together, although, as we shall see below, this is not always the case. Homonyms become part of the macrostructure of the dictionary, whereas polysemy usually affects the microstructure. Though long discussed and debated by linguists and lexicographers, there is no consensus about how to determine homonymy.[5] Although etymology is often mentioned as a criterion, it is an uncertain guide, as etymologically disparate words have sometimes evolved associated meanings, and words that can be traced back to the same root have often evolved distinct meanings, such that the modern speaker does not regard them as being related.[6] Zgusta sensibly remarks, "Homonymy begins at the point when the speakers of a language are unable to conceive different senses as connected . . ."[7] Divergence of sense must be the overriding factor in determining homonymy, and there is no sure standard by which to determine in every case whether the divergence is sufficient to warrant separate headword status as a homonym rather than status as a definition in a polysemous entry. In bilingual dictionaries, there are other considerations as well: "With languages having overt gender markings, . . . practical arguments favour separate entries for homonyms of different genders."[8]

In the day-to-day practice of lexicography, especially commercial lexicography, no one is concerned about the theoretical imperatives of distinguishing between homonymy and polysemy. The editors are solely concerned with representing the language in a way that will be seen as sensible and comprehensible by the dictionary user. Accordingly, some types of dictionaries, notably school dictionaries and ESL dictionaries, often do not distinguish the meanings of homonyms from other meanings that are polysemous senses of the headword. This is distressing to some scholars who have studied homonymy. One comments, "Thereby the differences between homonymy and polysemy are effaced, which misrepresents the real situation in the language."[9] But there is no "real situation" in the language. The situation is whatever the lexicographers believe it to be, based on their best understanding of both the language and the needs of their intended audience. To make matters more complicated yet, some ESL dictionaries, such as the *Cambridge International Dictionary of English* (*CIDE*) and the *Cambridge Dictionary of American English* (*CDAE*), accord separate headword status to different meaning clusters. This treatment obscures rather than emphasizes homonymic status, but it was seen as a way to help foreign learners find particular meanings, since learners lack the knowledge and intuitive sense of native speakers that make them "unable to conceive different senses as connected."

Run-on entries

In order to conserve space, virtually all dictionaries, even very large ones, have adopted the practice of "running on" at the end of entries the canonical forms of grammatically related words. Many regularly formed adverbs and adjectives, called *run-on entries* (or *run-on derivatives*), are thus listed without definitions at the end of the entry for an adjective, noun, or verb. Thus *racially* may be run on to *racial* and *transferable* to *transfer*. The presumption is that if one knows the meaning of the entry word and of the suffix – which is defined in its own alphabetic place as a main entry – one will have no difficulty understanding the derivative word.

In an effort to cram as many entries as possible into a dictionary –

since the run-on derivatives also count as entries – many dictionaries include thousands of rarely used derivatives, such as *oppressingly*, *sluggardliness*, and *idioticalness*, which appear in the *Collins English Dictionary* (*CED*). Some run-on derivatives may never have been used. Words that could exist but for which no record exists to prove that they have ever been used are called *latent words*.[10]

Though the practice of using rare or latent words to enhance one's entry count is an unfortunate waste of space, it does not contribute to confusion or misunderstanding. But the failure to list semantically important words as main entries is more serious. *CED*, for example, runs on *oppression* to *oppress*. Given the heavy usage in recent years of *oppression* in various senses, this is an abuse of the presumption that derivatives do not require full definition.

The assumption that certain forms are more basic semantically because they happen to be more basic grammatically is not necessarily true. To regard adverbs ending in -*ly* or nouns in -*ness* as less important than the adjectival root indulges the convenience of the definer at the expense of the needs of the user. In many cases, -*ly* words and -*ness* words have acquired senses not adequately covered by the root words, and in some cases the -*ly* adverbs are far more commonly used than the adjectives to which they are run on. -*ly* is supposed to mean "in a – manner." -*ness* is supposed to mean "the state of being –." Thus *swiftly* and *swiftness*, run on to *swift*, can be understood to mean "in a swift manner" and "the state of being swift," respectively. Well and good. It is understood in theory, if not always observed in practice, that if a derivative has a meaning not covered by the senses of the form to which it is appended, or not applicable to the formulaic definitions cited, it should be entered separately and defined. As a result, adverbs like *hopefully*, *incidentally*, and *literally* are defined as main entries in all reputable dictionaries.

But the problem is much broader than that of defining derivatives separately because they include senses peculiar to themselves. To say that *oddly* means "in an odd manner" or that *obviously* – which is far more common than *obvious* – means "in an obvious manner" is both misleading and ambiguous. Yet this is routinely done to save space. A check of the Cambridge International Corpus shows that *obviously* occurs more than three times as often as *obvious* when speech is considered as well as written texts. (See Ch. 4, p. 192 and Ch. 6, p. 296 for information about corpus use in lexicography.) In written text, the frequency of *obviously* in both British and American English is only slightly less than that of *obvious*. In spoken material, *obviously*, which is often used as a sentence modifier ("Obviously, I was wrong") occurs about four times as often as *obvious* in American English and more than ten times as often in British English. Yet in all the American college dictionaries except for *Merriam-Webster's Collegiate Dictionary*, Tenth Edition (*MW10*), as well as in *CED*, *obviously* is run on to *obvious*, without a definition. Similarly, *fortunately*, which is also often used as a sentence modifier and which in overall frequency is about as common as *fortunate*, is run on without definition in every one of the above dictionaries except *MW10*. *Completely*, though slightly less common in British and American writing than *complete*, is far more common in speech in both varieties, so that its overall frequency is much greater. Yet *completely* is run on to *complete* without a definition in all the American college dictionaries, including *MW10*, as well as in *CED*. The gloss "in a complete way" cannot be said to give an adequate explanation of *completely* in such common examples as "I was completely exhausted" or "I forgot my umbrella and got completely soaked." The meaning here is rather "to a very great extent" or "altogether." Lexicographic practice has in the past not allowed one to run on an adjective to an adverb, so the poor adverb, no matter how widely used, is pushed to the rear of the entry where it is lucky to get a pronunciation, much less a definition. However, some ESL dictionaries, such as *CIDE* and *CDAE*, do allow an adjective to be run on to an adverb. Nonetheless, adverbs remain a neglected part of speech. Traditional dictionaries seem to be bound by a kind of linguistic primogeniture, rewarding only the oldest and leanest of words with full treatment, while regarding derivative forms as tainted with the marks of an indelible subordination.

Webster's Third New International Dictionary (*NID3*), the last of the unabridged dictionaries, defines *oddly* as "in an odd manner or to an odd extent" and cites three illustrative quotations, while the entry for *odd* occupies nearly an entire column of type and is divided into six main senses subdivided into thirty-two subsenses. Are we to understand that *oddly* can mean "in an odd manner or to an odd extent" in each of the thirty-two senses of *odd*? Obviously not. More, in which senses of *odd* is *oddly* most commonly used, and in which is it rarely used? This information is central to an understanding of the use of *oddly*, but it is not given. Many *-ly* words fall into this category: *openly, modestly, deliberately, centrally, strangely*, and so on. For example, to say that *strangely*, in "He was strangely silent," means "in a strange manner" does not explain it. In this context it means "inexplicably" and is not related to *strange* in the sense of "unfamiliar or alien," as in "It was a strange environment for her." Yet *NID3* defines *strangely* as "in a strange manner," without even an illustrative quotation, and all the American college dictionaries and *CED* run it on without definition. What makes these omissions peculiarly important is that the undefined words are very commonly used. I have suggested elsewhere that modern dictionaries have a bias in favor of scientific and technical terms, and I believe the neglect of common words such as adverbs is the other side of the coin.[11] Dictionaries have increasingly taken on an encyclopedic function that precludes full treatment of common words. Common adverbs are regarded as less important than even those scientific terms rarely used in general contexts.

In the past, the comparative frequency of particular words was unknown, so frequency could not be used as a consideration arguing for headword status. But with the development of large linguistic corpora, that is no longer the case. (See Ch. 6.) Relative frequency of particular senses in both speech and writing can now be discovered through an examination of very large collections of text stored electronically. Even very large citation files, because they are collected by a process of selection, cannot be used reliably for statistical studies of frequency because they are apt to be unrepresentative of the language as a whole. As James A. H. Murray had occasion to remark in connection with the *OED* files, citation readers all too often ignore common usages and give disproportionate attention to uncommon ones, as the seasoned birder thrills at a glimpse in the distance of a rare bird while the grass about him teems with ordinary domestic varieties that escape his notice. By contrast, a corpus that is sensibly developed will, by design, be representative, at least to a much greater degree than any citation file. There is no longer any excuse for dictionaries to ignore frequency when determining headword status. It is a far more reliable guide than a lexicographer's hunch.

I do not maintain that relatively high frequency ought to guarantee a word headword status, but it is obviously of great relevance and is one of the most important factors to be considered. I am not even sure that we ought always to be wedded to the canonical form as the headword if its inflections are far commoner, especially in dictionaries for foreign learners. Surely it is confusing for many learners to have to find the entry *be* for many examples including *is*, *are*, *was*, *were*, and *am*. Why not put the headword under a form the user is most likely to look up, such as *is*? Of course, a cross-reference at *be* would refer the readers who sought the word there to look under *is*, where one would find all the other inflected forms and the canonical form. Such exceptions would be extremely rare, limited to a few of the most common verbs in the language.

Dictionaries are already in a quandary about what to do with common comparatives of adjectives that have developed their own meanings, such as *worse* and *better*. These are inflections but are also considered as lemmas, and are usually given headword status, but with one definition referring to the word's status as a comparative or superlative. Thus, *worse* is identified as the comparative of *bad* and *ill* and then redundantly defined as "bad, evil, etc., to a greater degree," along with other definitions specifying particular ways of being bad to a greater degree. *Worse, more, most,* and *better, best* are just too common with too rich an assortment of meanings, connotations, and collocational environments to be treated simply as inflections. This is an entirely reasonable decision. Though the status of such adjectives is not exactly comparable to common verbal inflections like *is* – which no one would argue is a canonical form – the question it raises is the same: should the representation of the language's formal structure take precedence over the reader's ability to use the dictionary to best advantage? The answer depends on the type of dictionary and its intended audience.

Scientific nomenclature

Scientific and technical dictionaries have terminological difficulties of a different sort. A group of medical experts convened in 1968 to discuss the problems of medical terminology concluded:

Most diseases are described under several names, some under as many as 20 or 30 different synonyms. The same drug is often designated under numerous different names . . . Equal confusion reigns in such diverse fields as bacteriology, virology, chemistry, to name just a few of the basic sciences, and nearly all of the medical sciences. A Russian and a French psychiatrist, for example, could never be sure that when using the same term they were designating the same entity, and the same would be true of a German and an American dermatologist.[12]

The problem here is neither of spelling nor of paradigmatic model, but the absence of a standard nomenclature. It is not analogous to the lack of a standard language, as in a country with mutually unintelligible dialects. German and American dermatologists believe they understand perfectly well one another's words, but they attach different meanings to the same medical term. Two people speaking widely different dialects, on the other hand, know very well that they cannot understand each other. The differences in pronunciation, stress, and other features make the same word unintelligible, even though it has the same meaning in both dialects.

How does one go about standardizing nomenclature? In other words, how does one determine preferred terms when there is no agreement among the experts? Recommended criteria, in order of importance, are as follows:[13]

1. Usage, as in textbooks, medical dictionaries, and other reference works
2. Recommendations of authoritative specialist organizations
3. Self-descriptiveness, i.e., giving preference to terms that describe the nature of the concept, as opposed to eponymous terms (terms named after people, such as *Bright's disease*). However, some eponymous terms are so well established by usage that they should be retained.
4. Specificity, i.e., not vague or ambiguous
5. Simplicity, i.e., as short as possible
6. Conceptual relationships, i.e., related concepts should ideally be related in terminology. Two forms of pneumonia should both include the word *pneumonia*. This may seem self-evident to those unfamiliar with medical terminology, but it is very often not the case, sometimes for good historical reasons. For example, often the causes of a newly identified disease are unknown or misattributed. Thus, like many other disorders, *legionnaire's disease* was named after the group of people (*American Legion* members) who, it was mistakenly thought, were the first to contract it. One of the early names for AIDS (before *acquired immune deficiency syndrome* became the accepted name) was *gay immunocompromise syndrome*, because, when the condition was first described, it was associated only with gay men. A disease originally thought to be a form of tuberculosis and accordingly named may turn out to be more closely associated with pneumonia, but by that time the original name given to the disorder may be widely known and have been translated into numerous other languages. If the name of the disease were to be changed suddenly it would cause widespread confusion among scientists who had known it only by the original name – and had known very well that it was a form of pneumonia – and even more so among scientists of other countries, because the new translation might be quite dissimilar to the original one. In fact, it is impossible to obliterate forms in widespread usage, and the attempt to do so merely aggravates the problem by multiplying the number of competing usages in currency.
7. Linguistic relationships, i.e., ideally the translations of a term into other major languages should be similar in all languages, so that one can more easily recognize that the two terms are the same.

ALPHABETIZATION

Dictionaries usually alphabetize letter by letter rather than word by word. They place *power, powerful,* and *power of attorney* in that order, whereas a word-by-word arrangement would place *power of attorney* before *powerful.* Letter-by-letter arrangement has the great virtue that readers need not know whether a compound is spelled as one word, as a hyphenated word, or as two words. Since usage is often divided about compounds – witness *database* and *data base, e-mail* and *email* – and is constantly shifting, the ability to locate such terms is of considerable practical importance.

Verbal idioms are particularly troublesome. No form of alphabetization can successfully deal with all types of idioms without listing each in several places, and no dictionary can afford the luxury of such repetition. However, with the aid of a computerized database it is now possible to include an idioms index in which every idiom is listed under every potential entry word with a reference to the headword under which the idiom appears. *NTC's American English Learner's Dictionary (NTC)* includes such a list after its A–Z section, as does *CDAE.* In electronic dictionaries, finding idioms is no problem, since typing in the idiom in the prescribed way, usually within quotes, will generally take the user directly to it. In most print dictionaries, verbal idioms such as *land on your feet* are "run in" at the end of the entry for one of the key words of the phrase, in this instance *land* or *foot.* In dictionaries that give headword status to different senses, such as *CDAE,* the idiom falls within the entry giving the sense of the word under which the idiom appears, so *CDAE's* idioms index shows this idiom appearing at *land* in the sense of "arrive." This arrangement (or microstructure, to use the technical term) calls for a finer sense distinction of the components of the idiom than is necessary in other dictionaries, which can lump together idioms without regard to the meanings of their key words. For print dictionaries, the question of which word in the idiom is most likely to be sought by the user is still one that has to be addressed and that is sometimes impossible to answer. Should the idiom be placed under the first word, or the most important word? Sometimes the first word is variable, as in *shed* or *throw light on.* Sometimes it is not easy to say which word is more important, as in *hang fire.* Most dictionaries prefer to list idioms under the first word, though exceptions are common. Absolute consistency is purchased at the price of the reader's confusion and frustration. Idioms indexes can help a great deal if readers use them, but so far few dictionaries include them.

The problems of alphabetization in general monolingual dictionaries are minor compared to those in scientific and technical works, which usually have a much higher percentage of phrasal entries, often 50 percent or more of the total. Rather than try to alphabetize *nuclei nervi vestibularis* letter by letter, for example, medical dictionaries generally employ the main entry / subentry system (sometimes called *nesting*), alphabetizing under the canonical form of the governing noun and then alphabetizing (usually letter by letter) within the subentry field. The term quoted above is alphabetized under the entry *nucleus*. The fact that its form of *nucleus* is plural has no bearing on its placement amidst other subentries that begin with the singular form. Within the field of terms beginning with a form of *nucleus*, its alphabetic place is determined by the letters NERVIVESTIBULARIS. *Stedman's Medical Dictionary* lists the following words in this order:

Monakow's nucleus
motor nuclei
motor nucleus of facial nerve
nucleus motorius nervi trigemini
motor nucleus of trigeminal nerve
motor nucleus of trigeminus
nucleus nervi abducentis

The letter-by-letter alphabetization of subentries is modified by ignoring some prepositions (such as *of* in the examples above), connectives, and articles.

The treatment of chemical terms is particularly troublesome, because systematic chemical names (like *methylcellulose*) are formed simply by sticking together the parts needed to describe the terms chemically, and it is a matter of indifference whether they are written as one word or two. Should *methyl cellulose* be alphabetized under *methyl* or *cellulose*? *Stedman's Medical Dictionary* partially resolves this problem by making an exception to its usual entry/subentry method of alphabetization. It lists most *methyl-* terms, for instance, as headwords, whether one word such as *methylprednisolone* or two words such as *methyl red*. But it cannot list all *methyl-* terms as main entries. *Active methyl*, *methyl alcohol*, and a number of other terms still appear as subentries under *methyl*. In dictionaries, one soon finds, if there is a possibility that certain forms may occur that do not fit into any category, one can be sure that they will occur. The best advice I can give is to set policy only after having had some experience with the kinds of entries to be encountered. Having set it, make minor adjustments or major exceptions when necessary, but once the project is well under way, don't make any major systematic changes. The programming that would have to be done at that point, given the complexity of the rules of alphabetization in a work of this sort, would probably require so many adjustments before all the bugs were out that it would not be worth doing, and might well introduce problems where there were none formerly. One is better off sticking with a less-than-perfect system than risking disaster.

Another major problem of alphabetization in technical dictionaries is the ordering of non-English alphabetic characters; of different typefaces of the same letter; of the same letter with superior or inferior figures, letters, or symbols; of entries consisting wholly or partly of numbers; and of non-alphabetic symbols. Practice in these cases varies from one dictionary to the next and, all too often, within the same dictionary. The issue must be addressed in sufficient detail in the dictionary style manual, to be discussed in Chapter 7. (See p. 363.) The particular order in which the entries are listed is of little importance so long as the problem of determining an order of entries is appreciated early in the project and a start is made at elaborating a fixed sequence. Almost surely, new terms will have to be added to the list in the course of compiling the dictionary; but once the order of entries is established, it should not be changed mid-course. For example, consider the possible ways in which the following entries could be sequenced:

Hg hg^{-1}
hG hg_∞
HG $\sqrt{hg}$
hG HG
1hg h_g
hg1

This list is by no means far-fetched. In fact, it is simple compared to many technical glossaries.

ENTRY COUNTING

We must now approach the delicate subject of what is meant by saying that a dictionary has 50,000 or 100,000 or 180,000 entries. The current situation is clouded by the deliberately confusing nomenclature used by many dictionary publishers, eager to tout their books as bigger than their competitors'. They refer to "references" without specifying what they mean. In some cases, "references" does refer to entries, in other cases, clearly not. Sometimes claims are made about the number of definitions rather than entries – since there are many more definitions than entries

– in the hope that the user will not pay much attention to anything but the size of the number and will use this number to make comparison with another dictionary's entries. The tradition in British lexicography in the nineteenth century and for all but the last decade of the twentieth has been less competitive than in America, hence less dependent on publicizing invidious statistical comparisons, of which entry count is a favorite. During this period the entry count in British dictionaries was scarcely mentioned in publicity releases, and if it was, it usually referred unambiguously to the number of headwords. Unfortunately, British dictionaries have begun to play the numbers game of claiming more of *something* than anyone else. What is a dictionary entry?[14]

As developed in the competitive world of American dictionary publishing, entry counting is based on two presumptions:

1. Every word or phrase that is explicitly or implicitly defined, so long as it is clearly identifiable, is an entry. Typically such entries appear in boldface type.
2. The more entries one has, or can claim, the better.

The system is designed to maximize the number of entries one can claim, but it is neither illogical nor fraudulent so far as its rules are scrupulously followed. Unfortunately, they are not, and dictionaries have with disturbing frequency made claims that are hard to justify even by the rather liberal system I shall describe. I once had a critic take me to task for the small type of my dictionary and in the next breath praise the larger, more legible type of a competitor that claimed almost the same number of entries as my dictionary. Why, he wondered, could we not have produced a work of comparable legibility? The answer was that we had not lied about the number of entries, whereas our competitor claimed to have 30 percent more entries than his dictionary actually contained.

Here is a sample entry article from *Random House Webster's College Dictionary (RHWCD)*:

par.a.chute (par′ə sho͞ot), *n., v.,* **-chut.ed, -chut.ing.** *–n.* **1.** a folding, umbrellalike, fabric device with cords supporting a harness or straps for allowing a person, object, etc., to descend slowly from a height, esp. from an aircraft. *–v.t.* **2.** to drop or land (troops, supplies, etc.) by parachute. *–v.i.* **3.** to descend by parachute. [1775–85; < F, = *para-* PARA-^{2} + *chute* fall; see CHUTE^1] **-par′a.chut′ist, par′a.chut′er,** *n.*

The following items are entries:

1. The main entry, or headword, i.e., *parachute* as a noun, the first part-of-speech specified.

2. Any other defined part-of-speech of the headword, i.e., *parachute* as a verb.
3. Inflected forms that are actually shown, such as *parachuted* and *parachuting*, even if represented in shortened form. Verbs having identical past tense and past participle forms in -*ed* and present participle forms in -*ing*, such as *rush*, usually do not show any inflected forms following the main entry. In that case, no other entries should be counted, even though the reader can surmise by their absence what the inflected forms are. Implication is not enough. A dictionary entry must actually appear in the article.
4. Run-on derivatives, such as *parachutist* and *parachuter*.

Thus, the article for *parachute* above includes six entries, not one. It is worth pausing to consider what does *not* count as an entry. Transitive and intransitive verb uses, such as defs. 2 and 3 of *parachute*, do not count as two entries. Individual definitions never count as entries. A word like *run* may take up a whole page and count for no more than two entries, one for each part-of-speech. Pronunciations and etymologies have no bearing on entry count. Lists of synonyms and synonym discussions do not count as entries, nor do usage notes.

The following items do count as entries, though they do not occur in the entry for *parachute*:

5. Idioms or other defined expressions "run in" an article, such as *at sixes and sevens* in the following entry for *six* from *Webster's New World College Dictionary* (*WNWCD*):

six . . . **1** the cardinal number between five and seven; 6; VI . . . **–at sixes and sevens** [Informal] **1** in confusion or disorder **2** at odds; disagreeing

6. Run-in variant forms – sometimes called *hidden boldface entries* – that are an alternative or longer form of the entry word, as in the following example from *WNWCD*:

creeper . . . **1** a person, animal, or thing that creeps . . . **8** the lowest gear in a truck, as for use on steep grades: in full, **creeper gear**

7. Other variants, whether alternative spellings or lexical variants, as in the following examples from *RHWCD*:

oys′ter.catch′er or **oys′ter catch′er** *n.* any of several heavy-billed shorebirds . . .
NFD. or **Nfd.** or **Nfld.,** Newfoundland.
tea′ serv′ice, *n.* a set of chinaware, silver, etc., for preparing and serving hot beverages, esp. tea. Also called **tea′ set′.**

Abbreviations provide a plethora of entries in very little space; thus *RHWCD* earns three entries for the abbreviations for Newfoundland. Geographical entries, which abound in most dictionaries, have many variants; biographical entries are usually short and are also a fertile field for adding to one's entry count. Even when such lists appear in a separate section following the A-Z section, they count as entries.

8. Words in lists following an entry for a common prefix, such as *un-*. Each of these words is a valid entry only if two conditions are met: first, that the prefix is defined in the sense in which it is used in the word; second, that the word sans prefix (in this case, the affirmative sense without *un-*) is defined in the dictionary. If these two conditions are met, the sense of the word can be surmised. Good dictionary practice also requires that if a word has any additional meanings not covered by the basic form that is defined, it should not be entered in a list, although this is not a condition for entry status. For example, the usual meaning of *unexceptional* is "ordinary," although it can also mean "not exceptional." Therefore, it would be misleading to enter *unexceptional* in a list of *un-* words even if *exceptional* were entered and defined.

Lists of this sort may be found in many dictionaries under *non-* and *re-* as well as *un-*. Although sometimes ridiculously inflated to include terms that seldom if ever occur, in principle such lists are legitimate. Because such prefixes can be applied to so many words and because the meanings are clear, including entries for all of them would be a waste of space. Many people believe wrongly and naively that if a word does not appear in a dictionary, it does not exist and may not be used. Lists may serve the purpose of comforting such people by including many forms that the compilers could not otherwise include. The same arguments, by the way, apply to the inclusion of run-on derivatives. In run-on derivatives the stress pattern, which is shown, often differs from that of the headword. For these reasons, both run-on derivatives and lists are useful space-saving devices if used with restraint, and it is perfectly proper to count them as entries.

The main entry form in a dictionary serves a number of different purposes:

- It indicates the preferred spelling.
- It indicates the usual printed form of the lexical unit, i.e., whether capitalized or not; whether considered foreign (and italicized) or naturalized.

- In the past, syllabication was routinely indicated with a centered bold-face period, a light vertical rule, or by some other symbol. Some dictionaries still provide this information, but more and more are abandoning it. In truth, syllabication is much less useful now than in former years. Most texts are composed on a computer using wrap-around technology that avoids the need for a carriage return, as in the old-fashioned typewriter. One therefore rarely has to hyphenate text, except in uncommonly long words where the division is obvious. Moreover, when syllabication is given in dictionaries, it is often mis-leading. The purpose of syllabication is to tell the reader where a word can be divided. Why, then, do some dictionaries – even some ESL dictionaries addressed to non-native speakers of English – persist in syllabicating **an.y** or **man.y**, which should never be divided? Showing syllabication is not necessary for pronunciation, which is separately indicated. Inertia and inattention are the only answers. Nobody has paid the matter any notice in years. In my view, syllabication is no longer necessary and takes up space that can be better used in other ways. For foreign learners, especially, it can be confusing, because a word division within a word can be mistaken for a word space, and the reader sees the entry as two words when it is in fact one. Multiword lexical units, where there are actual word spaces, are particularly likely to be misunderstood. In ESL dictionaries, the one exception where syllabication might still be useful is in closed compounds such as **east.bound** or **school.mate**, because division here reveals the composition of the word, which might not otherwise be obvious to foreign learners.

Almost every criticism made of dictionaries comes down at bottom to the lexicographer's need to save space. The elements of style that so baffle and infuriate some readers are not maintained for playful or malicious reasons or from the factotum's unthinking observance of traditional practice. They save space. Every decision lexicographers make affects the proportion of space their dictionaries will allot to each component. It is perfectly fair for critics to question these decisions, but they must realize that the length of a dictionary is finite, and as large as it may appear to them, it is never large enough for lexicographers.

In most American college dictionaries, less than half of the total number of entries are headwords. A ratio of close to 50 percent is high, demonstrating that the dictionary does not have an excessive number of run-on derivatives, lists, or other entries with implied meanings. For many years, *WNW* maintained a policy of having no run-on derivatives, but the smaller entry count this policy assured eventually compelled the editors to abandon it for competitive reasons.

It cannot be assumed that smaller dictionaries necessarily have lower ratios, since they also have fewer total entries, and there are limits to how many words can be run on as derivatives or entered in word lists. Their ratios are apt to be similar to those of college dictionaries and in some instances higher, depending on the policy of including derivatives. School dictionaries have far fewer derivatives, hence higher ratios, than adult dictionaries. ESL dictionaries, which are less concerned with total number of entries than native-speaker dictionaries, include no run-on derivatives or very few. Among ESL dictionaries, coverage of idioms, phrasal verbs, and collocations is more important than beating the competition in number of entries. This is one reason why even large ESL dictionaries contain on the whole fewer entries than native-speaker dictionaries of comparable size. What they include, they generally define.

GRAMMATICAL INFORMATION

Grammatical information is more essential for the person who is trying to speak or understand a foreign language than for the native speaker. It is not surprising, then, that ESL dictionaries should provide considerably more grammatical help than dictionaries for other audiences. In the 1960s and '70s, ESL dictionaries – then all British – gave very extensive and detailed grammatical information, particularly about verb patterns. The complexity of some of these systems baffled many readers, and the 1980s saw a trend towards simplification of grammatical coding, with the notable exception of the *Collins Cobuild English Dictionary*, which includes a wide outer margin on its pages for detailed grammatical coding and other information. Still, all the ESL dictionaries include a good deal of grammatical information. All distinguish between count nouns and mass nouns, for example, and give information about common verb patterns, the gradability of adjectives and adverbs, and the kinds of complements (such as *that* clauses) typically following certain verbs.

There is good reason to include such information in ESL dictionaries and in bilingual dictionaries, especially when the translation in the target language is a count noun whereas the source-language term is a mass noun, or vice versa. Some scholars have argued that it would be useful to include similar information in native-speaker dictionaries. New grammars of the English language are being prepared with the help of language corpora that will change the way grammatical information is treated in dictionaries, beginning with ESL dictionaries but eventually affecting every type of dictionary.[15] However, the needs and purposes of ESL dictionaries, which are essentially pedagogical, will always demand a more specialized treatment of grammar than in other dictionaries. Even the basic distinction between count and mass nouns is given to many exceptions among native speakers, who can and do pluralize nouns that ESL dictionaries call "mass." I have in my files "count" examples for the following mass nouns: "a tiresome *arrogance*," *Englishes* (now fairly common), *evidences, frightfulnesses, harms, impacts, knowledges, musics, nonsenses, poetries, politenesses, publics, resistances* (in nontechnical usage), "There is not one but many *silences*," *softnesses, surgeries* (in American English use), *unknowabilities, violences.* It is unlikely that even very large corpora will contain evidence of examples for all of these words, yet they exist. We must therefore be wary of presuming that practical guidelines for the foreign-born student have any theoretical basis or practical utility for the native speaker, who should not be constrained against using novel forms because of their rarity.

Context and variety of usage determine whether a noun can be made plural. In poetry, anything can happen. In scientific contexts, some words, like *etiology*, are often pluralized, though in ordinary usage they are generally considered noncountable. My experience as a dictionary maker convinces me that it is rash to suppose that any grammatical form cannot occur. Not the least value of lexicography is that one learns to be humble about one's own knowledge of the language.

General dictionaries provide basic grammatical information. Adult dictionaries indicate the part-of-speech of each entry, and the senses of the verbs are usually distinguished as to whether they are transitive or intransitive. Illustrative phrases serve to show the usual collocations or contexts in which each sense is used, thus providing a variety of grammatical information, such as whether a word takes an indirect object or whether it is usually used in the passive voice. Often other grammatical information is explicitly given. For example, the reader is advised that words like *economics* that are plural in form are construed as singular and that some words like *barrack* are usually used in the plural. Indication of the form of a word, especially capitalization, is also a common feature of dictionaries.

I can hear the reader protesting at this moment, "Doesn't the same argument you made about count versus mass nouns apply equally to any grammatical information given in a dictionary? If a dictionary says, 'usually used in the plural,' isn't it being equally factitious for the native speaker?"

My response is that the two cases are dissimilar. When a dictionary says, "usually used in the plural," it may be assumed that the only evidence that the word was ever used in the singular is a single fifty-year-old, smudged and partially illegible citation slip of questionable authenticity. Its statistical incidence in a corpus search approaches zero. When a dictionary says "usually," one may assume it to mean "almost invariably." The count/mass distinction is hardly so reliable for native speakers. Secondly, all nouns can be distinguished by countability, whereas other kinds of grammatical information given by dictionaries (except for part-of-speech) are highly selective. They are not given at all unless the evidence in their support is overwhelming. Foreign learners need guidance in the mass/count distinction and should not be concerned about rare exceptions, but native speakers do not need such guidance, and I am afraid that descriptions of prevailing usages, even if based on overwhelming statistical predominance, will be taken – perhaps even conveyed – as if exceptional uses are errors when in fact they are simply deviations from the prevailing norm. In every endeavor one finds people who have violated all the formal rules of preparation for success, yet defy all predictions – and confound their more traditional competitors – by excelling. Remote probability is an avenue of discovery, and though often fruitless, such statistically invisible efforts may add up in the aggregate, as particles of matter in the vastness of the universe are said collectively to have more mass than all the heavenly bodies combined, to something grander than well attested generalization.

Beginning children's dictionaries often do not include part-of-speech indications, because such labels would serve only to confuse the child who had not learned the rudiments of grammar. Even intermediate children's dictionaries deemphasize part-of-speech labels. Scientific and technical dictionaries provide little grammatical information. Most do not indicate part-of-speech, although irregular plural forms, as for Latin terms, may be included. Since the study of grammatical usage of technical terms is spare or nonexistent, there is little basis on which to provide information or guidance. Given the encyclopedic nature of such works, grammatical data are of marginal relevance in any case.

In bilingual dictionaries, the grammatical categories of the source-language vocabulary and its corresponding translations should be consistent. "The reader has the right to expect," one linguist observes, ". . .

that if Japanese verbs are usually translated as English verbs, an adjective will not turn up without some compelling reason." If a Japanese adjective is translated as "is dark," for example, it would be misleading to translate a Japanese verb the same way; rather, it should be translated as "gets (becomes) dark, cloudy, etc."[16]

The use of the word *compelling* in the above quotation illustrates one of the most difficult grammatical problems for monolingual lexicographers, namely, how to decide when the present or past participle of a verb should be considered an adjective and entered as a canonical form in its own right. The case for *compelling* is compelling, but the status of many other words is less clear cut: *domed* (stadium), *marbled* (veneer), *tempered* (steel), *hardened* (criminal), *flourishing* (vegetation), *pleasing* (performance). There are thousands of such terms that seem to defy all attempts to place them in lexical categories by which to judge their fitness for entry status. Many, for example, do not have any meanings that are not already well covered by their underlying verbs. Because any verb participle can be used adjectivally in English and many nouns can be used attributively, the mere fact of occurrence with such grammatical functions obviously does not sustain the argument to include them as separate entries. But some participles are used adjectivally much more commonly than others, and by the use of grammatically-tagged corpora containing many millions of words, lexicographers can now compare the relative frequencies of participles used adjectivally. (See Ch. 6, p. 296, for more information on corpus use.) They can thus determine with a high degree of reliability which participles merit entry status as adjectives. They can also see whether some participles have slightly different shades of meaning when used adjectivally in some contexts than one could impute to them simply by knowing their verbal meanings. Judgment still plays a part, of course, in determining the status of participles, but corpus use has provided a more scientific basis for making the decision than was formerly available.

Dictionaries also provide grammatical information about *function words*, so called because they function primarily as grammatical devices, as for example to link two words or introduce a phrase, rather than as lexical units. *Of, for, at, and, but*, and *to* are examples of function words. In a study of the function word *of*, John Sinclair shows that with the use of a corpus, function words can be defined lexicogrammatically, that is, by showing their grammatical functions and lexical contexts in which they occur, as in *a piece of wood, a cup of tea*, etc. If one has enough examples of each type, one can categorize the types.[17] Definition will be treated at length in the next chapter, but suffice it to say here that the requirement for substitutability – that the definition for a word be substitutable for the word itself in most contexts – cannot be met with function words. Dictionaries have long realized that function words could not be defined strictly lexically, but have not quite known how to handle them. When *MW10* defines *of* as " – used as a function word to indicate a point of reckoning <north ~ the lake>," it is employing a convenient style to get around the impossibility of stating what *of* means in "north of the lake" in a substitutable way. Other dictionaries employ different methods, but all end up trying to assign traditional definitions to them. Sinclair argues that the assignment of traditional meanings to function words is not helpful. Surely he is right, yet in practice it is not easy to describe meaning lexicogrammatically in a simple way, as we see in Sinclair's own *Cobuild* dictionary, one of whose definitions of *of* is: "You use **of** after nouns referring to actions to specify the person or thing that is affected by the action or that performs the action." To be sure, *Cobuild* then provides examples – "the kidnapping of the child," "the arrival of the next train" – to show what it means, but so do more traditional dictionaries that give more traditional definitions. The fact is that with respect to function words, neither *Cobuild*'s lexicogrammatical definitions nor more traditional lexical definitions can be understood readily without examples. What *Cobuild* does, however, is to provide guidance to the user by showing the grammatical frames in which particular meanings occur.

PRONUNCIATION

The pronunciation system favored by native-speaker American dictionaries – unlike British dictionaries – is one in which the entry word is respelled in alphabetic characters with diacritical marks over certain vowels and with primary and secondary stress marks indicated. Called a *respelling system*, it represents the meaningful, distinctive sounds in a language but is not based on how the sounds are produced; that is, it is not phonetic. It is based on *phonemes*, the smallest units of sound that can be used to differentiate meaning. Phonemes are theoretical constructs, composites of similar but variously articulated speech sounds. Phonetic sounds, or *phones*, on the other hand, are actual speech sounds classified by the manner and place of articulation, that is, by the way in which air is forced through the mouth and shaped by tongue, teeth, palate, lips, and in some languages by the uvula. The *r* of *run* and of *fur* is articulated differently, thus phonetically different, but belongs to the same phoneme in English and is represented by one symbol in most dictionaries. Likewise, the *p* of *pill* and *spill* and the *l* of *lean* and *feel* are not articulated identically, but are represented by the same phoneme. In some languages, the substitution of one of these sounds for the other in the same context would result in two different words; they are phonemically distinct in such languages, though not in English.[18] In the speech of many American southerners, the vowel sound of *pen* and *pin* is in free variation; such speakers are unaware whether they use the high front vowel [ɪ] or the mid front vowel [ɛ] in either context, though in other contexts, such as those of *slept* and *slipped*, a distinction is observed. In contexts like *pen/pin* the difference is not phonemic to southerners, though it is to most other Americans, who interpret the two utterances as different words. If a dictionary were designed to represent only the American English of southerners, [ɪ] and [ɛ] in these contexts would be represented by the same symbol; but since American dictionaries seek to represent American English pronunciation in general use throughout the country, they use two different symbols, usually /i/ and /e/, to represent these sounds. Parallel situations exist in the dialects in many other regions. No phonemic pronunciation system can cope very well with this kind of dialectal variation.

The chief difficulty in representing pronunciation is that the letters of the alphabet often represent more than one sound, as *a* in *late, can, far*, and *care*, and sometimes two different letters represent the same sound, as *c* and *k* in *cool* and *kin*. Because the letter *a* is pronounced variously, different symbols must be used to represent its different sounds. That the distinction between the sound of *late* and the sound of *can* is phonemic can be demonstrated by comparing *can* and *cane*. A change in the vowel sound changes the meaning of the two words, which occur in the same environment. The vowel in *late* is usually represented in respelling systems by /ā/, that of *can* by /a/, that of *far* by /ä/, and that of *care* by /er/ or /â/. These sounds are then linked to "key words," familiar words in which these sounds can be distinguished. If readers see /ä/ in a pronunciation, they are supposed to look at the pronunciation key, usually printed on every two-page spread or in the front of the dictionary, and find /ä/ identified as the first vowel sound in *father*. The system works so long as everyone knows how to pronounce the key word and pronounces it the same way.

The most widely used alternative to a respelling system is that of the International Phonetic Alphabet (IPA), which is used in virtually all British monolingual dictionaries and in bilingual dictionaries. Because

IPA symbols are phonetically based, i.e., on the area and manner of articulation, they can be used either phonetically or broadly phonemically, that is, taking in a range of closely related articulations when these correspond to phonemes. The actual distinction between the IPA and respelling systems is that, though both may be used phonemically, the IPA is phonetically based, and respelling systems used in dictionaries are not. Since the sound of *late* is a diphthong – composed of two sounds – it is represented in the IPA by two symbols [eɪ], not one as in respelling systems. To avoid relying on the phonetic values of any one language, the IPA uses both alphabetic and nonalphabetic symbols, representing the sound of *can* by [æ], that of *far* by [a], and that of *set* by [ɛ].

A system based on the manner of articulation can be used to produce the sounds of any language, even a language with which one is entirely unfamiliar. However, the notation to represent such sounds exactly must be much more elaborate than for a phonemic system. A purely phonetic system must indicate whether the tongue is high, mid, or low; front, mid, or back; whether a vowel sound is long or short, rounded, diphthongal, or retroflex (made with the tip of the tongue curled up toward the palate). In addition, the movement from one position to another, or glides, must be represented, stress pattern and pauses must be exactly indicated, and pitch or intonation may also be noted.

Because a purely phonetic description would be far too complicated for most dictionary users, all phonetically based systems used in general English dictionaries are broadly phonemic. For example, even though the *p* of *pill* and *spill* and the *l* of *lean* and *feel*, as I have noted above, are not phonetically identical, dictionaries whose systems are based on the IPA nevertheless use the same symbols – [p] and [l] – in each pair of words because the differences are not phonemically significant and distinguishing between them phonetically would serve no useful purpose. In technical language, they are *allophones* of the same phoneme. Foreign speakers will have to learn the slight differences in articulation through practice and by listening to native speakers, not through reading dictionary transcriptions.

Although a respelling system can work rather well among native speakers who are all familiar with the basic quality of English sounds, however they may differ in a few particularities, it does not work at all among foreign learners of English, who may not know how to pronounce *late* or *can* and who may bring into play their own foreign-language equivalents of these vowel sounds rather than use the English sounds. The phonemes in their own languages are not likely to be those found in English. For ESL and bilingual dictionaries, then, it is obvious that a phonetically based system is necessary. In recent years, the IPA has been adopted by some American ESL dictionaries, notably *LDAE* and *CDAE*. But the American college dictionaries have so far resisted using the IPA (except for the introduction of the schwa [ə]), much to the consternation of linguistic scholars, and even a dictionary that boasts of its representation of "global English," the *Encarta World English Dictionary*, opts for a respelling system rather than the IPA for its pronunciations.

A panel of American lexicographers convened by the American Dialect Society to discuss this very issue offered a number of reasons for the reluctance of American dictionaries to use the IPA.[19] Victoria Neufeldt, then of *Webster's New World Dictionary*, said that "the audience for a general dictionary [has] . . . an internalized, generally unconscious understanding of the relationship between English pronunciation patterns and the standard orthography," hence a respelling system is better. She also pointed out that the values of IPA symbols, which were based on the sound systems of the languages of Europe, would result in transcriptions like [fit] for *feet*, which most native speakers would find confusing since the transcriptions resemble other English words. Enid Pearsons of Random House agreed. Both maintained that pronunciations in general dictionaries should be kept simple and should limit the number of variants shown; an IPA system would be more complicated than necessary. Frederick Mish was not "optimistic about the chance of expanded use of the IPA in . . . [Merriam-Webster's] general dictionaries," as distinguished from learners' dictionaries. As a member of the panel, I offered the opinion that the expanding market for foreign learners' dictionaries would be the vehicle for growth by which the IPA might make inroads in the native-speaker dictionary market. ESL students, who are highly motivated to learn English pronunciations, are generally familiar with the IPA through their language courses. But in native-speaker lexicography there is a populist counter trend to make respelling systems even simpler, because studies have shown that the respelling systems currently in use are widely misunderstood. The simpler systems, which may be called "newspaper respellings," because they are commonly used to represent pronunciations in the popular press, would even abjure use of the schwa, substituting [uh] instead, and use [ee] for IPA [i] and [ah] for IPA [a].

The real question at issue is, "What's a dictionary for?" Does a dictionary for native speakers of the college size or smaller have a pedagogical or heuristic function as well as an information-giving function?

Should we tolerate some probability that a dictionary user will not understand everything perfectly in order to give reasonably accurate and exact information, or should we sacrifice that for a low level of basic comprehensibility for everyone? Is a dictionary essentially like a telephone directory, or is it more like a textbook? In a textbook, the reader often is challenged to take in more than can be easily assimilated. Learning does not come without a price. A directory poses no challenges but gives the merest amount of information. What is wrong with newspaper respellings? They rely on script – letters – rather than sound to convey sound. Respelling representation uses familiar letters but at least signifies through its use of diacritics over many that these symbols are not really letters. They are symbols for sounds. But when one renders *attention* as [uhtenshun] or *extravagant* as [ekstrahvuhgunt], one is using many different combinations of letters to represent the same sounds: sometimes *uh*, sometimes *u*, sometimes *ah*, sometimes *a*, etc. In rendering pronunciation, ideally one wants to represent each sound with one and only one symbol. Newspaper respellings are back-of-the-envelope and are not consistent; the same respelling can refer to two or more different pronunciations. They are also often inaccurate because the spellings often unduly influence the rendering of the pronunciation. Sympathetic as I am with readers who have difficulty with dictionary respelling systems, I am not in favor of simplifying pronunciations any further. In fact, I would like to see the IPA, which as we have seen can be used phonemically, gradually replace the respelling systems.

The arguments made by the lexicographers quoted above in defense of their dictionaries' use of respelling systems have some merit, but one must bear in mind that what was not stated was that marketing considerations play a very large role in making dictionaries reluctant to make this sort of change. The American college dictionary market is highly competitive, and no publisher wants to introduce a feature that might make his dictionary harder to use. The lexicographers argued that even the current respelling systems are widely misunderstood. But surely one of the reasons pronunciation is so confusing is that there is no consistency from one dictionary to the next in how pronunciation is represented. Some symbols are more or less uniform, but others such as the vowel sound in *fear* or the final sound in *very* are not, and even minor differences such as the use or absence of the breve over a symbol (for example, ă) can be confusing. The IPA would provide that consistency, not only among English native-speaker dictionaries but in ESL and bilingual dictionaries and dictionaries of other languages. In the current situation, one never knows whether the difference in rendering the pronunciation of the same word in two dictionaries using different respelling systems is an accidental artifact of the systems or whether it results from a different pronunciation. Apart from that, if people are already confused by the current systems, what have we to lose by introducing a new, better system? It isn't a case of "If it ain't broke, don't fix it." The system *is* broke. Although there are many IPA symbols, in practice, an adequate phonetically based system for a general English dictionary need not be much more complicated than a respelling system. The reluctance of American dictionary houses to use the IPA stems in part from the use of nonalphabetic characters, such as [ʌ] for the vowel sound in *hut* or [ɔ] for that of *law*, or the use of [ð], called the *eth*, and [θ], for the *th* sounds of *the* and *thread*, respectively. There really are not very many such characters; about a dozen IPA symbols would be needed for English dictionaries, and these, especially the consonantal symbols, could be introduced incrementally. A dictionary could proclaim the next year The Year of the Eth as part of a ten-year plan to convert to complete IPA representation. The IPA symbols for vowels would have to be introduced at the same time to avoid confusion with the existing alphabetic vowel symbols. Linked to a pronunciation key at the bottom of the dictionary page, the conversion process would not be an intolerable burden. There has been a great deal of publicity given to the "globalization" of English, but much of it is just talk. Here is something concrete that can be done to make the representation of English sounds understood throughout the world, and a clever publisher could make capital of this effort to promote his dictionary.

I would argue that as one learns to pronounce a foreign language little by little, through continuing use, increasing familiarity with the IPA will eventually lead to a recognition of a more exact phonetic value for each IPA symbol, even when it is used phonemically in a dictionary transcription. Although some IPA symbols may be redefined phonetically to embrace a degree of variation to avoid undue complexity, they will still have an essentially phonetic character and will be completely divorced from any alphabetic script – a fundamental distinction. Implicit in the arguments of the lexicographers in defense of respelling systems is the conviction that most users of their dictionaries are familiar only with English. This may once have been true, and may still be true to a great extent, but it is changing. It is bound to change. English will not always be the dominant language in the world, and in the age of the Internet and international business organizations, the knowledge of languages other than English will be seen as an essential part of one's education, as it already is in most other countries of the world apart from the US. In addition, the dictionaries I have been styling "native-speaker" are not just for native-born speakers. Many immigrants who have no difficulty speaking or comprehending English use "native-speaker" dictionaries for the same reasons native speakers use them, and they would benefit from the use of the IPA. It is time that we stopped defining the audience of native-speaker dictionaries as monolingual people too dumb to understand the IPA.

It is by now obvious to the reader that I do not view dictionaries as comparable to telephone directories, and, while I would not call them textbooks either, I do feel that a dictionary has an obligation to enrich the understanding of the user when it is possible to do so without interfering with the basic purposes of the dictionary. Indeed, in other respects all the college dictionaries recognize this obligation, for example by providing etymological information, usage notes, and synonym discussions. These are not essential parts of a general dictionary's purpose, but they are useful and dictionaries quite rightly include them. They should give the same attention to accurate pronunciation.

In a sense the whole debate about the IPA and respelling systems has been rendered moot by advances in technology that have made possible the audible pronunciations of dictionary entries by using a CD or an Internet connection. Although the use of audible pronunciations is an entirely welcome and exciting development in lexicography, in general only one pronunciation for each lexical item is given, and it may not accurately represent the pronunciations of all speakers. For ESL dictionary users, who basically need one representative pronunciation, the absence of variants will be of little account, and audible pronunciations work well.

One of the major problems in pronunciation parallels that of establishing the written canonical form: what pronunciation will be regarded as preferred, if any? In Britain, where dialectal variations are great, one dialect is preferred over others. The Received Pronunciation (RP) of southern England, based on the careful speech of educated speakers, especially those who are products of the best public schools and of Oxford and Cambridge, is still the standard. No general dictionary could possibly do justice to all the varieties in Britain. In the United States, on the other hand, there are fewer regional differences, and they are relatively minor. The most widely used pronunciation – whether it is acknowledged to be a standard or not – is the measure of priority. Perhaps the major national difference is that of *r*-pronouncers versus *r*-less speakers (in words like *sore* and *paper*). In American dictionaries, the form of the *r*-pronouncers is usually given priority, even though the front-matter guide may acknowledge that *r*-less speakers also exist in large numbers and are not speaking incorrectly. "I wonder," says James R. Hulbert, "how many users of our dictionaries realize that when they see [and I would add, "when they hear"] *färthar*, they are to understand that in the case of Virginians it means *fätha?*"[20]

There is no question that widespread variations such as the alternative ways of saying *either* with initial /aɪ/ or /i/ must be represented. What to do about *pen* and *pin*, or *father* with or without the /r/, is another matter. As one pronunciation expert acknowledges, rules for converting one symbol to another based on instructions in the front-matter guide are difficult to follow: "Moreover, the dictionary user requires information to be explicit at the point of entry and rarely consults the good advice given in the introductory sections, which are usually read only by other lexicographers."[21]

The alternative is to show each variation in the pronunciation of each word, the practice generally followed by *NID3*. A number of prominent lexicographers have criticized *NID3*'s pronunciations as too elaborate and cumbersome.[22] Some of the pronunciations are undeniably complex and difficult to follow, but it seems to me that the only synchronic, unabridged dictionary in English should record fully the variant pronunciations documented by regional linguistic atlases and by its own phonological records. Many of the criticisms that attended the original publication of *NID3* in 1961 showed that even professional writers had difficulty understanding many of the features of the dictionary apart from pronunciation, especially the presentation of usage information. But when one is trying to represent the language with a high degree of detail, some complexity is unavoidable. For the same reason, the *OED* is not the easiest dictionary in the world to use either.

Bilingual dictionaries generally show only one pronunciation. "[T]he foreign learner," one scholar comments, "would be at a loss when offered more than one variant."[23] Here as in ESL lexicography, audible pronunciations are generally to be preferred to written ones, but when transcriptions must be used, few variants should be included. Variant pronunciations are also kept to a minimum in school dictionaries. The student, whether native-speaking child or adult foreigner, needs direction. Both types of dictionaries are necessarily normative compared to general, adult, monolingual dictionaries.

Some scientific and technical dictionaries provide pronunciations and some do not. Because many technical terms are seldom pronounced outside of the lecture hall, it is often difficult to ascertain their pronunciations. Many pronunciations for scientific words are necessarily devised on the basis of analogy with other similar words whose pronunciation is known, since terms like *coccidioidomycosis*, for example, do not turn up frequently in conversation. The scientific vocabulary is preeminently written; numerous terms encountered frequently in print are rarely uttered. Thus, scientific and technical dictionaries necessarily adopt a normative approach to their pronunciations. Where a record of usage does exist, the pronunciations based on usage are given preference to those based on analogy, but in a large technical dictionary that situation is the exception rather than the rule.

James R. Hulbert remarks that dictionaries are less satisfactory in pronunciation than in spelling, meaning, or etymology.[24] The record of the spoken language is difficult to acquire, difficult to transcribe accurately and unambiguously, difficult to represent understandably in a dictionary transcription. Pronunciation remains a low priority in monolingual, commercial lexicography because lexicographers perceive that pronunciation is of marginal interest to their audience. Perhaps reflecting this state of affairs, one recent British dictionary, the *New Oxford Dictionary of English* (*NODE*), does not even give pronunciations for entry words it regards as too simple to warrant them, a policy that opens the door to the argument that simple words or definitions, too, might be omitted. But no one is ready to turn back the clock to re-embrace the "hard words" tradition of the eighteenth century.[25] The only comprehensive American pronouncing dictionary, John S. Kenyon and Thomas A. Knott's *A Pronouncing Dictionary of American English*, was published more than half a century ago (1944) and has never been revised. *NID3*'s full coverage of pronunciation may be interpreted as a gesture of atonement for its failure to revise Kenyon and Knott (published by G. & C. Merriam), a decision no doubt based on commercial considerations. For current pronunciations of American English, the reader has no choice but to consult general dictionaries. In ESL lexicography, the *English Pronouncing Dictionary* originally edited by Daniel Jones and revised by Peter Roach and James Hartman is the only general pronunciation dictionary in which both British and American English are given (almost) equal status, British English still being the default variety. The *Longman Pronunciation Dictionary* edited by John Wells covers mainly British

English, though some attention is given to American English. Both dictionaries use the IPA. These books, valuable as they are, are most at risk of being replaced by CDs in which pronunciations are given audibly.

ETYMOLOGY

Whenever the subject at a dinner or cocktail party among fresh acquaintances turns to what each of us does for a living, and I am introduced as a dictionary maker, inevitably the first response from my associates is that they find dictionaries fascinating, and in particular the derivation of words. From the number of cocktail party acquaintances who have in all seriousness, but with what sobriety I cannot say, affirmed that they loved to read – "yes, read" – dictionaries, one would suppose the nation to be studded with pockets of people neglecting their work and families to read dictionaries, especially etymologies. Somehow, I doubt it. I have never heard anyone say that he or she loved to read pronunciations. Although meaning is certainly most often sought by dictionary users, it does not have the cachet of etymology, which combines knowledge of other languages, especially the classical tongues, with arcane scholarship. It may come as a surprise to some readers, then, to learn that of all the elements included in modern dictionaries etymology has the least to do with the essential purpose of a synchronic dictionary. Etymology may be valuable in its own right, but it tells us little about current meaning and is in fact often misleading. Here is what a textbook on the development of the English language has to say on the subject:

> The belief is widespread, even by some quite learned people, that the way to find out what a word means is to find out what it previously meant – or, preferably, if it were possible to do so, what it originally meant . . . [S]uch an appeal to etymology to determine present meaning is as unreliable as would be an appeal to spelling to determine modern pronunciation. Change of meaning – semantic change, as it is called – may, and frequently does, alter the so-called etymological sense, which may have become altogether obsolete . . . [¶] Certain popular writers, overeager to display their learning, have asserted that words are misused when they depart from their etymological meanings. Thus Ambrose Bierce . . . declared that *dilapidated*, because of its ultimate derivation from Latin *lapis* 'stone,' could appropriately be used only of a stone structure.[26]

By the same token, Pyles and Algeo observe, we should have to confine the use of *eradicate* to roots, since it is derived from Latin *radix* "root"; *calculation*, from Latin *calx* "stone," to counting pebbles; *sinister* to leftists; and *giddy* to those divinely inspired, since *gid* is derived from *god*.

The error of associating current meaning with past etymological meaning is commonplace also in the sciences, particularly medicine, where devotion to tradition and a belief in the sanctity of Latin combine to reinforce the fallacy. As the medical lexicographer A. Manuila points out,

Many words, whether technical or in ordinary use, have departed so widely from their original meaning that the latter can be of interest only to medical historians and linguists. Thus, etymologically, *thalassaemia* means "sea in the blood," *gonorrhoea* "a flow of semen," *artery* "an air vessel," *asphyxia* "a weak or suppressed pulse," *autopsy* "self-seeing," *embryo* "a young animal," *diploma* "anything folded twice," and *anatomy* "a cutting through."[27]

Nathan Bailey's *An Universal Etymological Dictionary* of 1721 was the first English dictionary to treat etymology with consistent purpose and seriousness. Etymology was sometimes included in earlier dictionaries, but in a rudimentary way, often consisting simply of a language designation such as *L* for Latin. Bailey gave the Latin etymon and often more immediate sources, as in Italian or French. Though he too was inconsistent, Bailey is credited with having established etymology as "one of the requisites of any reputable dictionary."[28]

How far we have come in our expectations of what general dictionaries should provide by way of etymology is illustrated by criticisms of recent dictionaries. Patrick Drysdale, a British lexicographer formerly active in Canada, lists the following etymological desiderata:
1. Source language or language family
2. First English form and/or immediate source
3. Date or period of entry into English
4. Changes in form and meaning in English
5. Intermediate stages
6. Ultimate known source
7. Semantic development
8. Ultimate underlying or hypothetical form, e.g., an Indo-European root
9. Cognates in related languages also derived from the underlying form
10. Other English words derived from the same base.[29]

In the eighteenth century and the early part of the nineteenth, no one could have fulfilled Drysdale's standard for good etymological treatment, because the great advances in philology that were to transform it into a science had not occurred or were yet relatively unknown. What are the principles that the famous philologists of the nineteenth century – Rasmus Rask, Franz Bopp, August Friedrich Pott, Jacob Grimm, Karl Verner, Ferdinand de Saussure, Karl Brugmann, and others – elaborated? Essentially, they discovered and proved that sound change was regular rather than hit or miss. Henry Cecil Wyld, in the introduction to his dictionary, *The Universal Dictionary of the English Language*, which gives exceptionally full attention to etymology, describes the discovery:

We soon learn to appreciate the truth of the great principle which guides all philological study, that a given sound is always changed, in one and the same dialect, in the same way, under the same conditions. Thus, for instance, in Greek initial *s* becomes the aspirate *h*, and between vowels is lost altogether; in Celtic initial *p* is lost; in Sanscrit, Persian, and the Baltic-Slavic families a sound which appears as *k* in Greek and Latin and as *h* in Germanic, develops into the sound of *sh* or *s*; Germanic has changed old *p, t, k* into *f, þ* ("thorn"), *h*, respectively, and so on. These changes take place everywhere, in all words containing these sounds, not in only isolated words here and there.[30]

The importance of the last sentence above can scarcely be exaggerated, for up until this time etymologies had depended on chance similarities between words in different languages or on wildly speculative theories based on biblical stories to determine the derivation of words. As we have seen, Noah Webster devoted ten years of study to the world's languages with the aim of mastering the science of etymology, but since he was contemptuous of the principle of regularity of sound change and ignorant of the discoveries based upon it, his etymologies were worthless.

The modern etymologist must explain how every sound in the current canonical form of each word developed from older forms. If he cannot explain certain changes on the basis of systematic sound change according to established principles, he must have some other plausible explanation to account for them. Merely saying that the sounds of /d/ and /t/, for example, are similar will not do. Common sense, however, still plays an important role in good etymologizing. As the famous etymologist Walter Skeat declared, "observe chronology." "The word *surloin* or *sirloin*," he points out, "is often said to be derived from the fact that the *loin* was knighted as *Sir Loin* by Charles II, or (according to Richardson) by James I. Chronology makes short work of this statement; the word being in use long before James I was born." Borrowings are due to actual contact. "The history of a nation generally accounts for the constituent parts of its language. When an early English word is compared with Hebrew or Coptic, as used to be done in the *old* editions of Webster's dictionary, history is set at defiance . . ."[31]

The importance of etymology for historical dictionaries is beyond dispute. The main purpose of a diachronic dictionary such as the *OED* is to trace the development of form and meaning over an extended period of time for each word in the language. In this sense every historical dictionary is a work of etymology, although it is not an etymological dictionary. An etymological dictionary shows a word's form and meaning when it first appeared in English, from what other languages the form may have derived, and often describes its intermediate and ultimate forms and meanings, but the meanings given are usually simple glosses used to distinguish the sense from past or future meanings. Its attention is directed to the evolution of the form, and in order to distinguish one form from another, meanings must sometimes be distinguished. The attention of a historical dictionary is directed to the evolution of meaning, and it must therefore show the various forms having the same meaning.

Synchronic dictionaries need not deal with etymology at all and some do not. Small paperback, general dictionaries usually omit it. Desk dictionaries include only very brief etymologies. American college dictionaries give more extensive etymologies. The British native-speaker dictionaries vary rather widely in their coverage, but the *New Oxford Dictionary of English* (*NODE*) stands out for giving more thorough etymologies than the others, and they are written in plain English without abbreviations. Many lexicographers have been skeptical about the public's appetite for dictionary etymologies. Clarence Barnhart states, with characteristic honesty, "Most dictionary users have little interest or use for etymologies."[32] How does one square this with my acquaintance with untold numbers of people reading dictionaries and fascinated by the derivations of words? The people who think they love etymology regard etymology as stories – *interesting* stories – about word histories. Books recounting remarkable word histories – or histories that seem to be relevant to recent social or political events – have always been popular and successful with the public. In the nineteenth century, Dean Trench wrote a series of extremely successful and erudite works for a popular audience which, while not exclusively etymological, often included etymological information. In the early part of the twentieth century Ernest Weekley's books on etymology were very popular. H. L. Mencken's *The American Language* derived much of its popularity from its etymological information. Later in the century the works of William and Mary Morris and of Stuart Flexner drew wide and appreciative audiences, and more recently still William Safire's books have found a wide audience. Such books naturally select just those words and expressions that will provide material for entertaining accounts and are often highly speculative. This is not meant in criticism – who would be churlish enough to disparage books that are both educational and fun to read? – but they are not comparable to the treatment of etymology in dictionaries, which must provide histories for many thousands of words, the great majority of which do not have charming anecdotes associated with their histories but which instead consist of an uninspiring list of foreign words and a handful of glosses. Nor can dictionaries indulge in clever speculation.

Children's dictionaries either omit etymologies entirely or include brief statements when the derivation is particularly interesting. For example, they may say that *iconoclast* comes from Greek words meaning "breaker of images." Subjecting children who are in the process of mastering their own written language to unfamiliar words in other languages does not make a great deal of sense. Etymologies are not included in ESL dictionaries or in bilingual dictionaries. To use space on this subject for a foreign learner, given the many other more profitable uses to which the space could be put, would be foolish, especially when dictionaries for native speakers cover the ground so much better than any ESL or "translation" dictionary could.

Etymologies are often included in scientific and technical dictionaries, especially those for the older sciences such as medicine, because they are mistakenly believed to be essential to an understanding of meaning. In fact, what is important in medicine is not a knowledge of Latin or Greek but of the modern meanings of combining forms derived from Latin and Greek. It certainly helps, if one has never encountered *nephroureterocystectomy* before, to be able to divide the word into its components – *nephro-*, *uretero-*, *cyst-*, and *-ectomy* – rather than perceiving it as an alphabetic blur. But to know that *nephro-* has to do with the kidney implies no knowledge of the Greek *nephros* underlying it, and a knowledge of the underlying Greek or Latin can be misleading, as we have already seen, by implying a relationship that no longer obtains. If one understands the limitations of etymology in conveying modern meaning, it is surely of value to know how the ancients perceived conditions such as *thalassemia* and *gonorrhea* and may even, in rare cases, throw light on some aspect of modern meaning. Etymology's chief value lay in its historic and linguistic interest, not in its relevance to the modern meanings of scientific terms. However, curiosity about etymology is widely held to be a sign of keen intelligence. It suggests interest in, if not familiarity with, study of the classical languages, and Latin and Greek strike awe in the hearts of most people. Thus, by giving considerable attention to etymology, the compilers identify their dictionary with the prestige of the classical tradition and with a species of scholarship regarded reverentially by many potential customers.

Are etymologies useful to anyone? If they do not contribute to an understanding of current meaning, shouldn't they be omitted altogether from non-historical, general dictionaries? It is a question worth pondering. Patrick Drysdale considers the question and cites three reasons for including etymologies:

1. to provide raw material for the scholar and the student of the history of the English language;
2. to increase understanding of, and stimulate interest in, both language in general and one language in particular;
3. since a dictionary is a record of the culture of those who speak the language it describes, to provide clues to the history of the culture and its relationships to others.[33]

Without etymologies, the entries in a dictionary appear to have been granted their present shapes by divine right, without relation to any other language and without relation to the past. To divorce a language from its past misses the opportunity to show language in its context, even though particular words may be very well defined without etymology. It is the difference between seeing a lion on the African plains and seeing it in a zoo. The zoo may afford a better look at the lion – but a much inferior view of lions. I come back to my view that a dictionary should be more than a telephone directory in which you search for a datum and find it. A dictionary should give one the opportunity to expand one's view of language by offering more than is necessary, even if by doing so it includes some material that some readers will have difficulty understanding. A book, incidentally, performs this function better than an electronic database because a book is easier to scroll when one doesn't know exactly what one is looking for, in the marvelously efficient process of data retrieval called turning the pages. And I do mean "exactly." Who hasn't been frustrated in a computer search by not realizing, after fifteen minutes of enduring brusque messages accusing one of complete and final failure, that the computer wanted one to type, for example, "N.Y." rather than "NY," or vice versa, without ever giving the slightest clue as to why one's original input had been rejected? I know it is easy for programmers to anticipate such variations, but the point is they don't, because programmers aren't editors, and people who edit books are.

Etymologies demonstrate that language changes in form and meaning. Even the brief etymologies in synchronic dictionaries remind people of this process and sometimes give glimpses of the way other cultures, or our own in times past, viewed particular words. The processes of semantic change, coinages of new words, and linguistic borrowing from other languages (*loan words*) have been thoroughly explored and discussed in fascinating detail in a number of studies.[34] Dictionaries have sought ways to exploit the public's broad interest in new words and meanings, but have so far failed to come up with a successful formula. Conventional dictionary treatment of etymologies does not usually shed much light on semantic development, for two reasons: first, because often there has been too little scholarly research and there is uncertainty or ignorance about the subject; and secondly, because dictionaries have better uses for the space and have usually compressed their etymologies as much as possible. In this respect *NODE* is exceptional in spending an unusual amount of space on etymologies, and perhaps its treatment will inspire other dictionaries to take a fresh look at presenting etymologies in a more readable way for the general user. However, etymological scholars seem anything but sanguine about the future of etymology as a discipline or as a feature in general dictionaries. Drysdale remarks, "In recent times, the emphasis on descriptive linguistics has resulted in a downgrading of the importance of the history of words, while the wider availability of etymological dictionaries has made a full statement of etymology in the general dictionary seem less important."[35] Yakov Malkiel, in a survey of the history of etymological research, laments, "With the rarest of exceptions, the best of our universities hesitate to offer at any level lecture courses or seminars on etymology," although they offer instruction in every other aspect of language study. Malkiel lists numerous reasons for this neglect and notes with evident regret the priority given dictionary-style compilations as opposed to scholarly monographs.[36] Etymologists engaged by synchronic dictionaries, and by most historical dictionaries for that matter, do very little original scholarly research but rely mainly on etymological dictionaries, which in turn rely on scholarly monographs and on other etymological dictionaries. Most dictionary etymologists, while often conversant with the classical tongues and modern languages, are not professionally equipped to do original scholarly research, and they wouldn't have the time to do it if they were. If the well of original research in etymology dries up, dictionaries will simply go on repeating past suppositions, right or wrong. Whereas we can expect the treatment of dictionary meaning to improve with corpus use, and the representation of pronunciation to improve because of the recording and transcription of authentic speech, not to mention its audible presentation, the future of etymology is problematical.

In the eighteenth century and for most of the nineteenth, dictionaries of English placed the etymology near the beginning of the dictionary article, before the definition. This practice is still followed by the *OED* and other historical dictionaries, as well as by *NID3*, which presents its definitions in historical sequence. The Funk & Wagnalls unabridged *Standard Dictionary* of 1893 was the first dictionary to place the etymology after the definition, and since then the practice has been adopted by most other dictionaries. The reasoning was that since the definition is more often sought than etymology, it should appear earlier in the entry. The early placement of etymology within square brackets is seen as a kind of moat that the reader must leap across to reach his quest. I do not think it makes very much difference where the etymology is placed. If it is clearly marked as etymology, one loses no time sweeping ahead to its definition. Commercial dictionaries will, of course, go on declaring that they have shattered all precedent and opened communication to millions of frustrated dictionary users by their ingenious innovations, but often it's a matter of Tweedledum and Tweedledee.

SYNONYMS

One of Dean Trench's criticisms in his paper *On Some Deficiencies in Our English Dictionaries* (1857) was the scant attention given to "distinguishing of synonymous words." He calls for the discrimination of synonyms "likely to be confounded," such as *safe* and *secure*. The first dictionary to include a large number of such discussions was Joseph E. Worcester's great work of 1860, *A Dictionary of the English Language*, perhaps in heed of Trench's criticism. Worcester can be said to have established synonym discriminations as a standard feature of large dictionaries.

Dictionaries of synonyms

Dictionaries of synonym discriminations, variously known in the nineteenth century as *synonymicons* or *synonymies*, have a venerable history. The discussion of synonyms goes back to the ancients, and the earliest synonymies were of Greek and Latin during the Renaissance. French and German dictionaries of synonyms appeared in the eighteenth century. One of the earliest synonym dictionaries in English was John Trusler's

Difference between Words Esteemed Synonymous in the English Language (1766). Another very early synonym dictionary was that of Hester Lynch Piozzi, more widely known as Hester Lynch Thrale, the celebrated friend of Samuel Johnson. Her *British Synonymy: or an Attempt to regulate the Choice of Words in Familiar Conversation* appeared in 1794. William Taylor's small octavo *English Synonyms Discriminated* was published in 1813, and in 1816 George Crabb's *English Synonymes Explained*, the latter going through many editions. An edition of *Crabb's English Synonymes* was published in 1917, a century after the first edition.

The lack of any dictionary of synonyms in English before the end of the eighteenth century is not hard to explain. In the sixteenth and seventeenth centuries the extent of the entire English word stock was much smaller than it is now, and the problem then, as Taylor points out in the Preface of his book, was that the same word had to be used in a variety of contexts with different meanings. As the word stock increased, the lexicon absorbed words that were near synonyms of existing words, or words that evolved in meaning to become near synonyms. It was not until the word stock of English was sufficiently developed to embrace thousands of near synonyms that dictionaries of synonyms could be written with much effect.

As an example of the kind of discriminations given in such early books, here is part of Taylor's essay on *mirth* and *cheerfulness*, attributed to Addison: "Mirth is an effort, cheerfulness a habit of mind; mirth is transient, and cheerfulness permanent; mirth is like a flash of lightening, that glitters with momentary brilliance, cheerfulness is the day-light of the soul, which steeps it in perpetual serenity." Sometimes collocation was indicated, as in this essay on *brute* and *beast*: "Both these words are applied to animals, as distinguished from birds, insects, fishes, and man; but the term *brute* is confined to the untamed quadrupeds. [¶] We say, *beasts* of burden, never brutes of burden. The beasts of the field; the brutes of the forest."[37]

At this point we must backtrack a bit and determine just what is meant by synonymy, in the sense of the state of being synonymous. Zgusta specifies three aspects of lexical meaning: the designatum, connotation, and range of application. *Designatum* refers to the essential properties of the thing or concept that define it; *connotation* refers to associated features; and *range of application* refers to the variety of contexts in which the word may be used.[38] Zgusta defines absolute synonymy as occurring when two terms correspond in all three aspects of designatum, connotation, and range. Absolute synonymy is rare among general terms but common among technical ones, especially in medicine. For example, *Creutzfeldt-Jakob disease*, a progressive degenerative brain disease, has at least ten absolute synonyms (which I prefer to call variants), including *Jakob-Creutzfeldt disease*, *Jakob's disease*, *Creutzfeldt-Jakob syndrome*, *Jones-Nevin syndrome*, and *spongiform encephalopathy*.

If the correspondence is exact in one or two of the three aspects but not in all, the two words are near synonyms. *Beast* and *brute* have the same designatum – an animal other than man – but are dissimilar both in connotation and in range of application. It is precisely the object of synonym discussions to distinguish the ways in which two words differ in one or more aspect, usually that of connotation, and often of range as well. Such discriminations are based on individual point of view and depend for their effect largely on quality of expression rather than cogency of argument. At the end of his discussion of *beast* and *brute*, Taylor adds of another synonymist: "Dr. Trusler gives an opposite account of these words." Today both words are probably used metaphorically of people more often than of animals; these uses would be considered separate senses from those applied to animals but they would certainly affect the connotations associated even with the literal senses.

In the second half of the twentieth century, books of synonym discriminations were not nearly as popular as thesauruses (described below), and since comparisons of synonyms are much harder to prepare, there are fewer of them than of thesauruses. Richard Whateley's *Selection of English Synonyms* appeared in 1851 and Charles John Smith's *Synonyms Discriminated: A Dictionary of Synonymous Words in the English Language* twenty years later. The second edition of Smith's dictionary (1890) is an impressive work of 870 double-column pages, including etymologies, many quotations from well-known writers illustrating the words discussed, and an index. Smith frequently compares three or more words, and even as many as eight. James C. Fernald's *English Synonyms and Antonyms* was published in 1896 and revised in 1914. Fernald's discussions often involve a dozen words and consist of a sentence about each. He is one of the few synonymists to pay any attention to antonyms, though he merely lists them alphabetically at the end of each essay. The book includes a full index and a question-and-answer section for teachers. An interesting and useful feature is the inclusion of notes "on the correct use of prepositions" with the verbs discriminated. The *Funk & Wagnalls Modern Guide to Synonyms and Related Words*, edited by S. I. Hayakawa and the Funk & Wagnalls dictionary staff, was first published in 1968. Apart from Funk & Wagnalls, which has passed from the scene and is now, one might say, defunked, the only dictionary house with a tradition of producing books of synonym discriminations is Merriam-Webster. Its latest collection is *Merriam-Webster's Dictionary of Synonyms* (1993). Collections of this sort are so difficult to prepare that no one wants to begin a new book from scratch; therefore, every existing collection is revised, abridged, supplemented, and used in every way possible to provide the bases of "new" books. Even the *Modern Guide to Synonyms*, for example, written in the mid-1960s, drew upon Fernald's synonym essays as a point of departure, although, since they were fifty years old, they provided little help in the main, and writing the book was an enormously time-consuming enterprise.[39]

The much more modest success of synonym discriminations, as compared with thesauruses, is not surprising as soon as one realizes that the former are not really reference works. They may discriminate a few thousand words in all, but even were they to include twice or three times that many, they would hardly be comprehensive enough to assure users that they will find the word they seek, as a dictionary or thesaurus does. Their appeal is therefore much more limited, and for such books to find an audience they must either be written on a very simple level indeed or assume a degree of familiarity with word usage and meaning that not every reader has. For the reader to appreciate the finer distinctions among synonyms, the grosser distinctions have to have been assimilated and there has to be a thirst for greater knowledge of subtle discrimination. Interest in such books is not likely to be strong unless they are packaged in a way that represents them as having direct practical utility, which of course isn't true.

ROGET'S THESAURUS

In speaking of synonym dictionaries, I have been referring to works devoted to brief essays in which synonyms were discriminated. In 1852, Peter Mark Roget's *Thesaurus of English Words and Phrases* was published. Roget was an English physician who had already made a name for himself with his studies in physiology. The *Thesaurus* was a different sort of book, with words arranged, to use Roget's own description,

not in alphabetical order as they are in a Dictionary, but according to the *ideas* which they express. The purpose of an ordinary dictionary is simply to explain the meaning of words . . . The object aimed at in the present undertaking is exactly the converse of this: namely, – The idea being given, to find the word, or words, by which that idea may be most fitly and aptly expressed. For this purpose, the words and phrases of the language are here classed, not according to their sound or their orthography, but strictly according to their *signification*.

Roget elaborated six classes of categories: abstract relations; space; material world; intellect; volition; sentient and moral powers. Within these broad classifications he placed numerous subdivisions, with subdivisions further divided. He recognized that many words would fall into more than one category and that the placement of a word in one or another category was a difficult decision. Even the first edition included an index to help readers find the signification they were looking for, but the presumption then was that the elaborate classification of thoughts would usually suffice without resort to the index: "By the aid of the table [of classification of subjects into divisions], the reader will, with a little practice, readily discover the place which the particular topic he is in search of occupies in the series . . . [I]f, during the search, any doubt or difficulty should occur, recourse may be had to the copious alphabetical Index of words at the end of the volume . . ." However ingenious the hierarchy of concepts, it was pure fantasy to suppose that any conceptual arrangement of the vocabulary of English was natural to most native speakers. It cannot be doubted that few readers could have found the meaning sought without recourse to the index, which has been expanded greatly through the work's many editions. The most recent edition, *Roget's International Thesaurus* (1992), edited by Robert L. Chapman, straightforwardly instructs the reader to begin with the index.[40]

Conceptually vs. alphabetically arranged thesauruses

So closely identified is *Roget* with this kind of synonym work that the name, now in the common domain, has been adopted by many other synonym dictionaries, some using a conceptual arrangement and others organized alphabetically with a list of synonyms following every main entry. Both kinds of works are now called *thesauruses*.[41] The claim made by proponents of the conceptual variety that theirs is the only true thesaurus is specious. "Thesaurus" was used long before Roget adopted it for his work in its Greek sense of a storehouse or treasure, with the specific meaning of an exhaustive survey of words, as in Ainsworth's *Thesaurus Linguae Latinae Compendiarius* (1736), and it has retained this sense in English. It was perfectly suitable for Roget to describe his own work by the word *thesaurus*, but there is no historical or logical basis for arguing that his use of the term is the only correct one and that *thesau-*

rus may not, with equal regard for its history, be used to describe other kinds of synonym dictionaries, and indeed other kinds of dictionaries.

Roget is used in the titles of dozens of different synonym books. The use or non-use of *thesaurus* and *Roget* (exactly like the use of *Webster* among dictionaries) is worth millions of dollars to competing publishers. The real conflict is between those who would like to reserve these words for their own exclusive profit and those who fear that their failure to use them would place them at an enormous marketing disadvantage. The unfortunate fact is that most buyers of reference books know very little about the merits of competing works but rely chiefly on a familiarity with their names. The argument that *thesaurus* has a true sense is merely a smokescreen to conceal the battle for commercial profit.

Both the alphabetical and the conceptual thesaurus rely on an alphabetical listing, but the conceptual arrangement leads the reader from an index to clusters of words centered upon a congeries of related meanings. Most alphabetical thesauruses do not have an index, the presumption being that any word the reader might want a synonym for will appear as a headword. (*The Oxford Thesaurus*, as we shall see, is an exception, as it does have an index.) Both systems involve a great deal of repetition of any given word. In theory the conceptual approach offers a greater likelihood that the reader will find the word being sought, because the words for similar concepts will be found in adjacent or nearby sections. The alphabetical arrangement, on the other hand, is easier to use, since the reader can often find synonyms by looking in one place rather than two or more.

Among the alphabetical thesauruses are *Merriam-Webster's Collegiate Thesaurus* (1988); and *The Oxford Thesaurus* (2nd edn., 1997) and *The Oxford Thesaurus, American Edition* (1992), ed. Laurence Urdang. To my mind these illustrate the weaknesses and strengths of an alphabetical arrangement. *Merriam-Webster's Collegiate Thesaurus* is evidently a revision of the *Webster's Collegiate Thesaurus* of 1976, though there is no indication of this on the copyright page. It, like the 1976 edition, is declared to be "a wholly new book" in exactly the same words. Both editions have entries for words that few would want a synonym for, such as *immaleable, immedicable, immingle, immix, plummetless, prodigalize, proemial, profusive, programma*, and many others of similar rarity. Surely anyone for whom these words sprang to mind would need no thesaurus. It seems apparent that the entry list and synonyms were created from a database and that the work was prepared with insufficient editorial intervention. However, this thesaurus does seek to make finer distinctions than other thesauruses by having categories for "related words" as well as synonyms, and for "contrasted words" as well as antonyms. In both editions of *The Oxford Thesaurus,* the text consists of an alphabetically arranged thesaurus and a long index in which every synonym is listed with references to the headwords under which it appears, or to the headword entry under which it is listed, or both. The references specify under which numbered sense the synonym appears – a necessity, as there are many numbered senses in the alphabetical section. Among alphabetical thesauruses, it is unique. Within the alphabetical section, every synonym that is itself a headword is marked with a small circle, so the reader can turn to that entry for further synonyms. The thesaurus also includes an illustrative sentence for every sense to help distinguish meaning and show typical context. *The Oxford Thesaurus* is certainly the most sophisticated of the current lot of alphabetical thesauruses.

The conceptual scheme is associated with extreme inclusiveness. Rarely used words, non-English words, names, obsolete and unidiomatic expressions, phrases that are not lexical units but pseudodefinitions: all are thrown in together along with common words without any apparent principle of selection. For example, in the fifth edition of *Roget's International Thesaurus* (1992) – one of the best of the conceptually arranged works – we find included under the subheading *orator:* "Demosthenes, Cicero, Franklin D. Roosevelt, Winston Churchill, William Jennings Bryan, Martin Luther King." Why not Pericles and Billy Graham? Why not Daniel Webster or John C. Calhoun? When one starts to include types of things, where does one stop? Another conceptual thesaurus, *Bartlett's Roget's Thesaurus* (1996), includes within its conceptual categories of synonyms many lists of types of things: styles of art and architecture, sporting activities, heraldic terms, and a lengthy list of phobias in which I was disappointed to find no phobia for dictionaries, only one for words (*logophobia*). It also includes a sprinkling of quotations. I just don't know why *giant sloth* should be in a thesaurus, but it appears in this one under the category **oldness** and the subdivision *prehistoric animal,* and appears alongside other synonyms like *woolly mammoth, pterodactyl,* and *trilobite.* At times these works seem to be a potpourri of everything the compiler can think of. The governing principle seems to be that the more there is, the more likely it is that something in the collection will prove to be useful.

The alphabetical arrangement is usually associated with more selectivity, although there are some exceptions. But, generally speaking, names, rarely used words, and types of things are excluded. Because of their arrangement, alphabetical thesauruses can follow the sense breakdown of a dictionary. *The Doubleday Roget's Thesaurus in Dictionary Form* (1977), for example, was modeled after the sense breakdown of *The Doubleday Dictionary* (1975). In a work based on selectivity, the compilers must have in mind a clear perception of their intended audience. Though the level of difficulty of the synonyms may vary somewhat, the necessity of excluding some words imposes a limited range upon most alphabetical works that is lacking in most conceptually arranged works. Alphabetical thesauruses tend to be more homogeneous than conceptually arranged works. The governing principle is that the compilers know best what the user is likely to need.

Dictionary treatment of synonymy

Because general dictionaries are truly reference works, the inclusion of synonym discriminations makes a great deal of sense. When they are not included, they are not missed; when they are included, they are a welcome superfluity. Some usage notes, such as that for *uninterested* and *disinterested*, may masquerade as synonym discriminations, and it is these the user is most likely to seek and find. The words included in true synonym discriminations are unpredictable. Dictionaries sometimes combine discriminations with brief lists of synonyms keyed to specific definitions. Both adult and children's dictionaries include synonymies, but the children's version is apt to be more didactic in keeping with its pedagogical purpose. Among general dictionaries, the discriminations of *The Century Dictionary* (1889–91) are outstanding for their quality and for the sensitive choice of quotations illustrating each word discriminated. They are neither wordy nor too slight but give fair attention to each word and show typical contexts in addition to the quotations.

ESL and bilingual dictionaries do not include synonym discriminations, since such rarefied distinctions are quite beyond the skills of their users and altogether irrelevant to their purpose. Their aim is not to provide exquisite sensitivity to another language but to provide the means for communicating competently with a native speaker of another language. That goal is tough enough without worrying about the fine distinctions of connotation. Synonym discriminations are strictly for the native speaker.

The larger question of synonymy and bilingual lexicography is a profound one beyond the scope of this book. For example, two words in English may be near synonyms, such as *brute* and *beast*, but their respective translations into another language may be completely unrelated.

Contrariwise, two words in English that are semantically unrelated may correspond in translation to two near synonyms in another language. This is an illustration of anisomorphism, discussed by Zgusta at length in his treatment of the bilingual dictionary.[42]

I have mentioned technical dictionaries and said they differ from other kinds of dictionaries in having numerous absolute synonyms. As the reader may have surmised, I am not entirely easy with this statement. Can we really call *Jakob-Creutzfeldt disease* a synonym for *Creutzfeldt-Jakob disease*? It is a mere variant, having close kinship with spelling variants. Even in the case of less similar forms, such as the *Jones-Nevin syndrome* and *spongiform encephalopathy*, the absoluteness of synonymy with *Creutzfeldt-Jakob disease* is of a different order than that of ordinary language. *Jones-Nevin syndrome* and *spongiform encephalopathy* were names given to this disease by medical scientists who subsequently discovered that the diseases they had described were identical to one previously described by Creutzfeldt and Jakob. In medicine, this happens all the time. Recall the initial skepticism in the early 1980s that the virus concurrently identified in France and in the United States as the cause of what we now call AIDS was the same virus. It was first called by different names in the two countries. In America it was known as *human T cell leukemia/lymphoma virus-3*, abbreviated *HTLV-3*. Only later, after much discussion, disagreement, and confusion, was the name *human immunodeficiency virus* (*HIV*) settled upon. Indeed, since the syndrome it caused manifested itself by many different symptoms, there was considerable doubt that HIV could be the cause for AIDS in all of its varieties, and a small but obstinate minority of scientists is still not convinced. No examination of the usage of these terms in their immediate linguistic contexts could have established their identity, as would be the case with synonyms used in ordinary language. Scientific and technical terms are *said* to be the same by investigators on the basis of their examination of the detailed data describing the circumstances that these terms are supposed to signify. Subsequent research may show that the conditions described are not in fact the same, in spite of their having been used as absolute synonyms, in which case the terms now called synonyms will have to be reclassified. Unlike the words used in ordinary language, scientific nomenclature depends upon a process of naming and on the external, physical circumstances or properties of the things named. I believe that different names for the same entity should be called variants; to call them synonyms masks their fundamental difference from ordinary language, in which usage determines synonymity.

ILLUSTRATIONS

Nathan Bailey's dictionaries in the early eighteenth century included a number of woodcut illustrations, but it was not until the publication of John Ogilvie's *Imperial Dictionary* in 1850 that a dictionary gave prominence to pictorial illustration. *The Century Dictionary*, based on Charles Annandale's revision of the Ogilvie dictionary, is justly famous for the quality and number of its illustrations. The *Century* used some of the Ogilvie illustrations, but many others were drawn expressly for it or for the *Century Magazine*. The dictionary was published by the Century Company, whose *Century Magazine* was prized for the excellence of its illustrations. Since the manager of the company's art department, W. Lewis Fraser, was put in charge of assembling the *Dictionary*'s illustrations, it is not surprising that their quality is so high. As Michael Hancher has observed, the *Century Magazine* broke new ground in the art of illustration both technically and artistically, and the publishers brought this expertise to bear in illustrating the *Dictionary*. Most of its illustrations are wood engravings, improved by a process involving the use of photography, but the *Century Dictionary* also includes a few halftones, a surprisingly early use of this form of illustration in a dictionary. Moreover, as Hancher shows, the choice of subjects and the manner of representation were unusually original for its time. For example, the *Century* illustrates a horse *bucking* (for the verb *buck*) with an illustration after a drawing by Frederic Remington, the popular Western artist and sculptor, whose art had already appeared in the *Century Magazine*.[43] Even today, lexicographers view the illustration of a verb as a bit daring. The illustrations of animals and plants are exceptionally fine and are often initialed by the artists, one of whom was Ernest Thompson Seton. Seton's illustrations of birds are particularly notable. No dictionary since – in a period of more than a hundred years – has come close to matching the elegance and sophistication of the *Century*'s art.

Nowadays in the United States one takes for granted that every general dictionary will be illustrated, but it has long been debated whether the space used for illustrations contributes much to the basic purpose of a dictionary. To what extent do pictures help the reader understand meaning? In Britain, at least, the jury is still out. None of the leading dictionaries for native speakers published by Oxford, Collins, or Chambers is illustrated, although the *Encarta World English Dictionary* (*EWED*) (1999) devotes a considerable amount of space to illustrations. To some observers it is obvious that concrete objects such as forms of architecture, animals, plants, and many other things marked by a specific shape, such as geometric figures, are more easily grasped by means of illustration than by verbal descriptions.[44] As a generalization, this is certainly true; but it is misleading and naive to suppose that an illustration makes the definition superfluous. A picture is at best a representative example of the type of thing defined, yet it does not encompass anything approaching the full range of possibilities defined by the term it is supposed to illustrate. It thus performs graphically what an illustrative phrase or sentence does verbally. To say that a picture obviates the need for definition makes the mistake of substituting an example representing a class of things – in Zgusta's terms the *denotatum* – for the qualities that define the object (the *designatum*). The idea that simple words like *dog* and *cat* need no definition will be discussed in Ch. 4; I find it primitive, ill conceived, and vacuous. I should say that simple words need no pictures; they certainly do need definitions.

Zgusta sees the primary purpose of illustrations as that of depicting unusual or unfamiliar things. I agree. No need to illustrate *dog* or *cat*, but *gnu* or *capybara* is another story. "The pictures should not be overspecific," he adds, "but only general lest the user accept a feature only accidental to the picture as criterial to the designatum."[45] In other words, if one's picture of a gnu has a peculiarly long neck, we may wrongly suppose that all gnus have necks that long. This is good advice that is not always easy to observe in practice. If one is depicting a rare animal or plant altogether foreign to one's own culture, one must necessarily base the illustration on a limited number of available photographs or illustrations. One collects what source material that is available. Ideally, an expert in zoology should review the drawings to see whether they are accurate; in practice, it is difficult to find experts in every category depicted, or to entrust them if they are found with the ultimate responsibility for warranting that the art is accurate. Some experts, alas, are not conscientious; others, from a misplaced desire to be obliging, are not critical enough to be a reliable help. Frequently the editor must rely on his own judgment based on the best information available. Nonetheless, Zgusta's advice is important to keep in mind. Although there may be some comparatively short-necked giraffes, we ought not to use them as our model for *giraffe*.

This raises the question of whether drawings or photographs are more useful for dictionary illustration. Photographs are necessarily of unidealized individual things, whether zebras, geese, or medieval churches. Drawings may combine features of many individuals and thus represent a composite distillation of elements regarded as typical. If a drawing is done well, it is usually more informative, with its details more readily apparent, than any photograph (or halftone, as it is called when processed for printing). On the other hand, photographs have – or had, before the age of digitized images – an undeniable attachment to reality. There was always, in viewing a photograph, a slight thrill of appreciation that was missing in viewing a drawing; we knew that the thing photographed was really there and not designed to illustrate anything. It was authentic. In the age of computerized images, however, photographs can be easily altered. Photographic tricks once confined to Hollywood moviemakers and touch-up artists are now available to everyone. The cachet of authenticity of the photograph has been fatally compromised. On the other hand, this very flexibility in image-making allows dictionary art directors to modify photographs to make them more generic and remove unwanted detail. (For information on the practical aspects of dictionary illustration, see Ch. 7, p. 388.)

Even so, halftones are more difficult to use than line drawings and often less satisfactory. For one thing, a photograph must be much larger than a drawing to convey the same sense of distance and space rendered in a skillfully executed drawing. A photograph of a group of people, for example, must be severely reduced in size for dictionary illustration; one feels one is examining a postage stamp. Before digitization, everything in a photograph had to be uniformly reduced, the important foreground as well as the unimportant background; that is no longer the case, but there are limits to how much juggling one can do with differential sizing without making the photo look absurd. In an artist's drawing, proportions can be doctored more subtly to highlight whatever one desires.

Dictionary illustrations can be useful, but they are most often used as a marketing feature to promote one's own dictionary at the expense of the competition. Until the publication of the *American Heritage Dictionary* (*AHD*) in 1969, line drawings were *à la mode*. The *AHD*, with thousands more illustrations than any other dictionary of its time, included both line drawings and halftones. Although some of the halftones were of poor quality – always a problem in large printings with relatively inexpensive paper – the overall effect was successful from a marketing point of view. *AHD4* (2000) has introduced full-color illustrations. No doubt these add to the appeal of the dictionary for many users, but it is doubtful that color adds much to the explanatory power of the illustrations. Dictionaries that give expansive coverage to encyclopedic items are more likely to use halftones – for example, for people or places – than those that do not. Thus *EWED*, with thousands of encyclopedic entries, includes many photographs. The *American Heritage College Dictionary*, Third Edition (*AHCD3*) (1997), the third-generation offspring of *AHD*, has many more halftones than line drawings, many of which to my mind are either not necessary to illustrate meaning or, if necessary, not as effective as drawings would be. They provide visual interest to the page; one's eye is drawn immediately to them. They are easier to obtain than line drawings and cheaper if one factors in the staff time required to plan and commission drawings. *Webster's New World College Dictionary* (*WNWCD*) (4th edn., 1999) has joined the trend towards using halftones as well as drawings.

School dictionaries include many more pictures in comparison to the number of entries than do adult dictionaries, and nowadays the illustrations in all the leading children's dictionaries are in color. Very often adults seek a definition merely to confirm what they think a word means; this is less often true of children, who may have no notion of the word's meaning. For example, an adult may know that a dormer is a kind of window in a house, though may be unsure just what *dormer* means. A definition that reads "a small, roofed structure extending out from a sloping roof and containing a window" may therefore evoke in his mind a picture of what he has previously seen but may evoke nothing at all in the mind of a child who has no preexisting visual idea of such a structure. But if a picture is included, the child may then recognize a dormer as something he has seen, or least be able to identify one in the future.

ESL dictionaries can also profit from pictorial illustrations but, unfortunately, pictures must compete for space with other more essential elements, such as grammatical and usage information and collocational aids. Because ESL dictionaries are often used in formal instruction, they must be of portable size. Therefore, although pictures are desirable and some are usually included, there is not much space for them. Also, because of the variety of cultures for which ESL dictionaries are intended, one has to be careful not to include anything in one's illustrations that would be offensive in cultures whose traditions are very different from those of the dominant cultures in America or Britain. A picture showing any casual contact between a man and a woman, for example, would be offensive in some Muslim countries, where such behavior is considered fitting only in the privacy of the home.

Pictorial dictionaries such as *Dudens* (see Ch. 1, p. 19) used for bilingual translation make excellent use of illustrations. For the most part, only line drawings are used. It is amazing how much information is packed into each page of the Duden picture dictionaries through the grouping of drawings and the detailed labeling of the various parts in each illustration. With the exception of the *Collins Cobuild English Dictionary*, which has no illustrations, the larger ESL dictionaries – the *Longman Dictionary of Contemporary English* (3rd edn., 1995), *Cambridge International Dictionary of English* (1995), and the *Oxford Advanced Learner's Dictionary* (*OALD6*) (6th edn., 2000) – all make occasional use of composite, schematic drawings with many labels to illustrate complex objects. *OALD6* also includes a number of color illustrations of types of things – such as foods, clothing, and animals – in addition to its black-and-white illustrations.

Technical and scientific dictionaries can and often do use pictorial illustrations, as well as charts and tables, to supplement their text. To what extent the pictures are useful is a matter of debate. The difficulty is that technical dictionaries are often intended to serve users on a variety of levels, from student to advanced research scientist. Whereas the student may find the illustrations helpful, the more advanced user may regard them as intrusive or oversimple and wish that the space had been used for additional entries. Generally speaking, dictionaries intended for a broad market, such as one-volume medical dictionaries, are helped by illustration. Charts and tables are obviously useful in such works, although as a rule they should not be used to omit entries but rather as a convenient reorganization of included terms. Chemical elements may be included in a table for purposes of comparison, but they should also be included as alphabetic entries. However, in some cases the table can substitute for certain terms. For example, a table of poisonous snakes may make unnecessary the inclusion of each poisonous species so long as the genera are entered with cross-references to the table.

Just how important are illustrations in a dictionary? The answer depends on the intended audience. The more elementary or pedagogical the work is, the more useful are illustrations. Scholarly or historical dictionaries have no need of illustrations. Bilingual dictionaries seldom include them, because pictorial illustrations of words in the source language are a monolingual function. Illustrations of some words in L2 (the language that is foreign to the user) – which is in effect what the Duden picture dictionaries do – would be helpful, though to my knowledge it is not done, undoubtedly because editors would rather use the space to add entries or expand translational equivalents.

Other graphic elements, such as type size and page layout – at least as important as illustration – will be discussed in Ch. 7.

FRONT AND BACK MATTER

Up till now we have been discussing only the A–Z section of dictionaries and have been ignoring the introductory material and appendixes, called in the book trade *front matter* and *back matter*, respectively. These sections vary greatly in importance depending on the nature of the dictionary. In adult native-speaker dictionaries, a guide to the use of the dictionary is now considered essential, but it is astonishing how little help was given the reader in early dictionaries. By the time of Johnson, however, it was traditional to include an essay on English grammar and a history of the English language in a dictionary's front matter. The trend in recent years has been to cut back on front matter because it is widely believed among lexicographers that no one reads it. Some dictionaries still have front-matter articles on the history of the language or of dictionaries, on current usage, or on the different varieties of English used throughout the world, but these, when they exist at all, are shorter than front-matter articles in the past. In the age of channel-surfing and Internet browsing, no one believes that users of general dictionaries will have the patience to read substantial articles in small type. Gone are articles about grammar, pronunciation, and, with rare exceptions, etymology.

Although front-matter articles are seldom read by dictionary users, they are often regarded as important by reviewers, who, faced with the daunting task of examining a 1,600-page book with two columns per page, seize on the most conspicuous elements to read. It takes less time and effort to comment on the jacket blurb and front matter, and perhaps to look up one or two favorite neologisms, than to make an informed estimate of the value of the dictionary as a whole. Many a dictionary that has been prepared by dozens of people and that consists of 1 to 3 million words written and revised repeatedly over a period of five to ten years has been judged on the merit of one or two short essays composed by consultants whose contributions to the dictionary did not extend beyond their own essays. One cannot fault critics for reviewing a dictionary's front matter; anything in the book is fair game. Yet compared to the overall effort of producing a college dictionary, front-matter articles are of negligible importance. The attention given by reviewers, however, makes them of considerable commercial importance. Thus front-matter articles are often written by prominent scholars or educators in an attempt to establish the authority of the work and lend it prestige. In some cases these scholars have been associated intimately with the work, as, for example, Kemp Malone was with the *American College Dictionary*; but as a rule the association is more distant, sometimes little more than window dressing.

Ironically, the guide to the use of the dictionary, which is the only part of the front matter of demonstrable practical importance and the only one most readers ever use, is almost always ignored by reviewers. In order to detect omissions or ambiguities in the guide, the reviewers would have to have spent some time studying the dictionary's content and style, and this they are disinclined to do. Most guides describe every part of the dictionary article: entry word, syllabication (if given), pronunciation, inflected forms, various kinds of labels, cross-references, variants, etymologies, synonyms, and usage notes. The purpose of the guide is to describe as clearly as possible all the kinds of information included in the dictionary, show the reader how to interpret the data given (i.e., how to read the dictionary's style), and provide clues for locating as quickly as possible particular items of information. To put the matter simply, the guide answers the questions, "what's in it?," "what does it mean?," and "how do I find it?" Often parts of several pages from the A–Z section are reprinted to highlight particular features, such as illustrative sentences or usage labels, which are shown in another color or in a shaded area (called a tint block) or bracketed, and are linked to captions that identify the part and refer to sections of the guide where the item is discussed. This is an excellent use of graphics to provide the reader with a simple and clear index to the guide.

In general the American college dictionaries include more back-matter material than their British counterparts, with the exception of the *Concise Oxford*, which has forty pages of appendixes on a variety of scientific and linguistic subjects. It was formerly the practice to include most encyclopedic material – especially biographical entries, geographical entries, and abbreviations – in separate sections in the dictionary's back matter, but the current fashion is to integrate all such entries within the main A–Z section. Only *Merriam-Webster's Collegiate Dictionary* (*MW10*) (1998) continues to maintain separate sections for these entries in its back matter. Among favored back-matter sections in general dictionaries are guides to writing and punctuation and a miscellany of encyclopedic material, such as a list of the US presidents, population statistics, scientific and technical data (chemical elements, weights and measures, signs and symbols, etc.). The *AHCD3* differs markedly from the pattern by including only a section on Indo-European word roots by Calvert Watkins, thus restoring a popular feature of the first edition of

AHD that had been cut from the second edition. In former times a list of US and Canadian colleges and universities was certain to be included in all the college dictionaries, but now, remarkably, it appears in none. College students are only part of the market for these dictionaries, and although the word *college* or *collegiate* remains a strong selling point, publishers have apparently concluded that lists of colleges and universities can be dispensed with.

In school dictionaries and ESL dictionaries, front matter is much more important. In both cases, student guides or workbooks that include guides to the dictionary may be published separately as booklets. For the child, the guide to the use of the dictionary must not assume any prior familiarity with dictionary use. A children's dictionary guide is really not just to one particular dictionary but a guide to dictionary use. It must therefore be more detailed, yet written in much simpler language than that of an adult dictionary. The task is by no means easy and should be undertaken only by a highly skilled writer familiar both with dictionaries and with school curricula used in teaching dictionary skills.

A children's dictionary guide begins at the beginning, with the alphabet, and instructs the reader how to look up a word and how to use the guide words at the top of the pages. It then more or less covers the same ground that adult dictionaries do, but with numerous examples taken from the A–Z section and sometimes with questions or exercises for the reader. Teachers' manuals may be useful (as they are also in ESL dictionary instruction) in helping the teacher use the front-matter guide or separate workbook for classroom instruction. Whether separate or part of the dictionary's front matter, the guide for children is usually printed in large, attractive type, often in full color to highlight features and invite attentive reading. Information about the history of the language, etymology, or usage, if included at all, is generally incorporated in the guide, which may run to fifty pages or more.

For the ESL dictionary user, the front-matter guide or separately printed students' workbook and guide is basic to the understanding and use of the A–Z material. Although ESL dictionaries no longer incorporate long, detailed sections on the grammatical patterns of verbs, grammatical verb patterns are often taught in ESL/EFL programs that include instruction in using the dictionary. The back matter of ESL dictionaries contains various linguistic aids specifically for the foreign learner: lists of irregular verbs, sections on word formation, advice on punctuation. Sometimes standard encyclopedic material similar to that found in native-speaker dictionaries is also included. The *Cambridge*

International Dictionary of English (*CIDE*) uniquely includes an index of phrases for discovering where to find multiword lexical units. Some ESL dictionaries that have controlled defining vocabularies list the words used in such vocabularies in the back matter.

Technical and scientific dictionaries usually do not provide full guides to their use. Technical dictionaries that include subentries, for example, may give the reader some guidance on how entries and subentries are alphabetized, but often it is inadequate and does not account for many exceptions. Such dictionaries generally give scant attention to pronunciation even if it is routinely included within the body of the book. Transcriptions of pronunciation may be necessary for competitive reasons but seem to be considered of slight interest to users of technical books. The back matter of scientific and technical dictionaries is often devoted to tables of technical data, such as (in medicine) a list of normal ranges of different substances in laboratory tests.

Some dictionaries, often called encyclopedic dictionaries, go much further afield than the ones discussed so far. They may include a glossary of mythology, a manual of usage, a selection of quotations, a chronology of World War II battles, a section of maps in full color, or whatever strikes the publisher's fancy as a feature that will attract interest and invite purchase. The tradition of including encyclopedic material in dictionaries is as old as lexicography and was one of the practices deplored by Dean Trench in his celebrated paper of 1857. Although separate encyclopedic sections have nothing to do with the dictionary proper, there are no compelling logical reasons for condemning them. Their chief effect on the dictionary is to make it heavier to carry and more expensive to buy. Those who find their dictionaries heavy enough as they are will not rejoice to find biographies of every US president and vice-president contributing to their bursitis.

There is, to be sure, a touch of fraud in many encyclopedic dictionaries because they usually promise more than they deliver. By attempting to give the reader a bit of everything, they do nothing well, and they encourage the misconception that theirs is a better dictionary because it includes all sorts of aimless irrelevancies. But we must be mindful that we are talking about degrees of irrelevancy, since even the most respectable of commercial dictionaries boasts of certain encyclopedic features. *MW10* proudly displays an index of charts and tables and other marginalia, a device used a half century earlier by the *American College Dictionary*. A glance at the jacket copy of the leading general dictionaries shows how important these peripheral features are to their successful promotion. *AHD4* boasts of having 4,000 photographs, drawings, and maps. *NODE* announces in yellow type that it has 12,000 encyclopedic entries. *EWED* simply says it has thousands of illustrations and thousands of geographical and biographical entries. To be fair, they also make claims about their coverage of the lexicon, but nonlexical features are an attractive feature for many buyers.

Yet there is a difference between these dictionaries and encyclopedic dictionaries, which are generally sold at substantially higher prices directly to the consumer through promotional mailings, TV commercials, or magazine ads rather than through bookstores. Encyclopedic dictionaries appeal to a different and on the whole less sophisticated market, and their promoters have to have material for their sales pitch for the large flyers that are sent out by the hundreds of thousands to potential buyers. These are no doubt being supplemented by Internet ads which may in the long run replace direct mailings. (However, judging by the contents of my mail, direct mail solicitations are anything but dead.) Whatever the medium, promoters want features to itemize, especially those that seem to distinguish their dictionary from all others ever made. No subtleties or qualifications of any kind are allowed to dilute the impact of blunt assertion. The idea that a statement in such an ad could be true or false would strike most mass-market promoters as the purest whimsy. They would, like Saint-Exupéry's businessman counting the stars, urge one to be serious.

CHAPTER 4

Definition

What do we mean when we say we have defined something? The question, an ancient one, has been addressed by Plato and Aristotle as well as by modern philosophers, especially logicians and semanticists.[1] Although the distinction is not always made, and when made not always observed, logical definition is not the same as lexical definition. Logical definition – Richard Robinson calls it real definition, because it attempts to analyze things in the real world, as distinguished from words – has been the chief preoccupation of philosophers. When Socrates explores the meaning of virtue or truth, he is not seeking to define the words *virtue* or *truth* but the concepts that underlie them and the way people interpret these concepts. Philosophers have also concerned themselves with lexical (or nominal) definition, the definition of words, the subject of this chapter.

The traditional rules of lexical definition, based on Aristotle's analysis, demand that the word defined (called in Latin the *definiendum*) be identified by *genus* and *differentia*. That is, the word must first be defined according to the class of things to which it belongs, and then distinguished from all other things within that class. Thus *child* is a person (genus) who is young or whose relation to another person is that of a son or daughter (differentia).

Among other rules sometimes promulgated for definition are that a definition be equivalent to or capture the essence of the thing defined, that the definiendum not be included in any form among the words used to define it (called the *definiens*), and that the definition be positive rather than negative. Philosophers are not ignorant of the nature of linguistics or dictionary making, but it is remarkable how little attention they pay to the users of dictionaries. By contrast, lexicographers – all of them – pay a great deal of attention to the needs of their readers. For lexicography is a craft, a way of doing something useful. It is not a theoretical exercise to increase the sum of human knowledge but practical work to put together text that people can understand. The editor of *A Dictionary of the Older Scottish Tongue* – hardly a commercial enterprise – described his readers, with only very pale irony, as "customers" and identified them as "philologists, textual editors, literary historians, and general historians and antiquarians."[2] Every lexicographer, like any good author, has his readers very much in mind. Whereas philosophers are concerned with the internal coherence of their system of definition, lexicographers are concerned with explaining something their readers will understand. The methods they use to achieve their goals only incidentally coincide.

Linguistic prescriptions for definition often proffer as a principle what is clearly desirable but what may not be possible or practicable.[3] The space allotted to each definition must be severely limited, else the total number of terms must be reduced. To one who has not struggled to cut a carefully crafted definition in order to save space, it is difficult to convey the intensity of the effort or the misgivings experienced at having to weaken a definition one had worked hard to perfect. But it is almost always necessary to trim the length of entry articles – which usually means cutting definitions and examples – during the editing stages of a dictionary. The first stage in the writing of any dictionary, as we will see in Ch. 7, is always relatively expansive; one of the chief tasks of the revision editors is to cut the text back so that it fits into the space allotted for it.

No dictionary is spared the necessity of saving space, but scientific and technical dictionaries generally have more flexibility both in the number of entries they must include and in the number of pages to which they can expand. General commercial dictionaries – both monolingual and bilingual – are under severe constraints, regardless of the intended size. The *OED* editors were pressed to save space, as were the editors of *NID3*. Large dictionaries have more space but they have more entries to cover, more illustrative quotations, fuller etymologies and pronunciations, and a more discriminating breakdown of sense. The task is not rendered easier but more complicated by such treatment, and the need for brevity is no less exigent. The process of determining the size of one's dictionary will be discussed in Ch. 7, but it must be said here that practical considerations do not admit of much adjustment to the projected size of a commercial dictionary once the project is under way. One cannot just add another 128 pages because one needs the additional space; the extra 128 pages of text must be cut to fit the space available. It is precisely to avoid such a disaster that dictionaries must be carefully planned in advance and closely monitored while in progress.

KINDS OF MEANING

Before we describe the actual process of dictionary defining, it may be well to examine various kinds of meaning. C. K. Ogden and I. A. Richards pictured the process by which a thing (or referent) is identified as a symbol by drawing a triangle, with Symbol and Referent at each of the base angles, connected by a dotted line, and Thought or Reference at the apex.[4] The idea is that somebody sees a mouse scurrying across the floor and thinks Mouse, which is translated into the word/symbol *mouse*. The dotted line signifies that the animal scurrying across the floor and the word/symbol *mouse* have no direct connection.

Ladislav Zgusta depicts a similar triangle based on the Ogden and Richards model. He calls the mouse/referent the *denotatum* and our perception of the properties of mouse or the class of things to which mice belong (mousedom?) the *designatum* (now and then he slips into English and calls it the designation). Thus his triangle consists of *expression* (form of the word) and *denotatum* at the corners of the base of the triangle connected by a dotted line, and *designatum* at the apex. The word, or *lexical unit* (which may consist of more than one word), "is used to express its designatum and together with it denote the respective denotatum."[5]

Connotation is said by Zgusta to consist of all aspects of lexical meaning that have "contrastive value" with the designation. The designation enables us to say what a thing such as a mouse is, to recognize it when we see it, and to attach a name to it. Although not identical with the lexical definition, it is the chief basis for the definition. Connotation may suggest a degree of formality or informality, or variety of usage, sometimes called *register*, signifying an adjustment in style or variety of language used for different social situations. The third component of meaning is range of application: how broadly can the lexical unit be applied? *Salary* has a broader application than *stipend* or *honorarium*. Some words, such as *shuck* (corn), have a very limited range of application in modern use.

Zgusta's use of connotation is unusual. First of all, it must be distinguished from the logician's use. Richard Robinson, for example, uses *connotation* to mean what Zgusta means by designation. In Zgusta's terms, connotation refers to the difference between "to die" and "to peg out."[6] Zgusta says that *to die* has no connotation, but that an expression like *peg out* does. I do not agree; I would say rather that the distinction between these two terms is that of variety of usage and range of application.

Zgusta wants to account for those properties of language that are reported by dictionaries but that are not part of their essential meaning. What kind of knowledge are we conveying when we call a word slang or vulgar? Zgusta calls this kind of knowledge connotation. In its more traditional sense, however, connotation refers to the whole store of associated attributes of a word, derived from centuries of use. Far from having no connotation, *die* in the common sense is much richer in connotation than *peg out* or *kick the bucket*, or any number of other slang expressions with the same meaning. *Die* suggests grief, pain, suffering, absence, sorrow, and loss. *Peg out* or *kick the bucket* convey a tone of callous vulgarity, which according to Zgusta falls into the category of connotation; on the contrary, I would say that such expressions are weak in connotation. Traditionally, connotation depended on the historical, linguistic contexts in which a word had been used, not on the immediate social impact of its use. To be sure, since the use of language is social, the recognition of meaning in any word depends in part on the social context in which it is used, and connotation is part of meaning. But *peg out* and *kick the bucket* have an impoverished linguistic history compared to *die*. Their connotation is narrowed to the focus of its expression, like that of an otherwise meaningless curse such as *Damn!* Dictionaries deal only with certain kinds of meaning and ignore other kinds no less important, such as the connotations of *die*, and we must not suppose that associated meanings cease to exist because dictionaries fail to note them.[7] Zgusta's use of connotation is so narrowly confined to dictionary practice that in the broader context of meaning it is unappealingly trivial.

Even if we accept Zgusta's definition of connotation, it is difficult to justify the notion that *die* or any other general word (excluding scientific terms) is always without connotation. To many people it is customary to use euphemisms when consoling someone on a death in a family; the use of *die* or *death* in the linguistic context of a note of consolation might be considered harsh and unfeeling. All that one can say is that connotation in Zgusta's sense depends upon how the word fits the social context in which it is used, and since *die* is much more widely used and fits more contexts than *peg out* or *kick the bucket*, it can be used in some contexts without connotation. So can *life*. The difference is one of generality and range of application. In some contexts, surely, *life* and *death* are rich in connotations, but in others, such as legal briefs – "The defendant is alleged to have caused the death of John Smith" – they can be free of them.

THE PRINCIPLES OF DEFINING

Zgusta enumerates the following principles of defining:
1. All words within a definition must be explained.
2. The lexical definition should not contain words "more difficult to understand" than the word defined.
3. The defined word may not be used in its definition, nor may derivations or combinations of the defined word unless they are separately defined. But one part-of-speech may be used to define another, as "to use a crib" if the noun sense of *crib* (in the sense of a secret copy of notes, etc.) has been defined.
4. The definition must correspond to the part-of-speech of the word defined.[8]

These are sensible guidelines, but I would like to distinguish between essential principles and good lexicographic practice. Occasionally the criteria of good practice must be compromised, either to save space or for some other compelling reason. But a few basic principles must never be violated, else they defeat the whole purpose of the dictionary. I list these principles in order of importance.

Avoid circularity

Since the primary purpose of a dictionary is to inform the reader what words mean, anything that absolutely denies the reader the opportunity to find out the meaning of a word he has looked up is the most serious defect a dictionary can have. Mind you, circularity does not just make things difficult – it makes them impossible. No amount of diligence on the part of the reader can penetrate the barrier of circularity.

There are two forms of circularity. One defines **A** in terms of **B** and **B** in terms of **A**, and the other defines **A** in terms of **A**. The first kind is illustrated by these definitions:

	LEXICAL UNIT	DEFINITIONS
A	beauty	the state of being beautiful
B	beautiful	full of beauty
A	bobcat	lynx
B	lynx	bobcat

Among ESL dictionaries with limited defining vocabularies, the rule prohibiting this kind of circularity is sometimes ignored, particularly in the definition of simple words. The reasoning seems to be that defining a simple word with harder words would cause more difficulty for the reader than using circular definitions, which assumes the reader knows the meanings of the words being defined. For example, the *Longman Dictionary of American English* (*LDAE*) defines *sleep* as "to be asleep," and *asleep* as "sleeping." Although the use of a controlled defining vocabulary assumes that the reader has some familiarity with these words, I cannot agree that this gives the lexicographer license to define circularly. Why bother to give definitions at all if they don't define? One might as well omit all such definitions and simply say about the word, "You know what it means." Admittedly, it can be extremely difficult to define basic terms like *be*, *do*, and *go* in noncircular ways when one is using a limited defining vocabulary, but no one ever said writing dictionaries was easy.

The second kind of circularity is illustrated by this definition:

LEXICAL UNIT	DEFINITION
fear	a state of fear, one of the basic drives of human beings, the others being . . .

Or, more commonly, by

LEXICAL UNIT	DEFINITION
fear	the state of being fearful

when *fearful* is nowhere defined in the dictionary and is perhaps run on as a derivative to the article for *fear*!

The rule may be stated thus: *No word can be defined by itself, and no word can be defined from its own family of words unless the related word is separately defined independently of it.* Therefore, if *fearful* were defined separately without reference to *fear*, the definition quoted above would not be circular, although it would be bad lexicographic practice to define *fear* in terms of *fearful*. In other words, no word can be defined by a word whose own definition depends upon the word it is defining. I do not say that **A**'s definition may not include **B**, and that **B**'s definition may not include **A**. Such a relationship is circular only if the meaning of **A** *depends* upon **B** and vice versa. For example, these two definitions from *The Doubleday Dictionary* are perfectly proper:

	LEXICAL UNIT	DEFINITION
A	lynx	any of several wildcats of Europe and North America, with a short tail, tufted ears, and long limbs; a bobcat
B	bobcat	the American lynx

There is no circularity, because the meaning of *lynx* does not depend on the inclusion of *bobcat* in its definition.

The avoidance of circularity is so elementary that its occurrence in any professional dictionary is usually a simple blunder and not a case of ignorance or policy (with the exception noted above for the first type of circularity). No such assurance is possible in many amateurish, special-subject dictionaries or in newspaper glossaries of fad words, where circularity is commonplace. Even in competent hands, however, circularity can creep in when a word's definition is changed and one fails to make sure that the new definition does not introduce circularity. For example, the *Longman Dictionary of Contemporary English* (*LDOCE3*) defines *around* as follows:

5 if you move or go around something, you move around the side of it instead of going through or over it: *If the gate is locked you'll have to go around the side of the house.*

In this defining style, the introductory clause uses the definiendum in a context, and the main clause defines it in that context. The first use of *around* is routine in this style, but in this instance the main clause also uses the word to be defined. Note that the definitional main clause would make sense if it read "you move along the side of it" so the use of *around* here is unnecessary and is simply the result of carelessness or fatigue. No one who has worked on dictionaries for any length of time can say with assurance that he or she has never made such a mistake.

LDAE defines *branch* as "part of a tree that grows out from the TRUNK (= main stem) and has leaves, fruit, or smaller branches, growing from it." One understands the problem, but this definition does not offer an acceptable solution. The definition is both circular and illogical, since its use of *branches* in "smaller branches" can only refer to the definiendum itself, which, as defined, grows from the trunk of a tree, but we are suddenly made aware that this branch does not grow from the trunk but from another branch. So it's a branch but not a branch. Instead of writing two separate definitions, one for the branch that grows from a trunk and one for the branch that grows from other branches, or omitting the second kind of branch entirely, the definer sought to combine them in one definition, with disastrous results.

Dictionaries are often unfairly charged with circularity when their definitions are not circular. As I have pointed out, definitions may include a form of the word being defined, provided the word in the definition is elsewhere defined. The editor of *NID3*, Philip Babcock Gove, has made the point that such treatment must be adopted by dictionaries to enable them to include many more words than they would otherwise have space for.[9] For most dictionaries, it is not only acceptable but imperative that they define one part-of-speech in terms of another. For example, the noun *dream* may be fully defined and the verb may be defined as "to have dreams." There would be no point in repeating the entire noun definition of *dream* in its verbal sense. The reader has only to let his eye pass to the adjacent entry to discover the sense in which *dream* is used. In many entries, as for *bicycle*, where the noun definition may require several lines of description, no purpose would be served by repeating it in the verbal definition, which is best given as "to ride a bicycle." In such cases the device of defining one part-of-speech in terms of another is the only sensible policy.

Define every word used in a definition
When using a monolingual, general dictionary, readers have a right to expect that if they do not know the meaning of a word used in a definition, they can look that word up and find it defined. The Word Not In (WNI, for short) rule is broken more often than the circularity rule. In the past it was simply too difficult to check the words in every definition. If one is working on line (see Ch. 7), it is no longer difficult to check to see if a word is entered, but since the word list of a dictionary is constantly being changed – entries are always being added and deleted – errors can still occur. Computerized checks of definitions are especially valuable in ESL dictionaries using controlled vocabularies of 2,000 or 3,000 words. If one uses a word that is not part of the controlled vocabulary, one can be immediately alerted to this fact. Unfortunately, no computer check can distinguish sense, so words may still be used in definitions in nonallowable senses, and this remains a problem in ESL lexicography.

Two-way bilingual dictionaries generally make an effort to include every target-language word of the first section as a source-language word in the second part, although it is not always possible to do so and is less important than the WNI rule in monolingual dictionaries. Culture-specific words such as *home run* and *grass roots* cannot be directly translated but must be paraphrased. Idiomatic phrases often have no counterpart in another language. Frequently, two different editorial groups prepare the two halves of a bidirectional work, thus rendering concordance of vocabularies that much more difficult. It remains nonetheless a desirable feature, however imperfectly achieved.

Although the circularity rule applies to all monolingual dictionaries, the Word Not In rule applies only with qualification to scientific and technical dictionaries. Since the vocabulary is restricted to a particular subject, only those words pertaining to the subject must be included as entries and defined. General terms used in definitions are excluded from the rule. Because of the great many variants in some sciences, notably in medicine, it is extremely difficult to ascertain that every scientific term used in a definition is entered in exactly that form. For example, *hyperosmolar hyperglycemic nonketonic coma* may be used in a definition but entered under *hyperglycemic nonketonic coma* or under some other slight variation. Technically, this is an instance of WNI, but it is not very serious since the reader should be able to locate the relevant term as a subentry under *coma* without much difficulty. More serious is the case where an altogether different variant is used in a definition. The variant is entered, but when readers look it up they find a cross-reference to another term to which they must turn to find a definition. This is bad lexicographic practice but not a violation of the Word Not In rule.

Without a computer check of every word, it is impossible to be sure that every word used in each definition is the preferred form. Frequent checks may be made, to be sure, but because any dictionary in preparation is continually changing, a definitive check for Words Not In cannot be made until the project has been completed. This can be tricky because of the need to recognize inflected forms of entries, which of course are legitimate. Generally, checking the results of a WNI program and making the necessary changes take a week or two for a college-size dictionary. Some items that are not entries, such as numerals, proper names, or taxonomical names, may also be legitimate, so the WNI check must be carefully screened.

Dictionary editors must be vigilant in checking to see how the changes they make affect other definitions. In the early stages of a dictionary, changes can be made with relative impunity; in the latter stages one learns to be reluctant to make any change that alters the status of a word, since the amount of checking this requires may be so onerous that it far exceeds any benefit accruing from the change. One might suppose that computerization has made it possible to carry out major changes at any stage of a dictionary project, but this is not the case, chiefly because the computer programming for a dictionary database is extremely complex, and any significant changes made during the latter stages of a project might well cause serious damage, delaying the project for many months and involving major additional expenses. No one has yet been able to foresee with sufficient clarity all or even most of the kinds of specific problems that have to be dealt with at every stage of lexicographic work. The success of dictionary projects still depends largely on the resourcefulness of lexicographers in using the structured database originally devised, albeit with many small changes made at early stages of the project, to meet whatever problems arise at later stages. (See Ch. 7 for a fuller discussion of how computers are used in dictionary making.)

In some smaller dictionaries the Word Not In rule must be deliberately breached. Such dictionaries may have to use some specified derivative words, formed with common suffixes or prefixes, such as *treelike* or *eyeless*, that are not entered. However, *tree*, *-like*, *eye*, and *-less* are entered, so presumably any reader could surmise the meanings of the words by consulting their elements. This device, like so many in dictionary practice, is not one lexicographers cherish but one they are compelled to adopt to save space. It is tolerable so long as the particular forms considered acceptable in definitions are clearly specified and the practice is rigidly confined to these forms. For example, the style manual for a children's dictionary of which I was the editor specified that

The words formed with the following affixes and combining forms may be used in definitions even if they are not entered:

-ish	as in	greenish, yellowish
-less		footless, eyeless
-like		treelike, shiplike, shell-like
-ly		chemically, experimentally
-ness		greenness, cheapness
non-		nonreligious, nonsocial (sense of "not")
-shaped		leaf-shaped, balloon-shaped
un-		unsympathetic, untired (sense of "not")

Needless to say, all of the affixes and combining forms listed above must themselves be entered and fully defined.

The list was not assembled at the start of the project but only when it was under way, and then it began with three or four terms. Each additional form was added grudgingly when it was clear that it could not reasonably be avoided.

Define the entry word

The definition must define and not just talk about the word or its usage. It must answer the question, "what is it?," directly and immediately. There are many other characteristics of a good definition, and different kinds of words must be defined differently, but if a definition fails in its basic purpose of giving readers enough immediate information to enable them to surmise, at least approximately, its meaning in context, it is of no value whatsoever. Beginning definers tend to say too much and yet often fail to say what is essential. For example, a specialist may define *diagnosis* as follows: "The physician takes the history of the patient, evaluates subjective symptoms, and conducts his own examination to determine objective findings before making the diagnosis."

We see at once that the definition violates the rule of circularity by including the word being defined, but even more important in this case is that the reader is never told what *diagnosis* is. The writer says what the physician does but not say that the diagnosis is a judgment about the nature of a disease.

The commonest cause of this error is a confusion between the concept and the word. Specialists sometimes feel that the concept underlying a word is more important than the word itself and merely use the word as a pretext for describing actions or procedures associated with it. It is a natural error for them to make, since they have spent their lives taking these actions and usually only a very short time writing about them. But they must be made to understand that dictionaries are about words, not essentially about the things described by them, and that in dictionaries words are indeed important. Specialists can be given numerous tips on how to define; yet unless they grasp that fundamental point and learn to abide by it, their definitions will never be any good, no matter how carefully they observe the tricks of the trade.

GOOD DEFINING PRACTICE

Priority of essence

The most essential elements of meaning come first, the more incidental elements later. Do not begin a definition with "a term meaning" or "a term referring to" or the like: begin with the definition itself. Definers must put themselves in the place of someone who hasn't the vaguest idea what the word means and try to anticipate the kinds of wrong assumptions such a person might make about each draft of their definition, until they have written a definition that cannot be misunderstood. In an effort to distance itself from terms it deems offensive, the *Encarta World English Dictionary* (*EWED*) has adopted the strategy of beginning many definitions with the phrase, "An offensive term for," in spite of the presence of labels calling attention to their offensiveness. *EWED* thus presents as the essential meaning of such words that they are words and that they are offensive, and only then – sometimes! – deigns to tell the reader what they signify.[10]

Substitutability

For many words, the definition should be substitutable for the word in context. Substitutability is often declared to be a principle of defining, but there are so many cases where it is impossible to apply that it is idle to insist that it be universal. As one lexicographer observes, the substitution rule cannot be applied to words like *be, damn, in, it, yes, ought, the, to, tut tut, what?*, and *yes*.[11]

ESL lexicography in particular has demonstrated an increasing willingness to experiment with other styles of defining that abandon the principle of substitutability. Some ESL lexicographers feel that the effort to make definitions broadly substitutable often impairs their helpfulness for foreign learners, who need a more specific identification of context than substitutable definitions give.[12] The *Collins Cobuild English Language Dictionary* (1st edn. 1987) pioneered by introducing sentence definitions for many words. For example, the definition for *inflammatory* in the second edition of 1995 (called *Collins Cobuild English Dictionary*) is: "If you accuse someone of saying or doing **inflammatory** things, you mean that what they say or do is likely to make people react very angrily." The introductory clause establishes the context and the main clause defines the word within that context. A substitutable definition might be, "causing or likely to cause an angry reaction." The editors of *Cobuild* decided that sentence definitions were easier for their readers to understand and gave them more assistance in learning how to use the word than a substitutable definition. Other ESL dictionaries have also adopted sentence definitions for some words, although not as systematically as *Cobuild*. I applaud this innovation in ESL lexicography; I believe it has improved the quality of definition in many cases, especially in the treatment of idioms. I will have more to say about this under "Innovative defining styles," p. 178.

Even in dictionaries which largely adhere to conventionally substitutable definitions, however, the many thousands of definitions of scientific terms are not substitutable. For example, one looks in vain for a definition of *rose* to fit the context, "How sweet of you to give me a rose!" One does not mean, "How sweet of you to give me any of a genus (*Rosa* of the family Rosaceae, the rose family) of usu. prickly shrubs with pinnate leaves and showy flowers having five petals in the wild state but being often double or partly double under cultivation!" (*MW10*, def. 1a). One could mean, "How sweet of you to give me the flower of a rose!" (def. 1b), except that it is really "How sweet of you to give me the flower of any of a genus . . . !" We want to know what *rose* means in "How sweet of you to give me a rose!" The other definitions for *rose* in *MW10* don't give us a clue. The common meaning of *feather* in "A pigeon feather fell on my windowsill" is not given in any substitutable way in dictionaries. What we are given are long, precise, scientific definitions, like that for *rose*, and sometimes the catch-all, "Anything resembling a feather," which declares that the definer is not interested in wasting much time on a nonscientific use of a precise term. But we do not mean, "A pigeon object resembling a feather fell on my windowsill." Although we do not have in mind the scientific meaning of *feather*, yet we mean *feather*, not an object resembling it.[13]

We must now distinguish between those definitions that are based on examples of actual usage, definitions *extracted* from a body of evidence, and those (like that of *rose* and other scientific terms) that are *imposed* on the basis of expert advice. The experts are not concerned with how scientific words are used nonscientifically, even if such nonscientific use is very common. "Their goal is ease and accuracy of communication between those versed in the language of science."[14]

When we talk about scientific and technical terms and definitions, we are not talking about an odd or uncommon phenomenon. A third or more of the terms in *NID3* are scientific and technical, and in its supplement, *12,000 Words*, scientific and technical terms far outnumber general expressions. Clarence Barnhart, the dean of American commercial lexicographers, has said that "Almost 40 percent of the content of general-purpose dictionaries, such as college dictionaries, consists of scientific or technical terminology."[15] Since dictionaries of the size of American college dictionaries now contain from 160,000 to 180,000 entries, Barnhart's estimate translates into something like 65,000 to 70,000 entries. Because imposed definitions are not based, or not based primarily, on a collection of citations of actual usage or on language corpora (which will be described below in this chapter), substitutability is not regarded as relevant and most such definitions are not substitutable. One must add to this total thousands of encyclopedic entries, such as *Rosetta stone*, that appear in virtually every dictionary, and to which the substitution rule also cannot apply. Finally, one must add the thousands of biographical and geographical entries that now populate general dictionaries. It is plain that a high percentage of the space in general dictionaries is not devoted to substitutable definitions of definienda in context.

Although I endorse the use of a variety of defining strategies and do not feel that we should be obliged to make every definition substitutable, I still feel that substitutable definitions are desirable when no other alternative is clearly better. I am therefore distressed to find that some ESL dictionaries have abandoned the principle of substitutability simply because it is easier to ignore it. For example, *LDAE* makes no distinction in defining transitive and intransitive verbs, routinely including the object as part of the definition even for transitive verbs, instead of including the object within parentheses or omitting it. This simplifies defining, and it can be argued that such definitions are easier to understand, but I don't buy it. Substitutability can still help learners and native speakers alike grasp the specific use and meaning of a word.

As we will see in the next section, when constructing a definition from citations or from corpus evidence, the definer constructs his definitions to fit as many contexts as possible. The meaning, being deduced from a relatively few contexts, should in turn substitute not only for the definiendum in those contexts but for those of a very large number of other theoretical and actual contexts. We can say, then, that whereas substitutability is natural and apt for many extracted definitions, it is incidental to imposed definitions. Always a virtue, it should nonetheless be pursued with discretion and abandoned if it can be purchased only at the expense of clarity or unambiguousness.

Reflection of grammatical function

If a definition can be substituted for the word defined, it must be written in accord with the grammatical function, or part-of-speech, of the word defined. Even if it cannot be exactly substituted, the definition should reflect the part-of-speech of the word defined. The definition of a noun begins with a noun, that of an adjective with an adjective, and so on. However, as noted in the discussion of substitutability, it is not always possible or wise to make definitions substitutable, such as those of the prepositions *to* or *of*. But in general this rule is faithfully observed and should not be ignored without good reason. (See p. 171, "How to define by part-of-speech.")

Simplicity

"Avoid including difficult words in definitions of simpler words" is a traditional rule that seems to make sense, but like so many lexicographic rules it is often impossible to apply. It is customary, if not obligatory, when citing the rule to quote with great glee Samuel Johnson's definition of *network*: "Any thing reticulated or decussated, at equal distances, with interstices between the intersections." But here is *MW10*'s definition of *feather*, written 237 years after Johnson's *net*:

any of the light horny epidermal outgrowths that form the external covering of the body of birds and that consist of a shaft bearing on each side a series of barbs which bear barbules which in turn bear barbicels commonly ending in hooked hamuli and interlocking with the barbules of an adjacent barb to link the barbs into a continuous vane

There is no simple way to define precisely a complex arrangement of parts, however homely the object may appear to be. One obvious solution is not to define it precisely; but modern dictionary users expect scientifically precise, somewhat encyclopedic definitions. If one is to criticize Johnson for using difficult words to define a common word precisely, contemporary lexicographers must not be spared for doing the same thing.

What do we mean by "simple"? The word *feather* is simple, but the structure of the thing is anything but simple. What about a simple word like *time*? Saint Augustine said, "What, then, is time? I know well enough what it is, provided that nobody asks me; but if I am asked what it is and try to explain, I am baffled."[16] Unfortunately, definers are baffled too and must resort to more difficult words to try to cope with such difficult concepts. *MW10*'s relevant definition of *time* is "a nonspatial continuum that is measured in terms of events which succeed one another from past through present to future," which would certainly not satisfy Augustine and which is not simple, but is nonetheless an excellent definition. If one's life experience were so limited that one had no idea what time was and had never heard of the word *time*, this definition would be of no help. However, in that event, what would be of help? How could a concept of this complexity – or those underlying the words *motion*, *being*, *life*, and many others – be comprehended in words by anyone who had never heard those simple words uttered? The answer is plain: they could not.

The meanings of many words, including these deceptively simple ones, are seldom learned from dictionaries. A practical appreciation of their meanings is acquired as part of the process of growing up. A child may be unable to define *life*, but he has a sense of what distinguishes living beings from nonliving things. Analogously, many words with concrete referents are learned as a baby learns to associate the physical presence of a dog with the word *dog*: by observing someone pointing at an object or at something happening and uttering a word. This is called "ostensive" definition. Dictionaries define ostensively when they include pictorial illustrations of objects corresponding to the words being defined. All of us learn by the ostensive method all the time. The defect of this method, as Richard Robinson shrewdly observes, is that the level of precision of definition is low. After many repetitions of *dog* when in the presence of the same dog, a child may associate the animal with the utterance and know the word *dog*. But when he first sees a different, much larger dog, he will not associate it with the same word. He will have to be exposed to many kinds of dogs, and also be able to distinguish dogs from cats and other animals, before he has learned the meaning of *dog*. As Robinson says, "No one could learn to apply the word 'dog' correctly from one ostensive definition of it."[17]

When the question is asked, then, "Why can't a dictionary leave out simple words like 'dog' since everyone knows what they mean?" I reply, "It is one thing to be able to recognize dogs, and another to know what *dog* means." Though the lexical definition of *dog* cannot describe what a dog is in words sufficiently simple to one who has never seen a dog, it can, precisely, define the word. It is a commonplace experience for a person to know the meaning of a word but fail to recognize the thing described by the word upon seeing the thing for the first time. We may have studied what a *clerestory* is, but if we have never seen one it must often be pointed out to us in a church before we associate the thing with the word. Does this make the lexical meaning superfluous? Far from it. It is precisely this interplay between lexical and ostensive definition that refines and specifies our knowledge. Lexical meaning cannot always be relied on to give any picture of the real world; but, on the other hand, ostensive definition alone provides only rough clues to the extent and limitations of meaning and is of no help at all in understanding how a word functions as a word, information that is vital if we ever intend to use the word.

We cannot use language either for scientific inquiry or for the play of wit in literature without standards, even if they are only employed as a measure from which to deviate. The standards are not established by doyens of grammar pontificating with pipe in hand. Extracted definitions are determined by an examination of usage. Although usage in scientific terminology is given much weight when it is available, in general imposed definitions are determined by a consensus of experts. The argument against the inclusion in dictionaries of simple words is really based on the idea that because everyone knows how to use these words, their meanings are not important. It is true that their meanings are not important to everyone. Not everyone is interested in sports terms either, and not everyone is interested in religious terms. But every word is a part of the picture of how we view the world, and, as in a pointillist painting, small discrete elements seen on close viewing are not trivial and cannot be omitted without changing the overall impression.

Difficult words invade a definition in direct proportion to the degree of scientific specificity required. Dictionaries that define simply are not necessarily better; their editors have made a policy decision to sacrifice some precision of meaning for increased ease of understanding. The decision depends on how they view their readership. School dictionaries and dictionaries for foreign learners place a high value on ease of understanding and willingly sacrifice some precision. Scientific and technical dictionaries place a high value on precision and are generally unwilling to compromise the difficulty of their definitions. College-level dictionaries fall between the two extremes and vary among themselves, but certainly the trend is towards precision. The two largest commercial dictionaries for native speakers, *NID3* and the *Random House Dictionary* (*RHD2*), are both very much oriented towards precision at the expense of ease of understanding for the generalist. In the past the *OED* has taken an entirely different tack, directing its definition always to the generalist, a policy which has been deplored by specialists who view such definitions as inadequate. Indeed, this policy has been modified in the *OED Supplements* and in *OED2*, but it remains to be seen how far in the direction of scientific precision the editors of the third edition of the *OED* intend to go. Because American dictionaries have never drawn a sharp line between encyclopedic and lexical information, there is no theoretical constraint in defining scientific words with encyclopedic precision. The *OED* has drawn such a line, and lengthy encyclopedic definitions may not fit well into the balance it seeks to maintain between lexical and encyclopedic material. In opening the door to scientific terminology, *OED3* may find it difficult to close.

The dictum that every word should be defined by simpler words is gratuitous and misleading. All expository writing should be simple. All definitions should be as simple, direct, and clear as possible. The simple-definition rule confuses simplicity of form and of usage with simplicity of sense, ignoring the fact that an adequate definition often demands exact description or complex statement, which must presuppose familiarity with other, antecedent terms in order to keep the definition from becoming a long textbook essay. Hard words are used not because definers want to show off their vocabularies but because these words have more exact meanings than simpler words; therefore, they do not have to be qualified and they save space.

Brevity

The need to save space in dictionaries leads naturally to the injunction, "Be brief." Dictionary definitions should not waste words. The art of defining depends not only on the ability to analyze and understand what words mean, but equally on the ability to express such meanings succinctly. Robinson writes, "A lexical definition could nearly always be truer by being longer."[18] A good definer learns how to lose the least measure of truth with each shortening of a definition.

The first draft of a definition is almost always too long – and should be. Definers begin by constructing the best definition they can devise. This work is often creative and rewarding, even if it is sometimes exasperatingly difficult. Then the task of cutting begins. Every definition must be pared to say the most in the least number of words. Often it is improved in the process. (Robinson's statement above refers to a definition's "truth value" – how well it describes the real world – not its excellence as a definition. It is therefore not inconsistent to say that some definitions are made better by being shorter.) For example, here is an expert's definition of a term used in obstetrics, *trial of labor*: "allowing labor to either begin or progress with the intention of allowing labor to proceed as long as satisfactory progress is being made and as long as no complications occur." It is thirty words long and it is obviously defective, defining a noun phrase as an adjective, but it does get across the meaning. The definition was revised to read: "nonintervention in either the initiation or continuation of labor as long as satisfactory progress is observed and no complications occur." It is twenty words long, clearer and without redundancy, and says the same thing as the wordier definition.

Avoidance of ambiguity

Words in definitions must be used unambiguously in the context of the definition. If a word used in a definition has more than one meaning (i.e., if it is polysemous), the particular sense in which it is intended must be made clear by the rest of the definition. This problem is most conspicuous in dictionaries that depend on synonyms for definition, such as bilingual and short monolingual dictionaries. One cannot define *back-yard*, either in English or its equivalent in another language, by the English word *lot*, since *lot* has a lot of other meanings.

HOW TO DEFINE BY PART-OF-SPEECH

Nouns

From a formal point of view, nouns are the easiest of all words to define, and in scientific and technical dictionaries they are by far the most common. The defining noun may relate to the appearance, purpose, or composition of the thing defined, but it should pinpoint that property of the thing that is viewed by most speakers as being essential to it. If that essential property were not present, the thing would not be regularly identified by the definiendum. Thus, if *mirror* is defined as "a polished or smooth surface (as of glass) that forms images by reflection" (*MW10*), one can say that if it were not a surface it would not be called a mirror. Moreover, the surface must be polished or smooth. These features describe a mirror's appearance. The purpose of a mirror is to form images by reflection; this also is essential, but the definer chose to describe the thing before stating its purpose. If one tries to recast the definition, one realizes why. "An object designed to reflect images from a polished or smooth surface" implies what a mirror is rather than stating it. It is stylistically convenient to put "polished and smooth" first even though these qualities are no more integral to the meaning than the mirror's purpose. That mirrors are usually made of glass is indicated by the parenthetical "as of glass." Since the word *glass* also means "mirror," this is useful information, but it is only incidental, since mirrors can be made of other substances and still be mirrors.

A noun definition must immediately answer the question, What is it? In order to answer that question it must use a noun, whether qualified or not, in the first part of the definition that identifies the class of things or kind of thing to which the definiendum belongs. If the term to be defined is a phrase, such as *infectious hepatitis*, and *hepatitis* is elsewhere defined, it is perfectly proper to use *hepatitis* as the defining noun, as in "hepatitis characterized by" or "an acute form of hepatitis in which." There is no need to repeat the definition of *hepatitis*, especially in a technical dictionary. The user of a medical dictionary is more likely to know what *hepatitis* means, and the arrangement of entry and subentries places the basic term close to its combinations. In a general dictionary, the extra space required to paraphrase *hepatitis* as "inflammation of the liver" may be worthwhile to spare the reader the effort of looking up a distant entry.

The use of a noun element in the definition of a phrasal entry is not confined to scientific and technical dictionaries but is quite common in general dictionaries. *Student teacher* is defined by *Webster's New World College Dictionary* (*WNWCD*) as "a college or university student who teaches school under the supervision of an experienced teacher as a requirement for a degree in education." *Puppy dog* is defined by *MW10* as "a domestic dog: *esp:* one having the lovable attributes of a puppy."

The latter definition illustrates one solution to the problem of conveying connotation. *Puppy dog* is appropriately used in domestic contexts; it is a diminutive and shares the intimate register of words like *daddy*, *mommy*, or *honey* (as a term of affection). These words would all be out of place in a board of directors' meeting or even in ordinary business conversation. They express a certain attitude on the part of the speaker towards the person or thing described, and for *puppy dog* "one having the lovable attributes of a puppy" is the method used to convey this attitude. The definition might well have read: "a domestic dog: conveying the speaker's affection for puppies." Alternatively, a citation illustrating such an attitude, such as "a cute little puppy dog," might have been included to show a typical use.

Adjectives

Every dictionary has its own recommended style for defining adjectives. Style manuals for dictionaries using conventional defining style list the particular introductory adjectives that may be used, often for particular kinds of situations, and others that are proscribed. Here are some of the introductory words and phrases used by these dictionaries in defining adjectives:

able to	exhibiting	likely to
apt to	expressing	made of
associated with	for	marked by
being	full of	of
belonging to	having	of the nature of
capable of	having the quality of	pertaining to
characterized by	having to do with	producing
consisting of	inclined to	relating to
denoting	indicating	showing
describing	involving	tending to
designating	like	used (for, with, in, etc.)

Some of these should be used with caution or avoided if possible. *Associated with* may be ambiguous; *pertaining to* is old-fashioned and has been dropped by some dictionaries; some of the other words are too formal for a children's dictionary or too difficult for an ESL dictionary. Sometimes it is convenient to combine two introductory adjectives, e.g., "of or designating the color yellow." But a whole string of introductory adjectives should not be used to combine various senses that have little in common, e.g., "of, for, characterized by, or resembling."

Dictionaries so often use *of* in their definitions of adjectives because it covers a multitude of senses and has the marvelous property of being only two letters long. Its common use depends on strictly observing the substitutability rule. How would one better define *yellow* in "a yellow color" than by "of yellow"? One could say, "denoting yellow," but that does not work so well in "a yellow shade" or "a yellow swatch," whereas "of yellow" works just as well in all three contexts. Almost every defining characteristic common to dictionaries can be traced to the need to conserve space. Indeed, although the principal function of the dictionary style manual (see Ch. 7, p. 363) is to assure uniform treatment of similar entries, a very important consideration is the need to establish styles, consistent with clarity, that are most economical in expression.

Verbs

Verbs are often considered – justly, I think – the most difficult words to define, in part because many verbs have numerous senses that must be discriminated, and partly because of the complex relationship between verbs and their objects. One could write a long monograph on the question of defining verbs, a disquisition more suitable for a dictionary style manual than for this book. I propose here simply to outline some of the problems and suggest some solutions, but my treatment of this subject must be sketchy.

The definition of a verb begins with the infinitive form, with or without *to*, or another verb. Thus, from *MW10*:

hinder   *vt* **1 :** to make slow or difficult the progress of **:** HAMPER **2 :** to hold back **:** CHECK

Def. 1 refers to slowing the rate of progress and def. 2 to stopping it entirely or preventing it from occurring. Def. 1 might have been phrased, "to make the progress of slow or difficult," but this was likely rejected on the grounds that the unexpressed object should follow the entire definition and not come in its midst. The awkward phrasing of

def. 1 was thus considered preferable to the ambiguity of the alternative. Both definitions refer to transitive uses. If the sense defined is transitive, the definition should substitute for the transitive use of the verb,
although, as I have noted above, some ESL dictionaries have abandoned this policy and use definitions that include the object even if the
verb is transitive. Other ESL dictionaries use sentence definitions that
exemplify the verb's object in context and are therefore not substitutable except in a narrow range of contexts; they rely on illustrative quotations to exemplify a greater variety of contexts than their definition
covers. In traditional defining styles, the form of the definition should
leave little doubt that an object is called for to complete it, and should
suggest, if possible, the nature of the object. Note also that any verb
used as a synonym, such as *hamper*, should also be transitive. In def. 2,
the range of application is wider and people are more often among the
objects, as in "Shyness hindered him from asking the question." *NID3*
gives the useful contextual clue that this sense is often used with *from*,
but this is omitted from *MW10*. *WNWCD* gives these meanings in
reverse order:

hinder   **1** to keep back; restrain; get in the way of; prevent; stop **2** to make
difficult for; thwart; impede; frustrate

Def. 2 of *WNWCD* and def. 1 of *MW10* apply to this use: "Their plan
was hindered by irresolution and bad advice."

The two styles of defining are very different. The Merriam-Webster
version calls for uninterrupted phrases laid out in logical sequence,
however much they may vary from typical English syntax. *WNWCD*'s
style calls for greater simplicity, marked by reluctance to offend normal
syntax and a much freer use of synonyms. *MW10* regards synonyms as
a kind of cross-reference and prints them in small capital letters.
However, synonyms in the definition of any dictionary can be regarded
as cross-references to those words.

The intransitive sense of *hinder* is defined as follows:

WNWCD: to delay action; be a hindrance
MW10:   to delay, impede, or prevent action

An intransitive verb must be defined intransitively. There are two ways
to define intransitively: by including the object as part of the definition,
or by using another intransitive verb as a synonym. One cannot use a
transitive verb as a synonym for an intransitive verb, because it will not
substitute and is therefore misleading.

Many verb definitions cannot be defined adequately without specifying the typical object or the range of permissible objects, but most native-speaker dictionaries have been slow to recognize this or have been unwilling to use the space to provide adequate treatment. The object of a verb has to be considered part of its meaning. Sometimes native-speaker dictionaries do specify the objects of verbs by enclosing them in parentheses. *RHWCD* defines *interpolate* (def. 1) as:

1. to introduce (something additional or extraneous) between other things or parts; interject; interpose . . . **3. a.** to alter (a text) by the insertion of new matter, esp. deceptively or without authorization. **b.** to insert (new and spurious matter) in this manner.

By this device the kind of object usually taken by the verb can be indicated, as well as a restricted range of application. The trouble is that parentheses are used for a variety of information, even in the same dictionary. In some definitions it is not clear whether the parenthetical object refers to the word as a word or as a thing. *RHWCD*'s def. 2 of *doff* is "to remove or tip (the hat), as in greeting." Is one to assume that the word *hat* is the usual object of *doff*, or that *hat* means "any hat"? Dictionaries should have some way of distinguishing between *hat* and "the class of objects denoted by *hat*." In this instance the object is often "hat" but can be a kind of hat: one can doff a homburg or a derby.

RHWCD defines *prohibit* as follows:

1. to forbid (an action, activity, etc.) by authority or law. **2.** to forbid the action of (a person).

The objects are specified to distinguish the sense that takes a person as object from that which doesn't. Def. 2 refers to a use such as "He was prohibited from entering by a guard." Clearly, in these cases the parenthetical objects are not to be taken as words but as denoting the class of things defined by the words. We would hardly ever say, "An action is prohibited here." Readers are not told this; they must surmise it. When the indicated object is as vague as "an action, activity, etc.," it serves no useful purpose to state it, especially when an illustrative sentence is also provided. The real meaning of the parenthetical object is: "This sense does not take people as objects." Dictionaries should state this rather than trying to provide negative information by giving vague, nonhuman classes of objects that readers are not likely to interpret correctly. What does "etc." mean in this context? One can say, "Idleness and absence are prohibited in this school." Are idleness and absence actions or activities? Perhaps they are "etc." The use of parentheses can be defended as a means of indicating collocation and range of application in less space and in less equivocal form than by illustrative quotations. Nonetheless, its ambiguity is a defect.

In the traditional defining style for verbs used by native-speaker dictionaries, the class of objects is often not given at all in the definition but may be indicated by a brief illustrative phrase. *WNWCD* defines *hit* as follows:

1 to come up against, usually with force; strike *[the car *hit* the tree]* **2** to give a blow to; strike; knock

By contrast, *Cobuild*, a dictionary for foreign learners that employs a non-traditional style, defines these two senses (in reverse order) as:

1 If you **hit** someone or something, you deliberately touch them with a lot of force, with your hand or an object held in your hand. *Find the exact grip that allows you to hit the ball hard . . . She hit him hard across his left arm . . . Police at the scene said Dr Mahgoub had been hit several times in the head.*
2 When one thing **hits** another, it touches it with a lot of force. *The car had apparently hit a traffic sign before skidding out of control . . . She hit the last barrier and sprawled across the track.*

Cobuild devotes much more space to these verb senses, as do other ESL dictionaries, than dictionaries for native speakers of comparable size. Native-speaker dictionaries are more concerned about providing extensive vocabulary coverage than depth of treatment of what they do cover. Because verb use is critically important in language learning, ESL dictionaries devote particular care to their coverage of verbs. Note that the real distinction between the two senses of *hit* consists in the intention associated with the performance of the action and, to a lesser extent, with the kinds of objects affected by the action. In def. 1 of *WNWCD* and def. 2 of *Cobuild* the action described is accidental and the object is usually a thing. In def. 2 of *WNWCD* and def. 1 of *Cobuild* the action described is intentional, and the object is often a person. The essential physical act described may be the same in either case. Virtually all ESL dictionaries, even those for intermediate-level students, are better at defining and illustrating verb use than native-speaker dictionaries. *Cobuild*'s illustrative quotations have an authentic feel to them because they *are* authentic, based on actual language use. All high-quality ESL dictionaries are now based on the use of language corpora (described below), which have particularly improved their coverage of common verbs.

ESL dictionaries do not feel bound by many of the traditional rules of defining and are willing to experiment with new techniques. For example, *LDAE*, probably on the basis of frequency, defines some verbs under the participial (or adjectival) form, such as *embarrass:*

embarrass   to make someone feel EMBARRASSED: *I hope I didn't embarrass you in front of your friends.*
embarrassed   ashamed, anxious, or nervous, especially in front of other people: *I felt **embarrassed about** how dirty my house was.*
embarrassing   making you feel EMBARRASSED: *He asked a lot of embarrassing questions.*
embarrassment   the feeling that you have when you are EMBARRASSED: *Billy looked down and tried to hide his embarrassment.*

It is extremely unusual, at least in monolingual lexicography, to define a verb in terms of one of its inflections or derivative forms.

By contrast, *CDAE*, also innovative in its way, defines *embarrass* and enters the derived forms without definition, but with examples, as below:

embarrass   to cause (someone) to feel anxious, ashamed, or uncomfortable ·
He knew that letter would embarrass him and later he tried to get rid of it.
   embarrassed · *They sat in embarrassed silence.*
   embarrassing · *It's embarrassing to be caught telling a lie.*
   embarrassingly · *an embarrassingly poor performance*
   embarrassment · *She forgot her lines and blushed with embarrassment.*

CDAE does define derivative forms that are run on when there is a change in meaning but otherwise omits the definition, relying on illustrative quotations to show typical usage. In this it follows its parent dictionary, the *Cambridge International Dictionary of English* (*CIDE*), but *CDAE* more often includes definitions for derivatives than *CIDE*.

Observers may differ on the success of such strategies for defining (or not defining) particular forms, but they are certain to be influential in other branches of lexicography, especially as the use of corpora (described below, and in detail in Chapter 6) becomes more widespread. Access to large bodies of authentic text has emboldened lexicographers to introduce new methods which in the past they would have been unwilling to undertake, because they now have the research tools to determine the relative frequencies of particular inflections and derivatives, and they have a much clearer idea of how they are used.

Other parts-of-speech

Adverbs are defined by other adverbs or by prepositional phrases that substitute in the context of the particular sense. For example, *well* is

defined by *CDAE* as "in a good way; to a high or satisfactory standard."
Interjections are defined by other interjections or by explanations of the
frame of mind of the user of the interjection or the effect it is intended
to have on others. *Damn* is defined by *RHWCD* as: "(used as an expletive
to express anger, annoyance, disgust, etc.)". Pronouns are sometimes
defined in terms of their grammatical function, sometimes by a substitutable phrase. *Who* is defined by *CDAE* as: "used as the subject or object
of a verb when referring to a particular person or when adding information about a person just mentioned." (A usage note is appended saying
that in formal usage *whom* is used as the object of a verb or preposition.
In fact, *whom* is rarely used in speech, and less and less in writing; the
definition as given accurately reflects usage.) *Which* is defined by
WNWCD as: "what one (or ones) of the number of persons, things, or
events mentioned or implied?" *MW10* defines *she* as: "that female one
who is neither speaker nor the one addressed" and *her* as: "*pron objective
case of* SHE." Dictionaries, as one can see, have to devise novel ways of
expression to define pronouns. Conjunctions are defined by whatever
works in the particular context: other conjunctions, adverbs, or prepositional phrases.

INNOVATIVE DEFINING STYLES

I have already given several examples of innovative defining styles used
by ESL dictionaries in treating verbs, but I have barely scratched the
surface. One of the biggest problems in all general dictionaries is finding
a way to represent all the senses of a very common verb like *take* without
burying the reader under a mass of undifferentiated numbered senses,
within which are phrasal verbs, set phrases, and idioms, which are
included in no particular order, whether marked off by boldface type or
not. ESL dictionaries have been far more innovative in seeking solutions
to this problem than have native-speaker dictionaries.

LDOCE3 sets off very common verbs like *take* within a special section,
at the top of which it lists the basic senses or subjects, such as "move sth,"
"do something," "need sth," "get something in your possession," etc.,
and also has sections for "spoken phrases," "other phrases," and
"phrasal verbs." Each of these numbered sections correspond to one or
several individual definitions. For example, the heading "get something
in your possession" includes senses for *steal* ("She's taken my pen"), *get
control* ("Enemy forces have taken the airport"), *get sth* ("Jim took all the
credit, even though he hadn't done much of the work"), etc. Among the

spoken phrases listed are *take it from me, it takes all sorts . . .*, and *what do you take me for?* Among the phrasal verbs defined are *take after, take back, take in, take off, take on, take out,* etc., with numerous senses given for some of these entries.

CIDE and its American offshoot *CDAE* separate major clusters of meaning with "guidewords," a single word or short phrase that is used to distinguish broad areas of sense. Thus *CDAE*'s coverage of *take* includes separate articles distinguished by the guidewords *move, remove, accept, think of, hold, catch, need, act,* etc. Under each separate article it provides a definition and numerous illustrative examples, along with idioms and set phrases containing a form of *take* that reflects the meaning under which it appears. *Cobuild*'s technique of using a sentence definition has been adopted in one form or another by a number of other dictionaries because it is particularly well adapted for defining idioms which can be awkward to define in a traditional style. For example, here is part of *CDAE*'s entry for *take [ACCEPT]*:

People say **take care** instead of saying good-bye. · To **take care of** someone or something is to be responsible for them or do whatever needs to be done: *She took care of her little sister all afternoon . . .* · If you **take charge** of something, you accept responsibility for it or have control over it: *She took charge of the project and made sure it was finished on time.* · To **take** something **with a grain of salt** means to believe that it is not really important or completely true: *I've seen the article, which I take with a grain of salt.* · If you **take heart**, you feel encouraged . . . · When someone offers something and says **take it or leave it**, they mean that you must either accept it without any change or refuse it. · If you **take** something **lying down**, you accept it without complaint: *I can't take that criticism lying down.* · If you **take pains** to do something, you are very careful doing it: *He took great pains to dress appropriately.*

This style of defining has the virtue of immediately putting the usage in a social context as an interaction between people, whereas a traditional defining style is more abstract and less satisfactory. For example, *WNWCD* defines *take it or leave it* as "accept it or not." The definition is correct, but one is given no context that might explain how this expression is used or for what purpose. Incidentally, the use of the plural referent for "someone" in *CDAE*'s definition for *take it or leave it* is more or less standard in ESL lexicography, and at least one dictionary for native speakers, the *New Oxford Dictionary of English (NODE)*, has adopted it as well. *NODE* has been influenced by ESL dictionaries in other respects, as we shall see below.

Consider how well the sentence definition works for variable idioms.

Cobuild (1995) defines *kid gloves* in this way: "If you treat someone or something with **kid gloves** or give them the **kid glove** treatment, you are very careful in the way you deal with them, for example because they are very delicate or easily upset, or because they could be dangerous." This is followed by three quotations from authentic usage derived from linguistic corpora. (See Ch. 6 for the use of the corpus in lexicography.) The first example includes "treated with kid gloves," the second "handled with kid gloves," and the third "take off the kid gloves." By contrast, the native-speaker dictionaries which define this term conventionally (and which are not based on corpora) do not do nearly as well. *RHWCD* has an entry for *handle with kid gloves* (only one of many variants for this idiom), defining it as: "to treat with extreme tact or gentleness." All the other American college dictionaries and the leading British dictionaries for native speakers have similar treatments, although some enter the idiom as *with kid gloves*, which *MW10* defines simply as "with special consideration." The reader can judge for himself whose treatment best illustrates the meaning and shows the variety of possible contexts.

Nonetheless, the sentence definition has its limitations. It is not suited for defining realia, such as substances like *gypsum* or *iron*, nor for items that are part of a nomenclature such as *gynecology* or *archeology*, and various other types of entries. But for many verbs and phrasal verbs and, as *Cobuild* has shown, even for many adjectives and adverbs, the sentence definition can work well. It does require the use of more space than conventional definitions, and for this reason its use may be limited in all but the largest of dictionaries, but it has already proved itself to be a powerful new tool in ESL lexicography.

Phrasal verbs are another area to which ESL dictionaries devote special attention and for which they have devised innovative strategies. *CDAE* has separate entries for its phrasal verbs following the verb form, and these entries (as do the phrasal-verb entries for most ESL dictionaries) specify where the object falls. For example, one of *CDAE*'s three entries for *take up* is as follows:

take up *obj* [FILL], **take** *obj* **up** . . . *v adv* [M] to fill up (space or time) · *This desk takes up too much room.* · *My day is completely taken up with meetings.*

The symbol [M] means that the object is movable, and the form of the definiendum shows the possible positions of the object.

The corpus-based *LDAE*, like its parent dictionary *LDOCE3*, includes special treatment of "spoken phrases" that are used almost exclusively in speech. One such item under the entry *know* includes definienda for *you know* (in four different uses), *I know* (in two different uses), *as far as I know*, and *you never know*. The treatment for *you know* is:

a) said when you cannot quickly think of what to say next: *It has, you know, cherry pie filling.* **b)** said when you are trying to explain something by giving more information: *I have some clothes for Matthew, you know, for the baby, if Carrie wants them.* **c)** said when you begin talking about a subject: *You know, I worked in Arizona before I came here.* **d)** said in order to check if someone understands what you are saying: *I feel like New Mexico is really my home, you know?*

When *Webster's Third New International Dictionary* (*NID3*) was published in 1961, company publicity, seeking to capitalize on the dicta of structural linguistics, made much of the position that language is in a fundamental sense the spoken language. As we shall see in the next chapter, *NID3* was widely criticized for taking this stance, which was said to have shaped its "permissive" treatment of language. In fact *NID3* did not have the tools to examine the spoken language in any depth, and *NID3* like every dictionary before it is based almost entirely on the written language. Only with the development of large language corpora containing spoken material could lexicographers begin to take a look at enough speech to draw conclusions, and we are still at an early stage in our ability to examine different varieties of speech in sufficient volume to understand and describe spoken language with any confidence. *LDOCE3* and *LDAE* break new ground in their attempt to distinguish and describe spoken phrases that are extremely common but that are completely absent from our dictionaries. While the entry for *you know* strikes me as excellent, some of *LDAE*'s "spoken phrase" entries do not seem as surefooted and may be based on insufficient data. Nonetheless, *LDAE*'s attempt to cover spoken phrases is a commendable innovation and is an important step towards adequate dictionary treatment of the spoken language.

Among large native-speaker dictionaries, *NODE* is the first in a long time to change the way definitions have been organized and presented. The definitions themselves are traditional, but instead of presenting the reader with a long list of numbered definitions, as most other dictionaries do, *NODE* has grouped related meanings together in what it calls "core meanings," which are then broken down into unnumbered subsenses set off by a distinctive square symbol. Here is *NODE*'s entry for *machine*:

an apparatus using or applying mechanical power and having several parts, each with a definite function and together performing a particular task: *a fax machine* | *a shredding machine.* · [USU. WITH MODIFIER] a coin-operated dispenser: *a cigarette machine.* · TECHNICAL any device that transmits a force or directs its application. · FIGURATIVE an efficient and well-organized group of powerful people: *his campaign illustrated the continuing strength of a powerful political machine.* · FIGURATIVE a person who acts with the mechanical efficiency of a machine: *comedians are more than just laugh machines.*

NODE's use of "figurative" and other labels is an attempt to show the semantic relationships of divergent meanings instead of simply listing them independently. Since it only numbers "core meanings" – which may have been influenced by the clustering techniques used in ESL dictionaries such as *CIDE* – it has been able to cut down drastically on the quantity of numbered senses and simplify its presentation. It has not, however, cut back on the number of senses it covers, and its presentation demonstrates that it has made use of a corpus.[19] The native-speaker dictionaries have been slower to make use of corpora than ESL dictionaries, but the next generation of British native-speaker dictionaries are certain to be corpus-based now that the British National Corpus is available. (See Ch. 6, especially, pp. 288ff., for more information on the British National Corpus and on the development of an American corpus.) Widespread use of corpora by native-speaker dictionaries will undoubtedly lead to reevaluations of many of the standard features included in dictionaries, and the publication of new editions then would be an opportune time to introduce new defining techniques and styles of presentation.

STRATEGIES IN DEFINING

All definitions of things are compromises between specific accuracy and breadth of inclusiveness. The definition of a door as wooden is not wrong; it just leaves out too many doors. On the other hand, no definition can take in all of the particular things referred to by the word defined. There will always be marginal cases that are not covered by any definition: doors made of blasts of hot air, or doors that do not seem to lead into or out of anything. To include such disparate uses of *door* would so generalize the definition as to weaken its application to the vast majority of doors or so extend its length that it would try the patience of the reader. One can picture the definition of *door* as a circle around a dense, random collection of many thousands of dots, each dot representing a particular use. Beyond the perimeter of the circle there is also a smattering of dots. These are the uses of *door* that are not covered by the current definition; if such uses increase significantly, the circle will have to be expanded to include them, or as many of them as can be fitted in without making the circle too large. One must not assume that the uses of a word not covered by its dictionary definition are wrong; definitions merely abstract meaning from a preponderance of usage. The bigger the dictionary, the wider the scope of divergent uses its definition takes in, but there will always be some usages beyond the range of even the largest dictionary. I am not saying uses of language cannot be wrong, only that their wrongness depends on the opinions of other people. Their opinions may, of course, be influenced by dictionary definitions, but also by the failure of the usage to conform to facts or to real-world conditions.

In a general dictionary, specificity is less important than breadth of coverage, but usefulness demands the definition be as specific as possible consistent with a realistically broad compass of meaning. The challenge of defining is to learn how to weigh those two goals and intermix them in varying proportions for each novel situation. Let me illustrate this with an example drawn from my own experience. As a long-time fan of track-and-field (called "athletics" in the UK), I have observed how inadequately dictionaries have defined this sport. Most do not even call it a sport, but define it as a collection of athletic events. For example, the *American Heritage College Dictionary* (*AHCD3*) defines it as: "Athletic events performed on a running track and field associated with it." *WNWCD*'s definition is: "a series of contests in running, jumping, shot-putting, etc. performed on a track and on a field," with a reference to the sense of "field" used here. My definition in *CDAE* is: "a sport that tests a person's ability to run faster, jump farther or higher, or throw an object farther, when competing against others."

The definition can be criticized on several levels, but I wanted to make it broad enough to take in not only many running events but the jumping events, pole vault, the throwing events, and the decathlon. It leaves out race walking, which, incidentally, no definition of *walk* would cover, this being one of the dots outside the circle for *walk* and therefore requiring its own definition as a two-word lexical item. It arguably leaves out the pole vault, which is not a jumping event – imagine jumping 18 or 19 feet into the air! – but I hoped readers would not interpret "jump" literally. It also does not say that almost all the running events but the marathon, which is not a regular part of track meets, are conducted on a measured running track, although *CDAE*'s entry for *track*, under which *track-and-field* appears, does define a running track in this sport. In some ways, then, the definition is not specific enough – it omits some events – and it leaves out an important fact relating to the physical conditions under which the sport occurs. But it does capture the essence of what track-and-field is and has always been, even though the particular events and physical conditions have changed over time. In this case, I decided that breadth of coverage was more important than taking in all the relevant facts.

On the other hand, when defining the individual events in track-and-field, I felt I should be as specific as possible. The *pole vault*, for instance, is usually defined as an event in which an athlete uses a pole to vault over a bar. This is accurate, but it doesn't say how the pole is used. Constrained by using a controlled defining vocabulary which did not include *vault*, I defined *pole vault* in *CDAE* as: "a sports competition in which you hold a long, stiff pole near one end and force it to bend so that when it straightens, it pushes you up over a high bar." Although the definition describes how the pole propels the athlete over the bar, it could be improved by changing it to read "in which you run towards a high bar while holding a long, stiff pole," etc., although that would make it longer. One obviously can't get into all the technical details of the event, but one must try to give enough information so that the reader knows roughly what happens when someone uses a pole vault to get over a high bar.

I feel that it is possible to improve almost any definition. If a lexicographer begins to feel that he or she cannot improve existing definitions, it is time to think about taking up another line of work. Take the case of *run* in its basic sense. *Run* is usually defined as to go forward by moving the legs faster than when walking. After mentally picturing someone running, I realized that one can't run unless one is leaning forward. In running, one's center of gravity is always at a point ahead of where it is when walking. It seemed to me this was fundamental to the action, because without it one couldn't move fast. I therefore defined *run* for *CDAE* as: "to move your legs faster than when walking with the weight of your body pressing forward with each quick step," which I liked because the flow of words seemed to move at a pace analogous to running. Alas, "with each quick step" was cut in the final editing stage, a decision I can understand because since walking involves taking steps, the phrase can be seen as redundant; but the definition was better with it. One soon learns in dictionary work to give up too keen a proprietary interest in one's own words or one would live a life of continuous despair.

Defining abstractions poses a very different challenge from defining real objects. If one is defining *shopping cart* or *shovel*, there is no difficulty over determining the genus of the definition, and usually not much difficulty in describing what it is used for, but it may not be easy to describe its shape or structure. A shopping cart is a container; a shovel is a tool. But if one is defining an abstraction such as a legal *right*, the hardest part of the definition is often determining precisely what the genus is. A degree of specificity is necessary in describing a real object because one has to say what it looks like – even though it may come in many varieties – or what it is made of. However, as H. Bosley Woolf has pointed out, it is wise to be cautious about specifying precisely what materials something is made of.[20] Nothing dates a dictionary so rapidly as definitions that specify wood or iron or silk when the object or garment described can be made of plastic or synthetic materials. Of course, the obsolescence of some definitions is unavoidable. The pace of technological change is so rapid that no one can predict what new materials, designs, and uses will be devised for things. Definers must be well informed and imaginative. They must keep abreast of recent technological advances and be able to guess when they ought to be cautious about being specific. Here are the definitions for *shopping cart* and *shovel* in *CDAE*. The definer felt it was safe to say that shopping carts are made of "metal" rods. I think this is still generally true. But note that no material is mentioned in the definition for *shovel*.

shopping cart   a large container made of metal rods that rests on a wheeled base and has an open top and a handle at the back that you push
shovel   a tool consisting of a wide blade attached to a long handle, used for digging up or moving loose material, such as earth or snow

In defining abstractions, specificity is a snare – and here is where the use of a corpus is so important – because no one can summon up through one's own limited experience even a fraction of the variety of ways such words are used. Without being exposed to such variation, one cannot adequately define these words. What is the common thread running through *right* when used in "civil rights," "human rights," "a right to trial by jury"? My solution was to call it an opportunity. *CDAE*'s definition is:

right   your opportunity to be treated in particular ways that the law promises to protect for the benefit of society

The other key to this definition was the use of *promises*; the opportunity has to be backed by a promise with the weight of law behind it, implying that breaking the promise can have serious consequences for society.

Defining technical terms

Science editors on dictionary staffs sometimes make the mistake of demanding specificity even when some ambiguity is part of the meaning. Many terms, even scientific and technical ones, are flexible in application by design and serve an excellent practical purpose in defining an area calling for the user's judgment. For example, *arrested labor* was defined by one contributor to a medical dictionary as "labor that has failed to progress at an expected rate, given the particular characteristics of fetus and mother." The definition was criticized on the grounds that "expected rate" was not specified. But "given the particular characteristics of fetus and mother" implies that the expected rate will vary depending on the maternal pelvic shape, the position of the fetus in the uterus, and so on. The meaning of the term depends on the judgment of the user as to what the "expected rate" is, and thus the specific meaning of *arrested labor* will vary too. The critic's belief that all scientific terms must describe invariable and measurable phenomena is simply not the case. The term *arrested labor* could be applied to the same birth at different times by different speakers. There is a continuum of situations during which different speakers will use the term; some will use it sooner, some later, but a large majority will roughly agree on what "expected rate" means in a particular set of circumstances.

Defining scientific terms often involves defining a basic term, or main entry, and a great many subentries that include the entry word, such as the various forms of *nephritis* (inflammation of the kidney). The technical definer should group together all of the terms sharing a common element and construct a hierarchy of definition starting with the basic term, which may be compared to the trunk of a tree, which is gross, encompassing and profoundly implicit. The branches of the tree, or subentries (forms of *nephritis*), deal with increasingly nice distinctions, are of narrower compass, and are progressively more explicit. The flow of elucidation, compass, and explicitness normally goes in one direction only; one must define *acute interstitial nephritis* in terms of *nephritis*, not the other way around.

In dictionary work there are exceptions to every rule, and there are exceptions to this one also. Some entry words, such as *ounce*, are really only short (or *clipped*) forms of specific subentries, and they must be defined with reference to the subentries, such as *ounce avoirdupois, ounce troy, fluid ounce*. The entry/subentry arrangement cannot allow subentry definitions to be repeated under the main entry word, else thousands of definitions would appear twice. One cannot define *ounce avoirdupois* fully as one definition at *ounce* as well as at *ounce avoirdupois*. One must say simply that def. 1 of *ounce* is a variant of *ounce avoirdupois*. But in general the flow of definition does proceed from entry to subentry and from shorter subentry to longer subentry. This may be construed as an example of the rule that difficult terms may not be used to define simpler words, and in the context of scientific terms the rule has a certain validity.

One lexicographer lists the following mistakes as the most common in scientific and technical dictionaries:[21]

1. Failure to understand that a textbook type of description is not a definition.
2. Failure to indicate all the meanings of a term in the field covered by the dictionary. The definition should not represent one point of view only.
3. Failure to understand that self-explanatory entries are not legitimate lexical units, e.g., "fractures of the tibia." Hierarchical nomenclatures of scientific terms are seldom of much use in constructing a dictionary's word list because they are based on an arrangement of concepts rather than of words. They include many terms, such as "fractures of the tibia," that are not lexical units though they may be useful conceptual categories.
4. Failure to understand that in scientific usage a synonym (or variant) is a word that is an exact substitute for another.

The fourth point is a very common error, because in practice many pairs of terms that are not exact variants are used interchangeably. An obstetrics editor defined *vertex presentation* as a variant of *cephalic presentation*, which he defined as "a presentation of the fetus in which the lowest part that appears first in the uterine cervix is the fetal skull. This is the most common presentation of a human fetus during labor." Since *vertex* refers to the top of the head, I realized that *vertex presentation* is a kind of cephalic presentation (in technical terms, a *hyponym*), and the other presenting parts of the head – the brow, face, the occiput (back of the head), etc. – are identified as different kinds of cephalic presentations. The obstetrics editor was surely well aware of this fact, but since a vertex presentation is the most common, and since it is cephalic, in ordinary usage when a baby is born vertex first, I suspect that is often called a cephalic presentation. Thus "cephalic presentation" is an extracted meaning of *vertex presentation*. But in a technical dictionary, technical definitions are wanted. We could have included a sense of *cephalic presentation* with the meaning of vertex presentation; but this sort of situation occurs so frequently in medicine that it would have opened a can of worms which we wanted to avoid.

The editor's definition was also faulty because the important fact that *cephalic* refers to the skull or head appeared last instead of early in the definition. I therefore rewrote the two definitions as follows:

cephalic presentation   a presentation of the fetus in which the fetal head is the lowest part and appears first in the uterine cervix. This is the most common presentation of a human fetus during labor.
vertex presentation   a cephalic presentation of the fetus in which the vertex of the fetal skull is the lowest part and appears first in the uterine cervix. This is the most common cephalic presentation.

I would add to the list of common mistakes a fifth error: failure to realize that the context of a definition may not provide any frame of reference for the reader. An editor who is defining a whole series of definitions about fetal length, for instance, may occasionally neglect to mention that the object being measured is a fetus. But dictionary users read one entry at a time, and if the context does not specify what is being measured, they will be at a loss to understand the definition. This common error illustrates why dictionary defining is so demanding: each definition is entirely separate from every other definition and must constitute a tiny, discrete essay of its own, providing enough clues to context so that even in the briefest definition the readers know whether we are measuring fetuses or wavelengths, head sizes or reflexes. In an article or book one can skip along from sentence to sentence and presume that readers will keep pace with one's train of thought. Not so in a dictionary, where every definition must stand by itself.

Many mistakes do not fall clearly into any one category. For example, an expert on measures wrote the following definition of *meter* for a technical dictionary:

the SI base unit of length equal to the distance traveled by electromagnetic radiation through a vacuum in $1/299\,792\,458$ second. Between 1960 and 1983, the meter was defined as being equal to $1\,650\,763.73$ wavelengths in vacuum of the radiation corresponding to the transition between the levels $2p_{10}$ and $5d_5$ of the krypton-86 atom. [SI refers to Système International d'Unités, the metric system of decimal measures.]

It is a marvelously exact definition with one flaw: it gives absolutely no clue to the observable length of a meter! If one said to the expert, "But you have not told us what a meter is," he would reply, "On the contrary, I have told you exactly what it is. Since the meter is the standard by which all other SI measures of length are described, the meter cannot be described by comparing it to any other metric length and should not be compared to any nonmetric length because such measures are scientifically inexact." He is right, of course, yet from a practical point of view – and the lexicographer must always take the practical view – he must be overruled. One must include in the definition, and very early on, the fact that a meter is approximately 39.37 inches, however this pains the expert. It will not do to give a pure definition that does not answer the basic needs of many readers. The lexicographer, even of a technical dictionary whose definitions are far beyond his expertise, must insist upon exercising the ultimate judgment of what is useful. The technical data provided by the expert who defined *meter* are certainly useful in a technical dictionary, but because the lexicographer is *not* an expert he is able to recognize the needs of a wider variety of users than the specialist-definer.

The definition of *frog test* in *Butterworths Medical Dictionary* is my favorite medical definition. I quote it in full:

frog test   a test used to indicate pregnancy, in which a frog is used

This definition has an engaging simplicity and directness that I find charming. But one wonders how the frog is used. Do woman and frog stare at one another to see who blinks first? (If the woman, she's pregnant.) Is the test positive if the woman's touch turns the frog into a prince? My hopes for such a delightful pregnancy test were dashed and I was dumped right back into a seamy hospital lab with this definition from *Blakison's Gould Medical Dictionary*:

frog test   a pregnancy test in which urine containing chorionic gonadotropin is injected into the dorsal lymph sac of the male leopard frog (*Rana pipiens*). If spermatozoa are demonstrable in the frog's urine within 3 hours after injection, the test is positive.

When *frog test* is used, the context will rarely yield more information than that given by *Butterworths'* definition. If technical definitions were all extracted from usage, such definitions would be typical; fortunately, they are not, and this is an example of why they would not be adequate. *Gould's* imposed definition, prosaic as it is, is clearly more useful.

THE CITATION FILE

We have been describing the principles and techniques of defining, but we have not yet described the chief sources of definitions, the citation file and the electronic corpus. Up until recent years, dictionary makers relied mainly on the citation file for information about new words and meanings, but, with advances in computer technology, the electronic corpus is now much more important as a source of definition and other kinds of information about language use. (See Ch. 6, p. 273, for a fuller description of the electronic corpus.) Nonetheless, citation files continue to play an important role in compiling a new dictionary.

A *citation file* is a selection of potential lexical units in the context of actual usage, drawn from a variety of written sources and often some spoken sources, chiefly because the context illuminates an aspect of meaning. Citations are clipped from the source and pasted on a card or slip of paper, or retyped, and nowadays are routinely converted into a computer file by optical scanning or rekeyboarding. Citations are also collected to provide illustrative quotations that will be printed in the dictionary, especially in historical dictionaries and in the past in the larger synchronic dictionaries. Vast citation files still exist only in paper form because some of the citations cannot be scanned (the type is too faint, or too large, or the citation is handwritten, or there are important handwritten notes attached, or the paper is too fragile, etc.) and because keyboarding would be prohibitively expensive.

A *corpus* (plural *corpora*), Latin for "body," is a collection of different texts or of recorded speech, nowadays stored electronically on a computer and indexed so that any particular word can be found quickly in the context in which it has been used. Some corpora run to many millions of words, and may include all or parts of the running text of newspapers, books of fiction and nonfiction, magazines, scholarly and literary works, transcripts of television or radio programs, and unscripted speech.

The earliest English lexicographers by and large copied the definitions of their predecessors. Gradually, influenced by foreign-language dictionaries, some eighteenth-century lexicographers began to cite examples drawn from literature as evidence of usage. Although Samuel Johnson is often credited with having originated the use of illustrative quotations, he was not the first to adopt the practice even in English, though he did greatly expand its use and refine it. Nowadays, general dictionaries depend on citation files and electronic corpora primarily to provide them with the basis for defining new words and new meanings of established words. For established meanings of established words, they generally depend on older editions of their own work, acquire the right to use an earlier dictionary, or base their definitions on the definers' own

sense of the language with the help of definitions used in other dictionaries. They rely on specialists to define the large percentage of scientific
and technical terms. They stock their libraries with specialized dictionaries and reference books on a wide variety of subjects. It can be said
with some assurance that the only English dictionary ever created wholly
on the basis of citations was the *Oxford English Dictionary*, which took, by
the most charitable reckoning, fifty years to prepare. Every dictionary
after it has drawn upon its enormous store of information. In the past,
a large ongoing citation file was considered essential for the preparation
of any new general dictionary or for the revision of an existing dictionary, but it is now rather needed to supplement an electronic corpus and
to provide a way to collect odd or unusual or up-to-the-minute lexical
items, especially current slang and new scientific and technical terms
passing into the general vocabulary, which a corpus might not contain,
or which the definer would not think to look for. As Nelson Francis has
observed, *NID3* is the last great dictionary to be created without computer assistance.[22]

Some dictionary citation files are vast, numbering in the millions, but
with the availability of corpora, they will chiefly be of value for their historical information – that is, for evidence of uses that predate the development of electronic corpora. Citation slips are cumbersome to deal
with in large numbers because they take up a lot of space, and it is
difficult to examine many at the same time. The digitization of large
citation files has made them far more valuable, because not only is the
editor able to see more citations at a glance on the computer screen, but
every word in every citation can be indexed – not just the one cited – to
increase vastly the scope of the citation file. Thus, in the following citation for "over the top," *protests, threats, declined, answer,* etc., will also be
accessible if the file is digitized and indexed. (See Fig. 6, p. 192.)

This citation demonstrates that an item that is usually considered as
being a feature of British English is also used in America. As this
example illustrates, there are many reasons apart from definition for
citing a word or phrase. The context can illustrate whether a word is
slang, informal, or taboo, or is used with a particular connotation. Some
citations contain information about etymology or pronunciation.
Citations are often collected simply to show that a particular form exists;
this is most often the case with new scientific and technical terms,
although general words may also be cited for this reason if no better citation is available or if the term has been previously regarded as obsolete
or foreign.

ITEM   over the top

SOURCE NY Times   **DATE** Aug. 24, 1999

PAGE   A12   **AUTHOR** Irvin Molotsky

Yielding to protests from animal rights organizations and celebrities like Sir John

Gielgud and Bea Arthur, the Smithsonian Institution today canceled a panel discussion

and tasting of foie gras, the fattened liver of a duck or goose, that had been scheduled for

next month. . . . [¶] When asked whether the protests had taken the form of threats, Mr.

Umansky declined to answer. But he did say, "Some were way over the top."

6 Citation for "over the top"

The electronic corpus and how it differs from the citation file

Unlike a citation file, which usually consists of lexical items that an individual has seen fit to select, a corpus is a collection of running words from a variety of sources with the aim of including many different types of language use – mainstream newspaper reporting, popular and literary fiction, offbeat and avant-garde writing, and transcripts of speech in a variety of situations. A corpus is designed to cover many different subjects, such as politics and government affairs, business and economics, religion, science, sports, etc.

Although the texts to be included in a corpus are selected, the individual lexical items represented are not, as they typically are in citation collections. The quality of a corpus therefore does not depend on the collective judgments of a large number of people over an extended period of time. Because the size of the corpus is so large – some corpora now run to more than 300 million words, and are growing larger all the time – the quantity of information is of an altogether different magnitude from that of any citation file, such that the selection of texts, if it is at all sensible, has no measurable effect on the quality of the information obtained. Anomalies will be buried and invisible in the massive amount of mainstream texts included, whereas, in a citation file, every item is essentially equivalent. Citation files are therefore likely to give extraordinary importance to unusual items, because they have been noticed by the collector, whereas corpora give useful information about high-frequency words as well as low-frequency words, and the quality of evidence does not depend on the fortuitousness of selection, but chiefly on the size of the corpus and the tools available for using it. A good corpus can provide solid evidence of language use that is not available in any other way, and that would not occur spontaneously to even an experienced lexicographer. For a typical *key word in context* (**KWIC**) printout (for the word "conspicuous"), see Fig. 7, p. 194.

If a corpus is equipped with standard tools for statistical analysis, it is much easier to use than any citation file and can provide far more reliable information about meaning and use. Although there is still a role for individually collected citations in dictionary work, with the development of high-speed, desk-top computers capable of storing enormous amounts of text and the software to run them, the electronic corpus has replaced the citation file as the essential research tool in general lexicography.[23] In the past, the existence of an ongoing citation file is what distinguished reputable general dictionaries from purely derivative works; in the future, it will be the existence of sound electronic corpora. As always, having the tools needed will not guarantee they are used well, but not having them at all will guarantee that the dictionary does not measure up to a minimal standard of competence. No modern dictionary can pretend to cover the meanings and uses of its lexicon adequately today without the use of a corpus.

See Ch. 6, p. 273, for information on the history, planning, and design of corpora, as well as a description of their uses in lexicography.

Collecting citations

However important corpora are, they cannot be as up-to-the-minute as citation files, because it takes time to convert and process text and to incorporate it into the rest of the corpus. So citation collection is still important for finding new words and senses and for spotting trends in usage, such as British usages appearing in America or Americanisms in Britain. It is best to hire as citation readers people who have had experience working on dictionaries. One cannot expect everyone who is fascinated with words to have the necessary judgment to select good citations. Some people, however, who have never worked on a dictionary staff have somehow developed a gift for discerning good citations.

```
                    His conspicuous consumption, variously refer
's interesting that the most conspicuous and well publicized case of
e agents, and the Epilogue's conspicuous absenting of woman are devic
tory-solicitation includes a conspicuous display of foreknowledge reg
enty minutes where you're so conspicuous and you're really being show
ican military power was less conspicuous than most European countries
egan to exhibit an increased conspicuous consumption that percolated
; and his deformity was more conspicuous when he walked.
                     It was conspicuous far to sea both on the east
hen, foreign policy has been conspicuous by its absence from Oval Off
 some species include a very conspicuous broad band of silk across th
s bloody arm offers the most conspicuous instance of this in the Good
reoccupation with profit and conspicuous consumption.
n the attentions paid her by conspicuous individuals.
ill park their vehicles in a conspicuous spot alongside the freeway a
                    Conspicuous consumption makes way for a
mulation provided by certain conspicuous static patterns, this can be
ed by the flying corks, were conspicuous in the window of the Princes
e wealth of new material - a conspicuous slight as far as he was conc
                    Conspicuous splendor was what Piero de'
       .' This rather less conspicuous item noted
mporaries, however, its most conspicuous innovations were in style ra
truments of self-injury were conspicuous by their absence, and the ro
 less well defined or not as conspicuous, involving such variations o
ve been able to determine, a conspicuous absence of gift exchange in
bling that was intentionally conspicuous rather than disguised.
rliament in 1874, and became conspicuous in 1880 as the leader of a g
 who have, broadly, rendered conspicuous service to the nation, and r
ip of Elizabeth's entry, his conspicuous mention here, forty-five yea
rifle and his clipboard in a conspicuous place where they would be qu
ssive woman, substantial and conspicuous.
wingspan up to 30 cm/12 in; conspicuous eyespots and banded markings
ing its mark here, filling a conspicuous cultural gap for opera lover
ly re-examined, usually with conspicuous success.
s, Irish-American women were conspicuous at its meetings and especial
e No. 4 U.S. automaker, such conspicuous terrain at a dealer lot brin
iod, made, if anything, more conspicuous during the Regency Crisis of
 cities in Europe - the most conspicuous being the French Revolutions
, one of the rarest and most conspicuous plants in Britain, is now kn
hat dissenting words will be conspicuous by their absence; both shows
ings is to carry it out with conspicuous diligence and the minimum of
                    36 `Conspicuous in the symposium is a lack o
poisoning are as a rule more conspicuous in chronic, low-grade cases
    Ironically, given this conspicuous distortion of sources, one o
rawn, and we didn't have any conspicuous traumatic history that could
e certainly among their most conspicuous assets and absorb a great de
                    A conspicuous example of inaction is the K
ollowing the Equator is most conspicuous perhaps in Mark Twain's preo
                    Now a conspicuous example of tension in the Ro
```

7 Corpus printout for "conspicuous"

Among those without dictionary experience, it is simply not possible to predict who will be good and who won't; one must give a trial to any likely candidate and judge from the results.

To assure that one gets citations of good quality, one must spell out in detail the rules for citation collection. Here are the basic points that should be covered.

- How to prepare citations. The reader must be shown samples and told exactly where to put each item of information. Preprinted slips or cards, such as the one shown in Fig. 6, are helpful, although these may have to be retyped to be entered into a computer data file. Nowadays some system of electronic transfer should also be explored, such as transmission by e-mail or as attachments to e-mail, or in diskettes on which one can easily duplicate (as by a macro code) the requisite information fields of author, title, date, etc., required in a citation. Any system that makes rekeyboarding unnecessary is highly desirable.
- Length of citations. It is best to keep the citation reasonably brief, consistent with clarity and meaningfulness. As a rule, an entire sentence should be included, occasionally more. But nonessential material should be excised. Here is another example for "over the top":

Attitudes elsewhere in print were epitomized by Anne McElvoy, a columnist for The Independent, who concluded, "Diana is yesterday's princess." [¶] J. Mallory Wober, a social scientist who has just completed a book on the news media and the monarchy, said he was not surprised at this year's diminished commemoration. "When Diana died, we allowed ourselves to go over the top for a bit, but now we have gone back to normal," he said. "We have discharged all the grief at her death, which has thrown up all sorts of emotion – including embarrassment."[24]

The person quoted here is evidently British, so this is a typical use of the expression. The quotation might have been limited to the two sentences, "J. Mallory Wober . . . he said" without much loss of sense. But the first and last sentences may be necessary to show, long after the circumstances and aftermath of Diana's death have been forgotten, that Diana was someone associated with the monarchy and that there were widespread public expressions of grief at her death.

- Purpose of the file. Readers must be made to understand that their role is to collect raw data, not to make judgments. Free-lance readers should be discouraged from making notes about what they collect or from trying to define the term cited.

ITEM dot-coms

SOURCE New York Times   **DATE** Feb. 20, 2000

PAGE A36   **AUTHOR**

It is not just the fact that tax shelters are being created faster than dot-coms on the

Internet that worries Mr. Langdon and others, it is which companies are embracing them.

---

8 Citation for "dot-coms"

ITEM dot-comer

SOURCE New York Times   **DATE** Feb. 22, 2000

PAGE A23   **AUTHOR**

If Ronald Reagan were running today, he'd focus on these problems and a different

audience. He'd be more at home in Silicon Valley than Macomb County. His optimistic

message of individuality, distrust of government and reliance on markets would

undoubtedly make him a dot-comer.

---

9 Citation for "dot-comer"

- The criteria for selecting citations should be spelled out. If well-established senses of standard forms are not being sought, this should be stated. One should provide numerous examples of the kinds of words to be cited and enclose samples of a variety of citations. Not all the samples should be superb; some should be run-of-the-mill, lest the reader become too selective. The kinds of desired citations should be listed, as follows:
1. New words and phrases that constitute lexical units, such as *dot-coms, dot-comer,* and *dot* (see Figures 8, 9, and 10) or *coursepack* (a collection of photocopied material bound in a soft-covered book for a university course), or productive combining forms such as *cyber-* (as in "cybersex," "cyberspace," etc.).
2. New or unusual meanings and uses of well-established forms, such as

ITEM   dot

SOURCE   New York Times   **DATE**   March 15, 2000

PAGE   A22   **AUTHOR**   Christopher M. Clark

[Letter to editor]

American universities are in far more danger from failing to sustain the conditions of

high quality face-to-face education than they are from dot-competition.

---

10 Citation for "dot"

ITEM   raves

SOURCE   New York Times   **DATE**   Feb. 25, 2000

PAGE   B4   **AUTHOR**

The investigation began in July when the Phoenix Police Department's Juvenile

Enforcement squad infiltrated giant parties known as raves where they estimated that 90

percent of the youths were buying and taking Ecstasy, a stimulant that has become an

illicit favorite in nightclubs . . . .

---

11 Citation for "raves"

---

grow as a transitive verb ("We've got to figure out a way to grow the business.")

3. Slang, colloquialisms, taboo words, new trade or occupational jargon (such as advertising or computer terms). See, for example, Figure 11: "raves."
4. Special or technical vocabularies (especially scientific terms)
5. Foreign words and phrases if used without translation in predominantly English contexts, thus presupposing the reader's familiarity with them. Any representation of a foreign term in regular roman type (as distinguished from italics) is particularly citable, since it suggests the word is well along in the process of becoming naturalized.

6. Information on etymology, pronunciation, or grammar
7. Information on spelling or form, especially if the term's form is undergoing change, e.g., from capitalization to lower case or vice versa. These must be limited rigorously to specific areas of interest, because by and large an electronic corpus is far better at establishing common forms than a citation file.
8. Americanisms, Briticisms, Canadianisms, Australianisms, etc.: terms whose context reveals a meaning restricted to a particular English-speaking area. Also worth citing are instances of the use of an Americanism in Britain or of a Briticism in America (as the citation in Figure 6 for "over the top").
9. Trademarks other than in ads, whether capitalized or lower case, when used generically.

This is not an exhaustive list, and readers should be encouraged not to be limited by it once they have proved themselves. They should be provided with a copy of a recent dictionary to use as a basis of selection in questionable cases. As a rule, they should not cite a word in a particular sense if that sense is included in the dictionary provided them. The readers will not have time to check every citation – and indeed should be discouraged from doing so – but they should have it available nevertheless.

Dos and don'ts of citation reading

- Limit the number of allowable citations of the same item from the same source, for example, to two or three.
- Don't cite a word unless the context sheds some light on meaning or usage. "A scrumple approach to city planning was recommended by the mayor" gives no indication of what "scrumple" means and is useless.
- Do not cite words in eye dialect (spellings that try to represent common pronunciations), such as *uv* for "of" or *ya* for "you," unless there is some specific item of interest.
- Don't cite hyphenated words and phrases unless they have a distinctive meaning as a unit that the separate words would not convey separately. "Brown-and-black" (hat), "tired-looking," and "light-colored" (hair) are not good cites. This practice, incidentally, is the commonest source of poor citations. There are borderline cases, however; an ordinary phrase may have developed a distinctive sense

ITEM E-commerce

SOURCE New York Times   **DATE**   Sept. 6, 1999

PAGE C4   **AUTHOR** Bob Tedeschi

The problem for Internet retailers is how to harness the opinions of those real people without letting the negative comments chase prospective buyers away. The solution, some E-commerce companies are finding, is to allow customers to have their say, and hope that it ultimately builds sales.

12 Citation for "E-commerce"

ITEM skorts

SOURCE   New York Times   **DATE**   Sept. 4, 1999

PAGE B1–2   **AUTHOR** Lynette Holloway

The mother of 8-year-old Sheena Fray prefers skirts, but Sheena's 16-year-old sister , Tracy, found a way to skirt that issue. While their mother sat at home, they picked out a pair of "skorts," a combination of a short skirt and shorts . . .

13 Citation for "skorts"

as a compound, such as "self-medicate" (to take medicines without consulting a physician), and hyphenated words with new and productive combining forms are welcome, as in Figure 12 of "E-commerce."

- Look especially for citations that actually include a definition of a word. Often such citations are of *realia*, that is, actual objects as distinguished from conditions or abstractions, and may define a newly coined word. Figure 13 is an example of this type of citation.

ITEM   like

SOURCE   New York Times   **DATE**   Sept. 4, 1999

PAGE   B3   **AUTHOR**   David Barstow

Ms. Pescosolido declined to say how much Master P donated to last year's event. She

said Master P thought he was simply supporting an event to educate and energize young

black teen-agers. . . . [¶] "P's like, 'What? I'm not a racist—I don't even know that

guy,'" Ms. Pescosolido said.

---

14 Citation for "like"

For this type of citation, the citation file is still superior to an electronic corpus, though once one has identified a potential new word, the corpus can be used to search for other uses. A corpus search for these items will turn up many examples, so that further citations will not be necessary. For example, "skorts" is a commercial item and is advertised with pictures on many websites. Even the slang sense of "raves" cited in Figure 11 can be found in a corpus search in spite of its being a common word in another sense. Because corpora can now be tagged by part-of-speech, one can look for "raves" only as a noun, thus limiting the search so that one can home in on the sense being sought. Figure 14 for *like* illustrates the difficulty of using a traditional citation file for this kind of item.

This type of item can be far better researched by means of a corpus – especially if the corpus includes unscripted speech – than any citation file. One can not only get many more examples, but can see them in sufficient context to get an idea of what they mean and how they are used.

DEFINING FROM THE EVIDENCE

"For the lexicographer," says Allen Walker Read, "the crucial question about meaning is how to slice it up into manageable units . . . [He or she] collects large bodies of documented quotations, studies them for similarities and difference, and puts them into various piles."[25] A celebrated baseball umpire once silenced a belligerent player by saying that before he called a player "safe" or "out," he wasn't anything. Before a definer decides whether a collection of usages is one sense or four, it is nothing but a collection of usages. Both are imposing order as they see it on reality and both make errors. Unquestionably, the umpire is more important to baseball than lexicographers are to language, but both are in the business of interpreting behavior, and their interpretations, which are intended to be unbiased and true to the facts, have consequences for the game on the one hand and for the way we perceive the use of language on the other.[26]

The definer's task is not just to say what a word means, but to say whether there is a new meaning to be distinguished at all, or two or three. Bosley Woolf asks, "When do irony and metaphor cross the boundary between rhetorical divide and new meaning?"[27] The case of *ghetto* can be used to illustrate how a basic meaning can be extended to new situations and contexts.

Ghetto was first used in English to mean a part of a European city where Jews were compelled to live. The meaning was extended in America to a rundown or overcrowded part of a city where a minority group, particularly blacks, lived. Though not physically confined to the place, their opportunities were so restricted by prejudice or poverty that they were in effect forced to live in that part of the city. Perhaps concurrently with this extension, however, the word was also used to refer to any place of metaphorical confinement; by the early 1970s one began to see phrases like "suburban housewives locked in middle-class ghettos," where *ghetto* had no implication of poverty or any relation to cities. Because of a large number of such citations, I added a third sense of *ghetto* to *The Doubleday Dictionary*: "Any community or group separated physically or culturally from the rest of society." This sense now appears in most college dictionaries.

According to one provocative analysis of the treatment of metaphor in ESL dictionaries, metaphorical senses are not necessarily figurative extensions of the literal meaning. They retain at least part of the literal meaning but apply it in circumstances totally different from those in which the literal sense is normally used. In his discussion of the uses of the word *morass*, Geart van der Meer challenges the decision of *LDOCE3* to give a separate figurative definition – "a complicated and confusing situation that is very difficult to get out of" – to cover metaphorical uses. He points out that many of the figurative uses of *morass* in this sense include some allusion to getting stuck or getting pushed or pulled down into something, so that while *LDOCE3*'s definition does cover a part of the meaning, the actual uses one sees on consulting the corpus evidence nevertheless retain an image applying to the literal sense, which *LDOCE3* gives as "a dangerous area of soft wet ground." Van der Meer acknowledges that some metaphors do develop new meanings distinct from the literal meaning, but argues that dictionaries are too quick to split the literal meaning and should devise some way to represent meanings that have reached a transitional stage when the context in which the literal sense is used still has force, even while it is applied to novel situations unrelated to the original sense.[28] *LDOCE3* and other ESL dictionaries actually give the figurative sense first on the basis of the greater frequency of this sense compared to the literal sense. Quite apart from whether there should be a separate figurative sense, if, as van der Meer shows, the figurative meaning cannot be fully understood without understanding the literal sense, surely it is a mistake to give the figurative sense first. This is an area in which the use of the corpus will allow a more sensitive treatment of metaphorical meaning.

DECIDING WHAT TO PUT IN THE DICTIONARY

The citation file and the corpus are vital not just for determining what new words and new senses mean, but for providing evidence that they exist in sufficient numbers to warrant inclusion in a dictionary. Clarence Barnhart has estimated that 800 or so new words come into the "common or working vocabulary" of English every year, and that of these about 500 find their way into dictionaries of various sizes and types.[29] Rapidly growing use of the Internet has spawned a host of new words, as seen in the following excerpt from a *New York Times* article:

Network service providers said that the recent assaults included two types of attacks . . . Both are what are known as denial of service attacks because they prevent the targeted site from serving its customers. [¶] In the first, known as a SYN flood, attackers hack into – and install software on – a large number of computers, then use those machines to bombard the victim site with requests to start an e-commerce session. The large number of requests overwhelms the victim's servers, preventing customers from gaining access to the site. [¶] To prevent any tracing of these requests, the vandals employ a practice called spoofing, which alters the initiating address. [¶]The second type, known as a smurf attack, again involves the use of compromised machines, but it also employs a large third-party network of computers to "amplify" the data.[30]

What are the criteria for deciding whether to put new words and new senses in a dictionary?

The number of citations for a word or sense collected over a period of time from a variety of sources determines whether it will be included. The evidence obtained from a corpus is far more reliable than a citation file in making this kind of decision, because a citation file is too much influenced by the conspicuous nature of the items selected, whereas a corpus does not depend on such selection and will therefore yield a more accurate picture of the frequency of particular items. Moreover, it will often also suggest in what contexts it is most frequent, for example, in speech as opposed to writing, or in newspaper articles rather than in fiction or popular writing. The number of corpus *hits* (separate occurrences) of a lexical item, especially hits per million words in the corpus, is a very good way to make comparative judgments about which items to include. (This will be discussed more fully in Ch. 6.) If a balanced and up-to-date corpus is available, I would trust the corpus rather than citation files in determining which words should go in the dictionary; however, for very recent slang, or for technical and scientific words used in popular contexts, a citation file may still provide evidence that might be difficult to obtain easily from a corpus. Regardless of the source of one's information, the number of cites or corpus hits tells us little about a word if they are all from the same or a few sources. If we are preparing a general dictionary, we want to be assured that the use of the word is not confined to a narrow specialty, so we will check to see that it is used in a variety of sources.

The *OED*, following the Johnsonian tradition, gave special attention to the uses of the established writers of the literary canon, even when these were eccentric. Robert Burchfield, editor of the *OED Supplements*, writes of his concern to cover the works of T. S. Eliot, Virginia Woolf, Evelyn Waugh, W. H. Auden, and "even Dylan Thomas and James Joyce (except for most of *Finnegans Wake*)," and cites his decision to include the apparently unique use of *unleaving* (to lose or shed leaves) in the verse of Gerard Manley Hopkins.[31] With characteristic brio, Vladimir Nabokov once remarked in a letter to his publisher that though some of the words used in *Lolita* were not in "Webster," they would be in its later editions.[32] Perhaps so, but the *OED* is unique, and few other dictionaries would include a lexical item peculiar to one writer. Indeed, the *OED*'s policy can also be challenged. Unless the literary usage peculiar to one writer has become famous and is often quoted, I don't think there is any justification for including it, no matter how prominent the author is.

Even if a new word is used with great frequency over a short period of time, we want to know that it will not be obsolete by the time the dictionary is published. Fad words (or vogue words) may have enormous density of usage for a period of months and then disappear except for an occasional nostalgic use. For example, a number of new terms such as *chat group* (for a group of people exchanging opinions via the Internet), which dictionaries will surely add to their next editions, may be replaced in a few years by some newer term, perhaps because of technological changes in the way chat groups operate. When in the early 1970s young men took to racing through public places after shedding all their clothes, the event was dubbed *streaking.* As the number of such events multiplied, so did the word's use in its various manifestations. At the time, I was editing a dictionary that was just about ready to go to the printer, and I astonished my publishers by wondering aloud whether it ought to be included. I had more citations for it than I needed, but they were all from the very recent past and I was unsure how long the word would remain current. (It took no sociological genius to realize the event would soon die out – but that did not mean the word would cease to be used.) In the end I decided to put the word in, and in this case it was the right decision, since *streak* is still used in this sense, but much less often, because the event is less often practiced. At the time, the decision to put the word in was little better than a guess.

Unfortunately, dictionary editors have everything to gain and nothing to lose by inserting every new word (or *neologism*), faddish or not, that comes along, since the popular view is that the ultimate test of every new dictionary is that it has the very latest words. No attention is paid to the older, established words and meanings it has omitted to make room for the current crop of ephemera. Competitive dictionary publishers themselves encourage the notion that it is fair to judge a dictionary by how many new words it includes; they trumpet facts about how many new words they contain and send lists of the choicest morsels to newspapers. Even language societies have joined in the fun because of the publicity generated by novel words: the staid American Dialect Society, which publishes the academic journal *American Speech* and a series of esoteric publications on subjects such as trends in changes in the regional articulation of a vowel, has its moment in the journalistic firmament once a year when its members choose the "new word of the year." This exercise in frivolity will be defended as harmless or as bringing needed public attention to a neglected industry, but it mischievously exaggerates the importance of neologisms in lexicography (as opposed to their importance in marketing dictionaries, about which there is no argument), to the detriment of a better understanding of the qualities that make for a good dictionary. Certainly having new words and senses is important, but dictionaries commonly make no distinction over the commonness of the new words they choose to include, and the evidence for including them is often flimsy and influenced by the need to have a more bountiful list of neologisms than one's nearest competitor. In the face of intense pressure to include every item that one's competitor might have, many terms are included in dictionaries that will soon vanish from sight; indeed, their presence in many cases was never more than dimly felt, and only by those searching to find them. It is much easier to fill a dictionary with novel words than to prune it of obsolescent ones. Because a particular item is not collected in one's citation file does not prove that it does not exist. As Zgusta rightly observes, it is always difficult to draw negative conclusions from a citation file.[33] However, it *is* possible to draw negative conclusions from an electronic corpus. If the corpus is large and balanced (see Ch. 6 for what I mean by "balanced"), one can get a fairly good statistical idea of the relative frequency of any particular word or group of words. If the frequency of an item falls below a certain standard, one may have legitimate grounds for dropping it from the dictionary. Unfortunately, unless one has a good corpus and uses it for this purpose, there is no reliable way to uncover the last few decades' detritus of new words, which will continue to take up space, like weeds hidden in a luxuriant garden of vibrant flowers.

HOW USEFUL ARE CITATION FILES?

The underlying presumption of citation files is that, though infinitesimally small compared to all the uses of language, they truly represent the state of the language. We shall see that *representativeness* is a major goal of the corpus, and even if imperfectly realized, a corpus can achieve a far greater degree of representativeness than any citation file. However, it must be admitted that neither a citation file of millions of words nor a corpus of hundreds of millions of words can represent more than a tiny fraction of the immense volume of speech and writing that occur every single day. Since speech occupies a much greater role in the use of language than writing, and since citation files are based predominantly on writing, it is clear that traditional citation files cannot accurately represent all uses of language. All of the general dictionaries in both America and Britain are based almost entirely on the written word.[34]

In a seemingly simple but brilliant study in 1940, Kemp Malone tested the assumption that citation files are representative of actual usage by assembling a much larger sample for a single word, *mahogany*, than any dictionary had to date. He and his associates collected 1,500 citations for *mahogany*; even the *OED*, he pointed out, averaged only ten citations per term. Even today, no existing corpus could come up with anything like this number of hits for *mahogany*. For example, the Cambridge International Corpus of British and American English (then consisting of nearly 100 million words) turned up only 150 hits for *mahogany*. Malone's analysis of the citations showed that the chief meaning of the word, attested by 70 percent of the citations, was for a sense not included in *NID2*. *NID2* had included the term only in its scientific sense, and defined it primarily as a species of *Swietenia*, particularly *S. mahagoni*. Malone asks, "But what of the man who speaks of mahogany wood without having in mind any particular botanical species or genus?"[35] There are many kinds of wood called "mahogany," as Malone demonstrates. *NID2*'s definition was not based on the facts of English usage but on scientific sources or earlier dictionaries. Malone's analysis bears directly on the inability or unwillingness of dictionaries to define scientific terms on the basis of ordinary usage.

The definition for *mahogany* that Malone constructs from the preponderance of his citations does not mention any particular species:

A more or less hard and heavy wood derived from various related and unrelated tropical trees; the wood usually has interlocked or crossed grain, varies in color between reddish brown and brownish yellow, seasons well, and takes a high polish; it is much used for fine cabinet work and in making other articles of luxury or superior quality, as yachts and fine furniture.[36]

Whether this sort of definition is more helpful to the reader than the more precise botanical definition, which indeed covers some of the same information as this one, is beside the point. That question merely has to do with the most helpful mix of encyclopedic and lexical information. (Malone's article evidently did not persuade *NID3* to adopt his strategy, though it modified *NID2*'s definition considerably.) The point is that Malone's article presents evidence for doubting that citation files fairly and fully represent even the written language, let alone the spoken language. We must face the fact that citation files are flawed, particularly in their representation of technical words in widespread popular use. Their usefulness is limited by the impracticality of coping with thousands of citations for every word, even if such large numbers of citations could be assembled. (In using a corpus there are software tools available that make it possible to deal with a very large number of hits. This will be discussed further in Ch. 6.) Citation files are collected by many different people who necessarily applied different standards at different times and who were influenced by their own biases as well as those of their sponsors. The collection of citations is subject chiefly to the availability of certain written materials, which are overrepresented compared to other written material and all speech.

The written materials forming the core of citation files tend to be those of the educated and upper classes. *NID3* tried to broaden its scope and was roundly denounced for having done so, but the enlarged breadth of its coverage, though more than token, did not change its bias in favor of educated writing. I am not proposing that it should; I merely state the fact. Dictionaries act as a conservative force on the language because they tend to overrepresent the volume of conservative speech and writing, which is that of the educated classes, and underrepresent the volume of speech and writing by and for people who are relatively uneducated. I believe this imbalance serves most dictionary users better than a more balanced coverage would, but certainly the point is arguable. Dictionary users are not necessarily educated or of the upper class, but they are most interested in the usages of this class. *NID3* was criticized because it dared to give – *boasted* about giving – some attention to the usages of the less well educated. Its innovation was mild and utterly benign, about as threatening to established usage as New York City's latest antinoise campaign is to taxi drivers, which is to say, for those unfamiliar with New York, of no consequence whatever. From this point of view, citation files should be weighted to some extent in favor of educated usages. But certainly the larger dictionaries should make an attempt to cover a broad variety of usages, and in this respect *NID3*'s coverage, however imperfectly it may have been presented, should be applauded as a step in the right direction.[37] Nonetheless, with all of its imperfections, a citation file is still perhaps the best source for new words, and a valuable complement to a corpus as a source of new senses and new uses.

ILLUSTRATIVE QUOTATIONS

The illustrative quotations or invented phrases that exemplify the usage of particular senses are a critical part of the dictionary definition and should not be regarded as mere appurtenances. Illustrative quotations can convey a great deal of information about collocation, variety of usage (degree of formality, humorous or sedate context), connotation (affective implications), grammatical context (if a verb, does it take an indirect object?), and, of course, designative meaning. Often there is no better way to provide this information than by an illustrative quotation, and, for many common words, short illustrative phrases are essential to tell the reader how the definition is used in ordinary contexts. For example, consider how important the quotations are in *MW10*'s treatment for a verbal sense of *mean*:

to have in mind as a purpose; INTEND <she means to win> – sometimes used interjectionally with *I*, chiefly in informal speech for emphasis <he throws, I mean, hard> or to introduce a phrase restating the point of a preceding phrase <we try to answer what we can, but I mean we're not God – Bobby Ann Mason>

Zgusta argues that in larger dictionaries quoted examples are to be preferred over invented ones.[38] More recently, John Sinclair, the editor of the *Collins Cobuild English Dictionary* and a pioneer in the use of language corpora in ESL lexicography, has been a strong advocate of the use of only authentic examples. He argues persuasively that "human intuition about language is highly specific, and not at all a good guide to what actually happens when the same people actually use the language . . . However plausible an invented example might be, it cannot be offered as a genuine instance of language in use."[39] Indeed, Sinclair adds, intuition is important precisely *because* it differs from the actual record of usage. Although I am in essential agreement with this view, there are times when for good practical reasons one has to modify a quotation for the particular readership of the dictionary in question, and sometimes even invent a quotation based on what the corpus evidence has told one about the likely context and syntax of the use of the word. In dealing with actual quotations, one is constantly frustrated by their inclusion of words that are needlessly difficult or irrelevant to the usage being illustrated but that are integral to the quotation. Thus, even an unabridged dictionary such as *NID3* commonly uses invented illustrative phrases as well as quotations. Part of the genius of Samuel Johnson lay in the artfulness with which he modified his quotations.[40]

We have seen already how important collocational aids are to foreign learners of English. Traditional citation files are of limited usefulness in providing information about collocation of words. Far more useful are corpora, which are discussed in Chapter 6. Those ESL dictionaries that continue to rely entirely on invented examples to illustrate meaning and usage fail to take advantage of the available evidence of actual language use. Even when real-language examples must be modified for the sake of simplicity or to save space, the use of a corpus is essential in guiding the editor to form realistic examples. The British ESL dictionaries have pioneered in the use of corpora, and some American ESL dictionaries are now also corpus-based, but other American ESL dictionaries continue to include made-up examples that are altogether improbable; examination of a 100-million word corpus will turn up no comparable examples. To illustrate *conciliatory*, one American dictionary gives the example: "After arguing with her, he made conciliatory remarks about how much he loves her."[41] Another offers: "In a gesture of peace, the leader made a conciliatory speech about the war."[42] One cannot imagine a real-life context in which such a sentence would occur; it is a textbook illustration that may help to define the term, but it is not representative of actual usage. Here are some other improbable, non-corpus-based examples of *facetious*: "The teacher didn't appreciate Bob's facetious comment" and "Many people at the party were offended by his facetious comments."[43] Admittedly, it isn't always easy to come up with an actual corpus-based example, but one can do better than this. For example, the corpus-based *Cambridge Dictionary of American English* illustrates this word with: "She said she was never nervous on stage, but she was being facetious, of course."

In the field of ESL lexicography, simple enough examples cannot always be found for every level of learner, no matter how big the corpus. In arguing for the superiority of authentic examples over invented ones, Gwyneth Fox, a colleague of Sinclair's on the *Collins Cobuild Dictionary*, observes, "For a sentence that is to be looked at in isolation to make sense, it has to contain much more information than you are likely to find in real language where sentences do not occur alone but come before or after other sentences, and so are a small part of a longer text."[44] We have seen this observation confirmed in the artificial invented examples quoted above, such as, "In a gesture of peace, the leader made a conciliatory speech about the war." To make sense of much real language, one needs to look at more than one sentence, but the dictionary editor hasn't the space available to give examples of five or six lines. Compromises have to be made for the sake of understandability. I completely agree with Fox's remark, but rather than see this as proof of the necessity of rigidly adhering to the doctrine of authentic examples, I see it as justification for judiciously amending quotations when necessary. I believe this can be done more successfully than in the examples about the conciliatory leader or about Bob, the facetious student. These citations were written without the benefit of any corpus. Even when a corpus cannot yield a verbatim quotation for a dictionary, it very often provides one with a range of contexts that are entirely plausible. It may not be "genuine" in Sinclair's terms, but if genuineness is to be purchased at the price of understandability, I will forgo it.

School dictionaries are much shorter than adult dictionaries and tend to be revised abridgments of adult dictionaries, to which a specialized citation file focused on children's literature is considered a useful supplement. There is really no point in laboriously constructing every sense of *get* from a citation file when one is concerned with brief, simple definitions. The assumption, however, that the supplementary citation file should be based on books designed for children, even if one includes classic works as well as comic books, needs to be questioned. A citation file for a children's dictionary must take in much of the same material collected for an adult dictionary, for a child is exposed to extended senses of common words, like that of *ghetto*, just as an adult is. If the aim of a school dictionary is simply to help children understand the words used in their textbooks and other assigned school reading, a specialized citation file will meet the purpose admirably. If, however, a children's dictionary is designed to represent the language of children, a specialized citation file will fail utterly. The file for such a work would have to monitor television, movies, and the words of popular songs as carefully as it scrutinizes the language of *Huckleberry Finn* and *David Copperfield*.

Whenever actual citations can be used, they should. Actual usage has the weight of authority behind it. It provides documentation for the definition, which is really only an interpretive claim made by the lexicographer. He or she says the definition means thus-and-so based on the citations available, of which the one or two quoted are presumably exemplary. Readers are free to form their own conclusions as to whether the citations are apposite and justify the definition. Using invented examples is like fixing a horse race: the lexicographer invents an example to justify his definition instead of devising a definition to fit the examples. But the illustrative quotation does more than support the definition; it can indicate its range of application and show whether it is used metaphorically as well as literally. Often a metaphorical use does not justify a separate definition but can be clearly shown in an example. Judiciously selected quotations can substitute for part of a definition by indicating, to the reader who knows how to interpret them, what the limits of literalness of a definition are. For example, here is *NID3*'s def. 2 for the adjective *suspect*:

having the nature or status of a suspicious person or thing: provocative or worthy of suspicion: SUSPICIOUS <hold one suspect until his innocence is proved> <treat all innovations as suspect –A. T. Quiller-Couch> <he has been suspect to many members of his own party –*Time*>

The first citation, which is invented, gives the most common literal usage, that relating to legal guilt. The second citation illustrates that *suspect* is not confined to people but may be used abstractly, and in this sense the word suggests skepticism on the part of the person suspecting rather than culpability of the thing suspected. The third citation is again of a person but illustrates that it can be applied metaphorically to suggest that the person suspected is untrustworthy, unreliable, or unfaithful; the metaphor equates the official party position with right behavior and stigmatizes dissent as morally culpable. These citations do more. No two are alike in collocation. *Suspect* in the first and third is followed by prepositional clauses introduced by *until* and *to*, respectively. We see that someone can be "held suspect" in the first citation and that something can be "treated as suspect" in the second, and we see from the second that *suspect* need not be followed by a clause. One of the quoted citations is British, the other American. Such considerations are not accidental but were weighed by the definers to convey as much information as possible.

THE DEFINITION OF NAMES

The decision as to whether a name is generic or not is often difficult to make, even with the help of a citation file. As one English lexicographer asks, "If musicians say 'What this country wants is a Bayreuth,' does that amount to generalization?"[45] The question may be resolved, one would suppose, by an analysis of the citation file or corpus to see whether the generic use of *Bayreuth* meets the criteria for any term's inclusion. If it does, it should go in. But it is not that simple.

What does one do with terms like *Chomskyan* and *Kafkaesque*, or *Watergate* or *Disneyland*? Terms derived from names fall into three categories. Some, like *Chomskyan*, refer to a person and the work done by that person, or to a place or a person from that place (*Virginian*, *Londoner*), and should be defined only in relation to the person or place. They are essentially encyclopedic entries and, if the dictionary contains an entry for the person or place in question, could well be run on without a separate definition.

The second category, within which *Kafkaesque* falls, has developed one or more senses distinct from any necessary relation with the person after whom the word was formed, as in "Sometimes the humour becomes sinister and Kafkaesque" (from a 1965 work of Canadian fiction). The sense is "nightmarish, threatening in an obscure way." Such words are usually defined independently. As Randolph Quirk has remarked, words like *Freudian* and *Kafkaesque* have true dictionary meanings, "in respect of which Freud and Kafka are of only etymological relevance."[46] However, if the dictionary includes enough encyclopedic information under the entry for the person, it may not be necessary to include a separate entry for the lexical item. *The New Oxford Dictionary of English*, for example, includes an entry for Franz Kafka in which his work is characterized as portraying "an enigmatic and nightmarish reality where the individual is perceived as lonely, peripheral, and threatened." *Kafkaesque* is run on to the entry for *Kafka* without further amplification; it seems to me this treatment clearly conveys the sense of *Kafkaesque*. But it will not work for *Disneyland* (a place of fantasy or unreality) and other similar cases where the word's generic meaning has diverged significantly from the name after which it was formed.

The third category consists of words that allude to a specific public event and that are invested with many complex associations. It would be impossible to define such associations, since they differ from person to person, are often emotional, and depend on nonlinguistic cultural phenomena, but the central fact of the event is shared by many people, and because of the importance and frequency of such allusive words in the language, dictionaries cannot ignore them. They have to be included and defined as encyclopedic entries, and the entry should include enough information to suggest the importance of the event. Even British dictionaries, for example, include an entry for *Watergate* because it led to the resignation of a US president. Though very common, such words have not developed a separate generic sense distinct from the original event. An examination of the 423 corpus hits for this word in the Cambridge International Corpus confirms this. Even uses like "another Watergate" ("'Irangate,' as it was sometimes called, was widely billed by various pundits and media commentators as 'another' Watergate") are not generic, as reference is made to the original event, and if the reader does not know the nature of the original event, he will not understand the reference. There is no evidence for uses such as, "It was a kind of Watergate," as contrasted with *Disneyland*, which does occur in such frames. Dictionaries that include a separate generic sense for *Watergate* and similar terms have no basis for doing so, and are inventing senses that do not exist.[47] Allusive meanings tend to be restricted nationally or geographically and to be topical, and only the most sensational such as *Watergate* continue in use for many years. Even *Teapot Dome*, a major US scandal of the administration of President Harding in 1922, has disappeared from dictionaries. Its rich allusive meanings find a response in fewer and fewer people as that generation and the major events of its day are forgotten by all but historians. So, one day, will *Watergate*, but so far it is still with us.

OTHER SOURCES OF DEFINITION

As we have seen, no citation file can provide the right kind of data for all dictionary entries. Even a corpus, though more versatile than a citation file, will not meet all of the needs of a dictionary. Most scientific and technical terms must be defined by specialists on the basis of their judgments about preferred scientific usage. (See "Defining technical terms," p. 186.) Technical dictionaries do not, therefore, depend primarily on citation files. The pedagogical purpose of school dictionaries calls for greater flexibility in the choice and presentation of material than a rigorous dependence on citations could accommodate. The advice of educators and teachers must be solicited in order to insure that the dictionary gives sufficient coverage to school subjects, and, from a practical point of view, to promote the acceptance of the dictionary by other educators and teachers who will pass judgment upon it.

Citation files, although in this respect better than corpora, cannot be relied on to turn up new scientific and technical terms in any systematic way. They provide a great many scientific terms for dictionaries of neologisms, such as *12,000 Words*, the supplement to *NID3*, which is filled with words like *fenfluramine, fentanyl, fenthion, ferredoxin, ferricyanide,* and *ferrocyanide*. But they will not provide adequate or consistent coverage of various scientific fields for a general dictionary. For that one needs specialists, who compile lists of terms in their own subjects which they regard as essential.

Existing dictionaries have their scientific and technical terms categorized and coded by subject, and can easily print out computerized lists of terms for any subject along with the definitions. When preparing a new edition, each such list is sent to the respective specialist along with suggestions for additions that may have come from editors or other outside sources. The specialist is asked to review and revise the list, deleting obsolete terms and proposing new ones for inclusion. The same practice may be employed to update terms in many other special subjects such as law, business, sports, theater, music, and so on. However, the prudent reader will regard a dictionary's long list of experts on everything from archery to zither playing with a certain skepticism. Many experts, even some prominent ones, are not averse to having their names listed in a dictionary for a modest fee, provided they do not have to do anything. The practice was begun in 1658 in Edward Phillips' *The New World of English Words* and has continued without let-up ever since. It is not known whether Phillips paid his consultants anything, or even whether they knew their names were to appear in his dictionary. Modern consultants are paid, though meagerly, and, if they have sinned, we may at least have the satisfaction of knowing they have not profited much by it.

Another important source of new words and new senses is reference books, including other dictionaries. Dictionary makers acquire every significant new dictionary as soon as it is published. One's direct competitors' works are examined with due care to see what new terms they have included – or failed to include. Though definitions are protected by copyright, the listing of new terms and new senses is fair game for all comers. Once having discovered the existence of new words by seeing them in another dictionary, nothing prevents one from seeking more information about them from other sources and writing one's own definition. Facts cannot be copyrighted, only the specific way in which they are represented. Another dictionary's definition must be considered along with other citations for the word being defined. In Johnson's day and long afterward, dictionaries openly cited other dictionaries in print as the source for certain terms, quoting their definitions as illustrative quotations. Historical dictionaries still do, but commercial dictionaries are now loath to admit to having relied on a competitor. For marketing reasons, every dictionary is represented as being unaffected by every other. Nothing could be further from the truth. I doubt that anyone has the time to go through a competitor's dictionary entry by entry, or that such an exercise would be worthwhile if one did. Rather, the dictionary is examined under key terms, as a physician who from long familiarity with a patient knows where to look and what to look for. Copies of the new dictionary are kept close at hand and used by several staff members, for from such use new terms and senses will be found.

Dictionaries of new words and new word supplements are a good source of potential new entries and senses. The criteria for inclusion in such works are, however, much more lax than those for a general dictionary, so they are not quite as rich a source as one might suppose. If one has an ongoing citation file, one should already have some record of many of the terms listed, and the chief benefit of dictionaries of neologisms may well be the chance to see additional citations and compare the definition given with one's own.

When one defines a new term one is truly in uncharted waters. The intellectual effort is analogous to that employed in deciphering a message in code, except that, unlike cryptographers, definers never know whether they have the message right. Therefore, they seek what aid and comfort they can get by comparing notes with whatever else is available. When working from original sources, whether citations or corpus text, one should compose one's own definitions before looking at comparable definitions in other dictionaries. Otherwise, one is likely to be too much influenced by the other dictionaries' definitions. However, it is wise to check. Sometimes on reading another's definition of a new sense one may see that one's own has missed the essential point. Every definer has had this experience. It is for this reason, as we shall see in Chapter 7, that each definition passes through a number of critical reviews before it is adjudged to be final.

When there are gaps in the record of citations, as when one is revising a dictionary that has been allowed to become far out of date, other recent dictionaries are consulted as a matter of course. The latest edition of the *OED* is an essential resource for any such revision. Often definers must construct their own definitions based on the facts conveyed in other dictionaries' definitions, but without using the wording of the other dictionary. The definers' own knowledge of the language, their familiarity with the word and its use, and their *Sprachgefühl* (feeling for the language) play a decisive part in framing their own definition in their own words.

Specialized dictionaries and encyclopedic works are also useful to definers. Such references are not a primary source of new words and senses but are valuable as a means of checking to see whether new technical words or senses turned up by the citation file are really new, or whether they are well established in technical nomenclature but only now beginning to enter the general vocabulary. Slang dictionaries are valuable for the same reason: words that at first blush seem novel may

turn out to have been in use for half a century in the argot of a particular group, such as among southern black jazz musicians.[48] Also of
immense value is the *Dictionary of American Regional English*, which gives an
enormous amount of information about words that are restricted in use
to a particular region within the United States. Many of these words are
used mainly by older people in rural areas and are becoming increasingly rare. This dictionary is discussed at greater length in Ch. 5 (see p.
221). Current citations still determine current meaning, but a word's
earlier uses may contain important clues about more recent usage.
Without a good reference library, one might easily mistake mere extensions in meaning or variations in form of an existing word for an entirely
new word.

I have been speaking about the citation file and the defining process
as though definition depended simply on following a set of rules, and I
hope I have not given the impression that anyone willing to faithfully
follow the rules can learn to define. The qualities of a good definer are
discussed in Chapter 7, but it must be made clear that aptitude in
defining is an uncommon skill and that it cannot always be taught, even
to those with excellent formal educations. The best citations, the finest
specialists, and the most exhaustive reference library will go for nought
if the staff is unable or unwilling to use them. Good definers are precious; one puts up with their foibles and eccentricities as impresarios put
up with those of their leading performers. They are not replaceable. It
takes years of training and experience to make a really good definer, and
without a small cadre of such people no dictionary of quality can be produced.

CHAPTER 5

Usage

Usage refers to any or all uses of language, spoken or written. Usage bears the same relation to other aspects of language as the bloodstream does to the endocrine hormones. As the bloodstream circulates the hormones, which affect every aspect of growth and development, so does the vast flow of words in sound and writing constitute the medium through which speech is perceived as intelligible, meaning is discerned, and grammar is understood. *Usage* is used in another sense as well: the study of good, correct, or standard uses of language, as distinguished from bad, incorrect, and nonstandard uses. *Usage* may also take in the study of any limitations on use, whether geographic, social, or temporal. This chapter deals with those aspects of usage (in its broadest sense of all uses) that are singled out by dictionaries as being limited to some part of the universe of speakers or writers, past or present, either by special notes or labels or by qualifications within definitions.

No discussion of usage can be meaningful without giving some attention to why people regard certain usages as good or standard and others as improper, ignorant, or offensive. Controversies over good usage have a long history in English and continue to the present day. I will therefore devote a considerable part of this chapter to a discussion of attitudes towards usage. Finally, I will propose methods that might be employed in the future to identify and mark those examples of usage that need to be qualified in dictionaries. We shall see that an examination of usage cannot easily be confined to an examination of language and its contexts but turns us around towards the world of behavior in general, where our grounds for making assertions often leave us feeling uncomfortable and uncertain and sometimes even a bit foolish.

Here are the most common kinds of usage information given by general and ESL dictionaries, along with typical dictionary labels:
1. Currency or temporality: *old-fashioned, dated, archaic, obsolete, old use*
2. Regional or geographic variation: *U.S., British, Canadian, Australian, New Zealand, South African*, etc. Sometimes regional areas within a

country are specified, and sometimes *regional* or *dialect* is used as a label.

3. Technical or specialized terminology: *astronomy, chemistry, physics, sports,* etc.; these are called *field labels.* Sometimes *technical* or *specialized* is used as a label. *Trademark* is also used as a label.

4. Restricted or taboo sexual and scatological usage: *offensive, taboo, vulgar, obscene, rude;* sometimes combined with *slang,* e.g., *rude slang, vulgar slang*

5. Insult: *offensive, insult, disparaging, derogatory, disapproving, contemptuous, sexist, racist*

6. Slang: *slang*

7. Style, functional variety, or register: *formal, written, informal, spoken, colloquial* (now rarely used), *literary, historical, poetic, humorous, facetious, jocular, approving, euphemistic, baby talk* or *a child's word*

8. Status or cultural level: *nonstandard* or *not standard*

CURRENCY

When a word has completely disappeared from use but is retained for historical purposes, it is labeled "obsolete," such as *purchase* in the sense of pillage or plunder. "Archaic" is applied to words that are no longer in regular use, but which may occur occasionally in historical contexts, such as *damsel.* General monolingual dictionaries, which must be selective in their choice of entries, have relatively few archaic words and fewer still obsolete ones. An unabridged dictionary, even one synchronically focused like *Webster's Third New International Dictionary* (*NID3*), must pay considerable attention to older forms, as *NID3* does in reporting all usages from 1755. In bilingual and ESL dictionaries, accurate currency labeling is essential, since the user with limited familiarity with a language might otherwise use a word in altogether inappropriate contexts. Some bilingual lexicographers try to match the currency of the translations with the terms in the source language; if this can be done accurately, no label is necessary.[1] ESL dictionaries, which place much more emphasis on current usage than usage of the past, often apply a label such as *dated* or *old-fashioned* to words that are still in use but are associated with an earlier time and are not used, or not used in a particular sense, by the contemporary generation of young people. Thus, among the words that the *Cambridge Dictionary of American English* (*CDAE*) labels as "dated" are *asylum, coed* (for a female student), and *gay* (in the sense of happy).

Dictionaries with large, historical citation files can document reasonably well that a word or sense is archaic or obsolete, and dictionaries without them rely on the *OED*. If no occurrence of a particular sense has been found in 200 years, we can say with some assurance that the sense is obsolete. If we have none for the last 50 years, we cannot be so sure, and we might call such a sense archaic. Although language corpora can shed much light on whether a word is still in use, particularly in written use, they can tell us nothing about earlier periods for which adequate corpora are not available. Until we have better historical corpora, and until our current corpora have been maintained over a sustained period, we will be unable to determine when a particular usage has declined or is declining to the point of obsolescence. Since dictionary publishers are interested mainly in current usage, especially in new words and senses, they are unlikely to bear the expense of maintaining huge corpora based on language use 10 or 20 years ago, let alone 50 years ago, and I suspect they will be retired and discarded to make room for more contemporary coverage. It is certainly possible that universities will preserve language corpora over an extended period for linguistic research. But if dictionary publishers do not maintain such corpora themselves, or do not join together in a consortium to maintain them, I doubt that they will make use of them to track the frequency of usage of particular forms over time. Tracking obsolescence is not a high priority for commercial dictionary houses.

Specialized dictionaries have particular difficulties in applying currency labels accurately, because no large historical citation files of technical terms exist. Yet it is of great practical importance to label archaic and obsolete usages to alert the user that these terms should not be naively employed in a present-day scientific paper. There are some specialized, historical corpora, notably the legal databases *Lexis* and *Westlaw*, and the JSTOR Journals database – a computerized, full-text archive of many specialized journals – which Fred Shapiro has described as "a gold mine for studying the terminology of the humanities, social sciences, and natural sciences."[2] These should be used as much as possible, but for the most part one may still have to rely on the opinion of experts. When dealing with a large number of specialists, some of whom may have only a primitive grasp of dictionary practice and little intuitive feeling for the use of language, uniformity of treatment of currency is impossible.

REGIONAL VARIATION

Forms of expression and pronunciation limited to a particular region have long been regarded as objects of contempt and ridicule. Harold B.

Allen cites Edmund Coote's *The English Schoolmaster* of 1596 as providing "the first wholesale indictment of provincialisms." Although Nathan Bailey included dialectal terms in *Dictionarium Britannicum* (1730), Johnson did not. "Even the scholarly acceptance of the legitimacy of dialect studies in the last third of the 19th century did not affect the general notion that dialectalisms are substandard if not plainly incorrect."[3] One is exempt from such aspersions only if one's regional speech happens to coincide with that of the prestige dialect of the country or part of the country where one lives. *Prestige dialect* refers to a dialect widely accorded respect by all social levels in a community because it is identified with well-educated people of high social and economic standing.

Prestige immediately calls into play social and economic considerations of class. Randolph Quirk points out that uneducated speech is more closely identified with regional dialect, while educated speech conforms more nearly to a national variety.[4] In Britain, educated speech has been traditionally identified with "BBC English," in the United States with "network English" – that is, with national broadcasters of radio and television. The observation is more apt for Britain than for the United States, where there is no national standard, rather a different prestige dialect for each of the main dialectal regions of the country. Even in Britain the use of the pure BBC English of the postwar decades 1950–1980 is no longer an absolute requirement for public broadcasting – mild regional accents are increasingly heard – though it is still the norm.

Dialect, states one linguistic scholar, is "neither crude nor quaint speech; it is a national variety of a base language, possessing characteristics that may identify the speaker with a region, an era, another language in his background, or even . . . his social class or his race."[5] This discussion will deal mainly with regional dialect, but it is well to be reminded that dialect is any feature of speech that serves to identify the speaker as a member of a particular speech community, past or present.

Dictionaries in the US have had an indifferent record in reporting regional usages. *Webster's New International Dictionary*, Second Edition (*NID2*), often labeled definitions as "Dial. or illit.," as did college dictionaries after it, thus perpetuating the notion that dialectal forms were an illiterate form of speech. Moreover, many of the forms labeled dialectal were not in fact regional, and others labeled "illiterate" or "nonstandard" were actually dialectal. In part, the poor performance of dictionaries was due to the dearth of available studies. Regional literature is unreliable, since authors tend either to misrepresent or grossly exaggerate regional features of speech. But scholars have complained with some justice that even those works that were available were not fully utilized.[6] Yet on one of the few occasions when a dictionary did rely on a scholarly survey to inform a usage note about a controversial word – *ain't* – it was widely attacked.[7] I shall have more to say about the reception given *NID3* below. (See p. 254.) Maybe the public isn't ready to accept accurate information about usage.

In defense of dictionaries, the purpose of linguistic atlases is to chart dialects by exemplifying divergences in use. They are not designed to serve lexicography. Thus their coverage of vocabulary is only one aspect, and usually not the chief one, of their effort. They are not concerned with recording a vast number of usages but in finding just enough differences to draw meaningful conclusions about regional dialects. Valuable as they are, atlases are not ideal sources for determining which words, among the hundreds of thousands that may be included in a dictionary, should be labeled with respect to region, or for determining what the labels should be.

The Dictionary of American Regional English

Happily, the ongoing *Dictionary of American Regional English (DARE)*, edited by Frederic G. Cassidy, Joan Houston Hall, and a staff of twelve, will go a long way towards providing systematic guidance for both identification and labeling of vocabulary items. *DARE* is based on a vast collection of regional materials and on painstaking interviews with over 2,700 informants in 1,002 carefully selected communities in all 50 states of the US. Each questionnaire contained more than 1,600 questions, and nearly 2.5 million responses were obtained. Each informant was categorized by age, type of community, race, education, and sex. In addition, *DARE* has drawn upon extensive dialectal notes collected by the American Dialect Society and a number of other collections and has made thorough use of the existing dialect atlases. *DARE* provides definitions and dated citations for each entry, along with etymologies, pronunciation, and usage information when called for. The entries for *bull* and *mincy* (see Figures 15 and 16 on pp. 222–23) show typical treatments. (*DARE*'s entry for *bull* is quite long, and only part is included here.)

To date three volumes of the five planned for the dictionary proper have been published: the first, A-C, in 1985; the second, D-H, in 1991; and the third, I-O, in 1996. A sixth volume will include the data

bull n, also attrib

1 Std sense—formerly often avoided as a taboo word esp in **Sth, S Midl.** ˙ Cf *DS* K22, 23 and **beast B2, brute, cowbrute, gentle-man cow, male-cow**

1913 Kephart *Highlanders* 295 sAppalachians, Critter and beast are usually restricted to horse and mule, and brute to a bovine. A bull or boar is not to be mentioned as such in mixed company, but male-brute and male-hog are used as euphemisms.   1943 *New Yorker* 23 Oct 66/2 cTX (as of c1905), It was largely cattle country, but the word "bull" was seldom used in the company of ladies; the less offensive word "male" was employed to get the idea over.   1949 Kurath *Word Geog.* 62, The plain term *bull* is current everywhere, and in the North Midland and New York State other expressions are rare. In New England, the South, and the South Midland, however, the plain term is not used by older folk of one sex in the presence of the other. Even many of the younger genera-tion prefer the veiled expressions of the Victorian era.   1953 Randolph *Down in Holler* 96, Schele De Vere says that many Southerners use ox, male-cow, or even gentleman-cow instead of bull, but the Ozarkers usually say *male, cow-critter, brute,* or *cow-brute.*   1954 *Harder Coll.*

15 Part of the entry "bull" from the *Dictionary of American Regional English,* vol. I

summary (a list of all the responses to the questions in the questionnaire), a map section, a bibliography, an index to the labels in the text, addenda, and errata. It is estimated that when the five volumes of the dictionary proper are published, *DARE* will contain about 70,000 entries and include more than 2,500 maps showing the regional distributions of vocabulary items. For selected entries *DARE* includes these oddly shaped, computer-generated maps of the United States in order to show the geographic distribution of responses. See Figure 17 on p. 224. The map is intentionally distorted to reflect state population densities; thus New York and Massachusetts appear larger than they are and many of the western states much smaller.[8] Figures 18 and 19 on p. 225 show the distributions of *gesundheit* and *scat* in answer to the question, "When somebody sneezes, what do people say to him?" Though *gesundheit* is more common nationally, one can see that *scat* is widespread in the entire southern half of the United States except for the far west. It does not occur at all north of southern Missouri, nor does it occur west of the Rocky Mountains.

    DARE is certain to become the basic source of information about regional variation for American dictionaries and is indispensable to lan-guage scholars, but as one can see from the short samples I have

mincy adj **esp S Midl** Cf **mince**
Finicky or overly fastidious, usu about eating.
  1913 Kephart *Highlanders* 289 **sAppalachians,** A remarkable word,
common in the Smokies, is dauncy, defined for me as "mincy about
eating," which is to say fastidious, over-nice. **1927** *AmSp* 2.360 **WV,**
Mincy . . particular in eating. "She is too mincy to suit me." **1952**
Brown *NC Folkl.* 1.565 **wNC,** *Mincy.* . . Over particular, over exact,
finicky. "You're mighty mincy about your breakfast today. Are you
sick?" **1960** Williams *Walk Egypt* 224 **nGA,** Her voice was mincy, a
child playing a woman. **c1960** *Wilson Coll.* **csKY,** *Mincy.* . . Dainty,
said of an eater. **1967–70** *DARE* (Qu. H12, *If somebody eating a meal
takes little bits of food and leaves most of it on his plate, you say he
_____*) Infs **IN3, OH41,** Mincy; **TX40, VA35,** Mincy eater. **1972**
Cooper *NC Mt. Folkl.* 94, *Mincy*—finicky. **1984** Wilder *You All Spoken
Here* 12 **Sth,** *Mincy:* Fastidious; finicky; picky; she's so persnickety she
wouldn't be happy in a pie factory.

16 The entry "mincy" from the Dictionary of *American Regional English*, vol. III

included, the material is fascinating and is of interest to a much wider
public than scholars. It is the first substantial American *dictionary* to
employ unassailably objective methods for assembling a vast quantity of
data on regional differences in vocabulary. Its publication should result
in significant improvements in the coverage of regionalisms in all reputable American dictionaries. To take one example, scholars have long
known and written about the use of the so-called double modal, such as
might could – meaning "probably could" or "might be able to," a usage
common in the South. *DARE*'s entry draws upon this scholarship but
adds new material, with dated examples such as "I might could look it
up in my notes," and defines the regions where the double modal is used
as the South and South Midland. Apart from all the original material
that *DARE* includes, its importance also lies in pulling together in one
place all the essential facts relating to a usage and presenting it in a clear,
coherent way. This makes the material much easier to find and use than
it was formerly, and for that alone we should all be grateful. Since the
"might could" usage is fairly common, it ought to be included in
American college dictionaries, but it is not. One hopes that they will
learn to make use of *DARE* to enrich their coverage of regional English.
  DARE's importance for dictionaries extends beyond regional dialect,
since it also tracks regional differences based on type of community or
the age, educational level, race, and sex of the informant. Differences in
usage based on these criteria may be reliably distinguished for many

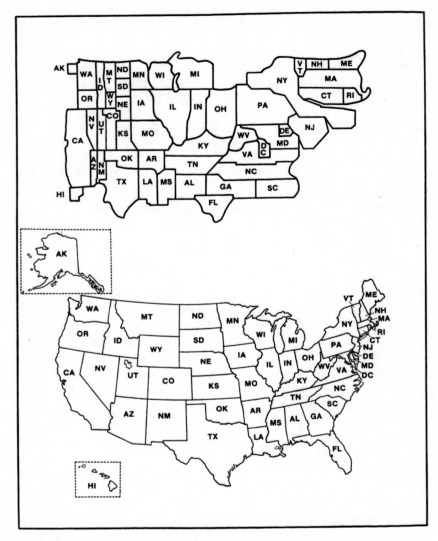

17 *DARE* base map showing state designations compared to standard map of the
United States

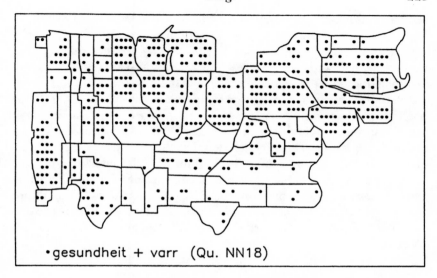

18 *DARE* distribution map for "gesundheit"

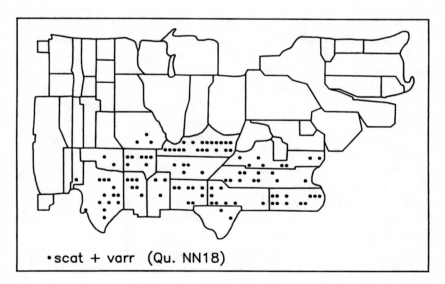

19 *DARE* distribution map for "scat"

lexical items for the first time. Apart from the actual data that dictionaries will be able to draw upon, the methodology employed by *DARE* is one they would do well to imitate. The percentages of informants falling into each subdivision of the five criteria were tabulated and recorded. For each question, the percentages of informants responding were compared to the percentage of that group giving a particular answer. If the percentage of young people, for example, giving a particular response was significantly higher than the percentage of young people responding to that question, *DARE* concluded that the response occurred especially frequently among young people. Thus it finds that *icky* is "esp freq among young and mid-aged speakers and among women," and that *klutz* and *dodo* are most commonly used by young speakers. Thus it finds that *beau dollar*, *curioussome*, and *funky* are especially used by Black speakers.[9] The relevance of this sort of information for general dictionaries is obvious.

SPECIALIZED TERMINOLOGY

Every general dictionary contains some words that have special meanings in a technical field or science. Field labels such as *astronomy*, *chemistry*, *medicine*, *physics*, *economics*, and *law* are applied to terms that are important in the field and in such widespread use that they have appeared in popular articles or in specialized magazines for the amateur rather than for the professional. Science digests, financial newspapers, health magazines, hobbyist publications of all sorts include a great range of technical terms, terms like *black hole*, *ester*, *quinolones*, *theory of relativity*, *margin* (in business and finance), and *voir dire*. Some dictionaries use field labels abundantly, others sparingly. Some incorporate the label within the definition with an introductory phrase, such as, "In astronomy . . ."

A label or qualifying phrase is essential when a word is used in two or more different disciplines with different meanings, or if it is used in one sense technically and in another popularly, such as *parameter*. Dictionaries continue to ignore many popular meanings of scientific terms. (See Ch. 4, p. 164.) For example, *DNA*, once restricted to scientific contexts, is now commonplace, especially in the context of forensic investigations. Dictionaries still define *DNA* only technically, which is a mistake. They should define it technically and label it as a technical definition, and define it generally in this sense without a label, as for example: "a chemical substance found in every organism and which is commonly used in forensic investigations because its particular structure within each individual is unique." Dictionaries do cover the forensic use of DNA under *DNA fingerprinting*, but *DNA* is quite commonly used in the sense in which I have defined it without reference to fingerprinting. Influenced by the fact that *DNA* is a familiar term and is widely used in nontechnical contexts, none of the American college dictionaries labels its technical definition of *DNA*. This stands logic on its head. The fact that a technical term is also used nontechnically argues all the more strongly that the technical definition be labeled. Only a British dictionary, the *New Oxford Dictionary of English* (*NODE*), applies the label *Biochemistry* to its technical definition.

NID3 was severely taxed in 1961 for dropping many of the field labels used in *NID2*, but its policy has been largely adopted by other dictionaries since. Critics missed seeing the copious use of such labels as *civil engineering*, *metallurgy*, and *manufacturing*; they should have reflected that the changes in many fields over the years had made such labels arbitrary and would have dated the dictionary. On the other hand, in its zeal to use few labels, *NID3* sometimes omitted one when it could have spared the reader confusion by including one. For example, def. 4 of *nothingness*, unlabeled, is as follows:

the conceptualization or reification of the affective content in an emotional experience (as of anxiety) that is negatively colored < ~ is . . . a distinctive metaphysical entity – J. A. Franquiz>; also: MEANINGLESSNESS <the utter ~ of not being – Jean Wahl>

The first illustrative quotation is supposed to tell us that the definition is a philosophical one, but the reader who innocently encounters this definition is likely to be baffled by it. A simple label or introductory phrase, such as "In existential philosophy" would have immediately made the definition intelligible and rendered the illustrative quotations, which are singularly unilluminating, superfluous. The introductory phrase would thus have saved space as well as clarified the definition.

As dictionaries acquire more experience in using large language corpora (discussed in Ch. 6), they will be able to determine in some cases whether a term is used chiefly in a particular range of activity (or *genre*, as it is called in corpus research). I have already described in the previous chapter how some ESL dictionaries are beginning to identify those words and expressions used mainly in speech. The next step is to define whether a term occurs preponderantly in one particular genre, such as business, entertainment, *belles lettres*, etc. This can be done in several ways. When using a corpus, the header information (the information at the top of the screen) identifies the source of the text displayed and usually the text category or genre in which it belongs. Even if the header information is not specific enough to identify "business" or "entertainment," the lexicographer can easily note from the source and the nature of the content whether the text is part of a business report, for example, or a review of a movie or a description of a sports event. If in scrolling down a whole series of corpus hits for a particular term, the lexicographer sees that they virtually all deal with the same subject, this can be noted. Alternatively, a corpus might include a number of subcorpora devoted to particular genres; the lexicographer could then compare the frequencies of the lexical item among the several subcorpora. For example, *apparel* is a word that rarely occurs in speech and is used almost exclusively in business or merchandising. It ought to be labeled in dictionaries with something like *mainly business use*. In time, corpus-based dictionaries will have enough evidence to label many such words. The labels will be somewhat broader than conventional field labels of older dictionaries, but they will be much more accurate and reliable than labels generated by expert advice. Eventually, I expect them to replace conventional field labels completely. (See also "Dictionary treatment of usage in the future," p. 268.)

SEXUAL AND SCATOLOGICAL TABOO

Although *NID3* did include many of the basic taboo words, those four-letter terms dealing with sex and scatology that once had the power to shock, no widely available, general dictionary in this century included *fuck* until a small British dictionary, the *Penguin English Dictionary* (1965), included it, followed by the much more prominent *American Heritage Dictionary* (*AHD*) in 1969. As reported by Herbert Morton, *fuck* was included in the galley proofs of *NID3* with the warning "obscene and usu. unprintable," but the president of G. & C. Merriam Company ordered the "f-words" deleted.[10] By the end of the twentieth century, the unprintable had become so printable that it was possible for a major publisher to issue a whole book about "the f-word."[11] It was not always so.

Allen Walker Read's classic article of 1934 entitled "An Obscenity Symbol" never once specified the word, but it nevertheless took considerable courage both on his part and on that of the editor, Cabell Greet, to print the piece. Read observes that its first occurrence in a dictionary was in John Florio's work of 1598. He also speculates on the nature of taboo. Neither sex nor excrementary functions are obscene, Read says. Attitude determines obscenity.

> [O]bscenity is any reference to the bodily functions that gives to anyone a certain emotional reaction, that of a "fearful thrill" in seeing, doing, or speaking the forbidden. Thus it is the existence of the ban or taboo that creates the obscenity.[12]

What is the origin of the ban or taboo? Read distinguishes between the taboo of thing (the sexual act) and the taboo of word (*fuck*). Attitudes towards taboo, he says, have been fostered by others' attitudes, engendered by punishment from parents and the thrill and hushed sense of daring and naughtiness from one's childhood peers. Taboo fulfills a deep human need, he argues, and societies preserve its usefulness as taboo by objecting to it. Doubtless Read is on firm anthropological ground in making these assertions, but I question whether taboo of thing is always separable from taboo of word. Even after *fuck* appeared in *AHD*, as I reported in 1974, none of the American college dictionaries (including *AHD*) defined *sexual intercourse*.[13] They preferred to abandon the basic principles of lexicography and tiptoe back and forth between aseptic scientific and veterinarian substitutes. If included at all, it was defined tersely as "coitus" or with the legalistic and baffling "sexual connection." These words were often defined circularly as "sexual intercourse."

Beginning with the free-speech movement of the hippies and flower children of the 1960s and continuing to the present day, there has been a growing public tolerance of taboo words, reflected in their expression in movies, popular magazines, cable TV shows, song lyrics, and other avenues of mass entertainment. Taboo words are increasingly part of the mainstream lexicon, particularly of young people. Though it took dictionaries some time to catch up with the public's mood, they now reflect this tolerance by including a much wider range of taboo terms than formerly. They also now define *sexual intercourse* in a noncircular way. It is a curious anomaly of the public's attitude towards taboo that uttering "sexual intercourse" in a public place today would turn more heads than uttering "fuck."

A number of seventeenth-century dictionaries contained taboo words, and Nathan Bailey included them in his *Universal Etymological English Dictionary* (1721). Johnson included some vulgar words, such as *bloody*, but by and large omitted them. In 1785, Francis Grose's *A Classical Dictionary of the Vulgar Tongue* appeared. In the nineteenth century, consciousness of taboo was stronger than ever. Read reminds us that in

America *leg* was not uttered before ladies, and *DARE* shows us that *bull* was similarly avoided in some parts of the country well into the twentieth century. One of the few consistencies in Noah Webster's behavior was his determination to exclude all vulgarities from his dictionaries, and the compass of vulgarity then was much greater than it is now.

The decision whether or not to include taboo words in a dictionary relates directly to the purpose of the work. If one conceives of a dictionary as purely descriptive, every word that can be documented as being in sufficiently wide use should be included, no matter how abhorrent. If a dictionary has normative or pedagogical aims, one must question whether taboo terms are useful. They should be included in ESL dictionaries for adults; a foreign learner has to be made aware of common taboo words to avoid the embarrassment of using them inadvertently. In a school dictionary, the inclusion of taboo words would probably cause much less harm than is commonly supposed, but there is no doubt that it would cause a great deal of hardship for their teachers. Young children cannot be expected to understand the dictionary's principle of objective selection of entries based on usage. Teachers would be confronted on the one hand by puzzled and titillated students and on the other by outraged parents. Life is too precious for sacrificial heroism to so little purpose; let us acknowledge the undesirability of including taboo words in children's dictionaries.

Difficulty arises in deciding whether to include taboo words in general dictionaries for adult native speakers, when the dictionaries will be used in schools. Educators view such dictionaries as normative; lexicographers do not. Even if the dictionary publisher is willing to compromise and omit those few taboo terms that are deemed most offensive, the educational censors are unlikely to be appeased. In 1976 the educational commissioner of Texas refused to list any of the four major American college dictionaries or *The Doubleday Dictionary* for purchase. It was not just the inclusion of the four-letter words that disturbed the commissioner; *Webster's New World Dictionary* (*WNW*) did not then include them but was banned anyway. The commissioner objected to terms like *bed, clap, deflower, john, G-string, slut, bastard,* and many others.[14] Newspaper accounts of dictionaries being banned from the school libraries and classrooms of small towns are commonplace.[15] The real decision facing a lexicographer who is asked to omit terms on the grounds of taste is not a matter of leaving out *fuck* and half a dozen other words. If that were the issue, its resolution would be fairly trivial. Scholarship will not languish because dictionaries omit *fuck,* and *NID3* was not fatally compromised by its original omission of the word. But the moment the lexicographer accedes to the principle of excluding any words on the grounds of someone else's taste, he has relinquished control of his dictionary and turned it into an instrument of privileged propaganda, like an American history text that omits all mention of slavery. Once he acknowledges that any criterion overrides that of use, how can he object to the exclusion of countless other words deemed objectionable to one group or another? For like other categories of usage, the offensiveness of various words is a continuum from the most objectionable sexual or scatological terms to mild profanities. Many a religious, fundamentalist family in America would still be shocked by hearing *Goddamn* or one of its many euphemisms. Shock value depends on circumstance and the attitudes of the audience. Nonetheless, as a rule, oaths, whether euphemistic or explicit, mild or savage, perform a different function from that of the sexual or scatological obscenities. The purpose of oaths can hardly be described better than in this passage from *The Golden Bowl* by Henry James:

His wife had once told him, in relation to his violence of speech, that such excesses, on his part, made her think of a retired General whom she had once seen playing with toy soldiers, fighting and winning battles, carrying on sieges and annihilating enemies with little fortresses of wood and little armies of tin. Her husband's exaggerated emphasis was *his* box of toy soldiers, his military game. It harmlessly gratified him, for his declining years, the military instinct; bad words, when sufficiently numerous and arrayed in their might, could represent battalions, squadrons, tremendous cannonades and glorious charges of cavalry. It was natural, it was delightful – the romance, and for her as well, of camp life and of the perpetual booming of guns. It was fighting to the end, to the death, but no one was ever killed.

INSULT

In the past several decades many of the sexual and scatological terms that were formerly taboo have become much more acceptable in public discourse and mass entertainment, and terms of insult have become more serious offenses. Whereas the sexual and scatological terms were seen as offenses against taste and decorum, which were in the past often considered to be particularly objectionable to women, terms of insult are viewed as morally repugnant, especially in the United States. As the status of women has changed from that of the vulnerable and more sensitive sex that had to be protected from crude language, many of the taboos about using the old-fashioned, four-letter words have dropped away. At the same time, minorities, homosexuals, and other groups have organized to raise sensitivity to discrimination against them and to exert pressure on government to do something about it. Their success has led to an extraordinary elevation in the public's appreciation of the gravity of the offense of using terms that offend these groups.

This change has not affected all groups equally. The degree of disapprobation given old-fashioned ethnic slurs – *wop, dago, yid, kike, mick, kraut, frog, Polack* – has not changed very much. The ethnic and religious groups represented by these words are well integrated into American society; the use of these words has been declining steadily and is no longer seen as much of a threat. But slurs directed against women, gays, and African-Americans are regarded with special outrage because the language of insult is seen to reflect attitudes that have resulted in the abuse of the rights – and in some cases even the loss of life – of people belonging to these groups. The few sexually taboo words that are still taboo, such as *cunt*, remain so largely because they are terms of insult, not because they offend decorum.

Dictionary labeling of insult is essentially political and moral. Every major English dictionary today takes a stand on the side of those who deplore racial and ethnic bigotry, oppose discrimination and abuse directed towards women and gays, and endorse tolerance of a diversity of opinion and life styles. Some take a stronger stand than others, using aggressive labels and adopting on occasion a tone of moral urgency, whereas some take a more detached approach, using labels that have the appearance of objective descriptions even when they are not. This position, although it is doubtless also the personal view of most lexicographers, essentially reflects the official views of the government under whose laws the business that produces the dictionary operates. English dictionaries are giving greater attention to the language of insult because governments have instituted laws that punish or suppress behavior against those groups that have organized themselves sufficiently to become an actual or potential political force, and because the weight of public opinion, influenced by corporate culture, university life, and mass entertainment, endorses this position. In the past, when governments did not recognize the equal status of certain groups, and when publishers did not account those groups a significant part of their market, dictionaries were much less likely to label terms that derogated those groups.

It is instructive to see how rapidly a formerly disenfranchised group can increase public awareness about language. *The Doubleday Dictionary* of 1975 was the first to label *queer* for "homosexual" as a contemptuous term; up till then it was unmarked, though it and other similar slang words were known to be offensive to homosexuals.[16] Homosexuals weren't then recognized as a group having independent social or political power, and they were therefore ignored. Ten years later one could not find a dictionary that did not warn the reader against the use of the term, and, as is the case with many such terms, some members of the in-group who were the object of disparagement have adopted the term *queer* as a gesture of defiance and to promote group solidarity. Eventually the word might lose its pejorative status.

Unfortunately, there are no agreed-upon criteria for finding some usages offensive or contemptuous or abusive. There are few studies that shed any light on the degree of offensiveness of specified terms under specified conditions. What matters is the relationship between the speaker and the spoken to, and between the speaker and the spoken about. Do they know each other well or not at all? Are they members of the same in-group? A woman who is speaking to a close female friend and who calls another woman a "girl" is not likely to cause offense, whereas a man's use of the word to a female business associate probably would. This kind of analysis depends upon usage notes, which dictionaries do try to include wherever possible. Labels cannot tell the whole story.

Insult can be affectionate. There is no basis for the flat assertion that *any* term is insulting under all conditions, no matter how offensive it may be under some. In practice dictionaries' labels of insult are based on the assumption that the speaker does not know the person spoken to well or that both do not belong to the same in-group. The advice is only about *public* behavior, since many reputable members of society routinely use terms of insult in private among like-minded people to whom these words are not in the least offensive. It is only when they miscalculate and use such terms when not among like-minded people that they offend.

How do dictionary editors decide what to label offensive or disparaging? It is based on the editor's judgment of society's norm for the limits of reputable public behavior. He consults slang dictionaries and other written sources, including other general dictionaries. Citation files and corpora are not of much help. Though the language of insult is common in fiction, the context in which it occurs is often between intimates who share the same prejudices; no one is insulted. Even when fiction does record the use of an insulting word said in anger, the brief context of a citation or a few lines of text in a corpus search is seldom sufficient to show that the person addressed is insulted. *Because* the writer expects us to understand that the language is insulting, the behavior of the characters often does not exhibit a shocked reaction. Indeed, one of the problems in using a corpus based on fictional speech is the high prevalence of insult. Often I have found myself unable to use an otherwise excellent corpus citation to illustrate a perfectly inoffensive term because it was embedded in a context that included disparaging or grossly insensitive comments about women or a minority group. To include such comments even within quotation marks would invite charges of bias and insensitivity from readers. In determining whether a particular usage is insulting or not, the lexicographer is compelled to use his own experience, moderated of necessity by his own moral views, whether consciously or not.

If, in the past, dictionaries were too slow to label terms of insult, they now seem too quick to do so. Many hundreds of terms are now labeled as *disparaging, contemptuous,* or *offensive* in dictionaries, often on the strength of dubious evidence but out of fear that they will be taken to be insensitive to some group. The *Encarta World English Dictionary* (*EWED*) has carried this trend to an extreme. *EWED* considers almost any word offensive that has to do with mental or physical incapacity, mental mistakes, sex, age, or race. It considers the word *madness* offensive, and one can't call someone a *nut* or *nutty* or a *nutcase* in its book without being offensive. *Weirdo* is off limits, and no one can be a *basket case* or a *vegetable* or *off his* (or *her*) *rocker, screwed up, schizoid,* or *handicapped.*[17] *EWED* makes no distinction between words used humorously or affectionately and words used to insult. So among the words it labels *offensive* are *jerk, slob, schnook, klutz, loony,* and *crazy.* It views the language as a fortified castle of virtue, and every battlement is equipped with a cannon loaded with warnings.

A racial taboo

Although most linguistic taboos deal with sex or scatology, in recent years taboo has been extended to the racial epithet *nigger.* For many years *nigger* had been labeled as a contemptuous term in dictionaries and treated similarly to ethnic and religious slurs. But a singular event in recent history has raised the consciousness of a wider public to the offensive status of *nigger* and made it unique, promoting it to the level of taboo.

No greater testament to the power of language use could be mooted than the televised trial of former football star O. J. Simpson, in a case that completely absorbed the attention of millions of Americans and others throughout the world from September 27, 1994, to October 3, 1995, when a verdict was rendered. Simpson, an African-American, was charged with the murders of his former wife and of a man – both white – who happened to be present during the alleged attack on his wife. Though many factors weighed in Simpson's acquittal of double murder, the most sensational issue in the trial was the admission by a Los Angeles detective, Mark Fuhrman, under questioning by one of Simpson's attorneys, F. Lee Bailey, that he had lied in asserting that he had not uttered the word "nigger" in the past ten years. Subsequently, Simpson's lead attorney, Johnny Cochran, hammered away at this issue, and so incendiary was the word that it could not be uttered even in neutral explanation but was referred to throughout the remainder of the trial as "the N-word" by the judge and prosecuting attorneys as well as by Cochran. As we have seen with the "F-word," the use of the first initial is a popular euphemistic device to avoid uttering a taboo word.

Cochran succeeded in so demonizing the use of "nigger" as to associate its utterance with the atrocities of the Nazi Holocaust. Incredible though it may sound at an interval of years, he managed to convey the conviction that anyone who said "nigger," no matter what the context, would be guilty of a crime worse than murder, and one felt, observing the judge, jury, and prosecution, that he had convinced everyone in the courtroom – and probably millions of TV watchers – that this was so. It was a brilliant use of the power of taboo to influence the way otherwise reasonable people think about issues of right and wrong. It not only discredited the witness, which helped Simpson's cause even though it could hardly exonerate him, it convicted the witness of a crime worse than anything Simpson was accused of. As a demonstration of the power of language to shape attitude, Cochran's handling of the use of "nigger" is without parallel in my experience. At the Simpson trial, utterance of the N-word was an offense so grievous as to make all other crimes, including murder, seem by comparison unimportant, a local event as opposed to a crime against an entire people.

After the Simpson trial, the pitch of anger and anxiety at its use increased, and dictionaries came under pressure to drop the word entirely. In 1997 the *Washington Post* reported a petition drive against Merriam-Webster to remove *nigger* from its dictionaries.[18] The company defended its treatment, which does state that it is "usu. taken to be offensive," and includes a usage note that says it often expresses "racial hatred and bigotry" when not used among blacks themselves. Rather than demanding that *nigger* be cut from dictionaries, I should rather call for more extensive coverage that includes in-group use by African-Americans, as in rap lyrics and ordinary speech, all unreported. Although general dictionaries cannot possibly represent all the meanings of every in-group usage of insulting terms, *nigger* (and a few other highly charged words such as *girl*) are special and merit such treatment.[19]

In 1998, New York City's Schools Chancellor, Rudy Crew, supported the decision of a principal to remove a "critically acclaimed book," *War Comes to Willy Freeman*, from classroom use because it contained the word "nigger" in a historical context. The book, which was to have been used by sixth-graders, was retained for library use and optional reading. The principal was said to have acted to avoid parental protest.[20]

The following year, David Howard, a white aide to the mayor of Washington, D.C., while speaking to a black colleague, said, "I will have to be niggardly with this fund because it's not going to be a lot of money." A co-worker reported that Howard had used a racial epithet, and the mayor of Washington, Anthony Williams, asked Howard to resign, which he did. Howard said that he had used "bad judgment" in selecting such a word. However, since Howard was the mayor's first openly gay appointee, the homosexual community came to his defense, and it was pointed out that *niggardly* has no connection to the odious N-word. Subsequently the mayor admitted he had acted hastily and invited Howard to rejoin his administration.[21]

A note in the *Encarta World English Dictionary* (*EWED*) counsels the reader to think hard before using *niggardly*. Although it is "in no way a racial slur," the note says, "the word sounds as if it might be one." Case closed.

I do not think that this is all foolishness. I do not think the people who are very upset at the use of "nigger" are crazy (sorry, *EWED*, to use an offensive word here), stupid, or tendentious. Given the history of the treatment of blacks in America and the entire black experience up to and including the present, no one should be surprised at the extreme level of sensitivity about racial issues. In such a climate, embarrassing mistakes can be made, and at least Washington's mayor realized his mistake and did something about it. But banning the word "nigger" from books or dictionaries, or banning any word, is an attempt to rewrite history or suppress truthful information about language use. It smacks of the treatment of Russian history during the Soviet era or the treatment in US textbooks before the civil-rights era of slavery and the history of African-Americans. It is doomed to fail. Certainly dictionaries should mark this word as offensive. The incredible level of hysteria associated with its use under any circumstances is a result of the adroit manipulation in the Simpson case of the emotions of a people who have been enslaved and oppressed so that they identify their oppression with the use of a word; the utterance of the word becomes their oppression. A word can cause hurt, but it's still no more than a word, and the wrongs a people have suffered will not be repaired nor their future secured if the word *nigger* falls from use and disappears from the language. The attitudes that gave the word its power to hurt will, unfortunately, survive, and it is these that should be the focus of our anger and outrage. The word is merely an incidental agent of its message and can change, like a mutating virus.

SLANG

Slang deserves a category all by itself. It is sometimes grouped with the style labels (*formal/informal*) and sometimes with the status labels (*standard/nonstandard*), but it does not fit comfortably with either. Slang does not represent a vocabulary that one can adopt to suit a social situation, as one can with terms on the *formal/informal* index. In fact, when slang is used appropriately it is on the way to becoming standard speech. Unlike other words restrictively labeled, slang is deliberately nonstandard. Much slang has been introduced by criminals, hucksters, and gamblers; how shall we characterize the cultural levels of these groups? They are off the beaten track, but are they necessarily of low cultural level because their occupations happen to be antisocial? Much slang derives also from the cant of musicians and soldiers and other groups that feel isolated or beleaguered. Their private vocabulary percolates through layers of language to become tomorrow's slang, then routinely peppers the conversations of young people everywhere. Some dictionary users mistakenly suppose that slang is necessarily in the category of taboo words. Although much slang deals with off-color subjects, taboo words are not necessarily slang and most slang words are not taboo. There is only an incidental correspondence between the categories.

Jonathan Lighter, the editor of the multivolume *Random House Historical Dictionary of American Slang*, offers this definition of *slang*: "an informal, nonstandard, nontechnical vocabulary composed chiefly of novel-sounding synonyms for standard words and phrases," but then immediately adds that it is inadequate because it leaves out the social dimension. He adds that slang "turns up especially in the derisive speech play of youthful, raffish, or undignified persons and groups" and therefore "often carries with it striking overtones of impertinence or irreverence." The use of slang also implies that the person to whom the slang is addressed "identifies fully with the speaker's attitudes."[22]

Although most slang is novel sounding, it is not necessarily new and can even be old-fashioned or archaic. Once upon a time, something really good was "swell" or "tops," usages now almost wholly defunct, though still slang. *Longhair* and *egghead* were two contemptuous slang words for intellectuals much in use during the early 1950s but now gone quite out of fashion. Nothing dates a person so quickly as using old slang in the presence of his children. Most slang is ephemeral, and often the same meaning is reincarnated anew with each generation, although the connotations may differ, as with *take it easy* and *chill out*, *it stinks* and *it sucks*, *blah-blah-blah* and *yada-yada-yada*.

Dictionary labeling of slang is notoriously inconsistent, as a number of critics have observed. In 1949, James B. McMillan compared five dictionaries with respect to the words *movie*, *razz*, *tycoon*, and *plug* (in the sense of a promotional mention). In no case did they all agree. *Movie* was called slang by one, colloquial by three, and popular by the other. *Plug* was called slang by one, colloquial by one, cant by a third, and was not labeled by the other two.[23] Similar inconsistencies, particularly noticeable in the treatment of slang, were found by Thomas J. Creswell in his analysis a quarter of a century later of ten dictionaries. He compared their treatment of 318 specific items in the *American Heritage Dictionary* (*AHD*), and concluded:

Every analysis presented in the preceding pages shows that as far as the 318 items under review are concerned, the ten modern dictionaries studied are far, far more often in disagreement than they are in agreement. As there is no well developed external criterion or bench mark currently available to evaluate dictionary judgments on usage, the dictionaries' claims of objectivity and authoritativeness in the treatment of usage must be rejected.[24]

Although I agree with Creswell's conclusion, the evidence he presents does not necessarily support it. If ten physicians arrive at ten different diagnoses of the same patient, we have no basis for impugning either their objectivity or their authority. The evidence available to each may have differed, as the linguistic evidence available to each dictionary certainly differed, and their interpretations of the evidence, even had it been the same, may have legitimately differed. We can conclude only that medicine and lexicography are inexact sciences and that some patients and some words are hard to diagnose.

The failure of *Webster's Third New International Dictionary* (*NID3*) to label many of its words as slang was the focus of innumerable protests and derisive newspaper editorials following the dictionary's publication in 1961. Herbert Morton reports that the policy established by *NID3*'s editor, Philip Gove, was to base judgments about slang on the citational evidence: was the word "used mostly in standard or nonstandard contexts"?[25] This begs the question. Often it is precisely the heavy use of slang that makes a context nonstandard in the first place. What else can make it nonstandard? Bad grammar? Misspellings? Incoherent expression? We aren't told. My own experience in using citational evidence and corpora tells me that in the vast majority of cases there is no way to determine objectively that a brief sample of text is nonstandard. For example, grammatical errors abound in speech in all kinds of contexts, including presidential press conferences and political debates. Are they then full of slang?

The policy of labeling very few words as slang has been continued in *NID3*'s collection of supplements. *12,000 Words* (1986) defines *ape* in *go ape* as "being beyond restraint: crazy, wild <went ape over another girl . . .>" without labeling it. Nor does it label *bag* in any of the following senses: "something suited to one's taste . . . an individual's typical way of life . . . a characteristic manner of expression." Its reluctance to take a stand on slang infuriated many critics, who felt the absence of a label stamped a word as approved and fit for use in all contexts. In this respect the critics were misguided. Inclusion of a word in a dictionary connotes no approval, and illustrative quotations were designed to show typical contexts. However, the absence of any qualifying label did suggest that the word was in standard usage. One may wonder that if *go ape*, which perfectly fits Jonathan Lighter's definition of slang and which is included in his slang dictionary, is not slang, what is?[26]

The controversy of *NID3*'s judgments merely highlights the difficulties confronting every dictionary editor. Creswell is right that there are no agreed criteria for making usage judgments, and it is this assertion, rather than the inconsistencies he found in dictionary treatment, that supports his claim of the lack of objectivity and authority in the treatment of usage. (Medicine, on the other hand, does have benchmarks for making diagnoses, in spite of which diagnoses differ.) How do editors decide what to label slang? They examine citations and corpus evidence and see if the context is slangy. (The alert reader notes some circularity, I hope, and begins to fidget in his chair.) This, after a fashion, was Gove's policy too. They look in other dictionaries and see what *they* have done. They look up the word or expression in slang dictionaries (discussed below). Most such dictionaries, though sometimes helpful, inevitably miss many slang expressions, and slang changes so rapidly that recently coined locutions will not be found in any slang dictionary. Even if the word sought is included, it does not necessarily merit being labeled slang. As Lighter has pointed out, slang dictionaries have universally fattened their coverage by including many terms that are by no conceivable definition slang.[27] Now at least we have the *Random House Historical Dictionary of American Slang*, and though it is a treasure of information, even it cannot cover everything, and since new slang expressions are constantly being coined and old ones are constantly losing their special focus as slang, it cannot keep up with the current situation, nor is it designed to. But it is immensely helpful. Chapman's *Dictionary of American Slang* (based on Wentworth and Flexner's work of the same title) and Green's *Cassell Dictionary of Slang* can help fill in some of the blanks. Nonetheless, many slang expressions cannot be found in any work.

One is tempted to throw up one's hands in exasperation, utter some loud, irreverent slang of one's own, and forget the whole business. Nothing elaborates theory so much as the need to justify practicality. It is easier to spend one's time constructing theories to explain why there is no such thing as slang than to identify and harness its peculiar energy and spice and stick a label on it. But that is what the dictionary editor must do, like it or not, for slang is a useful concept. Since there are no agreed external criteria for identifying slang, we must support efforts to establish them; but in the meantime we must rely on subjective criteria lacking in any authority save that of informed and educated people trained to be sensitive to language style. In day-to-day decisions, words are labeled slang by lexicographers or their advisers because the words are deemed to be extremely informal. This is unsatisfactory; slang is not simply very informal usage. But until we have agreed criteria by which to judge them, slang and informal words will appear in more or less free variation in dictionaries.

STYLE AND STATUS: AN INTRODUCTION

In 1948, John S. Kenyon drew a distinction between cultural levels, usually identified by the labels *standard* and *substandard* or *illiterate*, and functional varieties of English, describing the degree of formality or informality of a word or expression. He argued that whereas the degree of standardness depended on the social status and education of speakers – their cultural level – the use of familiar or formal speech depended on the social situation in which it was used. He said it was wrong to stigmatize informal usages as a "level" because that suggested a norm comparable to that of nonstandard usage. It was perfectly appropriate to use informal speech in informal situations. Moreover, both standard and substandard levels of speech had formal and informal varieties.[28] He also pointed out, as Charles C. Fries had in his introductory essay in the *American College Dictionary* (1947), that the label *colloquial* in dictionaries was widely misinterpreted to mean a localism, hence inferior to standard usage.

Although the label *colloquial* was intended to mean "more often used in speech than in writing," in practice it was often used to mean "informal," and the next generation of dictionaries replaced *colloquial* with *informal*. In fact, dictionaries of this period (prior to 1950) never had any evidence for labeling some words as "more often used in speech than in writing," since they were almost entirely based on writing, and no systematic studies of frequency of usage of speech existed. Not until Randolph Quirk's trailblazing Survey of English Usage – begun in 1959 but under development for many years – was any large-scale systematic attempt made to record speech. Indeed, it was only in the 1990s that the technology existed for developing corpora containing millions of words of speech. (See Ch. 6, pp. 284–86.) The decision to label some words *colloquial* was strictly a matter of the editors' own impressionistic sense of what was more appropriate to speech than to writing. In view of later studies that show how inaccurate are the perception and reporting of our own speech as well as the speech of others, one cannot have a great deal of confidence in the accuracy of these labels. Perhaps those who thought *colloquial* meant "Don't use this word in standard formal contexts" understood the lexicographers' judgments better than the lexicographers themselves.

Kenyon's article was instrumental in changing dictionary practice. What had been called "levels of usage" was from then on divided into a normative category (*standard/nonstandard*) and a stylistic one (*formal/informal*). In 1967, Martin Joos, in a short but important book, elaborated five styles that he compared to five clocks, each of which recorded a different time. Using another metaphor, he compared shifts in styles of speech (or *registers*) to the changes of clothes appropriate to different situations: "pajamas and overalls and committee-meeting suit."[29]

The five styles Joos specifies are, in order of decreasing formality: frozen, formal, consultative, casual, and intimate. The *consultative* style is used when it is assumed that one will not be understood unless one provides background information. The listener is treated like a stranger, though he participates fully, interrupting when necessary to ask questions or offer comments. The consultative style is normally used in business situations where a degree of informality is common, especially in America. In the *formal* style, "participation drops out," either because the assembly of listeners is too large or the speaker is too much given to command or too self-absorbed to tolerate listener participation. The formal style is also used for the first exchange between "urbane strangers," which Joos says, somewhat waggishly, lasts about six seconds. However, there are very few urbane strangers to be addressed formally, as Bergen Evans and Cornelia Evans note, writing for an American audience (in 1957!): "Forty years ago it was considered courteous to use formal English in speaking to strangers . . . Today it is more flattering to address strangers as if they were one's intimate friends. This is a polite lie, of course; but it is today's good manners. Modern usage encourages informality wherever possible and reserves formality for very few occasions."[30] British usage retained a more formal style between strangers far longer than American usage, but it too has adopted a more informal style both in business situations and in interactions between strangers. Joos' formal style is used to inform, and it is more detached (employing "one" rather than "I," for instance) and more cohesive in sentence structure than the consultative style. (This book is written mainly in the formal style, though now and then I lapse – as right now – into the consultative mode.) The *frozen* style is entirely written or declaimed without intonation. It is used in traditional formal situations and has all the warmth and spontaneity of a railroad timetable or a summons to jury duty. Car-rental forms and apartment leases are in the frozen style.

On the informal side, the *casual* style is typically used among friends and, unlike the consultative, requires no background information. It is studded with slang and with such ellipses as "can't find him" or "over here." In a passage that could well describe Internet or e-mail communication today – although written thirty years before it would become widely available – Joos describes the casual style as "for friends, acquaintances, insiders; addressed to a stranger, it serves to make him an insider simply by treating him as an insider." The description captures the implicit bond that people, even strangers, often feel when communicating over the Internet, enabling them to dispense with the traditional formulas used in paper transactions. The instantaneity of Internet communication gives it more of the quality of speech than of writing, though it is not speech. It is something in between. Perhaps we need another label for the virtual speech typical of electronic communication.

The *intimate* style is virtually in code, depending upon long familiarity, and is not often used to convey information. Whereas slang is used in the casual style to signal that both listener and speaker are insiders and are attuned to the same restricted vocabulary, slang is not used in the intimate style, because intimates do not have to be told they are insiders. "Each intimate group must invent its own code," or jargon, that individualizes it.[31]

In practice, the styles that dictionaries can distinguish correspond to some extent with Joos' formal, consultative, and casual styles. The consultative style is unmarked. The formal style is marked in some dictionaries (especially ESL dictionaries) with the label *formal*; other dictionaries do not distinguish it from the consultative style. The casual style, which corresponds to what used to be called *colloquial*, is now represented by *informal* or *slang* labels. The frozen style, if represented at all, is marked with a variety of labels: field labels (such as *law*), temporal labels (such as *archaic*), or style labels (such as *literary*). The intimate style is unrepresented in dictionaries.

The difficulty in determining style and status (*standard* vs. *nonstandard*) is that the criteria for both are not strictly linguistic but depend to a considerable extent on social context. This is the meaning of Joos' comparison of styles of speech to pajamas, overalls, or business suits. Neither lexicographers nor linguists are equipped to evaluate social context reliably. At pains to defend the decision to drop the *informal* label from *NID3*, Philip Gove cites the example of Leonard Bernstein, dressed in formal attire at the dedication of Lincoln Center in New York, asking Mrs. Bernstein, Mrs. John F. Kennedy, and Aaron Copland in an interview televised coast to coast, "Can you sweat it out?" Gove asks, "How much more formal in time and place can conversation get?"[32] Such a rigid standard for determining style suggests that no public utterance by any high government official or anyone in formal dress can be other than formal. That is to say, neither the president of the United States nor the British prime minister can speak publicly and informally. Certainly the social situation, including dress of the speaker, influences our perception of linguistic style, but no single criterion can be used to determine it. Gove's standard would preclude the possibility of deliberately using the warmth of an informal style to relax others, as Bernstein clearly did in the instance cited by Gove. Apart from that, much humor depends on the unexpected contrast of normally incompatible stylistic varieties.

What, then, determines style? The answer, even a partial, tentative answer, cannot be proffered without backtracking to review the historical forces that have shaped our attitudes towards usage, specifically to the status levels of standard and nonstandard. For although Kenyon's distinction between functional varieties and cultural levels is accepted by virtually all dictionaries, the public feels, and some well-known critics continue to argue, that style and status are related. Some linguistic studies suggest that they are not wholly wrong.

ATTITUDES TOWARDS USAGE AND THE NOTION OF CORRECTNESS

The teaching of English grammar in the seventeenth century was intended to prepare students for the study of Latin grammar. English was considered inferior to Latin, and approximations of Latin grammatical forms in English translation were used to drill students in Latin. Those English constructions were considered to be correct if they corresponded to the Latin equivalents and incorrect if they did not. For example, the rule of not ending a sentence in a preposition stems from analogy with Latin grammar. As Karl Dykema observes, the eighteenth-century grammarian was thoroughly conversant with classical grammar but had no basis for analyzing English in its own terms.[33] The tremendous interest in grammar in the eighteenth century is exemplified by the publication of about fifty grammars in the first half of the century and more than 200 in the second half. The prevailing theories governing instruction in English grammar assumed that there was an ideal English, now debased, and that English was a corrupt descendant of Latin and Greek.[34] Nineteenth-century textbooks were collections of rules based on these assumptions; they ignored actual usage. Many of the early grammarians were retired clergy, well versed in Latin, who expressed their disapproval of deviations from correct grammar in strongly moral terms. Popular commentators on usage are now more likely to be newspaper or television journalists, authors, literary critics, or professors of literature, but the tone of moral outrage has not changed. Verbal solecisms are frequently denounced as if they were morally indecent, not just trivial errors but fundamental assaults on dignified communication and the tradition of human civilization. This section will seek to explain why this is so.

Historical treatment of usage in dictionaries and grammars

Edward Phillips' *The New World of English Words* (1658) used symbols to mark certain words considered "hard words" or technical words, and in later editions Phillips compiled a list of words "to be used warily, and upon occasion only, or totally to be rejected as Barbarous, and illegally compounded or derived; the most notorious of which last are noted with an Obelisk."[35] Nathan Bailey's supplementary volume (1727) to *An Universal Etymological English Dictionary* (1721) employed a symbol to distinguish questionable usages from standard ones. Although Johnson proposed in his *Plan* (1747) to use a variety of symbols to denote questionable usages in his dictionary, in practice he appended a warning or brief notation, such as *low, barbarous, cant, ludicrous,* or *coarse.*

Robert Lowth's *Short Introduction to English Grammar* (1762), published in England seven years after Johnson's *Dictionary,* was based on the presumption that English grammar had been neglected and was in a state of disorder that needed correction and standardization, much as spelling had been by Johnson's *Dictionary.* He accused even the "best authors" of making mistakes and set about affirming rules and illustrations of proper use.[36] Although Lowth, later Bishop Lowth, recognized the principle that usage governs correctness, he held with other eighteenth-century grammarians that logic, analogy, and his own sense of proper form – moderated by Latin models – overrode the dictates of usage. His book was widely read and extremely influential.

For Americans, the most influential grammar of the early nineteenth century was that of Lindley Murray, an American living in England. His *English Grammar,* closely modeled on Bishop Lowth's work, appeared in England in 1795 and in Boston in 1800. It was enormously successful, going through more than 300 editions and selling 2 million copies in Britain and America. As Edward Finegan observes, Murray was a devoutly pious man with a sense of mission. He tended to view linguistic propriety as a matter of right and wrong. Like Bishop Lowth, he saw his grammar not simply as a work of linguistic guidance but as a moral instrument for correcting bad behavior. He adopted the unfortunate practice of illustrating the usage he deplored with invented sentences that no native speaker would ever use. For the rest of the century, millions of schoolchildren would have to endure the examination of countless illustrations of bad grammar in wholly fantastic sentences, such as "Never no imitator ever grew up to his author" and "The fields look freshly and gayly since the rain."[37] Two other important grammarians of this period were Goold Brown and Samuel Kirkham, both of whom, like Murray, viewed their grammars as morally inspired. Both included copious examples of proscribed usages, often from passages of each other's work that were not intended to illustrate error: they were bitter rivals. Goold Brown, while not equal to Murray in influence, was widely read and respected. Goold Brown's voluminous *The Grammar of English Grammars* (1851) delighted in pointing out putative errors of other grammarians. The petty and mean-spirited nature of the work – Johnson would have called it "peevish" – is apparent on every page, as in this quotation:

Dr. Webster gives us explanations like these: "CHINESE, *n. sing. and pl.* A native of China; also the language of China." – "JAPANESE, *n.* A native of Japan; or the language of the inhabitants." – "GENOESE, *n. pl.* The people of Genoa in Italy . . ." – "IRISH, *n.* 1. A native of Ireland. 2. The language of the Irish; the Hiberno-Celtic." According to him, then, it is proper to say, a Chinese, a Japanese, or an Irish; but not, a Genoese, because he will have this word to be plural only! Again, if with him we call a native of Ireland *an Irish*, will not more than one be Irishes? If a native of Japan be a Japanese, will not more than one be Japaneses?[38]

The minor style inconsistencies exhibited by these entries hardly merit Brown's heavy sarcasm, but the tone is typical of grammar books of his day. Brown continues, at great length, to expound the proposition that all such words are adjectives only, except in reference to languages. Brown cites innumerable examples of actual "incorrect" usages from Lowth's and Murray's grammars as well as from the great writers of English literature, such as Addison. From any rational view he would seem to have collected a vast body of evidence to refute his own argument, but to Goold Brown the usage of the greatest writers was of no account compared to his own peculiar appreciation of the logic underlying grammar.

There were nineteenth-century grammarians who disputed the views of Kirkham, Brown, and like-minded authors, but they were greatly overshadowed by the traditionalists and comparatively little known by the general public. Joseph Priestley in *Rudiments of English Grammar* (1861) accepted the principle that language change is natural and that current custom determines correctness. Noah Webster's views wavered between those of Priestley and Lowth; he endorsed usage in theory but in practice prescribed what was correct with little regard for usage. William Dwight Whitney, the Sanskrit scholar who would later assume the editorship of *The Century Dictionary*, wrote *Essentials of English Grammar* (1877), a school text, in which he maintained that the function of grammar was not to set rules but to describe actual usage "in an orderly way." This is the view of grammar now universally accepted by linguists. The grammarian seeks to uncover the principles and organization that underlie naive speech and make it coherent. Whitney defined good usage as the usages of the best speakers and of the best educated, and poor usage as the usages the best speakers disapproved of. He did not say how one would determine who the best speakers were. The definition thus appears to be circular, but it is still the one most commonly used. Nearly a century later, Morris Bishop, writing in an introductory article in the *American Heritage Dictionary* (*AHD*), states that those best fitted to determine good usage are "the enlightened members of the community . . . those professional speakers and writers who have demonstrated their sensitiveness to the language and their power to wield it effectively and beautifully."[39]

If we can tell who the best speakers are only by examining the quality of their usage, and if we cannot evaluate the quality of usage without knowing who the best speakers are, where are we? Clearly, there must be some independent means for determining either quality of usage or quality of speaker; they cannot be interdependent, no matter how cleverly one phrases the equation. Some scholarly studies, which we shall examine in the following section, have attempted by various means to address this question. The teaching of English, however, has until recently continued to follow the traditional pattern of Bishop Lowth and Lindley Murray and view all usages as either right or wrong. Thomas Pyles has written: "[The] inadequately educated, unsophisticated teacher of the near past . . . has to a large extent fostered the layman's confused notions about English usage, his belief that there are many rules governing English which must not be broken by those who aspire to write and speak well." The teacher is unfairly called upon to resolve trivial questions of usage in conformity with the popular notion that he (or, more frequently, she) is an expert arbiter of right and wrong usage. If she demurs, she is apt to be thought incompetent or disobliging. In short, if she wishes to retain the confidence and respect she must have to carry on her work effectively, she must "falsify the facts of usage as [s]he knows them from first hand observation."[40]

Studies of usage by linguists

Four major linguistic societies were organized in the United States in the fifty-year period beginning about 1870. The American Philological Society was founded in 1869, the Modern Language Association in 1883, the National Council of Teachers of English in 1911, and the Linguistic Society of America in 1924. Collectively, these groups would have a major impact on shaping scholarly attitudes towards usage and changing the way English would be taught in the US, although change has been much slower in the secondary schools and grade schools than linguists had hoped. The general public and some scholars in other branches of the humanities have been much less affected by and often hostile to the recommendations of linguists. The National Council of Teachers of English (NCTE) has been in the forefront in trying to change the attitudes of English teachers, but all have collectively strengthened the professional standing and influence of the linguist in lexicography as well as in education at all levels of instruction.

One of the earliest studies of usage to attempt an objective approach was that of J. Lesslie Hall, whose *English Usage* (1917) analyzed 125 disputed usages by consulting 75,000 pages of English and American literature. His determination as to whether a usage was acceptable was based on whether reputable authors used it.

Sterling Leonard's *Doctrine of Correctness in English Usage 1700–1800* (1929) not only presented a wealth of information about eighteenth-century grammars but suggested that their rules were intended to maintain distinctions of social class between gentlemen and the lower classes. It was not foreseen, he said, that the lower classes would imitate the usages that had been prescribed for their betters. It is hard to say whether usage guidance expressly for the privileged is any more elitist than the approach used by the *AHD*, in which "the ordinary user . . . can discover just how and to what extent his presumed betters agree on what he ought to say or write."[41] This instance of modern elitism recalls the demands of Swift and other eighteenth-century men of letters for an academy to "fix" usage.[42]

From its first publication in 1969, the *AHD* has relied upon a usage panel of "well-known writers, critics, and scholars" to serve as exemplars of educated writers who can guide the rest of us in matters of usage. In *AHD4*, however, Geoffrey Nunberg does not assert that the panel's task is to determine what correct usage is; the panel is not to be thought of as an Academy, he says. The panel's collective judgment "merely reflects the predominant practices of Standard English," which he defines as "the variety that happens to have been adopted by the educated middle-classes," but there is no reason to assume that the panel, an elite group of writers, scholars, and critics, share the predominant practices of standard English, or know what they are. The discovery of such practices is, precisely, the business of lexicographers. Nunberg admits that "the facts of use" must be taken into consideration, but argues that

"Whatever lexicographers may say they are doing, they invariably deal in critical evaluations of the raw facts of use."[43] Lexicographers do, indeed, evaluate "the raw facts of use," but their evaluation is not critical in the sense in which Nunberg uses it here. Lexicographers do not exercise any critical faculty or literary style or expression in evaluating the facts of usage. In its current edition, *AHD4* continues the policy of the previous edition in giving a balanced view of disputed usages rather than simply voicing the prejudices of conservative critics. Nunberg (or whoever composed the usage notes in *AHD4*) often performs the function of the lexicographer by making extensive comments on the comments of the usage panel members, and some of the best notes do not seem to be based on survey results from the panel.

Now, as in the eighteenth century, the emphasis is on preserving the significance of differences in usage that are linked to social class, but the market for usage guidance has broadened considerably. One must be forgiven for suspecting that, mixed with the concern for the ordinary user that underlies present-day attention to correct usage, is the awareness that insecurity about usage is good business. If nearly everybody thinks his speech needs to be monitored and corrected – or if nearly everybody thinks he or she is too fat and ought to lose some weight – nearly everybody is a potential customer. In Britain, where linguistic insecurity is less prevalent than in the United States, the market for usage guidance is much smaller.

Leonard next devoted himself to taking a survey of linguists, teachers, authors, editors, and others, and asked them to rate 102 usages. They were asked not for their own opinions but rather for their observations of actual usage. Nonetheless, as several critics have pointed out, the responses often reflected the opinions of the respondents. The study, sponsored by the NCTE and published in 1932 under the title *Current English Usage*, was undertaken to show that actual usage was less conservative than had been represented in textbooks. Ironically, the Leonard study set the precedent for soliciting the advice of presumed authorities about usage that *AHD* would adopt forty years later with the aim of showing that good usage was more conservative than commonly believed.

Although *Current English Usage* is widely viewed as a pioneering advance in the study of usage, it is seriously flawed. The presumption that those polled had enough facts at their command to give a meaningful response was unwarranted, and the assumption that their judgments would be uncolored by prejudice or the appeal of prestige forms was unjustified. Albert H. Marckwardt and Fred Walcott's NCTE study, *Facts About Current English Usage* (1938), attempted to objectify Leonard's data by comparing his conclusions with the recorded evidence of usage in various published sources, including the *OED* and *NID2*. Leonard had said that dictionaries tended to lag behind informed opinion of usage, but the Marckwardt and Walcott study shows that, on the contrary, the opinions of Leonard's respondents lagged far behind the record of usage as reported in dictionaries. The actual usage reported by these dictionaries was far less conservative than Leonard's experts said it was.[44]

Charles C. Fries' study of usage, *American English Grammar* (1940), is the first attempt to establish independent social criteria for categorizing style of expression.[45] It is one of the most original and thoughtful studies of English usage ever made. Fries obtained the right to use 2,000 handwritten letters and parts of another 1,000 letters addressed to the United States government, chiefly involving complaints and requests for some bureaucratic action to alleviate financial or other distress. Because the correspondents evidently had had to complete applications about themselves, Fries was able to identify most correspondents by age, schooling, occupation, place of birth, and in some cases by a confidential report describing the domestic conditions of the letter writer. All letters were those of Americans whose families were native to the country for at least three generations. He was thus able to classify the writers by social class before examining what they wrote. He divided them into three noncomprehensive groups: many people did not fit into any of the three groups.

Group III consisted of people with less than an eighth-grade education whose occupations were those of manual or unskilled laborer. Their letters showed a pattern of misspelling of simple words, no punctuation, and the violation of elementary conventions, such as the failure to capitalize the personal pronoun *I*. The writing of Group III was called "vulgar" and considered nearly illiterate.

Group I, at the other end of the scale, consisted of graduates of reputable colleges, members of professions, and army officers above the rank of lieutenant. Their letters showed a pattern of observing the conventions of spelling, punctuation, and capitalization. The writing of Group I was called "standard" and considered socially acceptable.

Group II, the majority of the correspondents, fell between these extremes. Their schooling consisted of from one year of high school to one year of college; their occupations, neither manual nor professional, included those of salespeople, skilled laborers, nurses, and noncommissioned officers in the army. Their letters conformed to the ordinary rules of capitalization and end punctuation and did not have misspellings of very simple words, but otherwise misspellings and departures from conventional form were tolerated. The writing of Group II was called "popular" or common.

It may be objected that Fries' use of the observance of formal rules of spelling and punctuation involved linguistic and not social criteria, thus impeaching the integrity of the study. But if the linguistic features used as group criteria are unrelated to the grammatical constructions under study – and that was the case – there can be no objection to their use. Indeed, the inclusion of a set of linguistic criteria unrelated to the linguistic criteria being studied is an ingenious tactic and may well be the single most important contribution of Fries' work to the future study of usage. One sign of standard English is a standard way of writing the language, "accepted (with some slight variations) all over the world as the 'right way' to spell, no matter what the English it represents sounds like."[46]

By placing each correspondent in a group, Fries could analyze statistically the differences in particular grammatical usages between one group and the next, and could thus call certain usages "vulgar" and others "standard" or "popular" without circularity. Fries does not imply any derogation of usages labeled "vulgar." He accepts the position that grammar is purely descriptive and that if any locution is in general use it is by definition grammatical. Usage and only usage, he says, is the basis of correctness. He defines standard English as that form of English "used in the conduct of the important affairs of our people. It is also the type of English used by the *socially acceptable* [his italics] of most of our communities and insofar as that is true it has become a social or class dialect in the United States." But it is not standard, he emphasized, because it is "more correct or more beautiful or more capable than other varieties of English."[47] Fries felt that it was the responsibility of the schools to teach this variety, since it was the means by which students could aspire to gain acceptance and prosper. In spite of all the hullabaloo over the supposed permissiveness of linguists, the great majority of linguists and linguistically informed educators still endorse Fries' position, though they may have differing views about the best way to teach standard English.

Largely as a result of the pioneering work of Fries, it was gradually realized that if we were ever to be able to make judgments about style or status we must know a great deal more about the social conditions in which language is used. The need for linguists versed in sociological techniques led eventually to the creation of a new branch of linguistics called *sociolinguistics*, which developed to record and analyze social rather than regional dialects – that is, dialects of social or economic class, ethnic background, or race.

William Labov's *The Social Stratification of English in New York City* (1966) employed much more sophisticated sociological criteria for establishing distinctions of social class than Fries had used.[48] Each informant was graded on a four-point numerical scale according to education, occupation, and income. The resulting numerical index placed each person in one of three groups: lower class, working class, or middle class which was in turn subdivided into lower middle class and upper middle class. Each informant was tested and recorded on tape recorders for five styles: casual, careful, reading, word list, and "minimal pairs." Labov's styles were selected along a continuum of self-monitoring, addressing the question, To what extent is the speaker aware of the style of his or her own speech? Casual speech defines a style used in relaxed conversation; careful speech is typical of a formal interview. The other three styles refer to reading a narrative, a list of words, and selected pairs of words (such as *guard* and *god* or *source* and *sauce*) designed to reveal particular phonological features such as the pronunciation of *r*.

Through ingenious techniques, Labov was able to test informants in all three categories. In one part of his study he spent hours pretending to be lost in three New York City department stores – catering respectively to the wealthy, the middle class, and the lower class – and asking employees where he could find an article that he knew to be on the fourth floor. When they said "Four" or "Fourth" he pretended not to have heard them to see whether the emphatic repetition – no longer casual – duplicated the feature being tested. He became friendly with black and white teenagers and young men and women who habitually socialized on the streets in sections of New York where poor people lived, and after being accepted as a familiar could engage them in conversation as well as subject them to more formal study. This took a great deal of time, tact, and the gift of a manner that would invite trust rather than suspicion. Whereas Fries worked from handwritten, unedited materials exclusively – the closest thing to speech he could get – Labov worked directly with people and recorded their speech. As important as Fries' work was, therefore, Labov's method cut away an intermediate step in the examination of usage. The recording of speech itself was nothing new; it had been used for many years in studying regional dialect. What was new was Labov's use of the technique for describing style variation by social class. Methodologically his work was far and away the most soundly crafted study of its kind.

One of the more interesting findings of his study is that the New Yorkers' report of their own usage is very inaccurate. What they actually report, he shows, is their norm of correctness. Labov suggests that the informant is not consciously lying. Rather, his "audio-monitoring norm" perceives his actual speech as if it were the norm. He hears the norm, not the speech. But Labov had the speech on tape and could verify that it was not what the speaker said it was. A series of words was read to the informant. Each word was pronounced several different ways. The informant was asked to circle the number corresponding to the way he pronounced the word; he could circle more than one number if he chose. Labov then checked the informant's choices against recordings previously made in which the informant had pronounced these words. If the choices corresponded to the actual pronunciations more than 50 percent of the time, the informant was considered to have accurately reported his usage. By this standard, few informants reported their usage accurately.

In another ingenious test, Labov determined the index of linguistic insecurity of his informants. "[T]he respondent is presented with a test which measures his tendency to consider his own pronunciation wrong, and to accept a pronunciation which he does not use, as right." It is a very simple test. Each of a series of words is pronounced two ways and the respondent is asked to circle the number of the pronunciation he thinks is correct. Then he is asked to mark the pronunciation he actually uses. "The number of items in which the respondent circles one form and checks another is the index of linguistic insecurity."[49]

Labov found that linguistic insecurity was highest among the lower middle class and much less among the upper middle class. About half of the lower and working classes had no measurable linguistic insecurity; they used the forms they regarded as correct. But the other half showed greater linguistic insecurity than the upper middle class. The working-class group was less insecure than the lower class. Women had a much higher index of linguistic insecurity – 50 percent higher – than men. Labov also showed in another test that women exhibit "a more extreme range of stylistic variation than men – a much greater degree of correction in formal style."[50] When we remember that the great majority of school teachers in America in the nineteenth and early twentieth centuries were drawn from the ranks of lower-middle-class women, Labov's findings help to explain the exaggerated emphasis on correctness taught in most traditional schools during this period.

Dictionary treatment of usage and the controversy over Webster's Third New International Dictionary

Clearly, the traditional approach to correctness in usage inherited from nineteenth-century grammarians was incompatible with that of twentieth-century linguists, and the two were bound to come into conflict. Dictionaries had always relied on scholars for guidance in etymology, but the *American College Dictionary* (*ACD*) broke new ground in 1947 by relying on a team of advisers who were among the most prominent linguists in the US. Its editorial advisory committee consisted of Leonard Bloomfield, Charles Fries, Cabell Greet, Irving Lorge, and Kemp Malone. The *ACD* was an enormously successful dictionary, and no college dictionary after it could afford to ignore modern linguistics.

In 1952 a commission of the NCTE published *The English Language Arts*, which presumed to advise teachers about structural linguistics. It specified five basic principles:
1. Language changes constantly.
2. Change is normal.
3. Spoken language *is* the language.
4. Correctness rests on usage.
5. All usage is relative.
It adopted the definition of "good English" of Robert C. Pooley, who had defined it as "that form of speech which is appropriate to the purpose of the speaker, true to the language as it is, and comfortable to speaker and listener. It is the product of custom, neither cramped by rule nor freed from all restraint."[51]

It was the apparent adoption of these dicta by *Webster's Third New International Dictionary* (*NID3*) in 1961 that so enraged many critics and set the stage for a public controversy.[52] Criticisms by Dwight Macdonald in the *New Yorker,* Jacques Barzun in *American Scholar*, and Wilson Follett in the *Atlantic* were often quoted in contemporary accounts. On the one hand, Merriam-Webster's aggressive and misconceived promotional efforts had aggravated the problem by exaggerating the degree of linguistic innovation in *NID3*. On the other, many of the criticisms were based on ignorance of the actual content of the dictionary or on misunderstandings of how dictionaries are prepared. But even when one has hacked away the luxuriant overgrowth of tangled misconceptions, biases, jealousy, spite, glory seeking, and plain muddleheadedness, there remains a kernel of truth in some of the criticisms. Here is Philip Gove, editor of *NID3*: "Not putting a label on a word even with hundreds of citations suggesting what the label might be does not mean that a reader is unable to do so mentally for its use in a particular context."[53] In spirit, this seems uncomfortably close to the abdication of responsibility with which *NID3* was charged. The reader does not have hundreds of citations at his disposal; the lexicographer does. Dictionaries had always assumed that their editors were better able to make decisions about usage than their readers were. If they weren't, what were they doing editing dictionaries?

What caused *NID3* to take this position? Why, to be specific, did it originally insist on not capitalizing any entries except *God*, on labeling very few words as *slang* or *nonstandard*, on omitting the *informal* label entirely? Why did it so often decline to provide usage guidance for the reader?

First of all, it must be remembered that older textbooks, often called derisively "Dick and Jane" textbooks for their stereotyped descriptions of white, middle-class America, were the near descendants of the highly moralistic textbooks of an earlier generation. Dictionaries were following the trend of other educational books by dropping – or at least moderating – traditional, middle-class biases in evaluating behavior. Secondly, the way publishers promoted dictionaries was – and is – often fundamentally at odds with the way the dictionaries were actually prepared. As Herbert Morton has pointed out, the publicity campaign for *NID3* encouraged the idea that everything in the dictionary was new and that the dictionary was revolutionary in design, emphasizing its practice of citing contemporary writers in its illustrative quotations. This was misleading at best. Its defining style, depending on a definiens with subordinate clauses buried within it without interior punctuation, was innovative, and its pronunciation system was certainly elaborate – many would say too elaborate – but to call them revolutionary was hyperbolic. The use of contemporary writers for illustrative quotations was not new, although *NID3* made greater use of them than previous Merriam-Webster dictionaries had done.[54]

For many years Merriam-Webster's unabridged dictionaries had been advertised as "the supreme authority." Although the slogan was not used for *NID3*, for promotional reasons the company had always encouraged the idea that people could look to the Merriam-Webster dictionaries to find out what was right. The advertising deliberately blurred the difference between standard English and correct English. The publishers "solicited, quoted, and disseminated the opinions of jurists and educators who said they looked to the Merriam dictionaries for the best answers to questions of meaning and usage. It invited the inference that Merriam editors and consultants were arbiters of what was correct and incorrect in the use of the English language."[55] Small wonder that some readers felt deceived when they discovered that *NID3* failed to note whether a term were informal or slang, standard or nonstandard, in contexts that suggested that some qualifying label was called for. Yet, to be fair, *NID3* did include some slang labels; it did give some usage guidance. By no means did it altogether reject the needs of the user. Though Gove's insistence on evidence was admirable, he was inflexible in not permitting his staff to interpret it more often for the benefit of users. Too often one feels that *NID3* would rather be unhelpful than risk being wrong.

The user expects guidance on many aspects of usage, but unfortunately the description of attitudes towards usage can never be entirely factual. One group may regard a particular usage as informal or nonstandard, whereas others may use it and regard it as entirely natural for any conceivable circumstance. When we talk about disputed usage, or what I should rather call "class markers," we are not marking the class of those who use them so much as those to whom their usage is objectionable. For example, the record plainly shows that most people of all classes customarily make no distinction between *disinterested* and *uninterested* or between *nauseated* and *nauseous*, yet critics continue to note the alleged differences in urgent or melancholy tones. Such a fastidious attitude serves to mark the critic as belonging to a high social class. The situation is analogous to that of a guest remarking on transposed forks in the place settings at a dinner table. As Dwight Bolinger puts it: "The *lie-lay* distinction is fragile and impractical, and the price of maintaining it is too high. But that is exactly what makes it so useful as a social password: without the advantage of a proper background or proper schooling, you fail."[56]

We cannot say that the principal motive of those people who pass judgment on others' usage is to mark their own class as higher than those they criticize, but their criticism certainly has that effect. When an action always produces certain results, it is safe to say that some people will perform the action to produce the effect. Indeed, since American society is in theory egalitarian, the evident superiority of usage critics must be formally denied even while it is patent. Usage critics commonly confess that they themselves have been guilty of many of the same infractions they deplore in others. (Just so, the dinner guest may laugh and say, "Oh, I always forget which way the forks go too!") It is a way of lessening the severity of the charge, of *noblesse oblige*, a token acknowledgment, even though both parties know it to be false, that speaker and critic are of the same social class. The difference between critics of table settings and usage is that critics of usage often act as though their objections were mainly moral rather than a matter of social grace. The dinner guest may or may not be a snob. The mere recognition of a social error does not make anyone a snob; it merely reflects breeding. It is the importance one attaches to the error and the way it affects one's behavior towards the culprit that makes one a snob. Likewise, the mere recognition of stigmatizing usages convicts one only of having had an old-fashioned education or of being sensitive to language use. But to accuse those whose usage differs from one's own of corrupting the language or of being sloppy thinkers, as the panjandrums of correctness routinely do, is quite another matter.

If usage cannot be determined without reference to social class, which class will be the standard? Pooley had described the informal style as one including words and phrases used by people "in their more informal moments, but which are generally excluded from formal public address, social conversation with strangers, and formal social correspondence."[57] Apart from the difficulty of determining socially informal moments, the very wording suggests a strong bias towards the upper class and upper middle class. Except for listening to an occasional formal public address, such as a political speech on television or an educational lecture, most people do not hear any formal speech. Social conversation with strangers, especially in the US, is not usually formal except among the very privileged and in elegant shops or restaurants that cater to the wealthy. For most people, formal social correspondence is mainly a matter of weddings, graduations, and deaths, and when compared to their overall use of language plays no role whatsoever. There is no real distinction between formal and informal usage except among the privileged and highly educated. To the extent that dictionaries of the past were created by and for this class, the distinction was possible and meaningful. But if dictionaries are to be directed towards a wider – though still not all-inclusive – group, they cannot in good faith mark out some usages as informal without saying to whom they are informal. *Informal* actually means "informal for those of the higher social classes, especially older, well-educated authors and professors in the humanities." We ought not then to be surprised that dictionaries differ so in their treatment of this label, since their estimations of the attitudes towards usage of a loosely defined educated class are also apt to differ.

Perhaps we can now understand why *NID3* omitted the *informal* label. The editors may have felt they could not define or know the attitudes of the class of people to whom some usages would be informal. They also knew that the proposed definition of *informal* as "more often used in speech than in writing," i.e., colloquial, was entirely specious. No one knew in the 1950s – when *NID3* was being written – what usages were more often used in speech than in writing. In deciding not to use the *informal* label, *NID3* simply declined to represent a particular social class. For an unabridged dictionary committed primarily to describing the language fully, it was a sound decision, though unpopular with critics who belonged to the social class thus disenfranchised. On the other hand, criticisms of *NID3* for using the *slang* label so sparingly seem to me justified. Smaller dictionaries are probably unwise to dispense with the *informal* label, though it needs better definition, and with the development of corpora of spoken English, more accurate labels may now be possible. (See "Dictionary treatment of usage in the future," p. 268.)

Gove's inflexible policies are also evident in the decision not to capitalize any entry (except for *God*) in the original edition of 1961. This resulted in thousands of absurd entries like that for *american*, labeled *usu. cap*, and for all the compounds with *american* in them. It is hard to fathom the reasoning behind this bizarre decision. Perhaps Gove felt that to capitalize an entry would signify that it was a name, and since no names or encyclopedic items were to be included in the dictionary, none should be capitalized. Perhaps he felt that since the "spoken language *is* the language" (in the view of structural linguistics), the form of the entries should not be modified by any graphemic convention that would obscure its existence as a sequence of sounds. Whatever the reasoning, it was a mistake, justly criticized by almost everybody.

Status labels present some of the same difficulties as style labels, but it is more important to know when one is using a nonstandard usage than an informal one. Labov has said that all speakers shift styles depending upon the relationship of the speaker to listener, the social context, and the topic. Contrary to Kenyon's assertion that functional varieties and cultural levels are entirely distinct, Labov showed that they were related. For example, the use of /d/ for /ð/ in words like *this* and *then* varied both by class (lower, working, lower middle, and upper middle) and by style (casual speech, careful speech, reading style, word list reading). The use of /d/ occurred in all classes in casual speech, though more frequently in the lower classes than in the upper. It occurred in all classes with decreasing frequency as the style became more formal. Labov remarks that if Kenyon's view were right, "no matter how casually an educated person spoke, we would have no trouble in recognizing him as an educated person," since all of his usages, formal or casual, would be standard usages. But this is not the case. "In actual fact, the same variables which are used in style shifting also distinguish cultural or social levels in English."[58]

For years lexicographers had been assuring dictionary users that style labels like *informal* suggest no animadversion against such usages. Informal usages are perfectly standard, they said and reiterated whenever possible. Well, they are standard – but not perfectly, for if Labov is right, the more informal the variety of style, the more likely it is that the style will include nonstandard usages *in every social class*. We cannot simply say, as many have, that standard English is the usage of the better-educated, higher social classes of a community, for at least in their casual speech these classes, too, use forms – though less frequently than lower classes – that are widely regarded as nonstandard. In the most formal style – the reading of word lists – the nonstandard form /d/ tended to disappear entirely in the lower middle and upper middle classes and diminished sharply in the lower class and working class. Informal speech is thus more apt than formal speech to include nonstandard forms. The degree of self-monitoring is greater as formality increases and usages perceived as incorrect are suppressed. As Martin Joos remarks, "Since usage differences call for efforts to keep them under control, there must be rewards for the efforts. They must have survival values."[59] Indeed they must.

Since all social classes use nonstandard forms casually, we cannot rely on the actual usage of any social class for determining standard English. Rather, we must rely – as with style levels – on the attitudes towards usage of a particular range of social classes. *NID3*'s modest and probably futile attempt to enlarge the range of its coverage of social classes was interpreted by critics as a rejection of any standard. The critics were right to assert that by including without comment a greater range of social and educational classes than had previously been recognized by *NID2*, *NID3* was broadening its definition of *standard*, but *NID3* was right to do so. The world had changed since 1934 when *NID2* was published, and has changed even more since 1961 when *NID3* was published. Radio and television had vastly increased the penetration of forms that would previously have remained local. Standard English can no longer be based on the elitist writing approved by authors of usage handbooks. If tens of millions of people hear and use certain locutions, apparently without disapproving of them, by what right can a dictionary charged with the responsibility of describing usage say they are wrong?

It is a mistake to regard standard English as a rigidly definable category. As Pooley has observed, standard usage describes a range of acceptable variations. What may be standard for one social context would be improper for another.[60] Moreover, even within the same social context, the point at which standard usage becomes nonstandard usually cannot be detected. A cultural level represents a continuum and its divisions, like the arbitrary divisions of taxonomy, are merely a human convenience imposed upon nature. Standard usage is an artificial construct that is immensely helpful in teaching English and in guiding people who are ambitious to adopt forms that are more generally acceptable among those people who have the power to reward them. It is not heaven-sent truth.

The sciences, too, are largely composed of concepts that upon close analysis have no beginning and no end but, like standard English, are useful because they are of great practical importance. The more fundamental the idea, the harder it is to define. Dr. J. L. Burton, writing in a dermatological journal, had occasion to make these remarks on the nature of *disease*:

It is difficult to define the general concept of "a disease." J. G. Scadding has given considerable thought to this problem . . . and he now defines the term as follows: "in medical discourse, the name of a disease refers to the sum of the abnormal phenomena displayed by a group of living organisms in association with a specified common characteristic by which they differ from the norm of their species in such a way as to place them at a biological disadvantage." . . . Dermatologists may be interested to note that, according to this definition, acne vulgaris is not a disease. Acne patients do not differ from the norm since the majority of the age-matched population suffers from the same condition. Moreover, those individuals who never get any sign of acne are more likely to have a decreased level of androgens and a correspondingly decreased libido. If one regards a tendency to decreased reproductive activity as a biological disadvantage, therefore, it is the lack of acne, rather than its presence, which constitutes a disease.

Homosexuality on the other hand, by this definition is a disease, and considering homosexuals do not reproduce, it is amazing that there are so many of them! The desire to go rock-climbing would similarly be a disease, unless the increased mortality of the rock-climber is counter-balanced by his increased fecundity, and so a homosexual rock-climber who had never had acne would be suffering from three diseases. Fortunately, such a patient would be unlikely to seek dermatological advice for his diseases, and so we will confine ourselves to the question of diagnosis of disease in those patients who do seek our advice.[61]

In spite of such criticism, the medical profession is not likely to abandon the notion of disease, nor should we abandon the notion of standard usage because it cannot be defined precisely.

Nonstandard varieties of English, notably Black English, have been studied by sociolinguists so that teachers might be better able to teach standard English to inner-city black children. If teachers could be made to understand that the black child's speech is not random or "illiterate" but conforms to grammatical rules that differ, often slightly, from standard grammar, they would not regard that speech with contempt and the children themselves would not regard their speech as inferior. Such, at least, is the theory underlying the sociolinguistic study of Black English, eloquently and persuasively presented by Labov in *The Study of Nonstandard English*. Familiarity with the structure of Black English can minimize conflict between teacher and student, such as that caused by confusing a difference in pronunciation with a mistake in reading. Some differences are typical of most southern American, rural speech, and others are apparently unique to Black English. But because most studies so far have dealt principally with pronunciation and grammar rather than with vocabulary, the study of Black English has had little impact on dictionaries. The *Dictionary of American Regional English* will provide the basis for recognizing those regionalisms used mainly by black speakers, but general dictionaries include few regional terms.

Modern usage guides

Usage guides are the twentieth-century descendants of the eighteenth- and nineteenth-century grammars discussed earlier in this chapter. They purport to instruct and caution us on the proper usage of language and are largely an American phenomenon, even though the greatest of them all, H. W. Fowler's *A Dictionary of Modern English Usage* (1926), is British. Fowler's work is distinctive because he brought to it a background in lexicography, considerable writing skill, and, at least occasionally, a sense of humor. He does not seem to have believed that the fate of the world hung in the balance of disputed usages, and his work is noteworthy for the large number of illustrative quotations shown for both "right" and "wrong" usages. He was the editor, with his brother, F. G. Fowler, of the first *Concise Oxford Dictionary* (1911) and the sole editor of the second edition (1929). Writers on both sides of the Atlantic have found his engaging style and the sheer volume of material encompassed irresistible, and his admirers are legion. In spite of a few instances where his interpretations can be called progressive, he was a defender of the attitudes of the well-educated, upper-class Englishman. The usages he recommended, however, do not reflect the usages of educated people in Britain or America today. Fortunately Robert Burchfield, the editor of the *OED Supplements*, has skillfully and sensitively revised Fowler's guide to do just that, in an edition retitled *The New Fowler's Modern English Usage* (1996). Called the Third Edition in order to keep Fowler's name in view, the book, as Burchfield says, "has been largely rewritten" (p. xi). This is no mere updating; Burchfield, though a great admirer of Fowler, well understood the limitations of the original work and has systematically examined, rejected, replaced, and rewritten everything in it. The citations adduced to support Burchfield's comments reflect current usage, and his judgments are more balanced and less idiosyncratic than Fowler's, without the caustic *hauteur* that many of Fowler's admirers so enjoyed. The book is really much more Burchfield than Fowler, and is a much better book.

The popularity of usage books in the United States reflects the degree of insecurity Americans feel about their use of language. We have seen in Labov's study that linguistic insecurity is felt most intensely among the middle class, the class most characterized by ambition to move up the scale of social acceptability. The mastery of a particular kind of language use is perceived, correctly, as important and usually essential for upward movement. Since American society is more fluid than British and movement between classes is more common, Americans are naturally more highly motivated to acquire the skills that will help satisfy their ambitions. In Britain, pronunciation alone (received pronunciation or an approximation of it) still serves to mark off the better-educated, privileged classes from others; but in America, every region has its own variety of standard pronunciation. Thus the distinctions that Americans look for and that usage guides help them find must depend on an arbitrary set of conventions dealing with particular items and involving chiefly diction (the choice of words) and grammar, with attention to pronunciation confined to a relatively few items.[62]

While linguists may deplore the attitudes expressed in usage guides, there is no doubt that such books are popular, and with good reason. The attitudes of others towards one's own use of language must be considered seriously by anyone who hopes to achieve practical goals. To deplore such attitudes, to argue that such attitudes ought not to exist, is to indulge in fancy and usually means that one is fortunate enough not to need ambition but wants to show one's sympathy for those who do. Since those who are ambitious and insecure are the great believers in prescriptive attitudes and buy the usage books that perpetuate them, scholars who are scornful of such attitudes must realize sooner or later that they are addressing only each other.

Most usage books are akin to the publishing genre known as "how to" books, a genre that is arguably the most profitable of all kinds of books published. Such books appeal to various kinds of insecurities and ambitions – social, economic, moral, sexual, health related, religious – and purport to tell the reader how to have a successful social life, how to get a better job, how to invest money and become rich, and so on. Modern usage guides combine the direct appeal to personal interest of such books with the qualities of a reference book, and can perhaps best be viewed as a kind of etiquette book. They deal with the manners of discourse and writing. They share the implied promise that if one takes their advice one will have made oneself linguistically acceptable to a higher class of society than one's own. They cannot be reasonably criticized for giving advice any more than a book of etiquette can be criticized for giving advice. The difficulty, as John Algeo has noted, is that usage guides usually fail to specify even vaguely the group whose norms they seek to represent.[63] Furthermore, the authority of usage books must depend ultimately on the presumption, whether stated or not, that the usages recommended are actually used by educated or cultivated speakers. For if they are not typical of educated usage, the book becomes a linguistic memoir rather than a guide to better usage. It makes no promise but says simply, "This is the way I do it," and presumes with wondrous innocence or arrogance that no further argument is needed to establish correctness. Yet for the vast majority of the usages dealt with there is no evidence to support the judgment made, and where there is evidence, it often flatly contradicts the conclusions drawn.

Wilson Follett's *Modern American Usage* (1966) states: "This discussion draws its authority from the principle that good usage is what the people who think and care about words believe good usage to be" (p. 6). This comes very close to being an *ipse dixit* declaration, since we must depend upon the authors to reveal to us the thoughts of those who "think and care about words," and the suspicion deepens that it is the authors themselves who constitute the only secure group in that category. Follett's book, which was completed after Follett's death by Jacques Barzun and others, has been revised (1998) by Erik Wensberg, who says the new edition treats about 500 words not considered in the earlier edition. Some of Follett's long-winded essays have been mercifully shortened and some deleted; one's general impression of the new edition, however, is that it is still very much Follett's book. Many of the entries have not been materially altered.

Richard A. Lanham criticizes usage books for their pettiness and shrill vocabulary of dos and donts:

How do you cultivate an "ear" [for language]? [Jacques] Barzun knows the answer as well as the Harper panelists – wide reading. You cannot memorize rules, you will not even want to try, until you have an intuitive knowledge of language, until you have cultivated some taste. Now usage dictionaries, if you browse through them, can help you confirm and sharpen your taste, but they are unlikely to awaken it. They move, again, in the opposite direction, argue that intuitive judgments are not intuitive but conceptual, codify them, render them a matter of rules. They would keep us perpetually on our "p's and q's," and a love for language does not lie that way. The perpetual single focus on correctness kills enjoyment, makes prose style into one long Sunday school. Usage dictionaries, that is, can teach us only what we already know. They tend to be the affectation of, well, of people specially interested in usage. They are most useful as the central document in a continuing word-game played by sophisticated people.[64]

How often have we not heard a usage expert taken to task for using in his own writing one of the very usages he inveighs against? For example, Stuart Sutherland reviews John Simon's *Paradigms Lost*, a traditional lament that language use has gone to hell; in the course of the review he upbraids Erica Jong for having written, "Everyone lies about their feelings." Three weeks later in the same periodical, a correspondent points out that Sutherland, in the same review in which he had criticized Jong, committed the same solecism by writing, "When someone seeks to tell others how to use words, the temptation to expose their own verbal sins is strong."[65] Can anyone doubt that this sort of pastime is played by people who have the leisure to indulge endless whimsy or who, like Goold Brown, are grimly committed to humiliating their peers?

In the history of usage guides, Bergen Evans and Cornelia Evans' *A Dictionary of Contemporary American Usage* is unusual in taking a moderately permissive approach. The Evanses define their recommended usages as "respectable English," "the kind of English that is used by the most respected people, the sort of English that will make readers or listeners regard you as an educated person."[66] This is a rather less restricted standard than Follett's. It is based on the presumed effect such usages will have on "readers or listeners" – not necessarily *careful* readers or listeners, or readers or listeners who "think and care about words" – just "readers and listeners." Ordinary people will regard you as educated if you follow our recommendations. This is what the Evanses promise. Their book is not essentially different from other usage guides; it merely represents the norms of a different class. It is also informed throughout with good humor and good sense and a much keener appreciation than other books of the history of language use, with special attention to differences between British and American usage.

Margaret Bryant's *Current American Usage*, on the other hand, *is* essentially different from every other usage book, since it does not purport to be a guide at all but to describe usage on the basis of actual studies. Much of its data was collected by the distinguished scholar James B. McMillan for a committee of the NCTE on English usage. Standard English is defined as "the type of language employed by leaders of our society, those who command respect and esteem, such as important journalists, statesmen, political figures, scientists, and business and professional people."[67] Though always limited in its coverage and now outdated because of the development of linguistic corpora, *Current American Usage* is an early and significant attempt to place usage data on an objective basis.

There are numerous other usage guides, more in America than in Britain. Among the leading British guides is that of Sidney Greenbaum and Janet Whitcut (*Longman Guide to English Usage*). Among the American guides are those of William and Mary Morris (*Harper Dictionary of Contemporary Usage*), Theodore M. Bernstein (*The Careful Writer*), Roy H. Copperud (*A Dictionary of Usage and Style*), and the Reader's Digest (*Success With Words*). The last-mentioned, in spite of its mass-market title, is in many respects more sophisticated than the other works cited. Edited by Peter Davies and David Rattray, *Success With Words* is not just a usage book but has articles on dialect, literary subjects, special lexicons, and etymology as well as on usage questions. Its approach to dialectal variation is objective and tolerant, demonstrating an awareness of contemporary research and a willingness to go into detail that is surprising and even courageous in a popularization for the mass market. Best of all, it includes numerous citations illustrating different usages, but the usage recommendations themselves are generally timid reaffirmations of the traditional prescriptive doctrine. We should nonetheless be grateful for the down-to-earth tone in which the usage advice is given, which lacks completely the sense of moral superiority characteristic of many traditional guides.

Up till now I have referred to this genre as *usage guides*, though many of the books call themselves dictionaries, because, though arranged in dictionary format, they are chiefly devoted to giving advice and the information they convey is secondary. *Webster's Dictionary of English Usage* (1989) (*WDEU*), edited by Ward Gilman and the Merriam-Webster staff, though it gives advice, is a dictionary first and foremost. It is the largest and the best of all the usage books, providing copious, authentic examples drawn from Merriam-Webster's citation files to back up its assertions about usage. Its editors have consulted a very large number of previous usage guides and frequently refer to them, often to disagree with their judgments. (These guides, along with many other books, are listed in an excellent bibliography at the back of the book.) The presumption, unusual in usage books, is that it is really possible to find out what the predominant usage has been, and the editors of *WDEU* see it as their job to investigate it and report it. *WDEU*'s tone is reasonable throughout and not heavy-handed; the writing style is straightforward and occasionally even humorous. The editors are not afraid to give advice, but they give reasons for it, and their reasons are based on evidence which they provide in the form of dated quotations with full bibliographic information. In the study of usage, *WDEU* is in a class of its own.

The Columbia Guide to Standard American English (1993) by Kenneth G. Wilson recognizes that the appropriateness of usage always depends on the nature of a particular social context. Borrowing the five styles originally set forth by Joos in *The Five Clocks*, Wilson uses them (in amended form) to govern the advice he gives.[68] In practice it is hard to see how these style levels affect the presentation of most entries, few of which are amenable to this treatment. The advice is sensible and enlightened, and many invented examples are given to illustrate particular usages.

The American Heritage Book of English Usage (1996) is one of the few usage guides that is arranged topically rather than in a single alphabetical list. It contains sections on grammar, style, word choice, science terms, gender, names and labels, pronunciation, word formation, and (oddly) e-mail. Along the top of each page is a set of symbols that resemble a computer screen's line of symbols (or *toolbar*) which identifies the section one is in. A word index and a subject index at the back help readers navigate to find an item they may be looking for. The *Book of English Usage* draws upon the responses of the usage panels of the American Heritage dictionaries. Unlike *CDEU*, the *Book of English Usage* is not concerned with reporting actual usage; it reports the attitudes of writers it respects. The editors have done a careful job of reporting these responses, but this precision is only of value if one accepts the two assumptions that would make it meaningful: first, that the usage panel is representative of that elusive category of careful or educated speakers that all usage books list as their exemplars in determining acceptable usage; and secondly, that the attitudes of any group, rather than the predominance of usage, determine acceptability in language use. *WDEU* places more reliance on the predominance of usage. Though it does not ignore the opinions and biases of the educated elite, it is careful to distinguish opinion from fact.

Bryan A. Garner's *A Dictionary of Modern American Usage* (1998) (*DMAU*) is by far the most individualistic of the current crop of usage guides. Garner's Preface has a tone of barely repressed anger at "descriptivists" and "professional linguists," who have "hijacked" usage dictionaries and who are afraid to give good advice. He at least will not be reluctant "to show the confusions into which writers fall," but it will be based on "current linguistic evidence."[69] Garner is vigorously opinionated about style, and many of his discussions employ the standards of analogy and logic to recommend against particular usages, though, to be fair, he is aware of the risk of relying on logic excessively. An immense amount of diligent research has gone into this book, but almost all of his critical comments about style have nothing to do with the research. He does use authentic examples, however, to illustrate his judgments. For example, he calls *conceptualize* "a bloated word that can be replaced by *conceive, think, visualize,* or *understand.*" This is followed by a number of actual quotations in which *conceptualize* occurs, and in which one of the other words could be used as a substitute. The author's attitude is at once informed, aggressively confident, and didactic, but the advice he gives is often not so different from the descriptivist writers of usage dictionaries he complains about in his Preface. Garner is no Goold Brown, nor even a Fowler. His views are actually close to those of *WDEU,* but delivered in a louder voice, and with somewhat greater attention to stylistic issues.

In one important way, *DMAU* foreshadows the future of usage books (as I will enlarge upon in the concluding section to this chapter) by drawing upon two very large proprietary corpora, Nexis and Westlaw (a legal and business research tool), to provide evidence for its conclusions. These corpora consist largely of newspapers and journals and are not representative of language as a whole (see Ch. 6, "Representativeness,"

p. 331), but they are nonetheless useful. Garner cites the frequencies of certain words in these corpora, showing that *self-deprecating*, for example, is far more common than *self-depreciating*. Many of the entries in *DMAU* include authentic, dated citations with full bibliographic information, and Garner is thoroughly familiar with older usage guides, frequently citing them. The book has two bibliographies, one a historical bibliography of books on usage, the other a select bibliography of books on various aspects of language.

The basis for most judgments in older usage guides was analogy, logic, and etymology. The nineteenth-century grammars established these criteria, and many twentieth-century usage books have endorsed them in practice to justify their criticisms of many modern usages. In the last decade or so of the twentieth century, however, one could detect a trend marked by an increased willingness to examine the facts of usage before making judgments about acceptability. This is a welcome development. Merriam-Webster had a very large citation file at its disposal for *WDEU*, but others will rely (as Garner did) on language corpora that computer technology has now made available. Once one actually examines the record of usage, it is hard to ignore it. No matter how one feels about the logic of preferring *esthetics* in American English, for example, to *aesthetics*, if one examines an American English corpus and finds that *aesthetics* occurs about thirty times as frequently as *esthetics*, this information may check one's enthusiasm for recommending *esthetics*.[70] Although the recent crop of usage dictionaries reviewed here differ in tone and use different sources for their evidence, none rejects the relevance of linguistic evidence to usage guidance. The linguists whom Garner disparages in his Preface have waited a long time to see this happen, but it has, and even Garner embraces the essence of their message. When Margaret Bryant's *Current American Usage* appeared in 1962, it was largely ignored, but it can now be seen as the forerunner of the current generation of usage guides.

DICTIONARY TREATMENT OF USAGE IN THE FUTURE

As dictionaries become more adept at using language corpora, they will be able to refine their judgments about usage questions. Rather than having to rely on a selected cadre of "good writers," as the American Heritage dictionaries do, dictionaries will be able to cite percentages over a very wide spectrum of actual use. Apart from dedicated corpora, which remain the best source for lexicographic research, one can explore the Internet by means of a search engine such as Alta Vista and find in how many different sites a particular word or phrase appeared, and use that as a basis of comparison with a variant form. An even better search engine is called "Google" (www.google.com), because it shows search results with the keyword highlighted in context.[71]

In the future, instead of reading that, for example, 65 percent of a panel of experts objects to a given usage, we may read that a particular controversial use, such as *hopefully* as a sentence modifier, occurs with high frequency in all kinds of writing and speech, with the exact frequencies cited for newspapers and magazines in political, legal, or entertainment contexts, fiction and nonfiction, scholarly writing, scripted speech, and impromptu speech. We may indeed finally be able to jettison *informal*, following *NID3*, and give more specific labels to many words instead, labels such as *spoken, written, formal; news, business, financial, legal, entertainment, sports, academic,* etc.; *popular fiction, belles lettres, nonfiction;* or some combination thereof, with the usual qualifying labels *often, usually, chiefly,* etc. The labels that look like field labels – *news, business,* etc. – as used here are not conventional field labels. They would apply to words that happen to be used with a significantly higher frequency in that genre as distinguished from other genres; the meanings of the words would not necessarily apply specifically to the subject of the label. Moreover, future corpora will be able to track the changing frequency of words like *hopefully* in particular genres over time, so that dictionaries will be able to say, for example, that *hopefully* as a sentence modifier is declining in certain types of writing but remains as common as ever in speech. As corpora of speech grow, the same sort of historical information will become available for words used mainly in speech such as *like* as a conjunction or adverb.

Dictionaries will nonetheless continue to devote most of their attention to the written language because people usually consult dictionaries to settle questions dealing with writing. In this respect dictionaries have been remiss in not paying more attention to clues to language attitudes expressed by punctuation, but through the use of corpora they will be better able to discover the meanings of punctuation in writing. For example, many words are enclosed in quotation marks with special meanings. Quotation marks around a word can signify that the writer is citing its form rather than its meaning, as in "I think you spelled 'accommodation' wrong." Quotation marks can also convey the meaning of the word even while citing it as a word, as in "I think 'hate' is too strong to describe what I feel." Sometimes this kind of use expresses the speaker's attitude, as in "We really don't like the word 'midget,'" said Mr. McDonald, using the nonmedical term for a normally proportioned but very short individual. He added that 'pituitary dwarf' was the accept-able term for such a person."[72] Quotation marks can also mean, "I do not normally use this locution, but use it now for special effect," as in "They wanted us to fail; they just 'set us up.'" Quotation marks are also used for words used in a novel sense and for words about which the writer feels insecure; they can thus mean "I do not care for this word but cannot think of a better one." Or they can express contempt for those who do use the expression and mean "I refuse to accept responsibility for using this word; its use here is to be taken as a quotation of other, inferior writers."

One of the major problems in the selection of a dictionary word list is determining whether a loan word like *barrio* (in American usage meaning a part of a town or city largely occupied by Spanish-speaking people) has been naturalized or not. Since it is customary to print foreign words in italics, the appearance of a loan word in roman type (like this, as opposed to *this*) is evidence of its acceptance as an English word. Unfortunately, when texts are converted electronically to corpora the type codes are often stripped out, and typefaces like italics are lost. Corpus software has to be improved to allow for the recovery of italics. Even if lexicographers do not know why a particular word is usually ital-icized, it would be helpful to label it *usually italic* or the like just as dic-tionaries now often label a word that is usually capitalized in writing. But often the use of italics will be clear, and the lexicographer can label the word accordingly, such as *not naturalized usu ital*, or *name usu ital*.

Dictionaries have never confronted the basic question of whether a style of usage is characterized as formal or informal because of its use or because of the people to whom it is addressed. We have seen this con-fusion in children's dictionaries, where books written for children are regarded as the stuff of a children's dictionary. Similarly, when we regard the writing of the *New York Daily News* or London's *Daily Express* as infor-mal, and the writing of the *New York Times* or *The Times* (of London) as rather more formal, are we making a judgment about the use of lan-guage or about the intended audience of each newspaper? How can we presume that the readers of the *News* or of the *Express* speak in the same vernacular with which these newspapers are written? Or, indeed, that the readers of the *Timeses* do? The styles are intended to reflect, we presume, the uses of their readerships. But do they? If they do not, but merely represent the misconceived journalistic traditions of a relatively few people, are we not giving such usages weight out of all proportion to their due? Is a usage informal because it is directed at working-class people, and not informal because it is directed at middle- and upper-class people? Does widespread exposure to a particular style of writing imply widespread use?

With the advent of computer corpora, one can have a subcorpus that reflects the language of the *Daily News* and the *Express* and another of the *New York Times* and *The Times* of London, and compare them to see how similar or different their lexicons and frequencies are. The *informal–formal* cline may not be suitable for a description of these varieties of language, and more specific labels such as *tabloid news* and *broadsheet* might be more meaningful descriptions. Similarly, when comparing the language of a popular movie magazine with that of the *New York Review of Books* or the *Times Literary Supplement*, labels like *pop mag* and *lit mag* might be better than *informal* and *formal*. The reader will recall Kenyon's distinction between cultural level (degree of standardness) and functional variety (degree of formality). In spite of Labov's finding that there may be a linkage, I still find the distinction a useful one, and I would argue that the difference between the language used in popular magazines and literary magazines is cultural, relating to the educational level and degree of literacy of the presumed readership, as well as to the kind of subject matter, and has nothing to do with the level of formality of the language used. We must abandon the notion that "standard" is one kind of language only, and that the only alternative to "standard" is "nonstandard." Both the language of popular magazines and the language of literary magazines are standard, but they are different, and within each variety there may well be different levels of formality. It is more important to identify the kind of publication or subject context in which words are typically used than to try to identify the degree of formality or informality within those contexts. I have been discussing print publications exclusively, but clearly in the future more and more publications will not be in print, and no doubt varieties of usage that are typical of certain types of Internet communication will have to be identified and characterized as well as those fitting the various print media.

The editing process has had a tremendous and incalculable impact – up till now completely unacknowledged – on dictionary treatment of usage as well as on the treatment of usage questions in usage guides. Copy editors, like teachers, are devotedly conservative in matters of usage; they are paid to be. Usage dictionaries along with other references form a wall of stolid, authoritative opinion on their desks. Just as usage dictionaries are changing, so, very gradually, is copy editing. The growing use of language corpora will dilute the impact of the tightly edited text of mainstream publishers, as corpora take in a much greater variety of sources: offbeat and counter-culture publications; text made available electronically, which is often lightly edited or unedited; fiction; and speech, including the transcripts of radio and TV talk shows and unscripted political discussions. Up till now the language that dictionaries have described has been that of edited copy. As the use of corpora makes its mark on dictionaries, that will change, and when it does dictionaries will have to make use of many more labels to define the varieties of language they are describing.

Many terms, especially slang usages, are age related. As we have seen, one part of the definition of slang may be its association with young people, but we should not assume that this is always the case. Slang dictionaries such as Chapman's *Dictionary of American Slang* often specify *students* or *teenagers* or the like, and, as we have seen, *DARE* sometimes identifies the age of its informants with respect to the use of regional words. Some expressions are used typically by older people, such as *youngster*, and some by younger people, such as *Yuck!* A similar situation applies to sex, and a corpus can reveal which terms in particular contexts are more often used by men or by women. If the so-called "header" information of corpus samples – that is, the bibliographic information about each sample – is sufficiently precise, dictionary editors will be able to make reasonable conclusions about typical users of certain forms without having to rely on their own limited experience. The description of usage and the application of usage labels will depend on the evidence before them, and this will be new in the history of lexicography.

CHAPTER 6

The corpus in lexicography

In language study, a corpus is any body of text collected with the aim of analyzing its features. Nowadays when one speaks of a corpus in lexicography, it is understood to refer to an electronic corpus, often one containing a vast number of words from many different sources. However, long before the age of computers, corpora were created to study various texts, such as the Bible and the works of Shakespeare, and make concordances from them. This process involved an immense human effort, because every word had to be copied out by hand to specify its position and to make possible frequency counts. In spite of this, some early corpora are of impressive size.[1]

HISTORY OF DEVELOPMENT OF LINGUISTIC CORPORA

The first, modern, large-scale corpus of English compiled for lexical study, as distinguished from literary analysis, was Edward L. Thorndike's word count of 4.5 million words, published as the *Teacher's Word Book* in 1921 and subsequently enlarged over the following decades in several stages to a corpus of 18 million words, which produced *The Teacher's Word Book of 30,000 Words*, by Thorndike and Irving Lorge. Based on texts from magazines and from juvenile reading, it consists of several lists of words showing their relative frequency. The book is designed to help educators and teachers determine which words are common enough to be used at particular grade levels.

Another early corpus of considerable size is Ernest Horn's *A Basic Writing Vocabulary: 10,000 Words Most Commonly Used in Writing*. This monograph, published in 1926, was compiled mainly from letters, both personal and published, from many different sources and in many different fields of endeavor. It is quite a sophisticated study. Some sense of the effort involved can be surmised from this description of the procedures used:

273

The actual tabulation of words was made as follows: the first recording of words was done on sheets $8^{1}/_{2}'' \times 13''$ indexed on the left hand side of the sheets with the beginning letters of key words such as *ab, acc, add, aff, ag,* etc. Experience with earlier tabulations made it possible to estimate rather closely the space which should be left between the guides so that words could be written in alphabetical order. A series of sheets indexed and spaced to hold 10,000 words was found to be most satisfactory.[2]

Since the study consisted of 5,136,816 running words of text, more than 500 such packets had to be painstakingly prepared.

Some early corpora were designed to study the frequency of speech sounds. Godfrey Dewey, an advocate of simplified spelling, published *Relativ Frequency of English Speech Sounds* (deliberately dropping the silent "e" from *Relative*) in 1923. He analyzed the speech sounds of 100,000 words from a wide variety of sources. Others before him, as he describes, had made similar studies, among them one by William Dwight Whitney in 1874, later to establish himself as a leading grammarian and the editor of *The Century Dictionary*.[3]

The pre-electronic corpus studies destined to have the most impact on lexicography were undertaken to help in the teaching of English to foreign learners, the field of education now known broadly as *English Language Teaching* (ELT), and more specifically as *English as a Second Language* (ESL) and *English as a Foreign Language* (EFL). Strictly speaking, ESL is the study of English in an English-speaking part of the world by people whose native language is not English, whereas EFL is the study of English by people living in their own non-English speaking countries. Nowadays dictionaries for foreign learners are intended for both of these groups, but the earliest were EFL dictionaries, and they originated in Japan. In this connection, the corpus work of Michael West, Harold E. Palmer, and A. S. Hornby of the 1930s is seminal, and has had a lasting impact on ESL dictionaries to this day. "At the Tokyo Institute for Research in English Teaching, where Hornby's research activities were centred from the mid-1930s, no activity had a deeper or more lasting effect on the early history of the learner's dictionary than the so-called 'vocabulary control' movement."[4] Harold Palmer was the leading figure in the movement to limit vocabulary for foreign learners, and as early as 1930 had issued a report on vocabulary selection.[5] In October, 1934, at the initiative of Michael West, who had been teaching English in India, the Carnegie Corporation sponsored a conference in New York City on the selection of vocabulary in the teaching of English.[6] Among those invited were Palmer, and Edward Thorndike as a consultant.

Subsequently, Palmer, West, and Lawrence Faucett, with help from Hornby, prepared *The Interim Report on Vocabulary Selection*, published in 1936, an extremely influential study. *The Interim Report* was more sophisticated than Thorndike's vocabulary studies, as it took grammatical function and meaning into consideration, distinguishing, for example, between *fly* (the insect) and the various verb senses of *fly*. Subsequently, Michael West, with the help of a semantic frequency count made by Irving Lorge, used part of *The Interim Report* in revised and expanded form in *A General Service List of English Words*.[7] This work divides the senses of the words according to the breakdown in the *OED* and shows the relative frequency of each sense. Because it does not contain a very large number of words, it has been of limited practical use in lexicography, but as a model of what could and should be done to improve corpus research in lexicography, it is of major importance. Michael West and James Endicott published the first EFL dictionary, *The New Method English Dictionary*, in 1935, which, we are told on the title page, explains the meaning of 24,000 items "within a vocabulary of 1,490 words."[8]

The work of Charles C. Fries, discussed in Ch. 5 (see p. 250) in connection with the study of usage, was also an early and original advance in corpus research. His *American English Grammar* (1940) studied the texts of several thousand letters, and his subsequent book, *The Structure of English: an Introduction to the Construction of English Sentences* (1952), used the analysis of transcribed telephone conversations for a description of grammar. The reader who thinks all of this far-flung research is all very interesting but has had no practical effect could not be more mistaken. Fries' studies show, as Graeme Kennedy points out, that 4,000 to 5,000 different words (or *types*) account for 95% of most written texts, that 1,000 types account for 85%, that 50 very high frequency function words account for about 60% of speech, and that nouns make up about 40% of the most frequent 1,000 words in English. Before corpus-based studies showed the importance of focusing on high-frequency words, textbooks and grammars for teaching English had often devoted enormous attention to uncommon words. The new studies, however limited, shed much needed light on the actual state of language use.

Chomskyan hostility to quantitative analysis

A number of linguists, reflecting on the period from the 1950s to the 1980s, have commented on the widespread hostility to quantitative analysis of language, especially in the United States, because of the pervasive influence of Noam Chomsky's theories. Chomsky's *Syntactic Structures* and subsequent books were based on the premise that since the potential uses of language (what he called "performance") were infinite, the ability ("competence") of the native speaker to generate such an infinite variety could only be explained by an intuitive grasp of the grammatical rules underlying such generation of utterances. *Syntactic Structures* set forth some of those rules, or "transformations," which, properly understood, could account for the particular form of every possible utterance. It was – and is – a bravura performance, a brilliant intellectual theory that sought to explain all possible utterances, and it was enormously influential in most university departments involved with the study of language. It became so influential, indeed, that linguistic scholars who did not share the essential tenets of transformational grammar often found themselves with dim futures.

Chomskyans were hostile to any quantitative approach to language study and sometimes ridiculed it because it could not account for the infinite variety of potential uses of language. Only the native speaker, they said, could do that. Graeme Kennedy remarks that Chomsky's influence suppressed statistical approaches to language study, and as a result corpus-based study of vocabulary "declined in influence from the 1950s until its revival . . . [in] the 1980s."[9] Another scholar, discussing this period from the vantage point of the 1990s, writes, "Chomsky argues that linguistics is a branch of cognitive psychology . . ., that it can be based on intuitive data and isolated sentences, that corpus data is unrevealing, [and] that the study of language in use is essentially uninteresting."[10] He adds, "The Chomskyan position has not significantly changed in over 25 years."[11] Geoffrey Leech, one of the pioneers in corpus research, talks of a discontinuity in the study of linguistics that "can be located fairly precisely in the later 1950s. Chomsky had, effectively, put to flight the corpus linguistics of an earlier generation. His view on the inadequacy of corpora, and the adequacy of intuition, became the orthodoxy of a succeeding generation of theoretical linguists."[12] Leech quotes a paper Chomsky gave at the University of Texas in 1958 in which he said that any natural corpus would be so badly skewed, omitting some expressions because they were obvious, others because they were false, and still others because they were impolite, that it would be little more than a list.[13]

The term *corpus linguistics*, Leech observes, did not exist in the 1950s. The linguists who called themselves *structuralists* (from *structural linguistics*) went into eclipse for twenty years until the computer revolution. *Corpus linguistics*, Leech says, was first used in the 1980s, and he defines it as a method of doing research, not as a branch of linguistics.[14] I would define it as the study of language using collections of text in a computerized file that can be analyzed by applying statistical procedures. In fact, nowadays *corpus linguistics* is sometimes considered a branch of *computational linguistics*, which may be defined as the study of natural language using the techniques of computer science. Although it is not quite true, as we shall see, that the development of linguistic corpora ceased entirely from the late 1950s to the 1980s, the climate in American universities in particular was hostile to this line of intellectual inquiry, and few corpus-based studies were undertaken either in the United States or in Britain.

Of all the particular events of this period, none sums up so perfectly the changing intellectual climate confronting experientially-based language study as Chomsky's celebrated review of B. F. Skinner's book, *Verbal Behavior*, published in 1957, the very same year as Chomsky's *Syntactic Structures*. The review appeared in the most prestigious journal in linguistics, *Language*, the official organ of the Linguistic Society of America, and even in a journal known for its exhaustive reviews, Chomsky's, at thirty-three pages, is one of the longest.[15] Skinner was already well known as the leading behavioral psychologist of his day; his experiments with pigeons had demonstrated that by "operant conditioning" their behavior could be controlled, and in *Science and Human Behavior* he had sought to show how the basic tenets of operant behavior apply to human beings. Skinner had long been interested in language, and his book on the subject was eagerly awaited. It was obviously intended to be a major statement by one of the leading experimental psychologists of his time on a subject of major importance. Skinner was in his mid-50s, at the height of his fame; Chomsky was just over 30.

The review was devastating. It was not simply meant to show, as it certainly succeeded in doing, that many of Skinner's basic assumptions were suspect and therefore his conclusions did not hold up. It was intended to take the book apart so thoroughly that there would be nothing left to salvage. The review goes beyond the usual constraints of criticism and even at this early date shows the rigid adherence to a single way of viewing language study that was to exclude corpus-based study as a legitimate tool of linguistic research. Near the end of the review, Chomsky wrote: "It is evident that more is involved in sentence structure than insertion of lexical items in grammatical frames; no approach to language that fails to take these deeper processes into account can possibly achieve much success in accounting for actual linguistic behavior."[16] Chomsky also wrote: "It appears that we recognize a new item as a sentence not because it matches some familiar item *in any simple way* [my italics], but because it is generated by the grammar that each individual has somehow and in some form internalized."[17] Why must the recognition occur in a simple way? Why can we not recognize a new item as a sentence in an extremely complicated way? The conclusion that each individual has to have internalized the grammar by which sentences are generated does not seem warranted just because the process of recognition of matching sentences is not simple. The success of corpus-based lexicography, in fact, leads us strongly to conclude that something very much like this – the recognition of a new item because it matches in some way, often not in any direct or simple way, a familiar item – is precisely what does happen in language acquisition and use. This is why linguists have in recent years devoted so much attention to the use of metaphor in ordinary language use.

Chomsky's review had the effect of permanently squelching any further approaches to language study along the lines of *Verbal Behavior*, and of staking the claim, loud and clear, that there was only one acceptable way to study the acquisition and use of language.

The emergence of corpus linguistics

The first major, computer-based study designed to be representative was the *Standard Corpus of Present-Day Edited American English* (better known as "the Brown Corpus"), assembled by W. Nelson Francis and Henry Kučera in 1963–64 at Brown University. It consists of 500 text passages of 2,000 words each, representing different categories (or *genres*) of writing. The corpus thus totals slightly more than 1 million words (*tokens*) in which about 50,000 different words (*types*) are used. The Brown Corpus was done in the face of widespread skepticism and indifference by a few determined and far-seeing scholars. It has come to be recognized throughout the world of English lexicography and language study as a groundbreaking event, one that demonstrated that a representative collection of texts could provide insights into language use not available in any other way. Intuition will not provide the kind of contextual clues that a corpus can give.

The Brown Corpus paved the way for similar studies of British English and for much larger corpora in the decades that followed. Although nowadays a corpus of 1 million words is small, in the 1960s it was considered large, or in any event large enough to be representative. No one would seriously argue today that a corpus of this size could be representative of present-day American English, because there is abundant evidence that many familiar words and phrases are not likely to occur very often or at all in a corpus of a million words. As Richard Venezky has pointed out, among those words occurring only twice are *abysmal, checkup, landslide,* and *rap.* Those occurring once include *ballistics, gnaw, invert,* and *radiate.*[18] Although American dictionary houses soon became aware of the Brown Corpus and many acquired copies of it, it did not have any immediate impact on the way lexicography was conducted. Rather, it served as a model for how a representative language corpus could be put together, and because of the extraordinarily generous policy of the compilers in making it available in various formats at cost to whomever wanted a copy, the Brown Corpus has been widely imitated. Modeled on the Brown Corpus, a study of British English was undertaken by Geoffrey Leech in 1970 at the University of Lancaster and completed in 1978 by the University of Oslo in collaboration with the Norwegian Computing Centre in Bergen; it has come to be known as the *LOB Corpus* (for Lancaster-Oslo/Bergen). The texts used in the Brown Corpus were all published in 1961, and those collected for use in the LOB Corpus were also published in that year; the selection of genres also match, with only slight differences in the number of samples assigned to each genre. Here are the genres used by the Brown Corpus along with the number of 2,000-word samples in each[19]:

A.	Press: Reportage	44
B.	Press: Editorial	27
C.	Press: Reviews	17
D.	Religion	17
E.	Skills and Hobbies	36
F.	Popular Lore	48
G.	Belles lettres, Biography, etc.	75
H.	Miscellaneous	30
J.	Learned and Scientific Writings	80
K.	Fiction: General	29
L.	Fiction: Mystery and Detective	24
M.	Fiction: Science	6
N.	Fiction: Adventure and Western	29
P.	Fiction: Romance and Love Story	29
R.	Humor	9

The miscellaneous category includes government documents, foundation and industry reports, college catalogs, and industry house organs. Each of the broad categories is subdivided to insure that no one type (such as sports or politics under press reportage) is accorded too much coverage at the expense of others.

The creation of the LOB Corpus allowed direct comparison of the contemporary usage of British and American English, so that one can say which words occur with statistically reliable greater frequency in one variety or the other. *Membership, college,* and *campus* occur far more frequently in American than in British English, whereas *introduced, introduction,* and *pupils* occur more frequently in British than in American English.[20] Moreover, in both the Brown Corpus and the LOB Corpus, it is possible to learn the frequency of particular words within particular genres, so that British and American English can be compared with respect to the same genre. You may find, for example, that an American word is commonly used in political writing, but in British English it occurs mainly in fiction. Clearly, such information is valuable for linguistic research and in particular comparisons between the two varieties, but the real significance of these two corpora was in establishing a benchmark for much larger corpora that would eventually follow from their precedent. The larger corpora used by dictionary makers today could not have been created, or would have been created with many avoidable mistakes, had it not been for the farsightedness of Francis and Kučera.

In Britain, even before the Brown Corpus had got underway, Randolph Quirk of University College London had begun his *Survey of English Usage,* which like the Brown Corpus was destined to become a landmark in the development of corpus linguistics, although it was not done with computers and still exists in the form of endless trays of 4 × 6-inch paper slips stored in file cabinets. In 1959 Quirk set out to collect 200 samples of British English, each of 5,000 words, to form a corpus of a million words. Half of the samples would be spoken and half written. The corpus was to be used to study the grammar and usage of educated British speakers and writers. What was really unusual was the attention given speech, which had been and is still neglected in comparison to written material. Also unusual was the painstakingly detailed annotations of the grammatical features of each word, and, for the spoken material, the prosodic features, such as a rising inflection or a pause. The vast amount of work of transcribing and marking each item, work that could only be accomplished by highly trained people, took twenty-five years to complete; it was finished in 1989. However, in 1975 another pioneer in corpus linguistics, Jan Svartvik of the University of Lund in Sweden, undertook to computerize the spoken portion of Quirk's *Survey*. This was a complex undertaking to begin with because of the conversion of the prosodic markings; but because the *Survey*'s spoken portion only added up to 435,000 words, Svartvik added new spoken material so that the corpus would total more than 500,000 words. The resulting computer corpus of spoken material is called the *London-Lund Corpus*, and was completed in 1980. It remains one of the largest computerized corpora of spoken material. Quirk's *Survey* was the first systematic collection of texts and spoken material to be subjected to careful grammatical analysis, and was later used as a basis for the largest modern grammar of English along with the Brown Corpus and the LOB Corpus.[21] "The grammatical features identified provided the basis for later . . . automatic tagging and parsing of corpora," which would become a routine part of corpus development in the 1980s.[22] The *Survey of English Usage* has been consulted and studied by scholars from around the world, and remains an invaluable resource especially for the study of grammar.

There was in Britain another tradition of language study based on evidence that was never extinguished, as it was virtually in the United States, by the dominance of Chomskyan-influenced linguists in the 1960s and 1970s. This tradition stems from the work of J. R. Firth and his followers.[23] Firth believed that language study should be based on actual instances of language use in whole texts and not on isolated sentences invented on the basis of intuition. As early as 1935, Firth wrote that "no study of meaning apart from a complete context can be taken seriously."[24] Absolute rejection of alternative points of view appears to have a rich tradition in language study. Firth also believed that the words used in a language (*lexis*) and the way in which they were arranged in the context of other words (*syntax*) were interdependent and could scarcely be distinguished. Grammar and meaning were closely intertwined. He also rejected the famous dualism of Ferdinand de Saussure that drew a distinction between *langue* (language) and *parole* (the particular way in which language is used by the individual), a duality reflected in Chomsky's distinction between *competence* (knowledge of the underlying rules governing language use) and *performance* (the particular expression of those rules).

"It is easy to forget or ignore how little data, either invented sentences or real texts, is actually analysed in the most influential literature in twentieth century linguistics," writes Michael Stubbs, going on to observe that in Chomsky's *Syntactic Structures* only twenty-eight invented sentences are discussed. Even among those linguists who professed to rely on evidence during the 1960s, '70s, and '80s, as he observes, invented utterances were the rule. Quirk's *Grammar*, though it used the million-word *Survey of English Usage* corpus as a source of information, apparently did not draw upon it for citations, but used mainly invented sentences.[25] According to the neo-Firthians, especially Michael Halliday and John Sinclair, no description of language can be adequate if it is not based on real language in context, and if it does not show the close interrelationships between meaning and grammar. Halliday has written, "grammar and vocabulary are not two different things; they are the same thing seen by different observers. There is only one phenomenon here, not two."[26] In the work of Sinclair especially, these ideas are expressed with a determined vigor that may lead to a radical reassessment of the nature of dictionaries and grammars. Sinclair maintains that words are not usually selected individually but are selected as groups; they come to mind in context and are spliced together with other groups to form sentences. Native speakers have no reliable intuitions about grammatical probabilities. Only the corpus can tell us what the probabilities are. Stubbs remarks, in summing up Sinclair's thought in the Firthian tradition, "[I]f the relation between lexis and syntax is rethought, then the whole relation between dictionaries and grammars must be rethought."[27] Sinclair is working towards the idea that there can be no fundamental distinction between a dictionary and a grammar: that in order to say what words mean, one must describe how they are used in sentences, and in order to describe how they are used in sentences, one must say what they mean.[28] In the context of doing dictionaries, Sinclair's commitment to authentic language is absolute. "Sinclair is suspicious of any sentence being mentioned in evidence that has not first been used in earnest. He has drawn attention on many occasions to the undesirability of using or discussing made-up examples."[29]

What, exactly, are the key features of computer corpus linguistics? According to one of the pioneers in corpus research, Geoffrey Leech, they are:

- A focus on linguistic performance rather than competence
- A focus on linguistic description rather than linguistic universals
- A focus on quantitative, as well as qualitative, models of language
- A focus on a more empiricist, rather than a rationalist, view of scientific inquiry

Each of these features contrasts, Leech says, with the "Chomskyan paradigm which has dominated much of linguistic thinking since the 1950s."[30]

Douglas Biber, one of the leading American corpus linguists, has studied different genres to show how the language used varies in specific ways. For example, he has studied the use of *that* clauses, first-person and second-person pronouns, demonstrative pronouns, *wh-* questions (*who, what, where, why, when,* and *how*), etc., and how they vary in written genres (press reporting, editorials, academic prose, various kinds of fiction, etc.) and spoken genres (face-to-face conversation, telephone conversation, public debates, planned speeches, etc.). He based his work on two corpora, the LOB Corpus of written texts and the London-Lund Corpus, a transcription of spoken English.[31] To Biber, the goals of corpus analysis are not to make "judgements of grammaticality" – an oblique reference to Chomskyan linguistics – but "to uncover typical patterns" of language use.[32] "In many cases," he observes, "humans tend to notice unusual occurrences more than typical occurrences, and therefore conclusions based on intuition can be unreliable."[33] Corpus linguistics thus emphatically rejects the central assumptions of Chomskyan linguistics: that the intuition of the native speaker is a reliable guide to language use; that competence in Chomskyan terms is discoverable by careful, rational, examination of the rules underlying one's own speech. Even more profoundly, corpus linguistics questions the existence of competence. It says, in effect, all the evidence that can be attested to is the actual performance of speakers and writers. Biber defines the central research goals of corpus study as "assessing the extent to which a pattern is found" and "analyzing the contextual factors that influence variability."[34]

Note how far this position is from that of Chomsky's, and how close to that of B. F. Skinner, the great empiricist. When Skinner ran his experiments with pigeons he looked for a pattern of behavior and analyzed the factors that influenced its variability. Although Skinner's *Verbal Behavior* is indeed seriously flawed in many ways, modern corpus linguistics owes more to the rigorous traditions of experimental biology in which Skinner was a pioneer than it does to the theoretic linguistic studies of Noam Chomsky.

Even before the logjam was broken and new corpora started to stream along on the current of corpus linguistics, the American tradition of compiling corpora for the study of vocabulary frequency for childhood education continued. In 1971, the creators of the American Heritage dictionaries produced a computerized study of some 5 million words collected from more than 1,000 different sources, mainly textbooks for grades three through nine, but with some selections from ungraded magazines.[35] The result, which was used in the preparation of the *American Heritage School Dictionary*, is a list of 86,741 different words printed alphabetically and in rank order, with their overall frequencies and frequencies in grades three through nine. Since the sources for the corpus are mainly school textbooks presumably written in controlled vocabularies, the frequency ranks only tell us what assumptions the writers of these textbooks made. Because the study is not based largely on the books and periodicals – not to mention movies and television shows – that children read and listen to, no one could deduce from it the vocabulary that children of various age groups actually use or are exposed to. One of the editors, Peter Davies, writing in an introductory essay, claims that the corpus represents "the printed language of the American elementary educational system," and can therefore be considered "a culturally marked subset of the total lexicon of English."[36] I cannot agree. The *Word Frequency Book* simply reflects past assumptions of previous textbook writers about the vocabulary suitable for children of various ages. The same textbook authors on whose works the *Word Frequency Book* was based could have used the *Word Frequency Book*'s findings as justification for composing new texts with the same grade-level vocabularies! Nonetheless, the *Word Frequency Book* is notable as one of the earliest, large computerized corpus studies, and as statistical analysis it is an impressive work.

Technological changes

As this review of the history of corpora has made clear, computers have been used in vocabulary studies and in lexicography for several decades. As early as 1970 an electronic concordance of Old English texts was being prepared for the Dictionary of Old English project in Toronto, and since 1980 it has been available on microfiche.[37] In the early to mid-1980s computers were used more extensively, but the expense and size of mainframe computers made them impractical for dictionary makers to use in-house. While doing a large medical dictionary for John Wiley & Sons in the 1980s, our staff had to edit definitions on paper printouts which were then sent to St. Louis where they were batch-processed in a large mainframe, printed out on forms of the same type, and returned to us for further editing. Jeremy Clear, the Senior Computing Officer for the *Collins Cobuild English Language Dictionary*, has written, "At the beginning of 1987 as I write this, it is still the case that the technology of microcomputers and network communications is unable to offer an economically competitive system which will allow a large team of lexicographers to compile dictionary entries without using pen and paper."[38] This was not exactly true, as by 1984 we were able to edit on screen, but we still had to send our tapes to St. Louis to be processed. Since then, however, the capacity of the hard disk of an individual computer has grown exponentially, and continues to grow, as has its speed of operation. Along with this has come an incredible degree of miniaturization, so that a computer that might have occupied a large-sized room in the 1970s is now far outperformed by something smaller than Johnson's two-volume folio edition. With miniaturization and vastly greater power, the prices have dropped, and continue to drop. A whole new generation of people have come along who learned how to use computers in grade school and are completely comfortable with them, unlike most people of my own generation, who are still frustrated by our inability to understand what makes them work, or why they stop working at inexplicable moments.

Unless the publishing industry had also changed to make computerized composition the norm, the acquisition of large electronic corpora would have been immeasurably more difficult. People have been interested in corpora for a long time, but they hadn't the means to create them without employing an army of workers copying texts by hand. With the increasing use of electronic composition and storage of texts, it became possible to acquire texts in electronic format for use in corpora. (See below, "Compiling a corpus," p. 323.) Although many texts were produced on floppy disks before the early 1980s, comparatively few publishers or composition houses were then prepared to make use of them. The changes have taken longer than predicted because composition houses saw, correctly, that moving to electronic composition would put many of them out of business. This is exactly what happened. Many compositors have gone out of business. Those that remained were forced to lay off most of their compositors and hire programmers and others familiar with electronic files. Today, one would be hard pressed to find any compositor who wouldn't be happy to use a disk in any word processing or page-formatting program. Many organizers of academic conferences and journal publishers now require texts on disks and often specify the programming language, and most book publishers now expect all of their manuscripts to be submitted on disk. With the vastly greater storage capacity of file servers, it became possible to store ever larger bodies of text. Ordinary individual computers now have storage capacities measured not in megabytes but in gigabytes (billions of bytes), and we will soon be talking about terabytes (trillions of bytes).

The broad availability of text in electronic form and the ability to store large amounts of data economically are the twin factors that have changed the face of lexicography. Concordancing software has also been greatly improved to speed the process of accessing items, and has also brought into play a number of sophisticated tools for linguistic analysis, for example in organizing collocational searches and in grammatical tagging. (See pp. 308 and 333.) Very large electronic corpora that not so long ago remained a gleam in the eye of madcap visionaries have become a reality. With such a corpus, serious dictionary makers will have the capacity to base editorial decisions on good evidence rather than guesswork or intuition. Whether they *will* has more to do with corporate priorities than with lexicography. Major changes because of language corpora have already occurred in ESL lexicography, first in Britain and more recently in the United States. Native-speaker dictionaries have been slower to adapt to the new technology, especially in the US, but no new major dictionary, whether for native speakers or foreign learners, can hope to be taken seriously if it is not based on corpus research, and I have no doubt that soon enough every new dictionary will claim, whether truly or not, that it is based on a huge corpus of texts.

Second generation corpora

The emergence of corpus linguistics as an applied discipline in lexicography can be linked to the COBUILD Project begun in 1980 and directed by John Sinclair. COBUILD was a joint venture of Collins, the British publishing company, and the University of Birmingham, and originally the corpus was called the Birmingham Corpus. (COBUILD stands for "Collins Birmingham University International Language Database.") COBUILD began compiling texts that would later become recognized as the second generation of language corpora, the so-called megacorpora, of much larger size than the first generation corpora like the Brown Corpus and computerized vocabulary studies. In 1982 the Birmingham Corpus amounted to 7.3 million words, seven times larger than the Brown Corpus, and was compiled primarily for the creation of a new advanced-level dictionary for foreign learners. Given the pioneering tradition in vocabulary studies in ESL and EFL studies, it is not surprising that the first large computer corpus assembled specifically for a dictionary should be one for foreign learners, the *Collins Cobuild English Language Dictionary* (*Cobuild ELD*).

The Birmingham Corpus was not only larger but much more broadly based than the Brown Corpus. The texts collected were written in 1960 or later. Seventy percent were British, 20% American, and 10% other, from a wide variety of sources. Twenty-five percent of the corpus was of spoken material. By the time the *Cobuild ELD* was completed in 1987, the corpus had grown to 20 million words. It has kept growing. Given a new name as the Bank of English, by 1997 it had surpassed 300 million words.

This and other very large corpora are styled "monitor corpora" by John Sinclair because they are open-ended and monitor the changes in a language over time. In his view, only this kind of very large corpus, constantly updated, can serve the needs of a general synchronic dictionary. Sinclair contrasts this type of corpus with a "sample corpus" such as the Brown Corpus, which seeks to be representative by including samples of limited extent from a variety of genres. The assumption is that if the selection is broad enough, the sample size does not have to be very great, but as lexicographers have gained more experience using corpora, they have discovered that this assumption is not true. Many words and expressions do not occur frequently enough to provide the lexicographer with enough evidence in a sample corpus. However, this objection does not mean that a sample corpus might not be better for purposes other than dictionary compilation, such as for some kinds of linguistic research.

The *Cobuild ELD* had a more defined theoretical basis than most new dictionaries. Given Sinclair's commitment to the principles of corpus linguistics, it had more purity of focus, for better or worse, than any dictionary since *NID3* in 1961, which had made an issue of its commitment to structural linguistics. Whereas *NID3*'s commitment to structural linguistics was mostly hype to show its superior linguistic sophistication, *Cobuild ELD*'s was genuine. It was betting the farm on the use of authentic language to inform its research and to furnish its definers with examples. As the reader will see below, I am somewhat critical of the insistence of the *Cobuild* editors on using only authentic examples without alteration, but I do admire their integrity and am certain that they have advanced the discipline of lexicography in no small way.

The Longman ESL dictionaries were also early on the scene in making use of corpora. The Birmingham Corpus was followed in the late 1980s by the Longman Lancaster English Language Corpus, like the COBUILD project a collaboration between a publisher and a university. Begun by Della Summers of Longman, it was developed by Geoffrey Leech of Lancaster University, and like the Birmingham Corpus it was designed to be used to edit dictionaries for foreign learners. It and two other companion corpora – one of spoken English and another of learners' English – comprise the Longman Corpus Network, which was used as the primary source for the third edition of the *Longman Dictionary of Contemporary English* (*LDOCE3*), like the *Cobuild* dictionaries, an advanced-level work for foreign learners. The Longman corpora contain selections of about 40,000 words each from over 2,000 books, periodicals, and other sources written after 1900, with a relatively high percentage of fiction (42%) compared to other corpora.[39]

For many years the field of linguistics was almost entirely independent of lexicography, even while lip service was being paid (along with modest honoraria) to prominent linguists to serve on committees listed on the mastheads of new dictionaries. But the emerging field of corpus linguistics, particularly in ESL lexicography, has changed all that. Indeed, as more lexicographers become corpus linguists and more corpus linguists become lexicographers, the distinction between these two groups is apt to become more and more problematic in the years ahead.[40] A parallel development is a partial blurring of the lines between software engineer and language specialist. Previously – and unfortunately this is still sometimes the case – software engineers were recruited who knew nothing about language study or dictionaries, and the lexicographers who recruited them knew next to nothing about software systems.[41] This is changing, as the data systems that are now required to build and manage a corpus for a modern dictionary require the services of a team of linguistically sophisticated software engineers as well as lexicographers who know more than which button to press to save their work.

The third major British publisher of ESL dictionaries, Oxford University Press, has been one of the main contributors to the British National Corpus (BNC), begun in January 1991 as a collaborative effort involving major academic centers, commercial publishers, and publicly funded institutions. It is thus not proprietary but publicly owned. The British government paid for half of the cost. (Would that the US government were so enlightened!) The BNC, according to Graeme Kennedy, "has set new standards in the way it has been designed to be representative" and "will become an international benchmark for corpus linguistics."[42] It consists of 100 million words, all British English, compiled from over 4000 texts, 90% written and 10% spoken. Ten million words of spoken English is a very large corpus of spoken English, and the spoken part includes some transcriptions of spontaneous conversation, which is not easy to acquire. The written portion, of texts after 1975, consists of 75% "informative" prose and 25% "imaginative" or literary. Most text samples are of less than 40,000 words. Sixty percent of the written corpus is from books, 25% from periodicals, and the rest from other sources, published and unpublished. The initial version of the BNC is available only within the European Union owing to copyright restrictions, but a new version in preparation will be made available outside the EU as well. The BNC is thus a worldwide resource for the study of British English, and the fifth and sixth editions of the *Oxford Advanced Learner's Dictionary* (1995 and 2000, respectively) make use of it. Complete information about the BNC, along with user fees and restrictions on its use, can be obtained from the website (http://info.ox.ac.uk/bnc) of the Oxford University Computing Service, the official agent handling its distribution.

As the BNC was being developed, Cambridge University Press was developing its own large corpus, called the Cambridge International Corpus, of both British and American English, and in 1995 Cambridge published still another advanced-level dictionary for foreign learners based on corpus research, the *Cambridge International Dictionary of English*. Since then the Cambridge corpus has grown to over 300 million words, matching the Bank of English in extent.

While all this activity in corpus research in ESL lexicography was going on in Britain, what was happening in the US? Not very much. In 1989 I wrote:

It is now apparent that some time in the 1970s the focus of innovative work in commercial lexicography shifted from the United States to Great Britain . . . During the 1960s, '70s, and early '80s, a great many major new American dictionaries issued from the American publishing houses of Funk & Wagnalls, Random House, Houghton Mifflin (American Heritage dictionaries), Simon & Schuster (Webster's New World dictionaries), and Merriam-Webster . . . But in spite of showy graphics and ballyhooed usage notes, there have been very few meaningful advances in commercial American lexicography in the past twenty years. American dictionary publishers are afraid to take risks because of the intense competition and because, being in the main publicly owned corporations, they must show constant growth in revenue. Really innovative works almost always take years to develop, and the investment period is therefore greatly protracted.[43]

The corporate environment in which the leading American dictionary houses find themselves is simply not conducive to large investments in the future. Merriam-Webster, the leading US publisher of dictionaries, has not revised its unabridged dictionary since 1961, after many years of revising it every 25 years.[44] (See "The unabridged dictionary in America: the passing of an era," p. 84.) Every one of the four leading commercial dictionary houses in the US (Merriam-Webster, Webster's New World, Random House, and American Heritage) is owned by another company, in most cases by a much larger company. To get some idea of the real place of dictionaries in the corporate firmament, here is what the *New York Times* reported about the sale of the Macmillan branch of Simon and Schuster to an investment company called Hicks, Muse, Tate & Furst:

In partnership with Kohlberg Kravis, Hicks Muse also controls the nation's largest chain of movie theaters . . . Michael J. Levitt, a Hicks Muse partner . . . described the purchase as consistent with the firm's other areas, including branded foods . . . From Simon & Schuster, Hicks Muse will receive titles that include the Betty Crocker cookbooks, Webster's New World Dictionary, Frommer's travel guides, and Macmillan computer books including the Idiot's Guide series.[45]

Since then, Hicks Muse apparently decided that *Webster's New World Dictionary* was not that good a fit, and has sold it to another company.

The trend towards corporate takeovers in the 1970s resulted in a loss of purpose among dictionary houses. They were swallowed up by huge enterprises. Since then many of them decided this was a big mistake, that the profit margins were so low they could make more money putting it in the bank, and sold off the book publishers they had acquired – but the damage had been done. Although the costs of the making of a dictionary are significantly higher than those of making most other kinds of books, to these goliaths the costs are trivial. In 1963 I worked for Funk & Wagnalls when it was bought by Reader's Digest, which wanted a dictionary for a mailing slot destined to go to its 11 million direct-mail customers. Its market research showed that such a dictionary with some attractive features added, selling for $11.95, would do very well. It had tried unsuccessfully to buy another college dictionary, but when that deal fell through, it bought us. We did a substantial updating and added new encyclopedic material, and our dictionary, called *The Reader's Digest Great Encyclopedic Dictionary*, did indeed do well, selling about 2 million copies. But after that, Reader's Digest lost interest in dictionaries and wanted us to do other sorts of books for its audience – gardening books and home repair books. It had other slots to fill, and dictionaries didn't fit into them any more. Now the name Funk & Wagnalls exists only for an encyclopedia and a mass-market paperback of uncertain provenance. As a dictionary house, Funk & Wagnalls has ceased to exist.

Because all the leading American dictionary houses are part of larger enterprises, there is little willingness to take risks. The big decisions are not made by dictionary editors, who have very little power in the corporate hierarchy, but by executives who control many other parts of the business of which the dictionary unit is just one, and often not a major one. Their goal, to use business argot, is to leverage their assets, that is, to use their dictionary staffs to produce books other than dictionaries that can be produced fairly quickly and bring a more immediate return on their investment. There is nothing wrong with the production of other books – nothing wrong with gardening books or home repair books – but it deflects the dictionary staff from its core business to other uses. On a personal level, if the alternative is for the staff to be laid off, one can only support doing other kinds of books. But it doesn't do much to advance the cause of lexicography or improve the skills of lexicographers. In my experience, top corporate executives all believe that lexicographers are a fungible commodity and can be replaced at will with no loss of quality. They believe that any bright recent college graduate can do the work of a seasoned lexicographer.

One of the constant pressures in lexicography that has had a tremendous impact on the production of American commercial dictionaries – and a major factor in making unabridged dictionaries obsolete – is the cost of labor. As the cost of labor has gone up, publishers have tried every available means to pare down their labor force. Even if an excellent corpus were available to commercial native-speaker dictionaries in America, it is not yet clear how they would make use of it. Having a huge corpus at one's disposal is wonderful, but it takes time to use it, and dictionaries that operate on a tight time-frame with a skeleton staff do not have the resources to make use of it.

Under such conditions, is it any wonder that American dictionary houses are reluctant to make the investment to build their own American corpus? It isn't that the cost would be so great; it wouldn't. But it would involve a commitment of people over time for a project that is not designed to produce immediate income, and publishers are not accustomed to spending money on research, especially when they will still have to make a substantial additional investment to use this material to produce a dictionary. Furthermore, the copyright issues that would dog a commercial publisher who sought to build a corpus are not trivial. For these reasons, the preparation of a corpus of American English that might be used by commercial presses will only become a reality if undertaken by an independent entity consisting of a consortium of publishers and other business organizations.

Fortunately, a series of preliminary steps have already been taken along these lines, with the goal of creating an American national corpus comparable to the British National Corpus. A meeting to discuss a proposed American national corpus was held on May 26, 1999, in Berkeley, California, prior to the regular biennial meeting of the Dictionary Society of North America. All the leading American dictionary houses were invited to send representatives, and most of them did so.[46] The Linguistic Data Consortium of the University of Pennsylvania, a nonprofit organization already active in corpus creation used for speech recognition and linguistic studies, has been enlisted as the vehicle for providing the data and licensing use of the data. Catherine Macleod, the head of the organizing committee, has said that reports and documentation for the new corpus would be handled by New York University. Preliminary funding from publishers has been solicited to cover the costs of the early stages of preparation. The prospects are encouraging that within the next five years, a substantial American national corpus will be created, with the goal of having a balanced corpus of 100 million words on the order of the BNC. The corpus would be licensed to the sponsoring publishers and universities, and perhaps to other legitimate enterprises under certain conditions.

National and specialized corpora

The Brown Corpus inspired four other first-generation corpora of the English of India, New Zealand, Australia, and Canada, all structured more or less along the same lines as the Brown Corpus. These are the Kolhapur Corpus of Indian English, the Wellington Corpus of Written New Zealand English, the Australian Corpus of English (also called the Macquarie Corpus of Written Australian English), and the Corpus of English-Canadian Writing. The Canadian corpus, undertaken at Queens University in Ontario, is three times as large as the Brown Corpus and has added a few genre categories in its collection.[47] Such parallel corpora are useful for comparative studies among the varieties of English used throughout the world.

Another important new corpus designed to include texts of many different regional varieties of English is the International Corpus of English, proposed by Sidney Greenbaum in 1988 and still in preparation. Each of the varieties is to consist of one million words, composed of 2,000-word samples from 500 different texts written from 1990 to 1993. In addition to contributions from countries where English is widely used as a native language for most residents, samples are to be obtained from India, the Caribbean islands, Singapore, Hong Kong, the Philippines, Nigeria, and other regions in Africa.[48]

A corpus of spoken American English of 200,000 words is in preparation at the University of California at Santa Barbara. The goal is to have thirty half-hour conversations in "standard American English" from various regions of the United States, and to provide simultaneous access to the results both in transcription and sound on a CD.[49] Part 1 of this corpus is now available from the Linguistic Data Consortium. (See below, p. 295.)

In the field of ESL and EFL, learners' corpora have been developed by various institutions, including Longman and Cambridge University Press. A learners' corpus usually consists of the texts, often writing assignments or test papers, composed by speakers of languages other than English. Data about each informant are carefully encoded, because speakers of Mandarin, Arabic, and French, for example, are likely to make different sorts of errors, and teachers may then profitably focus on the kinds of errors they are likely to encounter with each group. In addition, the age and sex of the informant may be relevant to some kinds of mistakes. The mistakes in the texts are categorized by type and marked in the text, so that word order errors, for example, can be distinguished from errors in subject-verb agreement. Some categorizations can be quite elaborate, and the markup can therefore be a time-consuming operation which can only be done by highly trained editors. Learners' corpora are used more by teachers, educators, and writers of ESL textbooks than by lexicographers, because ESL dictionaries cannot focus on the mistakes of any one group. Nonetheless, the broader conclusions that may be derived from studying learners' corpora – the kinds of errors that most learners are apt to make – do influence ESL dictionaries.

Up till now, all the corpora I have described are essentially synchronic, dealing with the modern period only, but there are diachronic, or historical, corpora, which include texts over long periods of time. The Helsinki Corpus of English Texts contains 1.5 million words and consists of 400 samples of continuous text from the eighth century to the eighteenth century, and includes elaborate information about each contributor (age, sex, social status, etc.) as well as identifying the period in which the sample was written.[50] "Some of the earliest applications of corpus-based analytical techniques were for the study of literary style," but while literary scholars have generally focused on the works of a single author, historical linguists need a range of texts from different genres extending across historical periods.[51] The problem is assembling such texts in machine-readable form. This is a lively area of linguistic study, and we can expect many more and better diachronic corpora in the years ahead. Linguists are interested in how language use changes over time, for example, the declining use of the semimodals "need to" and "ought to" and the increasing use of "have to."[52]

Many large corpora have been created for research of various kinds, such as the Bell Communications Research Corpus (also called the Bellcore Corpus) of 200 million words, chiefly of newspaper wire service stories. Nexis is a vast proprietary collection of a wide range of texts that can be searched, and Lexis is the most widely used database for legal research. In addition, the Alta Vista search engine on the Internet provides access to a vast range of texts. However, such undifferentiated text collections are of limited use to the lexicographer, although they can provide evidence that a particular item exists, and in some cases can give an idea of the relative frequencies of competing forms. They are fundamentally limited because, first of all, the texts included were not selected with a view to their linguistic representativeness (see p. 331); the frequency information from such corpora will be much less reliable than from a balanced corpus. Secondly, they lack the tools of analysis that a dedicated language corpus has. Thirdly, they seldom have adequate information concerning the date and source of each text in the collection (the so-called "header" information). In addition, most such corpora are expensive to use on a regular basis. Also, one cannot have complete confidence in the accuracy of either the texts or the header information. In some corpora, errors abound.

Although the subject of this chapter is English-language corpora, the reader should not get the impression that corpora exist only in English. There are corpora of many other languages. One of the earliest large corpora was a historical corpus of French, compiled for the *Trésor de la langue française*, a massive historical dictionary dealing with the period from 1789 to 1960. For information on corpora of many languages including English, visit the website of Michael Barlow, a professor of linguistics at Stanford University (http://www.ruf.rice.edu/~barlow), and click on "Corpus linguistics." He also includes much other useful information, such as on parallel corpora, corpora in two (or more) different languages that correspond in translational equivalents or some other way. Parallel corpora are useful in developing systems for machine translation and for scholars studying the relationships between different languages. The Oxford Text Archive, whose directories are accessible at the website (http://ota.ahds.ac.uk/index.html), is a large collection of historical texts from many languages; some texts are available at no charge for scholarly research.

One of the best sources of information about English-language computer corpora is, oddly enough, in Norway. In 1977 a small group of corpus linguists formed the International Computer Archive of Modern English (ICAME) to further cooperation among corpus workers. Among those attending were Geoffrey Leech, Nelson Francis, Jan Svartvik, and Stig Johannson of the University of Oslo. They soon formed an alliance with the Norwegian Computing Centre for the Humanities at Bergen to serve as a clearinghouse for ICAME, distributing texts and information on English corpora, a function it continues to fill. It also publishes the ICAME Journal which gives current information about new computer corpora. The ICAME website is (http://www.hd.uib.no). Don't be alarmed by the opening screen, which is in Norwegian; just click on the icon for the British Union Jack to get an English translation. Some corpora, including the Brown Corpus, can be obtained directly from ICAME at very reasonable rates.

The Linguistic Data Consortium (LDC), which I have already mentioned in connection with the preparation of an American national corpus, is another valuable resource in corpus linguistics. Based at the University of Pennsylvania, the LDC includes more than 100 companies, universities, and government agencies. Up till now its collections, which include speech as well as written texts, have been used mainly by industries and educational institutions interested in (to quote its website) "speech recognition and understanding, optical and pen-based character recognition, text retrieval and understanding, machine translation, and the use of these methodologies in computer assisted language acquisition." Much of the data in its collections is copyrighted, so distribution of its corpora depends upon the particular terms of the texts in that corpus. Members of LDC naturally have access to corpora under better terms than nonmembers. Membership is not cheap for an individual or small company, but when measured against the overall investment in a new technology, it is reasonable. The LDC website is (http://www.ldc.upenn.edu).

CORPUS USE IN MODERN LEXICOGRAPHY

The traditional citation file provides evidence of the meanings of lexical items by showing how they are used in a variety of contexts. Because a corpus shows a much greater variety of contexts than a citation file, it is a better source of definitions for most words – always with the caveat that the corpus must be balanced and not just consist of 100 million words from the *New York Times* or any other single source – although, given the variety of writing in a large newspaper such as the *Times*, even 100 million words from the *Times* would be better than the source material most dictionaries have had to work with in the past. (How to achieve a balanced corpus will be discussed below, under "Compiling a corpus," p. 323.) A common problem when working with a citation file is not having enough examples of a particular usage; a common problem when working with a corpus is having too many. Instead of 15 or 20 examples, one can easily get 250 or 500, and for common words, thousands of examples (or *hits*, as corpus users call them).

Fortunately there are ways to deal with this problem. Corpus searches can be limited to the maximum number of hits the editor wants to work with; some editors limit the number to 200 or 250; others may want to see 500 for a broader range of uses. Corpus software can also randomize its selection, so that if the editor wants to see evidence for "whale," and the corpus happens to include *Moby Dick*, one can avoid having to scroll through all of the hits from *Moby Dick* because that happened to be placed in the corpus before anything else. Randomization is the use of stochastic methods that utilize laws of probability to insure that the selection is based on chance. In any event, every time editors look at the results of a corpus search, they will see the header information at the top of the screen, giving information about each hit as it is highlighted, so that they can see if a preponderance of the hits nevertheless come from the same source. If one seeks a word or expression that only rarely occurs, it may occur chiefly in only one source, so in spite of randomization techniques, the editor has to be aware of the header information, particularly when examining items that are not common. Anyone using even a very large corpus in lexicography soon becomes aware that many expressions occur rarely; that, after all, is why it is necessary to have a very large corpus. Many idioms and other fixed expressions that we might intuitively feel are very common are in fact not common at all. Indeed, some expressions – "kick the bucket" comes immediately to mind – seem to exist mainly in textbook discussions of idioms and rarely in genuine speech or writing. For some words and expressions commonly found in dictionaries, there is no evidence at all.

A good corpus is useful, then, not only for what it includes but for what it does not include. If one has a 100-million word corpus that is based on a wide variety of written and spoken sources of many different types, and it does not include a single example of a particular lexical item, this datum means something. It does not mean that the lexical item does not exist. No corpus can prove that a word or expression does not exist, and no corpus is perfect. But if the corpus has been put together carefully to be representative, one can conclude that the lexical item, if it exists, either is extremely uncommon or is used almost exclusively in a specialized field that the corpus does not cover. A low frequency for a lexical item is therefore sound justification for omitting it from one's dictionary. Conversely, a high frequency argues strongly for inclusion. Clearly, making such determinations depends upon one's faith in the representativeness of the corpus, a critically important concept in corpus lexicography. (See p. 331.)

Up until now I have been talking in general terms about what a corpus can do. Let me now give some specific examples.[53] The word "surgery" is used in different ways in American and British English. In both British and American English, it is a branch of medicine, but in Britain it also refers to a doctor's office. Most ESL dictionaries therefore indicate that the word is used as both a *mass noun* (a noun that typically cannot be pluralized or counted) and a *count noun* in Britain, but only as a mass noun in American English. An examination of our American corpus showed that this was not so. Although the American college dictionaries do include a countable sense, none gives an example of its use. Figure 20 (p. 298) is a display of 36 corpus hits for "surgeries" in the sense of a surgical procedure, e.g. "I've had 11 surgeries in 11 years." Many of these examples are from a spoken corpus. Intuitively, I would not have guessed the countable use of "surgery" would be this common in American English; I was surprised at the number of hits. Based on this evidence, we included this sense in *CDAE*, along with an example.

Adverbs are perpetually slighted in dictionaries because it is so easy to run them on to adjectives and pretend they are less important and that their meanings can be easily surmised from the adjectives. But this is often not so, and even when the general adjectival meaning is apparent, the particular aspects of that meaning implied by the adverb are often far from obvious. Take, for example, "significantly," which is almost never defined in dictionaries. Dictionaries define "significant" as important, worth

```
art attacks and gall bladder surgeries.
ey've done, he's had several surgeries.
-year-old girl who had three surgeries to correct a cleft palate and
  than here for some elective surgeries but
e but never had time between surgeries.
            Despite two major surgeries in the late '70s, she has this
nd so on and so on, but most surgeries can be done outpatient, but it
    She has undergone several surgeries and will require more, accordi
physicians who perform fetal surgeries.
s knee problem, despite nine surgeries since joining the team in 1979
the football field and seven surgeries.
  up having six or seven knee surgeries."
he's had, as I said, several surgeries on his hand and, and, uh, he's
ays, but treatments in-clude surgeries to remove abnormal cervi-cal t
ioneered various circulatory surgeries and procedures; his fame as a
her "humane parole" and two surgeries have improved the condition of
zation performed 4,113 major surgeries last year.
even if he did, experimental surgeries usually are not covered.
              " Surgeries are taking much longer than th
people who have had multiple surgeries.
                Two surgeries into a shoulder repair, she ca
partner do about 100 implant surgeries a year, but in the past 12 mon
sy and underwent a series of surgeries.
ybody should be able to have surgeries that will save their lives or
  storerooms and use them for surgeries that the rules do not official
  did not explore whether all surgeries were medically justified.
, especially with, you know, surgeries all the time.
it caused and the four major surgeries it necessitated.
nd so on and so on, but most surgeries can be done outpatient.
o there will be no more such surgeries until additional studies are d
ong time to get, for certain surgeries that aren't emergency, and you
                  first surgeries
in the operating room during surgeries.
p care, including additional surgeries, in the initial price.
  As she rightly claimed, her surgeries were not about "becoming beaut
          "I've had 11 surgeries in 11 years," said Risien, 32.
```

20 "surgeries" – American subcorpus

noticing, and meaningful. An examination of "significantly" in our corpus showed first of all that it was fairly common, occurring 18.6 times per million words, almost exactly the same frequency as the word "realistic," for example – hardly a rarity. The corpus evidence also showed that its most common meaning was not "importantly" but "by a noticeably large amount," as in these two corpus examples: "Our prison population has significantly increased in the last ten years" "Men are making significantly more money than women at the same professional level." By measuring relative frequency, the corpus told us that this word is worth including and its examples showed that meanings inferred from the adjective were insufficient; the word therefore merited separate-entry status and its own definition. Neither the lexicographer's intuition nor experience would have yielded enough information to make that decision.

The foregoing example illustrates the fact that in modern corpus use, frequency data are not just raw frequency counts (though these are available), which are often not terribly meaningful, but frequency per million (or ten million) words. Also, as we will see below, there are other statistical tools available for determining relative probability. Such tools are more often used to determine the importance of set phrases, idioms, and *collocations* (commonly co-occurring words such as "light a match" or "say hello").

Take the case of "colossal," shown in Figure 21 (pp. 300–1). Anyone scanning this list will soon be struck by one fact: the overwhelmingly negative contexts of the figurative examples. One sees "colossal failure," "colossal errors," "colossal collapse," "colossal mess," "colossal waste of time," and "colossal indifference." There are one or two exceptions, such as "Tolstoy's colossal genius." But as a generalization, one can say that when the word is not used in its literal sense describing an object that is huge, "colossal" usually refers to something bad or regrettable. In a learner's dictionary in particular, this is valuable information; but even in a dictionary for native speakers such information might be useful. Again, this is not something that the lexicographer would be likely to discover without a corpus.

The *lemma* of a word is its basic form, usually the infinitive form of verbs and the singular of nouns, the form under which most words are entered in dictionaries. Thus "ran," "runs," and "running" belong to the lemma "run." Nowadays the words in a corpus are routinely *lemmatized* (linked to their lemma) through sophisticated software programs. This is extremely useful. If the editor wants to do a search for the phrasal verb "run down" in its various senses (to hit someone with a car, to lose strength, to find out the facts about something, to criticize someone), it is clearly necessary to find also "ran down," "runs down," and "running down" as well as "run down," and one should not have to conduct four separate searches. In a lemmatized corpus, one search will capture all of the inflections of "run" in combination with "down." Likewise, the plurals of nouns and the comparatives and superlatives of adjectives and adverbs can also be obtained in one search based on the lemma.

Most corpora nowadays also have been subjected to automatic grammatical tagging to differentiate parts of speech, and often to further differentiate some parts of speech functionally. Figure 22 (p. 302) shows the "tag descriptions" of "run" in the Cambridge International Corpus. (The frequency under each heading is per 10 million words.) One can also make the search case sensitive. This is useful when one is working

```
lies in recumbent posture, a colossal but mutilated figure of Buddha
tle Challenger in 1986. Such colossal failures have been headline new
                        Colossal hokum like they don't makeanymo
            At these colossal close outs, $7,000 designer wed
rs call the grape boycott a "colossal failure" and doubt the union wi
table buffalo-horn chairs, a colossal pair of 18th-century tables ado
a phantasmagorical burden of colossal furry vines and great clumps of
fe on the Mississippi, as "a colossal combination of robbers, horse-t
        After eyeing the colossal copper woman crowned in front o
te "would be one of the most colossal blunders of any administration.
's just been such a enormous colossal failure
niversal assent to a "silent colossal National Lie."
to "this horrible event, the colossal historical defeat of Russia."
ts have been immortalized in colossal monuments to the triumph of hum
ceiling shelves for the most colossal collection of books, records, a
ny televised, really seems a colossal breach of decorum, an outbreak
pect the entire affair was a colossal misunderstanding.
they, side by side with this colossal nonsense?
            "Despite colossal economic inequalities, they hav
            The "colossal drama" features, therefore, a v
employs the figure of "some colossal drama" to portray the cultural
        A work of colossal tedium, it excited for a brief
    It makes me want to cook colossal meals that take forever to prep
ernal entity undertaking the colossal task of allocating supplies for
The damage and the ruins are colossal," Sangheli said in a radio addr
-so's inventive terms, was a colossal misunder standing leading simpl
ut there have also been some colossal errors.
            A colossal bungle.
nal, inherited lie with the "colossal national lie" is supported by t
eterminant of form - until a colossal failure forced a reconsideratio
wing 16), and the unfinished colossal heads found in quarries on East
invariably to culminate in a colossal failure that takes everyone by
t least 50 people and caused colossal damage, Prime Minister Andrei S
und stage of San Francisco's Colossal Pictures into the world's bigge
itics or the public, and the colossal expense of his Vietnam War film
e "legend-play" recalls the "colossal drama" of the 1872 Preface, and
interval between two of the colossal supports").
evolve (or devolve) toward a colossal failure.
reated more massive and more colossal productive forces than have all
n its shield that provided a colossal view of all the rest of Valpara
        I look at the colossal, mangled heap under the BMW's w
in the essay, as "the silent colossal national lie that is the suppor
rmous unfamiliar shrubs with colossal gleaming leaves and great swoll
lies a white sunken city, a colossal octopus rises out of the city p
too; the one who had had the colossal nerve and courage to walk away
        Some of the colossal limestone blocks of the three p
beads and bell-bottoms as a colossal waste of time.
going forward in having two colossal industries doing battle with on
the dust lifted off, as the colossal weight slowly nuzzled, a final
ould ever be, anything but a colossal failure.
wha- that they'd made a colossal mess out of the road
```

21 "colossal" – American subcorpus

```
a kind of incredulity at the   colossal  capacity for visualization that
th the belief that there was    colossal  material power in wind, earthqu
eir own or their colleagues'    colossal  financial improprieties, LDP po
at Ephesus, one of the first    colossal  Greek temples.
missed as unlikely given the    colossal  disparity in the countries' eco
-century after that bridge's    colossal  collapse, there is reason to be
nd opened the way for Wynn's    colossal  offer.
sent a prime candidate for a    colossal  failure around the year 2000 fo
w it is clear evidence of my    colossal  gullibility that I didn't see w
    wha- that they'd made a    colossal  mess out of the road
orary Dostoyevsky, Tolstoy's   colossal  genius is beyond dispute.
g, to the famous tale of the   colossal  national truth teller and stain
ions are called forth by the   colossal  societal lie that holds human b
first product at Comdex, the   colossal  trade show for the electronics
ization has resulted in the   "colossal  drama" of the United States.
e important because, in this   colossal  drama, they are unquestionably
  United States is an area of   colossal  potential for natural gas.
irie into the heavens like a   colossal  eye, a hollow circular structur
t from ethnic cleansing on a   colossal  scale in Russia, Ukraine, or Ka
cient state sector will be a   colossal  process.
ration, Carajas represents a   colossal  undertaking.
  job that gobbled water into   colossal  compressors and squirted it out
t from ethnic cleansing on a   colossal  scale in Russia, Ukraine, or Ka
phae was almost tripped by a   colossal  sailor with fiery eyes beneath
ally the same as that of the   colossal  Firth of Forth Bridge (see Fig.
nce to the other his size is   colossal.
  To Sifton that was "a most   colossal  endowment of sectarian educatio
  both more and less than the   colossal  Women's Movement statue of hers
be surprised to learn of my   colossal  indifference to that proposal f
  Railway Station, $800 is an   colossal  sum, more than six months' aver
emblematizes - conceals the   "colossal  national lie" with which it is
```

with a word that also happens to be a name. It would be impossible to search productively for "bush" in an American corpus, for example, without making the search case sensitive to avoid being buried under thousands of references to former president George Bush and other members of his family active in politics.

In working on the word "crazy," I checked our corpus to find how common the noun was. To my surprise, there were no corpus hits for the singular noun; all were plural. There were 17 plural hits, among them "The crazies are out there in numbers," "We're food crazies," "We're beginning to get the crazies," "there have been some crazies that killed people with guns," "We've got a bunch of crazies on this team," "There's a lot of crazies out there," and "You can't take care of crazies forever, like my mother." See Figure 23 (p. 303). Most of these come from the spoken corpus. Apparently "crazies" – which I think is usually said with a sort of exasperated shrug not devoid of humor – is essentially generic and relates to a type of person rather than to an individual.

Word	Tag Description	All	AMSPOK	AMWRIT	BRSPOK	BRWRIT	Keys
ran(FU)	unclassified word	4	0	0	17	0	ran(FU)
ran(JJ)	general adjective	0	1	0	0	0	ran(JJ)
ran(NN1)	singular common noun	1	4	0	0	0	ran(NN1)
ran(VVD)	past tense of lexical verb	741	639	991	355	977	Ran(VVD),ran(
ran(VVN)	past participle of lexical	14	23	6	17	8	ran(VVN)
ru-n(NN1)	singular common noun	0	0	0	0	0	Ru-n(NN1)
run(CC)	coordinating conjunction	0	0	0	0	0	run(CC)
run(FU)	unclassified word	10	0	0	38	0	run(FU)
run(JJ)	general adjective	1	2	1	0	0	run(JJ)
run(NN1)	singular common noun	431	589	554	243	338	Run(NN1),run(
run(NNU)	unit of measurement, neutr	0	0	0	0	0	run(NNU)
run(VV0)	base form of lexical verb	337	553	316	226	252	Run(VV0),run(
run(VVD)	past tense of lexical verb	5	14	2	3	0	run(VVD)
run(VVI)	infinitive	856	1298	875	578	671	run(VVI),RUN(
run(VVN)	past participle of lexical	490	541	502	435	483	Run(VVN),run(
run-ning(VVG)	-ing participle of lexical	0	0	0	0	0	run-ning(VVG)
run-s(VVZ)	-s form of lexical verb	0	0	0	0	0	run-s(VVZ)
running(FU)	unclassified word	4	0	0	17	0	Running(FU),r
running(JJ)	general adjective	134	135	205	69	126	Running(JJ),r
running(NN1)	singular common noun	141	253	123	55	133	Running(NN1),
running(VVG)	-ing participle of lexical	1040	1475	1035	808	840	Running(VVG),
runs(FU)	unclassified word	2	0	0	7	0	runs(FU)
runs(NN2)	plural common noun	112	165	146	31	105	Runs(NN2),run
runs(VVZ)	-s form of lexical verb	370	367	510	247	355	Runs(VVZ),run

22 Tag descriptions of "run"

Based on this evidence, we indicated that this word is usually used in the plural. I am sure that somewhere in the world, someone has used "crazy" as a singular noun, but the fact that we have no evidence for it shows that it is not common.

"Perhaps the single most striking thing about corpus evidence," say Michael Rundell and Penny Stock, two lexicographers "brought up on a diet of citation slips," is "the *inescapability* [their italics] of the information it presents. If you are confronted with not two or three but dozens or even hundreds of instances of a word being used in a particular way, there is really no arguing with what the corpus is telling you."[54] Rundell and Stock go on to illustrate this by looking at "represent," which the learner's dictionaries of the 1970s defined only as being a representative of something. Yet there was copious corpus evidence of its use as a copula in sentences like "The Mansholt Plan . . . represents a bold initiative" and "This strategy . . . represents the most promising yet suggested," with the meaning of "to amount to or constitute." In some genres of text, they observe, it was the commonest use of the word.[55]

Among the many advantages of using a corpus in lexicography, perhaps frequency counts are the most important. One of the first decisions lexicographers have to make is what lexical items to put in and what to leave out, and if they decide to put something in, under what

Word	Tag Description	All	AMSPOK	AMWRIT	Keys
crazier(JJR)	general comparative adjective	7	10	3	crazier(JJR)
crazies(NN2)	plural common noun	7	10	3	crazies(NN2)
craziest(JJT)	general superlative adjective	6	11	1	craziest(JJT),C
crazy(JJ)	general adjective	574	798	349	CRAZY(JJ),Crazy

```
ithout hauling a shipload of   crazies  along."
 because there has been some   crazies  that killed people with guns and
  assault-rifle extremists or  crazies," says Bill Dominguez, chairman
 ; that is, Mcveigh and those  crazies  who made the analogy to the mili
      Yeah, there's a lot of   crazies  out there that can just go in an
                      The      crazies  are out there in numbers.
 s eyes and says: "We're food  crazies."
 lum, all the hyperdex-zonked  crazies  grinning fixedly into the bright
                      The      crazies, the clowns, the "sports intelle
 mikaze Kempies and Robertson  crazies  try to change the rules every ti
     We're beginning to get the crazies, and that's what we tried to avo
 mates: "We've got a bunch of  crazies  on this team...
      "You can't take care of  crazies  forever, like my mother.
 really necessary to have the  crazies  that populate her life before an
               And A few       crazies.
               And A few       crazies.
 e will continue to always be  crazies?
```

23 Tag descriptions and search for "crazy" and "crazies" – American subcorpus

form? For both such decisions, the corpus is indispensable. If an item has a frequency below a certain value in a large, representative corpus, one can conclude that the item is relatively uncommon and omit it with some degree of confidence. The relative frequency of various inflections of a word or variants in its spelling can lead one to a decision about what to regard as the lemma or preferred spelling. It has always been difficult to decide whether a compound should be entered in open, closed, or hyphenated form, and also to decide whether or not a word should be capitalized. Is it "e-mail," "E-mail," or "email"? In some cases the situation is too fluid to admit of any clear answer, and this is probably the case with e-mail, but very often the corpus can provide a reasonable basis for making a decision.

In the past, frequency of sense was often a matter of guesswork. But by analyzing the results of a corpus search, one can determine the relative frequencies of particular meanings of words, and use this information to put the definitions in that order. To be honest, it is still not always possible to distinguish frequencies of meanings with any great certitude because so much judgment is involved in distinguishing between closely allied meanings in the first place. Where the divisions of sense are straightforward, it is possible. ESL dictionaries in particular are already using the corpus in this way, and some are also using it to alert the reader if a particular meaning or word has a very high frequency over all, or a high frequency in spoken English.

A corpus can show that a word or a particular word or sense is used mainly or exclusively in certain varieties or categories. For example, the Cambridge corpus shows that the spelling "catalog" is virtually nonexistent in British English, but that both spellings of the verb are about equally common in American English, with the noun occurring about twice as frequently as "catalog" than as "catalogue." (This may be a consequence of the preference for "catalog" in US libraries.) A search for the word "dietary" turned up 147 hits in the Cambridge full corpus, but none at all in fiction or in the subcorpus of spoken English. This is a word used almost exclusively in nonfiction and technical writing. Some words are common in business and advertising but not otherwise; some words are used mainly to or by children. The use of some words can be correlated to the age or sex of the user. In British English, "gorgeous" is three times as likely to be used by a female speaker as by a male, and "ever so nice" is typically used "by women over 45, and hardly ever by men of any age."[56]

A corpus is also an invaluable source for information about grammar, both for dictionaries and grammars. New grammars will be based on corpus evidence and may even be called *lexicogrammars* because they will link meanings and grammatical features more closely than traditional grammars have done in the past. For example, one editor of a grammar in progress points out that in frames such as "I find it hard to believe," "it" occurs 98% of the time with "find" or "make," and "it" is followed by a restricted range of adjectives that include "difficult," "hard," and "easy."[57] Analysis of grammatical inflections in a corpus can provide much more sophisticated information than was formerly available. In giving information about the inflections of adjectives and adverbs, for example, lexicographers follow conventional rules and will indicate that a word like "safe" has a comparative form "safer" and a superlative form "safest," and a word like "responsible" is compared by adding "more" or "most" before it. But some adjectives and adverbs have no comparative (like "mere"), only a superlative, and some adjectives that supposedly cannot be compared by adding -*er* or -*est* in fact can (such as "tireder" and "wickedest"). Dictionary corpus searches for verbs very often turn up examples of transitive uses of supposedly intransitive verbs and vice versa. The task of the definers is to calculate how common such uses are and decide whether they should include them. Another perennial problem is deciding whether the present or past participle of a verb

Word	Tag Description	All	AMSPOK	AMWRIT	Keys
escalate(VV0)	base form of lexical verb	3	2	3	escalate(VV0)
escalate(VVI)	infinitive	15	8	22	escalate(VVI)
escalated(VVD)	past tense of lexical verb	7	4	9	escalated(VVD)
escalated(VVN)	past participle of lexical verb	20	20	20	escalated(VVN)
escalates(VVZ)	-s form of lexical verb	3	1	4	escalates(VVZ)
escalating(JJ)	general adjective	26	17	34	escalating(JJ),
escalating(VVG)	-ing participle of lexical verb	6	5	6	escalating(VVG)

24 Tag descriptions of "escalate"

has acquired adjectival status and merits inclusion as a lemma in its own right. In the past lexicographers had no way to decide this. With a corpus that has been grammatically tagged, they do. See Figure 24 for the results of a search for "escalate." (All the numbers are frequency per 10 million.) At a glance one can see that the adjective is common, accounting for fully one third of all occurrences.

There is scarcely any area of dictionary work where a corpus cannot provide important evidence for the lexicographer. The corpus is of great value in deciding on the word list and on the form of each entry. It is vitally important in defining, first in determining the sense breakdown if the word is polysemous and then in discovering more particularly how best to define each sense. It is not as good in defining realia (what is a *power mower* or a *jigsaw?*) but it is excellent at providing authentic examples of how such words are used. Although a corpus, unlike a citation file, usually gives extremely good coverage of common words, including phrasal verbs and idioms, if the corpus is large enough it can also be very serviceable in covering uncommon words. To be sure, the evidence still has to be solicited and evaluated. Humans are still writing dictionaries, not corpora. But the corpus is a tool that has breathed new life into the art of lexicography. Wrong decisions are still being made, of course, and always will be, but for the first time lexicographers at least have a sound basis for making decisions and can no longer plead ignorance.

Selecting examples in ESL lexicography

In dictionaries for foreign learners, the use of examples is of paramount importance. Often the corpus can provide suitable examples or at least suggest an appropriate context – that is, a *likely* context – which the lexicographer can use to create an example. Take a word like "reconcile." *CDAE* defines it in one sense as "to adjust the way you think about (a fact or situation that is opposed to another fact or situation) so that you can accept both." Try inventing a likely example for that sense. It would be almost impossible, especially if one wanted to avoid using a complex vocabulary and wanted to keep the example relatively short. Yet some example is obviously necessary. Often the corpus will not come up with something suitable that can be used without change, especially in a dictionary that is not for advanced students, but in this case I was able to find an authentic example: "Hurston tells the story of a country preacher struggling to reconcile his love for his wife with his attraction to other women." On the other hand, I could not find a suitable corpus example for the other included sense of "reconcile": "to reconcile (yourself) to a situation is to accept it even though it is unpleasant or painful, because it cannot be changed." The invented example is, "After the death of her husband, she found it difficult to reconcile herself to a life alone."

Why couldn't I find a suitable example for the latter sense of "reconcile"? John Sinclair's comment on this issue is apposite:

One of the inescapable conclusions of studying real text is that the categories of description are so intertwined in realization that very few actual instances are straightforward illustrations of just one of the factors that led to the particular choice. [¶] This does not constitute an argument for inventing examples.[58]

But I think it does precisely that. Sinclair says, "The selection of suitable examples . . . requires only a sufficiently large number of instances to choose from."[59] I disagree. No matter how big the corpus, I am skeptical that simple enough examples could be found for every level of learner. We had many examples for "conciliatory," but this just isn't a word that is used simply or in short, revealing contexts.

Let me quote another Collins Cobuild lexicographer, Gwyneth Fox, who presents the issue cogently:

Learners, and unfortunately some teachers, often feel that they should be provided with language that is as simple as possible, . . . [but] If a word typically occurs in a sentence which is grammatically complex or alongside vocabulary items that are infrequent, it would be misleading of a dictionary to present that word in a very simple clause or sentence with easy vocabulary.[60]

To illustrate this difficulty, let me quote from one of our corpus hits for "conciliatory":

The quorum fell silent. Then my aunt sat bold upright. "You had The Club on?" she exclaimed in disbelief. And then she grew conciliatory. "Don't worry," she said. "You'll get a new car. A better car. One with power everything. A plush interior. Loaded."

A car has been stolen. The language used isn't particularly difficult, and the example does illustrate the word's meaning, but it is clearly unsuitable for a dictionary. Other examples were too context-specific, for example "His remarks matched Israel's conciliatory policy toward Jordan."

I agree with Gwyneth Fox's argument that many words do not occur in simple, self-explanatory contexts. Most authentic language is highly specific. Names and places abound. Although the language in the quotation for "conciliatory" is not difficult, in many written contexts such words occur in complex environments where the vocabulary is apt to be correspondingly difficult. The sentences in which they occur cannot usually be shortened to fit the limits of a dictionary example without becoming totally obscure. I am referring to words like "compensation" or "residual," "contingency" or "requisite," "arbitrary" or "respite." These are not extraordinarily difficult words; they are words that educated people recognize and feel comfortable using. The problem is particularly acute in ESL lexicography, which resembles bilingual lexicography in having a dual purpose: to explain the meanings of words that readers hear and read (the "decoding" function) and to help them produce correct forms in their own speech and writing (the "encoding" function). By contrast, monolingual dictionaries for native speakers generally are for decoding purposes only. Whatever help users get in encoding is adventitious rather than built in to the design of the dictionary.

In ESL lexicography there is a conflict between providing information that is understandable for decoding purposes and giving accurate information for encoding purposes. Noncorpus-based ESL dictionaries often give improbable, invented examples using simple language in illustration of difficult words, such as this one from the *Newbury House Dictionary* for "conciliatory": "After arguing with her, he made conciliatory remarks about how much he loves her." Here is an example from *NTC's American English Learner's Dictionary* for "arbitrary": "The supervisor made an arbitrary decision to promote an employee." The inauthenticity of this example is obvious because of the lack of specificity. If a supervisor arbitrarily promoted someone, the supervisor and employee would be named, and we could expect a pertinent criticism to accompany the observation. This neutral, bland observation about two generic people occurs in a social vacuum. It has no consequences and no history. Real language is not used in such ways. This is textbook language, and although it does convey the sense, it is misleading as a model of actual usage.

The availability of corpora can now enable us, for the first time, to reject such juvenile and improbable formulations and replace them with more credible examples. Sinclair and his colleagues argue that to simplify the examples of complex words is to misrepresent how they are used. However, if the reader cannot understand the authentic example given – that is, cannot decode it – he or she certainly will not be able to use it. I do regard decoding as primary, and however important the encoding function is, we have to face the limitations, especially in inter-mediate-level dictionaries, in helping the user encode difficult words. To the extent that we can provide a level of difficulty to the example that is realistic without sacrificing understandability, we should. We should at all costs avoid ridiculously simple, childish examples for difficult words. What a corpus can do above all else – even when it cannot provide ver-batim examples that can be used in a dictionary – is to give examples at the right level of complexity and in a framework that is typical so that the lexicographer can devise examples that are not silly, stilted, or clearly artificial.

Time and again one learns that native intuition does not suffice when faced with the problem of coming up with suitable examples. Della Summers writes, "It is commonly opined by corpus workers that although things that are discovered are 'obvious,' they only become obvious once the corpus has revealed them to us, i.e. they are not reli-ably recovered from the lexicographer's innate knowledge and under-standing of the language."[61] Take the case of "wicked," which means morally wrong or bad. The corpus shows that in modern American usage the word is as often used to mean impressive because of being for-midable or dangerous, as in "wicked-looking machetes." Sometimes the context expresses admiration, as in "a wicked parody or two of contem-poraries." Even when used in its literal sense the word is often used tongue-in-cheek ("a thespian in wicked New York," "they think I'm the Wicked Witch of the West"). The evidence does not support defining "wicked" simply as morally bad without showing how the word is actu-ally used today.

Collocation

I have defined *collocation* as commonly co-occurring words, such as "say hello," but as the reader may have surmised, that rather offhand definition is not the whole story. Collocations are important in corpus lexicography because they are largely invisible in citation files and can only be discovered through the use of corpora. Also, in a large corpus, statistical norms can be applied to them, as we will see, to indicate the relative significance of their association. Collocations are of great importance in ESL and bilingual lexicography, where readers are unfamiliar with the common associative patterns of the language they are trying to learn.

How does one distinguish a collocation from an idiom, and how often do the words have to co-occur? This subject has been much discussed and debated among linguists and lexicographers, and they are not in complete agreement. An *idiom* is usually defined as a group of two or more words whose collective meaning cannot be divined by someone who knows the meanings of the separate words. In "If we don't leave right now, we'll really be up the creek," *up the creek* is an idiom. Many phrasal verbs, such as *turn up* in "I hope she turns up soon," are idioms, but not all.[62] Collocations have been described as habitual or as sounding natural, but, although true, this is too subjective a criterion to be useful. In practice, a collocation is any two or more words that are found together (that "co-occur") at a significantly higher frequency in natural speech or writing than they occur with other words. Collocations can be variable so long as they have some relatively fixed elements, such as "under (no, some, those) circumstances."[63] Corpus research has elaborated statistical methods for verifying relative frequency and the significance of such frequency.

The corpus allows us to measure the likelihood that two words have co-occurred by chance, and to compare this datum with the actual frequency of their co-occurrence. There are two statistical measures used to judge the significance of relatedness. *Mutual information* (MI) calculates the strength of the probability of each of two words occurring together, either consecutively or within a given span, as in the case of "under . . . circumstances."[64] A high MI score is evidence that the association of two words is greater than chance. As the span between the two words increases, the likelihood of their co-occurrence increases, but the statistical measure takes this fact into consideration. The MI score does not take frequency into consideration, so it may be misleading if one of the words is of very low frequency; if a low-frequency word occurs only with another word, it will receive a high MI score in spite of its low frequency. However, collocational search results always show the overall frequency (or *raw frequency*), so the editor can take low frequency into consideration. *T-scores* do not measure the strength of association between two words; rather, "the frequencies of the collocates for each word are analyzed and compared to each other."[65] T-scores are useful when comparing the collocates of two words, such as "begin" and "start." T-scores are also useful in analyzing high-frequency words such as prepositions; MI scores

Word	POS	Frequency	Modal %	MI	Mode	Count	C-Score
husky	adj	7	67	4.17	-1	19	3.80
hear	v	115	43	1.57	-2	4457	3.71
loud	adj	26	72	2.68	-1	333	3.69
hoarse	adj	7	43	3.98	2	25	3.57
his	dete	237	70	-0.07	-1	47351	3.14
tone	n	23	53	2.06	-2	549	3.03
gravelly	adj	2	100	4.33	-1	5	2.97
her	dete	168	73	0.04	-1	30099	2.94
shrill	adj	6	66	3.47	-1	34	2.94
low	adj	42	70	1.28	-1	2200	2.77
reedy	adj	2	80	4.49	-1	3	2.76
gruff	adj	3	74	3.80	-1	12	2.64
in	prep	373	31	-0.97	-3	184633	2.28
trail	v	5	94	2.66	1	70	2.28
raise	v	30	72	1.07	-2	1947	2.26
voiceless	adj	2	50	3.62	3	12	2.09
soft	adj	15	51	1.78	-1	461	2.08
whisper	n	6	49	2.42	4	103	2.07
of	prep	408	39	-1.36	1	298813	2.05
fricatives	n	2	50	3.87	1	6	2.02
sound	n	29	48	0.99	-3	2016	1.95
squeaky	adj	2	100	3.47	-1	10	1.94
hushed	adj	3	89	2.94	-1	27	1.85
authoritative	adj	4	79	2.54	-1	63	1.83
audible	adj	3	70	2.74	-1	42	1.81
high-pitched	adj	2	64	3.25	-1	15	1.72
boom	v	3	76	2.85	1	28	1.69
lower	v	16	91	0.96	-2	1169	1.68
speak	v	34	29	0.80	-4	2830	1.62
muffled	adj	3	79	2.63	-1	39	1.59
tremble	v	6	62	2.08	1	138	1.58
crack	v	5	89	2.00	1	134	1.57
sound	v	22	70	0.57	1	2318	1.46
resonant	adj	2	79	2.79	-1	24	1.35
be	v	308	43	-1.72	1	322869	1.34
lone	adj	3	79	2.34	-1	52	1.30
disembodied	adj	2	92	2.63	-1	27	1.26
nasal	adj	2	77	2.68	-1	25	1.24
shout	v	9	47	1.53	1	351	1.21
murmur	n	3	47	2.57	-2	41	1.12
trembling	adj	3	96	1.91	-1	96	1.12
deep	adj	12	57	0.90	-1	913	1.11
rise	v	13	84	0.64	1	1282	1.11
tremor	n	2	70	2.80	-3	17	1.07
own	dete	32	69	-0.18	-1	7160	1.03
tenor	n	2	94	2.14	-1	53	0.98
gentle	adj	6	45	1.64	-1	209	0.97
their	dete	59	58	-0.80	-1	24486	0.97
authorial	adj	2	85	2.40	-1	33	0.96
my	dete	50	65	-0.64	-1	17779	0.96
female	adj	10	88	0.73	-1	902	0.91
fade	v	5	57	1.57	1	176	0.90
say	v	85	36	-1.07	1	46518	0.89
familiar	adj	9	62	0.98	-1	637	0.81

25 Lemmatized collocation search for "voice"

soprano	n	2	75	2.43	-1	30	0.81
concern	n	13	36	0.59	1	1362	0.78
subdued	adj	2	69	2.05	-1	58	0.76
to	prep	235	20	-1.74	-3	249875	0.71
chorus	n	3	39	1.84	3	103	0.62
dissent	n	2	73	1.94	2	61	0.58
hum	n	2	55	2.20	-2	34	0.57
listen	v	10	57	0.44	-3	1183	0.54
your	dete	30	74	-0.59	-1	10018	0.53
from	prep	68	33	-1.14	1	39867	0.51
stern	adj	3	42	1.80	-1	89	0.51
with	prep	99	23	-1.21	-2	61958	0.51
booming	adj	2	87	1.79	-1	71	0.50
come	v	39	54	-0.71	1	14791	0.48
harsh	adj	4	46	1.52	-1	148	0.48
silence	v	2	29	2.46	3	34	0.48
agitated	adj	2	77	1.91	-1	55	0.46
ear	n	5	47	1.08	4	307	0.45
male	adj	8	87	0.47	-1	943	0.45
hiss	v	2	91	1.97	1	43	0.44
echo	v	3	73	1.43	1	149	0.39
muffle	v	2	45	2.08	2	39	0.35
have	v	119	25	-1.61	1	111745	0.33
narrative	adj	7	95	0.48	-1	770	0.31
sweet	adj	6	39	1.10	-1	386	0.31
opinion	n	8	78	0.34	2	1008	0.24
quiet	adj	6	53	0.67	-1	580	0.24
shaky	adj	2	80	1.96	-1	40	0.23
call	v	22	58	-0.50	1	6808	0.19
emotion	n	3	50	1.16	3	195	0.18
shake	v	6	68	0.59	1	583	0.18
distinctive	adj	3	43	1.25	-1	187	0.16
human	adj	11	84	-0.10	-1	2291	0.16
inner	adj	4	96	0.82	-1	323	0.15
ring	v	3	89	1.18	1	165	0.14
sing	v	7	27	0.92	1	497	0.13
bass	adj	2	93	1.41	-1	97	0.12
poetic	adj	4	88	0.88	-1	294	0.09
break	v	7	86	0.30	1	922	0.06
singing	n	4	85	0.81	-1	341	0.06
that	conj	92	50	-1.92	1	117883	0.06
mail	n	4	89	0.76	1	358	0.05
angry	adj	5	80	0.70	-1	422	0.03
cry	v	7	50	0.58	1	702	0.01
strong	adj	11	51	0.07	-1	1894	-0.03
behind	prep	12	38	0.01	1	2153	-0.04

are better at finding ordinary collocations, phrasal verbs, idioms, and open compounds. Some corpus software engineers have devised other statistical measures in an effort to take low frequency into consideration as well. Figure 25 shows a lemmatized collocational search for "voice," therefore including "voices," "voiced," and "voicing." Each collocate at the extreme left is also lemmatized, so "hear" includes "hears," "hearing," and "heard." The *C-score* is a modification of the MI score that gives some weight to the frequency.[66] *Frequency* is the number of co-occurrences per 10 million words with the lemmatized "voice." *Count* is raw frequency per 10 million words. *Mode* indicates the position of the collocate, with a negative value meaning that the collocate precedes "voice" or its inflections, and a positive value meaning it follows them. Therefore, the −2 Mode score for "hear" means that when "hear" occurred as a collocate for "voice" and its inflections, it preceded it and was the second word before it (i.e., with one intervening word) 43% of the time (indicated by the *Modal %*), as in "She heard a voice" or "We heard loud voices."

It is possible to do searches for more than one word and to lemmatize one or more of the words. If one wanted to do a search only for the phrase "hear voices," one could search for a lemmatized "hear" + "voices" when they occurred together in that order with no intervening words. Multiword searches can take a long time, however, so it is ill-advised to do a search for more than two words in combination unless the words are all of low frequency, or of two words if one of the words is an extremely high-frequency word (such as a particle or preposition). Most searches can be done in a very short time, but if one simply must do a search that will take a long time – say, twenty minutes or so – some systems allow one to put it on a queue on the network, where it will be done at night when the workload is lighter. One can then claim it the next morning, like a newspaper dropped at one's door.

Once the editors have obtained the overall collocational picture, they can call up the actual hits within the selected span for the word being searched. "Husky" appeared immediately before "voice" 67% of the time it appeared as a collocate. The 43 hits for "husky" are shown as Figure 26. I am displaying only "Key Word in Context" (KWIC) displays, but most systems allow for sentences or whole paragraphs to be displayed on command, and sometimes even the whole text of the source, though it is seldom necessary to use this option. Ideally, editors should be able to select a particular quotation and transfer the sentence in which it occurs directly to the dictionary entry or to a buffer where they can edit it and transfer it to the dictionary entry. This is the system we employed in editing *CDAE*.

Collocational searches can show which adverbs or prepositions commonly are associated with particular verbs, and how their use affects meaning. Because a search allows for a span in either direction of the verb, editors can find collocations and phrasal verbs even when one or more words intervene, as we have seen. Figure 27 (pp. 314–15) shows a portion of the results of the search for the lemmatized collocate "hear" occurring with the lemmatized "voice." In a collocational search for "run," under the collocate "down" one will find examples of "ran it

```
d, in what I thought a husky voice, "Good night!"
nnes," Petra said in a husky voice.
sound of that slightly husky voice.
aid to him in that low husky voice of hers?
sive vulnerable heroine, her voice ranging from glorious husky chest
you are," said a deep, husky voice behind him.
                    His voice was husky.
        Caldwell's own voice has a husky quality gloved by soft
have to go back in," a husky voice commanded.
she did have that very husky voice when she said, `Hi, I'm Rula Lensk
true," he says in his husky voice.
    see Dell, to hear her husky voice, to smell the inside of her cab: 1
saying to herself in a husky voice as she gazed within - `It was best
fathers in him," - Walter's voice was indistinct and husky here, and
adio, heard D'Aquino's husky voice, he persuaded her to read statemen
nst me," she said in a husky voice.
ng you," she says in a husky voice.
                    Trang's voice had a husky, midrange tone, as if
confessed the gloomy, husky voice of Mr Verloc.
        He lowered his husky voice confidentially before the unmoved
                    His voice was husky with sleep.
erloc's husky conversational voice was heard speaking of youth, of a
home?' she asked, her husky voice tickling his ear.
        A smooth, husky voiced pebble of a man, he looks well in
han a seal, and with a husky voice.
e dining-room," he said, his voice sounding strangely husky.
e risk?' he asked in a husky voice.
is nose and asked in a husky voice, "Has the chaplain informed his fa
did she speak, and then her voice had a husky ring to it.
midating effect of her husky voice and vowel-stressing accent, she re
                    Her voice was husky.
    them!' he begged in a husky voice, unable to sustain the forms of me
                    Her voice grew husky.
he said in a pleasant, husky voice, cadenced and calm.
    Mr Verloc raised his husky voice slightly.
                    Her voice was husky with sleep.
    Diana called, her voice husky with emotion.
    She had a low, husky voice that seemed more of a purr.
    "Here!" answered a husky voice from above; and, running up, Meg f
h her feline grace and husky voice.
u want?" he asked in a husky voice while she kissed his face everywhe
diately recognized the husky voice as that of a Grassleggings girl.
                    But her voice is husky, betraying the thick, whe
```

26 "husky" as a collocate of "voice"

down" and "ran the report down," in the sense of tracking down hard-to-find information, and under the collocate "by" one will find examples of "run something by" someone, in the sense of letting someone vet a text to approve it or catch mistakes. Collocational searches are extremely useful in defining phrasal verbs, and will show, for example, whether the same adverb or preposition is used with the verb in both British and American English, or whether one form is preferred in either variety.

Collocations, as I have already noted, are especially important in

```
roaring ocean and hear only voices; even if the sounds of the wind a
        "I could hear her voice so clearly now that I flinched.
d hear him, I could hear his voice telling me the things he has alway
rwise you would never hear a voice just a solid noise that would beco
g all fear, and, raising her voice to make herself heard above the up
ore: "Today, if you hear his voice, do not harden your hearts."
nning to hear a strong inner voice urging change.
ng Audivi vocem : `I heard a voice from heaven, "Come all wise virgin
thing, or wanted to hear his voice first and not the other's blithe m
later she heard the sound of voices.
hat I could hear only my own voice, but my own voice was the voice of
  I gave a jump to hear that voice, knowing it well for Grace's, and
moved on, and heard the loud voice of a man who, with a glass in his
might hear and recognise his voice.
        Today, if you hear his voice,
s to their advocacy, Clare's voice continued to be heard.
nd; and I seemed to hear the voice of the captain piping in the choru
a thick fog and heard my own voice as if it were far distant.
            She heard his voice as if from a great distance.
        Then I heard a voice from heaven say, "Write: Blessed a
happened," he said in a soft voice barely heard in the courtroom.
ing to hear laughter or soft voices.
nuine poetry we can hear the voice of a distinctive personality; but
  see Dell, to hear her husky voice, to smell the inside of her cab: 1
      Suddenly I heard a voice behind me.
s not to hear the stentorian voice of Luce's secretary, Corinne Thras
  How might one hear a Crow voice when the mountain of records that
ing in his arms, hearing his voice, loving him, being loved by him -
I couldn't even hear my own voice.
to the last compelling male voice she hears.
rs," said Stephen, whose low voice was distinctly heard, "and my fell
ly surprised to hear his own voice in this language.
e heard his somewhat fuddled voice at the other end.
            "A voice is heard in Ramah, weeping and gre
        The voices we hear seem to belong to everyon
ntered in trying to make his voice heard.
raised each; heard a roar of voices; people already coming up from di
e for her, it's the author's voice we hear; Norman's infatuation amou
"What a relief to hear your voice, I'm told you were kidnapped after
is manner, had you heard his voice at that moment!
        He heard a very low voice coming from the higher central cro
way, she heard the murmur of voices.
ed too much: he had heard my voice falter, and might have seen me bru
mere fact of hearing another voice disconcerted him painfully, confus
  and to our delight we heard voices.
suddenly I heard a familiar voice behind me:
face she knew, this is not a voice she ever heard.
ll felt too soon to hear his voice again.
lad or irritated to hear his voice.
      YOU won't hear the best voices in the world singing those classi
o fugge', and the last human voice to be heard in Dante's poem, the v
```

27 "hear" as a lemmatized collocate of "voice"

here long when she **heard** the **voices**.
ope / That the dead **hear** the **voice** of witch or wizard" (R 3. 1. 23 -
ure that a wide diversity of **voices** are **heard**.
ave a tendency to raise your **voice** in order to **hear** yourself speak."
                    She **heard voices**.
              Atlanta **voices** will be **heard** during festivities
  left, your ears will **hear** a **voice** behind you, saying, "This is the w
n and Elealeh cry out, their **voices** are **heard** all the way to Jahaz.
use men to **hear** his majestic **voice** and will make them see his arm com
store, I had neighbors whose **voices** I could **hear**, whose faces I could
ks of raucous laughter and a **voice** was **heard** shouting, `You'll need a
, as once-authoritative Tory **voices** are **heard** begging for jobs on the
she asked, I could **hear** her **voice** especially clearly because I'd mar
Fish could **hear** the excited **voices** of some of the soldiers organisin
  They could **hear** the raised **voices** only yards from the cottage.
        What I **hear** is your **voice** calling to children in these photo
litting a beat you **hear** this **voice** say, `Who gives a crap.'
          I'd **hear voices** coming from the people in the bea
      We must make our **voice heard** every way we can, not just l
in and said that you **heard** a **voice**, we have to pray about it.'
hard eyes and **heard** a rough **voice** speaking to me.
vision, maybe, when you **hear voices** but see no lips moving, I could h
lma a glass of water I **heard voices** coming from the porch.
n field you could **hear** their **voices** bellering like blowhorns clear ov
ick it up again and **hear** his **voice**, laughing, rich with desire, refus
ndays when he **heard** his lone **voice** among certain hard words of the Ps
that last sentence, **hear** the **voice** murmuring, "Better strike it out,
amn loud I can't **hear** my own **voice** singing along.
 Augustine reports **hearing** a **voice** telling him "Take and read!" -
n Rachael's face or **hear** her **voice**.
trap me and then I **hear** this **voice** saying.
 meant that he **heard** so many **voices** in his head that it became imposs
word `chivalry', I **hear** the **voice** of Edward Johnson declaring My nam
hurried on, "I've **heard** your **voice** although I've never had the pleasu
 for sure that the old man's **voice** we **hear** passing over the words slo
m his wife; when he **heard** my **voice**, he cleared his throat.
could **hear** the clear angelic **voices** from heaven above, calling upon t
he cried out, and he **heard** a **voice** by his ear.
d to **hear** doors slamming and **voices** calling all over the house.
and the need to **hear** his own **voice**, the last possession he had.
       The little boy **heard voices** and a shuffling of feet on the gr
 bordering a river, we **heard voices**: "Yank.
   She **heard** laughter in the **voices** around her, and the occasional lo
           That's your **voice** we **hear**.
d to make A lot more diverse **voices heard**.
minx - He longed to **hear** her **voice** again.
is is what the LORD says: "A **voice** is **heard** in Ramah, mourning and gr
       I can still **hear** his **voice**.
her lips were moving but her **voice** was not **heard**.
ieve that their, they, their **voice** is **heard**.
gling to make their creative **voice heard**, and gives it strength and a
          He often **heard voices**, which he didn't keep to himself.

dictionaries for foreign learners. There is usually very little logic behind the choice of a particular combination of words forming a collocation, and one of the commonest mistakes learners make is to use an inappropriate combination. Why do we say a *heavy* smoker or drinker rather than a *big* smoker or drinker? Why does a building *fall* into disrepair rather than *go* into disrepair? Why do we say we are *a little* tired or we were *a little* late or we have *a little* time left but not "We are a little sorry"? Why can two people eat *in silence* but not *in quiet?* Why does one sometimes get a *busy* signal when making a telephone call? The signal isn't busy. The signal means that the connection is in use. All of these examples are collocations, and they are learned as one learns a language, simply by hearing others use them and imitating other speakers, at first consciously, finally without thinking. Many linguists now believe that speech is generated in groups (or "chunks") of words rather than by stringing together separate words.[67] Only a corpus can uncover patterns of co-occurrence that reveal collocational usage. Citation files are essentially designed to uncover unusual usages, not usual ones. Sinclair goes so far as to say that individual works of genius or of outstanding literary merit are of little value in a language corpus, which should rather include "what is central and typical in the language . . . If we are to approach a realistic view of the way in which language is used, we must record the usage of the mass of ordinary writers, and not the stray genius or the astute journalist."[68]

Collocational searches are also vitally important in uncovering idiomatic usages, whether in the form of phrasal verbs or otherwise. The difficulty for the definer is deciding whether a collocation is an idiom. Is it fixed enough, and does it have a meaning that is different from the meanings of its composite elements? Complicating the matter even more, many idioms are variable themselves. For example, I searched for the idiom "put something on the back burner" (to delay considering it) only to find that this idiom is highly variable. I discovered that one could move something to the front burner (to consider it before other matters) as well as moving it to the back burner, so did a search for both "back burner" and "front burner" (Figure 28, p. 318). The search generated 43 hits, 11 of which, more than 25 percent, are for "front burner." Moreover, very few of the hits use "put something on" a burner. Items are instead moved, pushed, relegated to, or are just on the back or front burner. The idiom has been stripped down to "the back burner" or "the front burner," and there are even examples which do not include "the," such as "Washington's back burner" and "Quebec's front burner." In the end, the idioms went in my dictionary as "the back burner" and "the front burner." Here is a case where the verb preceding "the back/front burner" is really part of the idiom semantically but not morphologically, conveying the meaning of movement or position, but not depending on any one verb form to complete the idiom. I believe this situation applies as well to many other idioms in English. It is a common experience when using a corpus to find that expressions one regarded as fixed are not fixed at all but have many variations. Only the existence of very large corpora has allowed us to discover such variability, but now that we know it, we realize that one cannot get an accurate picture of the variability of language use unless one has a very large corpus.

Here is how John Sinclair explains why size is important:

Language is very complex, and people use it for their own ends, without normally being conscious of the relation between their verbal behaviour and the way that behaviour is characterized. They are creative, or expedient, or casual, or confused; or they have unusual matters to put into usual words, so they have to combine them in unusual ways. [¶] It is, therefore, necessary to have access to a large corpus because the normal use of language is highly specific, and good representative examples are hard to find.[69]

Many familiar fixed expressions, idioms, and collocations that we might suppose to be extremely common do not occur in natural language all that frequently. Graeme Kennedy observes that a corpus must be very large to contain a sufficient number of collocations; even 20 million words is not big enough.[70] He writes, " corpus studies have shown that a large proportion of the forms or elements of a language occur very rarely in actual use."[71] Jeremy Clear observes, "By far the majority of lexical items have a relative frequency in current English of less than 20 per million."[72]

How large is large? The meaning of "large" seems to be changing minute by minute. Less than a year ago, when I wrote the first draft of this chapter, I had no hesitation in considering a corpus of over 50 million words as large. Now I am not so sure. When the British National Corpus of 100 million words was created, it was at first regarded as immense, but now that both the Bank of English and the Cambridge International Corpus have over 300 million words, it seems slightly less immense, and one can imagine it some day appearing downright puny. In the early 1960s, we recall, a corpus of 1 million words was large. If the size of a large corpus increases by a factor of 50 every forty years, by

```
e happy?" must be put on the back burner until after the campaign.
          It's kind of taking a back burner right now, but I'm, I still
uisine may have moved to the back burner since the emergence of today
h planning isn't even on the back burner.
ter, he is putting it on the back burner."
orce was creeping toward the back burner.
's not, we'll move it to the back (burner).
in the city gets put on the back burner of the ol' ranch stove.
eplaced language on Quebec's front burner, a fascinating skeleton has
n, foreign policy was on the back burner.
e keep welfare reform on the front burner.
ble up much on the political front burner.
sue has kind of moved to the back burner," says Montana Gov. Marc Rac
has been boiling on Bryant's front burner ever since he discovered th
e was being relegated to the back burner, at least for the time being
eace drive from Washington's back burner.
eace drive from Washington's back burner.
the issue has come from the back burner all the way to the front," h
erns have been pushed to the back burner in terms of equality and civ
          "It's on the front burner now and the heat is up."
on, and it got pushed to the back burner," Grosvenor told a group of
rms seem to have gone to the back burner [recently]," says Ivan Denni
anctions against Iraq on the back burner while focusing on the more p
people and put myself on the back burner.
tly moved their cause to the back burner.
          Problem to sit on the back burner and not be there while it bu
t - or face being put on the back burner as international actors.
the program had been on the front burner for a couple of years.
nce put these doubts "on the back burner" and had left them there, al
alk will be relegated to the back burner for eight years," said Joe S
d 70,000 applications on the back burner, many to extort bribes.
ltural reform are going on a back burner.
deterrence has moved to the back burner.
e keep welfare reform on the front burner.
cerns are easy to put on the back burner.
ould keep the problem on the front burner.
          They can't put it on the back burner and just say, well, you know
Afghanistan has moved to the back burner.
to keep human rights on the front burner play into the hands of the
sident put this issue on the front burner through his statement in Ca
urners to check a pot on the back burner.
s managed to put Iraq on the front burner" and convince his people th
rhaps if we put money on the back burner
```

28 "back burner" and "front burner" – American subcorpus

2040 a corpus will have to be 2.5 billion words to be considered large. We are well on the way to the first billion-word corpus, so this estimate, no matter how bizarre it now seems, may well be conservative. It presumes a continuation of the incredibly rapid growth in computer speed and capacity we have experienced in the past decades, and much more advanced software tools to cope with such huge files, so that the user can make selections – or have the selections automatically made – to winnow any search to a manageable amount of data.

Other uses of the corpus

Machine translation, the automatic process by which one language can be translated into another, has made considerable progress through corpus research. Parallel corpora in two or more languages have been developed and have yielded important insights to help the translator. However, even in closely related languages, translational equivalents seldom mean the same thing in all contexts or are used in the same syntactic constructions; their connotations and degree of formality may differ also. Even when a lexical item in the target language can be used as the translational equivalent of the lemma in the source language – a situation that is not always possible – the translation of that lexical item will not always be the lemma of the original source language. Simple, two-way translation may be possible with realia – the names of animals or tools – and with some scientific terms, but rarely with more ordinary language. This is not to say that machine translation is not possible for ordinary language, only that it is beset with many problems requiring a high degree of linguistic sophistication to overcome. Where there are fewer problems, as in scientific and technical language, machine translation works best. But progress is being made in all areas.

Translation studies, the study of how language is used in translations from other languages into English, is an emerging field that will continue to benefit from corpus research. Access to corpora that include translations will provide the means of discovering patterns of language linked to specific source languages.[73] Such studies can help to improve translations and may result in new insights into the relationship between the two languages.

Speech synthesis and *speech recognition* are two very active areas of language study dependent on spoken corpora. Industry has spent and will continue to spend enormous amounts of its research funds to develop these areas further. The Linguistic Data Consortium mentioned earlier has much industrial support because it has spoken corpora that can be used in this area of research. Everyone who uses a phone to get information has already experienced some form of speech synthesis, which we readily recognize by the peculiar level inflections at the end of statements, when we would expect the voice to drop. We are left hanging, waiting for more, until we belatedly realize the message is over. By such means, all perfectly unintended by everyone, we learn the importance of inflection and pitch in human communication. As speech synthesis improves, we will lose even this. Early speech synthesis of this type depends upon slicing up the sounds real people make and recombining them acoustically. A more advanced stage, which is already a fact, is the creation of realistic speech entirely by the artificial production of sound. None of these advances would have been possible without corpora of recorded speech.

Speech recognition is also a very high priority in industry for many reasons. The goal is to be able to talk to one's computer, as, in some rudimentary ways, we can already talk to a machine at the other end of our telephone, which may understand numbers and "yes" or "no," but not much else. The benefits to the blind or otherwise disabled are obvious and significant, but there are many other uses that industry and government are eager to exploit.[74] Speech recognition is not just a matter of devising a machine that can interpret sounds acoustically. Whatever recognizes speech has to be able to distinguish between sequences of speech sounds that are possible or likely and sequences that are impossible or unlikely. To be efficient in real time, it has to narrow down the options for each expected sound in a sequence very quickly. It has to be programmed to know that in English (or any other language) certain phonemes do not follow one another, and be able to ignore misleading or adventitious acoustic features (a dog barking, a person clearing his throat or stammering) while "listening" for sounds that form a recognizable stream of speech. Computational linguists are very much involved in speech recognition.

With further advances in speech recognition, we may be able to say a word and immediately see its definition or translational equivalent displayed, or hear it. This would be especially helpful in ESL and bilingual lexicography, where the user may not know the canonical form that the dictionary regards as the lemma and uses as a headword. The utterance of any form of the word ought to generate the lemma and the information being sought. I am certain that speech recognition will advance to the point where a machine will be able to understand a wide variety of commands, and this capacity will have many excellent practical uses. It remains to be seen whether speech recognition will play a major role in dictionaries except for people with special needs.

One of the pioneers in corpus linguistics sums up the advantages of using a corpus in language study by making these points:[75]

- It is more objective; speakers often cannot report accurately what they say.
- It is verifiable.

- It is useful for the study of language variation, dialect, register, style; and for historical comparison.
- It establishes frequency of use.
- It is a theoretical resource.
- It is useful for machine translation, speech recognition and synthesis, and for software dealing with language use.
- It is more representative of language use than citation collections.
- The same corpus can be used for different purposes.
- It has the potential to be widely (sometimes freely) available for scholarly research.
- It is the only way to study the usage of non-native speakers – and there are a lot of them – because no other techniques will work.

All of this is true, and as the reader has surmised I am most enthusiastic about the use of computerized corpora in lexicography. Even so, it is wise to remind ourselves of the corpus' limitations lest we suppose it has solved all of our problems.

Limitations of the corpus

The main limitation of a corpus is that no matter how large it is and how carefully it has been assembled, it cannot possibly represent truly the myriad ways in which language is used spontaneously in speech and deliberately in writing. A corpus is always a selection and can only represent the speech and writing of those transcriptions and texts that are selected. This is something we would do well to remember, particularly when the audiences for which dictionaries are written have been expanded to take in a wider variety of social and educational classes than in earlier years. Whether admitted or not, a corpus is designed with various biases. Until recently, one such bias has been to favor writing over speech, largely because it is far more difficult and expensive to collect large samples of speech. Some types of writing have been favored over other types. Should the weighting given types of writing vary according to the estimated amount of each type that is produced or according to the size of the audience? See under *Representativeness*, p. 331, for a discussion of this subject.

Most existing lexicographic corpora are also limited in time, extending back perhaps to the 1970s, rarely much earlier. There are historical corpora (see p. 293 above), but as of now they only scratch the surface of past use. The entire Victorian period and the first part of the twentieth century is hardly represented at all in general language corpora. Until many books and other publications of these periods can be digitized and included in corpora – a process that would be labor-intensive and expensive, and therefore may never be done on a grand scale – citation files will continue to be the main source of information for these periods.

As corpora become larger and larger, lexicographers will have to depend more and more on the software tools to make decisions about frequency and form, and they will have to rely on the software to respond accurately to their searches, which will have to be more narrowly defined than they are now. Every dictionary is done under tight time pressures. No one will have the time to sort through thousands of hits or even many hundreds, in order to find a particular usage that has to be included. As Rosamund Moon has commented, corpus research is only as effective as the tools for retrieval, statistics, and linguistic analysis. If the grammatical tagging is not completely accurate, or if there are typographical errors, or if (for example) hyphenated compounds are not counted as single compounds, conclusions will be inaccurate.[76] Moon also questions whether dictionaries should even try to concentrate on representing speech because of the many difficulties of recording speech with fidelity in written form.[77] A great deal of judgment is brought into play during the process of transcription. If the quality of sound is not perfect, some words can be misheard; in actual speech, people often speak at the same time and interrupt one another, and they often do not speak clearly. Does the transcriber write "gonna" for "going to" if it is so pronounced? Moon also questions the capacity of software engineers ever to devise ways of automatically identifying so-called "fixed expressions," which include idioms, because her study indicates that fixed expressions are actually not very fixed, not common, and not predictable.[78]

Transcriptions of speech are written down by people listening to audiotapes. The spellings of words reflect decisions of the transcribers and represent only sound, not form. Spoken corpora should therefore be excluded from frequency counts that are made to determine preferred spelling or form (such as the hyphenation of compounds). Every corpus consisting of written and spoken parts segregates them into subcorpora (and often has other subcorpora as well) so that they can be searched independently, yet, because for most searches lexicographers need to use both written and spoken subcorpora, they may not always take the time to de-select the spoken corpus, and this will result in some skewing of the information on morphology. Given the relatively small percentage of spoken material in most existing corpora, this is not a serious problem, but as spoken corpora grow in size, it could become one unless editors become very disciplined in using only written text for decisions about form. Dictionary editors have to make many hundreds of decisions every day, each one involving a set of different keystrokes, and anything they can do to save a few keystrokes is welcome. Their dereliction isn't due to laziness, but to weighing the importance of getting more done against skipping a step that will rarely make any difference.

Dictionaries are not written in a vacuum, but by people working under the pressure of time. It sometimes seems to me that as technology has improved the speed and power with which we can examine the language, the pressures to produce quickly and with fewer staff have kept pace, so that on balance nothing is accomplished any faster or better. The expectations of management seem to rise at the same rate as the speed and power of the computer increase. There is no evidence that lexicographers now are better trained or more competent than they were in the past. Corpora can be used well or they can be used badly. Time pressures too often push the lexicographer to cut corners to avoid time-consuming analyses. It really doesn't do much good having a good corpus with marvelous analytical tools if they aren't used. Linguists who inveigh against lexicographers for not noticing or not recording this or that nice distinction often do not realize that lexicographers have strong incentives to work fast, even if working at home as free-lancers: namely, to earn enough money to make working worthwhile. The pressure for in-house staff is even greater, and continues day after day, often for years. This, of course, is not a limitation of the corpus itself but one imposed on it by the practical working environment of the lexicographer.

COMPILING A CORPUS

The first stage in compiling a corpus is to decide why it is needed and what its purpose will be. Even though we are concerned here only about corpora to be used in lexicography and not for other uses, the nature of the corpus will depend on the size and scope of the dictionaries for which it is to be designed, its intended audiences, and the resources (in both people and money) that can be marshaled for the effort of compilation. For the sake of efficiency, a corpus should not be any larger or more complex than it has to be to fulfill its functions. For example, if the corpus is to be used strictly for dictionaries of American English, there is no need to collect samples from other varieties, and in fact these should be avoided. The span of years to be covered by the corpus must be determined. If the corpus is for a general audience, whether for native speakers or foreign learners, a great deal of diversity of texts will be an important goal, and both written and spoken material should be sought. As we have already noted, a corpus designed for dictionary use should be large – at least 50 million words, and preferably more.

Text collection

One fundamental decision is the determination of how much of the corpus should be spoken and how much written. The spoken and written parts of a corpus are sometimes called *domains*. Because of the difficulties and expense of obtaining spontaneous speech, much spoken material consists of transcriptions of radio or television talk shows and political interview programs. This type of speech is called *semiscripted*, because it takes place in a controlled format in which certain spoken conventions are observed and in which the speakers are not free to say anything they please. Nonetheless, it is spoken and it is a valuable source of corpus data. Of even greater value is *unscripted* speech, such as conversations between friends or acquaintances or the chatting of two workers. Such material is much harder to acquire, requires a team of highly skilled people to prepare, and takes much longer to convert into a usable form than written text. One corpus linguist estimates that it takes ten hours to transcribe one hour's worth of recorded speech (usually 7,000 to 9,000 words) with minimal prosodic markup.[79] It is therefore much more expensive. Most dictionary houses content themselves with modest amounts of unscripted speech, though everybody wishes they had more of it. (As I have noted above, I expect this situation to change; a number of initiatives are underway to increase the coverage of unscripted speech.) But nobody's resources are unlimited; choices have to be made. If one wants to build a large corpus in a reasonable time at reasonable cost, it has to be predominantly written, with most of the spoken material being of the semiscripted variety.

The text types and size of each text selected have to be decided next. The parts of the texts that are selected (the *samples*) may consist of the whole text or a fixed number of words from each text, for example, the first 2,000; or samples can be selected at fixed intervals within the text, such as every other 2,000 words. The early corpora such as the Brown Corpus chose texts of limited size in part because the state of technology at the time made it difficult to imagine corpora much larger than a million words. But it was also believed that sample sizes of 2,000 words from each genre would be sufficient to represent that genre.[80] Now that technology permits large documents to be collected in their entirety, the only reasons to avoid whole documents are concern that their size would skew the entire corpus and because of copyright restrictions (discussed below). Concern over skewing the corpus is legitimate, but if the corpus is large, it is easily avoided. In making a selection of newspapers, for example, one would not want to include several years of the complete text of the *New York Times* or *The Times* of London, but for reasons of diversity of subject as well as size include only a part of each year over several years. Smaller newspapers and magazines might have the contents of an entire year included. One thing that computers do extremely well is to count; the size of any text is easily obtained, and corpus compilers can see that no single text becomes disproportionately large.

Before one decides what texts to include, one has to devise a system of categories for types of texts. These are sometimes broken down by *category* first and then by *genre* (sometimes also called *text type*). To avoid confusion I will use *text type* only in a general way and will use *genre* to refer to a specific text type.

Text *categories* refer to the types of sources from which the material has been obtained, such as newspapers, magazines and journals, documents, and personal communications such as private letters and diaries. By *document* I mean any type of miscellaneous printed material that is not a book, magazine, or newspaper; it includes, *inter alia*, junk mail (even though in the form of a letter), instructions for assembling a toy or piece of furniture, companies' annual reports, warnings on drug labels, signs and public notices, government pamphlets, legal notices such as jury summonses, and the ads on cereal boxes.

Genres usually applies to subject categories such as natural or applied science, politics and world affairs, business and economics, the fine arts, entertainment, *belles lettres*, and popular fiction. I do not find some of these text types very practical. Many nonfiction text sources are hard to qualify as belonging to any one subject. Not only are they difficult (in many cases impossible) to label accurately, but I am skeptical as to how useful they would be even if they were labeled. In examining the results of a corpus search, one can easily see from the header information and the text itself what the subject deals with. If all the hits one sees are in a business context, one knows that without having to rely on a code for that genre. Speaking from a practical point of view, I think coding by particular subject is a waste of time. While working on the American corpus for *CDAE*, I elaborated a system of categories and genres in consultation with the corpus acquisition editor, a system based on the actual day-to-day experience of receiving texts that did not fit into conventional text types. See Figure 29 (pp. 326–27).[81]

A PROPOSED ORGANIZATION OF CORPUS TEXT TYPES

<u>Domains</u>
- **Speech**
- **Writing**

<u>Text Categories</u>
- **Nonfiction**
- **Fiction**
- **Newspaper/Newsletter**
- **Magazine/Journal**
- **Document**
- **Personal Communication**

<u>Categories divided into genres</u>

1. Nonfiction

    1.1 How-to (including guides to home repair, advice on how to be a happier person, etc.)

    1.2 Biography (includes autobiography, published diaries, memoirs, obituaries)

    1.3 Narrative (chronological or topical histories of places or peoples, or historical monographs)

    1.4 Opinion (any argument seeking to explain a position, e.g., why we lost the war, why our children aren't being educated)

    1.5 General text reference (general references including encyclopedias, biographical dictionaries and general dictionaries)

29 A proposed organization of corpus text types

1.6 Specialized text reference (thematic references such as style manuals and technical manuals)

1.7 Educational (university textbook or high-level informational work). This could be subdivided into various educational levels if necessary.

2. Fiction

   2.1 Novel

   2.2 Short story

   2.3 Play

   2.4 Folklore

   2.5 Poetry

Note: for both nonfiction and fiction genres, a further distinction should be made if the text was translated, and the specific language from which it was translated should also be noted by a code. For example, the English text of the translation of a novel from German might be coded 2.1.1.2, with the third digit (1) referring to translation and the fourth (2) signifying German.

Many categorizations of text types are far more elaborate than this, but my advice is, "Keep things simple." An overelaboration of categories and text types is a waste of resources. In my experience many nice divisions of text types are of doubtful accuracy and rarely used. The input of unnecessary data is a waste of labor.

The actual process of compiling a corpus involves a great deal of contact by phone or fax between the corpus acquisition editor and the various owners of the texts, most of which are under copyright. One needs someone who is both persistent and patient in dealing with the owners, who are often busy and have other more important things to do than listen to someone who wants something from them but from whom they can expect little in return. Simply explaining *why* one wants copies of several books in electronic form from a publisher who has no idea about how dictionaries are compiled and very little interest in them to boot is no easy undertaking. One wants someone with both tact and charm – not an easy combination! In sales parlance, cold calls simply won't work. One has to contact prospective owners of texts first by letter, explaining as simply and briefly as possible why the texts are needed and to what uses they will be put. It is wise to mention that one would be glad to cover their costs for preparing duplicate disks of the material requested. In the course of events, some owners will demand additional fees, and there will be negotiation to come up with an acceptable amount. There are also commercial vendors who are licensed to provide some kinds of texts, notably newspapers and magazines, for fees, and, of course, these are not negotiable.

Most publishers and individual owners of texts do not read the initial letter explaining why one wants a copy of their texts. Constant follow-up is essential. In most cases, the corpus acquisition editor has to establish personal contact with the owner or the owner's representative and convince that person why the text is so important and also to allay any fears they may have that their text might be compromised and copied illicitly because of its inclusion in a corpus. Especially when dealing with a large company, it is often necessary to resend the initial explanatory statement with a personal note directly to the person one has spoken with. One must remember at all times that for most suppliers of texts, one's request is simply an annoyance, akin to receiving the fortieth request of the year to give money to an alumni association, and they must be persuaded why they should make this effort – however small – on one's behalf.

One must obtain written permission from every owner to use the copy of the text in specified ways and for specified purposes. The dictionary editor and corpus acquisition editor should create such a permission request, and it would not be a bad idea to show it to a legal counsel before putting it to use. If one happens to work for a nonprofit or educational institution, this should be emphasized because it will often make it easier to obtain permission, and at lower cost than would be the case otherwise. Some copyright owners may be willing to give permission only under certain conditions. One should be prepared to accommodate any reasonable request of this sort.

In addition to the category and genre coding, every sample should have a permission code, indicating first of all whether it is in copyright or out of copyright, or whether it is in the public domain (such as junk mail, recorded phone announcements, packaging information). If it is in copyright, a series of codes are needed to specify under what conditions permission has been granted. There are a variety of possibilities.

Sometimes the text acquired is not the final version that will appear in print; sometimes permission is granted for in-house research only but not for use in dictionary quotations; sometimes permission is granted only if some parts of the text are omitted from the corpus. One naturally will seek to obtain some texts published by one's own company, and these will have their own unique copyright code.

As the reader has by now begun to see, there is more to compiling a corpus than lifting up a phone and making a few calls. It represents a substantial commitment of time over an extended period. The corpus acquisition editor for *CDAE* worked half-time for more than a year, and was available after that for consulting. A clerical assistant devoted much of her time to helping the corpus acquisition editor by typing letters and, more importantly, by running time-consuming electronic processes to copy or convert disks that were received. Most disks that one receives from publishers have printing codes which must be stripped out. If the provider of the disk doesn't do it, one has to have someone on staff do it. It is usually a simple enough matter, though time-consuming, but on occasion it is not simple. It is important to have a staff editor knowledgeable about computer software and page formatting systems to give advice when the processing of a disk presents problems. Another job of the corpus acquisition editor is to keep complete records on every sample used. This is essential to answer any question that might arise at a later date about any aspect of the sample, such as one's right to use it; if for some reason the original disks have to be re-used, one has to know in what form they exist. Its more immediate use is to provide the *header* information during corpus searches, that is, the several rows of data that appear at the top of the screen when any corpus hit is highlighted for viewing. Typically, the header information includes the year the sample was produced, the language variety, the domain, text category, genre, author and title, and sometimes additional information. The sample records are more complete and should include the following items, although some items will not apply to every sample:

- Identifying sample number
- Number of disks
- Title
- Author
- ISBN
- Language variety
- Author's sex
- Software format

- Hardware format
- DOS or MAC
- Publisher
- Date
- Domain
- Text category
- Genre
- Extent in words
- Place of publication
- Permission code
- Notes

It may be the case that a national corpus, with the prestige of government backing it, can obtain almost any text it seeks, but for other, independent organizations, the success rate is not 100 percent. Many publishers or owners of material simply refuse to consider the request and will not respond, no matter how persuasive the corpus acquisition editor is. Others will demand fees that are completely out of line with any other cost associated with the corpus acquisition, and will not be open to negotiation. The key is to get the ear of an individual with a position of enough influence to get the permission needed. Most people will be sympathetic with the request if it is explained to them as an educational tool used for research in compiling dictionaries. It should also be made clear that their text will be part of a huge collection to which many others have also contributed, that the primary use will be to analyze language use, and that if any parts of their text are quoted, the quotations will be used to illustrate dictionary meanings and will be short. It also has to be emphasized that the corpus will be secure from unauthorized use and that under no circumstances will their texts be downloaded or printed out. There are some things one should not say. One should not specify a word limit to quotations. One should not promise the owners of texts reports or feedback of any kind or complimentary copies of one's dictionary. One should not promise that the entire corpus, of which their text will be a part, will not be copied – only that one's organization will remain in control of its use and the guarantor of its security. Because one cannot foresee the precise uses to which the corpus may be put, it is wise not to be more specific about such uses than one has to be.

Although one may begin compiling a corpus with exact ideas of the percentage needed for each text category and genre, one should be prepared to make adjustments. It may not be possible, given the practical restraints of time and money, to obtain samples in strict accord with one's original goals. Some material, especially that in the *document* and *personal communication* text categories, will not be available in electronic format, and will have to be optically scanned or keyboarded. Scanning has improved considerably but is still not perfect, and it is not possible in all cases, and keyboarding is slow and expensive compared to electronic transfer. For these reasons, the corpus acquisition editor has to be resourceful and take advantage of opportunities as they present themselves. Compiling a corpus is a practical enterprise; it has a budget and a schedule. If there is an opportunity to get a huge amount of perfectly good material at a negligible cost, even if it is not in an area one was particularly looking for, one should take it. Serendipity plays a significant part in most corpus compilations.

Representativeness

In spite of these exigencies, one should not compromise on the essential standard of representativeness of the corpus as a whole. A corpus is only good if it can be reasonably trusted to represent the way language is used by those people whose usage one is interested in describing. What are the ways representativeness can be achieved? One is by paying attention to text categories and genres. Another is size and number of samples. Still other considerations relate to the time period covered and to geographic distribution.

All the text categories should be well represented. Because it is easier to get a large amount of newspaper text from one or a few sources, this category is likely to be a large one in any corpus, but it should not overwhelm all the other categories. Big-city daily newspapers cover a great many different subjects: politics, business, sports, entertainment, cooking, book and movie reviews, fashion, etc. They are an excellent source in any corpus as they have been over the years for citation files. One should try to get a few small-city newspapers, if possible, as well as the national newspapers. Magazines tend to be more focused than newspapers, but for that reason give better coverage than general newspapers to major subgroups of the population, such as young women, teenagers, and hobbyists of various kinds. The language of magazines is rich in specialized terminology and current slang. The newspaper and magazine categories are productive, and reasonably constitute a large part of the written corpus. The nonfiction and fiction text categories are equally important. Nonfiction gives coverage to many different types of writing not well covered in newspapers and magazines – scholarly and scientific writing, for instance. Fiction is a goldmine of different registers, from formal, elevated descriptions to the intimate talk of lovers, covering language use in every conceivable social situation. Through the dialogue in novels and short stories, fiction helps to make up for the limitations of one's spoken corpus; it is an excellent source of regionalisms and taboo expressions.

Documents will yield a variety of styles. Commercial advertising, which occupies such a large part of our lives, cannot be ignored; think of television and radio commercials, display ads in magazines and newspapers, billboards and street signage; add to that the huge volume of sales letters and solicitations for money from charities and politicians, and one can see why the document category is important. Personal communication is less so, but it will give a historical and often regional dimension to the corpus that is valuable.

The size of the corpus is important. The authors of a recent textbook on corpus linguistics write: "[L]exicographic studies require particularly large corpora. Many words and collocations occur with low frequencies, and a corpus must be many millions of words, taken from many different texts, to enable investigation of their use."[82] Size is not sufficient, but it is necessary. It cannot make up for serious deficiencies, such as not having any fiction or any spoken material; but it can make up for quite a number of minor ones. A large corpus will contain a very diverse collection of combinations of words, and if one were satisfied with attending only to mainstream, reportorial level writing, with dollops of a more informal level from sports pages and gossip columns, 100 million words from newspapers would do fine. But dictionaries must cover a much broader spectrum of language than that.

Lastly, the time period and regions must be represented. Most modern corpora that are not historical have begun their collections in the late 1970s or early 1980s. It is not necessary to have samples representing every year in the period covered, but one should try to have the samples distributed throughout the period rather than concentrated in one part of it. Given the pressures on dictionaries to be up-to-date, however, corpora will usually be somewhat skewed towards the most recent years. Samples from different newspapers ought to be staggered rather than overlapping, as the news from any one period is very heavily concentrated on the politics or public event of the day (the Iraqi war, princess Diana's death, etc.) and there will be a tremendous amount of repetition in the language used to describe the same events. Corpora have to be kept up to date, so newer texts must be added at regular intervals.

Regional distribution is important, too. When we were compiling the American corpus for *CDAE*, we made special efforts to get newspapers from the west coast and from the southern US as well as from the east coast, and in collecting novels and other works of fiction we also tried to get texts from regional publishers who would reflect the language use of their area.

I have been talking rather glibly about *representativeness* and describing how it can be achieved, or, to be more honest, approximated, but it is not perfectly clear what is meant by *representativeness*. Just what or who is the corpus supposed to be representative of? Michael Rundell and Penny Stock address this point thoughtfully:

> To be truly representative of all language 'produced', a corpus would have to include a very high proportion of spoken language, a reasonable amount of newspaper text, and a tiny percentage of everything else; to be truly representative of all language 'consumed' the corpus would be dominated by popular newspapers and lowbrow fiction – other forms of text such as literary fiction or academic discourse would be only thinly represented on the grounds that they are not widely read. In reality neither of these interpretations of the term has been regarded as practical or desirable.[83]

Instead, corpus compilers aim to produce "a well-balanced collection of texts which collectively represent the full repertoire of spoken and written performance across the broadest possible range of contexts and genres."[84] The reason for this somewhat odd definition of *representativeness* is tied to the aim of the dictionary maker to find examples of as many different usages as possible. Having 40,000 corpus examples of "said," or of "Tony Blair," will not be of much help even though their inclusion in these numbers may be more truly representative of usage in both of the senses adumbrated by Rundell and Stock. That would be a waste of editorial effort, of computer processing time, and of computer storage space. It is scope of coverage rather than depth that lexicographers are after. A large corpus will provide plenty of depth of common terms without having to make any special effort to get them.

Lexical tools

Because of the huge size of modern corpora, many software programs have been written to speed and simplify research aimed at understanding language use. The first and most basic task after the samples have been processed is a concordancing program that will enable anyone seeking a particular word form to find it quickly. Concordancing programs are

So far, South Jordan and Riverton have emerged as clear front-runners, seeking creative ways to **tactfully** recruit the wealthiest of new move-ins.--

In fairness, it should be asked **tactfully,** not challengingly or angrily.--

When music leaders **tactfully** suggested that she not consider singing her forte, she was embarrassed and disappointed, she said.--------

The poem **tactfully** focuses on the lack of welcome to the bride not from Gregory but from her dead son, who being absent can cause no dissension between the newly-weds.--

The dynamics of heterosexual aggression are **tactfully** deflected into the less shocking nuances of female discourse.---

She can find no way to say this **tactfully,** but it_ 's the only fact that will explain their conversation, and she wants, for once, to have all the eddies and currents working on the surface instead of underneath.--

Attempting to lure her from what he saw as a decadent repertoire, he **tactfully** worked to separate Mrs. Pat_ 's acting from the dramatic texts in which she appeared.--------------------------------------

Those Z_ 's are still visible today, but the preservationists **tactfully** made no mention of them in their description of the beaded-board ceiling for the National Register.--------------------------------------

The bespectacled rabbit farmer **tactfully** disappeared.--------------------------------------

In a typical Hollywood production, we see a love scene on a cliff above a roaring ocean and hear only voices; even if the sounds of the wind and waves can be heard, the volume is **tactfully** lowered as the lovers speak.--------------------------------------

How she got pregnant is **tactfully** shrouded in mystery.--------------------------------------

Not knowing the policy, one husband offered me my only bribe ever: to get me to use his story, he slid a fifty-cent piece across my desk; I **tactfully** slid it back.--------------------------------------

He **tactfully** substituted the word condense for cut.--------------------------------------

We also have to work **tactfully** with the public.--------------------------------------

The way the publishers put it to us - only more **tactfully** - boils down to this: "_ Look, Hemingway, old shoe, you can't expect us to plunk out 10 grand in advertising your next book if you even refuse to appear at no cost at all on the David

30 Sentence search for "tactfully" – American subcorpus

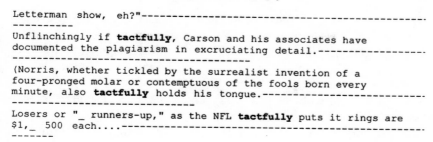

```
Letterman  show,  eh?"------------------------------------------------------
----------
Unflinchingly if tactfully, Carson and his associates have
documented the plagiarism in excruciating detail.-----------------
----------------------------------------
(Norris, whether tickled by the surrealist invention of a
four-pronged molar or contemptuous of the fools born every
minute, also tactfully holds his tongue.-----------------------
-----------------------------
Losers or "_ runners-up," as the NFL tactfully puts it rings are
$1,_ 500 each....----------------------------------------------------
-------
```

essentially indexes of every word that situate that word's position exactly with a set of numbers indicating the sample, the section within the sample, the paragraph, and the line on which the word appears. This information enables the program to avoid having to search through the entire corpus letter by letter for every word sought, a process that would be very time-consuming with a large corpus. It searches instead for the location of the word searched for, and since it has a record of every position in which that word exists, it can find all the occurrences very rapidly. Most concordancing programs, as well as virtually all other software used in corpus building, are custom-built and proprietary.[85] Every corpus has a unique structure and design, and it is therefore necessary to have one's own team of software engineers design the software tools in close cooperation with the lexicographers.

A typical concordancing program allows the researcher to find any word (or indeed any string of letters) and highlights that word in a Key Word in Context (KWIC) display consisting of single lines with the highlighted word in a different color in the center of each line, as in Figure 21 (p. 300), a monochrome version of the KWIC screen display. It is usually also possible to convert a KWIC screen to a display of sentences, as in Figure 30 for "tactfully," or full paragraphs. Some systems also provide access to the complete sample. (On occasion this is necessary because some paragraphs, as of dialogue, can be quite short, and one has to see more to understand the context.)

All modern lexicographical corpora are annotated with *tags* (specific sequences of codes, often within angle brackets) to mark certain features of the text. These are suppressed in displays of search results, so lexicographers do not see them. The process of tagging text (called *markup*) has been standardized so that everybody will designate that same part of a text, such as the end of a paragraph, with the same code. This system of markup, the *Standardized Generalized Markup Language* (SGML), has been further elaborated for the description of whole texts in the *Text Encoding Initiative* (TEI), which was devised and promoted by several organizations devoted to computing to make it possible to exchange texts from one system to another. Among other things, TEI divides a text into a header and the text itself.[86]

As we have already seen, in doing a corpus search, it is often convenient to capture all the inflections of a word along with the lemma, so that on searching for "run," one also finds "ran," "running," and "runs"; in searching for "child," one also finds "children"; in searching for "quick," one also finds "quicker" and "quickest." The linking of inflections to the lemma (*lemmatization*) is an important lexical tool for a number of reasons. First, it saves time in making separate searches for each inflection unnecessary. Secondly, by combining the related forms, the editor can immediately see which forms are commoner (often it is not the lemma) and how they differ in meaning as well as syntax. Dictionaries rarely distinguish meanings between inflections except when a participle of a verb is promoted to adjectival status ("an exciting concert," "dressed and ready to go"), but with lemmatization it is possible to observe many more distinctions and to write better definitions of those forms already considered to merit separate treatment. Thirdly, lemmatization makes frequency counts more meaningful. Lemmatization is not a simple process, but it can now be done extremely well, with virtually no errors. Of course, if the editor so chooses, he or she can still search only for a particular form; a lemmatized search is optional.

The order in which corpus hits are displayed is often subjected to a process of randomization, as noted above (see p. 296), to avoid a lop-sided presentation in which the editor has to wade through hundreds of hits from the same source before finding more variety.

Automatic grammatical tagging, developed in the 1970s, has improved a great deal. Early part-of-speech tagging had a reported success rate of 77%, but by the mid-1990s the success rate had climbed to 95%.[87] However, 5% is still not negligible, and in some systems the error rate is higher than that. Doing searches by part-of-speech has its share of surprises, but, over all, part-of-speech tagging is impressively accurate, and it is an immense help in dealing with a large corpus to be able to select just the part-of-speech that one is interested in. For example, if one is working on an adjective such as "right," which has many thousands of hits in its various grammatical forms, it is a marvelous convenience to be able to select just the adjective. See Figure 31. As

Word	Tag Description	AllAMSPOK	AMWRIT	Keys
right(JJ)	general adjective	5954	10183	1724 RIGHT(JJ),Right
right(NN1)	singular common noun	1101	708	1493 RIGHT(NN1),Righ
right(RR)	general adverb	14649	27484	1814 RIGHT(RR),Right
right(VV0)	base form of lexical verb	1	0	1 right(VV0)
right(VVI)	infinitive	0	0	0 right(VVI)

31 Tag descriptions of "right" – American subcorpus

this figure shows, coding goes beyond part-of-speech identification and gives other grammatical characteristics. For a full display of the types of grammatical discrimination now available, see the lemmatized search for "run," Figure 22 p. 302. This gives specific inflectional information beyond simple part-of-speech designations.

An even more advanced and complicated tagging procedure involves *parsing*, labeling parts of text according to their syntactic function, identifying subjects, objects, and complements, for example. Automatic parsing is extremely complicated, and in spite of a great deal of interest and effort in this area, parsing is still very much a work in progress. It would be of great benefit for grammatical research, and one can see important applications in translation studies comparing two languages, but its application to lexicography is less obvious.

Another area of great interest is semantic tagging, which *would* have an immediate impact on lexicography. In a sense semantic tagging has been with us for a long time, as the traditional thematic arrangement of a thesaurus, in which near-synonyms are linked by meaning, is a form of semantic tagging. Semantic tagging, also called sense tagging or word sense disambiguation, seemed to follow naturally from grammatical tagging, for example, in being able to distinguish homonyms automatically. The context surrounding *bank* as a financial institution differs significantly from the context surrounding the *bank* of a river, and it seemed sensible to try to devise programs to distinguish between them automatically. But the goals of semantic tagging are much more ambitious: the aim is nothing less than the elaboration of a system to link words according to specific aspects of meaning. This linkage might be especially useful in electronic dictionaries, permitting the user to move from one word to another related word easily, or enabling him to call up on command a whole set of words related in meaning with respect to one factor or another. At least this is the vision of those working in this area. This capacity would be particularly useful in ESL and bilingual lexicography. But semantic tagging is much less accurate than grammatical tagging, and much more subjective, so that the difficulty of accurate semantic tagging results not just from the difficulty of creating computer programs equal to the task of distinguishing between significantly different semantic environments – a tough assignment in itself – it results also from disagreements about the nature of the semantic distinctions being made.

The proponents of semantic tagging suggest that the process of defining will be simplified by assigning an entire cluster of related words to one definer, who can then make these meanings more internally coherent than would otherwise be possible. I find this presumption simplistic and unconvincing. It will not help the defining process if the same person who defines "kill" defines "murder," "assassinate," "bump off," and "sacrifice." (For some reason, death and dying seem to be popular subjects to illustrate semantic tagging.) For one thing, it is a simple matter for definers to access any other entry in the database and see how that word has been defined. They can then tailor their own work to be consistent with it. More fundamentally, defining a great many semantically related words at the same time may only serve to obscure their actual differences in authentic use, which often does not conform to our intuitive feelings about their semantic similarity. These words may *not* be as similar as we suppose.

Although all the words in this cluster have a meaning that is "to cause someone or an animal to die," they differ greatly in many other respects. A newspaper editor can kill a story, lack of interest can kill an idea, and a medicine can kill germs; partners in a tennis doubles match can say they were murdered by better players; characters are assassinated. It is naive to believe that these other meanings are irrelevant. In some cases, they may affect the presumed basic sense by adding connotations that a definer might have to recognize. The corpus may show that the sense we presumed was basic is not the most common. A definer who is assigned this cluster may be misled into thinking that their semantic linkage is significant when in fact it may not be. Death may not be as significant in linking all these words as theoreticians assume. Only corpus evidence can establish that, but the semantic tagging being done is not based on close corpus analysis but on intuition. Someone sits down at a desk and makes a list. The list is discussed and a number of people agree. If we are to give credence to such a system, we might as well abandon the corpus as a research tool and go back to relying on our intuitive knowledge of meaning. The capacity of an electronic dictionary to serve also as a thesaurus may indeed be useful, and I can see that semantic tagging might improve and expand this function – which, after all, is already possible – but I am not sanguine that semantic tagging will ever be of any use in writing dictionaries. Actual language is far too complex in its relationships to admit of any facile system of semantic connection. Dictionaries have more to lose by imposing a specious consistency on the treatment of supposedly similar words than they have to gain.

Most corpora are divided into different parts (*subcorpora*) because it is not necessary to search the entire corpus for every kind of information. The spoken material is kept in its own corpus so that it can be searched independently. Different language varieties, such as American English and British English, are separated as well. The corpus may have a historical component of older texts kept in a separate subcorpus. Copyright restrictions on some texts may mandate that they be maintained separately. A subcorpus of just newspaper text may be created, or one of fiction only. Editors can select which subcorpora to use in any search. The full corpus, then, is a composite of a number of separate corpora that can be searched separately or used in any combination as needed.

CORPUS USE IN THE FUTURE

Now that ESL dictionaries have shown how valuable the use of a corpus can be, working with a corpus is rapidly becoming indispensable in all branches of lexicography. Corpus use has been slower to develop in America than in Britain but, again through ESL dictionaries, it has established a beachhead, and the widespread use of corpora by all the leading American college dictionaries is inevitable. Though the development of an American national corpus on the order of the British National Corpus is clearly worthy of their support, the major American dictionary houses should create their own corpora as well, with their own research tools, to be able to tailor them to meet their particular needs. For competitive reasons, too, it would seem to make sense to have one's own dedicated corpus. In spite of the tradition of intellectual timidity in the American dictionary scene in the latter half of the twentieth century, one way or the other, large dictionary corpora will be developed in America as in Britain, because dictionaries that do not rely on corpora will not be able to compete at the same level as those that do. Once it is seen that the best dictionaries rely on a corpus, every dictionary will claim to use a corpus whether it does or not. The public will not know what "corpus" means and dictionaries will not tell them; they will only assure the public that a corpus is a very good thing to have and that they have it. Fraud has a long tradition in lexicography and there is no reason why it should cease in the age of corpora.

Nevertheless, I am confident that in the long run genuine use of corpora will become the norm in lexicography throughout the world, in bilingual as well as monolingual lexicography, in dictionaries for children as well as for adults, for native speakers as well as foreign learners. Their advantages are too manifest, and once they have been assembled and the software tools written, they are fairly inexpensive to maintain. In October 1998 I queried the leading American dictionary houses about their use of citation files and language corpora. Of those that responded, all said they used a corpus in the form of digitized citation files and made use of large databases such as Nexis. In some cases the searchable citation-file databases are quite large, but they are not the same as full-text corpora equipped with high-quality search tools.[88] The citations on which such corpora are based were selected because of the occurrence within each citation of a particular form, and therefore do not constitute a representative corpus as a collection of samples based on text categories and genres; they are not adequately representative of authentic language use. Citation files will remain useful in computerized form as part of a corpus, but the collection of citations will be narrowly focused on neologisms and special subjects. They will not be needed for the general vocabulary.

In the long run, the widespread use of corpora in lexicography will vastly improve the quality of dictionaries, but because of the financial investment involved in completely rewriting a dictionary, I do not expect a revolution in quality to happen overnight. As usual, Britain has led the way in extending the use of corpora to native-speaker dictionaries. The latest edition of the *Collins English Dictionary* draws upon the 323-million-word Bank of English to inform its research. Oxford University Press has published the corpus-based *New Oxford Dictionary of English* (*NODE*), even though it already has its venerable and highly popular (but pre-corpus) *Concise Oxford Dictionary*. In view of that, the publication of *NODE* was a strong statement of faith in the vital importance of a corpus for the future of lexicography. It was also a shrewd, competitive business decision. If the leading American college dictionaries do not begin investing in building and using corpora, they will soon be left behind, because Oxford and other publishers will begin to compete with them at all levels, and will capitalize on the use of corpora to offer a quality and depth of information that will be clearly superior to anything the American dictionaries can offer.

The publishers of the American college dictionaries find themselves in a bit of a bind. The compilation of a corpus, troublesome as that might be for them, is not a big expense, given the kinds of costs they have and the income they get from the sale of their dictionaries. The challenge is to change the mindset of top business executives, who will have to be convinced that a corpus is necessary. "Why spend money on a research tool?" they will ask. "Haven't you been doing dictionaries for years without one of these things? Why do you need one now?" But the really big expense will be when dictionary editors begin to *use* their new corpus and discover that they have to rewrite every word of their dictionaries, because much of that they said and kept printing, edition after edition, in some cases without change for ten or fifteen years, had little or no basis in fact. They will also discover a wealth of new material that is completely missing from their dictionaries – important new material including basic verb senses, phrasal verbs, idiomatic usages – which they must now find space for. The editorial cost of a complete A-Z revision will dwarf the expense of compiling a corpus, and the executives will wonder why they ever let themselves get talked into having a corpus compiled. But it will be too late. Once the cat is out of the bag and corpora come into play, every serious dictionary house will have to use a corpus if it wants to stay in business. Those that don't will have high profit margins on steadily dwindling sales, and will sooner or later fade away.

The upshot is that at the highest level, dictionaries will be better than ever – truer to the language, fuller in their descriptions, broader in their range of coverage, with far greater attention being given to speech than in the past. There will also continue to be dictionaries that do not use corpora and that copy those who do to improve their coverage; but even these unpleasant reminders of the weak integrity of the human spirit will be better than they would have been without the existence of corpora.

In the American dictionary scene, a long period of equilibrium will soon be over. There are certain to be major casualties and new players as the era of the corpus begins to take hold. Funk & Wagnalls was one of the leading dictionary publishers, a worthy rival to Merriam-Webster (then called G. & C. Merriam) for more than fifty years beginning in the 1890s, but when it failed to spend the money necessary – a great deal of money – to revise its unabridged dictionary, it declined. The decline took many years, but its course was inexorable once the fateful decision was made not to invest in fresh research. Now, although "Funk & Wagnalls" is still applied to a few small and obscure paperback dictionaries, there is no dictionary house of Funk & Wagnalls. Others now will make the same mistake and suffer the same consequences. But out of this ferment, the top surviving dictionaries will be better than ever.

CHAPTER 7

Dictionary making

Dictionary making is nothing less than the attempt to fashion a custom-made product on an assembly-line basis. Each dictionary project is unique and calls for its own set of specific rules, but the vast reach of the task demands rigorous organization to make the best possible use of one's resources and staff. The common belief that the making of a dictionary starts with defining words is as naive as the idea that the erection of a building starts with the purchase of construction materials. If one can imagine ordering tons of steel girders, cement, bricks, window glass, plumbing fixtures, and electrical wiring without having any plan of the building for which these materials are to be acquired, one will see the absurdity of the notion that dictionaries begin with defining.

The architect commissioned to design a building must know, first of all, to what uses the building will be put. A hospital requires an altogether different design from that of an office building or a church. Just so, the lexicographer is commissioned by a publisher to design a dictionary for a particular purpose or, as we should say, for a particular market. A general, adult, monolingual dictionary demands different qualities than one for children, for foreign learners, or for a special market such as physicians or electrical engineers. The design of a building reflects a vast number of decisions, some practical and some aesthetic, which are unique to that project, but it depends also on a large body of knowledge that all competent architects are expected to have at their command. These are the tools of the trade. In lexicography, too, a knowledge of the tools of the trade is crucial to meet the particular demands of each project.

Every dictionary has essentially three stages: planning, writing, and producing. In the precomputer age when composition houses set type, the planning stage usually required about 30% of the entire duration of a project, the writing stage at least 50%, and the production stage, which included composition, the remainder. Since composition is effectively

343

done now during the writing stage by lexicographers, whose coding will be later converted into printing codes, the production stage is now usually much shorter and the writing stage is longer. The planning stage still takes about 30% of the time, though it now absorbs a much higher percentage of the costs of the project because of the necessity of acquiring computer hardware and of hiring software engineers or consultants, who do not come cheap. The investment is now more front-loaded than formerly. The writing stage now consumes at least 60%, leaving 10% or less for the production stage.

At a very early stage, the structured database system that will be used to create and store the dictionary text must be designed. There are application software programs that can be leased to provide the basis for such a system, but they only provide a basis. A great deal of original programming has to be tailored to the particular system one wants to build. Most dictionary houses either have a team of software engineers on staff or contract with an independent company to create and service the software system. It is also essential for every dictionary house to contract with a computer hardware service, because the equipment has to process huge amounts of data and is used heavily. It will occasionally break down, and when it breaks down, the schedule suffers. One must plan for such contingencies and have someone who can be called upon to take immediate action.

The editor-in-chief and senior dictionary staff should be intimately involved with the creation of the features of the database, because they know the purposes to which it will be put. The temptation is always to create a database that can do all sorts of wonderful things that might be useful but that are really not necessary. The editor-in-chief has a budget and cannot agree to make the database more powerful and complex than it needs to be. When creating a database system, one has to define very specifically what one wants it to do, and to set priorities for how important each of these desired things is. A good software engineer will insist upon this exercise before he begins to design the system. For one who has not experienced the benefits resulting from going through the discipline of defining one's goals exactly, this exercise may seem needlessly fastidious and time-wasting; but it is not. If one does not go through this process methodically, one may wind up paying for a system that is far more complicated and costly than one will ever need. Such a system will also take longer to create and, because it is complex, will be apt to have bugs and to malfunction. Contrariwise, one may wind up with a system that is too primitive and that does not have the capacity to perform some key steps (such as making cross-reference checks of various kinds) that would save a great deal of time later on. Once a system has been designed and written, it is far more difficult to add such features than if they had been built into the system at the design level. It is therefore important not to stint on planning the design of the database system that serves as the framework for dictionary text.

PLANNING THE DICTIONARY

In general commercial publishing, the first consideration in evaluating any proposal is identifying the market: who will buy the book? This is the first consideration in dictionary publishing as well. Once it is established that there is a market for the dictionary, the size of the market is estimated and one's likely revenue from the dictionary's sale is projected. The particular features of the dictionary must be worked out to fit within that financial framework. In practice, the budget is neither a simple nor invariable calculation, since it depends on many assumptions subject to change.

The size of the dictionary is one of the earliest and most basic decisions to be made. How big is the book to be? How many entries should it contain? Dictionaries competing in the same market are compared, potential users are surveyed, and advice is sought from people who know the needs of the group to which the dictionary is addressed. Entry count is more important in some kinds of dictionaries than in others. College dictionaries generally vie with one another, at least in the United States, to claim more entries than their competitors. On the other hand, in dictionaries for foreign learners the size of the entry count is less important than clear definitions, copious examples, and good coverage of phrasal verbs and idioms. In technical dictionaries, too, matching a specific number of entries is less important than up-to-dateness and the quality of the definitions.

When the type of dictionary, size, and approximate budget have been established, the next major decision is scheduling, which in turn demands that one address the fundamental question of how the dictionary is going to be put together. On what materials will it be based? Who will write and edit the work? Will it be written entirely by an in-house staff or mainly by free-lancers? What role will outside experts play in providing definitions in special fields?

Sources

Once the size of the dictionary has been established, the word list must be selected and sources for definitions must be identified. Dictionaries are compiled from a variety of sources, as we have seen in Ch. 4 (pp. 189–93 and pp. 213–16) and Ch. 6 (pp. 296–321). Whether the predominant source is another dictionary, a citation file, or a corpus makes an enormous difference in the time required to do a dictionary. All commercial dictionaries are based to some extent on preexisting works. As James R. Hulbert notes:

We have noticed that Johnson used Bailey and that Webster used Johnson. . . . For commercial reasons it is natural that customarily dictionaries should minimise or even deny their use of competing books . . . Whether . . . explicit acknowledgement is made or not, anyone who consults a dictionary can be sure that its editor has considered what appears in preceding books of the kind and in his competitors, and used as much of it as seemed to him desirable for his own book.[1]

No one would dare risk overlooking an important sense because of having failed to check other dictionaries. However, citation files and corpora must supply new terms and new senses unless the new dictionary is to rely entirely on existing works. A corpus, supplemented by a citation file, grants the work an independent validity but requires substantially more time both to assemble and to use than other sources. The mix of old and new material is therefore of crucial importance in determining the dictionary's schedule.

Experts, whether on staff or not, can be called upon to draw up definitions in special fields such as law, music, sports, or cooking, as well as in scientific and technical fields. Reliance on outside contributors, however, makes the schedule vulnerable to the failure of one or more of the contributors to produce their material on time – or to produce it at all. There is little one can do to make outside contributors meet their commitments, since in most cases the fees are small and the threat of nonpayment would have little effect other than to suggest that the contributor resign. This is the last thing the lexicographer wants, since replacing such specialists would mean a longer delay than tolerating some tardiness. When a specialist resigns, the dictionary editor has not only to find a competent replacement – no small task in itself – but also to teach him or her to follow the dictionary's style, a process the editor has already gone through with the former contributor; at the end of it, there is no guarantee that the new contributor will honor the commitment any more faithfully than the last.

Reference books other than dictionaries are also used for various purposes, such as the assignment of usage labels. With respect to definitions in general dictionaries, reference books are used mainly to supplement or confirm information rather than as a primary source. In specialized dictionaries, on the other hand, reference books and textbooks often play a key role in assembling the word list, and in some fields they may provide standard definitions.

Scheduling and estimating expenses

Scheduling of dictionaries is notoriously inaccurate, most dramatically in the preparation of scholarly dictionaries but also of commercial ventures. Zgusta remarks, "I certainly do not know all lexicographic projects past and present; but of those I know not a single one was finished in the time and for the money originally planned."[2] He cites a Dutch dictionary that was planned to take 25 years but took 65, and Swedish and Danish works, planned for a dozen years, that required 65 and 49 years, respectively. When James A. H. Murray assumed control of the *New English Dictionary* (later the *Oxford English Dictionary*) in 1879, it was expected to take 10 years to complete. It took nearly 50, the last volume appearing in 1928, 13 years after Murray's death. The chief reason the *OED* took so long to write was its requirement that all of its vocabulary entries and definitions be based on original citations. If one counts the years during which the Philological Society collected citations, the work took 70 years to complete. No purely commercial dictionary, of course, could tolerate such a protracted period of preparation.

Why are predictions of scheduling so bad? Zgusta lists the "fragility of human nature," the difficulty of organizing teams of workers, and the mistaken idea that lexicography is simple and mechanical, whereas, on the contrary, "nearly . . .[every] context has something particular that defies generalization."[3] This is very true. In the context of commercial lexicography, I have offered these observations:

Usually the publisher is ignorant as to what's involved in preparing a dictionary, and the lexicographer is quite irresponsibly optimistic. I have often thought that no new dictionary would ever be undertaken if all parties knew in advance just how long it would take to do it . . . [L]exicography is truly the *writing* of a lexicon . . . And writing cannot be rushed without penalty. Moreover, dictionaries are

not easy to write, and they are very long . . . [A dictionary] is written simultaneously by a great many people who must be trained and supervised and persuaded to follow a set of consistent rules . . . [I]t's an awful job getting *any*
dictionary written, even a bad one. The idea that all of that work by so many
different people will one day be neatly compressed into one oblong book and
look as though it just fell out of a tree – that is really a wonder.[1]

Scheduling is by far the most difficult aspect of planning a dictionary
because it involves many factors that cannot be foreseen or properly
evaluated at the planning stage: the rate at which definers, etymologists,
and others will produce copy; staff turnover, a problem that is more
difficult to control when most of the staff is free-lance; the time required
to write and test the computer software programs, the complexity of
which is often greatly underestimated by everyone at the early stages of
a project; breakdowns in the computer hardware system once it is put to
the test of constant use; technological changes, such as upgraded computer hardware that necessitates additional programming to convert to
the new system; changes in the publishing management that may precipitate sudden changes in the policies of the dictionary; and, not least,
the need to take time to defend, promote, and explain the dictionary
within one's own company or university. In the case of scholarly dictionaries, the preparation of grant proposals and other fund-raising activities often consume a great deal of time and require the participation of
the top editors, thus having a major impact on the schedule.

Apart from the few publishers of major dictionaries, most book publishers have no idea of the cost or complexity of producing a dictionary.
Dictionaries are unlike any book they have ever published. They do not
fit into the usual pattern of financing; from an accountant's point of
view, dictionaries behave quite bizarrely. Most books cost comparatively
little to prepare (the plant cost, in publishing argot) but a great deal to
produce (paper, printing, and binding costs). The opposite is true of dictionaries, where the cost of production, though hardly negligible, is
small compared to the huge editorial development costs, which must be
amortized over a much longer period of time than book publishers are
generally familiar with. Data-management costs (systems analysis, computer programming and processing) are also much higher than they are
for other books.

The pressure is great to make the schedule of commercial dictionaries as lean as possible. Lexicographers who value continuous employment make concessions, even some they may have deep misgivings about,
while clinging to the cherished idea that they are not compromising their

integrity, not, to be blunt, lying to hold onto their job. For the lexicographer's vision is set on a distant goal, one that publishers cannot see and that they suspect will not occur, but which the lexicographer knows is worth reaching. It is almost a matter of faith, because at times it is quite impossible to see how the end of the task can ever be reached, even if all concerned work as hard as they are capable of working. David B. Guralnik made the same point in speaking about the preparation of the first edition of *Webster's New World Dictionary*: "There were times when ordinary prudence, good common sense, dictated the abolishment of the whole project. I am happy to report now that in this instance common sense did not prevail."[5] It must be added that this dictionary, like many another that was almost abandoned before its completion, has proved to be immensely profitable in the years since its first publication. The editor of a dictionary has to be absolutely bound and determined to finish the dictionary, or it will never be done. In a period when dictionaries were still written largely by in-house staffs, I wrote:

If from one end, he has the publishers tugging at him to finish more quickly, from the other he has people tugging at him to slow the pace to make certain improvements. These counter-pressures come sometimes from contributing scholars, but almost always from the staff itself – the people writing the definitions and all the other elements of each entry . . . The editor in chief is placed in the untenable position of appearing to defend a lower quality of work than his subordinates demand. But he must cope with the knowledge that unless he compromises to some extent by setting quotas, there will be no dictionary at all, and he and all of his staff will be out of a job.[6]

As we shall see, the role of the in-house staff has changed, creating a whole new set of problems, but the pressures to keep to one's schedule or accelerate it remain.

The situation has close parallels in other businesses, where considerations of quality must always be tempered by cost and by the price the customer is willing to pay. It is not widely appreciated to what extent these factors apply also to products having intellectual properties such as dictionaries. Every definition calls for scores of small decisions that the definer has little time to ponder but must make promptly. Dictionaries take so long not because they are done by perfectionists but because there is so much to be done. In fact, dictionary editors are far from perfectionists. They become expert in judicious compromise, weighing the cost in time against the possible benefit of an improved definition before undertaking any new research effort. Obviously, standards must be met, but every editorial step is measured against the time required to employ it.

How does one go about estimating the time required to compile a dictionary? One breaks down each step that can be foreseen, estimates how many definitions or entries each editor can do per hour or per day, and calculates how many editor days, weeks, months, and years will be required to complete the job. An *editor week* – the amount of work that one editor can do in one week – is the unit most often used. Two editor weeks equal the amount of work that two editors can do in a week or that one editor can do in two weeks. Of course, remembering the parable about the number of men needed to dig a ditch, we will not suppose that the work thirty editors can do in a week equals the work one editor can do in thirty weeks. In fact, no dictionary staffs have more than a handful of senior definers.

After one estimates the optimum rate of defining per editor week, one divides this number into the total number of terms to be defined, then inevitably finds that the dictionary can be done in something like 12,432 editorial weeks, which means that it would take 20 editors working 52 weeks a year (with no vacations or illness, and of course no turnover) almost twelve years (12,432 divided by 20 = 621.6 weeks divided by 52 = 11.95). If the editors averaged $40,000 per year, the editorial costs would be $800,000 per year or about $9.5 million overall. One turns pale, sits, asks for a glass of water. "Well," one says, after a time of limp reflection, "maybe they can work a little faster." Later, one may try working from the other end, that is, deciding how much money can be spent, how many editors can be afforded, and how fast each will have to work. But the result may be an impossibly fast rate of work. Ultimately, one works from both ends and seeks a compromise between what budget and time constraints allow and what one can reasonably expect editors to do, physically and mentally, every week, week after week.

Staffing

To what extent should one rely on a free-lance editorial staff rather than an in-house group? The attraction of free-lance editors is mainly financial. The cost of office space, equipment, administration, and employee fringe benefits makes in-house staffs many times more expensive than free-lance staffs. In-house staff workers who turn out to be poor editors or have personal problems that interfere with their work performance must be tolerated for a considerable period, whereas free-lancers who do not measure up are easily dismissed. Moreover, when work is slow in-house staff must be paid nonetheless, and when the project ends the employer may be forced to discharge part of the staff, a prospect neither side views with any satisfaction.

On the other hand, because one has less effective control over free-lance editors, the rate and quality of work are variable and the schedule vulnerable to delay. Free-lance editors can decide to take vacations whenever and for however long they wish, and there is nothing one can do about it. Whereas the in-house editor has all the incentive that ambition can fuel, the free-lancer is relatively uncommitted. Many free-lancers are engaged in more than one project simultaneously, and they will not be crushed by any single loss. If a better-paying opportunity comes along, they will quite naturally seize it, no matter what the consequences to one's project. The daily personal contacts between in-house staff and supervisor to correct errors as soon as they occur and the sense of teamwork and mutual respect of a staff can certainly inspire better work than that of an equal number of editors working independently, even if both groups are able and conscientious.

From 1890 to the 1930s, dictionary houses sometimes assembled very large in-house staffs, often numbering forty people or more. As labor costs increased in the ensuing decades, staff sizes decreased, but even in the early 1960s staffs of fifteen or more were still the norm. When a project ended, the staff was reduced through layoffs. In the 1970s and '80s the cost of employee medical benefits soared, and many employers began to look for ways to cut down on their full-time, permanent employees. As home computers became more widely available in the 1980s, some dictionary houses began to use more free-lancers and cut down on their staffs.[7] Although one or two dictionary houses in the US and Britain continue to maintain fairly large in-house staffs, they are not as large as they were in former times, and their days are numbered. Some companies also use contract workers, employees who work in the office either full-time or part-time for a stipulated period, generally for an hourly wage, and who usually receive some employee benefits. The employer benefits from having more control, and the employee at least has a job for the duration of the contract, generally for one or two years, but no job security after that. Nonetheless, contract workers still cost much more than free-lancers.

The trend is unmistakably towards using free-lancers working in their own homes, or to the hiring of independent editorial packagers (who in turn use free-lancers) to produce a particular work by contract. Some of the most prestigious dictionary houses on both sides of the Atlantic have published language reference books under their own imprints that were prepared chiefly by outside organizations, with their in-house dictionary editors acting more or less as commissioning editors. Computer technology now allows a system in which an editor working at home can use a modem to dial in to a central database and, using a secure password, transfer a section of a dictionary to his or her home computer, and then log off. So long as the software running the dictionary's system has been previously installed, the editor can edit the downloaded section whenever he or she wants to, and, when finished, dial in via modem and restore it to the central database. Though the dictionary's software editing tools can take up a lot of computer space, the capacities and speed of stand-alone computers have grown so much that they can easily handle them. Indeed, the new generation of computers have enough storage space to hold large corpora on their hard drives.

The social benefits of working at home are very considerable, and will help to enlarge the pool of qualified lexicographers. Parents with small children will obviously benefit by being able to work at home in accord with their own flexible schedules. Disabled people for whom travel would be a hardship will benefit. Older people who have retired from regular work but want to continue working on a part-time or irregular basis will benefit. Some social critics have deplored the growth of home workers in industry in general, maintaining that they are being exploited by being paid low wages and deprived of medical and other benefits. There may be substance to these criticisms in some cases, but in the rarefied realm of dictionary work, which calls for special skills that are in high demand when available, free-lancing seems to have many more positive than negative aspects. Free-lance editors are free to live wherever they want, thousands of miles from the dictionary house, and still contribute productively, and on a schedule tailored to their own needs rather than to their employer's. These are very great benefits. Moreover, there has never been job security in dictionary work for in-house staffs. Even those whose obligations demand that they work as a regular in-house employee now at least have the option in exigent circumstances of doing free-lance work until they can obtain another in-house staff position.

Periodically, even a free-lance staff should meet in the home office to discuss problems with their editing; it also helps morale for a group of people working as a team to meet one another, if only once a year, to associate faces and mannerisms with voices and e-mail messages. One gets better cooperation and commitment from a group if they have met one another. But even occasional meetings are not possible for everybody. I mentioned earlier that, in the past, in-house staffs often demanded a level of quality that might put the entire project in jeopardy, and that the editor-in-chief had to temper this zeal for perfection with the practical necessity of finishing the job. With the diminished role of the in-house staff and with little or no personal contact with the group of free-lancers, the pressure to maintain quality is now more often absent than present. It is all too easy to make decisions to speed the project that subtract from its quality in ways that most people (apart from staff) will not notice. The idea that electronic messages are just as good as face-to-face meetings is a convenient fiction. Although I appreciate the many benefits of home work for legions of people – including me – the daily interaction of staff editors working together in the same place certainly led to many useful improvements and corrections in dictionary work that were made spontaneously in conversation, that were too small, that seemed too fleeting or trivial and yet were too complicated, to bother explaining in writing. These small improvements in the aggregate added up to something not so trivial. We ought to face this, unpleasant though it is: other things being equal, dictionaries composed entirely by strangers will not be as good as dictionaries composed by people who work together and know each other. It can be argued, however, that other things never are equal, that the financial problems inherent in putting together and maintaining in-house staffs bring into play other pressures that have a damaging effect on a dictionary's quality.

It is very difficult to find highly skilled general definers. Losing even a single senior editor can set back a project significantly. Penny Silva writes in the introduction to *A Dictionary of South African English on Historical Principles*, "During 1990 the staff complement was expanded to five full-time and two-part researchers, two typists, and a clerical assistant . . . From 1991–4 the staff consisted of five editors . . ."[8] Really top-flight dictionary editors are about as rare as good poets. There are probably no more than a few hundred experienced general definers in all of the US and Britain combined, and not all of them are top-flight. Training new definers, which is usually necessary in any new project, takes much of the time of the skilled staff who act as teachers, thus cutting down sharply on their own productivity. If the in-house staff consists of three, and six or seven free-lancers have to be trained, it is safe to say that very little progress in the preparation of the dictionary will be made during the training period. Because of the complexity of dictionary work, the work of new editors has to be checked over an extended period, with particular intensity for at least six months, and sometimes much longer.

What are the qualities of a good definer? First and foremost, he or she must be able to write well and easily. Though called "editors," definers are primarily writers. They must have analytical minds that seek to chop things up into parts that can be understood separately and reassembled to fit their purpose. Poets are like that – good poets make good definers – but defining is not creative in the sense that writing verse is creative, and defining would bore most poets to death. Definers must have a broad, but not necessarily deep, fund of information; they must read the newspapers and be interested in the world, though they need not be – and seldom are – normal in their tastes and predilections. Special definers, on the other hand, who may work only on biological terms, for example, need to have a deep knowledge of that field but may know next to nothing about other subjects. Lastly, definers must have a feeling for the language, *Sprachgefühl*, a sense of aptness of expression, an appreciation of nuance, style, and idiom. This is to some extent implicit in the ability to write well, but not all good writers have it in equal measure. Many foreign-born writers, for example, can write English well but lack an appreciation of style, such that their writing may seem a bit heavy-handed even when they intend to be casual. Any such gap in intuitive understanding of style is disastrous in dictionary defining, and for this reason definers for general monolingual dictionaries are almost always native-born speakers. Bosley Woolf, former editor of the Merriam-Webster dictionaries, has said that it is a basic requirement that a definer for an English dictionary be a native speaker of the language.[9]

A word is in order about what definers do not have to be. They need not have enormous vocabularies or be polymaths, and I would never hire a person who said he or she enjoyed reading dictionaries as a hobby. They need not be linguists; in fact, knowledge of linguistics is of no particular help in dictionary defining. I say this from my own experience in working with definer trainees, and it is confirmed by the experience of other lexicographers. Patrick Hanks remarks, "I have not found that people with a sound theoretical understanding of current linguistic theory make good definition writers. It is a literary, not a scientific activity."[10] Bosley Woolf states that graduate study, while it may give the new definer an initial advantage, does not ultimately make him or her more fit for the job than "last year's college graduate."[11]

Woolf also says that defining requires humility. To those who have not worked on a project as vast and complex as a dictionary, the remark may be puzzling. Nothing cuts one down to size as quickly and finally as dictionary work. This has always been true, but using a corpus is an even more humbling experience than working from citations, because one is constantly confronted with abundant evidence of usages that are common but that one would not have thought of. One is constantly reminded of the infinite variety of language and sees example after example of cases that do not fit the pattern described in any dictionary. Novice definers with advanced degrees, whether in linguistics or another field, are apt to be overconfident, especially if those teaching them know less than they about the academic subjects they are freshly acquainted with. Such beginners often imagine that their academic training qualifies them for advanced work in lexicography and are chagrined and hurt when they discover that it doesn't.

The lack of humility of contributing specialists in a technical dictionary can be an acute problem. Medical specialists, for instance, have a great deal of confidence in their knowledge. Fine, one wants authoritative specialists. But they must also appreciate their relative ignorance of the vast majority of medical nomenclature, past and present. They must not, for example, exclude words from the dictionary simply because they have never heard of them; yet most medical experts would do just that unless countermanded by a nonexpert lexicographer. Apart from all other reasons, this illustrates why general lexicographers must be in charge of a specialized dictionary; only they know enough about language to be humble.

Most dictionary staffs are run by an editor-in-chief and a managing editor. The editor-in-chief has the ultimate responsibility for producing the dictionary on schedule and within budget. He often selects the policy advisers and takes an active part in the discussions that help to shape the decisions determining the dictionary's scope and market. Whether the editor-in-chief is invited to participate in the business decisions affecting the profitability of the dictionary – its pricing, production costs, and so on – depends more on his particular position within the company than on being editor-in-chief. In any event, much of his time is spent monitoring costs. If the dictionary is a contributed work, he deals with the contributors and is responsible for telling them what to do and for getting them to do it. He is also responsible for the quality of the work and does as much editing as time permits.

Although I have been speaking of the editor-in-chief as "he," there are now quite as many women heading dictionaries as men. Women have played a large role in lexicography for many years. I have in my possession a photograph of the "general editorial room" and of the "managing editor's room" during the editing of the 1913 unabridged dictionary, the *Funk & Wagnalls New Standard*, showing long tables with people seated side by side with propped-up dictionaries before them, and a significant minority of the editors are women. Some of the sub-editors for the *OED* were women, and women played a major role in providing the *OED* with quotations. Unfortunately, for many years women were denied the top positions in lexicography as in other areas, even while their numbers increased on dictionary staffs. There are now more women than men engaged in lexicography, and in recent years we have finally seen a number of women promoted to run dictionary programs. There are really not that many top positions in lexicography, and taking a poll of the sex of the chief editors wouldn't signify much of anything. But it is finally established in English-language lexicography that there are no barriers that would prevent a woman from becoming editor-in-chief of any dictionary. This is not to say that in any individual case prejudice might not still exist, but only that since there is ample precedent throughout the field for promoting women to run dictionaries, it would not take an act of singular courage to appoint another woman to such a post.

The managing editor's position varies greatly from publisher to publisher and from project to project. In some projects with an in-house staff, the managing editor, apart from doing his own editing, makes individual assignments, supervises their quality, sees that they are completed on schedule, trains new definers, keeps statistical data on the work's progress, and has a large hand in shaping the data-management program. The managing editor is thus turned inward towards the staff and the daily routine, while the editor-in-chief, Janus-faced, has to look inward and outward at the same time. In some cases the editor-in-chief is little more than a figurehead, with the managing editor doing most of the planning and all of the staff supervision. In other cases where the in-house staff is very small or nonexistent, the managing editor may be in fact little more than a staff editor who occasionally supervises a few freelance editors. In short, "managing editor" can mean a lot or a little, depending on the particular situation.

Selection of the word list

After the policies, scope, and market of a dictionary have been established and its schedule and costs estimated, the next step is the selection of the word list: all those terms to be included as dictionary entries, whether main entries or not. Although it is popularly believed that unabridged dictionaries contain all the words in the English language, as we have seen in our discussion of types of dictionaries, even an unabridged dictionary must have principles of selection and must exclude many thousands of words and expressions because they are obsolete, rarely used, or too specialized for a general dictionary. Considerations of available space always place practical limits on the number of entries that can be accommodated, especially in a one-volume dictionary. Clarence Barnhart has clearly explained the practical necessity for selectivity in deriving the word list for a college dictionary. If a college dictionary did not limit its entry count, it would run out of space somewhere in the letter D, about one-fourth of the way through an unabridged-size lexicon.[12] There are other compelling reasons why a word list must be selected before defining begins. As we have seen, one of the cardinal principles of defining is the rule that all of the terms used in definitions must themselves be entered in the dictionary. But how can this rule be observed if there is no word list? How can definers know when they are using a Word Not In in their definitions? Furthermore, one would have no way of insuring that parallel terms are defined in comparable ways, or that all the terms in a semantic cluster of equivalent or opposite meanings are included at all. Such a dictionary, if ever completed, would be a hodge-podge of inconsistencies and random omissions. The compiler of a glossary can afford to include whatever he feels will cause the reader difficulty, but a dictionary is self-contained, and within its stated scope it should be comprehensive and balanced in its coverage of comparable terms. This can be accomplished only by having a word list.

The time required to select a dictionary's word list may constitute a significant part of the entire project. Barnhart writes, "On my first high-school dictionary a staff of ten editors spent over five years combing the OED. Out of this mass of material we selected the meanings that were to be included in our high-school dictionary."[13] Barnhart also drew upon a large citation file for senses that appeared after *OED*'s publication. Frank Vizetelly stated that the compilation of the vocabulary for the Funk & Wagnalls *Standard Dictionary* (an unabridged work published in 1893) took twenty compilers a year. In my own experience, the compilation of the word list may take up to 20 percent of the entire duration of a new project, from beginning to bound books. However, a word list based largely on another dictionary, as in preparing an abridgment, would take proportionately much less time.

The particular selection of terms depends chiefly on the presumed user. There is no need to belabor the point made earlier that the vocabulary needed for a school dictionary will be different from that for adults, and that an ESL or specialized dictionary will have vocabularies different from either. However, a few comments may be in order on difficulties of selection that apply to almost all kinds of dictionaries.

What constitutes a legitimate dictionary entry? What is it, specifically, that makes a multiple lexical unit worth including? Two criteria have been cited. First, it must function like a unit so that its meaning inheres in the whole expression, as in *guinea pig*, rather than in its separate elements. No part of it can be replaced without the loss of its original meaning: one cannot call a *guinea pig* a *guinea hog*. The existence of semantically comparable one-word units (*rat, rabbit*, etc.) is further evidence that *guinea pig* is a unit.[14] Second, the stress pattern of compounds is usually distinctive, with primary stress on the first element and very little pause, if any, between the two elements, as in *blackbird* or *ladybug*. If one says aloud *guinea pig* and *large pig*, or *ladybug* and *green bug*, one will perceive the difference; both elements of the second expression receive equal stress, all the more noticeable because the pause between the two words is slightly longer than in the first expression. Thus, one can conclude that *guinea pig* is a compound, though written as two words.[15] The stress test does not work with every multiple lexical unit, such as *stress test*, a type of physical examination, or *safety glass*, or *school board*.

Although much attention is given to determining the lexical validity of multiple lexical units, every dictionary includes many phrasal entries that are not lexical units. The obvious cases of biographical and geographical entries need no elaboration; these are clearly encyclopedic terms. Less obvious, but bountiful in numbers, are terms like *Copernican system* and *listed building* (in *CED*) or *Jefferson Davis's Birthday* and *Riemannian geometry* (in *MW10*). Open a dictionary to virtually any page and one will find terms like these, which are included for a variety of reasons but principally because the reader expects to find them. *Copernican system* and *Riemannian geometry* provide useful historical and scientific information, but their status as lexical units is arguable. *Listed building* is an official designation in the United Kingdom and of national importance, but it is part of a specialized nomenclature. When one gets into the realm of nomenclature, where volume of usage is not a factor, one is hard pressed to find any theoretical basis for including one or a few elements of the nomenclature and omitting all others. Yet clearly one cannot admit more than a few, else one's dictionary would rapidly turn into a nomenclature.

The difficulty of distinguishing between lexical units and items in a nomenclature is especially nettlesome in specialized dictionaries, which are by their nature more encyclopedic than general dictionaries. For example, medical nomenclature may include many different terms for kinds of *agenesis* (absence of a part or organ resulting from its failure to develop in the course of embryonic growth) or *atresia* (congenital absence of a normal opening in a body vessel or part). It so happens that it is possible for virtually every part normally open to be closed at birth. We could thus have hundreds of *atresias* and thousands of *agenesis* entries. Some kinds of atresia and agenesis are more common than others and some are identifiable elements of complex genetic disorders; medical dictionaries try to confine their selection to terms that meet either of these criteria, but in many cases the decision is borderline if not arbitrary. Many diseases such as tuberculosis can afflict virtually every organ in the body. We may therefore reject *prostatic tuberculosis* along with many other like terms, but what about *pulmonary tuberculosis*? Logically, it should be omitted, yet no medical dictionary does so, even if the definition given is simply "tuberculosis of the lungs." In a specialized dictionary, the determination of whether a term is a lexical unit must depend on whether it is used often enough in preference to other phrases that mean the same thing to distinguish it as a name rather than as a merely fortuitous description. Unfortunately, few people are in a position to make that judgment, and those who are frequently disagree.

The selection of entries depends very much on the compiler's sense of what is wanted, and if what is wanted occasionally violates theory, so be it. My illustration of nonlexical terms in *CED* and *MW10* was not intended as criticism. Surely it is no fault to serve well the needs and expectations of the reader, provided one is faithful to the overriding purpose of a dictionary: describing the use of language. When the inclusion of nonlexical units becomes promiscuous and haphazard, merely serving the ends of marketing the dictionary rather than the needs of the user, we may fairly object to the practice. Dictionaries are *the* basic reference book in many homes, particularly in the United States, and it is hard to believe that the public would be better served by denying it nonlexical items in order to conform to a theoretical construct of a proper dictionary. The leitmotif running through Johnson's *Plan* of 1747 is that his dictionary beyond all else must be useful; to my mind that is still the first rule of good dictionary making.

In former years, the word list was compiled in a card or paper file, with each proposed lexical unit on a separate card or slip. This allowed space for other information, such as the source from which it was obtained, its part of speech, its status as a main entry or run-on derivative, an indication as to whether it was a general or a specialized word (and, if the latter, what specialty), and perhaps a symbol representing its degree of importance in the dictionary. Optional words could then be cut to conserve space at a later time.

Nowadays, needless to say, word lists are compiled and stored in computer files. Statistics on the total number of entries or the number in any particular category are easily obtained, since each of the items enumerated above (and probably several others) constitutes a separate field that can be searched independently. One can thus find all the items obtained from the same source, or all the phrasal entries, or all the verbs. One can find the ratio of main entries to total entries or the number of specialized entries, and then print out the terms of each specialty so that they can be sent out to consultants. Here is one area in which computerization has been an unequivocal blessing. Alphabetization is no longer a problem, and any number of people can work at compiling the word list without fear of duplicating their efforts so long as they all have access to the same database. Computerized files have cut the time needed for word-list preparation, and, even more important, they provide a continuous flow of information about the size and disposition of the word list.

To provide guidance in selecting dictionary word lists that accurately reflect the distribution of lexical units throughout the alphabet, Edward L. Thorndike prepared a study of the lexicon in the 1950s for the Thorndike-Barnhart dictionaries. On the basis of his study he divided the alphabet into 105 approximately equal units, called *blocks*.[16] (See Figure 32.) One can see that in English there are far more words that begin with S – which has 13 blocks – than with any other letter. The letter C, with ten blocks, is next. It is a truism in dictionary work that one is in sight of the end of the project on finishing S, but not before. The block system is helpful in providing a check on the criteria used by various compilers working in different parts of the alphabet. If one's word list shows that E has as many entries as S, for example, one should suspect that whoever selected the terms for E was far more permissive than the selector for S, and adjust the word list accordingly.

Language changes, of course, and the distribution of words according to their initial letters may have changed since this table was prepared and may change in the future; but I doubt that the overall distribution changes rapidly. I have used Thorndike's block system for several different dictionaries, adult and children's, and found it to be a helpful

Thorndike's block system of distribution of dictionary entries by initial letters

A–1	a–adk	F–36	fore–fror	P–71	post–prh
A–2	adl–alh	F–37	fros–fz	P–72	pri–prot
A–3	ali–angk	G–38	g–geq	P–73	prou–pz
A–4	angl–arak	G–39	ger–gord	Q–74	q–qz
A–5	aral–ath	G–40	gore–grouo	R–75	r–recn
A–6	ati–az	G–41	group–gz	R–76	reco–renn
B–7	b–basd	H–42	h–hav	R–77	reno–rhn
B–8	base–benf	H–43	haw–hh	R–78	rho–rotd
B–9	beng–bld	H–44	hi–horr	R–79	rote–rz
B–10	ble–bouq	H–45	hors–hz	S–80	s–sat
B–11	bour–buc	I–46	i–inam	S–81	sau–sd
B–12	bud–bz	I–47	inan–infn	S–82	sea–seo
C–13	c–caq	I–48	info–intn	S–83	sep–shio
C–14	car–cel	I–49	into–iz	S–84	ship–sinf
C–15	cem–chim	J–50	j–jz	S–85	sing–smd
C–16	chin–cled	K–51	k–kz	S–86	sme–sors
C–17	clee–col	L–52	l–ld	S–87	sort–spln
C–18	com–conf	L–53	le–lil	S–88	splo–stas
C–19	cong–coo	L–54	lim–louh	S–89	stat–stov
C–20	cop–cq	L–55	loui–lz	S–90	stow–sucg
C–21	cra–culs	M–56	m–marb	S–91	such–swar
C–22	cult–cz	M–57	marc–med	S–92	swas–sz
D–23	d–defd	M–58	mee–mil	T–93	t–tel
D–24	defe–deteq	M–59	mim–monn	T–94	tem–thq
D–25	deter–discol	M–60	mono–mz	T–95	thr–too
D–26	discom–dold	N–61	n–nif	T–96	top–trh
D–27	dole–dt	N–62	nig–nz	T–97	tri–tz
D–28	du–dz	O–63	o–oo	U–98	u–unl
E–29	e–elk	O–64	op–ou	U–99	unm–uz
E–30	ell–en	O–65	ov–oz	V–100	v–vim
E–31	eo–exb	P–66	p–par	V–101	vin–vz
E–32	exc–ez	P–67	pas–peq	W–102	w–wess
F–33	f–fem	P–68	per–picj	W–103	west–wis
F–34	fen–flah	P–69	pick–plea	W–104	wit–wz
F–35	flai–ford	P–70	pleb–poss	XYZ–105	x–zz

32 Thorndike's block system of distribution of dictionary entries by initial letters

guide in fashioning the word list. It will not work for every kind of dictionary, most obviously for specialized dictionaries, nor for dictionaries of very small size, but for general dictionaries of moderate to large size (between 30,000 and 200,000 entries) it is a fairly reliable guide to the alphabetic distribution of the lexicon. One should not be too rigid about the equivalence of all the blocks, however. The J block, for example, is actually shorter than any of the S blocks, but it was given its own block for simplicity's sake. Likewise, the XYZ block does not measure up to the size of other blocks. Frequently, too, the last block in a letter will comprise fewer terms than other blocks within the letter. In spite of these minor imperfections, the block system is a valuable tool not only in entry selection but in organizing the assignments to definers. Each definer can be given one block with the knowledge that it represents a fixed percentage of the entire work. Of course, some blocks contain words that are harder to define than other blocks, or words with many more definitions, so that the work involved in doing two different blocks is not strictly comparable. Nonetheless, the system does provide a rough guide to equivalence, and in assigning deadlines to individual definers the editor-in-chief or managing editor should make allowance for the degree of difficulty of each block and adjust the deadline accordingly. Because each block contains quite a considerable stretch of words, one might want to subdivide them into smaller units. There are other guides used in lexicography in which the alphabet is subdivided into many more separate units than in the Thorndike system. For example, the system used to produce *CDAE* contained 370 (obviously much smaller) sections. Now that numerous dictionaries are available in electronic form, some older dictionaries have been statistically analyzed by linguists and more accurate systems of alphabetic distribution may become available as a result. Until new systems have proved themselves, however, by being utilized to make new dictionaries, the Thorndike system will remain a useful guide to the relative weight of the letters of the alphabet.

As I have noted earlier (see p. 99), some lexicographers distinguish between the *macrostructure* of a dictionary and its *microstructure*. Decisions at the level of the lexical item deal with the dictionary's macrostructure, and include the word-list selection and the style of presentation of headwords and other features. Decisions at the level of particular meaning, such as the order and arrangement of definitions within an entry, are described as dealing with the dictionary's microstructure.[17]

The style manual

Most publishing houses have a company style manual that sets forth suggested rules for manuscript preparation, rules concerning capitalization, punctuation, spelling, footnote references, and so forth. But dictionaries are so specialized that they require their own style manuals, for many of the rules of regular manuals have no applications to dictionaries (such as footnotes), and literally hundreds of situations that must be resolved for dictionary work are not addressed at all, or not in sufficient detail, in regular style manuals. Moreover, etymologies have such a different set of problems that they often require a separate style manual, especially for large dictionaries. The etymological style may differ substantially from that used elsewhere in the dictionary.

The dictionary style manual is an alphabetically arranged reference guide to every aspect of editing dictionary copy. Though called a style manual, it is in fact also a teaching manual. It discusses the general defining style to be employed, with illustrations of various kinds of definitions. It explains, often in great detail, how particular grammatical forms (such as transitive and intransitive verbs) are to be treated. It illustrates how each part of the definition is to be coded. These codes not only identify that part, but many of them will be converted later to printing codes that will determine the type style of that part of the definition, and sometimes its placement on the page in relation to other text items. The editor-in-chief and senior staff are well advised to discuss any potential problems thoroughly and to deal with them in the manual, which should be as comprehensive as possible. It is difficult to find and impractical to correct inconsistencies once the defining stage is well under way. However, the variety of linguistic situations in which the rules must be applied cannot possibly be anticipated, and dictionary style manuals are frequently amplified and refined as novel situations are encountered. Every dictionary has unique problems; there can be no generalized manual that suits all dictionaries.

Although dictionary style manuals may now be stored electronically on a central database or on each editor's computer, I still believe it easier to use a printed manual with the sheets kept in a looseleaf binder or bound in a notebook with a spiral binding. In the latter case, it is best to print only on one side of every page to allow space for the many changes and additions that will inevitably have to be made in the course of the work. If the style manual exists in electronic form – or even if it does not

– changes and additions can be e-mailed to each editor as necessary. Indeed, as soon as each editor signs in to the dictionary database from his or her home computer, he can be given a style manual update or read a memorandum from the editor-in-chief. One may wonder why computer programs could not be created to detect and correct any style inconsistencies in the dictionary text. Dedicated software can provide numerous checks on the editing process, but these generally apply to the grosser forms of mistakes – such as omitting the part-of-speech label – rather than to any of the finer points of style. Constructing software to catch these errors would be immensely complicated and expensive, and might ultimately do more harm than good, for three reasons. First, because the style is in a constant state of flux, the programming could never keep pace with the changes, and programming errors would be apt to occur. Secondly, there are exceptions to almost every style rule, and unless the programming were flexible enough to allow for them, it would interfere with the editor's ability to make decisions. Thirdly, as each new style update was being implemented and the new software was being tested, all editing would have to be suspended, thus delaying the progress of the work.

A style manual I prepared for a children's dictionary ran to over eighty pages in typescript. The style manual for *CDAE* was over 150 pages initially, and with its many additions probably was the equivalent of 200 pages by the time the dictionary was finished. College and unabridged dictionary manuals, because of their complexity, can be even longer. To see the type of material covered, see Figure 33, "Typical headings in a dictionary style manual," pp. 366–71, but please understand that this outline is greatly simplified. The subjects covered and the emphasis given them depend to a great extent on the particular type of dictionary being prepared.

The style manual is designed for the use of in-house staff and free-lance editors. The situation is complicated when one must depend on outside contributors, as for a specialized dictionary. The specialists may need to know some of the items covered by the staff manual, but certainly not all. One must therefore prepare a simplified version of the style manual for contributors, omitting many of the finer points of style while leaving in most of the teaching aids. It is best to tell specialists only as much as they need to know to do their work. One must curb one's open-handedness not because of any proclivity for secrecy but because people unfamiliar with editing procedures tend to misinterpret the simplest editorial directions. The same person who can separate and suture microscopic blood vessels of the eye with perfect assurance falls into a state of mental collapse when instructed in the proper use of parentheses.

One of the chief differences in style between various kinds of dictionaries is the order of presentation of the entries. Almost all general native-speaker dictionaries, both in the US and Britain, now use a single alphabetical list, whereas other types of dictionaries employ a two-tier system, in which subentries appear, usually in boldface type within a paragraph introduced by a headword or indented below it. This arrangement is often used in specialized dictionaries, and is sometimes called *nesting* or *clustering*. Because most of the vocabulary entries in medical (and other specialized) dictionaries are multiword units, it is sensible to alphabetize them under the governing noun; it is easier to find a particular syndrome in an alphabetical list under the headword *syndrome* than to search for it throughout the dictionary. Even native-speaker dictionaries nest idioms and proverbial phrases (called *run-ins*), such as *make eyes at* and *an eye for an eye*, because there is no other convenient way to present them. Dictionaries for foreign learners typically nest a great many idioms and phrasal verbs under the main verb, and some ESL dictionaries also nest compounds. For example, in *CDAE*, *eyelash* and *eyelid*, among other compounds, are nested under *eye*, and *jet lag* is nested under *jet*.

In ESL lexicography, the argument for clustering is that it places semantically linked words together based on their morphological similarity, thus enabling the user to build on his previous knowledge of the headword's meaning and add new forms to his working vocabulary, enriching his ability to use them in conversation and writing (the encoding function). It may also help in decoding, because he may not know the exact form of a compound or other derivative but be able to locate it under the root form. Those who favor a single alphabetical format, on the other hand, argue that it can be hard to find nested words and phrases because they may appear out of alphabetical sequence, and if the user does not associate the headword with the compound form, he will not find it. There is merit to both arguments. Neither system works well in every case, but dictionaries have to make a choice and live with it for better or worse.

Another question that style manuals have to describe is the sequence of definitions. Dictionaries usually number each definition and arrange them either by frequency of use or in historical order. In either case, the result in some cases is a paragraph with many numbered definitions, in

---

Typical headings in a dictionary style manual (simplified version)

Abbreviations

    1. As main entries

    2. Used in the dictionary

Adjectives (defining style)

Adverbs (defining style)

Biographical entries

Capitalization

    1. What to capitalize

    2. Capitalized main entries

Codes (explanation of all codes in the text and keystrokes that will produce them)

Color terms

    1. Adj. + color ("light blue wall")

    2. Adj. + adj. ("light colored")

    3. Color + color ("blue-green")

    4. Use of black-and-white, etc. (set phrases)

    5. Colors as main entries

Combining forms

Contractions

Corpus

    1. Description

    2. How to do searches

    3. How to edit and copy in the dictionary text

---

33 Typical headings of a dictionary style manual (simplified version), pp. 366–71

Cross-references (This would be far more detailed than shown here.)

1. When required

2. Codes used to mark

3. As main entries

4. X-refs to specific defs.

Defining (Style of defining every part-of-speech, with examples shown of different problems. Particular attention is given to verbs.)

Defining vocabulary (if an ESL dictionary using a limited vocabulary)

1. When it must be used

2. How to style words not in the defining vocabulary in contexts normally restricted to it

The actual defining vocabulary would not be listed in the style manual, because that would be part of the database, which would automatically alert the editor when he or she was using an impermissible word in a field requiring its use. Editors can also easily check the database to see whether any word they intend to use is in the defining vocabulary.

Etymologies (often omitted because etymology is covered in a separate style manual)

Examples (or Illustrative examples)

1. Types (phrases and sentences)

2. Codes used (e.g., to mark off collocations)

3. Use of parentheses (or other punctuation) to show variability

Geographic entries

Grammar (especially elaborate in ESL dictionaries)

1. Grammatical types for each part-of-speech identified, with examples shown and codes used

2. Listing of grammar codes used with explanations and examples

Guidewords (sometimes used in polysemous entries to show basic sense concisely)

Idioms

Illustrations (pictorial)

Inflected forms

1. When to include

2. Which forms to include

3. When they must also be entered as x-ref headword entries

Labels (Types of labels, e.g., register, currency, language varieties; with their descriptions, codes, and keystrokes to produce them)

Main entries (or Headwords)

Numbers and numerals

Order of definitions

Order of entries

This describes the sequence in which entries spelled alike but differing in other ways will be entered, e.g., do capitalized forms precede lower-case forms? Do forms that are written solid precede hyphenated forms? A listing of theoretical possibilities is listed here, such as: sc, sc-, sc., s/c, s.c., -sc, Sc, Sc-, etc.

Parentheses (use of)

Parts-of-speech

Phrasal verbs

Preferred spellings

Pronunciations (often omitted because pronunciation is covered in a separate style manual)

Punctuation (allowable punctuation in specified fields)

Quotation marks (use of)

Quotations (if attributed illustrative quotations are included)

Run-in entries (entries such as phrasal verbs and idioms that often appear within the article of another entry)

Run-on entries (derivatives appearing usually without a def. at the end of a main-entry article)

1. Allowable suffixes in run-on entries

2. Form of presentation with POS label

3. When to pronounce

Scientific and technical entries

Sets (or Closed sets, Category entries, or Series entries)

These entries include series of terms that comprise semantic sets and therefore can all be defined according to the same or a similar formula. In practice, some members of the series require individual treatment, but the identification of sets and the establishment of a uniform style for each set of terms are important in saving time and in maintaining consistent treatment of like terms. Normally, one definer will be assigned to define all the members of a set. Dictionaries differ in how many kinds of entries they regard as belonging to sets. Some common sets are listed below. Each set is exemplified with one or several prototypes.

1. Alphabet
2. Notes of musical scale
3. Musical directions
4. Musical instruments
5. Numbers, cardinal and ordinal
6. Units of measure
7. Days of the week
8. Months of the year
9. Compass points and directions
10. Countries (and other geographic entries)
11. Colors
12. Nationality designations
13. Military ranks
14. Chemical elements
15. Geological periods
16. Signs of the zodiac

Syllabication

Synonyms

1. Use of in defs.
2. Lists
3. Discriminations

Trademarks

Usage notes

Variants

1. Variant spellings

2. Variant forms

Words Not In (list of prefixes, suffixes, and combining forms that may be used to form words in definitions even though the words are not separately entered, e.g., *-ish*, *-like*, *-shaped*)

---

college-level dictionaries sometimes twenty or more. Typographically, individually numbered definitions are striking, and the practice seems to encourage a finer breakdown of sense division, since each definition is easily distinguished from the others. From a different vantage point, this system sometimes encourages an artificial proliferation of senses that could be amalgamated at no great loss to understanding. Among modern native-speaker dictionaries, the *New Oxford Dictionary of English* is exceptional in clustering particular definitions under "core" meanings, the only definitions identified by number; this allows it to cut back sharply on its numbered definitions and in theory, at least, makes navigation of long, polysemous entries easier.[18] I am encouraged by *NODE*'s innovative defining system, as I believe that, except in the largest of dictionaries, the separate enumeration of very closely allied senses serves no useful purpose. Dictionaries are generally too timid to cut anything that gives the appearance of full coverage, because they fear (correctly) that reviewers who compare the numbered definitions for a word in two dictionaries will conclude that the book with more definitions is the better book. In very small dictionaries, in which definitions are often little more than synonyms, definition numbers are a waste of space. Numbering senses in a "vest pocket" dictionary is little more than a conceit.

Design specifications

Because dictionaries contain such an enormous amount of text in different type sizes and styles, copy fitting is complex, and the editor, who will surely be held responsible if the dictionary's length is not properly controlled, must take a dominant role in designing the type page. In most publishing houses, the interior design of books is set by the production staff; but production people, however skilled and knowledgeable they may be, seldom have any knowledge of the peculiar needs of a diction-ary. They have no inkling of the vast amount of material that must be compressed within its covers. The editor who leaves production to his company's production staff personnel risks disaster. To a large extent the dictionary handles its own production. In writing the text with specified codes, the editors are in effect composing the dictionary for printing. The editorial and composition processes have been amalgamated into one, so lexicographers are now more deeply involved in production than ever. Dictionary text is handled completely by the dictionary staff: it eval-uates copy, sends it out to referees if necessary, edits it, proofreads it, and, in controlling its length, performs the production task of copy fitting. The lexicographer certainly needs knowledgeable production people to advise and collaborate with on the selection of type and the design of an attractive but efficient page layout, and the opinion of marketing people should be solicited as well. The lexicographer should be open to all pro-posals to make the dictionary page more appealing; but he must insist that the design be economical of space and he should have the decisive say in what the final design is to be.

The relational database used in dictionary preparation gives a consid-erable degree of flexibility to the type style and size, to the design of the page, and indeed to the layout of the book. This flexibility has been tre-mendously important, as one of the hardest tasks in making a diction-ary is copy fitting, that is, getting the quantity of text that is actually written to fit in the space allocated for it. (See "Controlling length," p. 375.) If an ordinary book runs too long, the publisher may complain, but seldom will anyone's job be at risk, but if a dictionary slated to run 1,000 pages runs to 1,300 pages, the editor-in-chief will not have a bright future in that company. In dictionary work, everything depends on hitting the target number of pages (or getting very close to it), because the unit cost (the cost of manufacturing each book when a given number are printed) depends upon it, and a high unit cost will drive up the price. Also, the additional paper – given the large print runs of dictionaries – might not be available because it was not ordered early enough, and if paper is obtained on an emergency basis one pays a lot more for it.

Computerized composition in dictionary work allows the automatic implementation of many elements of style so long as the text is properly coded. Designated elements can be made to begin with a capital letter and end with a period, or be placed in a particular type style. Etymologies can appear automatically within square brackets and pro-nunciations within parentheses or diagonal lines. Numbers can be inserted automatically before a series of definitions. Any style feature automatically generated can be changed during the editing stage, such as the initial capitalization of definitions or the punctuation introducing illustrative phrases after them. If one's dictionary is running shorter than predicted, one can add more leading (spacing) between the lines, or slightly increase the size of type, or take a contrary action if one's work is running too long. Even small changes can have dramatic consequences. If one gains 1.5 characters per column-line over 300,000 column-lines, one has gained 450,000 characters, or the equivalent, at 5.5 letters per word, of over 80,000 words, the size of a modest book. This is a great advantage in copy fitting, but it is not always possible, and it is rarely advisable to make major style changes once the book is well under way. Decreasing the text type even slightly may make the type size appear smaller than the type of a competitor's book and thus be unacceptable. Increasing the text page even by a single column line may reduce the margins at top or bottom too much, and expanding column widths will take away space from the inner and outer margins and may make the type page unattractive or use up the margin space needed for thumb index tabs.

It is therefore no less necessary, even with computerized typesetting, to have all the type specifications fully laid out in the planning stage. Modifications may have to be made during the writing stage, but these should be minor adjustments. In any case the design must be settled by the time final editing begins.

The typography must not only be readable but must not be wasteful of space. "Readable" does not mean readable compared to novels but compared to other dictionaries. Some readable typefaces can set more characters per line than other faces. Most college dictionaries, for example, are set in a point size ranging from 5½ to 7. (Type is measured in picas, of which there are 6 to the inch. Each pica is divided into 12 points; thus there are 72 points to the inch.) Many novels (and this book) are set in 11 point type with 1½ points of leading between the lines (known in the trade as 11/12½), whereas even a readable dictionary may be 7/7 (that is, 7 point size with no leading between the lines). With computerized composition, one no longer is confined to set intervals of type sizes. A text type can be 7.35 or 6.98; round numbers are a thing of the past. A knowledgeable typographer can play tricks with type to give the appearance of greater size and legibility than one would suppose to be possible. The spacing between particular clusters of letters, for example, can be adjusted automatically by computer to a tighter or looser setting (called *kerning*) in order to save as much space as possible without compromising legibility. Also, various styles of type of the same point size differ greatly in their apparent legibility. The dictionary editor clearly needs a style that has maximum legibility and apparent size even in very small point sizes. This requirement limits the choice, especially since it is coupled with the demand for tight setting to save space and the need for a font with many different styles, sizes, and special characters.

Design choices depend to a great extent on the type of dictionary being prepared and on the competitive market for that type of diction-ary. College dictionaries have relatively small type because they have to fit an immense amount of text and pictures into about 1,600 pages. The number of entries and of other features of the dictionary are considered more essential than having larger type. School dictionaries, which have far fewer entries, have larger type: the lower the grade level, the larger the type. ESL dictionaries at an advanced level have text type compar-able in size to that of US college dictionaries but generally strive for an open appearance by providing generous margins or other text features such as boxed items that break up the text. ESL dictionaries at the inter-mediate level have larger type, comparable to that of upper-level school dictionaries.

In choosing the size of type one must also be mindful of column width. A type size of 7 points or less becomes unreadable if the line is too wide; the eye cannot easily make the transition to the next line. In unabridged dictionaries, however, which are usually set in three narrow columns, the point size can be quite small (5½ or 6 points, with minimal leading) and still be readable. The amount of leading between lines con-tributes at least as much to readability as the size of type. Text without leading can be harder to read than text in a smaller type with adequate leading.

If one's dictionary contains many illustrations, as children's diction-aries do, page layout requires the close attention of the art director to see that each picture falls on the same page as the term associated with it. Page layout, formerly done by pasting on boards the art and paper cut to the size of the text, is now handled by computer page-formatting pro-grams, which allow a much greater degree of adjustment in sizing of art than was possible in the past. Nevertheless, flexibility is not limitless. In children's dictionaries pictures occupy a much greater proportion of the total space available than in adult dictionaries, and if a picture happens to fall at the very beginning or end of a page, text has to be moved from one page to another. This can usually be done by computer without having to rewrite any copy, but in exceptional cases with very large pictures, rewriting copy may still be necessary.

In determining the design specifications of a dictionary, one must evaluate the need for printing an abbreviated pronunciation guide (or pronunciation key) on every two-page spread, a practice that takes up a great deal of space. School and college dictionaries routinely include pronunciation keys, but ESL dictionaries generally do not, presumably because grammatical and semantic information is considered more important and because most ESL dictionaries use the International Phonetic Alphabet (IPA) which foreign learners are taught in school. Technical dictionaries and bilingual dictionaries rarely include pronunciation keys throughout the text.

Controlling length

In the realm of copy fitting, the computer has been of enormous benefit. One thing the computer does extremely well is to count characters and spaces, so it is now a simple matter to learn exactly how long any part of the text is, and therefore to give fairly precise guidelines to editors on how long their sections should be or how much they have to cut. As an ongoing check on length, it is also possible to cast off, and to print out if necessary, rough pages that closely approximate the dictionary's final style. But unless one calculates in advance precise goals for the extent of the text, accurate counts along the way will have little effect.

In dictionary copy fitting, we are interested first of all in determining the total amount of text space available in the A-Z section, the main part of the dictionary exclusive of all front and back matter. Once the trim size (the outer dimensions) of the book has been established, the editors determine the layout of the text page, which in most dictionaries includes two or three columns of type. Various text types are experimented with until the style and size of the basic text have been agreed upon. (See "Design specifications," p. 371.) Along with the determination of type style, the margins of the book are set and the exact width and length of each column is fixed.

The basic unit of length is the column-line: the measure of the width of a single column of type. If a book has an A-Z section of 800 pages and has two columns of 60 lines per page, it has 96,000 column-lines (60 x 2 = 120 column-lines per page x 800 pages). Using the Thorndike block system (or some other system), one can then calculate approximately how many pages each alphabetic letter should contain. The letter

A, for example, would have 45.7 pages (6 blocks = 5.7% of the total space x 800 pages). The letter C would have 76.2 pages (10 blocks = 9.5% x 800). Each of the numbered blocks within each letter can thus be assigned a given number of text pages, and this figure can be converted to column-lines, since each text page has 120 column-lines. Once the type specifications and column-line length have been established, one knows how many type characters will fit on average on each column-line, and so can calculate the number of total characters (including spaces) that are available for text. The computer, as I have said, is very good at counting characters; therefore, it is no longer any problem getting accurate information about the size of a dictionary during the editing process. Controlling the length is still a problem.

To simplify matters, I have skipped an important stage in the copy-fitting process. Before determining the extent of the A-Z section, the editor has to calculate the amount of any space not used for regular dictionary text and subtract it from the total. This includes the following:

- pictorial illustrations
- special text items that are boxed or otherwise set off from the main text, such as synonym discussions, usage notes, etymological notes, etc.
- alphabetic breaks (Does each new letter begin on a new page? How much space will there be at the end of the text for one letter but before the beginning of the text of the next letter?)
- a pronunciation key (if it is part of the text page)

So in fact the editor in my example will not have 96,000 column-lines to work with but something less, depending upon how much space is used for these items.

In dictionaries for native speakers, the total number of entries is often a strong selling point, especially in the US, and the desired number of entries will influence the decision on how large to make the dictionary. If each entry on average takes two column-lines, and one wants to include 150,000 entries, one must have 300,000 column-lines available, or one must change one's defining style to reduce the average number of column-lines required for each entry. Let's suppose that the design of the dictionary calls for 80 lines per column or 160 column-lines per page. Such a book would have to have 1,875 pages to provide space for that many entries (300,000 divided by 160). However, if the average number of column-lines per entry could be cut to 1.7, the same number of entries would fit into fewer than 1,600 pages (1.7 x 150,000 = 255,000 divided by 160 = 1,593.8). Saving 280 pages of text in the huge print runs of most dictionaries represents an enormous saving of money. The dictionary could then be sold at a cheaper price than would otherwise have been possible. Of course, one could also cut the number of entries or reduce the size of the type so that more column-lines fit on each page, but there are drawbacks to both of those options. The number of entries cannot be reduced substantially without losing the market for which the book was designed. A dictionary with small type is apt to be less appealing than competing works, and its sales may suffer as a consequence. For these reasons, the space allotted to individual entries must be watched closely to see that no space is wasted and to make sure that the expected ratio of lines per block of entries is maintained. When definers are assigned a block of terms, they are not only given a deadline but are allotted a certain amount of text space in which to produce the requisite definitions. If they fail to meet their target by an appreciable amount, they are instructed to re-edit the text until they do. In the revision stage, editors are frequently told to cut the overall line length by a specific percentage. At the late editing stage, it is not possible to make consistent cuts of more than 10–15% without risking major errors, so it is essential to get close to the desired text length in the preliminary editing stages.

Assuming that the design specifications cannot be changed, what steps can be taken if a lexicographer does misjudge the length and finds it necessary to cut back? In general, native-speaker dictionaries, the lines per entry ratio is closely related to the ratio between main entries and total entries. As we have seen in Ch. 3, in college dictionaries less than half of the total entries are main entries. By converting main entries to run-on derivatives, the ratio of lines to entries will drop, since run-on derivatives take up very little space. But a dictionary with too many derivatives is not serving its readers well. Since definitions do not count as entries, another way to save space is to leave out definitions in polysemous words. Clarence Barnhart has estimated that college dictionaries have on average two definitions for every entry.[19] Another increasingly popular way to solve the problem is simply to report the number of definitions as well as (or instead of) entries, or to give the number of "references" without specifying what a reference is.[20] Such subterfuges are used, usually by marketing specialists with the connivance of dictionary editors, to make a dictionary appear to be much larger than its competitors even when it is not. Finally, definitions can be cut in length. Each of these steps diminishes the value of the book and is demoralizing to editors who must undo their own carefully wrought definitions in order to save space. To avoid them, careful planning and control of the dictionary text length are essential.

In contributed works, controlling length is problematical at best. It is virtually impossible to get a large number of specialists to confine their definitions to a set length. First of all, some subjects must be defined at greater length than others, either because the subjects themselves are more important and central to the purpose of the dictionary or because they are more complex than other subjects. Second, contributing specialists, no matter how expert in their own fields, are not experienced definers and lack the judgment required for a sense of proportion in definition length. Inexperienced definers often treat a pair of terms of equivalent importance and complexity quite unequally. One is analyzed in enormous details: particles of matter are weighed and described, conditions that might influence them are assessed, theories that account for their behavior are cited. The other, of the same level of importance, is dismissed with a genus and differentia statement, such as "a Herpes virus." Why? The two terms were defined at different times, and by the time the second one's turn came around the contributor had grown forgetful, weary, or careless. Or the simpler definition was written at an early stage before the contributor had developed a better idea of what was wanted or the confidence to be expansive. Although the dictionary editor can sometimes cut lengthy definitions, they may be too technical for him to rely on his own judgment, in which case he must have recourse to another expert. Similarly, he must ask other experts to expand definitions that are too sketchy. In spite of these efforts, the results are often uneven. In a contributed dictionary, it is necessary to be flexible as to the overall length.

TECHNICAL VOCABULARIES AND GLOSSARIES

As an aid for those preparing technical vocabularies and glossaries, Alexandre Manuila has written a practical, step-by-step outline, originally prepared for the World Health Organization, that is summarized here.[21]

1. Define the field to be covered by the vocabulary. The mere statement of a subject area or the selection of the title is not enough. Fields to be included and omitted should be carefully delimited.
2. Identify the group to whom the vocabulary is to be addressed.
3. Decide on its size (i.e., the approximate number of terms).

4. Decide whether a classified arrangement or alphabetic order is to be used.
5. Even if alphabetic order is selected, draw up a scheme for classifying the entire vocabulary. This step is essential to ensure that important concepts are not omitted and that contradictory definitions are not drawn up.

Example: The preliminary classification scheme for a vocabulary of air pollution might be as follows (in practice, more divisions would probably be used, and certainly many more subdivisions; only a few are given here as an example).

air pollutants
    gaseous pollutants
    particulate pollutants
processes that cause air pollution
meteorological phenomena that affect air pollution
methods for measurement of air pollutants
    gravimetric methods
    volumetric methods
    electrical methods
    optical methods
effects of air pollution
    effects on health
    effects on materials, structures
methods for reduction of air pollution

6. Select the concepts to be defined. List the preferred terms for these concepts under the appropriate divisions and subdivisions of the classification scheme. Under each heading, list the terms in a logical sequence, not alphabetically. Do not invert the terms.
7. Circulate the completed classified list of terms to a number of experts for comment. These experts should be representative of (a) the different disciplines covered by the vocabulary; (b) different geographical areas; (c) (if the glossary is multilingual) different mother tongues.
8. After adjusting the word list and the classification scheme in the light of the comments of the experts, draw up an entry for each term . . . The only way to avoid contradictory definitions is to draw up entries for a group of related concepts *as a group*.

Manuila then describes the preparation of the text, which would clearly now be done in an electronic file, with each subject area uniquely coded so that definitions could be easily sorted by subject, printed out, and sent to the relevant expert for checking. "A glossary of air pollution," he warns, "... should be submitted not only to air pollution experts but also to chemists, meteorologists, engineers, etc., who may have specialized knowledge of air pollution."[22]

WRITING THE DICTIONARY

The use of staff

Assuming that one has an in-house staff, there are essentially two ways to dispose them. Each reflects a different philosophy, or at least a different emphasis. One can have a staff of generalists who define all but the most specialized terms and who have the final say over all definitions, or one can have a staff of specialists with very few generalists.

The first method reflects an older tradition, in which lexicography is seen essentially as an application of humanistic scholarship and in which the ideal lexicographer, modeling himself after Johnson, is the supreme generalist. The editors of the *OED Supplements* not only defined terms but wrote their own etymologies and prepared their own pronunciations. Science terms were defined by science graduates of Oxford University but reviewed by general editors.[23] Such dedication to the tradition of the broadly educated humanist as a master of every field has its drawbacks. The first edition of the *OED* was notably deficient in its coverage of scientific terms, a deficiency the *Supplements* (and the subsequent Second Edition) sought to correct. Burchfield estimated that 20–25 percent of the terms in the *Supplements* were scientific. Although the *OED*'s etymologies have been justly admired, its pronunciations were simply the transcriptions, inherited from older works, of what received pronunciation was supposed to be. Little or no attention was paid to speech.[24]

Implicit in an extreme generalist approach is the idea of what an educated person is. In this view, a narrowly educated person is not truly educated. He is half formed, suspect in his grasp of fundamental facts and ignorant of refined taste; the responsibility for compiling a dictionary should not be placed in the hands of such a person. Clearly, whether admitted or not, from this vantage point the role of status and authority lurks only slightly beneath the surface. The generalist view willingly tolerates certain deficiencies, such as a summary treatment of pronunciation, for the overriding benefit of placing the ultimate authority for the work in the hands of generalists. The absence or scant treatment of specialized terms has not always been regarded as a serious defect, for it was assumed that the dictionary was for people who shared the ideal of the broadly educated man or woman.

The generalist approach, historically British, has long been modified in America by the introduction of special editors assigned to special tasks, and this has more recently become the norm in most British dictionary houses as well. Etymologies are almost always done separately by special editors or by outside contributors. (The danger of relying on a generalist for all aspects of lexicography is perhaps best illustrated by the rejection of many of Webster's etymologies by C. A. F. Mahn for the 1864 edition of Webster's dictionary.) Pronunciations, too, are routinely done by specialists, as are biographical and geographical entries. Most scientific and technical terms are handled by special editors or are sent out to consultants. Although usage labels are written by the general staff in the course of defining, usage notes are normally assigned to a designated general editor in addition to his defining duties.[25]

The philosophy underlying an approach emphasizing specialization endorses the importance of doing as opposed to understanding. The specialist has greater practical experience than the generalist; he has actively studied the subject whose terms he is defining and therefore writes from the viewpoint of a professional rather than as an informed amateur. A dictionary composed entirely by specialists is often a collection of special points of view with no unity of approach; its usefulness may depend on whether the reader's particular interests coincide with those of the specialists.

As I hope Ch. 5 made clear, the dictionary staff cannot turn to outside experts for reliable help in reporting varieties of style or status. It must rely on its own resources.

The differences between British and American practice are outweighed by their similarities, and they are becoming more alike with each passing year. Although most general dictionary staffs are a mixture of generalists and specialists, the nucleus of almost all dictionary staffs is composed of generalists. As in-house staffs have decreased, more and more special subjects, and often a good deal of general material as well, are handled by outside free-lancers and consultant editors. My own view is that general editors should retain ultimate control of every element of the dictionary entry. They should rarely overrule a specialist acting within his own competence, but the authority to decide what goes in a general dictionary should be theirs, for they are free of the narrow focus that may blind the specialist to the needs of the nonspecialist user.

Stages of defining and editing

In a general monolingual dictionary, defining always requires at least two stages: preliminary or *first-run* defining, and review or final editing. The first run may include a number of editors who are relatively inexperienced definers as well as others who are experienced. No matter who did the first editing, all first-run definitions must be carefully reviewed by senior definers, in no case by the same editor who wrote the original definitions. The review, moreover, is not simply critical; the second definer actually redefines the word, using preliminary material however he chooses. In ESL lexicography, other elements of the dictionary entry, especially the examples, are as important as the definition, and take up a much higher proportion of text space, and these will be reviewed as carefully as the definition. Only rarely does the preliminary text pass unchanged; more often it is considerably altered, not infrequently entirely rewritten. The existing definition and examples serve as an impetus to hasten one's absorption of the particular problems of the word's meaning and usage. Often the very mistakes of the first definer are of immense help in pointing up these problems. Good first definers do not have to be polished; but if they have enough insight to address, even imperfectly, the real difficulties inherent in the definitions and example text, they will speed the work of the second definer and contribute no little to the dictionary's ultimate merit. A definition can be wrong in so many ways and right in so few that it cannot be left to a single writer, no matter how experienced a definer he or she may be. (For a discussion of definition, see Ch. 4, p. 153.)

Most books today are written by authors sitting in front of computer screens, and it should come as no surprise that dictionaries are written the same way. To say that computers have revolutionized lexicography, therefore, is true, but their revolutionary effect in lexicography is no greater than their revolutionary effect in every other aspect of work and daily life. When I wrote the first edition of this book in the early 1980s, I used a manual Royal typewriter (true, that was a bit of a dinosaur even then!), and taped together the sheets of paper that emerged to form endless skeins of accordion-folded paper, which I could then snip apart to insert a new page or part of a page. It was messy but it worked. As I write this, I sit dutifully in front of a computer screen, and I can cut and paste on screen, but I am using more paper than I used the first time around, not less, because I want to see each new version of the manuscript as I amend it. We have had a revolution of sorts, but we do not have a paperless society. My point is that there is continuity even in the midst of enormous change; some habits die hard. Just so in dictionary work.

Dictionary editors now edit on screen, and instead of marking up their printed copy with the standard insignia of the proofreader, as they once did – a straight underline for italic type, a wavy underline for bold-face, etc. – they have to master a far more intricate set of instructions for coding their copy. Either the style manual or a separate instruction manual will tell them what codes to use and when to use them. The codes typically appear in angle brackets. For example, <R>See <X>studio<><> might be the form for a "See" cross-reference to the word "studio." Each empty pair of angle brackets marks the end of a code containing information. Such systems typically allow one to create most codes with different function keys on the computer keyboard or with the "Ctrl" or "Alt" key plus a function key. As with any software program, inserting the codes eventually becomes second nature to editors who use the system on a daily basis.

Although the manner of writing and editing dictionary entries has changed dramatically – as has the manner of producing other books – writing definitions or composing examples of usage has not changed very much. It is still a matter of analyzing samples of text and of writing prose of a very special kind. It is demanding work, requiring intense con-centration. The use of a corpus, while holding the potential of greatly improving the quality of dictionaries, has made the work even more demanding. With a corpus, there is much more evidence to work with, much more information that has to be interpreted, and it comes in a raw, unfiltered state; the corpus may make dictionaries better, but it has not made dictionary work easier.

The database systems used to create dictionaries are often extremely elaborate. They provide separate fields for each component of the dic-tionary entry, so that one can access just those fields and none other. They provide the means for making statistical counts of various kinds in any component. They allow one to make global changes. Often they include a way of documenting the current status of every aspect of the dictionary's progress, and provide a record of the work each editor does and when it is done. They provide access to the corpus and usually a way to move text from the corpus to the dictionary entry one is working with, where the corpus extract can be edited. Often they are a vehicle of com-munication within the dictionary staff, whether in-house or free-lance. They provide security so that the dictionary text cannot be accessed except by those who know a series of passwords. Senior editors can be given greater access to text than more junior editors.

Every system has a basic editing screen, and each system's screen will reflect the particular nature of the dictionary as well as the particular choices made by the team of lexicographers and software engineers who created it. Figure 34 is a somewhat simplified version of the basic editing screen used to create *CDAE*, a dictionary for foreign learners. The *Edited* field shows the stage of editing for this entry. The *Keyword* is the string of letters that determines the alphabetic position of the entry, which appears under *Word*. *POS* indicates part-of-speech. *Codes* refers to intransitivity and transitivity. The *Label* field is used for various usage information (register, currency, regional restriction, etc.). *Pron* stands for pronunciation. In *CDAE*, entries having more than one definition are given distinctive guidewords; the *Guideword* field indicates that in this sense, the guideword is "shoot." The *Notes* field is used by editors to send messages to each other or to make a comment. In ESL dictionaries, the *Examples* field is very important and is the longest field. This screen just shows the first example, but on scrolling down there would be many more examples, some of which might contain codes to set off collocations, idioms, or phrasal verbs, or any other feature that the editors decided they wanted to mark specially.

Every dictionary database system allows individual entries or any series of entries to be printed out. The form of the printout approximates the type styles of the printed book. The *embedded codes* that are created while editing and that appear on the computer screen are usually suppressed in printouts as they will be in the book; headwords appear in boldface, and other items in the text that are appropriately coded appear in boldface, italics, or small capitals, whatever the style dictates. In other ways, however, the layout of the printouts does not ordinarily resemble the layout of the printed pages of the completed book. The type sizes and even the fonts may be different, and the printouts are printed in one column in a broader measure than they will be in the book. But the computer printouts do look enough like the finished entries to be easy to edit and to proofread. Mistakes in coding can be quickly detected and corrected. In the past, there were numerous proofreading stages in dictionaries: several galley proof stages and two or more page proof stages. According to Frank Vizetelly, the Funk & Wagnalls *Standard Dictionary* of 1893 went through at least eleven proof stages.[26] The use of computerized systems for implementing and checking style features has made proofreading less of a burden than it formerly was, though it still has to

Basic Editing Screen

EDITOR PeterN	**DATE** 08 AUG 2001 **EDITED?** 2	
KEYWORD fire	**DEF.NUM** 02 **RUNON.NUM** 00 **INCLUDED?** Yes	
WORD fire	**POS** v	**CODES** I/T **LABEL**
PRON		
SPELLINGS		
VARIANTS		
INFLECTIONS		
GUIDEWORD SHOOT		
DEFINITION to shoot bullets or other explosives from (a weapon)		
NOTES See Sylvia's comment at "shoot."		
EXAMPLES		
He fired his gun into the air.		

34 Basic Editing Screen

be done carefully. A college dictionary contains about 3 million words or in the neighborhood of 16.5 million characters, and the typography is complicated, including pronunciations, etymology symbols, and an uncommonly large variety of type styles. A great many things can go wrong, and though computer checks have helped, the first edition of a dictionary is bound to have a number of errors.

What are some of the style checks that a computer can do? If each element in the dictionary entry is properly coded, it can provide checks of omitted or incorrect cross-references. If term X is a cross-reference to term Y, and X should appear following the definition at Y after the word *also* (or a code that designates the word), the computer can check that it does so appear, and if it does not, print a list of those X terms that do not appear following *also*. Conversely, it can check to see that all those terms following *also* at *Y* terms appear in their own alphabetic positions as *X* terms. By this means it can catch many simple typographical errors, because unlike the human eye a computer will never be fooled into thinking that *pavilion* and *pavillion*, *état* and *etat*, or *world-wide* and *worldwide* are identical. It will never fail to notice when a term having a numbered definition 1 has no definition 2, or vice versa.

The editor always has the option of using codes that are strictly instructions to go into a particular type mode, but they are used only in special cases. Let us say that <sc> means "Go into small capitals." If one means eventually to put cross-references in small capitals, why not label them all <sc>? One should not because, since other elements will also be in small capitals and therefore introduced by <sc>, one could not then uniquely identify cross-references, and one's program could not do the kind of cross-reference checks described above. Thus, except in special circumstances, composition codes should be avoided in the input stage of dictionary preparation. Instead, a set of arbitrary codes is used to mark off every feature in a unique way.

One complication that occurs in preparing a dictionary database is that occasionally the systematic rules governing particular computer codes must be violated. For example, suppose that the dictionary's style does not allow a definition to include a complete sentence ending in a period, but that in a particularly complex case, the definition must begin with a complete sentence ending in a period. One needs an exception code, a code that means "Hold everything! All systematic rules are rescinded; style exactly as you see." One can then protect the period from being deleted during a style check. Of course, the best program is that which requires the fewest exceptions; but a dictionary is such a vast and complex undertaking that in the course of the entire project some exceptions are bound to occur.

Automatic style checks have become an important time-saving factor in lexicography, but I would offer two reservations about their use. First, and most importantly, do not create a data check that automatically corrects items without having an editor examine them first. Although the computer never misses an inconsistency, it has no judgment, and will make changes for the sake of consistency that may result in bizarre changes. Sometimes the sense of the text demands an exception to a stylistic rule. One should get a printout of the list of putative errors and go over them to determine which ones are indeed errors, and correct only those. Secondly, there is a trade-off, as in every computer program, between complexity and efficacy. If one is willing to spend enough money and take enough time, programs can be devised to check almost anything, but for many potential problems it is still best to rely on editorial oversight. The best data checks are fairly straightforward and involve a large number of items that could be wrong.

Once the dictionary is published, the database can be helpful in many ways in updating the text. For example, one of the taxing and generally fruitless tasks of updating is that of locating the names in biographical entries of those people who may have died since the last revision. The name of every living person can be tagged with a unique code so that one can obtain a list of all such names before any updating for checking. Like so many other computer functions, this is the kind of item that only an editor would identify as an item worth marking, and it illustrates why the editor-in-chief has to be fully involved with the design of the database system. Computer people can tell editors what is possible and what is impossible, but only editors can decide what is desirable.

In a specialized dictionary in which definitions are contributed by outside experts, the editors' task is quite different. Many of the problems confronting the specialized dictionary editor are problems of nomenclature rather than definition. For example, few specialists have any sense of the distinction between a lexical unit (for example, *hypopituitarism*) and its generic equivalent (*anterior pituitary hormone deficiency*), which is in fact a brief definition. They will quite commonly represent the two expressions as variants, leaving it to the nonexpert lexicographers to sort things out. This is done on the basis of analogy with similar sorts of terms, by analyzing the way the specialist himself uses these expressions in other definitions, by consulting other dictionaries and reference books, and by their own sense of how the language works. It comes as a surprise to many people that dictionary editors can quite competently edit a specialized dictionary in a field in which they are not experts. Of course, some familiarity with the terminology helps, but it is much more important that the editors of a specialized dictionary know the principles of lexicography than that they be experts in the subject of the dictionary. Long before they have finished editing the dictionary they will be expert enough in the terminology; but if they have not begun with an understanding of lexicography, they will not learn it from their editing, and the dictionary will suffer as a result.

I referred earlier to the deep knowledge of a subject required by a special definer for a general dictionary. The reader may be perplexed as to why the editor of a specialized dictionary needs no such knowledge, or at least much less of it. The explanation is simple. The special definer is *writing* definitions from scratch, and he is writing them for a general audience. The definitions in a specialized dictionary are written by outside contributors, and though the editor frequently must rewrite, this is quite a different matter from that of creating one's own definition. It is also harder to write a technical definition for a lay audience than for another group of specialists, since in the latter case one can assume that ordinary technical terms will be understood. For a lay audience nothing can be assumed. The writer must therefore understand the theoretical basis of the term so that he can have a number of options at his disposal for recasting it in simple language.

In most general dictionaries, as we have said, while the defining stages are under way, the pronunciation and etymologies are being written independently by specialists. Synonym discussions and encyclopedic material such as biographical and geographical terms are also prepared independently, as are lists of abbreviations, foreign terms, various tables and charts, and the illustrations.

Illustrations

The importance of illustrations varies greatly from one dictionary to another. The American Heritage dictionaries in the US and the *Encarta World English Dictionary* are exceptional in devoting an enormous amount of space to illustrations, but the selection and preparation of illustrations are no small matters for any illustrated dictionary. For children's dictionaries, in particular, they are of prime importance. One of the early decisions to be made in planning the dictionary is how much importance – and how much money – is to be allocated to illustrations.

Once that has been decided, the main question to be answered is: what will be illustrated? Although one would like to have the definers' advice, one cannot afford to wait until each definer comes to a term that would benefit by being illustrated. Also, few definers have the experience in working with illustrations to have good judgment about what can reasonably be illustrated in a small space, and free-lance editors, in particular, are not likely to devote time to anything other than what they are being paid to do. Essentially the choice of what to illustrate must be made early on, and it is usually made by three or four people. The best arrangement is to have a picture editor whose chief responsibility is to select – in collaboration with the editor-in-chief and the managing editor or another senior editor – those terms that will be illustrated and to determine *how* they will be illustrated. Large projects also have an art director, who is an artist in the business of managing other artists. He or she must be an expert in typography as well as illustration and should have experience in illustrating reference books. The illustrations for a school dictionary, for example, are drawn in a different style, with a more relaxed and freer quality, than those for an adult dictionary, and now all major school dictionaries have full-color illustrations.[27] The school dictionary should avoid the cuteness that may be suitable for children's storybooks but is jarringly discordant in a reference book. Whereas the picture editor is responsible for the choice of illustrative content, the art director is responsible for the clarity, style, and consistency of the art, as well as for seeing that the job gets done on time. However, in projects with relatively few pieces of art, the picture editor may assume the responsibilities of an art director and work directly with the artists.

In larger projects the picture editor may need one or two subordinates, including a picture researcher who assembles illustrative material (called *scrap*) from which the artists work. Many of us have a vague idea of the difference between an alligator and a crocodile, but how many of us could draw pictures of each that clearly distinguish them without having photographs showing exactly what they look like? The picture researcher digs out photographs or high-quality drawings of aardvarks, lacewings, cogwheels, bend sinister diagonals, Egyptian pyramids, and anything else that is to be drawn. If the dictionary includes photographs as well, he or she has to obtain permission from the owners or seek to acquire photos in the common domain. (For a discussion of the comparative advantages of drawings and photographs, see p. 144.) The picture editor should maintain a constant liaison with the managing editor and the art director to make sure that the terms used in labeling parts of an automobile engine, for example, are not only included in the dictionary but are the preferred forms.

A great many questions arise in the course of illustrating a dictionary. For example, criteria must be set on when, if, and how to show a groundline. Will a simple abstract line do, or need one show a hint of shrubbery? Must horizons be shown in panoramic views? Just how detailed should machinery be? Can it depict, even if it does not label, parts that are not defined in the dictionary, or must it be no more specific than the dictionary is? How will relative size be indicated? In small pictures, how does one show that an elephant is bigger than a gopher? One way is to have reference objects, such as trees or people, but these matters have to be discussed and decided in advance.

All dictionary art is drawn to scale, usually either 200% or 150% of the actual size in print, according to set dimensions that have been established by the illustration team. Some dictionaries have only a single size for picture space (for example, the column width and a fixed depth); others have several sizes, with some pictures being a full column width and others of narrower width with wraparound text. If the illustrations are of various sizes, each size is assigned a letter: "A" size is the width of a full column 10 picas deep, for example; "B" size is a space 6 picas wide and 9 picas deep, etc. The number of different sizes should be kept to no more than four or five to minimize the chance of error when they are reduced in preparation for printing. Once the picture editor knows what is to be illustrated, the artists are asked to draw preliminary pencil sketches for approval, a stage that should be part of their contract, which should specify a rejection fee. In the event a pencil sketch is considered irredeemably unacceptable, or the dictionary staff simply decides it does not want to use a particular illustration for whatever reason and it is dropped from the book at that stage, the artist should be compensated for his or her work. Often the rejection fee is about 50 percent of the agreed fee for the finished drawing. Once the illustration team has examined the pencil sketches and the picture editor (or art director) has indicated what changes should be made for the final art, the artists are directed to prepare it. Sometimes more than one pencil sketch is needed before the go-ahead for final art can be given.

Apart from maps and graphs (which are usually produced with the aid of computer programs), drawings are still made in the traditional way, by an artist using ink on paper. Finished drawings are pasted on boards and overlaid with a protective sheet of acetate or smooth paper. It is always wise to make good-quality copies of finished art as soon as possible and to keep the copies in a separate place from the originals.

Nowadays all art is scanned, digitized, and stored on magnetic tape. Even so, the basic quality and character of the original art are important. The style of the art drawn by different artists should be compatible. One style should not be fancy and another plain, or one cartoonish and another ultrarealistic. The great advantage of computerized art is that it has made touching up by hand – an expensive and time-consuming job – completely obsolete. Changes can now be made simply and easily, and often better, by computer. For example, if the art or photograph has too much detail, it can be eliminated. If the weight of line needs to be high-lighted in a particular area, the line can be strengthened.

In former times when dictionaries were typeset in hot metal or by photo-composition, one received printed galleys set exactly according to the type specifications. It was easy to determine whether the style had or had not been followed. Because the typesetting went much faster than the writing or editing of a dictionary, one waited until one was far advanced with the writing stage – at least half finished – before typesetting began. As the first galleys arrived for the letters A and B, one might still be writing definitions for R and S. After the initial proofreading of A and B, one would receive corrected second galleys for A and B along with first galleys for C through E, while still writing definitions for T and U. At any given time, one might have first and second – and perhaps third – galleys, and even first page proofs, while the basic manuscript was still being written. The mere logistics of handling so many overlapping stages of proofreading required an elaborate bureaucratic apparatus and the personnel to keep track of it. There are only so many simulta-neous things a dictionary staff can do, and it therefore made sense to handle some stages sequentially even though, with a larger staff, they might theoretically have been handled concurrently.

Proofreading

Editorial input of computer codes and computerized composition have completely changed the proofreading process, drastically shortening and simplifying the proofreading stages. In effect the initial proofreading of galleys now occurs during the final stages of editing on-line, when the final editor prints out and proofreads each completed section. Ideally, the printout should resemble as closely as possible the final printed pages in type styles and layout, without having any embedded codes to inter-pret. It is now usually possible to get a printout at an earlier stage that suppresses codes and gives a fairly accurate representation of the type styles of the printed book.

If codes do appear in the text, they have to be proofread, and the proofreaders must learn the language of the computer system – not an insurmountable problem, but a complication to be reckoned with. In practice, the coding systems for dictionaries are far more complicated than I can indicate here, and no two dictionary programs are the same. More errors are likely to result if codes are in the text, as mistakes in font and type size will often not be obvious. The editor will have to have a checklist of the translations of each code to make sure it is correct. (These codes may not be exactly the same as the codes used in the editing process.) Whatever the form of the initial proofs, eventually the embedded codes will be suppressed and the resulting proofs will reflect the typography of the printed book. These proofs must be read carefully, preferably twice, to catch errors overlooked at the earlier stage.

Since typesetting is now accomplished by the editors who write the dictionary, the reader may wonder what the compositors do. Composition software is used to format the database output into pages. Most publishers now have their own experts on staff to handle this, but some output it as coded text, letter by letter, and send it by electronic transfer – in technical language, via FTP ("file transfer protocol") – to an outside compositor. It can be sent via the Internet using a nonpublic FTP site. The compositor, whether in-house or not, converts the text to the specified dictionary page format, either through custom-made pagination software or through off-the-shelf software such as Quark, Pagemarker, or Adobe Acrobat, to create a document that can ultimately be printed. The text is now completely coded with the type specifications that will be used in the printed book. This text is suitable for second (and third) stage proofreading, as it will correspond exactly to the printed text.

Paper, printing, and binding

The final stage of any book is its manufacture, commonly referred to as paper, printing, and binding. Since a dictionary has a comparatively large number of pages and, if a commercial dictionary, must be competitively priced, the paper must be of light weight but sufficiently opaque so that type on the underside of a page cannot be seen. The inclusion of illustrations, and especially of halftones, influences the choice of paper. Some lightweight paper of high quality may actually have to be rejected, not so much because of price as because the dictionary appears too insubstantial if it is used. The *bulk* of the book – the breadth of the compressed pages measured at the spine – makes the dictionary appear too slight when compared with other dictionaries for the same market. Unfortunately, the public and reviewers judge dictionaries principally by their apparent size, not by an informed examination of their content. If two otherwise identical dictionaries of different bulk are presented to book buyers, nine of ten will select the dictionary with the greater bulk, even though the slimmer volume may actually have paper of superior quality. To market a dictionary successfully, it must not only be comprehensive, it must *look* comprehensive.

Many dictionaries are produced with thumb indexes, supposedly to provide easier access to alphabetic sections. These are quite expensive, and for that reason dictionary publishers hate them, but they are popular with most dictionary users in the US, and, to remain competitive, American dictionaries generally have a thumb-indexed edition. In fact, sometimes that's all they have. Since the vast majority of dictionary buyers prefer the thumb-indexed edition even if it costs a dollar more than the plain-front edition, some publishers have stopped producing plain-front editions. The problem is that a dollar hardly covers the cost of a thumb index (usually 13 index tabs with affixed labels). To the great relief of British publishers, thumb indexes have never caught on in the UK dictionary market. Whether to include thumb indexes or not is strictly a marketing decision, like the choice of color of the cover or the design of the jacket. They are popular principally because they appeal to the American public's view of what a dictionary ought to look like, not because they are of any intrinsic value. For the same purpose, some dictionaries, like Bibles, are provided with a tipped or stippled edge, to give the impression of permanence, authority, and dignity. Dictionary publishers are not unhappy to have their books look like Bibles.

The preferred cover and jacket design emphasizes the title of the work, in particular the word *dictionary* or, in the US, the word *Webster*, which is in the common domain and can be freely used by any publisher. (See Ch. 8, p. 410, for an account of various legal battles over the use of *Webster*.) In Britain, some dictionaries emphasize the word *English*, and Oxford, like Merriam-Webster in the US, gives prominence to the name of its own distinguished publishing house. Design elements are usually subordinated to the words of the title and descriptive material, and the typography is usually bold but neither subtle nor fancy. It may have a certain elegance, though that is more often due to the placement of the type on the cover or spine than to unusual typography. Dust jackets may be of somewhat freer design than covers and are of brighter colors. Academic dictionaries often do not have jackets, but commercial dictionaries do. There have been dictionary jackets (and paperback covers) that sought to project an image of newness rather than dignity, and that forsook the time-honored biblical approach in favor of brilliant colors and vibrant design. Since there is no single factor that determines a dictionary's ultimate success or failure, it is impossible to say whether such an approach, which has seldom been attempted, has helped or hurt. Although newness and up-to-dateness are powerful selling points for a dictionary, it seems likely that attempts to capitalize on these qualities by innovative design deter some people from buying the book because the design offends their sense of the dignity a dictionary should have. Of course, much depends on the particular market the publisher has in mind. If the market for a slang dictionary, for example, is thought to be predominantly young people, the absence of dignity may not be a defect; but most general dictionaries have a much broader market than any particular age group.

Electronic products

Nowadays the end product is not always a book, but may be a hand-held electronic dictionary, a CD, or an electronic dictionary accessible via the Internet. A dictionary may also be included as a supplement of word-processing software or to the text in a CD consisting of academic or popular writing. If one is reading a Shakespearean play, a modern novel, or a text on African history on-screen, one would then have only to click on a word to find its dictionary meaning. All such uses are likely to experience growth and greater acceptability as the technology becomes increasingly sophisticated. Whatever the end product, the basic editorial stages of planning and writing are similar, but the creation of an electronic dictionary requires close coordination among the lexicographic team, someone knowledgeable about the conversion of editorial codes to printing codes (often but not necessarily a compositor), the supplier of the electronic equipment, and the publisher's own software engineers. Usually the company supplying the equipment has its own programs and engineers to apply them, but the dictionary publisher must have its own software experts involved to monitor their performance.

Hand-held electronic dictionaries are increasingly popular tools in foreign-language learning and as travelers' aids, doing the service of pocket bilingual dictionaries. They have small screens and keyboards, and one can key in a word in one language to see its equivalent in another. As speech synthesis and speech recognition improve (see Ch. 6, p. 319), we can expect such devices to *say* the word in the language we want to hear it in, and even to respond to our saying the word in our own language.

Some dictionaries are also available in CD form, in which the dictionary is a hypertext so that items in the text are linked to provide access in a way that is impossible in a printed book. Typically, any entry can be found just by typing it, and any word can be searched throughout the text; often one can search by field, for example, by regional or register labels (such as *Australian English* or *slang*). A CD provides help for poor spellers, for it often begins to select the initial sequence of letters in the word before one has finished typing it. Many CDs now provide audible pronunciations for their entries, a substantial improvement over the transcriptions in printed dictionaries, which many dictionary users do not understand. Some CDs provide other benefits unavailable in books. For example, their illustrations and maps may be larger and more detailed than those in print. One may be able to click on part of an illustration to see the word naming that part, or to click on the callout of a part to be transferred to the dictionary entry for that word. In spite of these positive features, I do not believe all printed dictionaries will become obsolete any time soon, but some will. The largest of dictionaries, the unabridged dictionaries (as well as multivolume encyclopedias), arguably already have. (See Ch. 2, p. 84.) The use of dictionaries as an adjunct to word-processing programs or as a hypertext link to other texts – such as academic books in electronic form – may indeed have a major impact in the long run on the college dictionary market in the US and on comparable print dictionaries in the UK. College students, increasingly reliant on the Internet for information and study aids, may find that an electronic dictionary, accessible as they work on-screen, meets all their needs.

Some dictionaries are accessible on-line to those willing to pay a fee, and some provide free but limited access. For example, one may be able to look up any word to find out its meaning, pronunciation, etymology, etc., but one will not be able to scroll through the dictionary text. However, the *Encarta World English Dictionary* (*EWED*) does allow one to scroll entry-by-entry. My hunch is that, with the exception of the *OED* and multivolume bilingual dictionaries, paying for on-line access to dictionaries will appeal mainly to those having a specialized interest, such as in medicine or law or electrical engineering, and that its success will often depend on being combined with other related databases that are much larger. As broad-band cables take over the market and Internet access becomes a feature of television programming instead of one's computer, access to on-line dictionaries and other reference books may become part of the cable-television package. That's as far as I care to look in my crystal ball.

REVISING AND ABRIDGING A DICTIONARY

Making a dictionary is like painting a bridge: by the time one coat of paint has been applied, the bridge is in need of another. Just so, before a dictionary has been published one should start making plans for its revision. In spite of all the care that goes into its preparation, the first edition of any dictionary contains numerous errors. Computerized composition allows one to make changes at less cost and much later in the process than was formerly the case, but, even so, once the final text has been released to the compositor for preparation of the final tape with printers' codes, the time is past for going back to the database. From then on, any changes must be made the old-fashioned way, by cutting and stripping in text on film. This should be done only for very serious errors, as it is expensive, risky, and introduces a disparity between the printed book and the database which could cause trouble later on. Every change made renews the possibility of fresh errors, necessitating still further changes. Therefore, generally speaking, no further changes are allowed once the text has been released to the compositor for the conversion of editorial codes to printers' codes. Every dictionary should have an ongoing correction file, where no error is too trivial to be noted. Occasionally users will draw one's attention to an error, but most errors and omissions are observed by the dictionary staff itself. As in-house dictionary staffs are cut back, the discovery and correction of errors for subsequent editions will inevitably suffer as a result.

College dictionaries are revised every ten years or so, but they are updated every year or every other year, chiefly in order to provide themselves with an up-to-date copyright date. Commercial publishers tend to feel that their dictionary's copyright date must be as current as that of their competitors, and thus demand frequent updatings, some of which are merely cosmetic, involving only a few score of minor changes and perhaps updated population figures. On the other hand, some updatings are far more extensive, consisting of several hundred significant changes and including the insertion of many new words and new senses. Even such a revision, however, would be quite invisible to most dictionary users who compared the old edition with the new. Updatings, whether comparatively extensive or trivial, do not involve a rekeyboarding of the entire dictionary or a redesign of the dictionary's style. They consist of selective changes on certain pages, even if called extensive, and compared to the volume of material that is unchanged, the amount of altered material is minute.

A genuine revision is another matter.[28] A revision, as I use the word here, implies a complete reexamination of the previous edition, new keyboarding of substantial parts of the text, and frequently the alteration of some design elements. The new edition ordinarily does not have the same number of pages as the old edition, and the title usually indicates that the dictionary has been completely revised. This does not imply that every entry of the new edition is entirely different from the corresponding entry of the old; far from it. It implies only that every entry has been critically reexamined, exactly as I have described how the review editor reexamines the work of the first definer. In this instance, the work of the "first definer" is often finely polished and in need of nothing more than a slight shift in emphasis or a modernized phrasing. Sometimes it cannot be improved and is best left alone. The important point is that it *is* reexamined in light of current evidence in the corpus or citation file.

Why cannot dictionaries be continually updated instead of being revised, especially now that they exist as computer databases? As I wrote in the Preface to *The Doubleday Dictionary*:

Dictionaries may be updated by the substitution of some new entries for old entries, and for the first few years after publication, such a procedure may work very well. But when a dictionary passes the ten- or fifteen-year-old mark, updating takes on a desperate character. Substituting a few new entries for old entries in such a book is like bailing out a swamped boat with a sieve. The language has accumulated too many new meanings and new words; too many of the definitions in the dictionary have taken on new emphases or passed from slang to informal usage or from informal to standard; too much of the book is written with a vocabulary and in a style that seems odd or baffling to a new generation of readers. Only a fresh examination of the entire range of possible entries, with careful attention to examples of current usage and the assistance of special consultants in the sciences and other fields, can provide an adequate basis for a thoroughly up-to-date dictionary.[29]

Revisions follow much the same process that I have outlined in this chapter for new dictionaries, but are made immensely more manageable by having a solid basis from which material may be selected and used or rewritten, and especially by having a computerized database to work with. Perhaps in no other area of dictionary making has computerization made more of a mark than in revising and in preparing derivative works, which can now be edited much more quickly and efficiently. If every type of item in a dictionary is coded uniquely – for example, etymologies – that item can be very simply deleted, or presented in a separate file to be edited down to a shorter length. Many other changes of this sort can be made automatically or made much easier by segmenting precisely those items in need of revision or abridgment. Whereas in earlier years, abridged editions took years to prepare, it is now commonplace to see an abridgment appear the very next year after its parent volume. Nothing is more difficult to predict or control than a dictionary begun from scratch. Adding new meanings or words to a revision is no different from adding them to a new dictionary, but the revision of existing definitions is infinitely easier than creating them anew. Still, the work is exacting, often long term, and demands skills of the highest order.

Abridging without revision calls for somewhat different skills than those needed for writing definitions. Though abridgers must know a good definition when they see one, they need not be capable of creating them from a corpus or citations. Their skills are mainly critical: they must know how to reorder words, deleting as many as possible along the way, until definitions are stripped to their essence. They must, however, no less than definers, be good writers. Space limitations in an abridgment dominate the quality of the editing. The commercial imperatives that govern abridgments call for comparatively large entry counts in a much smaller space than the original volume. Typically, one has to retain two thirds of the entries of a larger dictionary but fit them into one half of the space. This results in a low ratio of lines per entry, often 1.5 or fewer. There is a law of diminishing returns in defining: after one has cut a definition to a certain point, it cannot be cut further without making it nonsense, and one would be better off using the space to list a few synonyms. Synonym definitions are not necessarily a mark of lazy or inept editing; they may be the best solution to the problem of too little space.

REFLECTIONS ON COMPUTER TECHNOLOGY IN DICTIONARY MAKING

Dictionary making does not operate in a vacuum. It is part of the world of publishing, and the publishing industry, like almost every other business, has been changed profoundly by computer technology. It is said that we are in the information age. This may be true, but the rewards for distributing information far exceed the rewards for those creating it. As information technology gets more powerful and it becomes easier to distribute more and more information faster to more people, the quality of the information tends to decline. Less attention is paid to quality because it becomes merely something needed to fill spaces, like late-night television reruns used to fill the spaces between commercials. Competition increases to find "content," as it is called, but less money is devoted to it. Instead, money is devoted to new technology and towards promoting the distribution of its products.

The business of book publishing depended to a great extent on the high cost of producing books – the cost of composition and other plant costs (fixed costs), and of paper, printing, and binding. These costs were inextricably tied to a discrete event and product, the publication of the book. Since the book was expensive to produce and could not be changed once produced, the quality of information in it was important. It was cost-effective to spend money to avoid mistakes. It still is, but less and less, because books are increasingly viewed as impermanent, easily replaced because the information is stored on computer and can be reproduced cheaply. One ESL dictionary now promotes a new edition every year.[30] Hence errors are of less consequence because they can be corrected soon and cheaply.

But are they? Because information is so easily changed, there is actually less incentive to monitor its accuracy. When a company had to spend a significant amount of money on a new edition of a dictionary, it tried to make sure it got things right before going to press. More fundamentally, it hired a staff to handle the new edition, even though, as we have seen, this often meant cutting back on the staff later on. Hiring a staff is expensive, but given the expense of producing the dictionary and the income to be generated, it was justified. Dictionary publishing was thus – as was book publishing generally – a cyclical, discontinuous operation controlled by the rhythms of printing. However, as publishing, and dictionary publishing in particular, have become more and more driven by computer technology, these rhythms have changed. Computers have made text editing continuous, at least in theory. Whether or not a printed book exists, the computer database is really the text, and it lives on, like a queen ant, long after the particular individuals it has spawned have done their duty and passed away. Once the huge expense of planning and setting up the database has been undertaken, maintaining it is relatively inexpensive. Publishers have not made such large investments in computer technology in order to maintain the quality and currency of their databases, however, but to save labor costs and to give them flexibility in using the database to produce a multitude of products. The promise made about every large reference work is continuous updating. This scenario gives the impression of a horde of zealous editors fastidiously sorting documentation, analyzing vast corpora, sifting through mountains of up-to-the-minute citations. If one could peek into the quiet enclaves of actual dictionary editorial offices, a different scene entirely would present itself. The probability is that none of the five or six editors, shall we say (to be optimistic), whom one would see working at their computers would be assigned the task of updating the database. They would be working diligently on various publishing projects based on the central database, whose improvement and correction would be mere velleities incidental to their effort. Free-lancers do not even have access to the database unless working on a particular project. If in the course of creating a new work, staff or free-lancers also improved the old one, so much the better. Editorial expenses are always charged to a particular project, not to an amorphous existing database. I therefore doubt that much money or effort is being devoted to it, or will be in the future.

Computer technology has made possible the use of vast corpora which hold the promise of greatly improving the quality of dictionaries. However, as computers have made the editorial operation more powerful – capable of doing more tasks – the time allotted for dictionary making has dropped because of the expectation that computerization would save time. In-house staffs are small and getting smaller. Even if doing each task takes less time than formerly, there is now much more to do. Management only sees computers as time-savers and expects fewer people to do jobs in the same time or less than in precomputer days. As computers become capable of performing tasks ever more quickly, they also generate the need to perform more tasks. In terms of scheduling, the upshot is a wash. In fact, to compensate for the time needed to perform the increasing number of tasks and still preserve tight schedules, some other stage, such as a proofreading stage, may be accelerated or skipped entirely, thus jeopardizing the quality of the book in another dimension. New dictionaries still take about as long as they used to, but have much smaller staffs, and the computer technology is often not fully exploited because there isn't time. One can also say, more positively and with equal justice, that without the many time-saving capabilities of computer technology, dictionaries would take much longer to do today than they did in the past. The problem is simply that we must do much more, and with fewer people.

It sometimes seems to me that as the capacity for research increases because of advances in computer technology, the capacity to use it decreases at the same rate. Less time is devoted to producing major new works, and fewer people are employed to do it. In ESL lexicography, technology has produced better dictionaries. With few exceptions in other branches of lexicography, it has not, in spite of its capacity to do so; it has saved money in producing them while creating books of roughly the same quality. If publishers are willing to invest the resources to use large corpora to improve native-speaker dictionaries and bilingual dictionaries, these dictionaries, too, can be made better, but only if the dictionary staffs are given sufficient time to use them properly. Otherwise, the quality of dictionaries may decline in the years ahead. When there were fewer tools to produce dictionaries, more time and far more people were devoted to produce them, and the results were often impressive. Publishers have never understood the specialized nature of dictionary editing, and computer technology has given new currency to the idea that the machinery of dictionary production is more central to successful lexicography than people. Believers in this idea underestimate the human effort and skill involved in dictionary making.

CHAPTER 8

Legal and ethical issues in lexicography

PLAGIARISM

Dictionaries have always copied from one another, but no reputable dictionary today would take over entire sections of another work and print them verbatim, a practice common in the seventeenth century. If one makes a definition-by-definition comparison of a number of competing dictionaries, one will find very few identical definitions apart from the short, formulaic ones of the "of or relating to" variety. There are only so many ways one can define *bovine* or *reptilian*. On the other hand, one will find few sharp discontinuities. Although phrased differently, the definition of a given sense usually covers the same ground in all major dictionaries. Dictionary editors look at each other's books, and though editors form their own opinions about what ground should be covered, they dare not depart too far from the area laid out by their competitors. The definition quality of the leading American and British dictionaries is high, and in the vast majority of instances any major variation in treatment would be unwise. In this respect, the Merriam-Webster dictionaries in America and the Oxford dictionaries in the UK are less influenced by other dictionaries than other dictionaries are by them, and the British dictionaries show greater variety among themselves than the American college dictionaries. All American and British dictionaries, however, owe a great debt to the *OED*, and one can find numerous similarities in wording as well as in sense division between the *OED* and later generations of dictionaries. When does similarity become plagiarism?

It must first be understood that neither facts nor ideas can be copyrighted – only the particular form in which they are presented. If one defines a word representing an object by saying what the object is made of, how it is used, and what it looks like, anyone can define the word with reference to those same three criteria, provided the new definition is written in different words. Moreover, the second definition can also agree entirely as to the particular facts describing the materials, use, and appearance so long as they are not described in the same words as the original definition. In very short definitions, two definitions may be identical without implying plagiarism. One should not have to contrive awkward circumlocutions simply to avoid charges of plagiarism when straightforward definitions can be given.

On the other hand, odd metaphors that crop up in definitions of two different dictionaries suggest that someone copied from someone else, or perhaps both copied from a third source. Though technically this might be plagiaristic, no dictionary is entirely free of occasional, too close correspondences with antecedent works. They are surely to be avoided and should be weeded out when discovered, but as a practical matter occasional lapses of this sort could not be the ground for legal action: it would be next to impossible to prove the origin of the disputed passage. For proof of plagiarism, one would have to show a pattern of close correspondence between two works. If two dictionaries consistently shared the same or similar wording in a large number of definitions, and if these definitions were of a complexity and size that suggested there might have been many ways to treat them, plagiarism might be provable.

It behooves all dictionary editors to take an indulgent view of the pilfering of ideas, since no one is innocent. Ideas are sometimes expressed similarly not from want of imagination but because any major alteration of form would use too much space. With this understanding, it can be asserted that none of the major dictionaries in the United States or Britain engages in plagiarism, but all use other dictionaries as sources or checks against their own work.

In 1984 Robert Burchfield, the editor of the *OED Supplements*, annoyed because of the heavy reliance of other dictionaries on the *OED*, showed how closely *Webster's Third New International Dictionary* (*NID3*) had relied on the *OED* for its sense breakdown for the phrasal verb *make out* and its assignment of dialectal or temporal labels. Burchfield's article appeared in the British magazine *Encounter* with the unfortunate title "Dictionaries, New and Old: Who Plagiarises Whom, Why and When?" and was subsequently republished in a book under the less inflammatory title, "The Genealogy of Dictionaries." In it he charged that the "direct dependence" of *NID3* on the *OED* was "substantial and . . . is not acknowledged."[1] He was right, although similar charges can be made of many other dictionaries. However, because *NID3* is an unabridged dictionary, its coverage is closer in some respects to that of the *OED* than that of smaller dictionaries. Burchfield treads on dangerous ground in making such complaints, as all dictionaries, including the *OED*

Supplements, profit from looking at other dictionaries, most particularly *NID3*. In another essay dealing with an early period in the preparation of the *Supplements*, Burchfield himself acknowledges his debt to *NID3*: "The sheer quantity and range of the material included in *Webster's Third* made it ominously obvious that I had seriously underestimated the task of collecting modern English vocabulary."[2]

Burchfield goes on to link the contents of three dictionaries: the *American College Dictionary* (*ACD*) (1947); a British dictionary, the *Hamlyn Encyclopedic World Dictionary* (*EWD*) (1971); and an Australian dictionary, the *Macquarie Dictionary* (1981). Burchfield represents their close relationship as if he had uncovered by careful scholarship a clandestine plot to fool the public, but in fact *EWD* legally acquired the rights to use *ACD* and made full acknowledgment of this in its front matter. Subsequently the *Macquarie Dictionary*, a dictionary of Australian English, legally acquired the rights to use a substantial part of *EWD*. The idea was that the basic English lexicon common to Britain and Australia would be covered by the *EWD* material, and the *Macquarie* editors could then devote themselves to adding usages peculiar to Australia. Again, this is acknowledged, though the extent of dependence might have been made clearer. For the first part of Burchfield's essay, no mention is made of the legal acquisition of rights or of any acknowledgment. Only after several pages in which Burchfield compares these three dictionaries and exhibits identical definitions as proof of a correspondence that could not be accounted for by chance does he casually remark, "The editors of *EWD* admitted their indebtedness to the *American College Dictionary*."[3] The use of "admitted" here suggests impropriety or guilt, and it is misleading.

Not surprisingly, the *Encounter* article elicited strong rejoinders from some of the principals involved with these dictionaries. In an exchange of letters in a subsequent issue, Laurence Urdang, a prominent lexicographer who was associated with *EWD*, said Burchfield's account of these books was "riddled with errors, misconceptions, and misinterpretations" and bordered on libel.[4] Burchfield denied any responsibility for the title used in the magazine but did not dispute any of the facts Urdang presented. Thirteen years later Urdang was still furious over the imputation of plagiarism.[5]

"FAIR USE"

The legal concept of "fair use" governs the use of quotations of copyrighted work as illustrative examples of definitions. There is no numerical guide to how many words or characters may be quoted without infringing another's copyright, and any reasonable use of quoted material in a dictionary seems secure against legal action. In practice, no more than a sentence is usually required to render the sense, and frequently a phrase will do. Quotations longer than a sentence may be justified if the quotation actually defines the term or if it illustrates a variety of usage. Because the use of a quotation in a dictionary is protected by fair use, the dictionary editor should never request permission to use any quotation. If he does so, his request can be used as evidence that the use of the material was not subject to fair use. If his request is denied, and he uses the quotation anyway, he might be liable for infringement of copyright. Even if his request is approved, the request itself establishes an unfortunate precedent should he be challenged for the use of other material. In short, if the use is covered by fair use, don't ask.

Generally, in order to win a suit for infringement of copyright, the copyright owner has to show that he has suffered some material damage by such infringement. If the quotation is so long that potential customers might decide not to buy the book in which it originally appeared, the author has been materially hurt and deserves to be recompensed for his injury. This possibility seems extremely remote in dictionary use, but quoting several lines of song lyrics – or even a single line – might well precipitate a threatening letter from a lawyer. Holders of the rights of song lyrics are extremely vigilant in protecting them. Lexicographers should be prudent in their use of any copyrighted material and strive to keep their quotations as brief as possible, consistent with the purpose for which they are used.

Fair use does not apply to the collection of texts for use in a corpus, for which it is necessary to copy all or substantial parts of texts. Permission must be obtained from each owner of copyrighted text. (See Ch. 6, "Compiling a corpus," p. 323.) However, unless the conditions of obtaining permission to use the text in one's corpus expressly prohibit quoting any part of it in print or electronic format in a dictionary, the same rules governing fair use of any copyrighted material apply also to text that forms part of a corpus.

TRADEMARKS

A trademark is a symbol or name used by a maker of a product to distinguish the product from others of its kind. *Coca-Cola* is a trademark, or trade name, for a brand of soft drink. Trademarks usually are written with an initial capital letter. Trademark owners are naturally protective of the exclusive use of their trademarks, since their business often depends upon the public's recognition of their trademark. When a trademark is commonly used, however, as if it were an ordinary (or generic) term, not for a brand of a kind of thing but for the kind of thing itself, it enters into disputed territory. To the lexicographer, the word has become generic and should be included in the dictionary and defined. If it is written generically with an initial lower-case letter, it may be entered in this form, although it is usually identified as a trademark. To the trademark owner, such generic treatment is illegal, based on ignorance of the term's protected status or contempt for his proprietary interest. If the linguistic evidence shows that a trademark is well accepted as a generic term, particularly if it has inflections that are commonly used, it may be identified as a trademark only in its etymology.

Some trademark owners are hostile to any inclusion of their trademarks in a dictionary, even if they are entered in capitalized form and identified as trademarks. Others object if their trademarks are not capitalized. Almost all trademark owners are concerned to have their trademarks identified as trademarks, and lawyers often try to specify to lexicographers the exact form which they find acceptable, one which defines the trademark as a brand for a kind of thing.

The concern of trademark owners is understandable, as many trademarks have been lost because they were not adequately protected. Competitors who are sued by trademark owners for infringement often defend themselves by maintaining that the alleged trademark is actually a generic word in common use. Therefore they have as much right to use it as anyone else. For example, in 1966 Eastern Air Lines registered the name "Air-Shuttle" for its New York – Washington, D.C., and New York – Boston flights. When New York Air introduced a similar service between these cities in December 1980 and promoted it with the name "shuttle," Eastern sued. New York Air claimed that its use of "shuttle" was generic and refused to stop using the term. Prominent lexicographers testified on both sides of the issue. The judge decided that "shuttle" was generic but also found that New York Air's advertising was misleading because it suggested that it provided all the services Eastern did, and enjoined New York Air from advertising in that way, although it could continue to use "shuttle" to describe its service.[6]

Dictionary treatments of trademarks can be used as evidence in support of the position that a trademark is generic, though such treatment would hardly be sufficient to jeopardize a trademark in the absence of other evidence. If there is enough evidence to support generic status, the trademark may be declared invalid, at potentially enormous cost to the original owner. Thus the Bayer Company lost *aspirin* as a trademark in the United States, though it remains a trademark in Great Britain. Many other once-valuable trademarks, such as *escalator, mackintosh,* and *zipper,* have lost their protected status. To the trademark owner, the case is clear and simple. He asks the lexicographer to omit his trademark from dictionaries or, if it must be included, to treat it in a way that fully recognizes its protected status. It's not generic, the trademark owner says. It is legally protected, like *Microsoft* or *Rolls Royce.*

But is it? When lexicographers review the corpus and citational evidence and see countless uses of *kleenex,* both capitalized and not, to mean a facial tissue; of *xerox* used both as noun and verb, often inflected as *xeroxed* and *xeroxing,* to refer to a xerographic duplicate or the act of making such duplicates; of *band-aid* to mean a makeshift and usually inadequate remedy – what are they to do? These words are as much a part of the language as any other word. If the object of a dictionary is to represent the language so that people unfamiliar with the meanings of words can find those meanings, doesn't omitting trademarks from the dictionary subordinate the interests of dictionary users to those of trademark owners? What gives their interests priority? More to the point, by what right can trademark owners or anyone else be empowered to dictate the facts of usage? If the facts so warrant, any word or set of words can be generic, and as such be subject to inclusion in a general dictionary. The lexicographer has no intention of depriving a trademark owner of the exclusive right to use a term; but he is in the business of writing dictionaries and his overriding obligation is therefore to dictionary users. He cannot allow any special-interest group to determine what goes in his dictionary or how it is represented.

As a hedge against the sometimes importunate demands, even threats, of trademark owners or their lawyers, some dictionaries have taken to including a statement on their copyright page disclaiming any intent to affect the copyright status of words they include. The *Random House Webster's College Dictionary* (*RHWCD*), for example, states:

A number of entered words which we have reason to believe constitute trademarks have been designated as such. However, no attempt has been made to designate as trademarks or service marks all words or terms in which proprietary rights might exist. The inclusion, exclusion, or definition of a word or terms [*sic*] is not intended to affect, or to express a judgment on, the validity or legal status of the word or terms as a trademark, service mark, or proprietary term.

Written by corporate attorneys, such nervous disclaimers are designed to dissuade trademark owners from suing the publishers. It has always been a wonder to me that so many lawyers make their living avoiding lawsuits. So long as there is documentary evidence to support the form of a dictionary's inclusion of trademarked items, I see no reason why publishers allow themselves to be intimidated.

In the past, dictionaries took a distinctly more standoffish approach to trademark owners. But now that many dictionaries are published by subsidiaries of large corporations, the influence of corporate legal counsels is more apparent. Large companies have their own trademarks to protect and are naturally more solicitous of those of others. Often the corporate vice-president overseeing a dictionary publisher cannot understand why the dictionary, which in comparison to the entire corporation is a tiny part, should take any unnecessary risk of legal action. The dictionary editor must do battle to include any trademarks, and he is under great pressure to distort the facts of usage by entering all such terms only in capitalized form, even though the record may clearly show they are often written in lower-case letters.

By far the most weaselly nonrecorders of generic meanings of trademark terms are the Merriam-Webster dictionaries. *MW10* defined *Band-Aid* as "*trademark* – used for a small adhesive strip with a gauze pad for covering minor wounds." But what about these uses?

And, while the old pedagogy has failed for many reasons, clearly one of them is that its fundamental principles are wrong. It has mistaken a band-aid for the science of medicine. (Richard A. Lanham, "The Abusage of Usage," *Virginia Quarterly Review* 53:1 (Winter 1977), 49)

Arofsky continues: "Everything the Knicks [a basketball team] try is a Band-Aid remedy. There's no real vision of the team concept." (*New York Sunday News Magazine,* January 1, 1982, 20)

"From my point of view, I've seen no change how we're doing business to get qualified controllers," Mr. Thorstenson added. "I don't see any light at the end of the tunnel. All we've had is a helter-skelter, Band-Aid, stop-gap type of approach. There's seemingly no plan to deal with the situation." (*New York Times*, April 30, 1982, A-10)

"I see this as a Band-Aid, not a long-term program," says Mr. Pratt. (*Wall St. Journal,* June 5, 1985, 33 – front page of second section)

The notion of production control, as it is usually called, is indeed an appealing one: Enough of the band-aids of interdiction and domestic law enforcement; we shall strike at the *fundamentals,* namely drug production itself. (Peter Reuter, *Public Interest* 79 (September 1985), 80)

"A minor near-term event like a Band-Aid on the budget deficit doesn't erase the five years of overconsumption and under-savings that contributed to the problem." (*New York*, November 30, 1987, 16)

According to published accounts, Bush apparently intends to use the money freed up by defense-spending cuts as an election-year Band-Aid for the health-care crisis. (*New York*, January 20, 1990, 22)

Some policymakers would rather use a year-to-year approach, providing only annual subsidies or rent vouchers for tenants. This kind of band-aid strategy has the advantage of masking the budgetary effect of any expenditures. (*New Republic*, January 25, 1997, 11)

How can it be that Merriam-Webster, which boasts of having millions of citations, has insufficient documentation to include this sense? The *American Heritage Dictionary* (*AHD*) included a second definition for *Band-Aid* in its first edition of 1969: "Any superficial or temporary remedy or solution." This definition was dropped from *AHD2* and *AHD3*. *AHD4*, while resolutely refusing to define a trademark generically, at least acknowledges the figurative sense and quotes two citations for it. *Webster's New World College Dictionary* (*WNWCD*) and *Random House Webster's College Dictionary* (*RHWCD*) both explicitly define the figurative sense, but only *WNWCD* also includes the common use of *Band-Aid* (and *band-aid*) for any small bandage of the type described for the trademark. The Merriam-Webster and American Heritage dictionaries have sacrificed the needs of their users in this respect for the goodwill of corporate trademark owners.

Lexicographers who hope to stay honest should keep their company's legal counsel at arm's length or persuade him or her that they needn't turn into jelly every time a trademark owner complains about the treatment of a term.

In the United Kingdom, dictionaries are now subject to European Union regulations on trademarks. In 1994 the EU approved regulations stating that if a reference work gives the impression that a registered EU trademark is generic, the owner of the trademark can request that it be identified as a trademark and the publisher is required to so identify it "at the latest in the next edition of the publication." This seems a reasonable compromise to the competing claims of the lexicographer and trademark owner, as there is at least no prior restraint on how the word is to be treated, and there is no specific stipulation of how the definition of the trademark must be worded. Trademark owners will nevertheless try to dictate how their marks are to be represented, but dictionary publishers with spine can resist such pressures.

THE NAME *WEBSTER* IN AMERICAN DICTIONARIES

On June 4, 1800, Noah Webster put a notice in the New Haven news-papers of his intention to produce three dictionaries, "a small Dictionary for schools, one for the counting-house, and a large one for men of science."[7] Thus began the history of the association of the name *Webster* with American dictionaries. (For a description of Webster's early diction-aries, see Ch. 2, p. 69.) The dominance of the G. & C. Merriam Company, which acquired the Webster dictionaries in 1841, made *Webster* a valuable trade name, but in the decades following the 1890s so was *Funk & Wagnalls*, and *Webster* did not acquire its unique iconic status until well into the twentieth century after Funk & Wagnalls had faded from the scene. Without any serious competitor, *Webster* became synon-ymous with "dictionary" in the minds of American consumers. Yet it wasn't until 1995 when *RHWCD* included it that any dictionary dared to define *Webster* as "a dictionary of the English language." Given the tortured legal history of the use of *Webster* in dictionary titles, this caution is understandable.

The copyright of the 1841 edition of Webster's *American Dictionary* expired in 1889, as reported by Herbert Morton, and when the Merriam company failed to secure the exclusive right to use *Webster's* as a trade name, other dictionaries began using it without the approval of the Merriam company. "By 1904, at least a dozen firms were using *Webster* in their dictionary titles." From the late 1920s to the 1940s, the World Syndicate Publishing Company of Cleveland produced a number of dictionaries with *Webster* in the titles, and because of various misrepre-sentations the Federal Trade Commission filed a complaint in 1941 charging it with misleading and deceptive trade practices. "The Merriam company entered the proceedings as *amicus curiae* in the hope that the FTC not only would find the World company guilty of decep-tive practices but would also order it to stop using the Webster name."[8]

The result of the FTC hearings from 1946 to 1949 confounded Merriam's expectations. They won the battle but lost the war. Though the FTC did enjoin World from engaging in deceptive trade practices, it also decided that the name *Webster* could not be considered the exclusive property of the Merriam company, because *Webster's* simply meant a dic-tionary, not the dictionary of a particular company. Thus World, now under new leadership, won the right to use *Webster* in the title of its dic-tionaries. The decision, according to David Guralnik, "was based not only on the grounds that Merriam had long applied the designation to works (including their general dictionaries) in no way derived from Webster's 1828 dictionary, but also on the testimony of many academics, librarians, and others that to the public, the word 'Webster's' simply means an American dictionary, without reference to any particular publisher."[9] The decision was appealed by Merriam and reached the US Court of Appeals, which reaffirmed the FTC decision. Guralnik recalls Justice Learned Hand's comment that Merriam's claim that other dictionaries calling themselves *Webster* were bogus or not genuine was "merely childish extravagance."

Though most of the dictionaries using *Webster* in their titles before the 1940s were of indifferent quality or worse, often adapted from older out-of-print works, *Webster's New World Dictionary* (*WNW*) of 1953, under the editorship of David Guralnik, was recognized from the start as a worthy competitor of the Merriam dictionaries. Following the FTC's decision, more and more publishers began to use *Webster* in the title of their dictionaries. Publishers increasingly felt that if they did not include *Webster* in the title, their dictionary would be placed at a considerable disadvantage in the marketplace. Eventually, even the publishers of the Random House dictionaries came to believe this, and in 1990 they decided to add *Webster's* to the title of their dictionaries.[10] In 1991 the *Random House College Dictionary* became the *Random House Webster's College Dictionary* (*RHWCD*).

The Merriam company, which had changed its name from G. & C. Merriam to Merriam-Webster, immediately sued Random House for "trademark infringement and unfair competition" under federal and state laws. They could not argue that using *Webster's* as such was prohibited, but they argued that Merriam-Webster had established a proprietary right to using *Webster's* in conjunction with *Collegiate*, and Random House's use of the words *Webster's College* in its dictionary's title was therefore an infringement of their trademark. (This seems a latter-day attempt to reestablish *Webster's* as a Merriam trademark.) They also alleged that Random House had engaged in unfair competition by borrowing the "trade dress" of the Merriam-Webster dictionaries, that is, it had unfairly copied their distinctive appearance. They said the red color of the jacket of *RHWCD* and the size and style of the typeface used for the word *Webster's* on the spine would have the effect of confusing dictionary purchasers who, intending to buy the latest Merriam-Webster collegiate dictionary, would end up with *RHWCD* instead. Random House vigorously denied any attempt to deceive customers, pointing out that the words *Random House* remained part of their book's title and appeared in large letters (though not as large as *Webster's*).

The case came to trial on September 1991, and the jury found for Merriam-Webster, awarding damages (after adjustment by the judge) amounting to more than $2 million, and including $500,000 in punitive damages. The judgment was based chiefly on the alleged violation of the trade dress of Merriam-Webster dictionaries, especially the design of the *RHWCD* jacket and the use of *Webster's* and *College* in a style that, the jury felt, could be confused with Merriam's collegiate dictionary. After consideration, the trial judge doubled the award to $4 million. Random House appealed, but in response to the ruling did alter the design of the jacket for *RHWCD*, replacing the huge *Webster's* that had been on the spine with the word *Dictionary.*

In 1994 the judgment was completely overturned on appeal and the money award rescinded. A federal appeals court decided that using *Webster's* with *College* did not violate any trademark, and that neither bookstores nor customers would confuse Random House dictionaries with Merriam-Webster dictionaries. Merriam-Webster thereupon appealed to the US Supreme Court, which let the appeals judgment stand.

The latest jacket for *RHWCD* is red and features a huge *Webster's* on the spine. The front of the jacket has *Random House* in black letters against the red background and *Webster's College Dictionary* standing out boldly in white, with *Webster's* more prominent than any other word.

CREDITING LEXICOGRAPHERS

As I have said elsewhere in this book, in dictionary work one cannot afford to take too much pride in authorship, because editing a diction- ary is a joint enterprise. This does not mean that lexicographers are indifferent to recognition. Far from it. When one has devoted years to a dictionary project, one has a right to expect some recognition on the staff page if not the title page when the dictionary is published. Sadly, this has often not been the case. Usually injustices of this sort are known solely by the neglected, their intimates, and a few erstwhile colleagues. They remain buried in the memories of powerless people, and disappear when they die. When a dispute over recognition does become public, it is usually years after all the principals are gone, when nothing can be done to rectify the injustice.

One such episode had to do with the publication of the first volume of Sir William Craigie's *Dictionary of American English* (*DAE*) in 1938. Mitford Mathews, who worked on the *DAE*, tells the story of George

Watson, a Scot who worked diligently on the *DAE* for years and who assumed a great deal of responsibility. Eventually Watson felt unappreciated and neglected by Craigie and demanded, among other things, that his name be on the title page of the dictionary. Craigie agreed, and when the proofs of Volume I of the dictionary first appeared in 1936, Watson's name was included along with others'. But the proofs were revised before publication and most of the names, including Watson's, were omitted. Although Watson believed this was a deliberate deception, Mathews is not so sure, since Watson did leave the project before 1938.[11] Watson's name appears in *DAE* only in the acknowledgments.

Allen Walker Read, who also worked on *DAE*, disputes Mathews' version and defends Craigie. He asserts that although Mathews and Watson thoroughly loathed one another, Mathews resented Craigie's patronizing attitude and used Watson's situation as a way to attack Craigie.[12] All of this has the distinct aspect of washing one's dirty linen in public. Alas, dictionary work in the past when staffs had to work together in close proximity, often in the same large room, not uncommonly engendered a feeling over time of being locked in a vast prison cell with an assortment of eccentrics. Antipathies grew and had nowhere to hide. But there were friendships, too, and not all dictionary staffs resembled the apparent state of mutual contempt of the *DAE*'s.

In recent years Michael Adams, after reviewing the record and assessing all sides of the *DAE* dispute, concluded that the criticism of Craigie was "not unwarranted," that the whole pattern of his behavior reflected a willingness to claim more credit than he deserved, and that "[t]he archival and printed record suggest that Craigie denied the other editors [Mathews as well as Watson] credit" that they had justly earned.[13] Although Mathews "earned others' respect and goodwill," and went on to win a measure of fame subsequently as editor of the *Dictionary of Americanisms* (1951), he was never accorded "his share of recognition for his contributions to the DAE."[14] It is easy to take a disdainful view of such ignominious squabbles when one is not an aggrieved party to them, but I suggest that if one has made the personal sacrifices necessary to complete a major dictionary project lasting years – the deferral of all vacations, the unvarying pressure to produce, day in and day out, where all the motivation for high performance that extends one's hours is self-imposed – one might see things more sympathetically.

I have long been dismayed by the policy of many publishers of not recognizing the contributions of dictionary editors, and in 1996 set my own proposal before the Dictionary Society of North America to establish guidelines for crediting the work of lexicographers. A draft of the proposal was circulated to all the members of the DSNA Executive Board; some minor changes and additions were made and are incorporated in this proposal, which was subsequently approved without further change. With the permission of the Dictionary Society, I reprint the proposal virtually in its entirety, with a few, minor elisions.[15]

A proposal to establish guidelines for crediting the work of lexicographers

I. Introduction

The first question to be answered is, Who needs such guidelines? Why are they necessary? A second and related question is, Don't the publishers of dictionaries own their works and have the right to do whatever they wish in extending or withholding credit?

To the second question, the answer is, Yes, they do, and because of that the extensive contributions of lexicographers have often been ignored. Sometimes this happens through the accident of corporate forgetfulness (and, it must be added, indifference) in the aftermath of changes in the managerial ranks above dictionary makers and sometimes through deliberate suppression (for one reason or another), but its occurrence is frequent and deplorable.

Almost all dictionaries are owned by their publishers, either because they are entirely staff-produced or because they are produced in part by independent contractors who sign "work-for-hire" agreements. We have no quarrel with this arrangement. Since the publisher must provide a very large investment and takes all the risk, it is reasonable for the publisher to demand that the work be wholly owned and that subsequent adaptations, abridgments, etc., belong to the publisher. Indeed, few dictionaries would be undertaken on any other basis. The publisher's right to credit whomever it wants is not in dispute.

However, publishers are often unaware of the history and current state of lexicography. Through lack of awareness more often than intent, the names of lexicographers who have devoted years to the development of a dictionary may be omitted from subsequent editions. If publishers had guidelines, they might better appreciate the importance of due recognition to lexicographers, dictionary users, and themselves. Consequently they might give satisfactory acknowledgment, which now is sometimes thought to be of no more importance than acknowledging the printer or specifying the type styles . . .

The anonymity in which lexicographers are too often forced to work is a serious impediment to their careers and thus to the ultimate best interests of publishers and the public. It is unfair. Something can be done about it. It is the responsibility of the DSNA to do that something. From whom else in the US should such guidelines come if not from the DSNA?

This brings us to the first question. Who needs such guidelines? Why are they necessary? The nature of dictionary work is highly unusual in a publishing company. Publishers traditionally rely on authors working on their own time, often for years, to produce texts which the publishers will only then consider for publication, and from which, in return for the service and expense of publication, they will derive substantial benefit. The value of the book in truth far exceeds what the publisher contributes to it, but this value is of course independent of whether or not the book makes or loses money. Since publishing is a business, the publisher's justification for its profit has to do with taking the risk that few individual authors would take.

A dictionary written by a staff of lexicographers on the payroll of a publisher has a unique status. Suddenly the publisher finds itself in the position of one of its authors, and moreover, not just an author of a short monograph but of an immensely long and complicated work that will take years to produce, one subject to delays and additional expenses not originally reckoned. In every case we know of involving a publisher's first entry into dictionary making, the enterprise was more than the publisher bargained for.

Unless a company or university or major division within it is entirely devoted to dictionary making and has a long history of publishing dictionaries, the lexicographers are looked upon as anomalous employees. No one knows what they do, since they seem always to be hard at work yet produce nothing, even after years of employment. Often corporate vice presidents or university provosts share this puzzlement.

The job of a lexicographer, even a staff position, is by its nature insecure. Since dictionary work is project related, the completion of a project often means that the staff will be "downsized" with all but a core of cadre laid off, and sometimes those as well. Even in mid-course, projects have often been suspended and staff summarily laid off.

Since dictionaries are publisher-owned, lexicographers have no equity in the work they may have spent eight or ten years working on, and must rely solely on credit being given for their dossiers. Their knowledge and experience have no tangible products except the dictionaries they have contributed to; the rest is in the lexicographer's brain. If lexicographers are deprived of credit, they have no basis for establishing their credentials in the future to obtain another job. They have no basis for making a career of lexicography. In fact, this is precisely the condition we are in today.

The insecurity of a lexicographer's career affects not only him or her personally, but dictionary publishers and dictionary users as well, in fact, the entire enterprise of lexicography. Good dictionaries require good and experienced lexicographers. And persons entering a career in lexicography need a modicum of assurance that they can point to past work well done as a basis for seeking future lexicographical opportunities. It is thus also in the interest of publishers and the dictionary-using public to have a pool of skilled and properly credited lexicographers.

II. The problem

Because dictionaries take so long to complete, the composition of the editorial staff at the initiation of a project is often very different from that at its conclusion. Also, since dictionaries are expensive undertakings, they often generate a progeny of derivative works, whose relationship with their parent varies but is inevitably diluted over time. Further, every dictionary, if successful, remains in print for a long time and undergoes numerous revisions, some small and some great.

It is obviously impossible to expect that everyone who has worked on a dictionary, even for a short time and in a minor capacity, will be accorded credit in perpetuity. We are not here concerned with some theoretical ethic but with the practical matter of assuring that proper credit is given to professional lexicographers pursuing careers in their chosen work. Although we all recognize that the contributions of clerical and other supporting staff can be crucially important and deserve recognition in simple human terms, such matters are not the concern of this paper. Our concern is with lexicographers.

It may be instructive to note how the *Oxford English Dictionary* coped with the problem of recognition. Herbert Coleridge was appointed editor in November 1859 but died in April 1861. Shortly after, F. J. Furnivall was appointed editor; he served from 1862 to 1879, when James A. H. Murray became editor. This is recounted in the "Historical Introduction" of the *OED*, which recognized the importance (p. xiv) "of giving credit where credit is due."

Part VII of the *OED*'s Historical Introduction is devoted to specific acknowledgment of the principal readers before 1884, sometimes with indication of the number of citations each was accountable for; to another list of readers after 1884; to sub-editors, with dates; to assistants, divided into three groups, the first of which worked for at least ten years and in more than a few cases for more than forty years. Two other groups of sub-editors are listed, followed by proofreaders and "other helpers." In a work spanning 75 years (1859–1933), we would expect nothing less.

Fortunately, few modern dictionaries will be faced with an enormous roster of contributors like that of the *OED*. It testifies to the integrity of Murray and his colleagues at Oxford University Press that an extensive catalog of the begetters of the *OED* was deemed essential, even to the particulars of dates and number of citations acquired, to "give credit where credit is due." The Dictionary Society could do worse than follow this precedent.

III. The proposal

Two separate but related issues are credit itself (that is, listing lexicographers' names on the staff page) and the form of the credit (the title under which lexicographers are listed). Our main concern is with credit itself, although at the very top level, the form of the credit is of concern as well. Below we consider the role of the top editor first, then the roles of the staff.

We suggest that the chief editor of a dictionary be called the "editor-in-chief" and that, if the editor-in-chief appointed at the beginning of a project retains that position at its conclusion, he or she should be accorded credit in the printed (or electronic) book as "editor-in-chief." This is the customary title for the chief editor, although there may be reasons in some cases for not employing it (as because of numerous changes among the top editors).

Complications arise when the editor-in-chief resigns, is dismissed, or dies before the end of the project. Obviously, we cannot account for every possibility, and we cannot argue that an incompetent or otherwise unsatisfactory editor-in-chief be credited simply because he or she was originally hired for the job. But if a person has held a position as editor-in-chief for one half the duration of a project, or for five years (whichever is less), he or she deserves to be recognized as the original editor of the project. Anyone who has been engaged at the highest level with a project for that long must have had a major impact on it and deserves to have his or her contribution noted.

The same rule of thumb would apply to any other managing editors and senior staff, regardless of their specific titles such as "supervising editor," "executive editor," "senior editor," or "editor."

If the project has run its course pretty much as originally planned, the original editor should be identified by his or her original title with the dates of activity specified. However, in those cases where the project has undergone a major restructuring following the departure of the first editor-in-chief, he or she might be more properly identified in some other way, such as "contributing editor" or "consulting editor." The principle here is the extent to which the first editor's original vision or plan of the work was carried through. If it was, he or she deserves to be recognized as the chief editor. However, if it was substantially reshaped by another, it is only fair to recognize that the succeeding editor was the creator of the plan for the completed dictionary, while not ignoring the contribution of the first editor.

Although we have proposed limits of five years or one half the duration of the project, publishers should be urged to recognize contributions of lesser duration, perhaps two years or more in similar fashion. We should regard the five-year criterion as essential, and any deviation from it a serious departure from the standards of professional reference publishing.

An abridged dictionary may have a different editor-in-chief and staff than those of the parent work. Clearly, they should be recognized by the guidelines stated above for the work in which they were engaged. In every case, however, the editor-in-chief ... of the parent work should be acknowledged, either on the staff page or in the introduction of the abridgment.

If an abridgment is almost entirely a straightforward reduction and not a substantial revision of the content, it would be appropriate also to list the entire senior staff of the parent dictionary. If, on the other hand, the derived work involves major changes in the content, only the editor-in-chief ... of the parent work need be given, since the staff of the derivative work in this case deserves more recognition than the staff of the original work.

How long after the initial publication of a dictionary should the editor-in-chief and staff be listed? In our view, the origination of a new dictionary is such a rare and difficult enterprise that the original editor-in-chief and senior staff should be listed on all succeeding editions, even if the placement of their names on the staff page descends gradually, like a helium balloon with a slow leak, until it nestles at the bottom of the page in small type. It should nonetheless remain.

However, if the dictionary undergoes a major revision (as, for example, *Webster's Third New International* compared with the Second

Edition), we are justified in regarding the new edition as a new dictionary, and accord its staff the same rights here adumbrated for any new
dictionary. In that case, the staff of the earlier edition need not be
immortalized, although, as is usually the case, the introduction would
cite the chief editor of the earlier edition. This is not our concern,
however, and is not part of our guidelines.

So far, we have considered the editor-in-chief and senior staff, but
credit should also be given to the junior staff, younger lexicographers just
getting their careers underway, sometimes designated "associate editors"
(though in some cases that title applies to relatively senior staff) or "assistant editors." We propose the following rules for staff generally, including
junior staff.

Anyone working in any lexicographic capacity on a project for two
years or more deserves to be given credit on the completion of the original edition of the work, with a job title that is commensurate with his
or her level of responsibility and the nature of his or her assignment.
However, it is unreasonable to expect that such credit be recorded on
every subsequent edition, revision, or abridgment based on the work in
which each editor was engaged. Such notice becomes impractical as new
contributions from new editors must be acknowledged. Few companies
can maintain accurate records of junior editors long after they have
departed, and it is impractical to expect that every editor be listed on
every subsequent edition.

If a young editor makes a career of lexicography, he or she should
graduate to a more senior position and be accorded the more permanent credit advocated in this paper. In the meantime, even the single
listing in the original edition to which he or she contributed will provide
potentially valuable evidence of his or her work.

The foregoing considerations have led to the following set of guidelines . . .

GUIDELINES FOR CREDITING THE WORK OF LEXICOGRAPHERS

1. It is the responsibility of publishers to give credit to the lexicographers
who edit the dictionaries they publish, even though those dictionaries are
wholly owned by the publishers. Because the professional livelihoods of
lexicographers depend on such recognition and because dictionary
makers, publishers, and users are best served by fostering a skilled pool
of lexicographers through recognizing their work, the Dictionary
Society of North America strongly urges all publishers to adopt these
guidelines as a standard.

2. The editorial staff, and particularly the chief editor, should be credited on the staff page of its dictionary, recognized with appropriate titles, especially "editor-in-chief" for the chief editor. Due consideration should also be given to listing the editor-in-chief and, where the situation merits, the managing editor on the title page of the dictionary.

3. Any member of the senior staff who works on a dictionary for half the time of its preparation or five years (whichever is less) should be credited. If the work is a first or unabridged edition, this credit should be in perpetuity, though it may be variously presented to allow for greater prominence to succeeding editors. If a senior staff member works for less than this time, the recognition may be like that of junior staff (see 4 below), i.e., it will apply to the first edition only.

4. Any member of the junior staff who works on a dictionary for more than two years should be credited in the first edition of the work to which he or she has contributed.

THE DICTIONARY AS A REFLECTION OF SOCIAL VALUES

Dictionaries are often accused of bias, particularly against women and minority groups, and certainly in the past one can find evidence of this in the treatment of certain definitions. Usually these accusations are mounted against dictionaries that have not been revised or updated in many years and that reflect the cultural attitudes and prejudices of a past era. The dictionary editors did not set out to belittle or disparage any group; they unwittingly shared and reflected the prejudices of the prevailing culture. Evidence of a dictionary's cultural bias was demonstrated in a study by Ann Ediger Baehr of the 1952 and 1962 editions of the *Thorndike-Barnhart Beginning Dictionary*. She showed, among other things, that its illustrative citations reflected a disproportionate emphasis on Christianity. "From *a* to *Yule*, we counted fifty-nine references to the word *Christmas* . . . [in illustrative sentences]."[16] She cites these illustrative sentences (with the word being exemplified in italic type) as typical:

The Star in the East was the *sign* of Christ's coming.
Christ came to *save* the world.
Christ is called the *Rock* of Ages.
Christ give His disciples power to *remit* sins.
Jesus touched the sick man. *Thereon* he was healed and arose from his bed.
Jesus died on the *cross*.
All Christians are not of the same *persuasion*.

Most people *adhere* to the church of their parents.
The *solemnity* of the church service was felt even by the children.
Two roads *met* near the church.

Baehr also shows that the dictionary's illustrative phrases consistently represented girls as good, honest, pure, truth-telling, and generally wonderful; whereas boys were represented as violent, cruel, and irremediably wicked. She cites examples:

That cruel boy *tortures* animals.
The cruel boy *stoned* the dog.

And so forth. In spite of some modifications, the disparity in treatment of boys and girls was still apparent in the 1962 edition. Baehr is also critical of the uncompromising ethical absolutism reflected in its illustrative sentences, which reflect a world of pure goodness and pure evil.

Eventually, we can be sure, these uneven and biased treatments were edited out of the Thorndike-Barnhart dictionaries, but we cannot be sure that they have not been replaced by others, and I am speaking now not only of the Thorndike-Barnhart dictionaries but of all dictionaries. The accepted truths and assumptions of every generation often appear as blatant biases to later ones. Even conscientiously edited dictionaries like the *Thorndike-Barnhart Beginning Dictionary* are apt to reflect the cultural backgrounds and habits of the editors, especially when these are concordant with the dominant ethos and prejudices of the period. In the 1940s, when the 1952 Thorndike-Barnhart dictionary was prepared, few questioned that America was a Christian country and prayer was common in the public schools. The stern didactic tone of the illustrative sentences that Baehr criticizes was simply a carryover of the tradition of the early schoolbooks. The real point of the criticism is not that the dictionary was biased, but that it had not kept up with the times. It reflected past biases rather than current ones.

We have had occasion elsewhere to allude to the role of dictionaries in reflecting the values of the predominant social class. We see now that as these values change in the course of time, what was formerly innocuous can become intrusive and objectionable. The bright paint used to color parts of ancient Greek statuary would strike us today as tawdry. Every established dictionary reflects, however it may strive to be impartial, the prevailing biases of its times, because the biases often inhere in the very manner of expression used in its definitions. They inhere in the choice of terms to be included and in the fullness with which they are treated. Yet the indignation shown by some critics, who allege that the biases are either deliberate or the result of uncommon insensitivity, are almost always wrongheaded and unjustified.

Taking a leaf from the Baehr study of 1964, I compared two later editions of the *Thorndike-Barnhart Beginning Dictionary*, those of 1968 and 1988, to see whether the changes in the treatments of illustrative sentences revealed any significant shifts in cultural attitudes.[17] The focus of my attention was references to family members: mothers and fathers, sons and daughters, grandparents, etc. The shifts in attitude towards many family members were dramatic and unmistakable. Ninety percent of all references to mother and father in the sections I examined in the 1968 edition were deleted from the corresponding parts of the 1988 edition.

In 1968 mother was often associated with her nurturing role and with household obligations, as reflected in these illustrative sentences:

Mother has taught me always to say "Please" and "Thank you."
Mother cut the pie into equal sections.
The care of the baby claims much of Mother's time.
Mother sensed that Father was tired.
One of Mother's plates has a chip on the edge.

Father was associated in 1968 with the support of the family, discipline, and business:

My father has an income of $8000 a year.
My father pays most of his bills by check.
After the guests left, the boy got a sermon on table manners from his father.
She coaxed her father to let her go to the dance.
The running of Father's bath water early in the morning woke up the children.

By 1988, the role of mother had been sharply reduced, and that of father almost entirely extinguished. For example,

In 1968 the illustration for *check* was, "When we finished eating, Father asked the waitress for the check." In 1988 it is, "After we finished eating, the waiter brought the check to our table." Not content with excising Father, who initiated the action described, the editors have been so sensitive to the relationship between Father and the waitress and about feminine-ending words in general that they have substituted *waiter* (now like most *-er* words usually defined as neutral in gender). Moreover, it is the waiter who now performs the action, apparently unsolicited by anyone.[18]

Mothers and fathers have been replaced by parents of neutral gender. Grandparents appear as frequently in illustrative sentences as mother, but neither appears very often. The price of the new sensitivity towards parental roles is a loss of specificity; since the sex of any person mentioned is seldom specified, we can form no mental picture of the people involved. The illustrative sentences all tend to look like models, exemplary of some abstract realm of possibility rather than examples of the actual usage of language.

In comparing the two editions, one notices also that the altered relationship between parents and children reflects a different ethos of family life:

Whereas in 1968 parents told children what to do, in 1988 children tell parents what they want. Thus "The lazy boy's parents hounded him to do his homework" (1968) has been changed to "The children hounded their parents to buy a color TV." . . . The illustration for *indifference* in 1968 was, "The boy's indifference to his homework worried his parents." This has been changed in 1988 to "The child's indifference to food worried his parents."

The 1968 examples imply a responsibility on the child's part; the later examples imply none. Not only have most gender references disappeared, but the role of parents is now seen as essentially passive. They respond to problems and demands; they do not initiate any action, let alone set standards of behavior or enforce rules. The changes in the two editions were generated by real changes in American life during the period encompassed and no doubt also reflect the views of most lexicographers, but they have no more truth value, I submit, than the 1968 examples that would strike most of us today as either quaint or offensive. There is no one representation of American life and mores that is more typical than any other; there are only media stereotypes that often reflect in a general way real trends. It is these new stereotypes that present us with a picture of American life that influences the way many publications, including dictionaries, view it.

One can no more pretend that dictionaries are culturally neutral than one can pretend that any other utilitarian object such as a doorknob or clothes hanger is culturally neutral and without any particular design. Our familiarity with such objects should not blind us to the truth that all such objects are designed in the context of history, whether we are ignorant of that history or not. Although dictionary treatment of social attitudes necessarily lags behind the present, dictionaries, in choosing to recognize one set of values over other possible sets of values, give the values they select stability and authority, and by subtly representing those values (i.e., in their illustrative examples), they can be a progressive influence in furthering social change, especially when social behavior has not kept pace with predominant social values.[19]

The dictionaries I have been describing in this section did not use language corpora as a basis for their illustrative examples, which were instead invented by the editors. But corpus-based dictionaries are not immune from the reflection of particular social values. In Ch. 5 I noted that the authentic language of a corpus contains many examples of offensive or otherwise unacceptable speech. Lexicographers will not include examples expressing these attitudes. This is understandable; it is even necessary: their jobs might be in jeopardy if they did. But it expresses a bias. It distorts an accurate representation of how real language is commonly used. In Ch. 5 I also remarked upon the extreme sensitivity of contemporary dictionaries towards terms of insult and their comparative acceptance of formerly taboo sexual and scatological terms. The use of corpora will not change the expression of this set of attitudes in dictionaries. Moreover, as I point out in Ch. 6, the choice of the texts to be included in corpora shapes the way language is interpreted by lexicographers, which will inevitably be reflected in one degree or another by the choice of examples cited in dictionaries.

If the composition of a corpus reflects predominantly the writings and speech of a particular class of society, so will the dictionary based upon it. Since not all classes of society equally participate in writing and publishing, no corpus based largely on writing can truly reflect how language is used by all people. To the extent that corpora are based chiefly on written texts, they will chiefly reflect the values and attitudes of the educated, privileged classes of society. Corpora of speech are being collected and expanded, and we will see far greater attention given to speech in some dictionaries in the future, particularly ESL dictionaries. But I do not expect the dominance of written text in corpora to disappear any time soon.

Dictionaries are subject to all of the complex social pressures that individuals and organizations of the twenty-first century are subject to. They are also articles for sale. Though they can (and do) occasionally offend that community's sense of decency or propriety by the mere inclusion of offensive terms, they dare not show that they are insensitive to the pitch and tone of the more profound social values implicit in modern life. These, like the numbing background music on airplane and elevator, intended to calm the fears of excited imaginations, we have learned not to notice. However, if the unheard music of our biases were suddenly stopped, the shock of silence would make us start, like a baby awakened from sleep, and the world would then indeed be strange and frightening.

Notes

1 WHAT IS A DICTIONARY?

1 See Martin Stark, *Encyclopedic Learner's Dictionaries: A Study of their Design Features from the User Perspective* (Tübingen: Max Niemeyer, 1999), pp. 6–20 for a detailed comparison of the features of dictionaries and encyclopedias. Although the book deals specifically with an encyclopedic type of learner's dictionary, the comparison in this section has general application.

2 Yakov Malkiel, "A Typological Classification of Dictionaries on the Basis of Distinctive Features," in Fred W. Householder and Sol Saporta (eds.), *Problems in Lexicography* (Bloomington: Indiana University; The Hague: Mouton, 1967), pp. 3–24. Malkiel's article is condensed and modified from his earlier two-part essay, "Distinctive Features in Lexicography: A Typological Approach to Dictionaries Exemplified with Spanish," *Romance Philology* 12:4 (May 1959), 366–99, and 13:2 (November 1959), 111–55. The Householder and Saporta book is a valuable collection of lexicographic papers presented at a conference held at Indiana University in November 1960 and originally published as a supplement to the *International Journal of American Linguistics* 28 (1962).

3 However, to my mind the perspective category is weakly defined; the method of organization could just as well be considered part of presentation. On the other hand, Malkiel is unjustly criticized by Ali M. Al-Kasimi in *Linguistics and Bilingual Dictionaries* (Leiden: E. J. Brill, 1977) for not providing categories of "discrete, mutually opposed dictionary types" (p. 16). That was not Malkiel's intention. Moreover, the typology advanced by Al-Kasimi for bilingual dictionaries does not provide for discrete, mutually opposed dictionary types any more than does Malkiel's.

4 An illuminating discussion of bilingual lexicography, including a description of this terminology, can be found in Hans-Peder Kromann, Theis Rijber, and Poul Rosbach, "Principles of Bilingual Lexicography," in Franz Josef Hausmann, Oskar Reichmann, Herbert Ernst Wiegand, and Ladislav Zgusta (eds.), *Wörterbucher, Dictionaries, Dictionnaires: Ein internationales Handbuch zur Lexikographie, An International Encyclopedia of Lexicography, Encyclopédie internationale de lexicographie*, 3 vols. (Berlin: Walter de Gruyter, 1989–91), vol. III, pp. 2713–28.

5 This point is cogently made in Kromann, Rijber, and Rosbach, "Principles of Bilingual Lexicography," p. 2713.

6 Mary R. Haas, "What Belongs in a Bilingual Dictionary," in Householder and Saporta (eds.), *Problems in Lexicography*, p. 47.

7 Ladislav Zgusta, *Manual of Lexicography* (The Hague: Mouton; Prague: Academia, 1971), p. 320.

8 Cited by Richard S. Harrell, "Some Notes on Bilingual Lexicography," in Householder and Saporta (eds.), *Problems in Lexicography*, p. 51.

9 A number of culture-specific culinary terms are cited by Dinh-Hoa Nguyen, "Bicultural Information in a Bilingual Dictionary," in Ladislav Zgusta (ed.), *Theory and Method in Lexicography* (Columbia, S.C.: Hornbeam Press, 1980), p. 166.

10 Morton Benson, "Culture-Specific Terms in Bilingual Dictionaries of English," *Dictionaries: Journal of the Dictionary Society of North America* 12 (1990), 43–54. The examples cited are on p. 43 and p. 47.

11 Cited by Harrell, "Some Notes on Bilingual Lexicography," p. 51.

12 Mary R. Haas, "What Belongs in a Bilingual Dictionary," p. 45.

13 Zgusta, *Manual of Lexicography*, p. 210. Zgusta's treatment of the problems of selecting entries and providing equivalents in bilingual dictionaries is particularly good. See pp. 298–336.

14 David Crystal, *English as a Global Language* (Cambridge University Press, 1997), p. 61.

15 *Ibid.*, pp. 3–4.

16 H. L. Mencken, *The American Language*, the Fourth Edition and the two supplements, abridged, with annotations and new material, by Raven I. McDavid, Jr. (New York: Knopf, 1967).

17 George Philip Krapp, *The English Language in America*, 2 vols. (New York: Modern Language Association of America, 1925).

18 Allen Walker Read, "Approaches to Lexicography and Semantics," in Thomas Sebeok (ed.), *Current Trends in Linguistics*, vol. X (The Hague: Mouton, 1973), p. 153.

19 The quotation is from the Introduction, p. xii.

20 The quotation is from the Preface, p. vii.

21 See in this connection M. Lynne Murphy, "Defining People: Race and Ethnicity in South African English," *International Journal of Lexicography* 11:1 (March 1998), 1–33. Murphy analyzes how various South African dictionaries treat terms describing race.

22 Crystal, *English as a Global Language*, p. 103.

23 For a thorough analysis of these two encyclopedic learner's dictionaries and a discussion of the merits of this type of dictionary based on a user survey, see Stark, *Encyclopedic Learner's Dictionaries*.

24 Tom McArthur, "Culture-Bound and Trapped by Technology: Centuries of Bias in the Making of Wordbooks," in Braj B. Kachru and Henry Kahane (eds.), *Cultures, Ideologies, and the Dictionary: Studies in Honor of Ladislav Zgusta* (Tübingen: Max Niemeyer, 1995), p. 388.

25 *Ibid.* The first edition of my book erroneously stated that the *Lexicon* was produced automatically from a database. I was so impressed by the elaborate alphanumeric system of interrelated subject fields that I assumed this was the case. The author subsequently informed me (personal letter, March 15, 1995) that this was incorrect.

26 Sidney I. Landau, "The Making of a Dictionary: Craft versus Commerce," *Booklist* (incorporating *Reference and Subscription Books Reviews*) 77:6 (November 15, 1980), 481. K. M. Elisabeth Murray is the author of *Caught in the Web of Words: James A. H. Murray and the Oxford English Dictionary* (New Haven: Yale University Press, 1977).

27 See Sidney I. Landau, "The American College Dictionaries," *International Journal of Lexicography* 7:4 (Winter 1994), 311–51.

28 Read, "Approaches to Lexicography and Semantics," p. 161.

29 Clarence L. Barnhart, "American Lexicography, 1947–1973," *American Speech* 53:2 (Summer 1978), 115.

30 See Zgusta, *Manual of Lexicography*, p. 203.

31 *Ibid.*, p. 349.

32 *Ibid.*, p. 217.

33 Read, "Approaches to Lexicography and Semantics," p. 149.

34 *The Random House Dictionary of the English Language, Second Edition*, although called unabridged, is not comparable in coverage to *NID3*. It claims to have 315,000 entries, but this includes thousands of names of people and places, and other encyclopedic entries, whereas *NID3* includes none. The quality of sense breakdown in *NID3* is also much finer.

35 Philip Babcock Gove, "Preface," *Webster's Third New International Dictionary.* The quotations are from pp. 6a and 7a, respectively.

36 John Simpson, "The *Oxford English Dictionary* Today," undated publication of Oxford University Press describing the need for a thorough revision. I obtained a copy of this document in 1999.

37 Publishers' claims of dictionary entries are rarely challenged. But when Bantam Books claimed in advertisements in 1979 that its paperback dictionary, the *Scribner-Bantam Dictionary*, contained 80,000 entries, more than other paperback dictionaries, Random House filed suit, claiming that Bantam Books had misrepresented the number of entries. It said the *Scribner-Bantam* really contained about 56,000 entries, far less than Random House's paperback dictionary. The two publishers eventually reached an out-of-court settlement and Bantam withdrew its advertising. See *Publishers Weekly*, August 27, 1979, 294. The original hardcover edition published by Scribner's in 1977 was essentially the same book but its claim of having 80,000 entries was never challenged.

38 Sidney I. Landau, "Of Matters Lexicographical: Scientific and Technical Entries in American Dictionaries," *American Speech* 49:3–4 (Fall–Winter 1974), 242.

39 *Ibid.*, p. 241.

40 Barnhart, "American Lexicography," p.115.

41 Alexandre Manuila (ed.), *Progress in Medical Terminology* (Basel: S. Karger, 1981), p. 58.
42 But they do not include "dictionaries" of biography or geography, which deal not with words but with encyclopedic facts. Although dictionaries often include such encyclopedic material, collections devoted exclusively to biography or geography are specialized encyclopedias.
43 Harold Wentworth and Stuart Berg Flexner (eds.), *Dictionary of American Slang*, Second Supplemented Edition (New York: Thomas Y. Crowell, 1975; first edn. 1960), p. xiii n.
44 See Manuila, *Progress in Medical Terminology*, pp. 13–14. For example:

> Myelofibrosis . . . has been described in the literature in English under at least 12 names, in German under at least 13, and in French under at least 31 . . . [An author] dealing with a French paper on *panmyélose hyperpasique chronique* may translate this into English as chronic hyperpasic panmyelosis. Many such neologisms, though not generally in use, persist in the literature, simply because once or twice they have found their way into reputable journals.

> What Dr. Manuila calls a neologism is also a ghost term.

45 "Dictionary of American Family Names: Report on Work in Progress," *Euralex Newsletter* in the *International Journal of Lexicography* 12:3 (September 1999), 7.

2 A BRIEF HISTORY OF ENGLISH LEXICOGRAPHY

1 The chief source of information for early, monolingual English lexicography is DeWitt T. Starnes and Gertrude E. Noyes, *The English Dictionary from Cawdrey to Johnson, 1604–1755* (Chapel Hill: University of North Carolina Press, 1946), to which I am much indebted. This book was reissued (Amsterdam and Philadelphia: John Benjamins, 1991) with an introduction by Gabriele Stein, who also has provided a chronological list of dictionaries with their editions and locations and a select bibliography to complement that given in the original printing. For dictionaries of the sixteenth century and earlier, my chief sources were DeWitt T. Starnes, *Renaissance Dictionaries: English-Latin and Latin-English* (Austin: University of Texas Press, 1954), and Gabriele Stein, *The English Dictionary before Cawdrey* (Tübingen: Max Niemeyer, 1985). Any opinions expressed about the dictionaries of this period are my own.

For a thorough popular treatment of the history of English lexicography, see Jonathon Green, *Chasing the Sun: Dictionary Makers and the Dictionaries They Made* (New York: Henry Holt, 1996), which gives special attention to slang and includes much biographical data. The book's title derives from a passage from the Preface to Johnson's *Dictionary*, which I quote on pp. 61–2.
2 Presidential Address, *Philological Society Transactions* (1882–84), pp. 509–10, quoted in K. M. E. Murray, *Caught in the Web of Words: James A. H. Murray*

and the Oxford English Dictionary (New Haven: Yale University Press, 1977), pp. 203–4.

3 Starnes and Noyes, *The English Dictionary from Cawdrey to Johnson*, p. 2. See also Starnes, *Renaissance Dictionaries*, p. 8, and Stein, *The English Dictionary before Cawdrey*, p. 92.

4 Stein, *The English Dictionary before Cawdrey*, pp. 81–82. See also Starnes, *Renaissance Dictionaries*, p. 31, who comments about the title page blurb of the 1509 edition, "This is the sort of lively advertising we might expect to see today on the jacket of a new book, and, like the skit on the jacket, the matter of this title page should be read with due caution. The claim that the *Ortus* contains all that may be found in the five books named is, of course, absurd." Plus ça change, plus c'est la même chose.

5 Quoted in Starnes, *Renaissance Dictionaries*, p. 374 n.

6 Stein, *The English Dictionary before Cawdrey*, p. 381.

7 David O. Frantz, "Florio's Use of Contemporary Italian Literature in *A Worlde of Wordes*," *Dictionaries: Journal of the Dictionary Society of North America* 1 (1979), 49, 53.

8 Starnes and Noyes, *The English Dictionary from Cawdrey to Johnson*, pp. 10–11. On prevalent attitudes of the time on the perceived barbarousness of English, see Richard Foster Jones, *The Triumph of the English Language* (Stanford University Press, 1953), pp. 1–31. Jones describes Mulcaster's views about the English language on pp. 157–67, and on borrowed terms on pp. 206–7.

9 Allen Walker Read, in his article on "dictionary" for the on-line *Encyclopaedia Britannica* (November 16, 1999), mentions a third source, a translation from Latin to English by an unknown Dutchman of *The Book of Physicke* (1599), by Oswald Gabelkhouer. The book contained glosses for poorly translated Latin words, and it was this list of errata that Cawdrey incorporated into his dictionary, Read says, adding that Cawdrey's dictionary "can rightly be called a plagiarism."

10 Joseph E. Worcester, *A Universal and Critical Dictionary of the English Language*, p. lxii. The earliest English dictionaries Worcester mentions are those of Bullokar and Cockeram.

11 The suggestion that Mulcaster may have been the inspiration for Cawdrey's dictionary is made by Starnes and Noyes, *The English Dictionary from Cawdrey to Johnson*, p. 18.

12 *Ibid.*, p. 27.

13 *Ibid.*, p. 28.

14 *Ibid.*, p. 35.

15 *Ibid.*, pp. 37–47, especially pp. 42, 46.

16 *Ibid.*, p. 54.

17 *Ibid.*, pp. 61, 63.

18 Read, "dictionary," *Encyclopaedia Britannica*. Only the initials "J. K." identify the editor of *A New English Dictionary*, but Read, Starnes and Noyes, and most other scholars attribute the work to John Kersey, a lexicographer

known to be active during this period. However, see Henry B. Wheatley, "Chronological Notices of the Dictionaries of the English Language," *Transactions of the Philological Society* (1865), 240. Wheatley expresses skepticism about the attribution.

19 Fredric Dolezal, *Forgotten but Important Lexicographers, John Wilkins and William Lloyd: A Modern Approach to Lexicography Before Johnson* (Tübingen: Max Niemeyer, 1985), claims that Wilkins' and Lloyd's *Alphabetical Dictionary* of 1668 was the first dictionary to focus its attention on common words. There are two difficulties with this claim. First, the *Alphabetical Dictionary* forms a part of Wilkins' *Essay towards a Real Character and a Philosophical Language* and is not an independent work. Second, though it contains many innovative features, as Dolezal shows, in its coverage of a number of multiword lexical units and in its inclusion of many common words, it has more of the character of a thesaurus than a dictionary. Anticipating Roget's system of classification by more than 200 years, it depends on tables by which terms are classified. This view is evidently shared by N. E. Osselton in *Chosen Words: Past and Present Problems for Dictionary Makers* (University of Exeter Press, 1995), who writes (p. 4): "In it there are no direct definitions for most monosemous words, and the alphabetical list depends very largely on use in conjunction with the Philosophical Tables in the book by Bishop Wilkins to which it is appended." Dolezal says that it is the first dictionary in which the words used in its definitions are themselves defined. I do not dispute the importance or the innovative character of this work. I just don't agree entirely with Dolezal's assessment of its place in the history of lexicography.

20 Percy W. Long, "English Dictionaries Before Webster," *Bibliographical Society of America Papers IV* (1909), 30, cited in Starnes and Noyes, *The English Dictionary from Cawdrey to Johnson*, p. 72.

21 Starnes and Noyes, *The English Dictionary from Cawdrey to Johnson*, pp. 88, 89.

22 *Ibid.*, p. 102.

23 This entry, alphabetized under "*rolling*," is quoted from the 1766 edition.

24 See Esther K. Sheldon, "Pronouncing Systems in Eighteenth-Century Dictionaries," *Language* 22 (1946), 27–41. Sheldon divides early pronunciation guides into three stages: the first, mere indication of stress; the second, stress placed so as to indicate "long" or "short" vowels; and the third, a diacritical system representing the pronunciation of different vowels and consonants. Bailey progressed to stage 2.

25 Some sources cite Bailey's expanded 1731 edition of *An Universal Etymological Dictionary* as Johnson's source, but James Sledd and Gwin J. Kolb, *Dr. Johnson's Dictionary: Essays in the Biography of a Book* (University of Chicago Press, 1955), p. 4, cite this work, as does Mitford M. Mathews, *A Survey of English Dictionaries* (Oxford University Press, 1933; rpt. New York: Russell & Russell, 1966), p. 28. Bailey's two dictionaries were closely related and published only a year apart.

26 This entry is quoted in Starnes and Noyes, *The English Dictionary from Cawdrey to Johnson*, p. 119.

27 *Ibid.*, pp. 146–47.
28 See Sledd and Kolb, *Dr. Johnson's Dictionary*, pp. 84–104 (especially p. 94), a chapter devoted to a detailed discussion of the *Plan* in its several versions and to Johnson's relationship with Chesterfield.
29 Quoted by Long, "English Dictionaries Before Webster," p. 43.
30 Starnes and Noyes, *The English Dictionary from Cawdrey to Johnson*, pp. 146–63, especially pp. 156–57.
31 The number of entries in Johnson's *Dictionary* is variously reported as 41,443 by Harold B. Allen, cited by J. E. Congleton, "Pronunciation in Johnson's *Dictionary*," in J. E. Congleton, J. Edward Gates, and Donald Hobar (eds.), *Papers on Lexicography in Honor of Warren N. Cordell* (Terre Haute, Ind.: Dictionary Society of North America and Indiana State University, 1979), p. 60; as 43,500 entries by Read, "dictionary," *Encyclopaedia Britannica*; and as 50,000 entries by Frank H. Vizetelly, *The Development of the Dictionary of the English Language* (New York: Funk & Wagnalls, 1923), p. 11. Since Allen's count appears to be actual rather than an estimate, I am inclined to take his figure as the most accurate.
32 Robert Ainsworth's *Thesaurus Linguae Latinae Compendiarius* (1736), a Latin-English dictionary often used by Johnson to cite the existence of terms.
33 I owe this observation to Patrick Hanks, from his lecture, "Samuel Johnson and Modern Lexicography," delivered to the Johnson Society, Lichfield, March 2, 1999.
34 Osselton, *Chosen Words*, p. 95. Reprinted from Robert Ilson (ed.), *Lexicography as an Emerging Profession* (Manchester University Press, 1986). Osselton believes Johnson derived his coverage of phrasal verbs from bilingual dictionaries, because they were not covered by earlier English dictionaries.
35 Sledd and Kolb, *Dr. Johnson's Dictionary*, pp. 42–43.
36 Congleton, "Pronunciation in Johnson's *Dictionary*," p. 73. Congleton credits Johnson with significant innovations in the representation of pronunciation. Sheldon, in her "Pronouncing Systems in Eighteenth-Century Dictionaries," takes a contrary view. Sledd and Kolb, *Dr. Johnson's Dictionary*, p. 34, agree with Sheldon: "Certainly he did not influence the sounds of English, for he did not mark pronunciation."
37 R. W. Chapman, *Lexicography* (Oxford University Press, 1948), p. 13.
38 Sledd and Kolb, *Dr. Johnson's Dictionary*, pp. 134–41.
39 *A Universal and Critical Dictionary of the English Language*, p. lxiv. The allusion is to John Walker. See below, p. 67.
40 Richard Chenevix Trench, *On Some Deficiencies in Our English Dictionaries* (London, 1857). Dean Trench's two talks before the Philological Society, published under this title, are usually credited with providing the key stimulus for formulating plans that led to the development of the *OED*. Trench's specific criticisms and recommendations are discussed below in connection with the *OED*.
41 My chief sources of information on eighteenth-century pronouncing dictionaries are two articles by Sheldon: "Pronouncing Systems in Eighteenth-

Century Dictionaries," pp. 27–41, and "Walker's Influence on the Pronunciation of English," *Publications of the Modern Language Association (PMLA)* 62 (1947), 130–46. Any opinions expressed, however, unless specifically attributed to others, are my own.

42 Sheldon, "Walker's Influence," p. 146; quoted from a 1928 textbook based on Walker.

43 See Richard L. Venezky, "From Webster to Rice to Roosevelt: The Formative Years for Spelling Instruction and Spelling Reform in the USA," in Uta Frith (ed.), *Cognitive Processes in Spelling* (London: Academic Press, 1979), pp. 9–30.

44 "Noah Webster," *The Columbia Encyclopedia*, Fifth Edition, ed. Barbara A. Chernow and George A. Vallasi (New York: Columbia University Press, 1993), p. 2942.

45 Joseph H. Friend, *The Development of American Lexicography 1798–1864* (The Hague: Mouton, 1967), p. 15. Webster's was not the first dictionary to be published in America. That distinction belongs to Samuel Johnson, Jr. (no relation to Dr. Johnson), whose small dictionary of about 4,000 vocabulary items, *A School Dictionary*, was published in 1798 in New Haven, Connecticut. I am much indebted to Friend's monograph for its detailed analysis of Webster's work and especially for its sensitive description of the conflict between Webster and Worcester, and their publishers.

46 Friend, *The Development of American Lexicography*, p. 23.

47 Sledd and Kolb, *Dr. Johnson's Dictionary*, p. 198.

48 Friend, *The Development of American Lexicography*, p. 55. The examples cited above are taken from Friend.

49 George Philip Krapp, *The English Language in America*, vol. I, p. 363. Cited in part by Friend, *The Development of American Lexicography*, p. 35. After comparing the faults of Webster's dictionary of 1828 with those of Joseph Worcester's *Comprehensive Pronouncing and Explanatory Dictionary* of 1830, Krapp concludes (p. 372) that "the totals are greatly in favor of Worcester. One must conclude that the success of Webster has been due largely to judicious editing, manufacturing and selling."

50 Friend, *The Development of American Lexicography*, p. 85.

51 James R. Hulbert, *Dictionaries: British and American*, rev. edn. (London: Andre Deutsch, 1968), pp. 31–32.

52 Friend, *The Development of American Lexicography*, pp. 102–03.

53 The G. & C. Merriam Co. of Springfield, Mass., had bought the Webster interests along with the 1841 edition from an Amherst firm that had acquired them from Webster's heirs: Friend, *The Development of American Lexicography*, p. 82n. The company name was later changed to Merriam-Webster.

54 See John D. Battenburg, "Pioneer in English Lexicography for Language Learners: Michael Philip West," *Dictionaries: Journal of the Dictionary Society of North America* 15 (1994), 132–48. Battenburg provides a full account of West's position in the vocabulary control movement and his eventually

antagonistic relationship with Charles Ogden, who devised a "Basic English" vocabulary of 850 words, and discusses the features of *The New Method English Dictionary.*

55 For information about Hornby's life and an account of his many contributions to ESL/EFL, see A. P. Cowie, "A. S. Hornby, 1898–1998: A Centenary Tribute," *International Journal of Lexicography* 11:4 (December 1998), 252–68.

56 See Michael Rundell, "Recent Trends in English Pedagogical Lexicography," *International Journal of Lexicography* 11:4 (December 1998), 315–42, for a summary of recent developments. The innovations of *LDOCE* are discussed on pp. 318–20.

57 A. P. Cowie, "Phraseological Dictionaries: Some East-West Comparisons," in A. P. Cowie (ed.), *Phraseology: Theory, Analysis, and Applications* (Oxford: Clarendon Press, 1998), p. 220. I found the entire paper, pp. 209–29, helpful; it describes Russian influences on Western phraseological lexicography.

58 Sledd and Kolb, *Dr. Johnson's Dictionary*, p. 183.

59 The search for a single, unitary meaning for each distinct form of a word has never entirely gone out of style, though it remains an aberrant branch of linguistic research. Modern exponents include Charles Ruhl, *On Monosemy: A Study in Linguistic Semantics* (Albany: State University Press of New York, 1989). Much of the work of Anna Wierzbicka, while not embracing monosemy as such, posits universal or quasi-universal meanings associated with every word. No modern language scholar, however, would link monosemy to etymology as Horne Tooke did.

60 There is an uncanny parallel between Trench's call of 1857 and the collaborative effort nearly 150 years later, using a new technology, to assemble the British National Corpus for the same purposes. See Ch. 6, p. 288.

61 The characterization of Furnivall is based on K. M. Elisabeth Murray's in *Caught in the Web of Words*. He was apparently both infuriating and charming. Too impatient to be an editor, he was nonetheless a driving force in the early years of the dictionary.

62 In the history of citation reading, the curious case of Dr. William Minor, who contributed thousands of quotations to the *Oxford English Dictionary*, is prominent. The story is entertainingly recounted in Simon Winchester's *The Professor and the Madman* (published in the UK under the title *The Surgeon of Crowthorne*) (New York: HarperCollins, 1998).

63 Martin J. Wiener, *English Culture and the Decline of the Industrial Spirit, 1850–1980* (Cambridge University Press, 1981), p. 17.

64 According to Friend, *The Development of American Lexicography*, p. 86, Webster's son-in-law, Chauncey Goodrich, published a dictionary called *Pictorial Quarto Unabridged* in 1859. Even in this period, critics complained about the ceaseless competition among dictionaries to add entries. In 1865 Henry B. Wheatley lamented the inclusion of many useless additions to dictionaries and wrote that each succeeding lexicographer prides himself "upon having added so many thousand more words than are in any other work of the

kind," specifically citing technological and scientific words: Wheatley, "Chronological Notices of the Dictionaries of the English Language," *Transactions* (1865), 292–93.

65 Whitney, *The Century Dictionary* (1889), vol. I, p. v.

66 Funk, *A Standard Dictionary of the English Language* (1893), p. vii.

67 Read, "dictionary," *Encyclopaedia Britannica*.

68 Robert Burchfield, *Unlocking the English Language* (London, Faber & Faber, 1989), p. 88.

69 *LEXeter Newsletter* 10 (July 1992) (Dictionary Research Centre, Department of Applied Linguistics, University of Exeter), 2, reported by Joan Dicks.

70 Erich Segal, *Times Literary Supplement*, December 11, 1992, 12.

71 Personal communication from Robert Barnhart, Dec. 15, 1999.

72 The account of the history of American college dictionaries is based in part on Sidney I. Landau, "The American College Dictionaries," *International Journal of Lexicography* 7:4 (Winter 1994), 311–51. It is used here with permission of Oxford University Press.

73 This actually overstates the number of students, since I am using figures for 1899–1900. There are no data available for the year 1898.

74 The years 1995–96 are the latest years for which statistics are available at this time. The US population figure is an estimate for September 1995 by the US Census Bureau, the last numerical census having been in 1990.

75 Only the American Heritage line of dictionaries has not succumbed to the appeal of *Webster*, but Houghton Mifflin, the publisher of the American Heritage dictionaries, also publishes *Webster's II New College Dictionary* (1999) and the *Webster's II New Riverside* line of dictionaries.

76 The *Thorndike-Century Senior Dictionary* (1941) was the first dictionary to use the schwa.

77 Laurence Urdang, "Review of *The American Heritage Dictionary of the English Language*, Third Edition," *International Journal of Lexicography* 6:2 (Summer 1993), 131–32.

78 The vicissitudes of the usage panels have been well documented, and subjected to critical scrutiny, by Thomas J. Creswell, *Usage in Dictionaries and Dictionaries of Usage*, Publication of the American Dialect Society Nos. 63–64 (Tuscaloosa: University of Alabama Press, 1975); and Thomas Creswell and Virginia McDavid, "The Usage Panel in *The American Heritage Dictionary, Second College Edition*," in William Frawley and Roger Steiner (eds.), *Advances in Lexicography*, Papers in Linguistics, 18, no. 1 (Edmonton, Alberta: Boreal Scholarly Publishers, 1986).

79 Allen Walker Read reminds us in his unpublished paper, "An Obscenity Symbol after Four Decades," given at the University of Louisville, Kentucky (May 7, 1976) that *The Penguin English Dictionary*, a British paperback dictionary published in 1965, included an entry for *fuck*. However, this work did not have nearly the popularity of *AHD*.

80 It is worth noting that Laurence Urdang, the distinguished American lexicographer, was editorial director of the first edition of the *Collins English*

Dictionary. Patrick Hanks was the editor, Thomas Hill Long the managing editor.

81 The licensing of electronic rights is a major source of income for some print publishers already, and will certainly become even more important in the years ahead. For example, the spell-checker used for Microsoft Word was first licensed by Houghton Mifflin, publisher of the American Heritage dictionaries, but was later superseded by a spell-checker based on the *Encarta World English Dictionary (EWED)*, the digital version of which was sold to Microsoft. This version of *EWED* is also included with some Microsoft software.

82 However, in the future, access to electronic dictionaries may be available by other means. See Włodzimierz Sobkowiak, *Pronunciation in EFL Machine-Readable Dictionaries* (Poznan, Poland: Motivex, 1999), who describes the advantages of phonetically accessible electronic dictionaries for foreign learners. Access could be by "using phonetic search keys rather than spelling" (p. 71). Ultimately, through automatic speech recognition and speech synthesis, the user may be able to say a word and get a menu of possible candidates, choose one, then see the entry and hear its pronunciation.

3 KEY ELEMENTS OF DICTIONARIES AND OTHER LANGUAGE REFERENCES

1 For a scholarly and entertaining account of the reform spelling movement in America, see Richard L.Venezky, "From Webster to Rice to Roosevelt: The Formative Years for Spelling Instruction and Spelling Reform in the USA," in Uta Frith (ed.), *Cognitive Processes in Spelling* (London: Academic Press, 1979), pp. 9–30.

2 James R. Hulbert, *Dictionaries: British and American*, rev. edn. (London: Andre Deutsch, 1968), p. 49.

3 Samuel E. Martin, "Selection and Presentation of Ready Equivalents in a Translation Dictionary," in Fred W. Householder and Sol Saporta (eds.), *Problems in Lexicography* (Bloomington: Indiana University; The Hague: Mouton, 1967), p. 157.

4 See, for example, Franz Josef Hausmann and Herbert Ernst Wiegand, "Component Parts and Structures of General Monolingual Dictionaries: A Survey," in Franz Josef Hausmann, Oskar Reichmann, Herbert Ernst Wiegand, and Ladislav Zgusta (eds.), *Wörterbucher, Dictionaries, Dictionnaires: Ein internationales Handbuch zur Lexikographie, An International Encyclopedia of Lexicography, Encyclopédie internationale de Lexicographie*, 3 vols. (Berlin: Walter de Gruyter, 1989–91), vol. I, pp. 328–60.

5 See L. V. Malakhovski, "Homonyms in English Dictionaries," in R. W. Burchfield (ed.), *Studies in Lexicography* (Oxford: Clarendon Press, 1987), pp. 36–51, for a description of the various ways dictionaries treat homonymy. The author remarks, "There are still no clear definitions of the main concepts of homonymy" (p. 36).

6 R. H. Robins, "Polysemy and the Lexicographer," in Burchfield (ed.), *Studies in Lexicography*, cites the three senses of "charge": to "charge (load) a gun, charge the enemy, and charge the bill," which, though etymologically from the same source, are very different in meaning.

7 Ladislav Zgusta, *Manual of Lexicography* (The Hague: Mouton; Prague: Academia, 1971), p. 74.

8 Robins, "Polysemy and the Lexicographer," p. 57.

9 Malakhovski, "Homonyms in English Dictionaries," p. 40.

10 See Yakov Malkiel, "A Typological Classification of Dictionaries on the Basis of Distinctive Features," in Householder and Saporta (eds.), *Problems in Lexicography*, p. 9

11 See Landau, "Of Matters Lexicographical," *American Speech* 49:3–4 (Fall-Winter 1974), 241–44.

12 Alexandre Manuila (ed.), *Progress in Medical Terminology* (Basel: S. Karger, 1981), p. 10. As a result of this situation, the *International Nomenclature of Diseases* was initiated in 1968 under the direction of Dr. Manuila to establish a uniform nomenclature of diseases. The effort is sponsored by the Council for International Organizations of Medical Sciences (CIOMS) and funded in part by the World Health Organization, in part by grants from participating governments.

13 These criteria follow Manuila, *Progress in Medical Terminology*, pp. 19–22.

14 See Sidney Landau, "Dictionary Entry Count," *RQ* 4:1 (September 1964), 6, 13–15. So far as I know, this remains the only published account describing in any detail how dictionaries count entries. The US government's General Services Administration's guidelines for purchases of dictionaries (Federal Specification G-D-331D, issued in revised form June 28, 1974) includes some description of entry counting, but it is sketchy and incomplete. The information was based on the recommendations of commercial lexicographers, including me, following several hearings in the 1960s, but much of the material was written in 1942.

15 See, for example, Douglas Biber (ed.), *Longman Grammar of Spoken and Written English* (Harlow: Longman, 1999).

16 Samuel E. Martin, "Selection and Presentation of Ready Equivalents in a Translation Dictionary," in Householder and Saporta (eds.), *Problems in Lexicography*, p. 157.

17 John Sinclair, *Corpus, Concordance, Collocation* (Oxford University Press, 1991), pp. 81–98.

18 The phonemic systems used by American dictionaries are based on the pioneering work of George L. Trager and Henry Lee Smith, *An Outline of English Structure*, Studies in Linguistics: Occasional Papers 3 (Washington, D.C.: American Council of Learned Societies, 1957; first ptg. 1951). For a discussion of the phonemic systems based on Trager-Smith, see Arthur Bronstein, *The Pronunciation of American English* (New York: Appleton-Century-Crofts, 1960), pp. 311–16. Bronstein gives an admirably clear description of the articulations of speech sounds in American English.

19 See Arthur Bronstein (ed.), *Conference Papers on American English and the International Phonetic Alphabet*, Publication of the American Dialect Society No. 80 (Tuscaloosa: University of Alabama Press, 1998). The panel discussion of lexicographers, "Should We Change the Ways We Represent Pronunciation in American English Dictionaries?" is on pp. 107–20. The conference at which the panel discussion took place was held at the University of California at Berkeley on May 6, 1989.

20 Hulbert, *Dictionaries: British and American*, p. 54.

21 A. C. Gimson, "Phonology and the Lexicographer," in Raven I. McDavid, Jr., and Audrey R. Duckert (eds.), *Lexicography in English* (New York Academy of Sciences, 1973), p. 119. The McDavid and Duckert book is a most valuable collection of papers presented at a conference held in New York on June 8, 1973.

22 For example, see Clarence L. Barnhart, "American Lexicography," *American Speech* 53:2 (Summer 1978), 110, where the author quotes approvingly the criticisms of Robert L. Chapman and R. W. Burchfield. See Chapman, "A Working Lexicographer Appraises *Webster's Third New International Dictionary*," *American Speech* 42 (1967), 202–10.

23 T. Magay, "Problems in Indicating Pronunciation in Bilingual Dictionaries with English as the Source Language," in R. R. K. Hartmann (ed.), *Dictionaries and Their Users*, Exeter Linguistic Series No. 4 (University of Exeter, 1979), p. 99.

24 Hulbert, *Dictionaries: British and American*, p. 55.

25 See Sidney I. Landau, Review of Judy Pearsall (ed.), *The New Oxford Dictionary of English*, in the *International Journal of Lexicography* 12:3 (September 1999), 250–57.

26 Thomas Pyles and John Algeo, *The Origins and Development of the English Language*, 4th edn. (Fort Worth: Harcourt Brace Jovanovich, 1993), pp. 239–40.

27 Manuila, *Progress in Medical Terminology*, p. 107.

28 De Witt T. Starnes and Gertrude E. Noyes, *The English Dictionary from Cawdrey to Johnson, 1604–1755* (Chapel Hill: University of North Carolina Press, 1946), p. 102.

29 Patrick Drysdale, "Dictionary Etymologies: What? Why? and for Whom?," in Gillian Michell (ed.), *Papers of the Dictionary Society of North America 1979* (London, Ontario: The School of Library and Information Science, University of Western Ontario, 1981), p. 45. The author makes the identical points in Drysdale, "Etymological Information in the General Monolingual Dictionary," in Hausmann *et al.* (eds.), *Wörterbucher*, vol. I, pp. 525–30. See also Louis G. Heller, "Lexicographic Etymology: Practice versus Theory," *American Speech* 40 (1965), 113–19, for examples of the deficiencies of etymologies in current dictionaries.

30 P. ix. This passage is quoted verbatim except that where the author has abbreviated language designations I have written them in full. The symbol (þ) is an Old English character called the *thorn*, representing the sound of *th*,

either voiced or voiceless. The digraph *th* was used in the earliest English texts but was replaced by the thorn from about 900 to 1400. The Old English character *eth* (ð), also used to represent the *th* sound, is used in the IPA to represent the voiced *th*, as in *this*.

31 Skeat, *An Etymological Dictionary of the English Language*, p. xxviii.

32 Barnhart, "American Lexicography," *American Speech* 53:2 (Summer 1978), 113.

33 Patrick Drysdale, "Dictionary Etymologies," in Michell (ed.), *Papers of the Dictionary Society of North America 1979*, p. 47. The same points are made in Drysdale, "Etymological Information in the General Monolingual Dictionary," in Hausmann *et al.* (eds.), *Wörterbucher*, vol. I, pp. 525–30.

34 See, for example, Pyles and Algeo, *The Origins and Development of the English Language*; Albert H. Marckwardt, *American English*, second edn, revised by J. L. Dillard (Oxford University Press, 1980); and John Algeo (ed.), *Fifty Years Among the New Words: A Dictionary of Neologisms, 1941–1991* (Cambridge University Press, 1991).

35 Drysdale, "Etymological Information in the General Monolingual Dictionary," in Hausmann *et al.* (eds.), *Wörterbucher*, vol. I, p. 526.

36 Yakov Malkiel, *Etymology* (Cambridge University Press, 1993), pp. 167–68. The quotation is from the Preface, p. xi.

37 Taylor, *English Synonyms Discriminated*, pp. 98 and 99, respectively.

38 Zgusta, *Manual of Lexicography*, pp. 89–118.

39 I managed and contributed to the preparation of this work by the Funk & Wagnalls dictionary staff in cooperation with Hayakawa, who is listed as the editor along with the dictionary staff. The rights to the book were sold to Reader's Digest and subsequently to other publishers, and the original essays, supplemented by new ones, have appeared in revised form under many different titles.

40 Robert L. Chapman (ed.), *Roget's International Thesaurus*, Fifth Edition, p. xi.

41 *Thesauri*, also used as a plural, seems to me both pedantic and un-English.

42 Zgusta, *Manual of Lexicography*, pp. 294–344, especially pp. 294–97 and 312–25.

43 Michael Hancher, "Illustrations," in the Centennial Celebration of *The Century Dictionary* in *Dictionaries: Journal of the Dictionary Society of North America* 17 (1996), 79–115.

44 See, for example, Hulbert, *Dictionaries: British and American*, p. 85; and R. W. Chapman, *Lexicography* (Oxford University Press, 1948), pp. 21–24. Hulbert writes, "As to pictures, it is so inane to point out that at a glance a picture makes many subjects . . . clearer than many words can do, that I blush to do so."

45 Zgusta, *Manual of Lexicography*, p. 256.

4 DEFINITION

1 The best modern work on the subject is Richard Robinson's *Definition* (Oxford: Clarendon Press, 1965; first edn. 1954)

2 A. J. Aitken, "Definitions and Citations in a Period Dictionary," in Raven I. McDavid, Jr., and Audrey R. Duckert (eds.), *Lexicography in English* (New York Academy of Sciences, 1973), p. 259.

3 For example, see "Forum on the Theory and Practice of Lexicography," organized by William Frawley in *Dictionaries: Journal of the Dictionary Society of North America* 14 (1992/93), pp. 1–159, in which a practical lexicographer, B. T. S. Atkins, and a theoretical lexicologist, Anna Wierzbicka, present their views, and six other practicing lexicographers or academic scholars provide critical commentary.

4 C. K. Ogden and I. A. Richards, *The Meaning of Meaning* (New York: Harcourt Brace Jovanovich, 1923), p. 11.

5 Ladislav Zgusta, *Manual of Lexicography* (The Hague: Mouton; Prague: Academia, 1971), p. 34.

6 *Ibid.*, pp. 38–39.

7 See David B. Guralnik, "Connotation in Dictionary Definition," *College Composition and Communication* 9:2 (May 1958), 90–93. Dictionaries do attempt to recognize connotation if it is widely understood by users of the language, as Guralnik shows, by incorporating it in the definition or by adding a usage note or label. Illustrative examples, too, are valuable in showing connotation.

8 Zgusta, *Manual of Lexicography*, pp. 257–58.

9 Philip Babcock Gove, *The Role of the Dictionary* (Indianapolis: Bobbs-Merrill, 1957), pp. 9–14.

10 See Sidney I. Landau, Review of the *Encarta World English Dictionary*, in *Dictionaries* 21 (2000), 112–24.

11 Patrick Hanks, "To What Extent Does a Dictionary Definition Define?" in R. R. K. Hartmann (ed.), *Dictionaries and Their Users*, Exeter Linguistic Series No. 4 (University of Exeter, 1979), p. 36.

12 See, for example, Michael Rundell, "Recent Trends in English Pedagogical Lexicography," *International Journal of Lexicography* 11:4 (December 1998), 330–31.

13 See Landau, "Of Matters Lexicographical," *American Speech* 49:3–4 (Fall-Winter 1974), 241–44, especially p. 243. See also Sidney I. Landau, "Popular Meanings of Scientific and Technical Terms," *American Speech* 55:3 (Fall 1980), 204–9. The point is also addressed in Kemp Malone, "On Defining Mahogany," *Language* 16:4 (1940), 308–18, discussed below.

14 Landau, "Of Matters Lexicographical," p. 242. Robinson uses the terms *lexical* and *stipulative definitions* for my *extracted* and *imposed definitions*, respectively. His discussion of stipulative definitions is full of keen insights into the nature of scientific definition. See his *Definition*, pp. 59–92, especially pp. 66–80 on the advantages and disadvantages of this kind of definition.

15 Barnhart, "American Lexicography," *American Speech* 53:2 (Summer 1978), 124.

16 Augustine, *Confessions*, trans. R. S. Pine-Coffin (Harmondsworth, Middx.: Penguin Books, 1961), p. 264.

17 Robinson, *Definition*, p. 124.

18 *Ibid.*, p. 56.
19 See Sidney I. Landau, Review of *The New Oxford Dictionary of English*, in the *International Journal of Lexicography* 12:3 (September 1999), 250–57.
20 H. Bosley Woolf, "Definition: Practice and Illustration," in McDavid and Duckert (eds.), *Lexicography in English*, p. 256.
21 Alexandre Manuila (ed.), *Progress in Medical Terminology* (Basel: S. Karger, 1981), pp. 110–12.
22 W. Nelson Francis, "Language Corpora, B.C.," in Jan Svartvik (ed.), *Directions in Corpus Linguistics: Proceedings of Nobel Symposium 82* (held in Stockholm, Sweden, 1991) (Berlin: Mouton de Gruyter, 1992), p. 22. The "B.C." in the title refers to "before computers." Francis points out that many corpora of English were assembled before the computer. He also reveals that in an effort to capture ordinary language, on the advice of W. Freeman Twaddell, Merriam-Webster at one time collected the tenth word of the first line of each page from which citations had been collected, excluding function words. This was a clever way to build a corpus, but extremely labor-intensive compared to an electronic corpus.
23 Scientific and technical dictionaries will continue to rely on the consensus of experts or the authorized definitions of an official organization, though even here the use of corpora is likely to be more helpful than citation collections in revealing extensions of meaning and competing usages. The corpus is extremely important in bilingual lexicography, where it can provide much help in translation; corpus linguistics, discussed in Chapter 6, has also led to major advances in machine translation.
24 *New York Times*, September 1, 1999, A4.
25 Allen Walker Read, "Approaches to Lexicography and Semantics," in Thomas Sebeok (ed.), *Current Trends in Linguistics* (The Hague: Mouton, 1973), vol. X, p. 171.
26 It also has consequences for the way we perceive reality, for in slicing up meaning one is implicitly expressing a view of reality. The unanswered question is, "Which comes first?" To what extent does the way we slice up meaning influence the way we perceive the world? The interaction between language and reality has been most notably analyzed by Benjamin Lee Whorf in a series of essays written in the late 1930s and early 1940s, based on his studies of Indian languages of the Americas. See especially *Language, Thought, and Reality* (Cambridge, Mass.: MIT Press, 1956).
27 Woolf, "Definition," p. 257.
28 Geart van der Meer, "Metaphors and Dictionaries: the Morass of Meaning, or How to Get Two Ideas for One," *International Journal of Lexicography* 12:3 (September 1999), 196–208.
29 Barnhart, "American Lexicography," *American Speech* 53:2 (Summer 1978), 99.
30 *New York Times*, February 11, 2000, C6.
31 Robert Burchfield, *Unlocking the English Language* (London: Faber & Faber, 1989), p. 173. The lines of verse quoted are: "Margaret, are you grieving / Over Goldengrove unleaving."

32 Vladimir Nabokov, letter to Walter Minton, March 7, 1958, displayed in an exhibit at the New York Public Library, June 1999.

33 Zgusta, *Manual of Lexicography*, p. 46.

34 This is apt to change in the years ahead, as more and more speech is transcribed and included in corpora. More attention is given to speech in ESL dictionaries than in other kinds of dictionaries, because the ability to understand the spoken language and to produce speech are fundamental parts of the English language-teaching curriculum, but ESL dictionaries too depend mainly on the written language.

35 "On Defining mahogany," *Language* 16:4 (1940), 308–18. The quotation is from page 312. Its innocent use of "man," standard for its time, strikes us now painfully, and illustrates how dramatically attitudes towards language have changed.

36 *Ibid.*, p. 313.

37 John Willinsky's *Empire of Words: The Reign of the OED* (Princeton University Press, 1994) makes the case that the *OED*'s citational evidence is elitist and excluded the usages of various nonpreferred groups, accusing the *OED* editorial team of "betrayal of its historical principles." Willinsky acknowledges this criticism is "to read their work in light of current concerns with issues such as gender, disenfranchised classes, and power," but says "these issues were hardly absent from the period in which the dictionary was edited" (p. 177). This is a dubious contention at best. I am not convinced that he has made his case about the extent of the *OED*'s exclusivity, and I am uncomfortable about applying contemporary social attitudes retrospectively. I do not believe we should denounce Kemp Malone as sexist because he used generic "man" in 1940.

38 Zgusta, *Manual of Lexicography*, p. 265.

39 John Sinclair, *Corpus, Concordance, Collocation* (Oxford University Press, 1991), p. 4.

40 See Gwin J. Kolb and Ruth A. Kolb, "The Selection and Use of Illustrative Quotations in Dr. Johnson's *Dictionary*," in Howard D. Weinbrot (ed.), *New Aspects of Lexicography* (Carbondale: Southern Illinois University Press, 1972), pp. 61–72. See also Allen Reddick, *The Making of Johnson's Dictionary, 1746–1773* (Cambridge University Press, 1990), p. 97: "If suitable, he marked the passage, probably amended the wording, wrote a number indicating the meaning under which it was to be inserted."

41 Quoted from *The Newbury House Dictionary of American English* (1996).

42 *NTC's American English Learner's Dictionary* (1998).

43 *NTC's American English Learner's Dictionary* and *The Newbury House Dictionary*, respectively.

44 Gwyneth Fox, "The Case for Examples," in J. M. Sinclair (ed.), *Looking Up: An Account of the COBUILD Project in Lexical Computing and the Development of the Collins COBUILD English Language Dictionary* (London: Collins, 1987), p. 141.

45 R. W. Chapman, *Lexicography* (Oxford University Press, 1948), p. 28.

46 *Times Literary Supplement*, January 7, 1977, 13.

47 For example, *Encarta World English Dictionary* includes a second, generic def.

for *Watergate*: "a public scandal involving politicians or officials abusing power, especially if a cover-up is also attempted."

48 In this connection, Jonathan Lighter's *Random House Historical Dictionary of American Slang* (1994–) is invaluable.

5 USAGE

1 N. E. Osselton, "Some Problems of Obsolescence in Bilingual Dictionaries," in R. R. K. Hartmann (ed.), *Dictionaries and Their Users*, Exeter Linguistic Series No. 4 (University of Exeter, 1979), pp. 120–26.

2 Fred R. Shapiro, "A Study in Computer-Assisted Lexicology: Evidence on the Emergence of *hopefully* as a Sentence Adverb from the JSTOR Journal Archive and Other Electronic Resources," *American Speech* 73:3 (Fall 1998), 285–86. See also Ch. 6, pp. 293–94, for information about other historical corpora.

3 Harold B. Allen, "Introductory Remarks," in Raven I. McDavid and Audrey R. Duckert (eds.), *Lexicography in English* (New York Academy of Sciences, 1973), p. 50.

4 Randolph Quirk, Sidney Greenbaum, Geoffrey Leech, and Jan Svartvik, *A Grammar of Contemporary English* (London: Longman, 1972), p. 15.

5 Audrey Duckert, "Regional and Social Dialects," in McDavid and Duckert (eds.), *Lexicography in English*, p. 51.

6 For example, the *Linguistic Atlas of New England, Word Geography of the Eastern United States, Linguistic Atlas of the Upper Midwest, Linguistic Atlas of the Gulf States*. For a survey of regional dialectology in the US, see Harold B. Allen, "Regional Dialects, 1945–1974," *American Speech* 52:3–4 (Fall-Winter 1977), 163–261. For an excellent overview of regional variation in all major countries and regions where English is spoken, see David Crystal, *The Cambridge Encyclopedia of the English Language* (Cambridge University Press, 1995), pp. 298–363. Lawrence M. Davis, *English Dialectology: An Introduction* (University, Ala.: University of Alabama Press, 1983), pp. 16–68, provides a useful introduction to studies in the US and in Britain; Walt Wolfram, *Dialects and American English* (Englewood Cliffs, N.J.: Prentice Hall, 1991) is a basic text dealing with all kinds of language variation, including regional variation.

7 Edward Gates, "Should a Dictionary Include Only the 'good' Words," in Karl Hyldgaard-Jensen and Arne Zettersten (eds.), *Symposium in Lexicography V*, Lexicographical Series Major 43 (Tübingen: Niemeyer, 1992) says *NID3*'s treatment of *ain't* was based on reports of dialectologists, including that of E. B. Atwood, *A Survey of Verb Forms in the Eastern United States* (Ann Arbor: University of Michigan Press, 1953), which showed that the phrase *ain't I?* was used by three fifths of cultured informants in New England and by nearly one third of the cultured informants in the Middle and South Atlantic states.

8 The state populations used are those of the 1960 national census, which accurately reflected the distribution of the population during the period

1965–70 when fieldworkers were sent out to complete the questionnaires. *DARE* tries to account for population shifts by including recent citations and by commenting that a term has spread beyond the region reported in the 1960s.

9 The American Dialect Society has published indexes by region, usage, and etymology to the three volumes of *DARE* published to date. Thus one can easily find all the entries used chiefly by Black speakers or by young or old people, as well as entries limited to a particular region or originating from a particular language. These are *An Index by Region, Usage, and Etymology to the Dictionary of American Regional English, Volumes I and II*, Publication of the American Dialect Society, Number 77 (Tuscaloosa: University of Alabama Press, 1993) and *An Index by Region, Usage, and Etymology to the Dictionary of American Regional English, Volume III*, ed. Luanne von Schneidemesser, Publication of the American Dialect Society, Number 82 (Durham, N.C.: Duke University Press, 1999).

10 Herbert C. Morton, letter in the *New York Review of Books*, January 12, 1995, 53. Morton is the author of *The Story of Webster's Third: Philip Gove's Controversial Dictionary and Its Critics* (Cambridge University Press, 1994).

11 Jesse Sheidlower (ed.), *The F Word* (New York: Random House, first edn. 1995, second edn. 1999).

12 Allen Walker Read, "An Obscenity Symbol," *American Speech* 9:4 (December 1934), 264–78.

13 Sidney I. Landau, "*sexual intercourse* in American College Dictionaries," *Verbatim* 1:1 (undated, issued June 1974), 4–5. Reissued in *Verbatim: Volumes I & II* (Stein and Day, 1978), pp. 9–12.

14 Edward B. Jenkinson, "How to Keep Dictionaries out of the Public Schools," *Verbatim* 5:4 (Spring 1979), 12.

15 For example: "The American Heritage Dictionary was removed from school libraries and classrooms in Eldon, Mo., because of objectionable definitions it offered for such words as 'bed,' 'tail,' and 'nut'" (*New York Times*, April 5, 1982, C-11). It may have been for that reason that Houghton Mifflin, the publishers of American Heritage dictionaries, produced a dictionary purged of all taboo, *Webster's II New Riverside University Dictionary*, two years later in 1984.

16 Julia Stanley reported in "Homosexual Slang," *American Speech* 45:1–2 (Spring/Summer 1970), 45–59, that "Of these four terms [*queer, fairy, faggot*, and *swish*], *queer* was cited by homosexuals as the one that has the strongest connotations of distaste or disgust," and the word was considered "the worst that could be used." Yet until 1978 no dictionary other than *Doubleday* labeled it as contemptuous or offensive in this sense.

17 These and other terms are cited in Sidney I. Landau, Review of the *Encarta World English Dictionary*, in *Dictionaries: Journal of the Dictionary Society of North America* 21 (2000), pp. 112–24.

18 *Washington Post*, October 8, 1997, A16.

19 Full treatment to *nigger* is indeed given in Jonathan Lighter's *Random House*

Historical Dictionary of American Slang, with copious examples in various senses, including a number in Black English.

20 *New York Times*, December 15, 1998, B3.

21 *New York Times*, February 4, 1999, A18.

22 Lighter, *Random House Historical Dictionary of American Slang*, pp. xi–xii. Lighter's introduction, which should be required reading for anyone interested in slang, also includes a brief history of slang. Jonathon Green, *Chasing the Sun: Dictionary Makers and the Dictionaries They Made* (New York: Henry Holt, 1996), provides much historical information about slang dictionaries and their makers on pp. 139–70 and 402–39. His comment about Lighter's advantages (p. 433) compared to Partridge do not do justice to the sacrifices Lighter made over many years, with little help and little money, and no guarantee of eventual publication, to bring his dictionary to completion.

23 James B. McMillan, "Five College Dictionaries," *College English* 10:4 (January 1949), 214–21.

24 Thomas J. Creswell, *Usage in Dictionaries and Dictionaries of Usage*, Publication of the American Dialect Society Nos. 63–64 (Tuscaloosa: University of Alabama Press, 1975), p. 85.

25 Morton, *The Story of Webster's Third*, p. 136.

26 Morton admits that Gove's failure to present any convincing rationale for cutting back on the slang label invited criticism. *Ibid.*, p. 137.

27 Jonathan Lighter, "Some Problems of Documentation in Slang Dictionaries," unpublished paper presented at the American Dialect Society meeting in New York City in December 1981. Lighter cited entries such as *ABC's*, *AWOL*, spelling pronunciations like *az iz* (for *as is*), and journalistic inventions such as *circuit clout* (for *home run*), as examples of nonslang terms found in slang dictionaries.

28 John S. Kenyon, "Cultural Levels and Functional Varieties of English," *College English* 10:1 (October 1948), 31–36.

29 Martin Joos, *The Five Clocks* (New York: Harcourt Brace Jovanovich, 1967; first edn. 1961). The quotation is from p. 7.

30 Bergen Evans and Cornelia Evans, *A Dictionary of Contemporary American Usage* (New York: Random House, 1957), p. vii.

31 Joos, *The Five Clocks*, p. 32.

32 Philip Babcock Gove, "Lexicography and the Teacher of English," *College English* 25:5 (February 1964), 350.

33 Karl Dykema, "Historical Development of the Concept of Grammatical Proprieties," in Harold B. Allen (ed.), *Readings in Applied English Linguistics* (New York: Appleton-Century-Crofts, 1958), pp. 2–9.

34 Robert C. Pooley, *The Teaching of English Usage*, Second Edition (Urbana, Ill.: National Council of Teachers of English, 1974), p. 8.

35 Quoted in DeWitt T. Starnes and Gertrude E. Noyes, *The English Dictionary from Cawdrey to Johnson 1604–1755* (Chapel Hill: University of North Carolina Press, 1946), p. 55. An obelisk is a symbol now more commonly referred to as an obelus or dagger (†). See also Virginia McDavid, "Dictionary Labels for Usage Levels and Dialects," in J. E. Congleton, J.

Edward Gates, and Donald Hobar. (eds.), *Papers on Lexicography in Honor of Warren N. Cordell* (Terre Haute, Ind.: Dictionary Society of North America and Indiana State University, 1979), pp. 29–30.

36 I am indebted to Edward Finegan's *Attitudes Toward English Usage* (New York: Teachers College, Columbia University, 1980), pp. 18–61, for this discussion of early English and American grammars. See also Dennis E. Baron, *Grammar and Good Taste* (New Haven: Yale University Press, 1982), pp. 119–68, for a survey of English grammars of the seventeenth to nineteenth centuries. Baron discusses usage guides from the seventeenth century to the present as well (pp. 169–241).

37 Quoted by Finegan, *Attitudes Toward English Usage*, pp. 47 and 51, the first example from Murray and the second from Samuel Kirkham.

38 Goold Brown, *The Grammar of English Grammars*, Tenth Edn. (New York: William Wood, 1875), p. 271.

39 Morris Bishop, *AHD* (first edn., 1969), p. xxiii.

40 Thomas Pyles, "Dictionaries and Usage," in John Algeo (ed.), *Thomas Pyles: Selected Essays on English Usage* (Gainesville: University Presses of Florida, 1979), p. 200.

41 Morris Bishop, *AHD* (first edn., 1969), p. xxiv.

42 For an exhaustive survey of this tendency in America, see Allen Walker Read, "American Projects for an Academy to Regulate Speech," *PMLA* 51:4 (December 1936), 1141–79. See also Baron, *Grammar and Good Taste*, pp. 99–118.

43 Geoffrey Nunberg, *AHD4*. The quotations are from pp. xxviii and xxvii, respectively.

44 Albert C. Marckwardt and Fred Walcott, *Facts About Current English Usage* (New York: Appleton-Century-Crofts, 1938).

45 Charles C. Fries, *American English Grammar* (New York: Appleton-Century-Crofts, 1940).

46 Randolph Quirk, *The Use of English*, Second Edition (London: Longman, 1968), p. 87. Quirk makes the astute observation that although most of us remain unfamiliar with the sound of our own voices and are often surprised when we hear ourselves in recordings, we know our handwriting very well (p. 90). Our consciousness of writing makes it much easier to use spelling as a standard rather than speech.

47 Fries, *American English Grammar*, p. 13.

48 William Labov, *The Social Stratification of English in New York City* (Washington, D.C.: Center for Applied Linguistics, 1966). For a detailed description of *Social Stratification* and a critique of Labov's work, see Davis, *English Dialectology*, pp. 87–100, part of a survey of social dialectology, pp. 69–132.

49 *Ibid.*, p. 476.

50 *Ibid.*, p. 478.

51 Pooley, *The Teaching of English Usage*, p. 12. The definition first appeared in Pooley's *Grammar and Usage in Textbooks on English*, Bulletin 14 (Madison: University of Wisconsin Bureau of Educational Research, 1933).

52 The best account of the controversy can be found in Morton, *The Story of*

Webster's Third, pp. 153–264. A contemporary account edited by James Sledd and Wilma R. Ebbitt, *Dictionaries and THAT Dictionary* (Chicago: Scott, Foresman, 1962), is also valuable.

53 Gove, "Lexicography and the Teacher of English," p. 350.
54 See Morton, *The Story of Webster's Third*, pp. 166–67.
55 *Ibid.*, p. 168.
56 Dwight Bolinger, *Language – the Loaded Weapon* (London: Longman, 1980), p. 168.
57 Pooley, *The Teaching of English Usage*, p. 16.
58 William Labov, *The Study of Nonstandard English* (Champaign, Ill.: National Council of Teachers of English, 1970), p. 22. Originally published in 1969 by the Center for Applied Linguistics.
59 Joos, *The Five Clocks*, p. 8.
60 Richard Allsopp addresses these issues with insight in "The Need for Sociolinguistic Determinants for Status-Labelling in a Regional Lexicography," in Donald Hobar (ed.), *Papers of the DSNA 1977* (Terre Haute: Indiana State University, 1982), pp. 64–77. Although his particular concern is Caribbean English, his analysis of status labeling is pertinent. Status labeling, he says, is "inevitably elitist" and "assignment to levels within it will be class-intuitive." Moreover, the homogeneity and stability in language implied by such labeling was probably never justified and certainly is not justified today. The effect on language of sociopolitical changes since the Victorian period has been to emphasize "*social appropriateness of discourse style as the basis of acceptability*" (p. 71, author's italics).
61 J. L. Burton, "The Logic of Dermatological Diagnosis," *Clinical and Experimental Dermatology* 6 (1981), 3.
62 See, for example, Creswell's analysis of *AHD*'s usage notes in *Usage in Dictionaries and Dictionaries of Usage*, especially appendix 5, pp. 193–95.
63 John Algeo, "Grammatical Usage: Modern Shibboleths," in James C. Raymond and I. Willis Russell (eds.), *James B. McMillan: Essays in Linguistics by His Friends and Colleagues* (University, Ala.: University of Alabama Press, 1977), p. 70.
64 Richard A. Lanham, "The Abusage of Usage," *Virginia Quarterly Review* 53:1 (Winter 1977), 47–48.
65 Sutherland's review appeared in the *Times Literary Supplement*, October 23, 1981; the subsequent comment in that of November 13, 1981.
66 Evans and Evans, *A Dictionary of Contemporary American Usage*, p. v.
67 Bryant, *Current American Usage*, p. xxii.
68 Wilson also cites H. A. Gleason, *Linguistics and English Grammar* (New York: Holt, 1965), which enlarged upon Joos' categories, as a direct influence.
69 Garner, *A Dictionary of Modern American Usage*, p. xi.
70 This was the result of a search on the American English subcorpus of the Cambridge International Corpus.
71 I owe this information to Patrick Gillard. I am grateful to him for supplying it.
72 *New York Times*, July 23, 1983, 7.

6 THE CORPUS IN LEXICOGRAPHY

1 B. T. S. Atkins, Beth Levin, and A. Zampoli, "Computational Approaches to the Lexicon: an Overview," in B. T. S. Atkins and A. Zampoli (eds.), *Computational Approaches to the Lexicon* (Oxford University Press, 1994), p. 21, cite a late-nineteenth-century study of the German language consisting of 11 million words.

2 Ernest Horn, *A Basic Writing Vocabulary: 10,000 Words Most Commonly Used in Writing* (Iowa City: College of Education, University of Iowa, 1926), p. 22.

3 Godfrey Dewey, *Relativ Frequency of English Speech Sounds* (Cambridge, Mass.: Harvard University Press, 1923). Reference is made to Whitney's essay on p. 7.

4 A. P. Cowie, "A. S. Hornby, 1898–1998: A Centenary Tribute," *International Journal of Lexicography* 11:4 (December 1998), 254–55.

5 *Ibid.*, p. 255.

6 Graeme Kennedy, "Preferred Ways of Putting Things with Implications for Language Teaching," in Jan Svartvik (ed.), *Directions in Corpus Linguistics: Proceedings of Nobel Symposium 82* (Berlin: Mouton de Gruyter, 1992), pp. 335–73.

7 Michael West (ed.), *A General Service List of English Words* (London: Longmans, Green, 1953). "The General Service List" was originally published as Part V of the *Interim Report* in 1936. The 1953 version utilizes Irving Lorge's *The Semantic Count of the 570 Commonest English Words* (New York: Institute of Psychological Research, Teachers College, Columbia University, 1949).

8 Kennedy, "Preferred Ways of Putting Things," p. 339.

9 *Ibid.*, p. 340.

10 Michael Stubbs, "British Tradition in Text Analysis: From Firth to Sinclair," in Mona Baker, Gill Francis, and Elena Tognini-Bonelli (eds.), *Text and Technology: In Honour of John Sinclair* (Philadelphia: John Benjamins, 1993), p. 3.

11 *Ibid.*

12 Geoffrey Leech, "The State of the Art in Corpus Linguistics," in Karin Aijmer and Bengt Altenberg (eds.), *English Corpus Linguistics: Studies in Honour of Jan Svartvik* (London: Longman, 1991), p. 8.

13 *Ibid.*

14 Geoffrey Leech, "Corpora and Theories of Linguistic Performance," in Svartvik (ed.), *Directions in Corpus Linguistics*, pp. 105–22.

15 Noam Chomsky, Review of *Verbal Behavior*, by B. F. Skinner, *Language* 35:1 (1959), 26–58.

16 *Ibid.*, p. 54. Skinner was just as intolerant of alternative explanations of behavior. He thought that spontaneously generated behavior had as much credibility as spontaneously generated matter.

17 *Ibid.*, p. 56.

18 Richard L. Venezky, "Computer Application in Lexicography," in Raven I. McDavid, Jr., and Audrey R. Duckert (eds.), *Lexicography in English* (New York Academy of Sciences, 1973), p. 290.

19 Henry Kučera and W. Nelson Francis, *Computational Analysis of Present-Day American English* (Providence: Brown University Press, 1967), p. xix.

20 Knut Hofland and Stig Johansson, *Word Frequencies in British and American English* (Bergen: Norwegian Computing Centre for the Humanities, 1982), is the source of this information.

21 Randolph Quirk, Sidney Greenbaum, Geoffrey Leech, and Jan Svartvik, *A Comprehensive Grammar of the English Language* (London: Longman, 1985), p. 33. A number of other grammars have been derived from this work.

22 Graeme Kennedy, *An Introduction to Corpus Linguistics* (London: Longman, 1998), p. 19.

23 Firth, who died in 1960, held the first Chair of General Linguistics in a British university, and was from 1944 at the School of Oriental and African Studies in London. The source of my information about Firth and his linguistic principles is Stubbs, "British Tradition in Text Analysis," pp. 1–33.

24 Quoted by Stubbs, *ibid.*, p. 9, from J. R. Firth, "The Technique of Semantics," *Transactions of the Philological Society* (1935), 36–72.

25 Stubbs, *ibid.*, p. 8. The observation about Quirk's *Grammar* is made by John Sinclair, *Corpus, Concordance, Collocation* (Oxford University Press, 1991), pp. 100–1.

26 M. A. K. Halliday, "Language as System and Language as Instance: The Corpus as a Theoretical Construct," in Svartvik (ed.), *Directions in Corpus Linguistics*, p. 63.

27 Stubbs, "British Traditions in Text Analysis," p. 18.

28 See especially Sinclair, *Corpus, Concordance, Collocation*, Chapter 6, "The Meeting of Lexis and Grammar," pp. 81–98.

29 Patrick Hanks, Review of John Sinclair, *On Lexis and Lexicography*, in the *International Journal of Corpus Linguistics* 2:2 (1997), 290.

30 Geoffrey Leech, "Corpora and Theories of Linguistic Performance," in Svartvik (ed.), *Directions in Corpus Linguistics*, p. 107.

31 Douglas Biber, *Variations Across Speech and Writing* (Cambridge University Press, 1988). This book has been enormously influential in corpus studies especially because of the rigorous statistical standards he applied.

32 Douglas Biber, Susan Conrad, and Randi Reppen, *Corpus Linguistics: Investigating Language Structure and Use* (Cambridge University Press, 1998), p. 3.

33 *Ibid.*

34 *Ibid.*

35 John B. Carroll, Peter Davies, and Barry Richman (eds.), *The American Heritage Word Frequency Book* (Boston: Houghton Mifflin, 1971). Another computerized vocabulary study of over 5 million words, compiled from eight basal reading series, is Albert M. Harris and Milton D. Jacobson (eds.), *Basic Reading Vocabularies* (New York: Macmillan, 1982). It includes "A Short History of Vocabulary Lists," pp. 8–11.

36 Peter Davies, "New Views of Lexicon," in Carroll *et al.* (eds.), *The American Heritage Word Frequency Book*, p. xli.

37 Richard Venezky and Antoinette diPaolo Healey (eds.), *A Microfiche*

Concordance to Old English (Dictionary of Old English Project, Centre for Medieval Studies, University of Toronto, 1980).

38 Jeremy Clear, "Computing," in J. M. Sinclair (ed.), *Looking Up: An Account of the COBUILD Project* (London: Collins, 1987; rev. edn., 1995), p. 47.

39 Kennedy, *An Introduction to Corpus Linguistics*, p. 48.

40 John Sinclair, who is a professor at the University of Birmingham, is a corpus linguist, and lexicographers like Rosamund Moon are getting academic degrees in linguistics. See Rosamund Moon, *Fixed Expressions and Idioms in English: A Corpus-Based Approach* (Oxford: Clarendon Press, 1998), based on the author's doctoral thesis at the University of Birmingham. B. T. S. Atkins, a lexicographer formerly with Oxford University Press, has joined forces with Charles Fillmore, a Stanford University linguist well known for his "frame analysis" studies, to produce several papers. See, for example, "Starting Where the Dictionaries Stop: The Challenge of Corpus Lexicography," in Atkins and Zampoli (eds.), *Computational Approaches to the Lexicon*, pp. 349–93.

41 See Henry Kučera, "The Odd Couple: The Linguist and the Software Engineer, the Struggle for High Quality Computerized Language Aids," in Svartvik (ed.), *Directions in Corpus Linguistics*, pp. 401–20.

42 Kennedy, *An Introduction to Corpus Linguistics*. The quotes are from p. 52 and p. 53, respectively.

43 Sidney I. Landau, "Preface to the Paperback Edition," *Dictionaries: The Art and Craft of Lexicography* (Cambridge University Press, 1989), p. ix.

44 In a personal communication (February 22, 1990), Frederick C. Mish, editorial director of Merriam-Webster, stated that *NID3* "was set in hot metal in the late 1950s and has never existed in machine-readable form," and that his staff would create a machine-readable version of *NID3*, which would be a necessary prerequisite to the creation of an *NID4*. In preparation for the revision of this book, I wrote to Mish again, and in his reply of February 12, 1999, he states, "We are working on a new edition of the unabridged, but still in fairly early stages, and we are not confident enough yet of how the rest of the work will go to project a publication date. It will most certainly not appear within the next two years."

45 *New York Times*, May 18, 1998, A16.

46 The organizing committee consisted of Catherine Macleod (Coordinator) and Ralph Grishman of the Computer Science Department of New York University, Charles Fillmore of Stanford, Nancy Ide of Vassar College, Daniel Jurafsky of the University of Colorado at Boulder, and Mark Liberman, Director of the Linguistic Data Consortium at the University of Pennsylvania. An advisory committee consisting of Frank Abate, Sue Atkins, Lou Burnard, Wendalyn Nichols, and Michael Rundell was also created.

47 See Kennedy, *An Introduction to Corpus Linguistics*, pp. 29–31.

48 Sidney Greenbaum, "The Development of the International Corpus of English," in Aijmer and Altenberg (eds.), *English Corpus Linguistics*, pp. 83–91. See also Kennedy, *An Introduction to Corpus Linguistics*, pp. 54–57.

49 Wallace L. Chafe, John W. Du Bois, and Sandra A. Thompson, "Towards a New Corpus of Spoken American English," in Aijmer and Altenberg (eds.), *English Corpus Linguistics*, pp. 64–82.

50 See Matti Rissanen, "The Diachronic Corpus as a Window to the History of English," in Svartvik (ed.), *Directions in Corpus Linguistics*, pp. 186–205.

51 Biber *et al.*, *Corpus Linguistics*, p. 203.

52 Discussed in *ibid.*, pp. 205–10.

53 All examples are taken from the Cambridge International Corpus, and most involved work done in preparing *CDAE*.

54 Michael Rundell and Penny Stock, "The Corpus Revolution," *English Today* 31 (July 1992), 22.

55 *Ibid.*, pp. 22–23.

56 Michael Rundell, "The Word on the Street," *English Today* 43 (July 1995), 33. The article is based on the spoken corpus of the BNC.

57 Gill Francis, "A Corpus-Driven Approach to Grammar: Principles, Methods and Examples," in Baker *et al.* (eds.), *Text and Technology*, pp. 137–56.

58 Sinclair, *Corpus, Concordance, Collocation*, p. 84.

59 *Ibid.*

60 Gwyneth Fox, "The Case for Examples," in Sinclair (ed.), *Looking Up*, p. 138.

61 Della Summers, "Computer Lexicography: The Importance of Representativeness in Relation to Frequency," in Jenny Thomas and Mick Short (eds.), *Using Corpora for Language Research: Studies in Honour of Geoffrey Leech* (London: Longman, 1996), p. 263.

62 See Moon, *Fixed Expressions and Idioms in English*, especially pp. 2–5, for a discussion of terminology and types of idioms.

63 Cited by Kennedy, *An Introduction to Corpus Linguistics*, p. 117.

64 My explanations of "mutual information" and of "t-scores" are based on the explanations given by Jeremy Clear, "From Firth Principles: Computational Tools for the Study of Collocation," in Baker *et al.*, *Text and Technology*, pp. 278–82, and on Biber *et al.*, *Corpus Linguistics*, pp. 265–68.

65 Biber *et al.*, *Corpus Linguistics*, p. 267.

66 The C-score is a unique feature of the Cambridge Corpus Tools.

67 See, for example, Sinclair, *Corpus, Concordance, Collocation*, Chapter 8, "Collocation," pp. 109–21. See also Igor Mel'čuk, "Collocations and Lexical Functions," in A. P. Cowie (ed.), *Phraseology: Theory Analysis, and Applications* (Oxford: Clarendon Press, 1998), pp. 23–53. Mel'čuk says, for instance (p. 24), "People speak in set phrases, rather than in separate words, hence the crucial importance of set phrases." See also Douglas Biber and Susan Conrad, "Lexical Bundles in Conversation and Academic Prose," in Thomas and Short (eds.), *Using Corpora for Language Research*, pp. 181–90. They examine extended collocations of three or more words that show a tendency to co-occur, such as "Do you want me to," "I said to him," "in the case of," etc.

68 Sinclair, *Corpus, Concordance, Collocation*, p. 17.

69 *Ibid.*, p. 101.
70 Kennedy, *An Introduction to Corpus Linguistics*, p. 117.
71 Kennedy, "Preferred Ways of Putting Things," p. 335.
72 Jeremy Clear, "From Firth Principles," p. 274.
73 See Mona Baker, "Corpus Linguistics and Translation Studies: Implications and Applications," in Baker *et al.* (eds.), *Text and Technology*, pp. 233–50.
74 For example, as reported in *Science News* 156:13 (September 25, 1999), 197, the US space agency, NASA, has developed a softball-sized robot that, with the aid of onboard computers, can synthesize speech and recognize language, among other things, while it floats around the interior of the spacecraft.
75 Jan Svartvik, "Corpus Linguistics Comes of Age," in Svartvik (ed.), *Directions in Corpus Linguistics*, p. 7.
76 Rosamund Moon, "On Using Spoken Data in Corpus Lexicography," in Thierry Fontenelle, Philippe Hiligsmann, Archibald Michiels, André Moulin, and Siegfried Theissen (eds.) *ACTES EURALEX'98 Proceedings, V. II* (University of Liège, 1998), pp. 347–55.
77 *Ibid.* See especially pp. 348–49.
78 Moon, *Fixed Expressions and Idioms in English*, p. 51.
79 Kennedy, *An Introduction to Corpus Linguistics*, p. 81.
80 Although too small and selective to meet the lexical needs of a dictionary, the text categories of sample corpora may be perfectly suitable to represent grammatical features. See Biber *et al.*, *Corpus Linguistics*, p. 249.
81 This categorization is designed strictly for dictionary use, and it is not typical of many of those used. More specialized purposes would demand a more specialized categorization of text types.
82 Biber *et al.*, *Corpus Linguistics*, p. 249.
83 Michael Rundell and Penny Stock, "The Corpus Revolution," *English Today* 32 (October 1992), 49.
84 *Ibid.*
85 There are a few concordancing programs commercially available, among them the WordCruncher program, developed at Brigham Young University, that are well regarded when used with corpora of limited size. See Knut Hofland, "Concordance Programs for Personal Computers," in Stig Johannson and Anna-Brita Stenström (eds.), *English Computer Corpora: Selected Papers and Research Guide* (Berlin: Mouton de Gruyter, 1991), pp. 284–306. For a brief survey of various concordancing programs available, see Kennedy, *An Introduction to Corpus Linguistics*, pp. 259–67.
86 For a detailed description of text encoding and annotation, see Tony McEnery and Andrew Wilson, *Corpus Linguistics* (Edinburgh University Press, 1996), pp. 24–57.
87 McEnery and Wilson, *Corpus Linguistics*, p. 39.
88 For example, Frederic C. Mish, editor in chief of Merriam-Webster, reported that Merriam-Webster's citational corpus consisted of 62 million words, 55 million of which were indexed. He also said that the company's

citation file totaled 15¹/₄ million, but most of that remained in the form of 3x5-inch slips. All current citations are collected in computerized form (personal letter, Feb. 12, 1999).

7 DICTIONARY MAKING

1 James R. Hulbert, *Dictionaries: British and American*, rev. edn. (London: Andre Deutsch, 1968), pp. 47–48.
2 Ladislav Zgusta, *Manual of Lexicography* (The Hague: Mouton; Prague: Academia, 1971), p. 348.
3 *Ibid.*
4 Sidney I. Landau, "The Making of a Dictionary: Craft versus Commerce," *Booklist* 77:6 (November 15, 1980), 481–82.
5 David B. Guralnik, *The Making of a New Dictionary* (Cleveland: World Publishing Co., 1953), p. 11.
6 Landau, "The Making of a Dictionary," p. 482.
7 See Barbara Ann Kipfer, "The Declining Role of the In-House Dictionary Staff," *Dictionaries* 7 (1985), 237–45. Kipfer talked to nine different dictionary houses to survey them on their use of editors working at home. Frank Abate, one of the lexicographers interviewed, said he had been lending computers to free-lancers for such work since 1982 (p. 241).
8 Penny Silva (ed.), *A Dictionary of South African English on Historical Principles* (Oxford University Press, 1996), p. xv.
9 Bosley Woolf, "Definition: Practice and Illustration," in Raven I. McDavid, Jr. and Audrey R. Duckert (eds.), *Lexicography in English* (New York Academy of Sciences, 1973), p. 253.
10 Patrick Hanks, "To What Extent Does a Dictionary Definition Define?" in R. R. K. Hartmann (ed.), *Dictionaries and their Users*, Exeter Linguistic Series No. 4 (University of Exeter, 1979), p. 37.
11 Woolf, "Definition: Practice and Illustration," p. 253.
12 Clarence Barnhart, "Problems in Editing a Commercial Monolingual Dictionary," in Fred W. Householder and Sol Saporta (eds.), *Problems in Lexicography* (Bloomington: Indiana University; The Hague: Mouton, 1967), pp. 162–73.
13 Barnhart, "Problems in Editing," in Householder and Saporta (eds.), *Problems in Lexicography*, p. 165.
14 My analysis is based in part on Zgusta, *Manual of Lexicography*, pp. 144–51. Zgusta lists a number of criteria but fails to mention stress pattern.
15 The best description of the sound pattern of compounds can be found in the celebrated work of Leonard Bloomfield, *Language* (New York: Holt, 1933), Ch. 14, pp. 227ff. Exactly what constitutes a compound is a vexed question in linguistics, but one not germane to this discussion.
16 I am grateful to Robert K. Barnhart for permission to print Thorndike's system, which has been used informally by other dictionary houses apart from that of the Barnharts.
17 See especially B. T. S. Atkins, "Theoretical Lexicography and Its Relation

to Dictionary-making," *Dictionaries* 14 (1992/93), 4–43. Atkins describes decisions about the format of the dictionary, the sources of evidence, and market to be "pre-lexicographic decisions" (10–16).

18 This arrangement is partly modeled on the *OED*, though *NODE* is not directly based on the *OED*.

19 Barnhart, "Problems in Editing," p. 162.

20 For example, the *Encarta World English Dictionary* says on its dust cover that it has "Over 400,000 references." This cannot refer to entries. I do not know what it refers to.

21 Alexandre Manuila (ed.), *Progress in Medical Terminology* (Basel: S. Karger, 1981), pp. 55–57. Reprinted by permission.

22 *Ibid.*

23 Personal interview with Robert Burchfield, April 19, 1982.

24 The Second Edition of the *OED* (*OED2*) completely redid the pronunciations to render the transcriptions in conformity with accepted modern usage, and corrected many of them along the way.

25 The American Heritage dictionaries are exceptional in having a consultant, Geoffrey Nunberg, take much of the responsibility for their usage notes.

26 Frank H. Vizetelly, *The Development of the Dictionary of the English Language* (New York: Funk & Wagnalls, 1923), p. 38.

27 Full-color illustrations in children's dictionaries are a comparatively recent development. Up until 1968 all authentic children's dictionaries, as distinguished from alphabetic storybooks or vocabulary builders (some of which might be called dictionaries), were printed in black-and-white only. The *Harcourt Brace School Dictionary*, ed. Harrison G. Platt (New York: Harcourt Brace, 1968), was the first dictionary to include a second color in its illustrations, although it was not full color. The Macmillan children's dictionaries were the first to adopt full color in the 1970s. One of the earliest was the *Macmillan Dictionary for Children*, ed. Christopher G. Morris (New York: Macmillan, 1977).

28 Unfortunately, there is no consensus of usage regarding the terms *revision* and *updating*; to complicate things further, some dictionaries list new *printings*, which may be the verbatim reissue of the previous printing or include a few emendations. A new printing, of course, does not imply a new copyright. Even more confusingly, some dictionaries list only the copyright date of the current edition on their copyright page even when it is not the first edition. Readers then have no way of knowing that the dictionary is not new.

29 Sidney I. Landau and Ronald J. Bogus (eds.), *The Doubleday Dictionary* (New York: Doubleday, 1975), p. vii.

30 *The Newbury House Dictionary of American English*, first published 1996.

8 LEGAL AND ETHICAL ISSUES IN LEXICOGRAPHY

1 Robert Burchfield, *Unlocking the English Language* (London: Faber & Faber, 1989), p. 157. The essay was first published in *Encounter* 63:3 (September/October 1984), 10–19.

2 *Ibid.*, p. 14.

3 *Ibid.*, p. 154.

4 *Encounter* 63:5 (December 1984), 71–73.

5 In a review by Urdang of John Willinsky's *Empire of Words: The Reign of the OED* in 1997, Urdang says that Burchfield's *Encounter* article had "libelous implications" and sees hypocrisy in Burchfield's use of quotations from other dictionaries in the *OED Supplements* while imputing plagiarism to a publisher who purchases the rights to a dictionary legitimately. *International Journal of Lexicography* 10:1 (March 1997), 81.

6 The case is described in *Dictionaries: Journal of the Dictionary Society of North America* 6 (1984), 53–65.

7 Harry R. Warfel, *Noah Webster: Schoolmaster to America* (New York: Macmillan, 1936), p. 289.

8 Herbert C. Morton, *The Story of Webster's Third: Philip Gove's Controversial Dictionary and its Critics* (Cambridge University Press, 1994), pp. 216–17. Both quotations are from p. 216.

9 Personal communication from David Guralnik, January 17, 1994. Guralnik was the editor of the 1953 *Webster's New World Dictionary.*

10 As reported in the *New York Times*, September 14, 1994, "Lawrence Rosenthal, a Random House lawyer, argued that anyone publishing a dictionary without the name 'Webster's' in its title was fighting a losing marketing battle."

11 See *Dictionaries: Journal of the Dictionary Society of North America* 7 (1985), 214–24.

12 Allen Walker Read, "Craigie, Mathews, and Watson: New Light on the *Dictionary of American English*," *Dictionaries: Journal of the Dictionary Society of North America* 8 (1986), 160–63.

13 Michael Adams, "Credit Where It's Due: Authority and Recognition at the *Dictionary of American English*," *Dictionaries: Journal of the Dictionary Society of North America* 19 (1998), 1–20.

14 *Ibid.*, p. 18.

15 The proposal appeared in the *DSNA Newsletter* 20:1 (Spring 1996), 1–4. For further information about the DSNA, one should contact Dr. Luanne von Schneidemesser, Secretary-Treasurer, Dictionary Society of North America, University of Wisconsin-Madison, 6131 Helen C. White Hall, 600 N. Park Street, Madison, Wisconsin 53706. The DSNA website is (http://polyglot.lss.wisc.edu/dsna/index.html); the telephone number is 608 263-2748; the fax number is 608 263-3817.

16 Ann Ediger Baehr, "An Evaluation of the 1952 and 1962 Editions of the *Thorndike-Barnhart Beginning Dictionary*," *Elementary English* 41:4 (April 1964), 413–19. The quotations are from p. 416.

17 Sidney I. Landau, "The Expression of Changing Social Values in Dictionaries: Focus on Family Relationships," in Greta D. Little and Michael Montgomery (eds.), *Centennial Usage Studies*. Publication of the American Dialect Society No. 78 (Tuscaloosa: University of Alabama Press,

1994), pp. 32–39. This paper was first published in slightly different form under the title "The Expression of Changing Social Values in Dictionaries," *Dictionaries: Journal of the Dictionary Society of North America* 7 (1985), 261–69. The 1988 edition I examined was the *Scott, Foresman Beginning Dictionary*, the school edition, whose A-Z text is identical to the corresponding trade edition entitled *Thorndike-Barnhart Beginning Dictionary*.

18 *Ibid.*, pp. 35–36.
19 *Ibid.*, p. 39.

DICTIONARIES MENTIONED IN THE TEXT, FROM JOHNSON (1755) TO THE PRESENT: A BIBLIOGRAPHY AND INDEX

1 The title on the cover, repeated several times on front and back, is "Oxford American Wordpower Dictionary," but on the title page "Oxford" is omitted.

Dictionaries mentioned in the text, from Johnson (1755) to the present: a bibliography and index

(*Note.* References in the text to dictionaries *before* Johnson's may be found in the general index under the name of the compiler. References to Johnson's *Dictionary* are given here, but see the general index for references to Johnson. This index includes usage guides. Page references in **boldface** refer to significant comment or description or include a critical evaluation.)

The Barnhart Dictionary of Etymology, ed. Robert K. Barnhart (New York: H. W. Wilson, 1988) **37**

Bartlett's Roget's Thesaurus, ed. Elizabeth Ward Pitha (Boston: Little, Brown, 1996) **140**

The BBI Combinatory Dictionary of English, ed. Morton Benson, Evelyn Benson, and Robert Ilson (Amsterdam: John Benjamins, 1986) **75–76**

The BBI Dictionary of English Word Combinations, ed. Morton Benson, Evelyn Benson, and Robert Ilson (Amsterdam: John Benjamins, 1997) **75–76**

Blakiston's Gould Medical Dictionary, Fourth Edition (New York: McGraw-Hill, 1979) 189

British English, A to Zed, ed. Norman W. Schur (New York: Facts on File, 1987) **15**

British Synonymy: Or an Attempt to regulate the Choice of Words in Familiar Conversation, ed. Hester Lynch Piozzi (1794) 135

Butterworths Medical Dictionary, Second Edition, ed. Macdonald Critchley (London: Butterworths, 1978) 189

Cambridge Dictionary of American English, ed. Sidney I. Landau (New York: Cambridge University Press, 2000) (*CDAE*) 1, **76**, 103, **107**, **177–80**, **183–85**, 209, 218, **297**, **305–6**, 312, 325, 329, 333, 364, 365, 384

Cambridge International Dictionary of English, ed. Paul Procter (Cambridge University Press, 1995) (*CIDE*) 76, 101, 103, 147, **150–51**, 177, **179**, 182, 289

Cambridge Word Selector, Inglés-Español, ed. Elizabeth Walter (Cambridge University Press, 1995) **21**

The Canadian Oxford Dictionary, ed. Katherine Barber (Don Mills, Ont.: Oxford University Press, 1998) **14**

The Careful Writer, by Theodore M. Bernstein (New York: Atheneum, 1965) 265

The Cassell Dictionary of Slang, ed. Jonathon Green (London: Cassell, 1998) **39**, 240

The Century Dictionary and Cyclopedia, 10 vols., ed. William Dwight Whitney (New York: The Century Co., 1889–95) **84–85**, 89, **141**, **143**

Chambers 21st Century Dictionary, ed. Mairi Robinson (Edinburgh: Chambers, 1996) 95, 143

A Classical Dictionary of the Vulgar Tongue, ed. Francis Grose (London, 1785) 229

Collins Cobuild Dictionary of Idioms, ed. Rosamund Moon (London: HarperCollins, 1995) **41**

Collins Cobuild English Dictionary, Second Edition, ed. John Sinclair (London: HarperCollins, 1995) (*Cobuild*) **114**, **118**, 147, **164**, **176**, **179–80**, 208, 209

Collins Cobuild English Language Dictionary, ed. John Sinclair (London: HarperCollins, 1987) (*Cobuild ELD*) 76, **164**, 284, **286–87**

Collins English Dictionary (formally *Collins Dictionary of the English Language*), ed. Patrick Hanks (London: Collins, 1979) **95**, 143

Collins English Dictionary, Fourth Edition, ed. Diana Teffrey (Glasgow: HarperCollins, 1998) (*CED*) **95**, **102–4**, **340**, 358–59

The Columbia Guide to Standard American English, by Kenneth G. Wilson (New York: MJF Books, 1993) **266**

A Compendious Dictionary of the English Language, ed. Noah Webster (Hartford and New-Haven, 1806) **69–70**, 71

A Comprehensive Etymological Dictionary of the English Language, 2 vols., ed. Ernest Klein (Amsterdam: Elsevier, 1971) **37**

Comprehensive Pronouncing and Explanatory Dictionary, ed. Joseph E. Worcester (Boston, 1830) **72**

Concise Oxford Dictionary, ed. H. W. Fowler and F. G. Fowler (Oxford: Clarendon Press, 1911; 2nd edn., ed. H. W. Fowler, 1929) **95**, 262

Concise Oxford Dictionary, Ninth Edition, ed. Della Thompson (Oxford: Clarendon Press, 1995) 95, **149**, 340

Crabb's English Synonymes, rev. edn., ed. George Crabb (New York: Grosset & Dunlap, 1917). See *English Synonymes Explained.*

Critical Pronouncing Dictionary and Expositor of the English Language, ed. John Walker (1791) **67–69**

Current American Usage, ed. Margaret Bryant (New York: Funk & Wagnalls, 1962) **265**, **268**

Davies' Dictionary of Golfing Terms, by Peter Davies (New York: Simon and Schuster, 1980) **34–35**

A Dictionary of American English on Historical Principles, 4 vols., ed. William A. Craigie and James R. Hulbert (University of Chicago Press, 1938–44)(*DAE*) **13**, **412–13**

A Dictionary of American Idioms, Third Edition, ed. Adam Makkai, Maxine Tull Boatner, and J. Edward Gates (Hauppauge, N.Y.: Barron's, 1995) **40**

Dictionary of Americanisms: A Glossary of Words and Phrases usually regarded as peculiar to the United States, ed. John Russell Bartlett (Boston: Little, Brown, 1848) 13

A Dictionary of Americanisms on Historical Principles, ed. Mitford M. Mathews (Chicago University Press, 1951) **13–14**, 413

Dictionary of American Regional English, ed. Frederic G. Cassidy and Joan Houston Hall (Cambridge, Mass.: Belknap Press, 1985–)(*DARE*) **23**, **39**, **216**, **221–26**, 261, 272

Dictionary of American Slang, Second Supplemented Edition, ed. Harold Wentworth and Stuart Berg Flexner (New York: Thomas Y. Crowell, 1975; first edn. 1960) **38–39**, 240

Dictionary of American Slang, Third Edition, ed. Robert L. Chapman (New York: HarperCollins, 1995) **39**, 240, 272

A Dictionary of Canadianisms on Historical Principles, ed. Walter S. Avis *et al.* (Toronto: W. J. Gage, 1967) 14

Dictionary of Caribbean English Usage, ed. Richard Allsopp (Oxford University Press, 1996) **14**

A Dictionary of Contemporary American Usage, by Bergen Evans and Cornelia Evans (New York: Random House, 1957) 242, **264–65**

A Dictionary of the English Language, ed. Samuel Johnson (1755) 29, 56, 59, **60–66**, 73, 98–99, 245

A Dictionary of the English Language, ed. Joseph E. Worcester (Boston: Hickling, Swan, & Brewer, 1860) **73–74**, **134**

A Dictionary of the English Language, ed. Noah Porter (Springfield, Mass.: G. & C. Merriam, 1864) (the "Webster-Mahn") **74**, 84

A Dictionary of First Names, ed. Patrick Hanks and Flavia Hodges (Oxford University Press, 1990) 42

A Dictionary of Idioms for the Deaf, ed. Maxine Tull Boatner (Hartford, Conn.: American School of the Deaf, 1966) **40**

Dictionary of Jamaican English, Second Edition, ed. F. G. Cassidy and R. B LePage (Cambridge University Press, 1980; 1st edn. 1967) **14**

A Dictionary of Modern American Usage, by Bryan A. Garner (Oxford University Press, 1998) *(DMAU)* **267–68**

A Dictionary of Modern English Usage, ed. H. W. Fowler (London: Oxford University Press, 1926) **261–62**. See also *The New Fowler's Modern English Usage*.

The Dictionary of New Zealand English: A Dictionary of New Zealandisms on Historical Principles, ed. H. W. Orsman (Oxford University Press, 1997) 14

Dictionary of the Older Scottish Tongue (Oxford University Press, 1931–) **28**

A Dictionary of Slang and Unconventional English, Eighth Edition, original edn. Eric Partridge, rev. edn. Paul Beale (London: Routledge, 1984; first edn. 1937) **38**

A Dictionary of South African English on Historical Principles, ed. Penny Silva (Oxford University Press, 1996) **14**, 353

A Dictionary of Surnames, ed. Patrick Hanks and Flavia Hodges (Oxford University Press, 1988) **42**

A Dictionary of Usage and Style, by Roy M. Copperud (New York: Hawthorn Books, 1964) 265

Difference between Words Esteemed Synonymous in the English Language, ed. John Trusler (1766) 134–35

The Doubleday Dictionary, ed. Sidney I. Landau and Ronald J. Bogus (New York: Doubleday, 1975) 141, 158, 201, 230, **232–33**, **397**

The Doubleday Roget's Thesaurus in Dictionary Form, ed. Sidney I. Landau and Ronald J. Bogus (New York: Doubleday, 1977) **141**

Encarta World English Dictionary, ed. Kathy Rooney (London: Bloomsbury, 1999); US edition, ed. Anne H. Soukhanov (New York: St. Martin's Press, 1999)*(EWED)* 31, **121**, **143**, 146, **152**, **163**, **234**, 236, **388**, **395**

English Dialect Dictionary, 6 vols., ed. Joseph Wright (London: H. Frowde, 1898–1905) 35, 39

An English Pronouncing Dictionary, ed. Daniel Jones (London: J. M. Dent, 1917) 37

English Pronouncing Dictionary, ed. Daniel Jones, Peter Roach, and James Hartman (Cambridge University Press, 1997) **37**, **126**

English Synonymes Explained, ed. George Crabb (London, 1816), later published as *English Synonymes* and as *Crabb's English Synonymes* 38, 135

English Synonyms and Antonyms, ed. James C. Fernald (New York: Funk & Wagnalls, 1896; rev. edn. 1914) **136**

English Synonyms Discriminated, ed. W. Taylor (London, 1813) 38, 135

An Etymological Dictionary of the English Language, ed. Walter W. Skeat (Oxford: Clarendon Press, 1879–82, rev. 1909) **37**

An Etymological Dictionary of Modern English, ed. Ernest Weekley (1921; rpt. New York: Dover, 1967) 37

Explanatory Combinatorial Dictionary of Modern Russian, ed. I. Mel'čuk and A. Zholkovsky (Vienna: Wiener Slawistischer Almanach, 1984) **75**

Fifty Years Among the New Words: A Dictionary of Neologisms, 1941–1991, ed. John Algeo (Cambridge University Press, 1991) **40**

A selective bibliography of nondictionary sources

Aijmer, Karin and Bengt Altenberg (eds.), *English Corpus Linguistics: Studies in Honour of Jan Svartvik* (London: Longman, 1991)

Atkins, B. T. S. and A. Zampoli (eds.), *Computational Approaches to the Lexicon* (Oxford University Press, 1994)

Baehr, Ann Ediger, "An Evaluation of the 1952 and 1962 Editions of the *Thorndike-Barnhart Beginning Dictionary*," *Elementary English* 41:4 (April 1964), 413–19

Baker, Mona, Gill Francis, and Elena Tognini-Bonelli (eds.), *Text and Technology: In Honour of John Sinclair* (Philadelphia: John Benjamins, 1993)

Barnhart, Clarence L., "American Lexicography, 1947–1973," *American Speech* 53:2 (Summer 1978), 83–140

"Problems in Editing a Commercial Monolingual Dictionary," in Householder and Saporta (eds.), *Problems in Lexicography*, pp. 161–82

Béjoint, Henri, *Tradition and Innovation in Modern English Dictionaries* (Oxford University Press, 1994)

Biber, Douglas, *Variations Across Speech and Writing* (Cambridge University Press, 1988)

Biber, Douglas, Susan Conrad, and Randi Reppen, *Corpus Linguistics: Investigating Language Structure and Use* (Cambridge University Press, 1998)

Bloomfield, Leonard, *Language* (New York: Holt, 1933)

Bronstein, Arthur, *The Pronunciation of American English* (New York: Appleton-Century-Crofts, 1960)

Burchfield, Robert, *Unlocking the English Language* (London: Faber & Faber, 1989)

(ed.), *Studies in Lexicography* (Oxford: Clarendon Press, 1987)

Chapman, R. W., *Lexicography* (Oxford University Press, 1948)

Chomsky, Noam, Review of *Verbal Behavior*, by B. F. Skinner, *Language* 35:1 (1959), 26–58

Congleton, J. E., J. Edward Gates, and Donald Hobar (eds.), *Papers on Lexicography in Honor of Warren N. Cordell* (Terre Haute, Ind.: Dictionary Society of North America and Indiana State University, 1979)

Cowie, A. P., "A. S. Hornby, 1898–1998: A Centenary Tribute," *International Journal of Lexicography* 11:4 (Dec. 1998), 251–68

(ed.), *Phraseology: Theory, Analysis, and Applications* (Oxford: Clarendon Press, 1998)

Creswell, Thomas, *Usage in Dictionaries and Dictionaries of Usage.* Publication of the American Dialect Society, nos. 63–64 (University: University of Alabama Press, 1975)

Crystal, David, *The Cambridge Encyclopedia of the English Language* (Cambridge University Press, 1995)

The Cambridge Encyclopedia of Language, Second Edition (Cambridge University Press, 1997)

English as a Global Language (Cambridge University Press, 1997)

Drysdale, Patrick, "Dictionary Etymologies," in Michell (ed.), *Papers of the Dictionary Society of North America 1979*, pp. 39–50

Finegan, Edward, *Attitudes Toward English Usage* (New York: Teachers College, Columbia University, 1980)

Fox, Gwyneth, "The Case for Examples," in Sinclair (ed.), *Looking Up*, pp. 137–49

Friend, Joseph H., *The Development of American Lexicography 1798–1864* (The Hague: Mouton, 1967)

Fries, Charles C., *American English Grammar* (New York: Appleton-Century-Crofts, 1940)

Gove, Philip Babcock, *The Role of the Dictionary* (Indianapolis: Bobbs-Merrill, 1957)

Green, Jonathon, *Chasing the Sun: Dictionary Makers and the Dictionaries They Made* (New York: Henry Holt, 1996)

Hartmann, R. R. K. (ed.), *Dictionaries and Their Users*, Exeter Linguistic Series, No. 4 (University of Exeter, 1979)

Hausmann, Franz Josef, Oskar Reichmann, Herbert Ernst Wiegand, and Ladislav Zgusta (eds.), *Wörterbucher, Dictionaries, Dictionnaires: Ein internationales Handbuch zur Lexikographie, An International Encyclopedia of Lexicography, Encyclopédie internationale de lexicographie*, 3 vols. (Berlin: Walter de Gruyter, 1989–91)

Hobar, Donald (ed.), *Papers of the DSNA 1977* (Terre Haute: Indiana State University, 1982)

Householder, Fred W. and Sol Saporta (eds.), *Problems in Lexicography* (Bloomington: Indiana University; The Hague: Mouton, 1967)

Hulbert, James R., *Dictionaries: British and American*, rev. edn. (London: Andre Deutsch, 1968)

Ilson, Robert (ed.), *Lexicography as an Emerging Profession* (Manchester University Press, 1986)

Johannson, Stig and Anna-Brita Stenström (eds.), *English Computer Corpora: Selected Papers and Research Guide* (Berlin: Mouton de Gruyter, 1991)

Jones, Richard Foster, *The Triumph of the English Language* (Stanford University Press, 1953)

Joos, Martin, *The Five Clocks* (New York: Harcourt Brace Jovanovich, 1967; first edn. 1961)

Kennedy, Graeme, *An Introduction to Corpus Linguistics* (London: Longman, 1998)

Kenyon, John S., "Cultural Levels and Functional Varieties of English," *College English* 10:1 (October 1948), 31–36

Krapp, George Philip, *The English Language in America*, 2 vols. (1925; rpt. New York: Frederick Ungar, 1966)

Labov, William, *The Social Stratification of English in New York City* (Washington, D.C.: Center for Applied Linguistics, 1966)

  The Study of Nonstandard English (Champaign, Ill.: National Council of Teachers of English, 1970)

Landau, Sidney I., "The American College Dictionaries," *International Journal of Lexicography* 7:4 (Winter 1994), 311–51

  "Dictionary Entry Count," *RQ* 4:1 (September 1964), 6, 13–15

  "The Expression of Changing Social Values in Dictionaries: Focus on Family Relationships," in Little and Montgomery (eds.), *Centennial Usage Studies*, pp. 32–39

  "Of Matters Lexicographical: Scientific and Technical Entries in American Dictionaries," *American Speech* 49:3–4 (Fall–Winter 1974), 241–44

  "Popular Meanings of Scientific and Technical Terms," *American Speech* 55:3 (Fall 1980), 204–9

  Review of the *Encarta World English Dictionary*, in *Dictionaries: Journal of the Dictionary Society of North America* 21 (2000), 112–24

Leonard, Sterling A., *Current English Usage* (Chicago: National Council of Teachers of English, 1932)

Little, Greta D. and Michael Montgomery (eds.), *Centennial Usage Studies*. Publication of the American Dialect Society, no. 78 (Tuscaloosa: University of Alabama Press, 1994)

Malkiel, Yakov, *Etymology* (Cambridge University Press, 1993)

  "A Typological Classification of Dictionaries on the Basis of Distinctive Features," in Householder and Saporta (eds.), *Problems in Lexicography*, pp. 3–24

Malone, Kemp, "On Defining mahogany," *Language* 16:4 (1940), 308–18

Manuila, Alexandre (ed.), *Progress in Medical Terminology* (Basel: S. Karger, 1981)

Marckwardt, Albert C. and Fred Walcott, *Facts About Current English Usage* (New York: Appleton-Century-Crofts, 1938)

Mathews, Mitford M., *A Survey of English Dictionaries* (Oxford University Press, 1933; rpt. New York: Russell & Russell, 1966)

McArthur, Tom (ed.), *The Oxford Companion to the English Language* (Oxford University Press, 1992)

McDavid, Jr., Raven I. and Audrey R. Duckert (eds.), *Lexicography in English* (New York Academy of Sciences, 1973)

McEnery, Tony and Andrew Wilson, *Corpus Linguistics* (Edinburgh University Press, 1996)

McMillan, James B., "Five College Dictionaries," *College English* 10:4 (January 1949), 214–21

Michell, Gillian (ed.), *Papers of the Dictionary Society of North America 1979* (London,

Ont.: School of Library and Information Science, University of Western Ontario, 1981)

Moon, Rosamund, *Fixed Expressions and Idioms in English: A Corpus-Based Approach* (Oxford: Clarendon Press, 1998)

Morton, Herbert C., *The Story of Webster's Third: Philip Gove's Controversial Dictionary and Its Critics* (Cambridge University Press, 1994)

Murray, K. M. E. *Caught in the Web of Words: James A. H. Murray and the* Oxford English Dictionary (New Haven: Yale University Press, 1977)

Osselton, N. E., *Chosen Words: Past and Present Problems for Dictionary Makers* (University of Exeter Press, 1995)

Pooley, Robert C., *The Teaching of English Usage*, Second Edition (Urbana, Ill.: National Council of Teachers of English, 1974)

Pyles, Thomas and John Algeo, *The Origins and Development of the English Language*, fourth edn. (Fort Worth: Harcourt Brace Jovanovich, 1993)

Quirk, Randolph, Sidney Greenbaum, Geoffrey Leech, and Jan Svartvik, *A Comprehensive Grammar of the English Language* (London: Longman, 1985)

Read, Allen Walker, "Approaches to Lexicography and Semantics," in Sebeok (ed.), *Current Trends in Linguistics*, pp. 145–205

"An Obscenity Symbol," *American Speech* 9:4 (December 1934), 264–78

"dictionary" in the on-line *Encyclopaedia Britannica* (November 16, 1999)

Robinson, Richard, *Definition* (Oxford: Clarendon Press, 1965; first edn. 1954)

Rundell, Michael, "Recent Trends in English Pedagogical Lexicography," *International Journal of Lexicography* 11:4 (December 1998), 315–42

Rundell, Michael and Penny Stock, "The Corpus Revolution," *English Today* 30 (April 1992) 9–14; *English Today* 31 (July 1992), 21–31; *English Today* 32 (October 1992), 45–51

Sebeok, Thomas (ed.), *Current Trends in Linguistics*, vol. X (The Hague: Mouton, 1973)

Sheldon, Esther K., "Pronouncing Systems in Eighteenth-Century Dictionaries," *Language* 22 (1946), 27–41

"Walker's Influence on the Pronunciation of English," *Publications of the Modern Language Association* 62 (1947), 130–46

Sinclair, John, *Corpus, Concordance, Collocation* (Oxford University Press, 1991)

(ed.), *Looking Up: An Account of the COBUILD Project* (London: Collins, 1987; rev. edn. 1995)

Sledd, James and Wilma R. Ebbitt, *Dictionaries and THAT Dictionary* (Chicago: Scott, Foresman, 1962)

Sledd, James and Gwin J. Kolb, *Dr. Johnson's Dictionary: Essays in the Biography of a Book* (University of Chicago Press, 1955)

Starnes, DeWitt T. *Renaissance Dictionaries: English-Latin and Latin-English* (Austin: University of Texas Press, 1954)

Starnes, DeWitt T. and Gertrude E. Noyes, *The English Dictionary from Cawdrey to Johnson, 1604–1755* (Chapel Hill: University of North Carolina Press, 1946); reissued with an introduction by Gabriele Stein (Amsterdam and Philadelphia: John Benjamins, 1991)

Stein, Gabriele, *The English Dictionary before Cawdrey* (Tübingen: Max Niemeyer, 1985)

Stubbs, Michael, "British Tradition in Text Analysis: From Firth to Sinclair," in Baker *et al.* (eds.), *Text and Technology*, pp. 1–33

Svartvik, Jan (ed.), *Directions in Corpus Linguistics: Proceedings of Nobel Symposium 82* (Berlin: Mouton de Gruyter, 1992)

Svensén, Bo, *Practical Lexicography: Principles and Methods of Dictionary-Making* (Oxford University Press, 1993)

Thomas, Jenny and Mick Short (eds.), *Using Corpora for Language Research: Studies in Honour of Geoffrey Leech* (London: Longman, 1996)

Trench, Richard Chenevix, *On Some Deficiencies in Our English Dictionaries* (London, 1857)

Vizetelly, Frank H., *The Development of the Dictionary of the English Language* (New York: Funk & Wagnalls, 1923)

Weinbrot, Howard D. (ed.) *New Aspects of Lexicography* (Carbondale: Southern Illinois University Press, 1972)

Zgusta, Ladislav, *Manual of Lexicography* (The Hague: Mouton; Prague: Academia, 1971)

Index

This general index includes references to dictionaries before Johnson's *Dictionary* (1755), which are listed here under the name of the editors except when the editors are unknown; in that case they are listed under the title. For titles of books, look under the author's name. References to dictionaries after Johnson's *Dictionary* (and including his dictionary) may be found under their titles in "Dictionaries mentioned in the text : a bibliography and index," beginning on p. 456.